W9-AFQ-553

Dog-Friendly NEW ENGLAND

A Traveler's Companion

THIRD EDITION

WITHDRAWN

© A KATZ/SHUTTERSTOCK.COM

Dog-Friendly NEW ENGLAND

A Traveler's Companion

THIRD EDITION

Trisha Blanchet

The Countryman Press
Woodstock, Vermont

Copyright © 2003, 2006, 2014
by Trisha Blanchet

Third Edition

All rights reserved. No part of this book may be reproduced in any form by any electronic or mechanical means, including information storage and retrieval systems, without permission from the publisher, except by a reviewer, who may quote brief passages.

Dog-Friendly New England
ISBN 978-1-58157-224-7
ISSN 1559-2545

Book design by Hespenheide Design
Composition by Chelsea Cloeter

Maps © The Countryman Press

Published by The Countryman Press,
P.O. Box 748, Woodstock, VT 05091

Distributed by W. W. Norton & Company, Inc.,
500 Fifth Avenue, New York, NY 10110

Printed in the United States of America

10 9 8 7 6 5 4 3 2 1

For Duncan and Oly

Heartfelt thanks

to Scott, Mom, Dad, and Tricia
for your help and company
on the road

CONTENTS

Introduction

Admit it—you buy birthday presents for your dog. You have a picture of him in your wallet and another one, framed, on your desk. You say the words shmoopy, woopy, or poopie at least once a day (and don't mind). Maybe it's a poodle that you pine for, or a bloodhound, or a mutt. The breed doesn't really matter. The truth is, you're a dog lover. And the dog you love the most is your own.

But you're also a normal, social human being, one who wouldn't mind getting away once in a while to see new places, meet new people, and escape the daily grind. So you try to make vacation plans and quickly learn a hard truth: There are some people in the world, in fact many people, who don't enjoy the company of a 75-pound shedding, drooling canine. These people may say they would rather you *didn't* bring Fido to their hotel, B&B, campground, or cottage. They may be very adamant on that point. You make call after call, continue to come into contact with this strange breed of humans, and finally come to the conclusion that you've got two choices: You can give in to those chocolate-brown, sad eyes and skip the vacation altogether, or you can hit the road and leave your furry friend in a (gulp) kennel. For a whole week. Alone.

Luckily for us, it doesn't have to come to that. From the Green Mountains of Vermont to the posh digs of Boston, there are many small and large, inexpensive and extravagant accommodations in New England that allow and even welcome animals. There are also bookstores, outdoor restaurants, tour boats, and countless other businesses that cater to furry, scaled, or feathered clientele. The only problem is that many don't advertise their pet-friendly status, so they have, in the past, been difficult to find. But not anymore.

Dog-Friendly New England is designed to take you on a four-legged tour of every region of Connecticut, Rhode Island, Massachusetts, Vermont, New Hampshire, and Maine. Within each region, you'll find pet-friendly overnight accommodations in every style and price range, restaurants that offer outdoor seating or take-out service, parks and historic sites where animals are allowed, and even doggie day-care centers, groomers, and pet shops. From here on in, your family vacations can include every member of the family—even the one that likes to stick his head out the window on the way there.

ACCOMMODATIONS

Few things can make or break a vacation like the roof over your head. Each of us has a different expectation of the "perfect" accommodation: Some prefer to be left on their own, cook their own meals, and bask in a rustic, unadorned atmosphere. Others want pampering, personal attention, gourmet breakfasts, and a concierge. Or maybe you're searching for something in between.

Bringing an animal along changes the equation a bit, but it shouldn't alter your plans and hopes for a great trip. Many hotels, B&Bs, and inns welcome your four-legged family members, although you should be aware that some do charge an additional nightly fee or a one-time cleaning fee. This book divides them into the following categories:

Hotels, Motels, Inns, and Bed & Breakfasts

This is the largest group and includes everything from luxury and chain hotels to the tiniest B&Bs with one or two guest rooms. In general, inns are more intimate than standard hotels but don't include breakfast in the rates (though some do). Rates are comparable at all three types, depending on the location. Hotels typically appeal to those who prefer to

MANY INNKEEPERS HAVE RESIDENT DOGS THAT WELCOME CANINE GUESTS.

know in advance precisely what they're getting and enjoy their privacy and anonymity. With a B&B or inn, you can expect to get to know the hosts, share a main entrance and living areas, and perhaps sit down to breakfast with other guests. Motels, motor inns, efficiencies, and "housekeeping cottages" (meaning that you do your own cleaning) are the most affordable accommodations in each region—and you'll notice that some regions have more to offer than others. Efficiencies and cottages are usually rented by the week, though you can also sometimes rent them by the night upon request.

Campgrounds

Always a popular standby with pet owners, New England campgrounds offer a surprisingly diverse range of experiences. Some simply provide a place to park your RV; others are full-fledged "resorts" with daily scheduled activities, recreation halls, hot showers, and heated swimming pools. Privately owned facilities tend to cater to families; state-run campgrounds have fewer amenities and usually appeal to those seeking a more secluded, quiet escape.

Homes, Cottages, and Cabins for Rent

If you're seeking a getaway of a week or longer, renting a private home, cottage, cabin, or apartment can be a convenient and comfortable alternative to staying in a hotel. In most cases, the renter will have to contact the homeowner directly to check on availability and may have to answer a few questions about the number of people in the party and the personality and type of pet that's coming along. Most owners require a standard

A Note about Camping Fees

The camping fees listed in *Dog-Friendly New England* reflect each campground's "base fees" (for example, $18–23 per night). The exact definition of a base fee, however, can vary from site to site. Some campgrounds intend this charge to cover only two adults, with children adding to the total tally. Other properties include a family of four or five in their base rate. In most cases, the campground managers will prohibit more than four unrelated adults from sharing a single campsite.

A Note about Rates

Few things change more quickly in the tourism industry than rates. Often, they vary from season to season and year to year. The rates shown in each listing of *Dog-Friendly New England* range from lowest to highest (for example: $59–139 per night). The lower end of that scale usually reflects the off-season rate and the most budget-friendly (read: small) rooms, while the higher end reflects the price of the best rooms/suites during the high season. You can anticipate the high season of each accommodation based on its locale: In a beach town, summer rates will set you back; at a ski resort, wintertime fetches the highest prices. In addition, be aware of the omnipresent "weekend jump"—your room can double in price as weekdays roll into weekend days. All rates were accurate at the time of this writing, but always confirm the charges before handing over a credit card.

security deposit; many ask for an additional deposit against pet damage. Here are a few international Web sites that specialize in vacation home rentals:

www.homeaway.com
www.vacationhomerentals.com
www.vacationrentals.com
www.newenglandvacationrentals.com
www.vrbo.com

You can also find privately owned rentals on the area's local Craigslist, and local visitors bureaus or chambers of commerce often list vacation rentals.

Rental Agencies

Perhaps you have special requests or requirements or are just having trouble locating the type of lodging you want: In either case, rental agencies can often help. Some are simply listing services; others are traditional real estate agencies that also dabble in vacation rentals. Costs vary from nothing at all to a hefty finder's fee—make sure you're clear on the charges before starting the search process.

IN THE DOGHOUSE

So why don't all hotel/motel/B&B owners allow pets? The majority cite "guests' allergies" as the main reason for their humans-only policies. But many also point to factors that have nothing to do with physical health and everything to do with quality of life. Among those who used to permit pets but stopped, those who allow pets now but are considering changing that policy, and even those who happily allow pets, there are several common complaints that come up again and again during discussions about traveling animals. These mistakes made by some pet owners lead to anger on the part of innkeepers and frustration on the part of conscientious pet owners, who are left to bear the brunt of others' irresponsibility. There are other concerns, of course, but these rank as the top five:

1. Not cleaning up after your animal. Few things are more disconcerting or disgusting than stumbling across a little "present" left by an animal—especially when you're in your own yard, driveway, or walking path and you don't own a pet. This is far and away the greatest complaint that lodging owners and the general public have with pets in their communities. There's a simple solution, of course; nevertheless, some pet owners still refuse to carry pooper-scooper bags and dispose of the mess. We've all seen it happen, even on trails with posted fines where scooper bags are provided.

A Note about Breeds

You may have heard it said that there are no bad breeds, only bad owners. Nevertheless, many campground and hotel owners maintain pet-friendly policies that exclude certain breeds, most commonly pit bulls (Staffordshire bull terriers), rottweilers, German shepherds, and, more recently, huskies. In some cases, the innkeepers are adhering to insurance policy restrictions; in other cases, they chose to initiate the restrictions on their own. Owners of these particular breeds might want to double-check breed-specific policies before arriving with Rover in tow. Fairly or not, it is possible to be turned away at the door. In most cases it is better to be up front with the innkeepers than to have vacation plans ruined at the last minute.

A Note about Pet-Friendly Policies and Fees

Like rates, pet-friendly (or -unfriendly) policies can undergo subtle or dramatic changes over time. An innkeeper may have a bad experience with a four-legged guest and abruptly reverse his animal-friendly rules, despite his listing in this book. One hotel owner might decide to raise her fees for pet guests, while another might choose to do away with pet fees altogether. It is always a good idea to ask directly about fees and policies before making a reservation. It also never hurts to ask if the owners have any specific requests or requirements (pet beds, crates, etc.) for their animal guests. One noticeable change from the first edition of *Dog-Friendly New England* is a subtle rise in pet fees: Many hotel managers and innkeepers have raised their fees from $5 and $10 per night to $15 or $25. Inflation? Perhaps. Cashing in on the dog-travel trend? Who knows. But be prepared to pay a little more than you used to when you bring your pup along for the ride.

2. Leaving your pet alone in the room or at the campsite. "My dog doesn't bark." "My Fluffy would never claw at the furniture." Uh huh. We'd all like to think that—and maybe it's true, when we're around. But who knows what our pets do when they're alone in a strange place? Lodging owners say *they* know, and they've learned the hard way. This is one of the most common reasons lodging managers give for changing their pet-friendly policies: No one wants to pay $150 per night to listen to someone else's dog whine, whimper, and bark for hours on end.

3. Letting your animal sleep or sit on the furniture. For many of us, it is perfectly acceptable and natural to let our dog curl up next to us on the couch or sleep at the end of the bed. But for innkeepers trying to control dander and allergens, pet hair and upholstery usually don't mix. (Many maintain hardwood floors in designated pet rooms specifically for this reason.) In addition, many B&Bs and hotels pride themselves on providing a décor filled with fine furnishings and priceless antiques—most likely, they didn't intend for them to be used as doggie beds or scratching posts. If you anticipate a problem in this area, bring along your own bedspread and

CANINE RESIDENT MEGHAN TAKES A BREATHER IN ONE OF THE PET-FRIENDLY ROOMS AT THE LAZY DOG INN IN CHOCORUA, NEW HAMPSHIRE. (PHOTO COURTESY OF LAZY DOG INN)

towels to cover and protect your host's furniture.

4. Not adhering to leash requirements. Most innkeepers who require dogs to be on a leash on their property have a good reason: Maybe they have cats. Maybe the home has residents or visitors who are afraid of animals. Maybe they have a prized flower garden to protect. In any case, letting your pooch have free rein isn't likely to endear you to the owners. Some innkeepers, on the other hand, don't mind—but be sure to ask before setting Fluffy free.

5. Leaving the place in a shambles. At best, this can result in disarray. At worst, total destruction. One B&B owner described a situation in which a guest's large dog knocked over a television set, smashing it, and left mud caked all over the furniture. The guest then checked out and drove away quickly before the owner could discover the damage. A manager of a large chain hotel described a guest who washed his dog in the tub and clogged the drain with hair, causing the bathwater to flood the floor. Another innkeeper said he was shocked to discover that two dogs staying with him had never been treated with flea and tick preventive medication; he spent hundreds of dollars ridding his home of fleas after they left. Of course, these strange cases are the exception to the rule. But we can all do little things to make cleanup easier on our hosts—and make them more likely to continue inviting animals into their homes, hotels, and campgrounds.

If enough of us avoid these common mistakes, hopefully the list of pet-friendly accommodations choices will grow as we change naysayers' minds about the joys—and feasibility—of traveling with a furry friend in tow.

OUT AND ABOUT

You've done it: You've found a great pet-friendly place to stay, unloaded the car, and unpacked your bags. Now what?

Each region of New England is filled with fascinating, fun, and historic things to do and see. Some of them, like museums, boutiques, and go-cart tracks, are unfortunately off-limits to your pet. But others, including parks, walking tours, and old-fashioned sightseeing, are not. The "Out and About" section is designed to be a starting point in your animal-friendly explorations of each region. Only attractions that allow pets are included. It is not, by any stretch, a complete listing of all there is to explore (we'd need one book per region to cover that). For each attraction, you'll also find a phone number, address, and, in some cases, a Web site to visit for more information. These are only the highlights; by starting down the big roads, you'll inevitably stumble upon the quiet corners and fascinating people that make New England such an intriguing place to visit.

QUICK BITES

If you've ever tried to travel with your pet, you may have noticed that one of the most difficult aspects of your trip was eating—or not eating, as the case may be. Unless you've lined up a pet-sitter or kennel, you can pretty much rule out dining in any restaurant that requires you to sit inside and order from a waiter or waitress. And in most cases you can also rule out leaving your favorite pooch in the car. (Heat and cold can reach extremes inside a vehicle and cause severe injury and even death.) Fasting is probably not an option. So where does that leave you? The

"Quick Bites" section lists places in each region that offer outdoor seating and takeout: In some cases, that means running inside a restaurant to order sandwiches or pizza; in others, it might mean ordering ice cream or fried clams from a take-out window or sitting at an outdoor café.

Like "Out and About," this section isn't intended to be a complete listing of all dining choices in a region, but simply a place to get started. While some outdoor eateries do offer upscale and even gourmet items, it's important to note that these are, in most cases, truly "quick bites." Also, it's always a good idea to check with the manager or host/hostess before seating yourself and your pet, even in outdoor areas; just because a restaurant has sidewalk tables, that doesn't necessarily mean the owners will let your pooch sit there. Pet-friendly policies change frequently, and local health codes may prevent the restaurant from serving you and Rover together.

HOT SPOTS FOR SPOT

Like traveling with young children, vacationing with animals comes with a unique set of challenges. Running out of dog food isn't a reason to panic—unless your finicky canine eats only one hard-to-find brand. Or maybe you have your heart set on visiting the renowned art museum at your vacation destination, and pets aren't allowed inside. Perhaps your cocker spaniel got sprayed by a skunk on one of your hikes at the state park and you're suddenly in need of a groomer. Fast.

FLYBALL IS ONE OF THE POPULAR POOCH ACTIVITIES AT CAMP GONE TO THE DOGS IN PUTNEY, VERMONT. (PHOTO BY STEVE SURFMAN)

You've worked long and hard to plan this vacation, and there's no need to let any of these or similar scenarios ruin your day or your trip. In the "Hot Spots for Spot" section, you'll find specialty pet shops, doggie day-care centers, pet-sitters, groomers, kennels, and other animal-centered businesses in each region. These pet professionals will be happy to keep an eye on your animal or provide much-needed supplies. Pet owners should note, however, that a listing in this book is not tantamount to a recommendation: Whenever possible, take the time to speak with the staff, check out the Web site, tour the facilities, and form your own judgments before leaving your animal in the care of others.

ANIMAL SHELTERS AND HUMANE SOCIETIES

These are the hardworking folks throughout New England who are taking in lost, abused, and neglected animals and helping them find new families (or reconnect with old ones). If, heaven forbid, your dog gets lost on your trip, these agencies are good places to contact when you start your search. They also typically host fund-raisers, festivals, and other events where visitors and their pets are welcome.

IN CASE OF EMERGENCY

You probably, hopefully, won't need them. But in case of an accident or illness, the veterinary hospitals listed in each region should help you locate a nearby veterinarian. Although they represent just a sampling of the total number of animal clinics available, the listings provide a geographically scattered selection; no matter what part of the region you're in, you should find a veterinarian not too far away.

MUST-HAVES

Your animal no doubt has a favorite toy, treat, or blanket that you wouldn't dream of leaving behind. While you're packing it away, stash these ever-important items, too:

- **Vaccination certificates and/or vet records:** Many hotel, campground, and kennel owners require vaccination certificates and/or vet records as a condition of admittance, but not all will let you know that beforehand. (Strange, but true.) A certificate of rabies vaccination is the most commonly requested record, although some lodging and kennel owners also ask to see proof of protection against heartworm and kennel cough. It's almost a sure bet that at least one person will ask to see your pet's health records at some

A Note about Motion Sickness

Pets unfortunately can suffer from this dreaded travel affliction as often as people do. If you've never hit the road with your animal before, you might want to speak to your veterinarian beforehand about possible medications and strategies to combat queasiness. In addition, it never hurts to have paper towels and upholstery cleaner somewhere in the car, just in case.

point during your trip. Most pet owners assume that their animal's collar tags will be proof enough of vaccinations, but that's not usually the case. To be on the safe side, have copies of your records made and bring them with you in case the innkeeper is required, by an insurance company for example, to keep the records on file.

- **Crate/kennel:** Even if your dog hasn't stepped foot in a crate since the day she was house-trained, it's always a good idea to have one along. For safety reasons, some innkeepers require that pets be crated when left alone in the room (though many don't allow pets to be left alone at all). As with other policies, you might not learn this one until you arrive at your destination, so having a crate on hand can alleviate a lot of aggravation. The folding kind is especially convenient for cases like these.

- **Towels, towels, towels:** Simply stated, you can never have enough. Aside from the fact that it's just courteous to wipe your pet's feet before he muddies up your innkeeper's Oriental rugs, some accommodations' owners actually require this. And you'll be happy to have them after Rover finishes up his romp in the pond or his run through dubious puddles on city streets. Some pet owners find it helpful to line their car seats with towels or other coverings before hitting the road—especially if their animal has a tendency to suffer from motion sickness.

- **Water and water bowls:** You can buy fancy water totes and portable bowls at a pet store or simply carry a couple of plastic bottles and a plastic bowl: Either way, make sure to always have an ample supply of H_2O and something for Spot to drink out of. (Water is equally important in winter as in summer.) It sounds like common sense, but it can be easy to forget this detail in the flurry of packing and traveling.

- **Pooper-scooper bags:** This is undoubtedly one of life's least-pleasant chores. Still, unless you want to be public enemy number one, make sure to have the necessary picker-upper tools when your pet takes bathroom breaks. Squeamish animal owners can take advantage of the newer bags with wire rims: Your hand never gets too close to the yucky stuff.
- **A spare bag of food:** This can become especially important if you're visiting rural areas, if your travel plans have an indefinite length, or if your pet is a finicky eater. It's better to return home with an unused bag than to be stuck with a hungry pooch in a one-stoplight town.
- **Treats and chew toys:** Traveling brings many lulls, both anticipated and unwelcome. If your dog is used to running around a yard, she might have a hard time being cooped up in a car for hours on end or spending the evening quietly sitting in an antiques-filled guest room. Rawhide bones and other chewy treats may help to keep your pet occupied and happy.
- **Temporary ID tag:** In addition to your pet's regular tags, you might also want to think about adding a short-term identifier while you're away from home. This can be as simple as a piece of masking tape placed over the "regular" tag and scribbled with the name of your hotel, your cell phone number, or anything else that might help someone find you in the event that your dog gets lost.

Now that all the details are taken care of, just roll down the window, turn up the radio, and enjoy the New England welcome waggin'. From covered bridges to majestic mountains, seacoast shanties to urban adventures, America's six northeasternmost states are always surprising, always welcoming, and always full of adventure—for any species. After all, dogs love chowdah, too.

Connecticut

1

A STAFFER HELPS VISITING PUPS HAVE A GOOD TIME AT THE DOGGIE DAY CAMP AT BEST FRIENDS PET CARE IN ROCKY HILL. (PHOTO COURTESY OF BEST FRIENDS PET CARE)

Eastern and Central Connecticut

This multifaceted region offers the best of both worlds for urbanites and solitude seekers: In just a few days you can visit the busy capital city of Hartford, the farms and orchards of the state's northeast Quiet Corner, and the tourist attractions of Mystic and the seacoast—not to mention Connecticut's famous (or infamous?) gambling meccas: Foxwoods and Mohegan Sun.

With the exception of the casinos, where pets are not allowed in any of the hotels or on the property, animal owners will have a fairly easy time getting around and seeing the sights. A good number of chain hotels, motels, and independent B&Bs welcome four-footed travelers, and the area's parks and attractions offer more than enough natural diversions to fill a relaxing and fun vacation. (One of the region's best-known attractions, the Mystic Seaport living-history museum, welcomes companion animals; see "Out and About.") Connecticut isn't traditionally a big tourism draw for New Englanders—vacationing Boston-area residents, for example, tend to head north to the ski hills or south to the Cape. But the state's proximity to New York City makes it popular with visitors from the Big Apple looking for changing leaves, campgrounds, quiet getaways, and colonial charm.

ACCOMMODATIONS

Hotels, Motels, Inns, and Bed & Breakfasts

Avon

Residence Inn Hartford-Avon, 55 Simsbury Rd., Avon (860-678-1666; www.marriott.com); $129–199 per night. For an extra $100 one-time fee, your pooch is welcome to stay with you in your studio, one-bedroom suite, or two-bedroom suite at this Residence Inn. Guests can also enjoy an outdoor swimming pool, complimentary hot breakfast buffets each morning, free high-speed Internet access, fireplaces, and full kitchens.

Cromwell

Quality Inn Cromwell, 111 Berlin Rd., Cromwell (860-635-4100; www.choicehotels.com); $84–125 per night. The Cromwell Quality Inn (formerly the Comfort Inn) offers free daily continental breakfast, free high-speed Internet access, cable television, meeting rooms, free coffee in the lobby, and plenty of parking. Two pets are permitted per room for an extra $25 per night.

Dayville

Comfort Inn Dayville, 16 Tracy Rd., Dayville (860-779-3200; www.choicehotels.com); $79–135 per night. Guest rooms, suites, a restaurant and lounge, cable television, a fitness center, and an indoor swimming pool are available at this Comfort Inn (formerly a Holiday Inn Express) in eastern Connecticut. Pet owners sign a pet-policy form at check-in and pay an additional $15 per room, per stay (not per night).

East Hartford

Econo Lodge East Hartford, 490 Main St., East Hartford (860-569-1100; www.choicehotels.com); $58–109 per night. This Econo Lodge has cable television, exterior corridors, free coffee in the lobby, irons and ironing boards, a wake-up service, in-room coffeemakers, air-conditioning, and a multilingual staff. Pet owners pay a refundable $50 deposit and a pet fee of $10 per night.

Enfield

Motel 6, 11 Hazard Ave., Enfield (860-741-3685; www.motel6.com); $49–59 per night. No matter where you travel in the region, you'll find a Motel 6 nearby; the economy Motel 6 chain offers amenities such as cable television with premium movie channels, free coffee and local phone calls, swimming pools at some locations, laundry facilities, and "kids stay free" programs. Your pets are always welcome.

Red Roof Inn, 5 Hazard Ave., Enfield (860-741-2571; 1-800-RED-ROOF; www.redroof.com); $55–74 per night. Guests at this Red Roof Inn location can enjoy cable television, free newspapers and local calls, alarm clocks, express check-out services, 24-hour front desks, and smoking and nonsmoking rooms. Pets are welcome, and numerous restaurants are nearby.

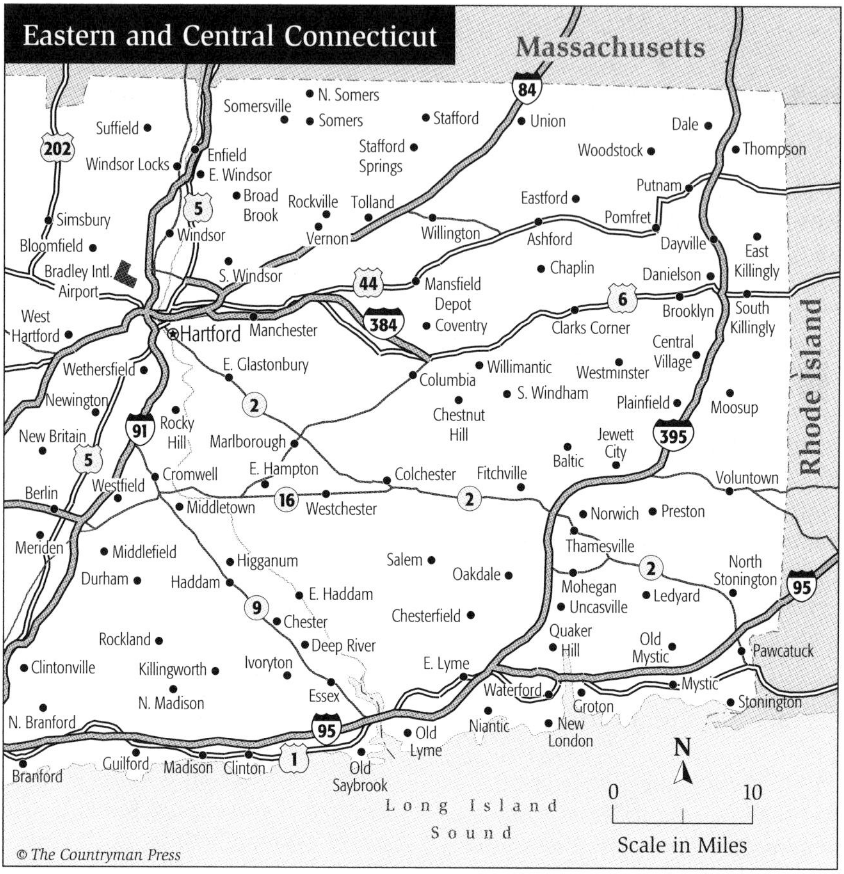

Farmington

Farmington Inn, 827 Farmington Ave., Farmington (860-269-2340; 1-888-720-9755; info@farmingtoninn.com; www.farmingtoninn.com); $79–139 per night. Located in the historic district of Farmington, this luxury hotel has 72 guest rooms and 13 suites, four-poster beds, bathrobes and feather beds in some rooms, cable television and VCRs, desks, in-room irons and hair dryers, marble bathrooms, and an on-site café. Pets are welcome in designated rooms for an additional $20 per night.

Homewood Suites by Hilton Hartford-Farmington, 2 Farm Glen Blvd., Farmington (860-321-0000; www.hilton.com); $110–149 per night. This all-suite facility has 121 include a fitness center and an indoor swimming pool. Pets up to 75 pounds are allowed with prior notice and an additional $75 nonrefundable fee.

Groton

Ramada Groton, 156 Kings Hwy., Groton (860-446-0660; 1-888-215-2756; www.wyndham.com); $59–179 per night. Air-conditioning, a restaurant and lounge, an indoor swimming pool, room service, and in-room movies are some of the amenities offered at this coastal Ramada (formerly a Clarion Inn). Guests can also enjoy complimentary breakfasts and newspapers. Dogs (sorry, no cats) are allowed for an additional $15 per night.

Hartford

Ramada Plaza Hotel, 50 Morgan St., Hartford (860-549-2400; www.wyndham.com); $123–219 per night. This upscale hotel (formerly a Crowne Plaza) offers room service, a concierge desk, a gift shop and newsstand, a swimming pool, wake-up service, a restaurant, complimentary continental breakfasts, cable television with premium movie channels, and in-room coffeemakers, hair dryers, irons, and ironing boards. Pets weighing less than 50 pounds are allowed for a one-time fee of $50 per stay.

Residence Inn Hartford, 942 Main St., Hartford (860-524-5550; www.marriott.com); $179–269 per night. The Residence Inn locations in Hartford, Manchester, Mystic, and Windsor offer lodging for long- and short-term stays, with studios and one- and two-bedroom suites. Most have amenities such as swimming pools, cable television, fitness centers, in-room coffeemakers, laundry facilities, and 24-hour front desks. Your dog is welcome with a one-time fee of $100.

Ledyard

Abbey's Lantern Hill Inn, 780 Lantern Hill Rd., Ledyard (860-572-0483; info@abbeyslanternhill.com; www.abbeyslanternhill.com); $110–159 per night. For an additional $20 per night, pets and their owners can enjoy this inn's Cottage, which comes complete with a private fenced-in patio, hardwood floors, a queen-size bed, ceiling fans, air-conditioning, and cable television. Although the inn is located on a quiet road with a large

ABBEY'S LANTERN HILL INN, JUST DOWN THE ROAD FROM FOXWOODS RESORT CASINO, IS CLOSE TO ALL THE MYSTIC-AREA ATTRACTIONS.

lawn and picnic area, Foxwoods Casino is within walking distance (1/3 mile), and Mystic Seaport and Mohegan Sun Casino are located 6 miles away. Rates include a continental breakfast on weekdays and a full homemade breakfast on weekends.

Residence Inn Hartford Manchester, 201 Hale Rd., Manchester (860-432-4242; www.marriott.com); $174–214. Pets are welcome for an additional $100 "sanitation fee" at this Residence Inn location, where you'll find free on-site parking, 96 suites on three floors, cable television with premium movie channels, daily buffet breakfasts, fireplaces, and an outdoor swimming pool. Each suite also comes equipped with voice mail, feather or foam pillows, a coffeemaker, an alarm clock, and a fully equipped kitchen.

Meriden

Hawthorne Suites by Wyndham Hartford/Meriden, 1151 East Main St., Meriden (203-379-5048; www.wyndham.com); $109–139 per night. Guests at this Hawthorne Suites hotel (formerly a Candlewood Suites) can enjoy high-speed wireless Internet access, a fitness center, laundry facilities, 124 spacious suites with kitchenettes, free local telephone calls, and business services. Dogs weighing less than 60 pounds are permitted for an extra fee of $75 (up to six nights) or $150 (more than seven nights).

Milldale

Days Inn Hartford/Southington/Waterbury, 2109 E. 16th Ave., Milldale (860-621-9181; www.wyndham.com); $69–99 per night. Pets up to 55 pounds are permitted at this Days Inn for an additional $10 per night, where guests will find hair dryers, ironing boards, and coffeemakers in all the rooms, and a fitness center, cable television, free daily continental breakfasts, free newspapers, vending machines, and free parking.

Mystic

Hyatt Place Mystic, 224 Greenmanville Ave., Mystic (860-536-9997; 1-800-833-1516; www.hyatt.com); $179–299 per night. Animals weighing less than 50 pounds are allowed for a one-time fee of $75 for a stay of 1–6 nights. The ideally located hotel has a 24-hour front desk, cable television, a fitness center, and laundry facilities; all the suites have living rooms, coffeemakers, microwaves, refrigerators, and alarm clocks.

Econo Lodge Mystic, 251 Greenmanville Ave., Mystic (860-536-9666; www.choicehotels.com); $75–90 per night. Formerly known as the Old Mystic Motor Lodge, this centrally located motel has 25 rooms, an outdoor swimming pool, Internet access, cable television, exterior corridors, free local telephone calls, free coffee in the lobby, microwaves, irons and ironing boards, and free continental breakfast each morning. Animal owners pay an extra $10 per dog, per stay (not per night). Movie fans may want to grab a bite at nearby Mystic Pizza.

MOVIE BUFFS AND PIZZA FANS WILL ENJOY A "SLICE OF HEAVEN" AT MYSTIC PIZZA. (COURTESY OF MYSTIC COUNTRY)

Harbour Inne & Cottage Bed & Breakfast, 15 Edgemont St., Mystic (860-572-9253; harbour inne@earthlink.net; www .harbourinne-cottage.com); call for rate information. This unique accommodation offers four guest rooms with private bathrooms, a cottage that can accommodate up to six people, and amenities such as air-conditioning, continental breakfasts, cable television, and a location that is central to all the Mystic attractions, including the train station just a block away. Quiet, well-behaved dogs are welcome with prior approval.

Residence Inn Mystic, 40 Whitehall Ave., Mystic (860-536-5150; www.marriott.com); $199–359 per night. This all-suite accommodation offers high-speed Internet access, a swimming pool, on-site parking, meeting rooms, daily buffet breakfasts, free coffee in the lobby, laundry facilities, and a picnic area. Guests can choose from studios and one- and two-bedroom suites. Those traveling with a canine will pay a one-time nonrefundable fee of $100.

New London

Red Roof Inn–New London, 707 Colman St., New London (860-444-0001; 1-800-RED-ROOF; www.redroof.com); $49–89 per night. The New London Red Roof Inn is located near plenty of restaurants. Standard amenities include smoking and nonsmoking rooms, free local telephone calls, alarm clocks, Internet access, free coffee in the lobby, and cable television with premium movie channels. One "well-behaved family pet" is welcome per room.

Niantic

Motel 6, 269 Flanders Rd., Niantic (860-739-6991; www .motel6.com); $49–89 per night. This clean-and-simple motel welcomes your well-behaved dog and offers amenities such as laundry facilities, cable television with premium movie channels (including HBO and NESN), a "kids stay free" program, Internet access, free local telephone calls, and free coffee in the lobby each morning.

Simsbury

Ironhorse Inn, 969 Hopmeadow St. (Rte. 10), Simsbury (860-658-2216; 1-800-245-9938; www .ironhorseinnofsimsbury.com);

$75–160 per night. Guest rooms at the Ironhorse Inn have balconies, voice mail, cable television, microwaves, refrigerators, and mini stoves. Guests can also enjoy a picnic area, a swimming pool, a sauna, walking paths, high-speed Internet access, free daily continental breakfasts, and nearby shops and restaurants in downtown Simsbury. One pet per room, up to 40 pounds, is welcome in designated rooms for an extra $15 per night.

Southington

Motel 6, 625 Queen St., Southington (860-621-7351; www.motel6.com); $49–79 per night. It might not be fancy, but this Motel 6 is part of a dog-friendly chain that will provide you and your pet with a welcome mat and a good night's sleep. The amenities at the Southington location include smoking and nonsmoking rooms, free local telephone calls, free coffee in the lobby, laundry facilities, and cable television with premium channels. Kids stay for free.

Residence Inn Southington, 778 West St., Southington (860-621-4440; www.marriott.com); $179–209 per night. Your dog is welcome at this Residence Inn, although pet owners are asked to pay an extra one-time fee of $100. The all-suite hotel has a 24-hour Grab-n-Go Market with snacks and sundries, free high-speed Internet access, an indoor swimming pool, a hot tub, a fitness center, a complimentary breakfast buffet, and a weekly barbecue.

Stonington

Another Second Penny Inn, 870 Pequot Trail, Stonington (860-535-1710; innkeepers@secondpenny.com; www.secondpenny.com); $129–199 per night. Kelly (the dog), Hobo (the cat), and Tommy Dorsey (the horse) will welcome you to Another Second Penny, a 1710 inn surrounded by 5 acres of forests, fields, and gardens. A five-course breakfast is served daily. For an extra $25 per stay (not per night), one pet weighing less than 40 pounds is welcome in the Noyes Room, which has a private bath, garden views, a king-size bed, a walk-in closet, and a rocking chair.

Stonington Motel, 901 Stonington Rd. (Rte. 1), Stonington (860-599-2330; stoningtonmotel@aol.com; www.stoningtonmotel.com); $60–80 per night. Located within walking distance of trails, a boat ramp, and scenic coves, the Stonington Motel offers accommodations with cable television, air-conditioning, and in-room refrigerators and microwaves. "Small- to medium-size" dogs (call to see if yours qualifies) are welcome, provided they are housebroken, nondestructive, and well behaved. Dog owners pay an extra $20 per night.

Vernon

Howard Johnson Express Inn–Vernon, 451 Hartford Tpke., Vernon (860-875-0781; www.wyndham.com); $69–129 per night. Pets are allowed at this Howard Johnson Express Inn, which offers a 24-hour front desk, a swimming pool, a restaurant, room service, cable television, alarm clocks, nonsmoking rooms, free newspapers, complimentary continental breakfasts, interior corridors, and free parking.

Voluntown

Tamarack Lodge, 21 Ten Rod Rd., Voluntown (860-376-0224; www.tamaracklodgect.com); $50–65 per night. This rustic accommodation, once a former wagon wheel forge, and named for the profusion of tamarack trees on the property, welcomes families—including well-behaved, house-trained pets—to its 20-acre resort with cabins, a private beach, walking paths, a sauna, an outdoor swimming pool, and a lounge. There are no televisions on-site to disturb the peace and quiet, and there are no extra fees for companion animals. The lodge abuts the Pachaug State Forest.

Waterford

Rodeway Inn at Crossroad, 211 Pkwy. N., Waterford (860-442-7227; www.choicehotels.com); $49–149 per night. Formerly known as the Lamplighter Motel, this Rodeway Inn is situated on the central Connecticut shore and offers 38 guest rooms and efficiencies, an outdoor swimming pool, exercise equipment, and cable television. "Small- to medium-size" dogs (call to see if yours qualifies) are allowed with a $25 per dog, per night fee with a maximum of two pets per room.

Wethersfield

Comfort Inn, 1330 Silas Deane Hwy., Wethersfield (860-563-2311; www.choicehotels.com); $79–109 per night. For an extra $20 per night, your pup is welcome to stay at the Comfort Inn. Amenities include free daily continental breakfasts, a fitness center, free newspapers, evening cocktail receptions, interior corridors, meeting rooms, business services, high-speed Internet access, and cable television with premium movie channels.

Motel 6 Hartford–Wethersfield, 1341 Silas Deane Hwy., Wethersfield (860-563-5900; www.motel6.com); $56–75 per night. Located in quaint Wethersfield and convenient to downtown Hartford, this Motel 6 location offers all of the chain's usual amenities. Expect to enjoy free coffee in the lobby, premium movie channels, a "kids stay free" program, free local telephone calls, and laundry facilities. Your well-behaved pet is welcome.

Willington

Rodeway Inn Willington, 327 Ruby Rd., Willington (860-684-1400; www.choicehotels.com); $79–129 per night. If your dog weighs less than 30 pounds, she'll be permitted to stay at this Rodeway for an extra $20 per night. Two pets per room are allowed. The economy hotel has cable television, an exercise room, free local telephone calls, free continental breakfasts, free newspapers, laundry facilities, and voice mail.

Windsor

Residence Inn Hartford–Windsor, 100 Dunfey Ln., Windsor (860-688-7474; www.marriott.com); $99–229 per night. For an extra $100 "sanitation fee," your favorite fluffy friend can join you at this Residence Inn, part of the Marriott hotel chain. The all-suite hotel offers amenities such as a daily buffet breakfast, free local phone calls, a picnic area, a grocery-shopping service, and valet dry-cleaning services. Each suite has a full kitchen, high-speed Internet access, cable television with premium movie channels, and individual climate controls.

Windsor Locks

Baymont Inn & Suites Hartford–Windsor Locks, 260 Main St. East Windsor (860-627-6585; www.wyndham.com); $81–139 per night. Pets are permitted at this airport-convenient hotel offering free shuttles to your airline gate, free daily newspapers, complimentary continental breakfasts each morning, a wake-up service, and a "kids stay free" program. Up to two pets per room, under 50 pounds, are allowed for an additional $50 per stay.

Econo Lodge Inn & Suites, 34 Old Country Rd., Windsor Locks (860-623-2533; www.choicehotels.com); $79–139 per night. The amenities at this Econo Lodge include standard rooms and larger suites, cable television, free continental breakfasts, work desks, an outdoor swimming pool, free coffee in the lobby, free airport shuttles, and in-room coffeemakers. Dogs are permitted for an extra $20 per night with a two-dog-per-room limit.

Motel 6 Hartford–Windsor Locks, 3 National Dr., Windsor Locks (860-292-6200; www.motel6.com); $51–76 per night. Your pup is welcome at all Motel 6 locations, and this one is no exception. Choose from smoking and nonsmoking rooms and take advantage of free morning coffee in the lobby, free local calls, cable television with premium movie channels, laundry facilities, and Internet access. If you happen to have some children in tow, they'll stay for free.

Quality Inn at Bradley Airport, 5 Ella Grasso Tpke., Windsor Locks (860-623-9494; www.choicehotels.com); $115–200 per night. Guests at this Quality Inn can enjoy a complimentary hot breakfast buffet each morning, an indoor heated swimming pool, a restaurant and sports bar, a 24-hour front desk, room service, laundry facilities, and cable television. Canines are welcome for an extra $25 per stay with no weight limit.

Woodstock

Elias Child House Bed & Breakfast, 50 Perrin Rd., Woodstock (860-974-9836; 1-877-974-9836; afelice@earthlink.net; www.eliaschildhouse.com); $100–135 per night. Tucked away in Connecticut's Quiet Corner, this 1700s B&B has two guest rooms and one suite, all with private baths and fireplaces. The home itself boasts nine fireplaces in all, cooking hearths, a beehive oven, and antique furnishings; outside, guests can feel free to explore the B&B's 47 acres. Dogs are welcome for an extra $10 per night. This B&B is for sale, so be sure to call ahead to check the pet policy with the new owners.

Campgrounds

Ashford

Brialee RV and Tent Park, 174 Laurel Ln., P.O. Box 125, Ashford 06278 (860-429-8359; 1-800-303-CAMP; admin@brialee.net; www.brialee.com); $31–49 per night. Two leashed, well-behaved dogs are permitted per site at Brialee, a campground offering a recreation hall, lighted sports courts, three trails for hiking and biking, boat rentals, a sandy beach, a private lake, a heated swimming pool, planned activities, a camp store, a snack bar, restrooms with showers, laundry facilities, and wooded or sunny sites.

© AMMIT JACK/SHUTTERSTOCK.COM

Baltic

Salt Rock State Campground, 120 Scotland Rd. (Rte. 97), Baltic (860-822-0884; www.ct.gov/deep/saltrock); $33–40 per night. This is one of the few state-owned campgrounds where your pet is allowed: Two animals are permitted per site. The campground offers 71 sites for tents and RVs, access to the Shetucket River, restrooms with showers, a swimming pool, and 120 acres of land.

Bozrah

Odetah Camping Resort, 38 Bozrah St. Ext., Bozrah (860-889-4144; 1-800-448-1193; info@odetah.com; www.odetah.com); $45–62 per night. This large family campground is located on a 30-acre lake. The facilities include a beach, wooded sites, a swimming pool, tennis courts, a camp store, a snack bar, restrooms with showers, laundry facilities, a recreation hall, and a pavilion. Well-behaved, quiet dogs are welcome as long as they are leashed and walked off-site.

Chaplin

Nickerson Park Family Campground, 1036 Phoenixville Rd., Chaplin (860-455-0007; camp@nickersonpark.com; www.nickersonpark.com); $35–38 per night. This family-focused campground has 100 sites (some along the riverbank), modern restrooms with showers, laundry facilities, a lodge with a fireplace, a game room, and planned activities. Hiking, mountain biking, and fishing are particularly popular here. Most breeds of dogs are welcome, as long as owners use a leash.

Eastford

Charlie Brown Campground, 98 Chaplin Rd. (Rte. 198), Eastford (860-974-0142; www.charliebrowncampground.com); $37–52 per night. Two pets are permitted per site at Charlie Brown's, a campground offering amenities such as a playground, sports courts, a camp store, a recreation hall, laundry facilities, modern restrooms, tent and RV sites, and stocked trout streams. Dog owners are asked touse a leash, clean up any messes, and bring proof of vaccinations.

Peppertree Camping, Rte. 198, 146 Chaplin Rd., Eastford (860-974-1439; trudy@peppertreecamping.com; www.peppertreecamping.com); $30–35 per night. Well-behaved dogs are welcome at Peppertree, a campground offering sites for RVs and tents, a pavilion, restrooms with showers, a camp store, picnic tables and fire pits, laundry facilities, seasonal sites, and hookups.

MURPH TAKES A BREAK AT THE ELIAS CHILD HOUSE BED & BREAKFAST IN WOODSTOCK, CONNECTICUT. (PHOTO BY TONY FELICE)

The campground is located on the Natchaug River.

East Haddam

Wolf's Den Family Campground, 256 Town St., East Haddam (860-873-9681; information@wolfsdencampground.com; www.wolfsdencampground.com); $45 per night. Campers at Wolf's Den will find 205 sites, an Olympic-size swimming pool, a camp store, laundry facilities, restrooms with showers, a recreation hall with a stage, and special activities like Christmas in August, Country Western Weekend, and lobster bakes. Leashed dogs are permitted in all areas except the playground and the pool area.

East Killingly

Stateline Campresort, Rte. 101, 1639 Hartford Pike, East Killingly (860-774-3016; www.statelinecampresort.com); $28–58 per night. Stateline provides campers with a private lake, a swimming pool, a recreation center, a camp store, a teen center and an adult clubhouse, a snack bar, a playground, boat rentals, and laundry facilities. A full schedule of planned activities includes barbecues, dances, and softball games. Leashed, quiet pets are welcome for an additional $3 per night.

Lebanon

Lake Williams Campground, 1742 Exeter Rd. (Rte. 207), Lebanon (860-642-7761; 1-800-972-0020; lakewilliamscampgd@lwcg.net; www.lakewilliamscampground.net); $33–59 per night. Campers choose from

Pets in Connecticut State Parks

Connecticut has more than 100 state parks, 32 state forests, and 14 state camping areas. While leashed pets are allowed in most parks (except Sherwood Island and Squantz Pond between April 15 and September 30), only four areas allow camping with pets: the three state forest campgrounds allow one pet per site, and Salt Rock Campground allows two pets per site (www.ct.gov/deep/lib/deep/regulations/23/23-4-1through5.pdf).

sunny, wooded, or waterfront sites at Lake Williams, a campground with a boat launch and boat rentals, a playground, a camp store, a recreation hall, laundry facilities, scheduled family activities, hayrides, and modern restrooms. One leashed pet per site is allowed, as long as owners clean up after their animals.

Lisbon

Ross Hill Park Family Campground, 170 Ross Hill Rd., Lisbon (860-376-9606; 1-800-308-1089; rosshillpark@snet.net; www.rosshillpark.com); $43–48 per night. The Ross Hill Park facilities include wooded and sunny sites for RVs and tents, restrooms with showers, three playgrounds, boat rentals, a snack bar, a camp store, breakfast on weekends, laundry facilities, and a pond with a beach. Animal owners are asked to keep their pets on a leash, clean up after them, and not leave them unattended. Two pets are allowed per site.

North Stonington

Mystic KOA Campground, Rte. 49, 118 Pendleton Hill Rd., North Stonington (860-559-5101; 1-800-624-0829; www.koa.com); $42–53 per night. The Mystic KOA, formerly known as Highland Orchards, has sites for RVs as well as tents; guests can also rent on-site camping cabins. The campground's amenities include two swimming pools, restrooms with showers, a miniature golf course, a basketball court, a fishing pond, and a camp store. Located on the site of one of Connecticut's oldest farms, this campground has a fenced dog park for off-leash play.

Old Mystic

Seaport Campground, Rte. 184, 45 Campground Rd., Old Mystic (860-536-4044; www.sunrvresorts.com); $31–42 per night. This campground offers a location that's close to all the Mystic and casino attractions, as well as amenities such as a camp store, laundry facilities, a swimming pool, restrooms, a fishing pond, miniature golf, and organized children's games and entertainment. A maximum of two pets are allowed at each RV site; pets are not allowed at tent sites.

Stafford Springs

Mineral Springs Family Campground, 135 Leonard Rd., Stafford Springs (860-684-2993; www.mineralspringscampground.com); $35–45 per night. Mineral Springs's facilities include a heated recreation hall, modern restrooms, a swimming pool, laundry facilities, a playground, hiking trails, horseshoe pits, a dump station, a camp store, and a fishing/ice-skating pond. Leashed, quiet dogs are welcome as long as owners clean up any messes; canines are not allowed in the pool area or at the playground.

Voluntown

Pachaug State Forest Campgrounds, Rte. 49, Voluntown (860-424-3200); $17–27 at Green Falls and $14–24 at Mount Misery per night. Though dogs are not allowed in Connecticut's state park campgrounds, they are welcome, on a leash, in a few state forest campgrounds like those at Pachaug. The forest offers two distinct camping areas: **Green Falls,** which has 18 sites and a pond; and **Mount Misery,** which has 22 sites and a stream for fishing. One pet per site is allowed.

Willington

Wilderness Lake Campground & Resort, 150 Village Hill Rd., Willington (860-684-6352; info@wilderness-lake.com; www.wilderness-lake.com); $30–45 per night. The facilities at Wilderness Lake include a sandy lake beach, modern restrooms, a recently renovated banquet hall, a miniature golf course, trails for walking and biking, sports courts, an arcade, a playground, canoes, and paddleboats. Two leashed pets are permitted per site; owners must bring proof of vaccinations and clean up after their animals.

Woodstock

Beaver Pines Campground, 1728 Rte. 198, Woodstock (860-974-0110; www.beaverpinescampground.com); $26–47 per night. "Controlled pets are always welcome" at Beaver Pines, where campers will find restrooms with showers, laundry facilities, a camp store, a game room, sports courts, a propane filling station, and planned activities like Bingo Night and picnics. Two leashed dogs are permitted per site.

OUT AND ABOUT

Annual Fur Ball, Protectors of Animals, 144 Main St., East Hartford, Glastonbury (860-569-0722; www.poainc.org). This yearly event is usually held during the winter months at an upscale location such as the Glastonbury Hills Country Club. Put on your finery and help support Protectors of Animals, a nonprofit organization that helps local homeless pets. The group holds other fun fund-raising events throughout the year, including the **"Playin' for the Animals" Golf Tournament** in fall.

Bigelow Hollow State Park and Nipmuck State Forest, Rtes. 171 and 190, Union (c/o Shenipsit State Forest, 166 Chestnut Hill Rd., Stafford Springs 06076; 860-424-3200). Together, these adjoining state preserves provide more than 9,000 acres of open space for exploring. Popular activities include cross-country skiing, hiking, boating, dog walking, snowmobiling, fishing, and wildlife-watching. Canines are welcome but must be leashed at all times.

Bluff Point Coastal Reserve, Depot Rd., Groton (c/o Fort Trumbull State Park, 90 Walbach St., New London 06320; 860-444-7591). Visitors to Bluff Point can experience salt marsh and forest ecosystems while walking along this rocky shoreline and bluff in Groton. It's a great spot for wildlife-watching, hiking, saltwater fishing, cross-country skiing, mountain biking, or just relaxing with an ocean-view picnic. Leashed pets are welcome.

Chatfield Hollow State Park, 381 Rte. 80, Killingworth (860-663-2030). Have a picnic, hike the trails, swim, fish, skate, ski, or just relax at this 355-acre park centered on artificial Schreeder Pond. Park facilities include a restroom, a concession stand, parking areas, and a picnic shelter. Neighboring **Cockaponset State Forest** provides additional miles of trails. Dogs are welcome on a leash, although they are not permitted on the beach or in the water at the swimming pond.

Comstock Covered Bridge, Comstock Bridge Rd., East Hampton. One of the last remaining covered bridges in the state, this 90-foot span has an original Howe truss; it was first built in 1791 and rehabilitated in 1840. The bridge crosses the Salmon River and carries foot traffic only. After crossing, you can enjoy a walk and picnic in the nearby state forest.

Day Pond State Park, Day Pond Rd., Colchester (c/o Eastern District Headquarters, 209 Hebron Rd., Marlborough 06447; 860-295-9523). Fully stocked with trout, Day Pond attracts fishing enthusiasts, history buffs, and hikers with 180 acres of land and water. Parking, flush toilets, telephones, and picnic areas are available. Dogs must be leashed.

Devil's Hopyard State Park, 366 Hopyard Rd., East Haddam (860-873-8566). Your pet won't be permitted at the on-site campground in this state park, but you and your furry friend are nonetheless welcome to roam the site's trails and relax in the picnic area. The origin of the park's interesting name is a bit of a mystery: One legend speculates about the creation of perfectly cylindrical round holes at Chapman Falls. Early settlers, finding it hard to believe that nature could have created the holes, looked instead to a more sinister source.

Fort Griswold Battlefield State Park, 57 Fort St., Groton (860-

449-6877). Leashed dogs can join their owners in exploring this unique commemorative park, the site of a Revolutionary War battle in which notorious traitor Benedict Arnold led a massacre. Parking is free, and amenities include picnic tables, restrooms, and a small museum.

Fort Saybrook Monument Park, Rte. 154, Saybrook Point, Old Saybrook (860-395-3123). This scenic 18-acre city park has a boardwalk, views of the Connecticut River, and displays detailing the history of the original Saybrook Colony and the Algonquin Nehantic Native American tribe that once lived here.

Fort Trumbull State Park, 90 Walbach St., New London (860-444-7591). Although leashed pups are technically allowed within this park, they are not permitted in the fort or on the impressive fishing pier—taking away most visitors' reasons for visiting at all. Dog lovers are probably better off sticking with one of the other nearby parks for a fun outing.

Gay City State Park, Rte. 85,Hebron (c/o Eastern District Headquarters, 209 Hebron Rd., Marlborough 06447; 860-295-9523). One of Connecticut's most interesting parks, this 1,500-acre gem surrounds an abandoned 18th-century village. You can still see the foundations of the houses and mills as you walk the trails and cross-country ski. Visitors can also swim, fish, and picnic. **Meshomasic State Forest** is right next door. Pets must be leashed and are not allowed on the beach.

Gillette Castle State Park, 67 River Rd., East Haddam (860-526-2336). Gillette Castle is one of Connecticut's most popular tourist stops. The 24-room mansion was designed and built by William Hooker Gillette and is open for tours. As you might guess, doggie visitors are not permitted inside the castle, but you and Rover can enjoy a picnic on the grounds and admire the building's impressive architecture from the outside.

Haddam Meadows State Park, Rte. 154, Haddam (c/o Chatfield Hollow State Park, 381 Rte. 80, Killingworth 06419; 860-663-2030). This is a popular spot from which boaters and others can access the Connecticut River. The 175-acre property has open spaces for sports, picnic areas, a boat launch, parking areas, walking paths, and an access road for vehicles that winds around the perimeter. Leashed pets are welcome.

Hammonasset Beach State Park, 1288 Boston Post Rd., P.O. Box 271, Madison 06443 (203-245-2785). One of the state's most-loved parks, Hammonasset boasts 919 acres, 2 miles of sandy beach, nature trails, an environmental education center, a bike trail, sport fields, saltwater fishing opportunities, picnic areas, restrooms, a pavilion, and a concession stand. Companion animals, unfortunately, are not permitted on the beach or in the campground. They are welcome in other areas as long as they're leashed.

Heritage Trail Vineyards, 291 N. Burnham Hwy., Lisbon (860-376-0659; vintner@heritagetrail.com; www.heritagetrail.com). Stop by this eastern-Connecticut vineyard for a peek at the production of wines made with estate-grown grapes. The scenic property encompasses 38 acres with a pond and deck for relaxing. Leashed dogs are welcome, though Heritage Trail president Diane M. Powell advises caution on the vineyard's busy two-lane road.

Hopeville Pond State Park, Rte. 201, Griswold (860-376-2920). This 544-acre park provides opportunities for nearly every conceivable recreational activity, including hiking, canoeing, mountain biking, fishing, boating, and picnicking. Visitors can also take advantage of restrooms, parking areas, a boat launch, and a concession stand. Dogs must be leashed and are not allowed on the beach or in the campground.

Mansfield Hollow State Park, Bassetts Bridge Rd., Mansfield (c/o Mashamoquet Brook State Park, Wolf Den Dr., Pomfret Center 06259; 860-928-6121). Fishing and hiking are the two most popular pursuits at Mansfield Hollow, where visitors can enjoy a boat ramp, picnic tables, and numerous trails for walking, mountain biking, and exploring. An Army Corps of Engineers dam created the park's 500-acre lake; because it is used as a public water supply, no swimming is allowed.

Mashamoquet Brook State Park, 147 Wolf Den Dr., Pomfret Center (860-928-6121). According to the Connecticut DEP, this state park offers "hiking, camping, fishing, and swimming for the whole family." That's not quite true—if one member of your family happens to have fur and a tail. Dogs are prohibited from the campground, the beach, and the picnic shelter at Mashamoquet, but they are allowed, on a leash, on the hiking trails and at the outdoor picnic area.

Millers Pond State Park Reserve, Foot Hills Rd., Durham (c/o Chatfield Hollow State Park, 381 Rte. 80, Killingworth 06419; 860-663-2030). With a 30-acre pond and more than 170 acres of woods, you and Spot can easily spend a pleasant afternoon at Millers Pond. Facilities are minimal, although you will find a parking area and pit toilets. Anglers come here for the healthy population of trout and smallmouth bass. Dogs must be leashed.

Mystic Seaport, 75 Greenmanville Ave. (Rte. 27), Mystic (860-572-5315; 1-888-9-SEAPORT; visitor.services@mysticseaport.org; www.mysticseaport.org); $15–24 per person. Sneak a peek at Connecticut's maritime past at this living-history museum with tall ships and a 40-acre re-created village with a one-room schoolhouse, a general store, a chapel, a meetinghouse, a bank, a printing office, a tavern, a ship chandlery, and other relevant buildings. Leashed pets are allowed on the grounds, though not on the ships or in the exhibit buildings and restaurants.

Natchaug State Forest, Pilfershire Rd., Eastford (c/o Mashamoquet Brook State Park, Wolf Den Dr., Pomfret Center 06259; 860-928-6121). Natchaug is well known among horse lovers, who enjoy riding on the forest's many equestrian trails. But you don't have to have a horse to visit the park, which also provides hiking and cross-country skiing trails, fishing opportunities, and picnic areas. Your dog is welcome on a leash.

Nehantic State Forest, Rte. 156, Lyme (c/o Gillette Castle State Park, 67 River Rd., East Haddam 06423; 860-526-2336). Visitors to Nehantic State Forest will find picnic tables, water views, and plenty of opportunities for boating, swimming, and hiking. Leashed dogs are welcome. One note of caution: So-called Lyme disease gets its name from this very town, where those troublesome ticks cause no end of trouble for locals and their pets. Be sure to check your pets, your kids, and yourself carefully for clinging ticks when it's time to go home.

Northwest Park, Lang Rd., Windsor (860-285-1886; www.northwestpark.org). This town-owned property boasts 473 acres with 12 miles of trails, concerts, nature programs for adults and children, picnic areas, cross-country ski and snowshoe rentals, and community gardens. Pets are welcome on a leash. For more information and a trail map, visit the Friends of Northwest Park Web site, listed above.

Olde Mistick Village, junction of Rte. 27 and Coogan Blvd., Mystic (860-536-4941). This charming outdoor shopping center has tree-lined walking paths, flower gardens, a pond, shady greens, a gazebo, clothing boutiques, toy stores, maritime gift shops, candle makers, a movie theater, bakeries, and restaurants. Several of the shops have animal themes, from wildlife critters to dogs and cats (see **Raining Cats and Dogs** under "Hot Spots for Spot"). The village is open daily year-round.

Pachaug State Forest, Rte. 49, P.O. Box 5, Voluntown 06384 (860-376-4075). Animal lovers will appreciate this preserve's dog-friendly campgrounds (see "Accommodations"), along with its scenic views, picnic areas, and trails for hiking, snowmobiling, and horseback riding. You can also swim, fish, access the on-site boat launch, or explore the park's rhododendron sanctuary. Pets are allowed on a leash.

Penwood State Park, 57 Gun Mill Rd., Bloomfield (860-242-1158). Penwood offers more than enough activities to keep everyone in the family busy: The 787-acre park has a bike trail, cross-country skiing and hiking trails, a nature center, scenic views, picnic areas, parking areas, and restrooms. Pets are welcome on a leash in the picnic areas and on the trails.

Prudence Crandall Museum, Canterbury Green, Canterbury (860-546-9916). Leashed pets are allowed on the grounds (but not in the house) at this notable site, a National Historic Landmark and the location of New England's first academy for young black women, established by Prudence Crandall on April 1, 1833. Crandall and her students were forced to close the academy shortly thereafter in 1834, having endured harassment and violence from protestors in the community. In 1995, Connecticut named Crandall as the official State Female Hero. The museum is also a stop along the Connecticut Freedom Trail.

Quaddick State Park, 818 Town Farm Rd., Thompson (c/o Mashamoquet Brook State Park, Wolf Den Dr., Pomfret Center 06259; 860-928-6121). This former Native American fishing village has a reservoir, parking areas, public telephones, restrooms, sports fields, and a boat launch. Popular activities include boating, fishing, swimming, and picnicking. Dogs must be leashed and are not allowed on the beach.

Rocky Neck State Park, 244 W. Main St. (Rte. 156), East Lyme (860-739-5471). The two highlights of this park—the beach and the campground—are decidedly unfriendly to dogs. But canine-loving visitors can still enjoy an outdoor meal in the picnic area and explore the diverse hiking trails.

Salmon River State Forest, Rte. 16, Colchester (c/o Eastern District Headquarters, 209 Hebron Rd., Marlborough 06477; 860-295-9523). Your leashed pet is welcome at Salmon River, a popular fly-fishing and hiking spot. Visitors can also access hiking, mountain biking, horseback riding, and cross-country skiing trails, explore remnants of historic buildings, fish, or have a picnic. The preserve adjoins neighboring **Day Pond State Park** (see page 35).

Shenipsit State Forest, Rte. 190, Stafford (860-424-3200). The facilities are limited at this 6,100-acre forest—just a parking area and pit toilets—but the property provides ample opportunity for solitude and wildlife-watching. Hike the trails, take in the views, fish, have a picnic, or just enjoy the quiet. Dogs must be leashed.

Stratton Brook State Park, 194 Stratton Brook Rd., Simsbury (860-658-1388). Completely handicapped accessible, Stratton Brook features a railroad-bed-turned-bike path, babbling brooks, swimming and fishing opportunities, and 148 acres of woods. Cross-country skiing is allowed in winter; dogs must be on a leash.

Wright's Mill Farm, 65 Creasy Rd., Canterbury (860-774-1455; info@wrightsmillfarm.com; www.wrightsmillfarm.com). This

Christmas tree farm and popular wedding site welcomes pets on leashes; the farm hosts activities throughout the year, including farm tours and hayrides, and annual events like Oktoberfest, and a Father's Day picnic. Visitors are also welcome at the on-site 300-year-old mill complex and 20-acre pond.

QUICK BITES

Harry's Place, 104 Broadway, Colchester (860-537-2410; www.harrysplace.biz). Always busy, this seasonal take-out restaurant isn't fancy: You'll eat your burgers, hot dogs, ice cream, lobster bisque, and fish sandwiches on disposable plates at picnic tables in the parking lot. But no one in the long lines ever seems to mind.

Hot Tomato's Ristorante at Union Place, 1 Union Pl., Hartford (860-249-5100; www.hottomatos.net). Reservations are recommended at Hot Tomato's, a long-standing favorite in Hartford with an indoor dining room and a large patio seating area with views of Bushnell Park. Diners will find menu items such as "world famous garlic bread," Three Devil Shrimp, salmon, Osso Buco, New York strip steak, and swordfish.

North End Deli and Catering, 991 Poquonnock Rd., Groton (860-448-0600; www.northenddeli.com). Create your own sandwich combination or choose from the North End's specialties. At dinnertime, pasta, chicken, and seafood meals are available for takeout; call ahead and they'll have your order ready when you arrive. One-of-a-kind sandwich creations include The Hanover Street, The South Street Seaport, and The Empire.

The Place, 901 Boston Rd., Guilford (203-453-9276; www.theplaceguilford.com). The first sign you see here says PUT YOUR RUMP ON A STUMP, and they really mean it! UCLA (that's the United Clam Lovers of America, of course) gave this ultracasual outdoor restaurant its top vote for Best Non-Fried Clams on the Planet. That's a pretty big endorsement for such a low-key spot—diners sit on stumps (literally) at round tables and choose from menu items on a large wooden sign reading "This must be THE PLACE." In addition to steamers, you'll also find rib-eye steak, bluefish, roasted corn, lobster, and a great big outdoor barbecue. Well-behaved dogs are permitted with responsible owners.

Pump House Grille, 63 Elm St. (Bushnell Park), Hartford (860-728-6730). Open seasonally, this outdoor café is located in Bushnell Park and serves casual fare such as sandwiches, soups,

MYSTIC SEAPORT AS SEEN FROM ACROSS THE MYSTIC RIVER (PHOTO BY MICHAEL MELFORD, COURTESY OF MYSTIC COUNTRY, CONNECTICUT)

salads, wraps, fruit salads, and burgers. Don't be surprised if you hear live music in the afternoon or evening.

Rein's New York–Style Deli and Restaurant, 435 Hartford Tpke. (Rte. 30), Vernon (860-875-1344; www.reinsdeli.com). You'll see the signs for Rein's along I-84; many travelers have been happy they took Exit 65 and tried one of the sandwiches at the Connecticut institution. You'll find a plethora of take-out options, including bagels with cream cheese, pastrami reubens, meat knishes, cheddar fries, triple-decker sandwiches, salads, and even bread pudding.

Sea View Snack Bar, 145 Greenmanville Ave. (Rte. 27), Mystic (860-572-0096; www.seaviewsnackbar.com). This decidedly casual spot offers wonderful views of the water, and picnic tables with umbrellas. You can order treats like fried seafood and soft-serve ice cream from the take-out window.

Vanilla Bean Café, 450 Deerfield Rd., P.O. Box 206, Pomfret 06258 (860-928-1562; www.thevanillabeancafe.com). This popular café has indoor and outdoor seating, hot and cold sandwiches, soups, baked treats, and cold drinks, including beer and wine. Breakfast is served on weekends and full dinners are served Wednesday through Sunday. For your browsing pleasure, the café also has gallery space.

HOT SPOTS FOR SPOT

Best Friends Pet Care, 60 Harris Rd., **Avon** (860-673-0555); 1511 Silas Deane Hwy., **Rocky Hill** (860-721-8080; www.bestfriends petcare.com). These two Best Friends locations (the Avon site is also known as Mountain View Kennel) offer overnight boarding, pup playgroups, grooming, doggie day care (aka Doggy Day Camp), training services, and multiple-pet discounts. For more information on all the Best Friends Pet Care locations, call 1-888-FOR-PETS or visit the Web site.

Candlewick Kennels, 2811 Hebron Ave., Glastonbury (860-633-6878; www.candlewick kennels.com). Animal guests at Candlewick can take advantage of grooming services at The Spa, sniff out some new toys in Bartholomew's pet shop, or check in for boarding. Playtime sessions, which can include anything from a brushing to walk in the woods, are available for an extra charge. The kennel recently began to offer training services, as well.

Creature Comforts Animal Inn, 454 Providence New London Tpke. (Rte. 184), North Stonington (860-599-1784; www .ccanimalinn.com). The "innkeepers" at Creature Comforts strive to make your pet's stay with them fun and stress free: Dogs have access to indoor/outdoor runs and enjoy supervised playtimes in fenced-in areas, while cats relax in 4-by-6-foot kitty condos with skylights and scratching posts.

DJ's Grooming and Pet Supply, 119 Oakland St., Manchester (860-649-0485). DJ's staffers have been washing, clipping, and beautifying pets in the Greater Hartford area for more than 20 years. The shop also sells food and supplies for companion animals. Reservations are recommended for grooming.

Maple Ridge Kennels, 270 Rogers Rd., Groton (860-445-4999; mrkbark@aol.com). Maple Ridge provides grooming and boarding services for both dogs and cats. Canine visitors enjoy heated and air-conditioned indoor/outdoor runs, while felines have a separate, quiet boarding area. Optional dog-walking services are available upon request. Reservations are recommended: Bring vaccination records with you at check-in.

Pawsitive Park, 261 Asylum St., Norwich (860-367-2660; www .pawsitivepark.com). Managed by the City of Norwich, Pawsitive Park is an off-leash dog park that was renamed the Estelle Cohn Memorial Dog Park. With walking paths, off-leash areas, and wading pools, your pooch will have a ball. **Raining Cats and Dogs,** Building One, Old Mistick Village, Rte. 27, Mystic (860-536-2280). Located within the popular Old Mistick Village shopping area, this fun shop stocks everything an animal lover could want, including breed-specific gifts, clothing, welcome mats, mugs, and books. You'll also find water bowls, key chains, wind chimes, greeting cards, magnets, and other items emblazoned with images of dogs and cats.

ANIMAL SHELTERS AND HUMANE SOCIETIES

Animal Friends of Connecticut, P.O. Box 370306, West Hartford 06137 (860-232-1393; www.afocinc.org)

The Animal Haven, 89 Mill Rd., North Haven (203-239-2641; www.theanimalhaven.com)

Animal Welfare and Rights Entity (AWARE), P.O. Box 598, Tolland 06084 (860-871-2315)

Connecticut Humane Society Fox Memorial Clinic, 701B Russell Rd., Newington (860-666-3337; www.cthumane.org)

Connecticut Humane Society Headquarters, 701 Russell Rd., Newington (1-800-452-0114; www.cthumane.org)

Connecticut Humane Society Waterford Branch, 169 Old Colchester Rd., P.O. Box 41, Quaker Hill 06375 (860-442-8583; www.cthumane.org)

Helping Paws, P.O. Box 476, Colchester 06415 (860-267-0496; www.helpingpawsinc.org)

Meriden Humane Society, 311 Murdock Ave., Meriden (203-238-3650; www.meridenhs.petfinder.com)

Whiskers Animal Shelter, 342 Lathrop Rd., Plainfield (860-564-7138; www.petfinder.com/shelters/whiskers)

IN CASE OF EMERGENCY

Clinton Veterinary Hospital, 93 Old Post Rd., Clinton (860-669-5721)

Companion Animal Hospital, 801 Poquonnock Rd. #1, Groton (860-449-9800)

Connecticut Veterinary Center, 470 Oakwood Ave., West Hartford (860-233-8564)

Dayville Veterinary Clinic, 21 Putnam Pike, Dayville (860-779-2700)

Norwich Animal Hospital, 439 Salem Tpke., Bozrah (860-889-1387)

Tolland Veterinary Hospital, 70 Hartford Tpke., Tolland (860-875-5748)

TWO FRIENDS ENJOY THE VIEW FROM THE LOOKOUT AT WEBB MOUNTAIN PARK IN MONROE.

Western Connecticut

Though geographically small, this region nonetheless seems to have something to please every personality and taste. Drive a half hour in any direction and you'll stumble upon communities that are as different from each other as, well, cats and dogs. Down near New York City, exclusive waterfront towns like Greenwich, Darien, and New Canaan are home to sprawling mansions, gated neighborhoods, and country clubs. Travel north and you'll find lakes, quiet suburbs, and the friendly working-class cities of Danbury and Waterbury. Places like Fairfield and New Haven, meanwhile, provide diverse populations, great restaurants, world-class universities, and lots of green space.

As lively and interesting as southwestern Connecticut is, its visitors tend to come more for business than for pleasure. If you're looking for a vacation spot, however, the northern reaches of the Housatonic Valley and Litchfield Hills offer your best bet for a quiet getaway. Once you've found a place to stay (note: pets are not allowed in most state park campgrounds but are allowed in state forest campgrounds with a one-pet-per-site limit), you and your pet can set out to explore rivers, covered bridges, downtown shopping areas, town greens, vast natural areas, and state forests and parks. The region provides a unique blend of rural charm and urban sophistication; whether you want to join the crowd or keep to yourself, the sights, sounds, and smells offer a quintessential New England experience.

ACCOMMODATIONS

Hotels, Motels, Inns, and Bed & Breakfasts

Bethel

Microtel Inn & Suites by Wyndham, 80 Benedict Rd., Bethel (203-748-8318; www.wyndham.com); $72–119 per night. Choose from standard guest rooms and suites at this recently built Microtel; all rooms have coffeemakers, hair dryers, and cable television with premium movie channels, while suites also have microwaves, sinks, and refrigerators. Pet owners pay a refundable security deposit of $100 and an extra $11 per night, per pet.

Branford

Motel 6 New Haven–Branford, 320 E. Main St., Branford (203-483-5828; www.motel6.com); $39–80 per night. This Motel 6, located about 9 miles from downtown New Haven, offers the economy chain's standard amenities, including cable television with premium movie channels, free local calls, coffee in the lobby, a "kids stay free" program, and Internet access. Pets are welcome.

Bridgeport

Holiday Inn Bridgeport, 1070 Main St., Bridgeport (203-334-1234; www.ihg.com); $104–139 per night. This high-rise hotel is located near the new baseball and hockey stadiums and offers an indoor swimming pool, room service, free newspapers, a fitness center, alarm clocks, in-room movies, a florist, and a gift shop. Dogs weighing less than 20 pounds are welcome; pet owners will be charged a refundable $50 deposit and $15 per night.

Brookfield

Newbury Inn & Suites, 1030 Federal Rd. (Rtes. 7/202), Brookfield (203-775-0220; www.newburyinn.com); $85–125 per night. Recently renovated, the Newbury Inn (formerly the Twin Tree Inn) offers affordable luxury with spacious suites and spa-like bathrooms, some with Jacuzzi tubs. Located near Candlewood Lake, the inn provides a deluxe continental breakfast, included in the room rate, and pets are welcome for an additional $10 per night, with no weight restrictions.

Cornwall Bridge

Cornwall Inn & Lodge, 270 Kent Rd. (Rte. 7), Cornwall Bridge (860-672-6884; 1-800-786-6884; www.cornwallinn.com); $159–259 per night. This family-owned

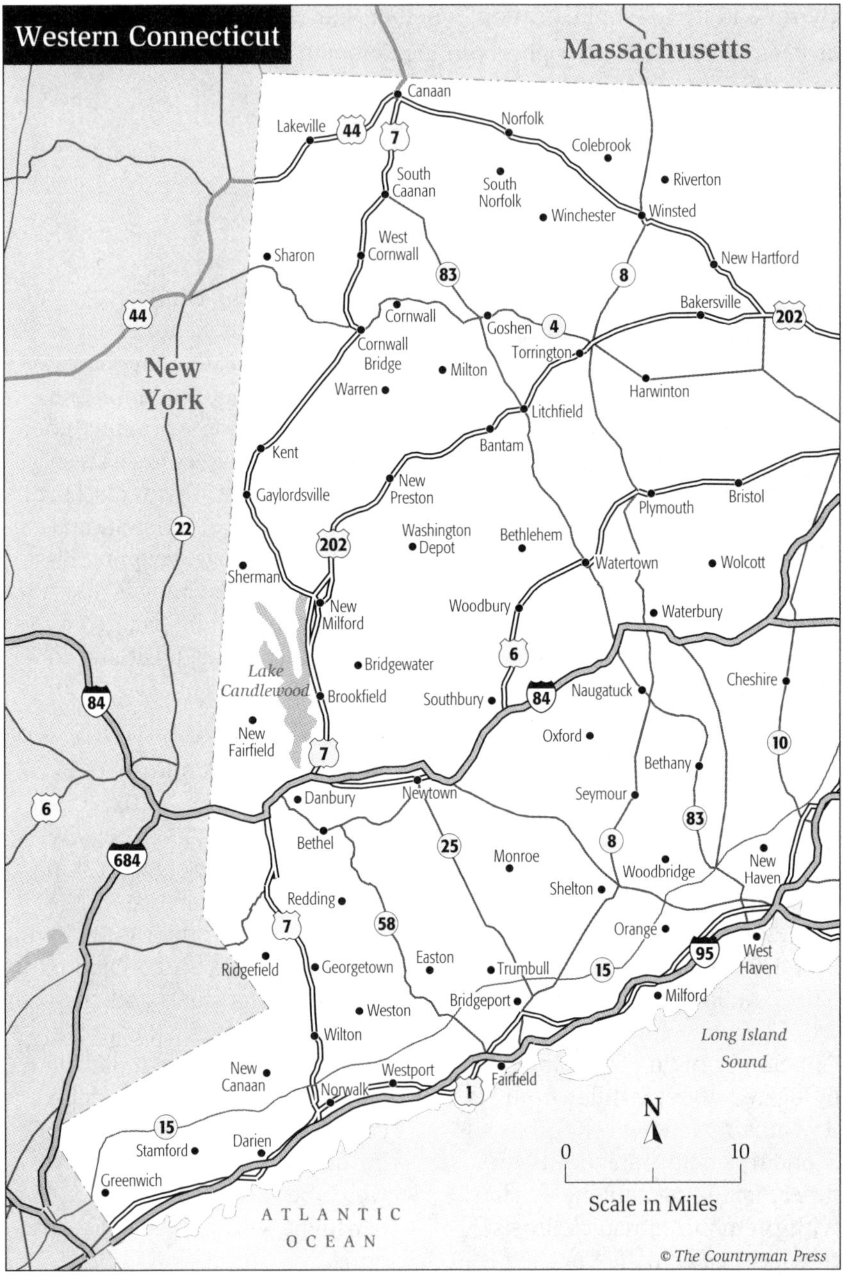

inn has an intimate atmosphere and 3 acres of grounds with a swimming pool, a hot tub, and a rambling stream. The inn is made up of two buildings: The pet-friendly Country Lodge building has eight rooms, all of which offer air-conditioning, private baths, and cable television. The main inn building houses a restaurant and tavern, along with more guest rooms. The rates include daily continental breakfasts. Pet owners pay an additional $20 per stay.

Danbury

Residence Inn Danbury, 22 Segar St., Danbury (203-797-1256; www.marriott.com); $139–179per night. Choose from studios, one-bedroom suites, and two-bedroom suites at this Residence Inn, where the amenities include a swimming pool, a hot tub, a fitness center, a complimentary daily breakfast buffet, and high-speed Internet access. Your pup will be welcome for an extra $100 per stay (not per night).

La Quinta Inn & Suites Danbury, 116 Newtown Rd., Danbury (203-798-1200; www.lq.com); $109–146 per night. Pets are permitted at this Danbury hotel (formerly known as the Wellesley Inn Danbury), which offers free newspapers, an indoor swimming pool, a "kids stay free" program, a business center, a wake-up service, free continental breakfasts, meeting rooms, and room service.

Lakeville

Interlaken Inn Resort and Conference Center, 74 Interlaken Rd., Lakeville (860-435-9878; 1-800-222-2909; info@interlakeninn.com; www.interlakeninn.com); $139–199 per night. This pet-friendly resort has been welcoming guests for more than 100 years with tennis courts, a swimming pool, an adjoining golf course, a game room, a fitness center with spa services, and 30 acres with two lakes. Animals are welcome in the Woodside Building rooms, which can accommodate up to four people; in the Townhouse Suites, which come with fireplaces and kitchens; and in the Townhouse Rooms. Pets are welcome with an additional $20 per-day fee, and the resort has numerous pet-friendly hiking trails, as well as off-leash play areas. The Pet Away Package includes amenities for both pets and their owners.

Wake Robin Inn, 106 Sharon Rd. (Rte. 41), Lakeville (860-435-2000; info@wakerobininn.com; www.wakerobininn.com); $149 per night. Surrounded by 12 hilltop acres, this historic inn was once the home of the Taconic School for Young Girls. Pets weighing less than 40 pounds are allowed in the inn's 15 summer motel units for an additional $10 per stay (not per night).

Milford

Red Roof Inn–Milford, 10 Rowe Ave., Milford (203-877-6060; www.redroof.com); $66–79 per night. This Red Roof Inn location has 110 rooms, exterior corridors, laundry facilities, cable television, a "kids stay free" program, alarm clocks, free local calls, daily newspapers, and express check-out services. One pet per room is welcome without extra charges.

New Haven

New Haven Suites, 3 Long Wharf Dr., New Haven (203-777-5337; 1-866-458-0232; www.newhavensuites.com); $119–209 per night. A short drive from downtown New Haven and Yale University, this all-suite hotel is the first "green" extended-stay hotel in the area. After a $4 million renovation, the hotel boasts modern rooms, many with fireplaces, free Wi-Fi, a swimming pool, a 24-hour front desk, cable TV, laundry services, and a complimentary breakfast buffet. Pets are welcome but must be crated when left in the room.

Omni New Haven at Yale, 155 Temple St., New Haven (203-772-6664; www.omnihotels.com); $161–425 per night. Just steps from the Yale campus, the Omni combines modern amenities with traditional New England charm. Pets 25 pounds and under are welcome for a $50 fee per stay. The hotel boasts a restaurant and fitness center and is steps from several walking trails for you and your four-legged friend to enjoy.

Norwalk

Homestead Studio Suites Norwalk, 400 Main Ave., Norwalk (203-847-6888; www.extendedstayamerica.com); $105–155 per night. Each suite is equipped with a kitchen, air-conditioning, cable television, voice mail, a desk, a coffeemaker with complimentary coffee, an iron, and an ironing board. Guests will also find laundry facilities on-site. One dog of any size is permitted per room for an additional $25 per night (with a $75 maximum charge).

Silvermine Tavern, 194 Perry Ave., Norwalk (203-847-4558; 1-800-693-9967; innkeeper@silverminetavern.com; www.silverminetavern.com); $135–160 per night. This inn and restaurant is a local favorite. Although pets are not allowed in the main building, they are welcome to stay in the rooms just across the street at no extra charge. The tavern serves hearty New England fare in indoor and outdoor seating areas overlooking a millpond; all of the inn's guest rooms are filled with antique furnishings.

Shelton

Hyatt House, 830 Bridgeport Ave., Shelton (203-225-0700; www.hyatt.com); $118–178 per night. The Hyatt House brand prides itself on residentially inspired décor to make guests feel right at home. Smaller than the traditional Hyatt Hotels, Hyatt Houses offer modern suites with kitchens and work areas, free Wi-Fi, plush bedding, and comfy seating areas with a complimentary Bistro breakfast with made-to-order omelets that adds to the luxurious feel on a moderate budget. One dog up to 50 pounds is welcome for a fee of $75 per stay. The hotel is located along the restaurant and retail corridor, just west of New Haven.

Homestead Studio Suites Shelton, 945 Bridgeport Ave., Shelton (203-926-6868; www.extendedstayamerica.com); $99–159 per night. Designed for long-term stays, these accommodations provide separate living areas and full kitchens in each suite, cable television, alarm clocks, free local calls, voice mail, business services, and air-conditioning. The extra charge for pets is $25 per night, with a maximum charge of $150. One dog of any size is welcome per room.

Residence Inn Shelton Fairfield County, 1001 Bridgeport Ave., Shelton (203-926-9000; www.marriott.com); $89–139 per night. Residence Inns offer larger-than-average accommodations, including studios and one- and two-bedroom suites with kitchens or kitchenettes. High-speed Internet access, fireplaces, free shuttles, a swimming pool, a hot tub, and free continental breakfasts are also offered. For an extra $100 per stay (not per night), your dog is welcome to join you.

Southbury

Crowne Plaza, 1284 Strongtown Rd., Southbury (203-598-7600; www.ihg.com); $109–180 per night. The Crowne Plaza provides its guests with amenities such as valet laundry services, a gift shop, room service, a business center, meeting rooms, Internet access, local shuttles, a lounge, and a multilingual staff. Pets are permitted with no weight restrictions for an additional $25 per stay.

Stamford

Hilton Stamford, 1 First Stamford Pl., Stamford (203-967-2222; www.hilton.com); $152–209 per night. This modern Hilton, close to downtown Stamford, welcomes pets up to 75 pounds with a $50 fee per stay. You'll find all the amenities you expect from this chain, including an indoor heated pool, fitness center, and full service restaurant with tasteful and comfortable rooms and suites.

Stamford Marriott Hotel & Spa, 243 Tresser Blvd., Stamford (203-357-9555; www.marriott.com); $109–299 per night. If you have a big buddy, the Stamford Marriott is a good choice, since there are no weight limits and a reasonable $49 fee per stay. Located in the heart of downtown, across the street from the Stamford Town Center Mall, this full-service hotel has an indoor/outdoor pool, restaurant, and bar that combine urban amenities with New England charm.

Campgrounds

Barkhamsted

American Legion State Forest and Peoples State Forest Campgrounds, W. River Rd., Barkhamsted (860-379-0922); $14–17 for residents, $24–27 for non-residents per site. Though pets are not allowed in any state park campgrounds, they are allowed, on a leash, in state forest campgrounds. The American Legion property has 30 sites, flush toilets, and trails for hiking and cross-country skiing. One pet is allowed per site. For more park information, see "Out and About."

White Pines Campsites, 232 Old North Rd., Barkhamsted (860-379-0124; 1-800-622-6614; www.whitepinescamp.com); $47–59 per night. Campers at White Pines can enjoy wooded and open sites for tents and

RVs, cabin rentals, a swimming pool, a pond, game courts and fields, a camp store, a snack bar, scheduled events and activities, paddleboats, and a game room. Leashed pets are welcome, provided they are walked in the designated area and are not left unattended.

East Canaan

Lone Oak Campsites, 360 Norfolk Rd., P.O. Box 640, East Canaan 06024 (860-824-7051; 1-800-422-2267; loneoakinc@aol.com; www.loneoakcampsites.com); $59–70 per night. Lone Oak Campsites offers its guests amenities like the Chipmunk Market & Deli, the Hayloft Lounge, two swimming pools, a kiddie pool, a hot tub, a recreation hall, and planned activities like table-tennis tournaments, swim races, bingo, and adult happy hours. Leashed dogs are welcome, as long as owners agree to clean up after them.

Litchfield

White Memorial Foundation Campgrounds, 17 Whitehall Rd., P.O. Box 368, Litchfield 06759 (860-567-0857; info@whitememorialcc.org); $14.50–17.50 per site. The White Memorial Foundation operates three campgrounds at its 4,000-acre conservation area: **Pine Grove Campground** is available for groups only and is free for nonprofit youth groups; the **Windmill Hill Family Campground** has 18 sites; and the **Point Folly Family Campground** at Bantam Lake has 47 sites. Dogs must be on leashes.

Note: Connecticut residents receive a significant discount on state park camping fees. If you're traveling with a state resident, they must make the reservation in order to qualify for the resident rate.

OUT AND ABOUT

American Legion State Forest, W. River Rd., Barkhamsted (860-379-0922; 860-379-2469). This 78-acre park offers hiking, snowshoeing, and cross-country skiing trails, picnic areas, restrooms, sports fields, a campground (see "Accommodations—Campgrounds"), and access to the Farmington River. The trails provide great views of the valley and the river. The park was named for the organization that donated the original plot of 213 acres.

Ansonia Nature and Recreation Center, 10 Deerfield Rd., Ansonia (203-736-1053; ansnaturectr@snet.net; www.ansonianaturecenter.org). This former farm is now open free to the public as a 104-acre nature center and park with more than 2 miles of trails, a pond, fields, wetland areas, a butterfly garden, a visitors center, picnic areas, and recreation fields. Dogs are welcome on a leash.

Bark Park, Governor St., Ridgefield (203-431-2755; www.fairfieldcountyonline.com). Scenic Ridgefield already has a lot going for it: Now it has a dog park, too. This fenced-in, leash-free area is divided into two sections (for small and large dogs), and also offers benches and water.

Black Rock State Park, Rte. 6, Watertown (c/o Topsmead State Forest, P.O. Box 1081, Litchfield 06759; 860-567-5694). This is a great park, but not necessarily for dog lovers—canines are not permitted in the campground or on the beach. However, it's loaded with artifacts from the Mohegan, Paugussett and Tunxis tribes, with scenic views and Indian legends galore. Black Rock could come in handy if you're passing through and want to relax with a picnic or give Fido a chance to stretch his legs, but note that there is a parking fee in season.

Burr Pond State Park, 385 Burr Mountain Rd., Torrington (860-482-1817). Most visitors to Burr Pond head first to the walking path that surrounds the site's 88-acre pond; other park activities include picnicking, boating, swimming, fishing, and hiking, and ice-skating in winter. While you're hiking, look for the bronze tablet that commemorates Connecticut's role in the Civil War and Industrial Revolution. You'll also find restrooms, a boat launch, and a concession stand. Dogs must be leashed.

Campbell Falls State Park Reserve, Tobey Hill Rd., Norfolk (c/o Burr Pond State Park, 385 Burr Mountain Rd., Torrington 06790; 860-482-1817). Leashed pups are welcome to join their owners in an exploration of the scenery at Campbell Falls, which gets its name from waterfalls that tumble into cold streams. The park is frequented by anglers, hikers, dog walkers, families, and bird-watchers. There are no developed facilities within the reserve.

Collis P. Huntington State Park, Sunset Hill Rd., Redding (c/o Putnam Memorial State Park, 492 Black Rock Tpke., Redding 06896; 203-938-2285). A favorite among mountain bikers, this 878-acre park is also one of the hottest spots around for local dog lovers. The walking paths are wide, flat, and easy to navigate, winding their way past ponds, small bridges, forests, fields, and a horse farm. Water-loving dogs will enjoy wading into the easy-to-access ponds.

Covered Bridges. Western Connecticut is home to two of these distinctly New England landmarks: **Bulls Bridge,** just off Route 7 in Kent, still carries vehicle traffic to and from New York. The **West Cornwall Bridge** up the road was rehabilitated by the state in 1973 and was originally constructed with a Town lattice truss.

Dennis Hill State Park, Rte. 272, Norfolk (c/o Burr Pond State Park, 385 Burr Mountain Rd., Torrington 06790; 860-482-1817). Looking for a great view? You'll find it at the top of this 240-

© ROBERT MANLEY/SHUTTERSTOCK.COM

acre preserve, a former private estate. On a clear day you can see Haystack Mountain, Mount Greylock, portions of the Green Mountains, and even portions of New Hampshire. Leashed dogs are welcome on the trails and in the picnic area, but not inside the summit pavilion.

DiGrazia Vineyards, 131 Tower Rd., Brookfield (203-775-1616; www.digraziavineyards.com). The resident cat and dog at DiGrazia hang out in the tasting room of this vineyard and winery where reds, whites, dessert wines, and ports are created. Your dog is also welcome on a leash. Because the vineyard sometimes hosts weddings and other special events, you might want to call ahead.

Hamden Dog Park, Ridge Rd. and Waite St., Hamden. Managed by the Hamden Parks and Recreation Department, this popular dog park has separate areas for large and small dogs, picnic tables, benches, a wheelchair-accessible trail, a patio, and lots of friendly pups and dog lovers. Locals host regular fund-raising events to help improve the park and keep it looking spiffy.

Haystack Mountain State Park, Rte. 272, Norfolk (c/o Burr Pond State Park, 385 Burr Mountain Rd., Torrington 06790; 860-482-1817). With 224 acres, this park offers great views for people of all ages and abilities: A paved road leads halfway up the mountain to a parking area. Once you reach the lot, you can stay for a picnic or continue farther up on foot to the summit on a half-mile-long trail. Dogs must be leashed.

Housatonic Meadows State Park, Rte. 7, Sharon (c/o Macedonia Brook State Park, 159 Macedonia Brook Rd., Kent 06757; 860-927-3238). Fly-fishermen appreciate the cold, fast waters of Housatonic Meadows; in addition to river access, the 450-acre park provides restrooms, parking, drinking water, public telephones, picnic areas, sports fields, and boating opportunities.

Indian Well State Park, Howe Ave. (Rte. 110), Shelton (c/o Osbornedale State Park, P.O. Box 113, Derby 06418; 203-735-4311). The biggest attractions of this park—the beach, recreation area, and main picnic area—are off-limits to your pet. Still, if you're looking for a woodsy hike, you are welcome to take Rover on the trails or in the Maples Picnic Area. The trails offer a few challenging hills and even some small but pretty waterfalls.

John A. Minetto State Park, Rte. 272, Torrington (c/o Burr Pond State Park, 385 Burr Mountain Rd., Torrington 06790; 860-482-1817). Open meadows and small ponds dot the landscape at this canine-friendly park. The wheelchair-accessible site also has picnic tables, trails for hiking and cross-country skiing, and opportunities for fishing. Parking is free; dogs must be leashed.

Kent Falls State Park, Rte. 7, Kent (c/o Macedonia Brook State Park, 159 Macedonia Brook Rd., Kent 06757; 860-927-3238). With open fields, picnic areas, streams, trails, and restrooms, this park is popular with local families as well as visitors. But the highlight of any visit is the waterfall itself: You can follow the cascade all the way to the top via pathways and stairs that allow views along each step of the way. Pets are welcome on a leash.

Kettletown State Park, Rte. 188, Southbury (860-424-3200). Native Americans traded this 490-acre swath of land to the settlers for one brass kettle: The area was then named Kettletown, and the moniker stuck. The park offers picnic areas, hiking trails, swimming and fishing opportunities on **Lake Zoar,** and sports fields and ice-skating in winter. Dogs must be leashed.

Lake Waramaug State Park, 30 Lake Waramaug Rd., New Preston (860-868-0220; 860-868-2592). The main attraction of this

95-acre park is the lake itself. Visitors come to fish, swim, scuba dive, ice-skate, and canoe, and also enjoy land-based activities like picnicking and hiking. Amenities include restrooms, a concession stand, parking areas, and a picnic shelter. Leashed dogs are allowed.

Macedonia Brook State Park, 159 Macedonia Brook Rd., Kent (860-927-3238). Although dogs are not permitted in the Macedonia Brook campground, they are welcome to sniff their way along the trails and through the picnic areas—on a leash, of course. The 2,300-acre park is popular with hikers; trails range from easy to challenging and offer views of nearby mountain ranges. Bring a picnic and spend the day.

Mohawk State Forest, 20 Mohawk Mountain Rd. (Rte. 4), Goshen (860-491-3620). Much of the land for this 3,350-acre park was donated to the state by the White Memorial Foundation (see **White Memorial Conservation Center** below). Hiking and snowmobiling are allowed on the trails, and visitors can also picnic, fish, bird-watch, enjoy scenic views, and wander through an unusual black spruce bog. Dogs must be leashed.

Mount Tom State Park, Rte. 202, Litchfield (c/o Lake Waramaug State Park, 30 Lake Waramaug Rd., New Preston 06777; 860-868-2592). There's plenty to do at this popular 230-acre park, including fishing, swimming, picnicking, boating, ice-skating, scuba diving, and hiking to the top of the 1,325-foot mountain for which the park is named. Visitors can also take advantage of restrooms, a concession stand, parking, and public telephones. Leashed dogs are welcome everywhere except the beach.

New Canaan Nature Center, 144 Oenoke Ridge (Rte. 124), New Canaan (203-966-9577; www.newcanaannature.org). Leashed pets are welcome at this 40-acre nature center with 2 miles of trails, a wetlands boardwalk, ponds, meadows, and an arboretum and gardens. For a trip map, visit the center's Web site, listed above.

New Haven Parks (203-946-8019). The city's famous green, surrounded by 17th-century churches, is host to outdoor concerts in summer and picnickers and walkers year-round; nearby, restaurants, boutiques, and galleries provide opportunities for window-shopping and people-watching. Other parks include **Lighthouse Point** on Townsend Avenue, 426-acre **East Rock Park** on East Rock Road, and **East Shore Park** on Woodward Avenue. Dogs must be leashed.

Peoples State Forest, W. River Rd., Barkhamsted (860-379-0922; 860-379-2469). Encompassing nearly 3,000 acres, Peoples State Forest is located just across the road from the **American Legion State Forest** (see above). Visitors to Peoples will find parking, restrooms, and a picnic shelter. Popular activities include fishing, hiking, picnicking beside the

Farmington River, cross-country skiing, and snowmobiling. Dogs are allowed but must be leashed.

Pequonnock River Greenway. Winding through the towns of Newtown, Monroe, and Trumbull, this railroad-line-turned-bike-path will eventually reach all the way down to Bridgeport. It's a quiet, flat, and wide path, frequented by families and dog walkers. One of the most popular stretches runs from Pepper Street in Monroe down to the town's Wolf Park (where pets are not allowed). You can park at the Pepper Street lot to make the hour-long trip up and back.

Putnam Memorial State Park, intersection of Rte. 107 and Rte. 58, Redding (203-938-2285). Archeologists still conduct regular digs at this fascinating site, which served as the winter encampment of the Continental army in 1779. Visitors can still see the remains of soldiers' fire pits as well as reconstructed log buildings and a museum. Leashed pets are welcome on the trails (some of which are paved) and in the picnic areas, but not inside any buildings.

Puttin' on the Dog, Greenwich. This tail-waggin' annual event, hosted by the nonprofit Adopt-A-Dog organization, is typically held in late September in Roger Sherman Baldwin Park. Activities include lighthearted dog competitions with celebrity judges, demonstrations, entertainment for children, pony rides, food, auctions, grab bags, and music. For more information on this year's dates and times, call Adopt-A-Dog at 203-629-9494 or 914-273-1674, send an e-mail to info@adopt-a-dog.org, or visit www.adopt-a-dog.org.

Seth Low Pierrepont State Park Reserve, Barlow Mountain Rd., Ridgefield (c/o Putnam Memorial State Park, 492 Black Rock Tpke., Redding 06896; 203-938-2285). This former private estate was a gift to the people of Connecticut from Seth Low Pierrepont, a millionaire and former diplomat who died in 1956. The reserve has a boat launch, hiking trails, and plenty of opportunities for wildlife-watching, fishing, boating, and hiking. Leashed pets are welcome.

Sherwood Island State Park, Sherwood Island Connector (Exit 18 off I-95), Westport (203-226-6983). Sherwood Island offers one of the area's only truly public beaches, making it a very popular spot with locals as well as visitors from other regions. The park features a moving memorial to the victims of the September 11, 2001, terrorist attacks in nearby New York City. Amenities include a nature center, salt-water fishing and swimming, a picnic shelter, bathrooms, sports fields, and interpretive programs. Leashed dogs are permitted only during the off-season, from October 1 to April 14. Expect to pay a $9–13 for residents ($15–22 for non-residents) entrance fee, depending on the time of year.

SoNo Arts Celebration, South Norwalk. Otherwise known as South Norwalk, SoNo is home to an annual arts festival each August in the bustling downtown area. The normally busy streets are roped off to make room for more than 150 exhibits, food carts, and vendors selling everything from sculptures and photographs to clothing and handcrafted furniture. Grab a fresh-squeezed lemonade and wander with Rover—there's always something to see. Check dates and event schedules at www.sonoarts.org.

Southford Falls State Park, Rte. 188, Oxford (860-424-3200). Like **Kent Falls State Park** (see above), the big draws here are the waterfalls, which tumble into the Eight Mile River near the south end of the property. Besides "fall-watching," visitors also enjoy fishing, hiking, cross-country skiing, and picnicking. Amenities include restrooms, parking, and a picnic shelter. Dogs must be leashed.

Squantz Pond State Park, 178 Shortwoods Rd., New Fairfield (203-797-4165). This extremely popular park has a beach, wooded areas, and plenty of opportunities for boating, swimming, fishing, hiking, ice-skating, scuba diving, picnicking, bird-watching, and leaf-peeping. Unfortunately, however, your furry friend is allowed to join the fun on the trails only during the off-season, from October 1 to April 14. Dogs are not permitted on the beach at any time during the year.

Topsmead State Forest, Buell Rd., P.O. Box 1081, Litchfield 06759 (860-567-5694). This once-private estate is now open to the public as a scenic spot where visitors can enjoy activities like cross-country skiing, bird-watching, picnicking, hiking, and relaxing. Dogs are welcome on the trails and in the picnic areas but are not permitted inside any of the estate's buildings.

Trout Brook Valley Preserve, Easton and Weston. Mountain bikers, horseback riders, hikers, and dog walkers all enjoy this scenic, quiet spot with more than 20 miles of trails to explore. Trout Brook Valley was scheduled to become a golf course and housing development until the Aspetuck Land Trust stepped in to save the property from development. To reach the preserve, follow Route 58 to Route 136 South. Take your second right onto Old Redding Road; follow to the end and then take a right onto Bradley Lane to the trailhead.

Walk-A-Dog-Athon, The Animal Haven, 89 Mill Rd., North Haven (203-239-2641; www.theanimalhaven.com). Usually held on the third Saturday in September on the North Haven Town Green, this lively event raises funds for the nonprofit animal-welfare organization The Animal Haven. Past festivities have included dog-obedience demonstrations, pet massage therapy, contests with prizes, and plenty of refreshments for pups and people. The entry fee includes a T-shirt and a doggie gift.

Webb Mountain Park, Webb

Circle, Monroe. It's a bit hard to find, but once you and Spot locate this fairly remote 136-acre park you'll be glad you made the effort. Trails are marked by color: Follow the red blazes to reach the Lookout, a rocky shelf with impressive valley and river views. To reach the park, take East Village Road off Route 111, take a left onto Webb Circle, then turn right at the park entrance sign. Dogs must be leashed.

West Haven Boardwalk, Captain Thomas Blvd., West Haven. This is a popular spot for local dog owners in warm weather: You'll see almost every breed of dog romping along the beach and the boardwalk. A restaurant with picnic tables is across the street (see **Chick's** under "Quick Bites"). Leashed dogs are welcome as long as their owners clean up after them. (The town imposes a heavy fine for violators.)

White Memorial Conservation Center, 80 Whitehall Rd., Litchfield (860-567-0857; info@whitememorialcc.org; www.whitememorialcc.org). This environmental education center and museum comprises about 4,000 acres of woodlands, meadows, and riverfront in the northwest region of the state. Visitors can enjoy 35 miles of trails, several picnic areas, activity fields, boat launches, and campgrounds (see "Accommodations—Campgrounds"). The nature museum features exhibits on local natural history, conservation, and ecology. Dogs are welcome on a leash.

Winslow Park, N. Compo Rd., Westport. Winslow Park is the preferred spot for local canine lovers: Dogs are welcome to run off-leash in the northern end of this large grassy park with shady spots and paved walking paths. You'll also find a picnic area, gardens, and a parking lot located at the corner of North Compo Road and Post Road.

QUICK BITES

Chick's, 183 Beach St., West Haven (203-934-4510). Perhaps the best thing about this casual family restaurant—besides the fried seafood, hot dogs, take-out windows, and picnic tables—is its location, right across the street from a boardwalk and beach (see **West Haven Boardwalk** under "Out and About"), where dogs are allowed. Make an afternoon of it!

Dr. Mike's Ice Cream, 158 Greenwood Ave., **Bethel** (203-792-4388); 44 Main St., **Monroe** (203-452-0499). Renowned locally, Dr. Mike's shops serving homemade ice cream are busy year-round. The Monroe location has outdoor seating on the porch and a small grassy area; in Bethel, you can enjoy your cone while strolling past the quaint downtown shops.

Downtown Kent. This tiny strip of boutiques, restaurants, and bookstores along picturesque Main Street (Route 7) offers several choices for quick meals, and most have outdoor seating in the summer. The Kent Farmer's Market is held on Saturday from 9–1 on the Green.

Firehouse Deli, 22 Reef Rd., Fairfield (203-255-5527; www.firehousedelifairfield.com). Located in a former firehouse, this deli is popular with college students, workaday types, and visitors. Offerings include a salad bar, breakfast treats, quiche, and a huge variety of hot and cold sandwiches on wraps and fresh breads. Outdoor tables are available seasonally, and the deli is even located across the street from a park.

Fisherman's Net Seafood Market, 11 Old Kings Hwy., Darien (203-655-0561). At Fisherman's Net, you can reel in fast seafood meals like sea scallops, fish-and-chips, fried clams and shrimp, crabcakes, and fish sandwiches, all served with fries and slaw.

Glenwood Drive-In, 2538 Whitney Ave., Hamden (203-281-0604; www.glenwooddrivein.com). Open year-round, this well-loved drive-in/diner serves up its famous grilled hot dogs in one of three ways: normal, well-done, and "burnt." No matter how crispy you like it, you can top your dog with chili, cheese, sauerkraut, and any number of other gooey adornments. Fries, burgers, and seafood are also on the menu.

Katz's Deli & Restaurant, 1658 Litchfield Tpke., Woodbridge (203-389-5301; www.katzdeli.net). This popular New York–style Jewish deli offers traditional favorites like bagels and lox, egg creams, matzo ball soup, corned beef, pastrami, and other lunchtime treats.

Louis' Lunch, 261–263 Crown St., New Haven (203-562-5507; www.louislunch.com). Talk about longevity—this tiny lunch stop has been serving burgers and sandwiches to New Haven visitors and residents since the late 1800s and claims to be the birthplace of the hamburger sandwich. You won't find anything fancy here, but you will find the perfect midday treat for a picnic or a walk in the park with your pooch.

Meli-Melo, 362 Greenwich Ave., Greenwich (203-629-6153; www.melimelogreenwich.com). Take a moment while you're strolling down tony Greenwich Avenue to stop into this crêperie and juice bar serving sandwiches, salads, crêpes, and freshly blended smoothies made with fruits and vegetables.

Mexicali Rose, 71 S. Main St. (Rte. 25), Newtown (203-270-7003). If you're craving burritos, tacos, black beans, and homemade chips and salsa, this teeny-tiny restaurant is the place. Order your meal to go (most patrons do) and have a picnic at the Newtown green, known as Ram's Pasture, right down the street.

New Haven's Wooster Street. A haven for Italian immigrants since the 1920s, this popular section of New Haven abounds with famous coal-fired-oven pizza shops—most notably **Sally's** (203-624-5271; www.sallysapizza.com) and **Pepe's** (203-865-5762; www.pepespizzeria.com)—along with several upscale restaurants and bakeries. There's no outdoor seating at the pizza places, but you can pick up a pie to go. Expect a wait, especially on weekends.

Rawley's Hot Dogs, 1886 Post Rd., Fairfield (203-259-9023). This roadside stand has been keeping 'em coming for more than 50 years with dogs that are deep fried, then grilled. The cheese and chili dogs are especially popular.

Stillwater American Bistro, 3 Clifton St., New Haven (203-466-2200). The New Haven *Advocate* raves about this place (especially the views), so it's probably worth a try. Sitting beside the Quinnipiac River, the bistro has an indoor dining room as well as outdoor tables with umbrellas, where you can enjoy steaks, lamb, seafood, pasta, and even Sunday brunch.

HOT SPOTS FOR SPOT

Animal Welfare Society Pet Store, 8 Dodd Rd., New Milford (860-354-1350; www.aws-shelter.org. All the proceeds of the pet-supply shop benefit the Animal Welfare Society, a nonprofit organization helping local homeless pets. Shoppers can stock up on food, treats, water bowls, AWS T-shirts, pet-hair removal aids, and lots of other items.

Best Friends Pet Care, 528 Main Ave., **Norwalk** (203-849-1010); and Rte. 42, **Bethany** (203-393-3126; www.bestfriendspetcare.com). Overnight boarding, doggie day care, and grooming are all available at these two branches of the Best Friends pet-care chain. You can also sign your four-footed friend up for Canine College obedience classes or additional playtimes during boarding.

Dog Gone Smart, 15 Cross St., Norwalk (203-838-7729; www.doggonesmart.com). Dogs and dog lovers can appreciate the wide array of services available at Dog Gone Smart, including overnight boarding, doggie day care, group and private training classes, a large play area, a do-it-yourself dog wash, and grooming services. The center even has an indoor swimming pool for therapy and fun.

Earth Animal, 606 Post Rd. E., Westport (203-222-7173; 1-800-622-0260; info@earthanimal.com; www.earthanimal.com). This is a fun stop for two- and four-legged customers. Earth Animal stocks holistic supplements, organic foods, gourmet doggie treats, books, flea and tick remedies, toys, picture frames, and anything else an environmentally conscious pet lover could want. Those who aren't passing through Westport can shop at Earth Animal's online store.

Marta's Vineyard Canine Resort, 519 Federal Rd., Brookfield (203-775-4404; martas vineyard@aol.com; www.martas vineyard.com). Owned and operated by veterinarians, Marta's Vineyard offers rooms, luxury suites, junior suites, a "senior center" for geriatric pets, and a "petite center" for especially small canine guests. Each pet is exercised twice a day in fenced-in areas. Grooming services are also available.

PawPrint Market, 876 Post Rd., Darien (203-656-3901). Doggies are welcome to join their owners on a shopping trip to PawPrint Market, a pet-supply store offering food, toys, grooming supplies, gift ideas, and more.

Schulhof Animal Hospital Pet Spa, 199 Post Rd. W., Westport (203-226-1231; www.schulhof animalhospital.com). In addition to veterinary services, this animal hospital offers a "pet spa," overnight boarding, acupuncture, homeopathy treatments, nutritional supplements, dog-training classes, and full grooming services.

Sitting Service of Fairfield County, 1031 Post Rd. (Rte. 1), Darien (203-655-9783; sit serve@aol.com; www.thesitting service.com). The staffers at this unique company provide while-you're-away care for your house, your kids, and yes—your pets. For about $20–45 per day, the pet-sitters will provide food, water, exercise, medication, and TLC in your absence.

Thomaston Feed, 141 Watertwon Rd., Thomaston (860-283-9661; info@thomastonfeed.com; www.thomastonfeed.com). Specializing in companion animal supplies, this family business stocks food, leashes, collars, bowls, pet shampoos, holistic supplements, treats, chew toys, and more for dogs, cats, birds, gerbils, and even horses.

Town House for Dogs and Cats, 1040 Post Rd. E., Westport (203-227-3276; www.townhousefor dogs.com). Town House provides overnight boarding as well as doggie day care, pickup and delivery services, and grooming. Boarded dogs enjoy large indoor/outdoor runs and outdoor play sessions when the weather permits.

ANIMAL SHELTERS AND HUMANE SOCIETIES

Adopt-A-Dog, Greenwich, Connecticut, and Armonk, New York (203-629-9494; 914-273-1492; www.adoptadog.org)

SPCA of Connecticut, 359 Spring Hill Rd., Monroe (203-445-9978; www .spcact.org)

Animal Welfare Society, 8 Dodd Rd., New Milford (860-354-1350; www.aws-shelter.org)

Bridgeport Animal Shelter, 525 Asylum St., Bridgeport (203-576-7727; www.bptanimalcontrol.com)

Connecticut Humane Society Bethany Branch, 788 Amity Rd., Bethany (203-393-0150; www.cthumane.org)

Connecticut Humane Society Westport Branch, 455 Post Rd. E., Westport (203-227-4137; www.cthumane.org)

Danbury Animal Welfare Society (DAWS), 147 Grassy Plain St., Danbury (203-744-DAWS; www.daws.org)

Friends of Animals (advocacy group), 777 Post Rd., Suite 205, Darien (203-656-1522; www.friendsofanimals.org)

New Fairfield–Sherman Animal Welfare Society, P.O. Box 8232, New Fairfield 06812 (203-746-2925)

New Leash on Life, P.O. Box 171, Stratford 06615 (203-944-0171; www.geocities.com/newleashonlife)

Pet Animal Welfare Society (PAWS), 504 Main Ave., Norwalk (203-750-9572; www.pawsct.org)

Strays and Others, P.O. Box 473, New Canaan 06840 (203-966-6556; www.straysandothers.petfinder.com)

IN CASE OF EMERGENCY

Countryside Veterinary Hospital, 374 Leavenworth Rd., Shelton (203-929-0500)

Greenfield Animal Hospital, 212 Hillside Rd., Fairfield (203-254-0700)

High Ridge Animal Hospital, 868 High Ridge Rd., Stamford (203-322-0507)

Litchfield Veterinary Hospital, 286 Torrington Rd., Litchfield (860-567-1622)

Mattatuck Animal Hospital, 1095 Chase Pkwy., Waterbury (203-754-2105)

Noah's Ark Animal Hospital, 44 Mill Plain Rd., Danbury (203-743-9999)

Pet Shield Veterinary Hospital, 126 E. Pearl St., New Haven (203-776-7799)

Schulhof Animal Hospital, 199 Post Rd. W., Westport (203-226-1231)

Rhode Island

2

WESTERLY, RHODE ISLAND (© LARRY ST. PIERRE/SHUTTERSTOCK.COM)

Rhode Island

This small state is a big draw for New England visitors. From Providence gondolas to quaint East and West Bay waterfront hamlets and the quieter corners of Blackstone Valley and South County, the area packs agricultural, urban, and small-town attractions into one convenient package. Most Rhode Island tourists head first to Newport, a playground for the country's wealthiest captains of industry that now offers lodgings and fun for everyday folks wanting a peek at the "other half's" lavish lifestyle—past and present. Newport is one of the dog-friendliest towns around. From the downtown cobblestone streets and greens to the famed Cliff Walk, massive mansions, and abundant parks, you and Rover will find plenty of playing, hiking, and gawking opportunities. And you won't be alone: Lots of hands are holding leashes in this hopping, upscale spot.

The state's other main tourist attraction is Block Island, a pristine dot in Long Island Sound that offers breathtaking views from all sides and a classic maritime atmosphere. While Block Island is very pet friendly, accommodations are somewhat limited to small inns that book up well in advance. But despite the difficulty in finding a place to stay, Block Island still makes for an intriguing doggie day trip from your home-away-from-home base on the mainland. Grab an ice cream, rent a canoe, hike the bluffs, admire the Victorian architecture, and count your blessings that The Nature Conservancy and others are working to preserve the island's natural beauty for future generations.

ACCOMMODATIONS

Hotels, Motels, Inns, and Bed & Breakfasts

Block Island

Blue Dory Inn, 61 Dodge St., Block Island (401-466-5891; 1-800-992-7290; rundezvous@aol.com); $265–565 per night. This Victorian-style inn offers a variety of accommodation choices, from traditional guest rooms in the main house to luxury suites and cottages. Guests enjoy views of the ocean and downtown area. Pets are welcome in certain rooms and cottages for an additional $50 per stay (not per night), though they cannot be left unattended at any time.

The Darius Inn, 62 Dodge St., Block Island (401-465-6357; www.dariusblockisland.com); $195–525 per night. Just across the street from the Blue Dory Inn, the Darius is an all-suite inn that welcomes pets with a one-time $50 fee per stay. Breakfast and happy hour snacks are included in the room rate.

Gothic Inn, 440 Dodge St., Block Island (401-466-2918; 1-800-944-8991; info@thegothicinn.com; www.thegothicinn.com); $75–395 per night. Well-behaved dogs and cats are allowed in the two-bedroom apartments and one large guest room at the Gothic Inn, a cheery accommodation located in Block Island's historic district. Each room has a private entrance, making dog walks convenient. A continental breakfast is served each morning in the sitting rooms.

Island Home Inn, 585 Beach Ave., Block Island (401-466-5944; 1-888-261-6118; theislandhomeinnbi@gmail.com; www.theislandhomeinn.com); $125–295 per night. This hilltop inn has guest rooms in the main house and the carriage house, country furnishings, porches, large lawns

BLOCK ISLAND'S GOTHIC INN SIGN (COURTESY GOTHIC INN)

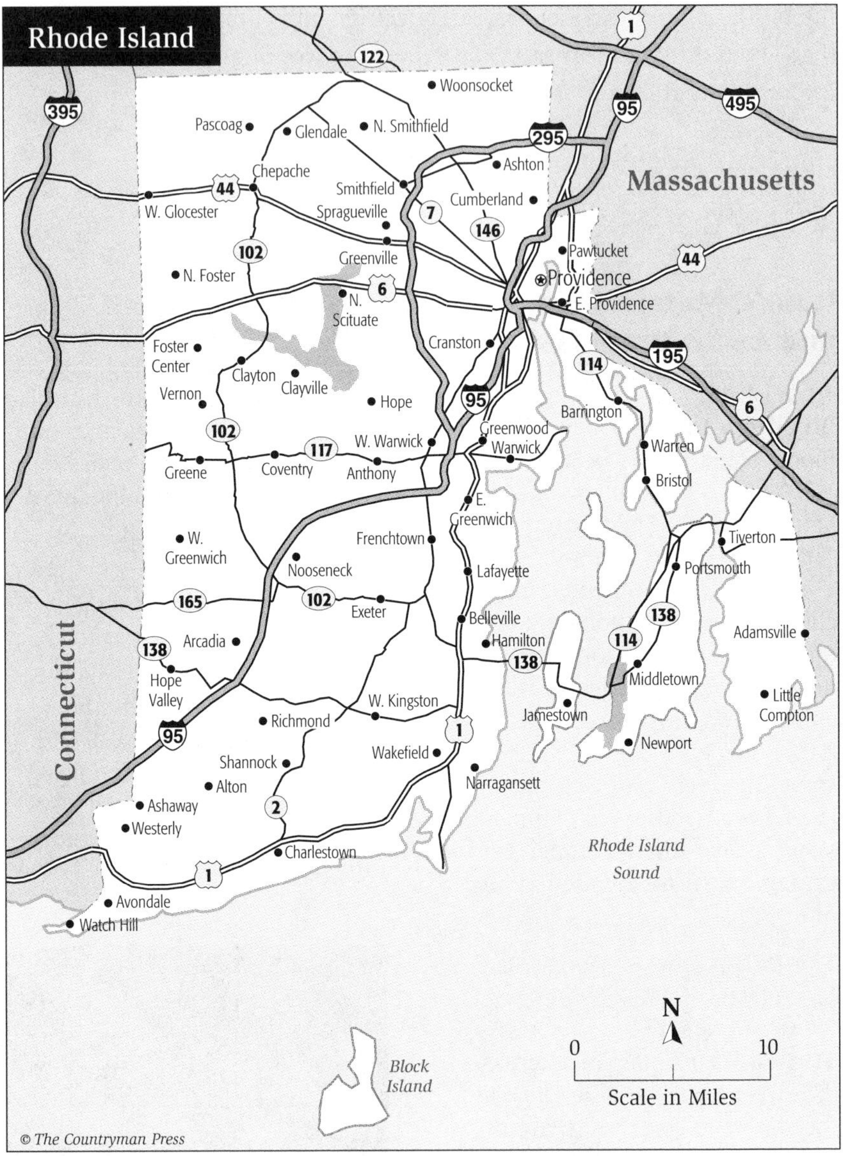

and views of the harbor, rolling hills, and Block Island's famous Great Salt Pond. Breakfast and afternoon tea are included in the rates; pets are welcome in two rooms (the Daylily and Sunflower Suite) with no additional fees, but must not be left unattended in rooms.

East Providence

Extended Stay America Providence–East Providence, 1000 Warren Ave., East Providence (401-272-1661; www .extendedstayamerica.com); $95–119 per night. The studio suites at Extended StayAmerica feature fully equipped kitchens,

Internet access, voice mail, cable television with premium movie channels, work desks, alarm clocks, free local telephone calls, and access to laundry facilities. Dog owners pay an extra $25 per night (not to exceed $75 per stay).

Middletown

Ambassador Inn & Suites, 1359 W. Main Rd., Middletown (401-849-2718; www.newportambassadorinn.com); $79–149 per night. This recently renovated hotel has a location that's close to Newport attractions, beaches, and the University of Rhode Island. Amenities include Internet access, continental breakfasts, alarm clocks, and hair dryers. Dogs are permitted for an extra $15per night, as long as they are not left unattended. A maximum of two pets allowed per room.

Howard Johnson Inn Newport, 351 W. Main Rd., Middletown (401-849-2000; www.hojo.com); $69–279 per night. Located close to Newport, this Howard Johnson offers an indoor swimming pool, a hot tub, a sauna, cable television with premium movie channels, a game room, a fitness center, and voice mail. The hotel also has an attached restaurant with outdoor seating in summer. Companion animals are welcome in first-floor standard guest rooms for an additional $10 per pet, per night fee. The hotel even offers useful information for out-of-town pet owners in the "Wags and Whiskers" section of its Web site, including directions to the local dog park and nearby pet-friendly businesses.

Quality Inn & Suites, 936 W. Main Rd., Middletown (401-846-7600; www.qualityinn.com);

Rhode Island Visitor Resources

The state and local tourism offices can help you find pet-friendly accommodations, restaurants, and attractions, as well as provide maps and other information you may need on the go or to plan your visit:

State of Rhode Island (800-556-2484; www.visitrhodeisland.com)

Providence (800-233-1636; www.goprovidence.com)

Newport and Bristol County (800-976-5122; www.discovernewport.org)

Warwick (800-492-7942; www.visitwarwickri.com)

South County (800-548-4662; www.southcountyri.com)

Block Island (800-383-2474; www.blockislandinfo.com)

Blackstone Valley (800-454-2882; www.tourblackstone.com)

BLOCK ISLAND'S GOTHIC INN, WITH ITS CHARMING GINGERBREAD TRIM, IS LOCATED IN THE HISTORIC DISTRICT. (COURTESY OF GOTHIC INN)

$99–139 per night. The Quality Inn has an indoor heated swimming pool, an on-site spa, 25-inch televisions with premium movie channels, a restaurant serving breakfast and dinner, a lounge, shuttle services, and a location that's close to Newport attractions. All 40 rooms, from the studio suites to the three-bedrooms, have Jacuzzis. Dog owners are welcome but must pay an extra $25 per pet, per night.

Newport

Bannister's Wharf Guest Rooms, Bannister's Wharf, Newport (401-846-4500; www.bannistersnewport.com); $75–340 per night. Pets are welcome for an additional $25 per stay at Bannister's, where guests can choose from rooms and suites, all with harbor views and a deck. The owners also rent out two-bedroom apartments nearby. There are few better locations from which to enjoy the downtown hubbub; all accommodations have air-conditioning and satellite television.

Motel 6 Newport, 249 Connell Hwy., Newport (401-848-0600; www.motel6.com); $49–69 per night. This economy motel offers cable television with premium movie channels, smoking and nonsmoking rooms, Internet access, and free coffee in the lobby. Kids under age 17 stay free with a parent, and well-behaved pets are welcome without extra fees.

Murray House Bed & Breakfast, 1 Murray Place, Newport (401-846-3337; murrayhousebnb@aol.com; www.murrayhouse.com); $99–255 per night. Children and well-trained pets are welcome at this ideally located B&B in the famous mansion district (Bellevue Avenue) of Newport. You'll find private entrances to each room, gourmet daily breakfasts in your room or patio area, an outdoor swimming pool, a hot tub, flower gardens, televisions, air-conditioning, and in-room coffeepots, refrigerators, microwaves, and toasters. The beach and a dog park are both a short walk away.

Sanford-Covell Villa Marina, 72 Washington St., Newport (401-847-0206; www.sanford-covell.com); $60–325 per night. Pets are allowed in designated rooms at Sanford-Covell, a harborside B&B and marina with great water views, a wraparound porch, an entry hall with a 35-foot ceiling, a reflecting pool, a dining room, and guest rooms furnished with four-poster beds and antiques. There are no extra fees for companion animals at this elegant 19th-century Newport house.

Knights Inn, 240 Aquidneck Ave., Newport (401-324-6200; www.knightsinn.com); $49–159 per night. With water views and a large lawn area with Adirondack chairs, this two-story inn attracts pet lovers from all over. All guest rooms have two double beds or one king bed, cable TV, and air-conditioning. Visitors can borrow kites or bicycles, enjoy daily continental breakfasts, and use the swimming pool and workout equipment at the fitness center next door—all free of charge. Downtown Newport, the Cliff Walk, and the mansions are a short drive away. Pets are welcome for an additional $10 per night with a maximum of two pets per room.

Victorian Ladies Inn, 63 Memorial Blvd., Newport (1-888-849-9960; info@victorianladies.com; www.victorianladies.com); $115–275 per night. The Victorian Ladies Inn offers the charms of yesteryear with today's modern amenities. Guests can enjoy 11 individually decorated guest rooms (categorized as standard, deluxe, and luxury), flower gardens, a dining room, and a parlor. Doggie guests are welcome in select rooms for an additional $25 per night.

Portsmouth

Founder's Brook Motel and Suites, 314 Boyd's Ln., Portsmouth (401-683-1244; www.foundersbrookmotelandsuites.com); $49–139 per night. Founder's Brook guests can choose from standard motel rooms or larger suites; some of the suites have whirlpool tubs. The motel offers a quiet, off-the-road location, in-room coffeemakers and refrigerators, and senior discounts. Pets are allowed in certain rooms for $10 per stay (not per night) for short stays, or $35 per month for longer stays.

ENJOY YOUR MORNING COFFEE ON THE PORCH OF THE GOTHIC INN. (COURTESY OF GOTHIC INN)

Providence

Marriott Providence Downtown, 1 Orms St., Providence (401-272-2400; 1-866-807-2171; www.marriott.com); $169–269 per night. With a one-time sanitation fee of $49, your pooch will be a welcome guest at this downtown Marriott. The full-service hotel has extras like concierge-level rooms, indoor and outdoor swimming pools, room service, express check-out services, a fitness center, valet laundry services, a 24-hour front desk, a restaurant and lounge, and cable television with premium movie channels.

Omni Providence, 1 W. Exchange St., Providence (401-598-8000; www.omnihotels.com); $179–379 per night. The Omni Hotel charges a one-time $50 fee per stay for pets but has no weight limit, which will come as welcome news to those of us with pups bigger than a dachshund but smaller than a Lab. This upscale, full-service hotel is attached to the Providence Mall and Dunkin' Donuts Center and offers an indoor pool, fitness center, city views, minibars, cable television, alarm clocks, voice mail, and writing/computer desks.

South Kingstown

King's Rose Bed & Breakfast, 1747 Mooresfield Rd., South Kingstown (401-783-5222); $125–175 per night. This 1930s-era Colonial welcomes well-behaved pets and their owners in its seven guest rooms, all with private baths. Antique furnishings provide a dignified and relaxed atmosphere, and the 2 acres of grounds allow plenty of room for exploring. "For those who packed too quickly, we have extra pet bowls, blankets, and food," says innkeeper Perry Viles.

ENJOY THE VIEW OF GREAT SALT POND FROM YOUR ROOM IN THE ISLAND HOME ON BLOCK ISLAND. (PHOTO COURTESY OF ISLAND HOME)

THE GOTHIC INN ON BLOCK ISLAND OFFERS OLD WORLD CHARM IN THE MIDST OF THE HISTORIC DISTRICT. (COURTESY GOTHIC INN)

Warren

Thomas Cole House, 81 Union St., Warren (401-245-9768; 401-751-9109); $125–175 per night. Innkeeper Marian Clark welcomes well-behaved dogs and cats to her guesthouse, located in the historic district. Guests enjoy a second-floor suite with a bedroom, a bathroom, a library, and a dressing area; other amenities include full daily breakfasts, a terrace with a fountain, a dining room with a fireplace, and flower gardens.

Warwick

Crowne Plaza Hotel Providence-Warwick, 801 Greenwich Ave., Warwick (401-732-6000; 1-800-439-4745; www.ihg.com); $136–249 per night. The Crowne Plaza is located about 10 minutes from downtown Providence, offering 266 guest rooms, meeting rooms, high-speed Internet access, a fitness center, a sauna, a hot tub, an indoor swimming pool, air-conditioning, and in-room coffeemakers, hair dryers, irons, and ironing boards. Those traveling with a pet pay an additional $50 per stay.

Hampton Inn & Suites Providence/Warwick–Airport, 2100 Post Rd., Warwick (401-739-8888; www.hilton.com); $129199 per night. Each morning, guests at this Hampton Inn can enjoy a complimentary hot breakfast, along with other amenities such as a swimming pool, a fitness center, free high-speed Internet access, business services, laundry facilities, cribs and high chairs, ATMs, and a gift shop. Dogs weighing less than 30 pounds are permitted without extra fees.

Holiday Inn Express Warwick-Providence, 901 Jefferson Blvd., Warwick (401-736-5000; 1-800-HOLIDAY; www.ihg.com); $102–159 per night. A $25 fee per stay is required for companion animals with a maximum of two pets per room at this pet-friendly Holiday Inn Express; just let the front-desk staff know at check-in that you're staying with a furry friend. Amenities include a complimentary continental breakfast, a business center, high-speed Internet access, an ATM, and a free airport shuttle.

Homestead Studio Suites Providence-Airport-Warwick, 268 Metro Center Blvd., Warwick (401-732-6667; www.extendedstayamerica.com); $104–149 per night. Formerly known as MainStay Suites Warwick, this all-suite accommodation offers full kitchens, complimentary breakfasts on weekdays, a basketball court, a fitness center, voice mail, alarm clocks, cable television, air-conditioning, a hot tub, and a location that's close to downtown Providence and T.F. Green Airport. One pet per room is welcome for an additional $25 per night, with a maximum charge of $150 per stay (not per night).

Motel 6 Providence-Warwick, 20 Jefferson Blvd., Warwick, (401-467-9800; www.motel6.com); $76–110 per night. This city motel is located 2 miles from T. F. Green Airport and has laundry facilities, free coffee, an outdoor swimming pool, cable television with premium movie channels, smoking and nonsmoking rooms, and a "kids stay free" program. One well-behaved pet is permitted per room.

Residence Inn Providence-Warwick, 500 Kilvert St., Warwick (401-737-7100; www.marriott.com); $149–219 per night. Designed for long-term stays, this Residence Inn features a swimming pool, a hot tub, complimentary breakfasts, meeting rooms, free local telephone calls, a picnic area, a tennis court, and studio and penthouse suites with full kitchens. Pet owners pay an extra $100 nonrefundable "sanitation fee."

A VISITING GOLDEN RETRIEVER PUPPY CHECKS OUT THE SIGHTS IN DOWNTOWN NEWPORT.

Westerly

Sea Shell Motel, 19 Winnapaug Rd., Westerly (401-348-8337; www.seashellmotel.com); $70–170 per night. The Sea Shell often posts photos on their Web site of their four-legged visitors, as well as their own canine host, Lucy. For an extra $10 per stay (not per night), your pet is welcome to join you at Sea Shell, an oceanfront motel with a hot tub, a lawn area, water views, air-conditioning, cable television with premium movie channels, and refrigerators. Pet owners should call ahead for prior approval.

West Warwick

Extended Stay America Providence–Airport–West Warwick, 1235 Division Rd., West Warwick (401-885-3161; www.extendedstayamerica.com); $75–129 per night. Extended StayAmerica offers roomy studio suites with kitchens, work desks, voice mail, wireless high-speed Internet access, laundry facilities, free local phone calls, irons, and ironing boards. Dogs are permitted for an additional $25 per night (not to exceed $150 per stay).

Campgrounds

Ashaway

Frontier Family Camper Park, 180 Maxson Hill Rd., Ashaway (401-377-4510); call for rate information. Located close to the Connecticut border, the Frontier Family Camper Park offers more than 100 sites for RVs and tents, a playground, a swimming pool, restrooms with showers, a dumping station, and a volleyball court. For an extra $3 per night, pets are permitted with size and breed restrictions; call for details.

Foster

Ginny-B Campground, 7 Harrington Rd., Foster (401-397-9477; www.ginny-bcampground.com); $34–35 per night. Leashed pets are welcome to join the fun at this family campground offering 200 sites, recreation halls, two softball fields, a basketball court, a volleyball court, a playground, a camp store, laundry facilities, modern restrooms with showers, dumping stations, a lending library, and opportunities for fishing and swimming.

Hope Valley

Whispering Pines Campground, 41 Sawmill Rd., Hopkinton (401-539-7011; wpinesri@aol.com; www.whisperingpinescamping.com); $39–53 per night. This full-service family campground has sites for tents and RVs, a swimming pool, a miniature golf course, free boat rentals, basketball and volleyball courts, a recreation hall, a camp store, laundry facilities, a playground, a snack bar, and a fishing pond. Quiet, leashed pets are allowed as long as their owners clean up after them.

Jamestown

Fort Getty Recreation Area, Fort Getty Rd., Jamestown (401-423-7211; 401-423-7264); $25 per night. Open seasonally, from May to October, this municipal campground has sites for tents and RVs, beaches, hiking trails, ocean views, and the remains of historic Fort Getty. Campers can also enjoy picnic areas and a sand volleyball court. Dogs must be leashed. Transient RVs are no longer allowed.

West Greenwich

Oak Embers Campground, 219 Escoheag Hill Rd., West Greenwich (401-397-4042; camping@oakembers.com; www.oakembers.com); $30–35 per night. Campers at Oak Embers can enjoy lots of family-friendly activities, including hayrides, barbecues, horseback riding, swimming, volleyball, romping in the playground, and hiking on the trails. Most breeds of pet dogs (call to see if yours qualifies) are permitted, provided they are leashed, attended to, and cleaned-up after.

West Kingston

Wawaloam Campground, 510 Gardiner Rd., West Kingston (401-294-3039; www.wawaloam.com); $42–55 per night. With 300 tent and RV sites on 100 acres, this large campground almost guarantees to keep everyone in the family occupied. Amenities include a swimming pool with a waterslide, a playground, a miniature golf course, restrooms with showers, picnic tables, a snack bar, and two recreation halls. Campers can bring pets, but their visitors cannot.

Homes, Cottages, and Cabins for Rent

Narragansett

Kagel's Cottages, 71 Kenyon Farms Rd., Narragansett (c/o P.O. Box 575, Wakefield, RI 02880; 401-783-4551; www.kagels.com); $850–1,598 per week. The Kagel family rents five waterfront cottages, ranging in size from one to three bedrooms, on its 63-acre property. Most are fully equipped with kitchens, televisions, and living areas; all sit on Salt Pond and offer island views and surrounding lawns and woods. Housebroken, leashed pets are welcome as long as their owners can provide proof of vaccination. Dogs are not allowed on the beach.

For more Rhode Island vacation rentals, check these Web sites:

- www.narragansettri.com
- www.homeaway.com
- www.vrbo.com
- www.vacationrentals.com

Vacation rentals are often listed on local chamber of commerce Web sites, as well as Craigslist.

OUT AND ABOUT

Arcadia Management Area (401-539-2356). Spread throughout four southern Rhode Island towns, this sprawling 14,000-acre park has wild areas and 30 miles of trails for mountain biking, hiking, horseback riding, and cross-country skiing. Trails are identified by colored blazes: Yellow-blazed trails include the 5-mile-long **Breakheart Trail** and the 1.6-mile **John B. Hudson Trail;** white-blazed trails include the 2-mile-long **Escoheag Trail** and the 3-mile-long **Mount Tom Trail.** The trails are managed by the Narragansett chapter of the Appalachian Mountain Club; for more information, visit www.amcnarragansett.org. Dogs are not allowed on designated cross-country skiing trails.

Beaches. Like most beach areas, Rhode Island's coastal region is not particularly wel-

Rhode Island Parks Pet Policy

You must have a pet certification form to camp with your pets at Rhode Island State Parks, which you can download from their Web site: www.riparks.com/PetPolicy.html. Pets are allowed at all parks except Charlestown Breachway and East Beach and must be leashed. Note that pets are not allowed in concession areas at any parks. While it's good to have a rabies tag on your dog's collar, also carry the veterinarian-issued certificate for proof of vaccination. A complete copy of Rhode Island State Parks' pet regulations is available on the Web site, and the official guide to state parks is available as a free app for smart phones and tablets.

coming to dogs. You will find a few opportunities to hit the sand with Rover, however: On **Second Beach** (aka Sachuest Beach), dogs are permitted from 5 AM to 7:45 AM during the high season, and anytime during the off-season. On **First Beach** (aka Easton's Beach), dogs are prohibited at all times during the high season but are welcome, on a leash, in the off-season. Dogs are permitted on all state park beaches, but only during the off-season. On **Block Island,** dogs are permitted on the beaches, year-round, as long as they are leashed and owners clean up any messes they leave behind.

Beavertail State Park, Beavertail Rd., Jamestown (401-423-9941; 401-884-2010). This 153-acre park is the home of one of America's earliest working lighthouses, Beavertail Light. Visitors come for views of the ocean and rocky coastline, open and sunny grass areas, hiking trails, and saltwater fishing opportunities. Dogs are welcome on a leash.

Blackstone River Bikeway (401-762-0250; www.blackstoneriverbikeway.com). This path runs through Lincoln, North Smithfield, Woonsocket, and Pawtucket. Some of the phases of this 17-mile-long biking and walking path have been completed, and some were still under construction at the time of this writing. The former railroad lines along the Blackstone canal are being converted to a 12-foot-wide paved path with picnic tables, restrooms, parking lots, public telephones, and access for walkers, cross-country skiers, joggers, and dog walkers.

Block Island Ferry (c/o Interstate Navigation, State Pier, Galilee, Wakefield 02880; 401-783-4613; 1-866-783-7340; info@blockislandferry.com; www.blockislandferry.com). As long as you use a leash or carrier, your dog will be welcome on board this convenient ferry. The trip takes one hour from the Point Judith dock and two hours from the Newport dock. Vehicle reservations must be made in advance by phone, but they are not necessary for walk-on passengers. Parking is available on a first-come, first served basis ($5–20 per day) across the street from the ferry dock in Point Judith. In Newport, you can park free of charge at Fort Adams State Park. Visit the Web site for directions to each dock, schedules, and fare information. Round-trip fare is $24.65 per person.

Block Island Greenways, Block Island. Just one of the pristine island's many walkable and scenic recreational opportunities, the Greenways are 25 miles of protected trails through open fields, woods, the Mohegan Bluffs, and wetlands. For more information and maps, call The Nature Conservancy's Block Island office at 401-466-2129, or visit www.nature.org.

Brenton Point State Park, Ocean Drive, Newport (401-849-4562; 401-847-2400). This is a popular spot for dog owners. Located at the site of one of Newport's former mansions, the park offers unbeatable views of the Atlantic, along with picnicking, fishing, and hiking opportunities. It's located about halfway down famous Ocean Drive.

Cliff Walk, Newport (www.cliffwalk.com). With the world-famous Newport mansions on one side and the ocean on the other, this 3½-mile-long paved path winds along cliffs and offers some of New England's best views—both natural and man-made. Your pup is welcome on a leash. The path officially starts at Memorial Boulevard, but you can find jumping-on spots elsewhere along the route. Expect crowds and lots of other dog walkers in all seasons.

Colt State Park, Rte. 114, Bristol (401-253-7482). With wide views of Narragansett Bay, orchards, 4 miles of bike paths, a wedding chapel, more than 400 picnic tables, wooded trails, a salt marsh, and flower gardens, this 464-acre park is one of the most popular in Rhode Island. Restrooms and public phones are available; dogs must be on a leash.

Downtown Newport. Thames Street and the various wharfs are lined with shops, restaurants, historic churches and greens, street vendors, and entertainers—and there's all the people-watching you can handle. It's especially crowded in the summertime and during the winter holidays, when Santa makes a visit by boat to Bowens Wharf.

Fort Adams State Park, Harrison Ave., Newport (401-847-2400). Located just off Ocean Drive and extending into Narragansett Bay, Fort Adams has 105 acres of open and scenic picnic areas, soccer fields, boat ramps, and concession stands. It's also the home of **Sail Newport,** a nonprofit sailing facility offering rentals and instruction. Every summer the park hosts blues, jazz, and folk music festivals.

© A KATZ/SHUTTERSTOCK.COM

Dogs must be on a leash and are not allowed on the beach.

Heart and Sole Walk for the Animals, Portsmouth. This fun annual event is the major fundraiser for the **Potter League for Animals,** an advocacy and sheltering organization located in Middletown. Visitors are welcome to take part in a 1- or 3-mile walk, canine obstacle courses, cat photo contests, and contests like best Tail Wagger, Stupid Pet Tricks, and Least Obedient Dog. The event is typically held in June at Glen Park in Portsmouth. Activities and times change from year to year; for updated information, call 401-846-8276, visit www.potterleague.org, or stop by the league's headquarters at 87 Oliphant Lane in Middletown.

Newport Dog Park, Connell Hwy., Newport. Located at the base of the Pell Bridge, this park is nothing fancy but provides Rover with a good opportunity to stretch his legs—leash-free. Be sure to bring pooper-scooper bags.

Photo Dog Art Gallery, Water St., Block Island (401-466-5858). Animal lovers and photography buffs will appreciate this gallery featuring black-and-white photographs of Block Island landscapes, buildings, and animals, with a focus on dogs. Photographer Jill T. Graziano is also available for private shoots.

Rhode Island North–South Trail. Have some extra time? This 75-mile-long byway is a great way to see the charming back roads, historic villages, and rustic hiking trails in the western part of the Ocean State. For maps, check out www.rigreenways.org. **Roger Williams Park,** 1000 Elmwood Ave., Providence (401-785-9650). Perhaps best known for its zoo, this 430-acre Providence park also has charming tree-lined walkways, gardens, waterways, a boathouse with paddleboats available for rent, a museum, and Carousel Village. Leashed dogs are welcome in the main park area.

Snake Den State Park, 2321 Hartford Ave., Johnston (401-222-2632). This park's ominous name doesn't fit well with its calm and inviting atmosphere, complete with 1,000 acres, forested walking trails, a working farm, and an impressive canyon. Enter through Dame Farm or park at roadside parking areas on Brown Avenue. Dogs must be leashed.

WaterFire, Providence. Join the crowds at one of Rhode Island's most unusual and popular events, where more than 90 bonfires are lit on specially designed floats on the waterways of downtown Providence. Artist Barnaby

Evans started this still-growing event/art exhibit in 1994; today a nonprofit organization keeps the fires burning with up to 19 lightings per year. For more information and a detailed schedule visit www.waterfire.org.

WaterPlace Park and Riverwalk, Providence. This recent Providence addition played a major role in the city's well-publicized renaissance. It's a truly impressive sight: Venetian-style footbridges cross the winding canal, where gondolas are available for rent in summer. Plenty of benches, walkways, and even performance areas make this a fun place to hang out. The park area also serves as the location for the popular WaterFire exhibit (see above).

QUICK BITES

Café di Mare, 11 Bowen's Wharf, Newport (401-847-2962). For a sweet treat or something more substantial, stop at this small café serving fudge, sandwiches, calzones, salads, wraps, and bottled drinks. The café's sandwiches are served on a choice of five different types of bread. Enjoy your bounty at one of the many tables outside.

Clockwork Deli & Catering Company, 446 N. Broadway, East Providence (401-431-1883). Take a load off at Clockwork Deli's outdoor seating area while enjoying stuffed deli sandwiches with turkey, chicken, roast beef, tuna, vegetables, and gourmet mustards on fresh-baked breads.

George's of Galilee, 250 Sand Hill Cove Rd., Narragansett (401-783-2306; www.georgesofgalilee.com). Although the locals would probably like to keep this place to themselves, the secret's out: George's serves fantastic seafood from a take-out window. The take-out menu offers Rhode Island clam chowder, baked stuffed quahogs, fish-and-chips dinners, lobsters rolls, fried clams, fried scallops, wrap sandwiches, and much more.

Marina Café & Pub, Marina Plaza, Goat Island, Newport (401-841-0999). This fun Goat Island eatery has lots of casual outdoor seating, live entertainment on weekends, and dishes like fried calamari, buffalo chicken salad, grilled tuna steak, baked sole, the Marina Grille burger, lemon chicken, and, of course, lobster and clam rolls.

Payne's Dock Snack Bar, Payne's Dock, Block Island (401-466-5572). Open seasonally, this is a great casual spot to enjoy breakfast, sandwiches, chowder, ice cream, and Payne's famous homemade donuts. The dock is also the place to rent boats and buy souvenirs.

Pier Pizza Company, 13 Pier Marketplace, **Narragansett** (401-792-9393; www.pierpizza.com);

328 Main St., **Wakefield** (401-788-8181); Post Rd., **Warwick** (401-738-8008); Post Rd., **North Kingstown** (401-886-9899); and 152 Gansett Ave., **Cranston** (401-944-9941). Pier Pizza has takeout and delivery services. Though the restaurant is best known for large, New York–style pizzas, the staff also cooks up pasta dishes, subs, salads, and rich desserts. The Narragansett and Wakefield locations have outdoor seating, as well.

Rocco's Little Italy, 124 Broadway, Newport (401-848-4556; www.roccosnewport.aquidneck.us). Popular with locals as well as visitors, Rocco's serves up a taste of the Old Country with huge pizzas, grinders, and dishes like shrimp parmigiana, linguine with clam sauce, chicken marsala, stuffed Sicilian eggplant, and fried calamari. Outdoor seating and free delivery are available.

Thames Street Eateries. This bustling Newport strip is lined with restaurants; many offer takeout, and a few offer outdoor seating. Try the gyros, tuna sandwiches, fruit smoothies, and ice cream at

THIS SWEET SHOT IS ONE OF MANY ON DISPLAY AT THE PHOTO DOG ART GALLERY ON BLOCK ISLAND. (PHOTO BY JILL T. GRAZIANO)

Blue Water Wraps, or the vegetarian and classic sandwiches served on gourmet bread at the **Panini Grill** next door. On East Thames Street, **O'Brien's Pub and Restaurant** has a huge outdoor seating area and serves crabcakes, fish-and-chips platters, steaks, and a variety of sandwiches.

White Horse Tavern, 26 Marlborough St., Newport (401-849-3600; www.whitehorsenewport.com). Serving travelers since 1673, the White Horse is one of the most recommended restaurants in Newport for both its fine dining, farm-to-table cuisine, and its great burgers.

HOT SPOTS FOR SPOT

Delmyra Country Club for Dogs and Cats, 191 Ten Rod Rd., Exeter (401-294-3247; www.delmyra.com). Pet owners are encouraged to take a tour of the facilities at Delmyra before dropping off their cat or dog for short- or long-term boarding. The Doggie Palace has indoor/outdoor runs, windows, heated floors, and air-conditioning; cats enjoy kitty condos with piped-in music. Pet food is included in the rates, and grooming and training services are also offered.

PROVIDENCE'S DOWNTOWN WATERPLACE PARK AND RIVERWALK

Doggie Styles Pet Spa, 1160 Charles St., North Providence (401-727-2270; www.doggiestyles petspa.com). Whether you need doggie day care or grooming services, Doggie Styles can oblige: Services include shampoos, cuts, teeth cleaning, and even canine massage and aqua therapy. Appointments are recommended, but walk-in service is available.

Metropet Dog Center, 2057 W. Shore Rd., Warwick (401-732-3647; info@metropet.net; www .metropet.net). If playing with other dogs, napping in the sun, and running through the yard are your dog's idea of fun, she'll love the doggie day-care facilities at Metropet. The center offers two large outdoor play areas, swimming pools, shady spots, two indoor playrooms with heat and air-conditioning, and even a daily nap time with crates.

Wag Nation, 92 William St., Newport (401-619-3719; www .wag-nation.com). This boutique's slogan is "where pets rule," and it's true. From organic food and treats to apparel, accessories, beds, bowls, collars, and leads, Wag Nation has everything you could possibly need for your pal.

ANIMAL SHELTERS AND HUMANE SOCIETIES

Animal Rescue League of Southern Rhode Island, 213 Robinson St., Wakefield (401-783-7606; www.arlsri.org)

Bristol Animal Shelter, Minturn Farm Rd., Bristol (401-253-4834)

Charlestown Animal Shelter, Sand Hill Rd., Charlestown (401-364-1211)

Cranston Animal Shelter, 920 Phenix Ave., Cranston (401-464-8700; www.cranstonri.com)

Defenders of Animals (advocacy group), P.O. Box 5634, Weybosset Hill Station, Providence 02903 (401-461-1922; www.defendersofanimals.org)

East Greenwich Animal Protection League, P.O. Box 184, East Greenwich 02818 (401-885-1158; www.egapl.org)

Friends of the North Kingstown Dog Pound, 105 Narragansett St., North Kingstown (401-295-5579)

Pawtucket Animal Shelter, Slater Memorial Park, P.O. Box 2567, Pawtucket 02861 (401-722-4243)

Potter League for Animals, 87 Oliphant Ln., Middletown (401-846-8276; www.potterleague.org)

Providence Animal Control Center, Providence Police Department, Ernest St., Providence (401-243-6040)

Providence Animal Rescue League, 34 Elbow St., Providence (401-421-1399; www.parl.org)

Rhode Island Animal Advocates, P.O. Box 3463, Peace Dale 02883 (401-247-4898)

Rhode Island SPCA, 186 Amarai St., Riverside (401-438-8150; www.rispca.com)

Volunteer Services for Animals, 27 Dryden Ln. (Rte. 1), Providence (401-273-0358; www.volunteerservicesforanimals.org)

Warwick Volunteer Services for Animals, P.O. Box 7544, Warwick 02887 (401-738-0605; VSAWarwickcoord@aol.com)

West Warwick Animal Shelter, 106 Hay St., West Warwick (401-822-9250)

Woonsocket Animal Shelter, 105 Cumberland Hill Rd., Woonsocket (401-766-6571)

IN CASE OF EMERGENCY

Hoffman Animal Hospital, 1338 Broad St., Providence (401-941-7345)

Newport Animal Clinic, 541 Thames St., Newport (401-849-3401)

North Rhode Island Animal Hospital, 21 Sayles Hill Rd., North Smithfield (401-766-7608)

Povar Animal Hospital, 15 1st St., East Providence (401-434-0106)

Tiogue Veterinary Clinic, 916 Tiogue Ave., Coventry (401-821-6927)

Turco Animal Hospital, 3 Ashaway Rd., Westerly (401-596-8910)

Warren Animal Hospital, 581 Metacom Ave., Warren (401-245-8313)

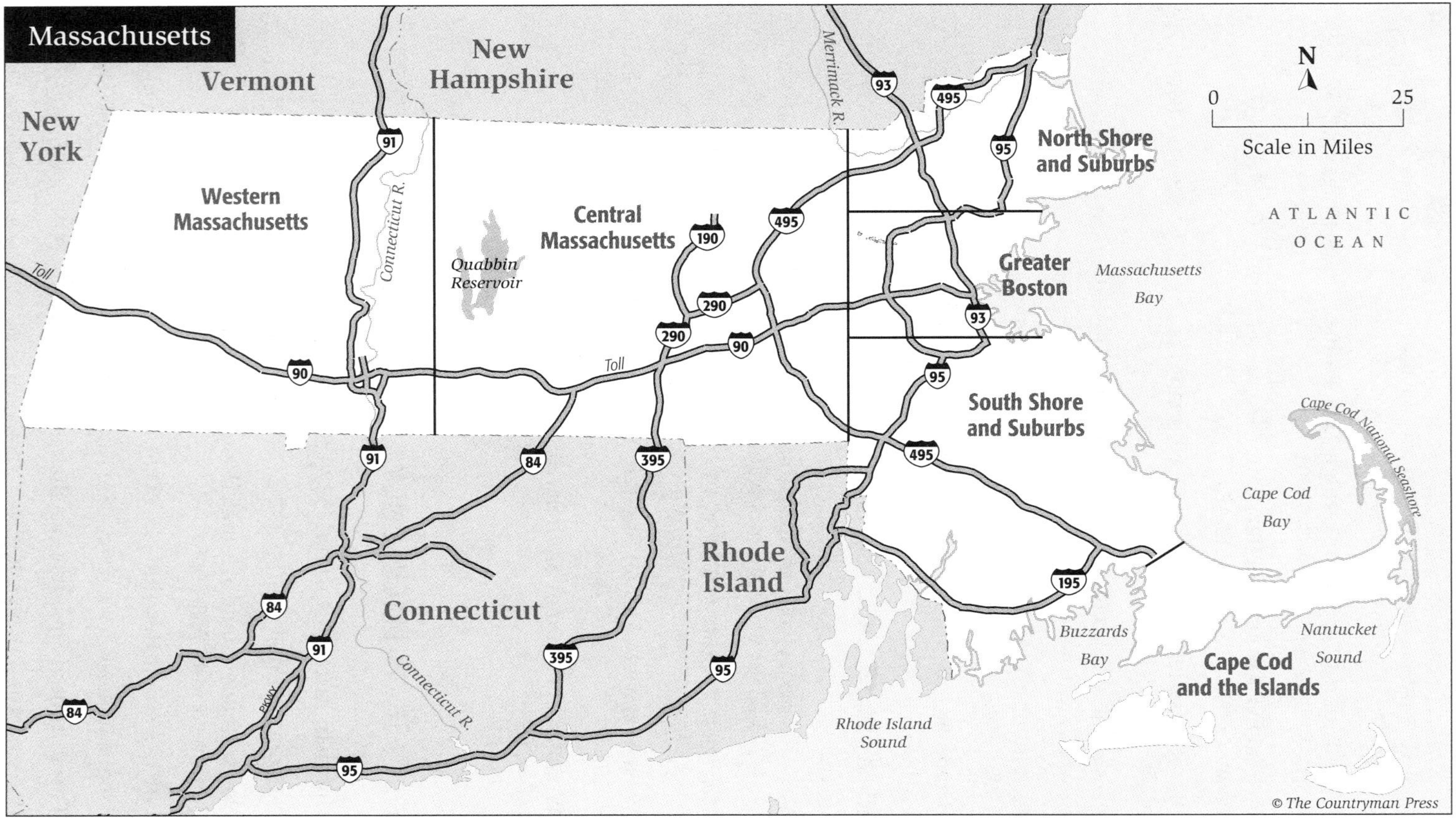
Massachusetts
New York
Vermont
New Hampshire
Western Massachusetts
Central Massachusetts
Quabbin Reservoir
Connecticut R.
Merrimack R.
North Shore and Suburbs
Greater Boston
South Shore and Suburbs
Cape Cod and the Islands
Rhode Island
Connecticut
ATLANTIC OCEAN
Massachusetts Bay
Cape Cod Bay
Cape Cod National Seashore
Buzzards Bay
Nantucket Sound
Rhode Island Sound
Scale in Miles
0
25
N
Toll
PKWY
91
90
84
395
290
190
495
93
95
195
© The Countryman Press

Massachusetts 3

North Shore and Suburbs

A curious mix of modernity and history, northeastern Massachusetts is home to top technology companies as well as many of the nation's most revered historic sites and monuments. From infamous witch hunts to Revolutionary War battles, the North Shore preserves the roots of American independence while also continuing to play a role in its advancement.

Along the coast, history and tourism take on a distinctly nautical flair. On Cape Ann, home of the country's first fishing ports, Gloucester and Rockport are havens for artists, weekenders, and seafood lovers. Nature buffs flock to Plum Island State Park, while Newburyport, Ipswich, and Essex offer plenty of upscale shopping and dining. In Lowell, riverfront mills document the early days of the Industrial Revolution. And to the south, Lexington and Concord stand as monuments to a nation's beginnings with parks, cemeteries, battle greens, and colonial-era homes and taverns. (Thoreau's famous Walden Pond makes for a wonderful day trip, but alas, pets are not allowed.) The inner suburbs are busy workaday places filled with commuters and longtime residents, many of whom can trace their ancestors back to those tumultuous times. About 3 million people live in the area, and they love to visit the seacoast and historic sites, too—expect crowds and parking hassles, especially in summer. Preparation and patience are the keys to enjoying any trip to this remarkable slice of Americana.

ACCOMMODATIONS

Hotels, Motels, Inns, and Bed & Breakfasts

Andover

Homewood Suites Andover, 4 Riverside Dr., Andover (978-475-6000; 1-800-527-1133; www.hilton.com); $99–149 per night. Choose from one-bedroom or two-bedroom suites at this hotel offering a free breakfast buffet, an outdoor swimming pool, a fitness center, and an outdoor barbecue area. Each suite has cable television, free local calls, laundry service, and alarm clocks. When checking in with Fido, you'll pay a fee of $25 per night, up to a maximum of $75, with a one-dog-per-room limit. The hotel was formerly known as Comfort Suites Andover.

Residence Inn Boston-Andover, 500 Minuteman Rd., Andover (978-683-0382; www.marriott.com); $119–169 per night. Pets are welcome guests in the suites at this Residence Inn, designed for long-term stays with separate bedrooms, kitchens, and living room areas. Each suite has cable television and a coffeemaker; amenities also include a workout room, meeting and banquet facilities, a swimming pool, and a 24-hour front desk. Animal owners pay a one-time nonrefundable fee of $100.

Staybridge Suites Andover, 4 Tech Dr., Andover (978-686-2000; www.staybridge.com); $109–149 per night. This hotel is an oasis for night owls and time-strapped travelers: The front desk, laundry facilities, workout room, and business center are all open 24 hours a day. You'll also get free food at breakfast time and during the Sundowner social hours, and the suites are fully equipped with kitchens, bedrooms, and living areas. Those traveling with a pet pay an additional $75 per stay (not per night).

Burlington

Candlewood Suites Boston-Burlington, 130 Middlesex Tpke., Burlington (781-229-4300; www.ihg.com); $99–149 per night. Pets are welcome guests at this Candlewood Suites location offering high-speed Internet access, 149 suites, a fitness center, air-conditioning, free local phone calls, laundry facilities, and in-room hair dryers and coffeemakers. Dogs weighing less than 80 pounds are allowed for an additional $75 (up to six nights) or $150 (more than seven nights).

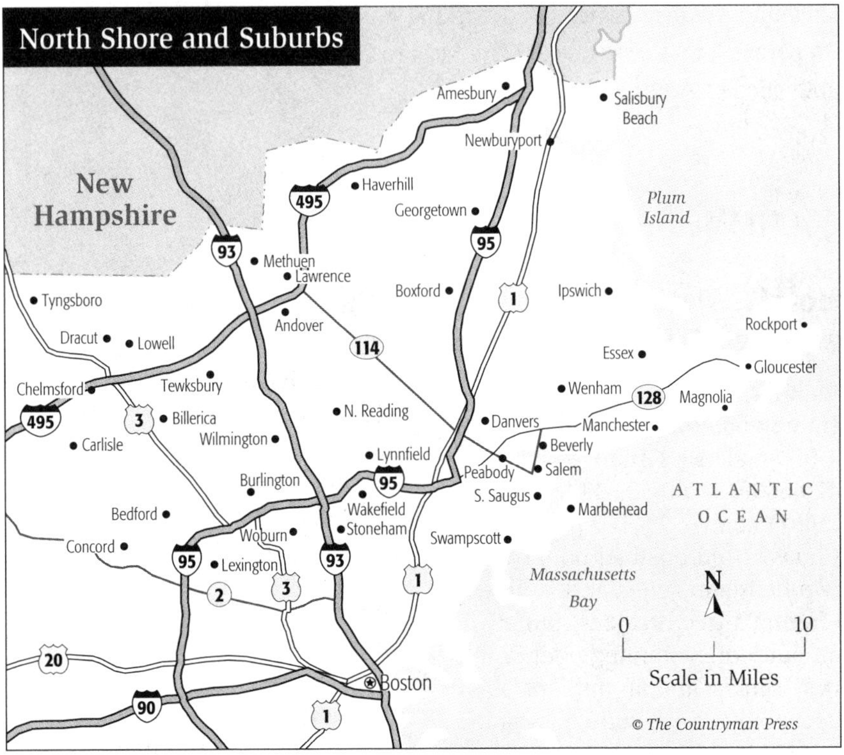

Extended Stay America Boston-Burlington, 40 South Ave., Burlington (781-359-9099; 1-800-804-3724; www.extendedstayamerica.com); $99–149 per night. The suites at this extended-stay hotel have full kitchens stocked with cutlery and cookware, computer workstations, separate bedrooms and living-room areas, and cable television. The Burlington Mall and its surrounding restaurants and shopping plazas are close by. Pets are welcome for an extra $25 per night, with a maximum charge of $75. One dog is allowed per room.

Staybridge Suites Burlington, 11 Old Concord Rd., Burlington (781-221-2233; www.staybridge.com); $119–169 per night. Frequented by business and leisure travelers, this all-suite hotel has complimentary full hot breakfasts, a 24-hour convenience store, a fitness center, a swimming pool, Internet access, free local telephone calls, laundry facilities, and a shuttle service to local businesses and attractions. Each suite has a full kitchen, cable television, and a DVD player. Animal owners pay an additional $15 per day.

Concord

Best Western at Historic Concord, 740 Elm St., Concord (978-369-6100; www.bestwestern.com); $99–159 per night. Just down the road from Concord's renowned bridge, churches, and historic homes, this Best Western offers an outdoor swimming pool, a fitness center, complimentary continental breakfasts, cable television with premium channels, hair dryers, and data ports. Pets are welcome for an additional $10 per night, although they cannot be left alone in the rooms at any time.

Danvers

Motel 6, 65 Newbury St., Danvers (978-774-8045; www.motel6.com). All Motel 6 locations are pet-friendly. The Danvers location has 109 rooms, interior corridors, an indoor swimming pool, cable television with premium movie channels, free local telephone calls, laundry facilities, and a "kids stay free" program. One well-behaved pet is permitted per room.

Residence Inn Boston North Shore–Danvers, 51 Newbury St., Danvers (978-777-7171; www.marriott.com); $129–189 per night. This Residence Inn location welcomes pets with a one-time cleaning fee of $100. Amenities include cable television with premium movie channels, a daily buffet breakfast, an outdoor swimming pool, a fitness center, safe-deposit boxes, and coffee in the lobby. All of the accommodations are suites of varying sizes, equipped with full kitchens, high-speed Internet access, and separate living and sleeping areas.

Town Place Suites by Marriott Danvers, 238 Andover St., Danvers (978-777-6222; 1-800-257-3000); $149–199 per night. This pet-friendly, all-suite hotel is located just behind the Chili's Restaurant on Route 1; each suite has separate living-room and bedroom areas, along with a kitchen. Other amenities include a swimming pool, a fitness center, laundry service, free parking, and a 24-hour front desk. Pet owners pay a one-time $100 cleaning fee.

Gloucester

Cape Ann Motor Inn, 33 Rockport Rd., Gloucester (978-281-2900; 1-800-464-VIEW; www.capeannmotorinn.com); $85–275 per night. You can relax in this motor inn's standard rooms or live the luxe life in the Honeymoon Suite ($170–225 per night). The building is located on the shorefront at Long Beach. Though dogs are welcome at the inn any time of the year, they're allowed on the beach itself only from Labor Day through Memorial Day.

Good Harbor Beach Inn, 1 Salt Island Rd., Gloucester (978-283-1489; www.goodharborbeachinn.com); $85–190 per night. This small red-and-white inn sits directly on the sand at Good Harbor Beach—you'd be hard-pressed to find a better location at a better price. In terms of pets, the inn welcomes them according to the same schedule as the beach itself: only during the off-season (after Labor Day to Memorial Day), and there's an additional $10 per-night fee.

Manor Inn, 141 Essex Ave., Gloucester (978-515-7386; www.castlemanorinn.com); $99–154 per night. Animals are allowed in certain motel rooms (but not in the main manor) at this historic accommodation overlooking the Annisquam River. Many of the motel rooms have water views, and all have cable television and air-conditioning. During the high season, guests can also enjoy free breakfast. Pet owners pay an additional $15 per night fee.

Ocean View Inn & Resort, 171 Atlantic Rd., Gloucester (978-283-6200; 1-800-315-7557; oceanviewwedding@gmail.com); $99–280 per night. This waterfront resort sits on nearly 6 acres with a restaurant, two swimming pools, and large decks; it's a popular spot for weddings and makes a picturesque home base for exploring the North Shore area. While not allowed in the main inn, pets are welcome in three adjacent motel buildings, Seaside, Ocean Terrace, and Cliffside, without extra fees.

Vista Motel, 22 Thatcher Rd., Gloucester (978-281-3410; 1-866-847-8262; www.vistamotel.com); $105–185 per night. For an extra $18 per day, guest pets are permitted in four of the Vista Motel's first-floor efficiencies overlooking Good Harbor Beach. The landscape includes an outdoor swimming pool and more than 3 acres of waterfront lawns and gardens—perfect for exploring with Spot. Pets cannot be left alone in the rooms at any time.

Lexington

Aloft Lexington, 727 Marrett Rd, Lexington (781-761-1700; www.starwoodhotels.com); $132–209 per night. A member of the Starwood Group, Aloft Hotels are super modern with cool amenities like an indoor splash pool, 24-7 fitness center, neon-laden lounge, and public spaces that sit up and beg you to hang out and socialize. All Alofts have an "arf pet program," greeting canine guests with the same exuberance as those on two legs: a bed, bowls, treats, and a toy await your pooch with no extra fees. Pets up to 40 pounds are welcome, but don't despair; if your dog is over 40 pounds, call the hotel and ask for a waiver of the size restriction. This Aloft even has a self-service car wash with eco-friendly suds.

Quality Inn & Suites, 440 Bedford St., Lexington (781-861-0850; 1-877-424-6423; www.choicehotels.com); $99–139 per night. Formerly a Holiday Inn Express, the Quality Inn welcomes dogs up to 50 pounds with a $25 fee per stay and a one-pet-per-room limit. Amenities include an outdoor swimming pool, in-room coffemakers and hairdryers, and free Wi-Fi. The hotel is located near the Minuteman Bike Trail and has spacious grounds for dog walking.

Marblehead

Seagull Inn Bed & Breakfast, 106 Harbor Ave., Marblehead (781-631-1893; host@seagullinn.com; www.seagullinn.com); $140–250 per night. Choose from the Lighthouse Suite, the Seabreeze Suite, or the Library Suite at this home-turned-B&B on the ocean. Each suite has

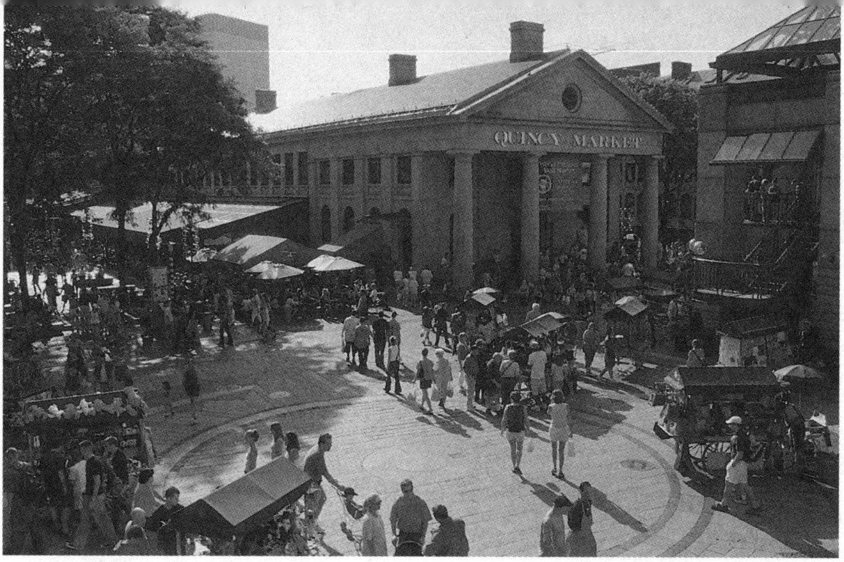

air-conditioning, a refrigerator, a TV/VCR, and a coffeemaker. Downstairs, the Harbor Room serves as a gathering place for guests. Dogs (sorry, no cats) are welcome as long as they stay off the furniture.

Peabody

Extended Stay America Boston-Peabody, 200 Jubilee Dr., Peabody (978-531-6632; 1-800-804-3724; www.extendedstayamerica.com); $99–139 per night. This newly renovated all-suite facility, formerly a Homestead Studio Suites, is located in the Centennial Business Park. Amenities include free Wi-Fi, in-room movies, an indoor swimming pool, laundry and valet services, babysitting services, air-conditioning, cable television, and continental breakfasts. Pet owners pay an extra $25 per night, with a maximum charge of $150.

Rockport

Carlson's Bed & Breakfast, 43 Broadway, Rockport (978-546-2770; carolhcarlson@verizon.net); $90–125 per night. This picture-perfect home and art gallery allows pet guests in one of the rooms, which has a private entrance, private bath, and double bed. "Animals are welcome," says innkeeper Carol Carlson. "We even had a parrot once." A full breakfast is served each morning in the dining room. All the sights and sounds of downtown are a walk away, and the beach is about a half-mile walk.

Rockport Inn & Suites, 183 Upper Main St., Rockport (978-546-3300; www.rockportinnandsuites.com); $170–225 per night. Freebies abound at the Rockport Inn with a complimentary continental breakfast, plus free Wi-Fi, daily paper, and local calls. The gorgeous indoor pool and hot tub may keep you inside, but there are also tennis courts. Up to two pets per room are welcome for an additional $30 per pet, per day.

Salem

Hawthorne Hotel, 18 Washington Sq. (on the common), Salem (978-744-4080; 1-800-SAY-STAY; www.hawthornehotel.com); $175–309

THE GRAND LOBBY AT THE HAWTHORNE HOTEL IN SALEM, WHERE CANINE GUESTS ARE WELCOME. (PHOTO COURTESY OF HAWTHORNE HOTEL)

per night. Just like the town that surrounds it, the 1925 Hawthorne Hotel boasts a long and fascinating history. Celebrities and a president have stayed at the Hawthorne, and your pooch will be treated like a VIP too with a welcome gift. For a special treat, order something from the canine room service menu. The guest rooms and dining room are decorated with antiques, lavish draperies, and period touches; there's also a fitness room, valet, and laundry service on-site. Upon check-in, animal owners sign a pet-policy agreement that outlines the rules and regulations, and the pet fee is an additional $15 per night.

Salem Inn, 7 Summer St., Salem (978-741-0680; reservations@saleminnma.com; www.saleminnma.com); $129–289 per night. Prepare to be bewitched: This luxurious inn on the National Register of Historic Places will take you back in time with fireplaces, four-poster beds, Oriental carpets, three separate historic buildings (ca. 1834, 1854, and 1874), and a flower-filled courtyard. Each guest room and family suite is individually decorated with period touches. Pets are welcome for an additional $15 per night.

Tewksbury

Holiday Inn Tewksbury-Andover, 4 Highwood Dr., Tewksbury (978-640-9000; www.ihg.com); $105–295 per night. Convenient to both I-93 and I-495, this hotel welcomes pets and offers a concierge desk, in-room movies, complimentary morning newspapers, a fitness center, a restaurant and lounge, an indoor swimming pool and a sauna, cable television, hair dryers, and alarm clocks. If you're paying in cash, the hotel will ask for a refundable security deposit of $50, plus a nonrefundable $50 cleaning fee per stay.

Motel 6 Tewksbury, 95 Main St., Tewksbury (978-851-8677; www.motel6.com); $59–79 per night. This is a very pet-friendly chain, welcoming you and your companion animal at all of its locations. It's kid-friendly, too—your child (under age 17) will stay for free. Other amenities at the Tewksbury location include free coffee in the lobby, laundry facilities, cable television with premium movie channels, and a swimming pool.

Residence Inn Boston Tewksbury/Andover, 1775 Andover St., Tewksbury (978-640-1003; 1-800-627-7468; www.marriott.com); $139–179 per night. The bedrooms at this all-suite hotel are separated from the living rooms with french doors; many also have fireplaces, balconies, and patios. All suites are equipped with full-size kitchens, but you can choose to let someone else do the cooking and enjoy the daily hot breakfast buffet, instead. Pet owners pay a one-time cleaning fee of $100.

TownPlace Suites by Marriott Tewksbury, 20 International Plaza, Tewksbury (978-863-9800; 1-800-257-3000; www.marriott.com); $104–154 per night. This all-suite hotel is popular with business travelers visiting nearby companies such as Raytheon, Hewlett-Packard, and Wang. Guests enjoy studio apartments and one- and two-bedroom suites with work areas, kitchens, and living rooms, a complimentary breakfast, and free high-speed Internet access. Pets are welcome with a one-time non-refundable fee of $75.

Westford

Residence Inn by Marriott Westford, 7 Lan Dr., Westford (978-392-1407; 1-800-331-3131; www.marriott.com); $131–209 per night. Close to the Nashoba Valley ski resort and a number of large corporations, this Residence Inn has one- and two-bedroom suites, a 24-hour front desk, a swimming pool, cable television, a fitness center, and daily free breakfasts. Pet owners pay $100 per stay.

Woburn

Residence Inn Boston-Woburn, 300 Presidential Way, Woburn (781-376-4000; www.marriott.com); $119–149 per night. For an extra one-time fee of $100, you and your pet are welcome to stay at this all-suite hotel offering express check-in and check-out services, daily buffet breakfasts, a barbecue area, a car-rental desk, and a fitness center. Each suite comes equipped with high-speed Internet access, a full kitchen, cable television with premium movie channels, and a fireplace.

Campgrounds

North Andover

Harold Parker State Forest—Lorraine Park Campground, 1951 Turnpike St. (Rte. 114), North Andover (978-686-3391); $12 per night Massachusetts residents; $14 per night out-of-state residents. The goal here was to provide a semiprimitive camping experience, so the sites allow for more privacy than you'll find at most other New England campgrounds. (There are no hookups for RVs.) Each site has a picnic table, fire pit, and barbecue grill, and restrooms are also available. Dogs must be on a leash and cannot be left unattended at the site. Owners should have a current license and proof of vaccinations ready at check-in. (See "Out and About" for more information on the state forest.)

Salisbury

Black Bear Family Campground, 54 Main St., Salisbury (978-462-3183; reservations@blackbearcamping.com; www.blackbearcamping.com); $40–50 per night. Tents, trailers, and RVs are all welcome at Black Bear, a busy family campground with a playground, a video arcade/poolroom, swimming pools, basketball courts, a camp store, laundry facilities, a large playground, and restrooms. "Small" pets (call to see if yours qualifies) are welcome, but must be on a leash at all times.

Rusnik Family Campground, Rte. 1, Salisbury (978-462-9551; 978-465-5295; rusnik2001@aol.com; www.rusnik.com); $32–42 per night. You'll find everything a family could need or want at this seacoast campground, including an outdoor swimming pool, shady and sunny sites, hookups for RVs, a miniature golf course, laundry and bathroom facilities, a duck pond, a playground, and sports courts and fields. Pets must be quiet and leashed, and owners must clean up after them.

Salisbury Beach State Reservations Campground, Beach Rd. (Rte. 1A), Salisbury (978-462-4481; 1-877-422-6762; www.salisbury-beach.org); $18 per night Massachusetts residents; $20 per night out-of-state residents. Horses are allowed during the off-season, and leashed dogs are welcome year-round at this popular campground. And though horses are allowed on the beaches, dogs are not. Campers can choose from 481 campsites and make use of the recently renovated restrooms. Reservations are required. (See "Out and About" for more park information.)

West Gloucester

Camp Ann Camp Site, 80 Atlantic St., West Gloucester (978-283-8683; www.capeann

campsite.com); $32–40 per night. This campground has a great location, spread out along 100 acres on the shores of Atlantic Ocean inlets. Tents, trailers, and RVs are welcome; hookups and daily/monthly rates are available.

Dog owners are asked to clean up after their animals, keep them on a leash, and not to leave them alone at campsites.

Homes, Cottages, and Cabins for Rent

Check the Boston Craigslist for vacation rentals, or these local rental agencies:

www.rockportusa.com
www.atlanticvacationhomes.com
www.weichertrents.com

OUT AND ABOUT

Annual Rock Run Motorcycle Ride. This benefit ride originated as a way to raise funds for the Massachusetts Society for the Prevention of Cruelty to Animals (MSPCA) at Nevins Farm. Riders collect pledges, wear one-of-a-kind T-shirts (with a different design each year), and enjoy the rush of the road as they raise money and see old friends. For more information on this year's event, visit www.mspca.org, call 978-687-7453, or visit the MSPCA Nevins Farm location at 400 Broadway in Methuen.

Downtown Rockport. Known for its picturesque location and resident artists, this hub of activity attracts almost every type of visitor with its myriad art galleries, cafés, specialty shops, and scenic lookouts. While you're there, make sure to check out "Motif #1," a red lobster shack covered in buoys that has been called the most photographed building in America. Parking is always tricky: While the downtown area hums all year long, summer is especially crowded. Wear comfortable shoes and expect to take a long walk to reach the action. Shuttles are sometimes available from municipal lots.

Gloucester Maritime Trail, Gloucester. The Cape Ann Chamber of Commerce (33 Commercial St., Gloucester; 978-283-1601; info@capeannchamber.com; www.capeannvacations.com) has created a "trail map" that outlines scenic and informative walks around the city's waterfront, downtown, and harbor areas. As the oldest fishing port in America (established about three years after the Pilgrims landed at the South Shore's Plymouth), the city offers more than its share of historical points of interest. Don't miss the famous *Fishermen's Memorial* statue on Stacey Boulevard.

Halibut Point State Park, Gott St., Rockport. This waterfront park offers some of the best views in Massachusetts; on a clear day, you can see the shore all the way up into Maine and New Hampshire. During your visit, you can hike the trails, stop for an ocean-view picnic on the cliffs, or take a self-guided tour to learn about the Babson Farm Quarry and the history of the Massachusetts granite industry. (Guided tours are also offered during the high season.) Pets must be on a leash.

Harold Parker State Forest, 1951 Turnpike St. (Rte. 114), North Andover (978-686-3391). With 3,000 acres of forestland and ponds, Harold Parker forest (named for the first chairman of the Massachusetts State Forest Commission) is a mecca for hikers, fishermen, boaters, hunters, campers, and day-trippers. The Berry Pond day-use area, open Memorial Day through Labor Day, offers restrooms and changing areas. Leashed pets are welcome everywhere except the beaches. (See "Accommodations—Campgrounds" for more information.)

Lexington Battle Green, Lexington. Each year on Patriots' Day (the Monday closest to April 19), actors gather on the green to reenact the events of April 19, 1775, when a ragtag group of local farmers armed themselves on this same patch of grass to try to keep British soldiers from advancing on Concord. When the first shots rang out, the first battle of the American Revolution had begun. Today, a *Minuteman* statue stands guard over the green, which is located in the downtown area near shops, restaurants, historic homes, and a bike trail.

Minute Man National Historical Park. The protected sites of this park are spread throughout the towns of **Lexington, Lincoln,** and **Concord** and detail some of the more fascinating happenings of the American Revolution. Highlights include the **Meriam's Corner** battle site; the **North Bridge,** site of the "shot heard 'round the world"; and the Paul Revere capture site. You can take a guided tour or wander at your own pace along the Battle Road Trail. Start at the visitors center at 174 Liberty St. in Concord (www.nps.gov/mima).

Plum Island & Sandy Point State Reservation, Parker River Wildlife Refuge Rd., Plum Island, Ipswich (978-462-4481). This park is named for the wild beach plum shrubs that grow on the dunes here. Pets (on a leash) are allowed here only during the off-season, between October 1 and April 1, but it's just as well: Summer is extremely crowded with beachgoers, and spring and fall provide more solitude with which to enjoy the spectacular scenery and wildlife. Nature trails include boardwalks to take you through the marshes at your own pace; don't forget the binoculars!

Dogs are not allowed on the beaches.

Rocky Neck Art Colony, 77 Rocky Neck Ave., Gloucester (978-282-0917; www.rockyneckartcolony.org). Located just off East Main Street, the nation's oldest working art colony has evolved into a fascinating area of galleries, shops, and eateries; on any given day, you might stumble across a poetry reading, painting demonstration, or historical lecture. The people-watching opportunities alone make it worth the trip.

Salem Walking Tours, 175 Essex St., second floor, Salem (978-745-0666). Your dog may not be allowed inside the museums, but there are several tour companies that can tell you all you need to know about the city's "haunted" past on guided walking tours—some during the daytime, some lit only by the light of a lantern at night. Contact one of these companies: **Salem Ghost Tours** (www.salemghosttours.com) at 978-741-1170; **Salem Historical Tours** (www.salemweb.com/guide/tours.php) at 978-745-0666; **Derby Square Tours** (www.derbysquaretours.com) at 978-745-6314; or **Spellbound Tours** (www.spellboundtours.com) at 978-745-0138.

Salisbury Beach State Reservation, Beach Rd. (Rte. 1A), Salisbury (978-462-4481; www.salisbury-beach.org). While not allowed on the beach itself, leashed pets are welcome to roam the rest of this 521-acre park, including hiking trails, a picnic area, and boat ramps. Bird-watchers should keep a lookout for loons, snow buntings, ducks, northern shrikes, and grebes, among other species.

QUICK BITES

Bedford Farms Ice Cream, 18 North Rd., **Bedford** (781-275-6501; www.bedfordfarmsicecream.com); and 68 Thoreau St., **Concord** (978-341-0000). Take Rover for a well-deserved ice cream, soft serve, or other treat at either of Bedford Farms's two locations. They're open year-round and serve more than 60 flavors of homemade ice cream and frozen yogurt. The farm itself has been running since 1880; today, it's a not-so-well-kept secret that locals would probably rather keep to themselves.

Boulevard Ocean View Restaurant, 25 Western Ave., Gloucester (978-282-2949). Outside dining is available at this well-known local restaurant serving Portuguese specialties and, of course, seafood. The specials board usually has something for everyone.

Carry Out Café, 155 State St., Newburyport (978-499-2240; www.carryoutcafe.com). "Home-cooked meals to go" are the specialty at this cute café offering daily specials such as southwestern chicken wraps, lasagna, vegetable napoleans, stroganoff, baked salmon with lemon and thyme, balsamic roasted chicken with red potatoes, chili, and New England clam chowdah.

Essex Seafood Restaurant and Fish Market, 143R Eastern Ave., Essex (978-768-7233; www.essexseafood.com). This casual "lobster shack" has a wide variety of seafood for takeout, including clam and tuna rolls, scallop and shrimp boats, and calamari, haddock, and lobster plates. Non-seafood eaters can order burgers, chicken fingers, and hot dogs. Go DIY and pick a lobster from the lobster pool.

Giuseppe's Fresh Pasta, 257 Low St., Newburyport (978-465-2225; www.giuseppesfreshpasta.com). Owner Giuseppe C. Masia cooks up Italian favorites to eat in or take out. "I have a lot of regular customers who are pet owners and order our dinners to go," he explains. "Some of them even get dinners for their dogs, because it's all they'll eat!" Beer and wine are served in the dining room; the entire menu is available at the Web site.

J. T. Farnham's Famous Clams, 88 Eastern Ave., Essex (978-768-6643). Paper plates and good old-fashioned heaping portions of fried seafood and lobster are just the ticket for hungry pet owners. Outside picnic tables are available.

Kimball Farm, 400 Littleton Rd., Westford (978-486-3891; www.kimballfarm.com). Friendly dogs are a common sight at Kimball Farm, a popular stop for families in the area. Most people come for the ice cream—heaping cones and sundaes made with more than 40 homemade flavors. But you can also get a sandwich, burger, and other treats at the outdoor luncheon grill (June through September). Picnic tables are available.

Treadwell's Ice Cream of Peabody, 46B Margin St., Peabody (978-531-9430; www.mytreadwells.com). Locals love the homemade flavors at this Peabody standby—for more than 50 years, they've been serving up great scoops. On any given day, you'll find about 25 flavors of ice cream, including butter crunch, mocha almond, chocolate, and vanilla, as well as low-fat frozen yogurt and sherbet. Bring a large group to try the Kitchen Sink: 12 scoops of ice cream, three toppings, whipped cream, nuts, and jimmies.

Victoria Station, Pickering Wharf, Salem (978-745-3400; www.victoriastationsalem.com). This restaurant has a scenic location on Salem Harbor and some outdoor tables on the brick patio. Seafood, prime rib, steaks, and all-you-can-eat salad are all on the menu, and locals rave about the haddock tacos and lobster ravioli. They also have a gluten-free menu.

Woodman's of Essex, 121 Main St. (Rte. 133), Essex (978-768-6057; 1-800-649-1773; www.woodmans.com). Woodman's is known for the best clam rolls, onion rings, and chowder in town. Not only does Woodman's have steamed clams, fried clams, clam cakes, and clam chowder, they also have a dog-walking area and picnic tables overlooking the salt marshes. Most customers order their lobster, shrimp, and frozen drinks from the pickup counter and enjoy their meal at the picnic tables or in their cars. The staff are happy to provide bowls of water for thirsty dogs.

HOT SPOTS FOR SPOT

Absolutely Canine Studio and Gallery, 38 Washington St., 1st Floor, Unit 2, Newburyport (978-462-6262). While you're in Newburyport enjoying all the shopping, restaurants, and water views, stop by this canine photography gallery and studio for a look at some candid and unique canine pics. Photographer Dawn Norris also provides on-location photo sessions throughout New England with your favorite pooch; visit the Web site to view the portfolio and to learn more about pricing and scheduling.

Animal Krackers, 232 Main St., Gloucester (978-283-1186). Food, toys, treats, and supplies are all available at Gloucester's only pet store. Food brands include Solid Gold, Science Diet, Eukanuba, Iams, and Breeder's Choice; nutritional supplements, flea and tick collars, leashes, collars, and doggie sweaters are also in stock.

Barking Boutique, 699B and 753 Boston Rd., Billerica (978-667-6868). Pet day-care services and professional grooming, including medicated baths and nail clipping, are available at this facility, open since 1977. Cats and dogs get their own individual boarding areas. The grooming salon and kennels are located at two different (but nearby) locations.

The Barking Cat Pet Emporium, 266 Essex St., Salem (978-745-BARK; www.thebarkingcat.us). The Barking Cat's Web site includes some adorable pictures of visiting canines and felines; this is the place for pets to see-and-be-seen in historic Salem. The homey store stocks fun toys and treats, Stephen Huneck prints, pet-related books and gifts, and a wide selection of all-natural pet foods. The owner is also happy to recommend nearby groomers, pet-sitters, veterinarians, and other service providers.

Best Friends Pet Resort and Salon, 394 Middlesex Rd., Tyngsboro (978-649-8585; www

.bestfriendspetcare.com). Best Friends is a chain with 41 locations throughout the United States, including Walt Disney World; the Tyngsboro location offers overnight boarding as well as doggie and kitty day care. You can choose extra services such as grooming, private one-on-one playtime, or walks for your buddy, for an additional fee.

Bone-Anza Doggie Daycare, 18 Bow St., Beverly (978-922-0117; www.boneanzadoggiedaycare .com). While you sightsee, your pooch can play, nap, go for walks, and socialize with the other animals and people at Bone-Anza. The staff will visit your house or hotel room ($10 per trip) to walk and water your dog, or you can bring your pet to their Cabot Street location ($20 per day) for fun and field trips to the beach and park with other pets.

Dawg City, 38 Pearson St., Andover (978-474-0655; www .dawgcityinc.com). Golden retrievers, Jack Russell terriers, shelties, Labs, and a host of other breeds are regulars at this Andover grooming salon. Make an appointment for a wash, cut, or clip when your pup needs a bit of freshening up. They also offer training classes.

Doggie Den, 16 Emerson St., Haverhill (978-373-0803; doggie denthe@aol.com). This business offers a little something for every pet owner, from grooming to training, supplies, and pet-focused photography. They even have a pickup service to save you the trip.

Beverly Dog Spa, 45 Enon St., Unit 5, Beverly (978-922-9227; info@dogspa.net; www.beverly dogspa.com). This upscale shop specializes in spoiling your pup, providing everything from nail trims to hydrosurge spa baths and aromatherapy treatments. The salon uses all-natural shampoos and conditioners and even offers a soundproof "quiet room" for its four-legged clientele. This is also a good spot to buy high-end collars, leashes, doggie coats, and handmade water bowls.

Dogville Dog Daycare, 120B Canal St., Salem (978-744-7840; woof@dogvilledaycare.com). Cape Ann offers more than its share of museums, restaurants, beaches, and boutiques; while you're visiting the sites, Dogville staffers can help keep an eye on your favorite four-legged friend. Dogville's owner, Claudia Siniawski, is a former animal control officer who has visited nursing homes and autistic children with her therapy dog, Tucker.

Good Dog! Gallery, 49 Bearskin Neck, Rockport (978-546-1364; www.gooddoggallery.com). Four-legged shoppers are always welcome at this hip gallery in the already hip town of Rockport. Visitors will find an impressive array of dog-focused artworks, including hand-hooked wool rugs, colored-glass creations, hand-painted ceramic lamps, woodcraft designs by Gloucester native Jim Lounsbury, water-color dog portraits, and Giclee prints by renowned Vermont artist Stephen Huneck. Dog treats abound!

Marblehead Animal Hospital, 19 Atlantic Ave., Marblehead (781-639-1300; www.marbleheadanimalhospital.com). In addition to providing medical services for companion animals, this pet hospital also offers complete grooming services using all-natural shampoos and skin treatments. Appointments are recommended.

Paws at Play, 210 Eastern Ave., Gloucester (978-281-PLAY; 1-866-360-PAWS). This doggie day-care facility is located in a renovated New England farmhouse. "There are climate-controlled inside playrooms as well as a large outdoor play yard," explains owner Gina Shlopak. "The dogs get lots of supervised group play and human interaction."

Paws Pet Boutique, 106 Main St., Amesbury (978-388-7297). This pet-centered shop sells animal-focused items such as SheaPet premium skin care products, Planet Dog toys and gear, Four Preppy Paws designer dog accessories, 1st CLASS Canine training aids, and RuffDawg toys.

Pawsitively Best Friends, 16 State St., Newburyport (978-499-9999; www.pawsitivelybestfriends.com). Newburyport is known for great shopping—this animal boutique put a four-legged spin on the town's upscale retail experience. Inside, you'll find items such as little brown cat photo note cards, Spotless Paw cleaning gloves, Furry Angel pet memorial candles, and Bowsers pet products.

Pawsitively Marblehead, 63 Atlantic Ave., Marblehead (781-639-0449). Monty Dog dog pillows, Dogz Togz, Marine Dog leashes, and Best Friend Bakery treats are just a few of the items you'll find at this Marblehead pet boutique.

Pet Companions Bed & Biscuit, 271 Main St., Reading (781-944-5445; www.petcompanionsinc.com). Pet Companions offers "pajama parties" (aka overnight boarding), doggie day-care services, and even playgroups for canines hoping to make friends. Doggie guests spend their days playing catch, swimming, running, and enjoying naps in the air-conditioned house. The company also offers a Somerville location (191 Broadway, Somerville; 617-623-2758).

Pet Source, 1173 Main St., **Concord** (978-371-7072); and 313 Marrett Rd., **Lexington** (781-676-0011; www.petsource.biz). This local chain of pet-supply stores sells carriers, crates, training equipment, toys, treats, leashes, collars, and of course plenty of pet food. Pet Source also has two locations in **Stow** and **Marlboro** (see "Central Massachusetts").

Pet Supplies Plus, 34 Cambridge St., **Burlington** (781-273-0200); and 400 Highland Ave., **Salem** (978-740-9788). These large stores are like supermarkets for pets, stocking a wide selection of chew toys; dog, cat, bird, and small-mammal food; books;

leashes and harnesses; pet beds; and more.

Unleashed, 12 Lothrop St., Beverly (978-922-8114; theteam @unleashthedog.com; www .unleasheddoggiedaycare.com). Unleashed offers everything a visiting or local pet might need, including doggie day-care facilities, at-home pet-sitting, complete grooming services, training classes, and even and a well-stocked shop with pet supplies and all-natural food. The day-care facility has indoor and outdoor play areas where visiting canines can play, nap, and enjoy plenty of TLC.

ANIMAL SHELTERS AND HUMANE SOCIETIES

Cape Ann Animal Aid, 4 Paws Ln., Gloucester (978-283-6055; www .capeannanimalaid.com)

MSPCA at Nevins Farm, 400 Broadway, Methuen (978-687-7453; www .mspca.org)

Northeast Animal Shelter, 347 Highland Ave., Salem (508-745-9888; www.northeastanimalshelter.org)

Strays in Need, Inc., 29 Ash St., Danvers (978-774-1409; www.straysin need.com)

IN CASE OF EMERGENCY

Andover Animal Hospital, 233 Lowell St., Andover (978-475-3600)

Beverly Animal Hospital, 303 Cabot St., Beverly (978-927-5453)

Cape Ann Veterinary Hospital, 2 Wildon Heights, Rockport (978-283-3238)

Clipper City Animal Hospital, 419 Merrimac St., Newburyport (978-462-7101)

Countryside Veterinary Hospital, 289 Littleton Rd., Chelmsford (978-256-9555)

Lexington-Bedford Veterinary, 476 Bedford St., Lexington (781-862-3670)

Linwood Animal Hospital, 1500 Gorham St., Lowell (978-453-1784)

McGrath Animal Hospital, 31 Lexington Rd., Billerica (978-667-2194)

Reading Animal Clinic, 1312 Main St., Reading (781-944-1699)

THE BOSTON HARBOR HOTEL IS A LUXURY ACCOMMODATION WITH GREAT VIEWS AND A POOCH-FRIENDLY ATTITUDE. (PHOTO COURTESY OF BOSTON HARBOR HOTEL)

Greater Boston

Like most urban centers, Boston has many more pet-friendly accommodations than you would find in the outlying areas of Massachusetts, and most of them are located in the city center within walking distance of historical attractions and serene parks. The luxury hotels, in particular the three Kimpton boutique hotels, the Fairmont, the Colonnnade, and the Eliot, have taken notice of all you pet lovers out there, promising to pamper your pooch with deluxe "pet packages," fluffy dog beds, and other extras. But don't worry if your budget won't accommodate the high-end hotels: There are plenty of moderately priced options, from chain hotels to charming inns, for you and pal to get a good night's sleep.

And the unprecedented canine welcome doesn't stop there: Visitors and locals will also find doggie happy hours, dog-adventure companies offering field trips for four-legged friends, "canine concierge" services, deluxe pet bakeries cooking up fresh-baked biscuits, and enough doggie day cares to entertain pups from one end of the city to the other. Best of all for pet owners, some of the region's most popular sites—from Faneuil Hall to the Freedom Trail—also happen to be outdoors. There is little you *can't* do with your pet here, except perhaps sample the cuisine at the city's many renowned restaurants, visit an art gallery, or poke around a museum. And for those occasions, there are plenty of pet-sitters and doggie day cares around (see "Hot Spots for Spot") to keep an eye on Fluffy. Animal owners should note that dogs are not allowed at Boston Harbor Islands State Park; luckily the mainland offers more than enough opportunities for peering into the city's enticing past and present. Tea, anyone?

ACCOMMODATIONS

Hotels, Motels, Inns, and Bed & Breakfasts

Boston

Boston Harbor Hotel, 70 Rowes Wharf, Boston (617-439-7000; www.bhh.com); $350–830 per night. Pets are welcome at this high-end waterfront hotel that features a health club and spa, a 60-foot lap pool, a staffed business center, on-site covered parking, an indoor gourmet restaurant and an outdoor café, and a water shuttle to Logan Airport. A recipient of the Forbes Five Star Award, the Boston Harbor Hotel is built on the site of a 17th battery. Pet amenities are provided at check-in, and a dog-walking service is available. Animals must be caged when left alone in the rooms.

The Colonnade, 120 Huntington Ave., Boston (617-424-7000; 1-800-962-3030; reservations@colonnadehotel.com; www.colonnadehotel.com); $330–1,000 per night. When it comes to making pet owners feel welcome, the Colonnade stands out from the rest. The hotel offers a VIPet program that features a dog-walking service ($15 per walk) and gifts for your animal. For its human guests, amenities include 285 contemporary rooms and 12 luxury suites, a shoeshine service, free newspapers, laundry and valet service, a rooftop swimming pool (the only one in Boston), and a restaurant. The four-diamond hotel recently received a $25 million renovation and is as sleek and stylish as its Back Bay neighborhood.

Eliot Hotel, 370 Commonwealth Ave., Boston (617-267-1607; 1-800-44-ELIOT; www.eliothotel.com); $395–750 per night. This all-suite hotel was built in 1925 and offers 79 suites, 16 guest rooms, room service, mini-bars, express check-in and check-out service, a fitness center, a restaurant and lounge, and a concierge service. This is old-school luxury at its finest with special amenities including a welcome gift, complimentary shoe shines and newspapers, and nightly turndown service. The Eliot has no weight or size restrictions for pets and doesn't charge extra fees for them, although the management asks that you not leave your animal alone in the room. Pet-sitting services are available.

Fairmont Copley Plaza, 138

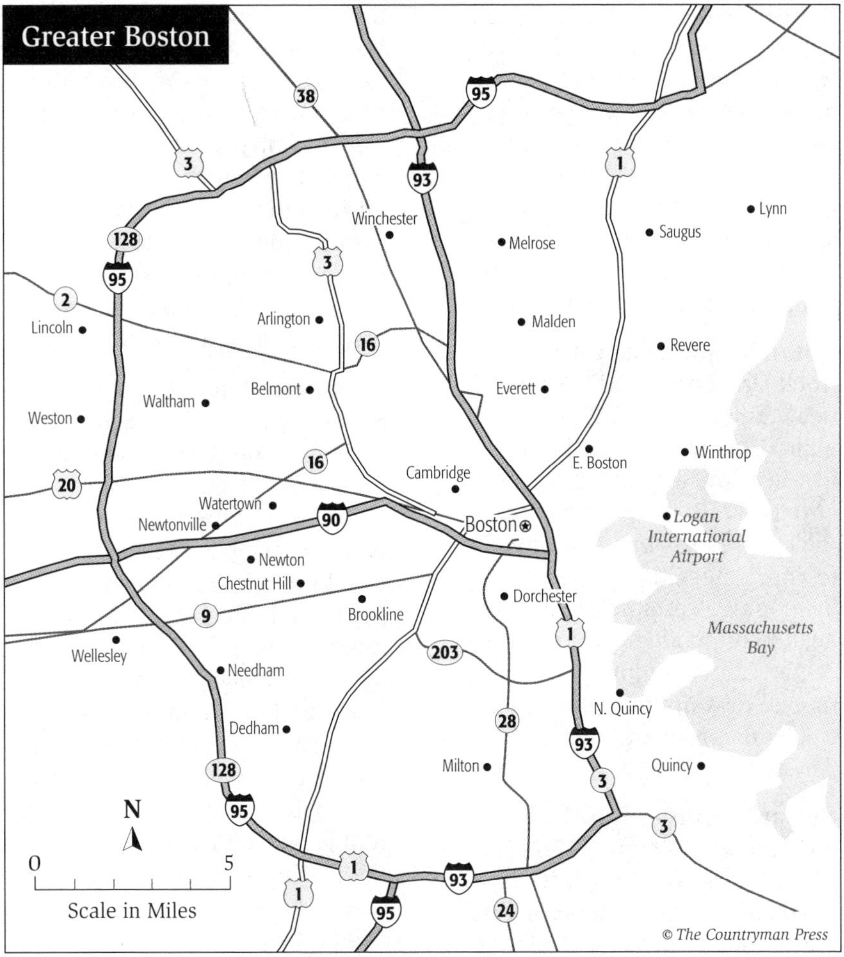

St. James Ave., Boston (617-267-5300; www.fairmont.com); $399–839 per night. The lavish Fairmont has been welcoming guests since 1912; on-site you'll find a fitness center, a beauty salon, 379 rooms and suites, in-room movies, 24-hour room service, desks with data ports, and babysitting services. Pets of all sizes are welcome for an additional $25 per night. Or, if you can't bring your own dog along, consider making the acquaintance of Cutie Copley, the hotel's Canine Ambassador, a black Labrador who was a guide dog before entering the hospitality industry. Cutie is available for walks, runs, or snuggling for out-of-town guests who find themselves missing their four-legged companions at home.

Four Seasons Hotel, 200 Boylston St., Boston (617-338-4400); $550–795. The Four Seasons' pet policy counts most dogs out: Only animals weighing less than 15 pounds are allowed.

But pet owners looking for posh digs for their small pooch or cat will undoubtedly enjoy the "pet menu," available through room service, as well as the indoor swimming pool, 24-hour front desk, and laundry and valet services. From most of the 273 rooms, you'll have views of the Public Gardens and Beacon Hill.

Hilton Boston Logan Airport, 1 Hotel Dr., Boston (617-568-6700; www.hilton.com); $299–395 per night. This 600-room Hilton isn't just near the airport—it's at the airport. Walk from your room to the covered skyway and directly to your gate. Other hotel benefits include two restaurants, a café, a health club and spa, a business center, and soundproofed guest rooms. Pets up to 75 pounds are welcome for an additional $50 per stay.

Howard Johnson Inn, 1271 Boylston St., Boston (617-267-8300; 1-800-I-GO-HOJO; www.hojo.com); $160–239 per night. This is one of the best in-city bargains for pet owners and Red Sox fans: Located next to Fenway Park, the HoJo Inn has many of the same services of the fancier hotels, including a concierge service, a 24-hour front desk, free parking, a restaurant, and babysitting services. Animals are welcome without extra fees, although they cannot be left alone in the rooms.

Hyatt Regency Boston, 1 Avenue de Lafayette, Boston (617-912-1234; www.hyatt.com); $299–499 per night. The Hyatt Regency is a deluxe 22-story hotel offering high-speed Internet access, a business center, a health club, massage therapy, 27-inch flat-screen televisions, and premium movie channels. Dogs are welcome. The hotel even offers an Extreme Pet Package that includes doggie treats, a neighborhood map, free valet parking, breakfast, a late checkout, a water bottle, and a Frisbee.

Nine Zero Hotel, 90 Tremont St., Boston (617-772-5800; www.ninezero.com); $322–800 per night. This is one of Boston's most pet-friendly accommodations, a member of the Kimpton Hotel group who pioneered the pet-friendly luxury hotel movement. Voted Best Boutique Hotel by *Boston* magazine, Nine Zero offers 24-hour room service, personal shoppers, valet parking, a fitness center, concierge services, therapeutic massage, and deluxe rooms and suites. The hotel's In the Doghouse package is free of charge to all guests and includes doggie treats, water and food bowls, and a pet bed. For doggie divas, the Tail in One City Package provides designer amenities for an additional charge.

Onyx Hotel, 155 Portland St., Boston (617-557-9955; www.onyxhotel.com); $180–500 per night. Another member of the pet-friendly Kimpton Hotel group, the Onyx Hotel will welcome your furry, finned, or feathered friend to join your vacation fun. Guests here enjoy concierge services, a complimentary wine hour each night, 24-hour room service, valet parking, and other luxuries. The hotel's "pet amenities" include gourmet treats, cleanup bags, and optional dog-walking and dog-sitting services. The Pampered Pet Packge includes gourmet pet menues, treats from the nearby **Polka Dog Bakery** (see "Hot Spots for Spot"), and a comfy bed.

Omni Parker House, 60 School St., Boston (617-227-8600; www.omnihotels.com); $459–799 per night. The historic Omni Parker House, founded by Harvey Parker in 1885, is the oldest continuously operating hotel in the United States, and is located in the heart of historic Boston on the Freedom Trail. It's also the birthplace of scrumptious Boston Cream Pie and sweet, pillowy Parker House Rolls. With 551 luxurious guest rooms, a fitness center, and all the modern amenities a traveler would want, the Omni welcomes dogs under 25 pounds with a one-time $50 fee per stay.

Ramada Inn Boston, 800 Morrissey Blvd., Boston (617-287-9100; www.wyndham.com); $149–198 per night. This Ramada is popular with tourists and business travelers, offering free shuttles to the airport, subway stations, Boston Medical Center, and New England Medical Center. Downtown attractions are located about 4 miles away. Pet owners must sign a release form and agree to follow the hotel's rules and regulations for animal guests.

Seaport Hotel, 1 Seaport Ln., Boston (617-385-4000; www.seaportboston.com); $279–450 per night. The Seaport's 426 guest rooms and suites have water views, handcrafted furniture, and a combination of classic and modern touches. The hotel also offers an indoor swimming pool, laundry and turndown services, airport shuttles, free shoe shines, a gift shop, and a florist. Pets weighing less than 50 pounds are welcome without extra fees, as long as they are not left alone in the rooms at any time. The hotel provides loaner beds, treats, and waste bags for your pooch, and hosts a weekly Canines & Cocktails on the Tamo Terrace.

Sheraton Boston Hotel, Prudential Center, 39 Dalton St., Boston (617-236-2000; www.starwoodhotels.com); $259–759 per night. With more than 1,200 rooms, the Sheraton Boston is one of New England's largest hotels. The Hynes Convention Center and the Copley Place Mall are just a skywalk away; inside the Sheraton, guests can enjoy an indoor swimming pool, a restaurant and bar, room service, concierge service, and a business center. Pets up to 40 pounds are welcome without extra fees; you'll be asked to sign a pet-policy waiver at check-in.

Brookline

Beech Tree Inn, 83 Longwood Ave., Brookline (617-277-1620; 1-800-544-9660; www.beechtreeinn.com); $119–179 per night. Well-behaved pets are welcome at the Beech Tree, a Victorian-style B&B with 10 guest rooms, air-conditioning, a sitting room, and a resident collie named Sophie. Guests enjoy a continental breakfast each morning. Animal owners must sign a copy of the pet policy outlining the house rules.

Bertram Inn, 92 Sewall Ave., Brookline (617-566-2234; 1-800-295-3822; innkeeper@bertraminn.com; www.bertraminn.com); $179–329 per night. Owned by a historic preservationist, this 1907 inn has 10 guest rooms on three floors; each room is individually decorated with touches like bookshelves, four-poster beds, antique walnut furniture, and cheery window swags. Air-conditioning, Internet access, and full daily breakfasts are also available. Pets are welcome with preapproval, though they can't be left unattended in the rooms.

Holiday Inn Boston-Brookline, 1200 Beacon St., Brookline (617-277-1200; www.ihg.com); $194–259 per night. For an extra $25 per night, pets can join their owners at this Holiday Inn, which features air-conditioning, an indoor swimming pool, room service, in-room movies, cable television, high-speed Internet access, in-room hair dryers, a "kids eat free" program, a fitness center, and a lounge. Downtown Boston is a few minutes' drive away. Parking is available for $15.

Cambridge

Charles Hotel Harvard Square, 1 Bennett St., Cambridge (617-864-1200; 1-800-3232-7500; www.charleshotel.com); $249–4,500 per night. This ultradeluxe hotel, a member of the Preferred Hotels group and a AAA four-diamond property, offers the finest of everything, including a great location right on Harvard Square. Charming New England décor, with special touches like custom handmade quilts, coexist with modern amenities, including Wi-Fi and flat screens. In addition to VIP rooms and services, a beauty shop, a fitness center, baby- and pet-sitting services, and room service, the hotel also has two on-site gourmet restaurants (see "Quick Bites") and an award-winning jazz club and bar. Pets are welcome with a $50 one-time fee but can't be left alone in the rooms.

Hotel Marlowe, 25 Edwin H. Land Blvd., Cambridge (1-800-825-7140; www.hotelmarlowe.com); $265–535 per night. This luxury boutique hotel, one of three Kimpton Hotels in the city, has concierge services, 24-hour room service, a fitness center, valet parking, and elegant rooms and suites. After staying at the Hotel Marlowe five times, your pooch becomes a VIP (Very Important Pet) and receives a lunch box full of treats from the **Polka Dog Bakery** (see "Hot Spots for Spot"). Pampered Pet Packages are also available, including the Man's Best Friend Pampering Kit, the Finicky Feline Pampering Kit, and Pet-Pourri Package. The hotel is adjacent to a park, and the concierge can arrange dog walks if you don't have time to stroll with your pal or want to relax at the nightly wine hour.

THE CHARLES HOTEL IS LOCATED IN THE HEART OF HARVARD SQUARE IN CAMBRIDGE.

Residence Inn by Marriott Boston Cambridge Center, 6 Cambridge Center, Cambridge (617-349-0700; www.marriott.com); $199–349 per night. Guests enjoy a complimentary buffet breakfast, free newspapers, fax and photocopying services, free high-speed Internet access, and laundry facilities at this all-suite, extended-stay facility. Each suite has a separate bedroom and living room and a full kitchen. Pet owners pay a $150 nonrefundable fee.

Charlestown

Bunker Hill Bed & Breakfast, 80 Elm St., Charlestown (617-241-8067; crawolff@cs.com; www.bunkerhillbedandbreakfast.com); $150–175 per night. A cozy alternative to the "big city" hotels, this Victorian-style B&B offers two guest rooms, an antiques-filled living room, free snacks and beverages, a hot tub, air-conditioning, televisions, bathrobes, slippers, and complimentary full breakfasts. The owners are very animal-friendly and allow pets for an extra $10 per day; they'll also be happy to point the way to the neighborhood dog park and the Freedom Trail. Parking is available for $15.

Dedham

Residence Inn by Marriott Dedham, 259 Elm St., Dedham (781-407-0999); $199–249 per night. Located in the suburbs south of Boston, this Residence Inn has suites with kitchens, a swimming pool, free parking and newspapers, a fitness center, cable television, free daily hot breakfasts, free Internet access, in-room coffeemakers, and a 24-hour front desk. Pets are allowed with a one-time $100 nonrefundable fee.

Medford

Hyatt Place Boston/Medford, 116 Riverside Ave., NE, Medford (781-395-8500; www.hyatt.com); $168–278 per night. Pets weighing less than 50 pounds are permitted at Hyatt Place for an extra $75 per stay. The Medford location, 4 miles from downtown, offers 158 suites, complimentary Wi-Fi, 24-hour room service, a fitness center, laundry facilities, meeting rooms, and limited shuttle services.

Newton

Hotel Indigo Boston-Newton, 399 Grove St., Newton (617-969-5300; www.newtonboutiquehotel.com); $140–250 per night. The Hotel Indigo chain is inspired by the modern design hotels of Europe and is both eco-friendly and pet-friendly. Two dogs per room are allowed with a $50 per-stay cleaning fee and a $50 refundable damage deposit. The hotel has a fitness center, in-room movies, room service, cable television, free high-speed Internet access, a wake-up service, coffeemakers and hair dryers in the rooms, air-conditioning, and a concierge desk.

Revere

Hampton Inn Logan Airport, 230 Lee Burbank Hwy., Revere (781-286-5665); $199–268 per night. As its name implies, this hotel is just north of the airport and 3 to 6 miles from most Boston attractions. On-site, you'll find an indoor swimming pool and a hot tub, satellite television, and a fitness club. The hotel also offers a free airport shuttle service. "Small" pets (call to see if yours qualifies) are welcome without extra fees.

Saugus

Colonial Traveler Motor Court, 1753 Broadway, Saugus (781-233-6700); $69–99 per night. This simple and clean motor inn is located about 6 miles north of Boston and offers standard rooms, one- and two-bedroom suites, cable television with premium movie channels, refrigerators, and coin-operated laundry facilities. Pets are welcome in designated rooms for an additional $10 per night.

Winthrop

Inn at Crystal Cove, 600 Shirley St., Winthrop (617-846-9217; ccove@tiac.net; www.inncrystalcove.com); $104–162 per night. Located on a peninsula just outside Boston, this inn has great views of the city skyline and harbor. Each of the 30 guest rooms has air-conditioning, cable television, and free local calls; some rooms also have balconies and water views. "We have lots of open spaces for dogs to run around," says manager Karl Sticker. "We also have parks nearby and a gigantic boulevard for dog walking." Pets are enthusiastically welcomed.

Woburn

Red Roof Inn Boston Woburn, 19 Commerce Way, Woburn (781-935-7110; 1-800-RED-ROOF); $85–145 per night. This suburban economy hotel is located close to the train and bus stations and makes a good home base for visiting Boston or any of the large companies in the surrounding I-95 corridor. Guests can take advantage of express check-out services, free local calls, cable TV, and free newspapers. Pets that weigh less than 80 pounds are welcome.

Rental Agencies

Bed & Breakfast Associates Bay Colony, Boston (1-888-486-6018; info@bnbboston.com; www.bnbboston.com). This reservations service can help you find short-term (three nights to a few months) housing in the Boston area; at any given time, a few of their accommodations allow pets.

OUT AND ABOUT

Arnold Arboretum of Harvard University, intersection of Centre St. (Rte. 1) and the Arborway (Rte. 203), Boston (617-524-1718; www.arboretum.harvard.edu). This is a fantastic destination for any visitor—one that just happens to allow your pets to come along, too. The 365-acre research and educational arboretum contains one of the best woody plant collections in the world. Highlights include a bonsai garden, a lilac collection, the Chinese Path, and 130 types of maple trees. (If you arrive in early October, you'll enjoy a fiery show of foliage.) Dogs must be leashed, and owners are expected to clean up after their animals.

Back Bay Fens. Designed by Frederick Law Olmsted, the Fens is the spot where a real-life police officer helped some ducklings cross a busy road. (Sound familiar? The *Make Way for Ducklings* statue is located on the Common.) Today visitors will find the Kelleher Rose Garden and the Victory Garden, which is the oldest remaining U.S. garden from World War II. Dogs are permitted, but must be leashed.

WATCH THE SWAN BOATS GLIDE BY AS YOU STROLL WITH YOUR POOCH AROUND THE BUCOLIC BOSTON PUBLIC GARDENS. (COURTESY OF GREATER BOSTON CONVENTION & VISITORS BUREAU)

Boston Common. Like many of New England's commons and greens, this one was once used to graze cattle. Today, of course, it is better known as one of the oldest public parks in America. Comprising 50 acres, it includes the **Boston Public Garden,** fountains, the *Make Way for Ducklings* sculptures, and the famous Swan Boats. Dogs must be on a leash.

Boston Harborwalk, various locations, Boston. The Boston Harborwalk is more of an idea than a particular place: Throughout the city, you'll find the walkway winding through neighborhoods, beside businesses, and along parklands, always offering a great view of the water. Many areas along the Harborwalk are dog-friendly, including Christopher Columbus Waterfront Park, Lewis Wharf, Rowes Wharf, and Puopolo Park, all in the **North End;** Belle Isle Marsh, Constitution Beach (off-season only), and East Boston Greenway, all in **East Boston;** Commonwealth Pier, Castle Island (off-season only), Carson Beach (off-season only), and Commonwealth Pier, all in **South Boston;** Paul Revere Park and the Charlestown River Dam and Locks, both in **Charlestown;** and Old Harbor Park, Tenean Beach (off-season only), Malibu Beach/Savin Hill Beach (off-season only), and Pope John Paul II Park, all in **Dorchester.** Dog owners must use a leash and clean up any messes their pooches leave behind. For more information, visit www.bostonharborwalk.com.

Carson Beach, Day Blvd., South Boston. As far as New England beaches go, this one is nothing special. But it's close (a half mile from the JFK-UMass/Boston station on the Red Line) and provides welcome ocean breezes on a hot day. A walking path borders the beach. Leashed dogs

HARBORWALK IS A GREAT CHOICE FOR A SCENIC DOG WALK ALONG THE WATER. (COURTESY OF GREATER BOSTON CONVENTION & VISITORS BUREAU)

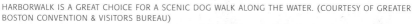

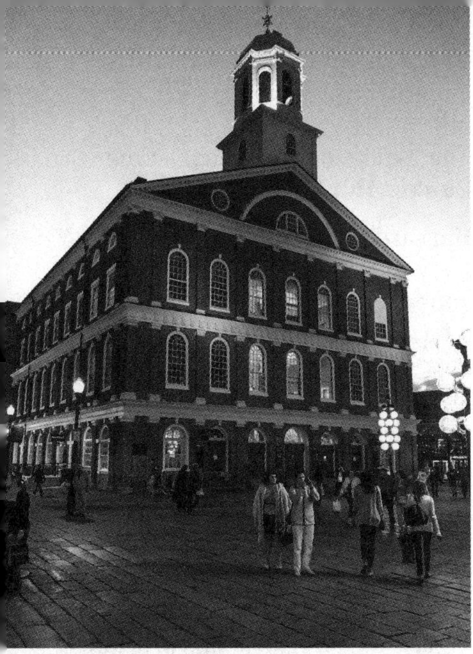
FANEUIL HALL (© MARCIO JOSE BASTOS SILVA/ SHUTTERSTOCK.COM)

are welcome, but only during the off-season.

Charles River Canoe and Kayak, 500 Broad Canal Way, Artesni Park (off Soldiers Field Rd.), Cambridge (617-965-5110). Rent a canoe and explore the harbor with your favorite adventurous canine. The waterway is typically crowded with kayaks, sailboats, motorboats, and the boats of rowing teams at practice, so use caution, especially near the Boston University Bridge.

Charles River Reservation, Boston. Managed by the Metropolitan District Commission, this 17-mile-long stretch of park winds its way around the river with views of rowers, sailboats, and the Cambridge and Boston skylines. The pathways, especially popular with joggers and dog walkers, run past the **Hatch Shell** (where the Boston Pops give their annual Fourth of July concerts), **Mount Auburn Cemetery,** and **JFK Memorial Park,** among other spots. The park runs alongside Storrow Drive, Memorial Drive, and Soldier's Field Road. It also includes the Esplanade on the Boston side.

Christopher Columbus Waterfront Park, Boston (www.foccp.org). After a visit to the North End, take a stroll over to this green and garden-filled area located between Commercial and Long Wharfs, the city's first waterfront park. Keep traveling south toward Central Wharf and the **New England Aquarium,** and you'll find plenty of spots to stop and enjoy the views. (If you're lucky, you'll also see the seals hanging out in the aquarium's outdoor habitat.) Dogs must be on a leash. Don't miss the Rose Kennedy Rose Garden in bloom.

Faneuil Hall and Quincy Market, Boston. This large outdoor gathering place and vendor area has cart after cart selling scarves, cookbooks, hats, oatmeal cookies, clam chowder, flowers, T-shirts, trinkets, rubber stamps, and a seemingly endless array of other items and foods. (There's inevitably at least one cart selling pet-related fun stuff.) Additions in recent years have included indoor shopping malls and chain stores, but there's still plenty to do outside with your pooch in tow. Walk the cobblestone streets, enjoy a hot pretzel from a vendor, or just relax on a bench and watch the world go

© COL/SHUTTERSTOCK.COM

by. The marketplace is tucked between North, Congress, and State streets.

First Night, Boston. The city streets fill with people, ice sculptures, and celebration every New Year's Eve in Boston and Cambridge. There are usually more than 250 indoor and outdoor shows, entertainers, and artists, along with fireworks. If your pooch doesn't mind crowds and loud noises, this is a must-see.

Freedom Trail, Boston (www.freedomtrail.org). This self-guided trail of Boston's historic sites is one of the city's most popular attractions—and, like all of the best things in life, it's absolutely free. Start at the Visitor Information Center on the Boston Common and follow the red brick/red paint line as it winds through the streets. Medallions on the ground mark each of 16 notable sites, including the **Old South Meeting House,** the **Boston Massacre site,** and the **Paul Revere House.** The 2-mile-long trail ends at the **Bunker Hill Monument.**

Harvard Square, Cambridge (www.harvardsquare.com). Park your car here and wander for a bit; this bustling commercial area has about 20 bookstores, 10 music stores, 9 museums, 5 theaters, and street performers around every corner. There are plenty of students around and over 8 million visitors annually, but people from every conceivable walk of life also find themselves drawn to the activity and discussions at the small cafés and sidewalk benches. To get there, just head for JFK Street and follow your nose around the winding and crowded streets.

Lynn Woods, Pennybrook Rd., Lynn (781-593-7773; www.flw.org). "Lynn Woods is dog's

TAKE A STROLL THROUGH HISTORIC BOSTON AND VISIT THE FAMOUS PAUL REVERE STATUE. (COURTESY OF GREATER BOSTON CONVENTION & VISITORS BUREAU)

HARVARD SQUARE (© COL/SHUTTERSTOCK.COM)

paradise," says park ranger Dan Small. "We have 40 miles of hiking trails and fire roads." Because the on-site ponds are part of the local reservoir system, dogs aren't allowed to swim, and they must be on a leash at all times. Popular landmarks include the stone tower, Dungeon Rock, the rose garden, and Wolf Pits. There are more than 100 species of birds in this 2,200-acre forest reserve.

MSPCA Walk for Animals, Boston. The **Massachusetts Society for the Prevention of Cruelty to Animals (MSPCA)** puts on this walk every autumn—2005 marked its 25th anniversary. The dates and locations change periodically; call 617-522-WALK, e-mail walkforanimals@mspca.org, or visit www.mspca.org for the latest information. Expect to enjoy games, raffles, and crazy contests like Best Trick and Mutt of the Year. The society also hosts a fun Animal Hall of Fame fund-raising dinner each year—all are welcome to attend.

Petiquette Pooch Concierge, Boston (617-733-3923; www.petiquettesouthboston.com). Winner of "Best Dog Walker" and "Best Pet Sitting Service' in the local dog lover community, this pooch concierge offers group and solo walks, dog sitting, and even overnights at their own doggie B&B (their home!).

The Pooped Pooch, Boston (617-755-3288; www.poopedpooch.com). A local award winner for their personal and hands-on walking and sitting services, The Pooped Pooch serves the areas of Dorchester, South Boston, and the South End.

The North End, Boston (www.northendboston.com). This Italian enclave is slowly becoming more of a melting pot of different peoples, but it's still the place Bostonians go to get a taste of Italy. In addition to myriad restaurants, cafés, and pastry shops, you'll also find the **Paul Revere house, Copp's Hill Burying Ground,** and the famous **Old North Church** on these narrow, historic streets. The neighborhood stretches throughout Hanover, Salem, Parmenter, Richmond, Fulton, and Prince streets, roughly located between Faneuil Hall and the wharfs.

Pine Ridge Animal Center/Pine Ridge Pet Cemetery, 55 Anna's Place at 238 Pine St., Dedham (781-326-0729; www.arlboston.org). Operated by the Animal

Rescue League of Boston, Pine Ridge is home to the oldest continuously operated pet cemetery in the United States. Visitors will also find a livestock rehabilitation center and the **Safford Memorial Animal Care and Adoption Center** at the 27-acre site.

Provincetown–Boston Ferry, Boston Harbor Cruises, Long Wharf Ferry Terminal, Boston (617-227-4321; www.bostonharborcruises.com); $38–59 per person, round-trip. Take a scenic shortcut from Boston to one of Cape Cod's most interesting towns. Boston Harbor Cruises' "fast ferry" welcomes animals on board for this 90-minute journey on the Atlantic; the boat is the biggest passenger ferry in the United States. (For more information on Provincetown, see "Cape Cod and the Islands.")

The T. Locals know the local MBTA subway system (www.mbta.com) simply as "The T" and take its colorful "lines" (the red, the green, the blue, etc.) everywhere they need to go in the city. Dogs are permitted, although owners are asked to avoid rush hours and always use a leash or crate.

QUICK BITES

Absolutely Asia, 864 Main St., Waltham (781-891-1700; www.absolutelyasia.com). Order your Chinese and Thai food to go or have it delivered; specialties include Yu Hsiang–style pork and beef, Hong Kong–style pan-fried noodles, jumbo shrimp in black bean sauce, sweet and sour chicken, Yanchow fried rice, and Thai-style spicy seafood soup.

Café Arpeggio, 398 W. Broadway, South Boston (617-269-8822; www.cafearpeggio.com). You'll find a few sidewalk tables at Café Arpeggio, a "Parisian-style" café offering homemade, hand-blended ice cream, soups, sandwiches, and baked goods. For more information on the company's **Fall River** location, see the "South Shore and Suburbs."

Davio's To Go, 10 St. James Galleria Atrium, Boston (617-357-4556; www.davios.com). This shop is the companion to Davio's Northern Italian Steakhouse on Arlington Street. The take-out location offers Davio's dishes in convenient take-home packaging—just unwrap and eat once you get back to the hotel. Selections include bagels, muffins, croissants, panini, and a variety of soups and salads.

El Pelón Taqueria, 92 Peterborough St., Boston (617-262-9090; www.elpelon.com). Locals love this tiny Mexican restaurant, where most of the items are available as takeout and everything is very reasonably priced. House specialties include fish tacos, grilled burritos, taquitos, enchiladas, and extra-hot sauce.

STROLL AROUND THE MARKETPLACE AT HISTORIC FANEUIL HALL IN BOSTON. (COURTESY OF GREATER BOSTON CONVENTION & VISITORS BUREAU)

Faneuil Hall Marketplace, 3 Faneuil Hall Marketplace, Boston (617-523-1300; www.faneuilhall marketplace.com). If you're craving it, you'll probably find it here. Many of the restaurants have outdoor seating on the cobblestones, and the marketplace itself has a huge selection of take-out-only eateries serving everything from seafood to pizza, gelato, and cheesecake. You can't bring your dog inside the walk-through marketplace, but outside there are plenty of benches to be found for enjoying your bounty.

Harvest Co-op and Café, 580 Massachusetts Ave., Cambridge (617-661-1580; www.harvest coop.com). This café is more of a store than a restaurant, with organic foods from meat and seafood to local produce, but those traveling with a pup will find the counter service, take-out choices, salad bar, and juice bar convenient. Options include smoothies, deli sandwiches, salads, and fresh produce, as well as a wide variety of options for vegetarians.

Henrietta's Table, 1 Bennett St., Cambridge (617-661-5005; www .henriettastable.com). Located at the dog-friendly **Charles Hotel** (see "Accommodations"), Henrietta's offers lots of outdoor tables and dining choices like baked Gloucester scrod, asparagus tart, seared salmon burger, Maine rock crab cake, and campfire s'mores with vanilla ice cream. This is classic New England on a plate.

Kinsale Irish Pub & Restaurant, 2 Center Plaza, Cambridge St., Government Center, Boston (617-742-5577; www.classicirish .com). The owners of Kinsale Irish pub offer you and your dog a traditional "Cead Mile Failte" (100,000 welcomes) at both this pub and their other establishment, The Asgard, in Cambridge. There will be plenty of opportunities for people-watching (and dog-watching) when you enjoy your meal at the sidewalk seating area of this classic Irish restaurant and pub. A full take-out menu is also available.

Mike's Pastry, 300 Hanover St., Boston (617-742-3050; info@mikespastry.com; www .mikespastry.com). This staple of the North End has been serving flaky, creamy, crunchy, and downright delicious treats since . . . well, seemingly since forever. Take a peek at the Old North Church and then stop by Mike's for cookies, biscotti, gelato, marzipan, fig squares, fudge, and endless other options on display in the long bakery cases. Locals swear by the red velvet cake and whoopie pies.

New England Soup Factory, 2 Brookline Pl., **Brookline** (617-739-1899); and 244 Needham St., **Newton** (617-558-9988; www.newenglandsoupfactory.com). When you're tired of sandwiches, stop by this take-out shop for a cup of chili or soup with every imaginable combination of ingredients. The menu changes daily. And if you're *not* sick of sandwiches, they have those, too, along with desserts. Locals (and visitors) give this place rave reviews.

Parish Café, 361 Boylston St., Boston (617-247-4777; www.parishcafe.com). In 1992, owner Gordon Wilcox begged Boston's best chefs to create a signature sandwich for his menu, so you can munch your way around the city in one spot. Located just around the corner from the Public Garden, this upscale café has some outdoor seating and serves sandwiches on gourmet bread with ingredients such as prosciutto, lobster salad, roast beef, pork medallions, halibut, and arugula. Appetizers include choices such as vegetable potstickers, spinach salad, and a cheese plate.

Picante Mexican Grill, 735 Massachusetts Ave., Cambridge (617-576-6394; www.picantemex.com). Located in Central Square, this counter-service restaurant serves burritos, enchiladas, and other Tex-Mex and vegetable dishes. Some outdoor seating is available, and the prices are more than reasonable.

Stephanie's on Newbury, 190 Newbury St., Boston (617-236-0990; www.stephanieson newbury.com). Stephanie's has a large sidewalk-seating area where you'll find businessmen, moms with high chairs, power shoppers, and yes, even the occasional well-behaved pooch. Enjoy sophisticated comfort food, from crab cakes and tuna tartare to pulled-pork quesadillas, or grab a quick bite and a drink while watching all the Newbury Street trendsetters walk by.

Tremont 647, 647 Tremont St., Boston (617-266-4600; www.tremont647.com). This unique and stylish restaurant regularly hosts Doggie Days on the Patio. Every Saturday from 2 to 5 PM, Tremont 647 welcomes canine diners of all sizes to enjoy treats from the **Polka Dog Bakery** (see "Hot Spots for Spot"), as well as "doggie delicacies," such as Martha's Meatballs, Lamb Rangoon, and even a Dogmopolitan made with lamb broth, beet juice, and a citrus twist. Whether you're a local or a visitor, this doggie happy hour is a can't-miss event in the city. Humans will want to try the pan-seared scallops, grass-fed beef, or the chef's five-course tasting menu.

The Upper Crust Pizzeria, 20 Charles St., Boston (617-723-9600; www.theuppercrustpizzeria.com). As you might guess from the name, this eatery specializes in pizza—but you'll also be able to choose from a wide variety of calzones, salads, and seafood dishes. The entire menu is available online, and they offer free delivery.

Veggie Planet, 47 Palmer St., Cambridge (617-661-1513; www.veggieplanet.net). This vegetarian restaurant and pizzeria in Harvard Square bakes its pizzas on organic pizza dough with varieties such as Mexican bean, caramelized fennel and onion, and red-peanut curry. Coffee, tea, and Italian sodas are also available, as are salads, waffles, organic breads, and rice dishes. The emphasis is on "ecological eating" and healthy options.

HOT SPOTS FOR SPOT

The Adventure Dog, Boston area (617-939-7407). The Adventure Dog offers canine adventures for small groups of dogs, as an alternative to kenneling and doggie day care. Field trips include Water Wonder (swimming and water play), Trail Hike (exercise and socialization), Sensational Snow Time (winter hikes), the Block Walk (designed for seniors, puppies, and less-active adult dogs), and the Park Adventure (Frisbee, fetch, and running). Overnight pet-sitting is also available.

Best Friends Pet Care, 15 Main St., Wakefield (781-245-1237; www.bestfriendspetcare.com). This branch of the national pet-sitting chain offers overnight boarding for dogs and cats. Doggie and kitty day care is also available, as are grooming services. You can purchase playtime sessions for your pet during her stay for an extra $5 per session.

The Common Dog, 57 Garden St., Everett (617-381-6363; more info@commondog.com; www.commondog.com). Local and visiting dog lovers have a great resource in this full-service dog care facility. One of the company's most popular services is its doggie day care, which includes plenty of attention and frolicking in indoor and outdoor play areas. You can also take advantage of "B&B" overnight care, shuttle bus transportation service, a doggie salon and spa, and even a training academy. Visit the Web site for pictures, schedules, rates, and information on making an appointment.

D'Tails Pet Boutique, 482A Columbus Ave., Boston (857-233-2672; www.dtails-boston.com). Located in the South End, D'Tails covers all the fine print, from dog walking, dog sitting, grooming and play groups to selling a wide variety of food, treats, and canine accessories.

Dog Day Afternoons, 1011 Harrison Ave., Boston (617-442-2682; www.dogdayafternoons

FOUR-LEGGED CLIENTS OF FOUR PAWS AND A LEASH ENJOY EACH OTHER'S COMPANY IN DORCHESTER. (PHOTO BY RICH COLICCHIO)

.org). Your pup will have plenty of room to run, play, and explore at this 5,500-square-foot doggie day-care facility. Located in the South End, the center has off-street parking and also offers dog walks, overnight boarding, a "limo service" for pets, and plans for an aquatherapy program.

Doggie Daytrippers, 214 Shawmut Ave., Boston (617-306-1863; info@doggiedaytrippers.com; www.doggiedaytrippers.com). Doggie Daytrippers specializes in keeping canines busy, entertained, and happy on field trips around the Boston area. In addition to offering swimming and hiking adventures, the company can also provide doggie day care and a B&B&B (bed, breakfast, and bone) service for overnight care. Visit the Web site for rates, schedules, field trip locations, and lots of pictures.

Downtown Dog, Boston (617-504-7750; info@downtowndog.net; www.downtowndog.net). Downtown Dog provides "affordable pet services for busy Bostonians," including at-home pet-sitting and transportation to veterinarian appointments. The company also donates a percentage of its profits to the MSPCA.

Especially for Pets, 444 Great Rd., **Acton** (978-264-4444); 1223 Chestnut St., **Newton** (617-964-7387); and 44 Main St., **Wayland** (508-647-6923; www.especiallyforpets.com). This Massachusetts-based chain has six locations (see "Central Massachusetts" for more listings) and offers a large variety of nutritional supplements, pet foods, and doggie treats by makers such as Bark Bars, Bow Wow Botanicals, and the 3C Baking Company.

Four Paws and a Leash, Dorchester (617-898-1206; dennis@fourpawsandaleash.com; www.fourpawsandaleash.com). Owner Dennis Saccoach runs his pet-caretaking business out of Dorchester and serves the entire Greater Boston area. Services include obedience training, dog walks, play sessions, and at-home pet care. Dennis is bonded, insured, and certified in Pet First Aid and CPR by the American Red Cross.

Hounds About Town, Roslindale (617-320-9285; info@houndsabouttown.com; www.houndsabouttown.com). Hounds About Town is co-owned by two Australian shepherds, Chloe and Duffy (with a little help from their human companion, Tina Alderman). The company offers group outings, daily dog walks, overnight pet-sitting, private overnight boarding, and a pet-taxi service.

Laundromutt, 489 Concord Ave., Cambridge (617-864-9274; www.laundromutt.com). As the clever name implies, this is the place to go when your well-traveled pooch needs a bit of freshening up. The self-service dog wash provides a place for you to clean your pup and leave the mess behind; full-service grooming and drop-off services are also available by appointment. Laundromutt even has a retail shop, where you'll find pet-care necessities and other fun items.

Linda's Critter Corral, 73 Bessom St., Lynn (781-599-7387; www.lindascrittercorral.com). If you run out of pet food or supplies on the road, stop by Linda's. This well-stocked shop has everything you might need for cats, dogs, gerbils, birds, and other animals, as well as toys, gifts, and collectibles for animal owners.

Paws Here, 320B Charger St., Revere (781-286-PAWS; www.pawshereinc.com). With more than 8,000 square feet of indoor space, a large fenced-in yard, a wading pool, and plenty of balls and toys, Paws Here offers cageless day care and boarding with plenty of activities to keep your dog entertained. The center also offers a small retail store, training classes, and pickup/drop-off services for canine clients.

Pawsh Dog Boutique and Salon, 31 Gloucester St., Boston (617-391-0880; www.pawshboston.com). Balki, the Boston Terrier, loves working at his parents' store in Back Bay, and will help you choose the best treats and trendiest accessories for your four-legged pal. Winner of a Best of Boston award from Boston magazine, Pawsh also has a grooming salon, but be forewarned, they're usually booked solid.

Pet-Estrian Services, Belmont (617-484-2489; petestrian@aol.com; www.pet-estrian.com). Based in Belmont, this animal-focused business offers daily dog walks, pet-sitting services, and daily Leader of the Pack playgroups that offer dogs a chance to socialize and exercise while their owners are otherwise occupied. Owner Lesley Sager Levine even publishes an online newsletter for her clients.

The Pet Shop, 165 Harvard Ave., Allston (617-787-0857; www.petshopboston.com). Stock up on food, treats, toys, and other necessities at this Allston pet-supply store, a family-owned business that also offers lots of aquarium supplies and fish.

Polka Dog Bakery, 256 Shawmut Ave., Boston (617-338-5155; www.polkadog.com). This South End "treat boutique for dogs" offers handmade, all-natural goodies, including Liver's Lane meat treats, Power Barks, Treatza Pizza, peanut butter oatmeal crunch cookies, and Tuna Yelpers. The on-site boutique also offers designer doggie sweaters, collars, and tons of toys. Would your dog forgive you if you *didn't* stop by for a visit? They also have a location in **Jamaica Plain** (617-522-1931).

The Pooch Palace, 18 Stanley Ave., Watertown (617-924-7790; www.thepoochpalace.com). Talk about a home-away-from-home: This pet-boarding facility is located in a converted two-family home, offering a cozy atmosphere with bedrooms, two fenced-in play areas, decks with awnings, and 24-hour care from live-in staffers. The company also offers doggie day trips, training classes, and a Pooch Boutique. The Pooch Palace is open by appointment only.

Raining Cats & Dogs, 368A Huron Ave., Cambridge (617-354-9003). You won't have to worry about quality control at this upscale pet boutique: All products are "Ernie tested" by the resident Jack Russell terrier. Shoppers can browse an animal-centered selection that includes items such as Kitty Kaviar, hand-knitted boiled wool sweaters, raw foods, and smoked bones. The store also offers a doggie day-care service; call for reservation information.

Red Dog Resort & Spa, 274 Southampton St., Waltham (617-505-1204; steven@skiptonpetcenter.com; www.bostonredddog.com). The owners of the Skipton Pet Center (see listing below) recently opened this boarding and day-care facility, formerly known as the Skipton Kennel, for local and visiting pups. Co-owner Karen lives 24 hours a day with the dogs in her care and provides lots of one-on-one attention. There's plenty for your pal to do at the aquatics center, or there's always a day of pampering at the "spa." The resort also offers pickup and delivery.

Skipton Pet Center, 274 Southampton St., Boston (617-427-2230; 1-800-PET-MENU; steven@skiptonpetcenter.com; www.skiptonpetcenter.com). This company offers a most unusual service in the pet-supply world—they deliver! You can call the 800 number and get dog and cat food, treats, toys, and other supplies delivered to your door, or you can visit their Southampton Street store Monday through Saturday from 9 AM to 8 PM.

'sPoochies, 400 Tremont St., Boston (617-357-7387; 1-888-DOG-SPA-8). Offering plenty of "services for the well-to-do canine," this doggie day spa and boutique has AKC-standard cuts, soapy baths, nail clips, tooth care, flea baths, hand scissoring, and a variety of other grooming services. In the boutique, you'll find brands such as Fab Dog, Wagwear, Gooby, and West Paw. An online boutique is also available.

ANIMAL SHELTERS AND HUMANE SOCIETIES

Alliance for Animals, 232 Silver St., South Boston (617-648-6822; www.afa.boston.org)

Animal Rescue League of Boston, Headquarters, 10 Chandler St., Boston (617-226-5605; www.arlboston.org)

Animal Umbrella, 320B Charger St., Revere (617-731-7267; www.animalumbrella.org)

City of Boston Animal Shelter, 26 Mahler Rd., Roslindale (617-635-1800; www.cityofboston.gov/animalcontrol)

Massachusetts Society for the Prevention of Cruelty to Animals (MSPCA), 350 S. Huntington Ave., Boston (617-522-7400; www.mspca.org)

Melrose Humane Society, P.O. Box 760668, Melrose 02176 (781-662-3224)

Pawsafe (foster care), Medford (adopt@pawsafe.org; www.pawsafe.org)

Quincy Animal Shelter, 56 Broad St., P.O. Box 88, Quincy 02169 (617-376-1349; www.quincyanimalshelter.org)

Stray Pets in Need (SPIN), P.O. Box 812143, Wellesley 02482 (781-235-1218; www.straydogsandcats.com)

Welcome Home Rescue, 25 Ridgeway Ln., Boston (welcomehome1@hotmail.com)

IN CASE OF EMERGENCY

Angell Memorial Animal Hospital, 350 S. Huntington Ave., Jamaica Plain (617-522-7282)

Arlington Animal Clinic, 191 Broadway, Arlington (781-646-0758)

Brookline Animal Hospital, 678 Brookline Ave., Brookline (617-277-2030)

Cambridge Veterinary Care, 1724 Massachusetts Ave., Cambridge (617-661-6255)

Charles Street Animal Clinic, 158 Charles St., Boston (617-227-0153)

Everett Animal Clinic, 456 Ferry St., Everett (617-387-6777)

Porter Square Veterinarian, 360 Summer St., Somerville (617-628-5588)

South Bay Veterinary Group, 587 Tremont St., Boston (617-266-6619)

Woburn Animal Hospital, 373 Russell St., Woburn (781-933-0170)

© KRIS HOLLAND/SHUTTERSTOCK.COM

South Shore and Suburbs

Visiting pet owners aren't likely to complain about the South Shore's peaceful scenery, quaint shopping villages, and lovely public parks—but they just might grumble a bit about the small number of pet-friendly accommodations offered in this busy corner of the state. Likewise, those who came to Massachusetts to delve into real-life history lessons will be disappointed to learn that many of the region's most popular attractions, including Battleship Cove, Edaville USA, and Plimoth Plantation, are off-limits to pets. (Luckily, you and your furry friends can still check out the *Mayflower II* and Plymouth Rock from the sidewalk: See Pilgrim Memorial State Park under "Out and About.")

Most of the South Shore's tourism appeal is centered along its coast, starting in the north with picturesque towns like Scituate and Duxbury and working down to the historically significant Plymouth; the near-Cape communities of Wareham, Marion, and Fairhaven; the southern havens of Dartmouth and Westport; and the bustling port cities of New Bedford and Fall River. Visitors don't typically venture into the suburbs, though there are more than enough parks and attractions there to keep you busy. Many first-time Massachusetts visitors find the South Shore's tourist-friendly location—midway between the Cape and Boston—to be an ideal home base for covering both ends of the vacation spectrum.

ACCOMMODATIONS

Hotels, Motels, Inns, and Bed & Breakfasts

Braintree

Candlewood Suites Boston–Braintree, 235 Wood Rd., Braintree (781-849-7450; www.ihg.com); $109–179 per night. Canines weighing less than 80 pounds are welcome to stay at this Candlewood Suites for an extra $15 the first night and $10 each additional night, up to a maximum of $150. The hotel's amenities include business services, a fitness center, high-speed Internet access, laundry facilities, air-conditioning, and in-room coffeemakers and hair dryers.

Hyatt Place, 50 Forbes Rd., Braintree (781-848-0600; www.hyatt.com); $127–164 per night. Hyatt Place hotels are designed to be your home away from home, and that includes your furry family members. Pets up to 50 pounds are welcome for an additional $75 per stay. The 204-room hotel features an indoor pool and fitness center and anchors the South Shore Place shopping center.

Motel 6 Boston South–Braintree, 125 Union St., Braintree (781-848-7890; www.motel6.com); $39–75 per night. Like other Motel 6 locations, the Braintree site (located about 10 miles from Cambridge) welcomes pets. The motel offers cable television with premium movie channels, laundry facilities, free coffee, a "kids stay free" program, and free local phone calls.

Brockton

Residence Inn Boston-Brockton, 124 Liberty St., Brockton (508-583-3600; 1-800-627-7468; www.marriott.com); $154–279 per night. Designed for long-term stays, the Brockton Residence Inn has suites with kitchens, desks, and separate bedroom and living-room areas. On-site, you'll also find a swimming pool, a fitness center, and valet service. Pet owners pay a one-time "sanitation fee" of $100.

Fairhaven

Holiday Inn Express Fairhaven, 110 Middle St., Fairhaven (508-997-1281); $89–149 per night. This Holiday Inn Express has 80 guest rooms, an on-site fitness center, air-conditioning, laundry facilities, photocopying and fax services, and free continental breakfasts. It's located on the scenic waterfront, close to restaurants, shops, and the Fairhaven Historic District. Pets are welcome for an additional $10 per night.

Huttleston Motel, 128 Huttleston Ave., Fairhaven (508-997-7655); $50–70 per night. This clean, quiet motel is family owned and operated, offering an affordable lodging alternative in the coastal community of Fairhaven. The motel is located right outside New Bedford and about 20 minutes from the Cape Cod Canal. Pets are welcome with prior approval for an additional $5 per day; animals cannot be left alone in the rooms

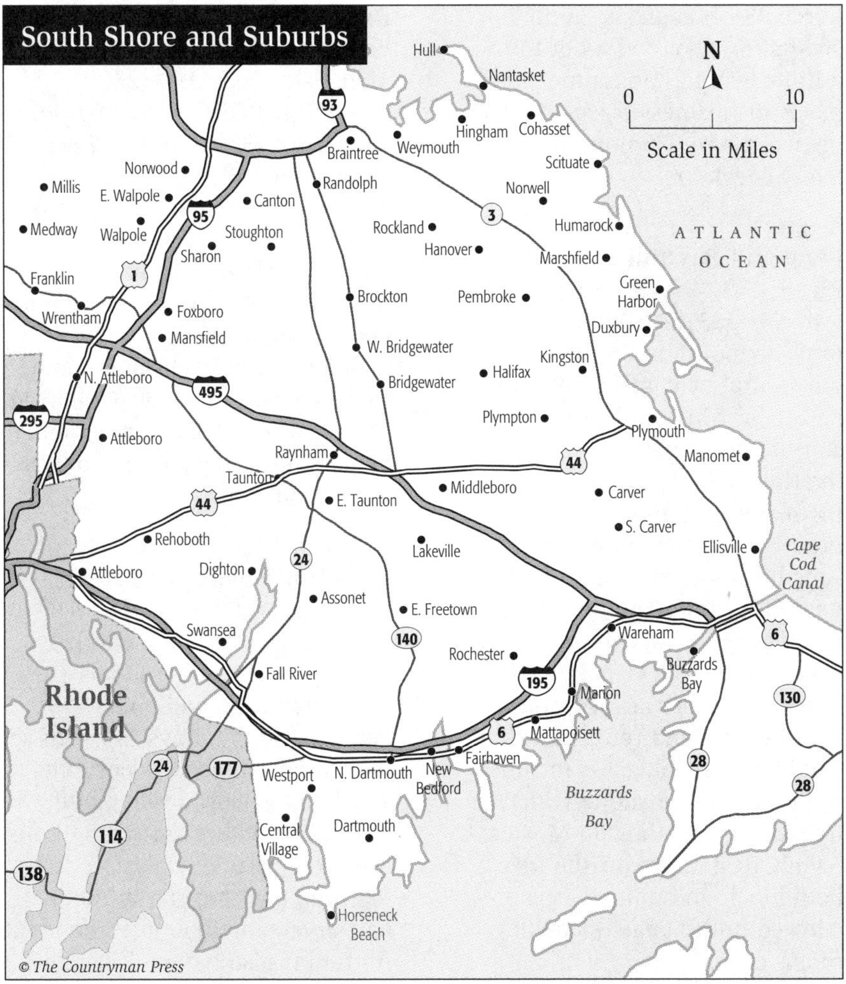

and must be leashed at all times on the property.

Foxboro

Residence Inn by Marriott Foxboro, 250 Foxboro Blvd., Foxboro (508-698-2800); $134–229 per night. You can choose from a studio or a one- or two-bedroom suite at this Residence Inn, which also offers a swimming pool, free breakfast buffets, laundry facilities, a barbecue area, high-speed Internet access, cable television with premium movie channels, and a rental-car desk. Pets are welcome with a one-time fee of $100.

Franklin

Hawthorn Suites Hotel, 835 Upper Union St., Franklin (508-553-3500; 1-800-527-1133; www.hawthorn.com); $118–249 per night. Choose from one- and two-bedroom executive or luxury presidential suites at Hawthorne suites, a full-service hotel offering free buffet breakfasts, an indoor swimming pool and a hot tub, a fitness center, and a meeting place for business travelers. Pet owners pay a $75 nonrefundable fee at check-in.

Kingston

Plymouth Bay Inn & Suites, Rte. 3, 149 Main St., Kingston (781-585-3831; 1-800-941-0075; inn@plymouthbay.com; www.plymouthbay.com); $119–199 per night. This inn is a movie star: it was transformed into the Galaxy Motor Lodge for the major motion picture *The Box,* starring Cameron Diaz. Amenities include indoor and outdoor swimming pools, a fitness center, a hot tub and sauna, 27-inch color televisions with free movies, private balconies, microwaves, and refrigerators. A continental breakfast is included in the room rate, along with free Wi-Fi. The Cancun Mexican Family Restaurant on-site serves both lunch and dinner. Pets are allowed in designated smoking rooms only.

Mansfield

Holiday Inn Mansfield, 31 Hampshire St., Mansfield (508-339-2200; www.ihg.com); $139–179 per night. The Mansfield Holiday Inn offers an indoor swimming pool, a hot tub and sauna, outdoor tennis courts, laundry and valet services, in-room movies, free morning newspapers, a restaurant and lounge, room service, and in-room coffeemakers and hair dryers. Pets up to 30 pounds are allowed for an additional $15 per night.

Red Roof Inn Mansfield/Foxboro, 60 Forbes Blvd., Mansfield (508-339-2323; 1-800-RED-ROOF; www.redroof.com); $69–89 per night. You can take in a Patriots' football game in Foxboro and then relax at this Red Roof Inn, part of the national chain of economy motels. Guests enjoy a swimming pool, cable television, laundry facilities, express checkout, and free local calls. One well-behaved pet per room is allowed, although owners have to sign a pet-policy agreement form.

Middleboro

Days Inn Middleboro, 30 E. Clark St., Middleboro (508-946-4400; www.wyndham.com); $89–129 per night. Animals are welcome for an additional $15 per night at this Days Inn with a maximum of two pets per room. The hotel is close to Plymouth attractions and features a 24-hour front desk, cable television, free morning newspapers, in-room hair dryers, and laundry services. All rooms also have refrigerators and microwaves. Guests enjoy a continental breakfast each morning.

New Bedford

Captain Haskell's Octagon House, 347 Union St., New Bedford (508-999-3933; stay@theoctagonhouse.com; www.theoctagonhouse.com); $65–155 per night. This extremely pet-friendly B&B welcomes animals of all shapes and sizes without extra charges; owners Ruth and Chuck Smiler even offer a discount to pet owners who have adopted their animal from a shelter. Doggie amenities include beds, bowls, treats, and pooper-scooper bags. The historic whaling captain's home features spacious antiques-filled guest rooms with sitting areas and private baths. Dogs are welcome in the parlor, dining room, conservatory, veranda, and garden. Ruth and Chuck also have plenty of suggestions for four-legged outings in the area, including beaches, walking tours, and eateries. Canine hosts Mick and Daisy will welcome your pal, but note that there are also resident felines here.

Plymouth

Auberge Gladstone Guest House, 8 Vernon St., Plymouth (508-830-1890; 1-866-722-1890; aubergegladstone@aol.com; www.aubergegladstone.com); $125–175 per night. Well-behaved dogs are welcome for an extra $25 per night at Auberge Gladstone, where guests will find mini kitchens en suite, an outdoor hot tub, bikes available for borrowing, Internet access, satellite television, fireplaces, a relaxed atmosphere, and a downtown location within easy walking distance to restaurants and historic sites. The 1848 house is located one block west of the waterfront on a serene tree-lined street and offers loaner bikes for touring.

Beach House Bed & Breakfast, 45 Black Pond Ln., Plymouth (508-224-3517; 1-888-BNB-CLIF; denise@beachhousebandb.com; www.beachhousebandb.com); $170–190 per night. Located directly on the ocean, this modern, weathered-shingle B&B has wicker deck furniture and lounge chairs, a private beach, bright interior furnishings, hardwood floors, cable television, and great views; in the fall and winter months you can often see seals, and in warmer weather you can watch the lobstermen bringing in their catch. Golf courses and other attractions are nearby. Pets are welcome in one designated room, and the room rate includes a full breakfast.

Hall's Bed & Breakfast, 3 Sagamore St., Plymouth (508-746-2835); $65–90 per night. For an extra $5–8 per night (depending on size), dogs can join their owners at this downtown Victorian B&B located close to the Town Green and everything Plymouth has to offer, including shops, restaurants, and historic sites. A full country breakfast is included in the rate, as is parking.

Rehoboth

Five Bridge Inn Bed & Breakfast, 154 Pine St., Rehoboth (508-252-3190; info@fivebridgeinn.com; www.fivebridgeinn.com); $98–150 per night. Dine on complimentary wine and cheese while you relax in your guest room or in common areas at this spacious and luxurious B&B. On-site, you'll also find a lap pool, a screened-in gazebo, a tennis court, and hiking trails on the inn's 80 acres. Five Bridge specializes in weddings and other events. Pets are welcome.

Scituate Harbor

Inn at Scituate Harbor, 7 Beaver Dam Rd., Scituate Harbor (781-545-5550; 1-800-368-3818; www.innatscituate.com); $125–307 per night. Guests at this contemporary inn can relax on the outdoor deck overlooking the harbor, walk to downtown shops and restaurants, or swim in the indoor swimming pool. All rooms have cable television, air-conditioning, and water views; two of them are available for pet owners for an additional fee of $20 per day, per pet. Grab a pint and some lobster fondue at The Dogwatch Tavern.

Seekonk

Motel 6 Providence-Seekonk, 821 Fall River Ave., Seekonk (508-336-7800; www.motel6.com); $53–75 per night. Your pet is welcome to join you at this Motel 6 location, where you'll find interior corridors, a "kids stay free" program, free coffee in the lobby, free local calls, laundry facilities, and cable television with premium movie channels. The Seekonk Speedway is located about 3 miles away.

Clarion Inn Seekonk, Rte. 114A, Seekonk (508-336-7300; www.clarionhotel.com); $79–149 per night. Close to Brown University and Providence College, this hotel is popular with campus visitors and business travelers alike. Amenities include an on-site restaurant, room service, a swimming pool, free local calls, and a 24-hour front desk. Pets are welcome for an extra $75 per stay with no weight limit.

SAGE, THE CAMP DOG, SPLASHES AROUND AT NORMANDY FARMS FAMILY CAMPING RESORT IN FOXBORO. (PHOTO COURTESY OF NORMANDY FARMS CAMPGROUND)

Somerset

Quality Inn Somerset, 1878 Wilbur Ave., Somerset (508-678-4545; 1-800-228-5151; www.choicehotels.com); $101–159 per night. Located across the water from Fall River, this Quality Inn has a restaurant and lounge, free continental breakfasts, an indoor swimming pool, laundry facilities, room service, and cable television with in-room movies. Animal owners will no doubt appreciate the hotel's pet-friendly policies (no extra fees) as well as its picnic area in the yard.

Campgrounds

East Mansfield

Canoe River Campground, 137 Mill St., East Mansfield (508-339-6462; www.canoeriver.com); $32–46 per night. Leashed, quiet pets are welcome at Canoe River, a family campground with 200 sites for tenters and RVers. The wooded grounds offer swimming pools, a pond, an arcade, boat rentals, Internet access, and lots of scheduled activities. The site is close to the Rhode Island border and about a half hour's drive from Boston in one direction and Plymouth in the other.

East Taunton

Massasoit State Park Campground, 1361 Middleboro Ave., East Taunton (508-822-7405; 1-877-422-6762); $12–17 per night Massachusetts residents; $14–19 per night out-of-state residents. Open from late April to Columbus Day, this campground welcomes leashed pets to its 120 sites for tents and RVs. Campers can take advantage of showers, flush toilets, a dumping station, and picnic tables and fire pits at each site. The state park (see "Out and About" for more information) also has a boat ramp and hiking trails. Pet owners must show valid rabies vaccination records.

Foxboro

Normandy Farms Family Camping Resort, 72 West St., Foxboro (508-543-7600; camp@normandyfarms.com; www.normandyfarms.com); $36–69 per night or $237386 per week. Bring your tent or RV to Normandy Farms for a full resort-style camping experience. Facilities include a gift shop, a snack bar, modern restrooms and laundry areas, scheduled children's activities, swimming pools, and the Recreation Lodge. Pets are always welcome but must stay on a leash and cannot be left alone. Inquire with the pet-friendly staff about the campground's dog-walking service.

Hingham

Wompatuck State Park Campground, Union St., Hingham (781-749-7160; 781-749-7161); $12 per night Massachusetts residents; $14 per night out-of-state residents. Choose from 262 campsites (140 with hookups) at this large campground offering restrooms with showers, a dumping station, fireplaces and picnic tables at each site, hiking trails, and a boat ramp. (See "Out and About" for more information about the park.)

Middleboro

Boston /Cape Cod KOA, 438 Plymouth St., Middleboro (508-947-6435; 1-800-562-3046; www.koa.com); $32–54 per night. Tenters and RVers are welcome at this centrally located campground; quiet, leashed pets are welcome at campsites but not in the Kamping Kabins. The KOA has a swimming pool and sundeck, volleyball and basketball courts, a game room, dances and movie nights, and a playground.

Plymouth

Sandy Pond Campground, 834 Bourne Rd., Plymouth (508-759-9336; www.sandypond.com); $30–44 per night. With 200 campsites, canoe rentals, sports fields, a beach, hiking trails, and a playground, Sandy Pond offers families plenty to do. The camp store stocks all the basics, including firewood and food. Quiet pets are welcome as long as they stay on leashes, although the campground bans certain breeds; call for details. There is a $5 per night fee for animals weighing more than 25 pounds.

South Carver

Myles Standish State Forest Campground, Cranberry Rd., South Carver (508-866-2526);

$12 per night Massachusetts residents; $14 per night out-of-state residents. This 14,000-acre park (see "Out and About") near Plymouth has nearly 500 campsites for tenters and RVers, along with hookups, a dumping station, restrooms with hot showers, picnic tables, and fire pits. There are also five "group camping" sites that can accommodate 50 persons each.

Westport Point

Horseneck Beach State Reservation Campground, Rte. 88, Westport Point (508-636-8817; 508-636-8816); $15 per night Massachusetts residents; $17 per night out-of-state residents. Run by the Massachusetts Department of Conservation and Recreation, the Horseneck Beach campground is open seasonally with 100 campsites, picnic areas, a boat ramp, restrooms with showers, and a dumping station. Pets must be on a leash and are not allowed at the beach. (For more information on the reservation, see "Out and About.")

Homes, Cottages, and Cabins for Rent

For rental cottages, check the Boston Craigslist, the local chamber of commerce and tourism Web sites, or some of these vacation rental agencies:

www.homeaway.com
www.vrbo.com
www.cyberrentals.com

OUT AND ABOUT

Feast of the Holy Ghost, Fall River. This huge street fair and celebration takes place during the last week of August each year in downtown Fall River. Visitors can enjoy a traditional procession, music, street performances, and of course *lots* of food. If you're not in town during the festival, you can still check out the **Maritime Heritage Trail** and the **Columbia Street Historic District,** where you'll find shops, restaurants, and historic brick architecture.

F. Gilbert Hills State Forest, Mill St., Foxboro (508-543-5850). Local mountain biking enthusiasts know the way to this 1,000-acre preserve spread throughout Foxboro and Wrentham; it was named for a former state park employee who created many of Massachusetts's first state park maps. The forest has 23 miles of trails for hiking, biking, horseback riding, and cross-country skiing. Dogs must be on a leash.

Fort Phoenix State Reservation, Green St., Fairhaven (508-992-4524). The first sea battle of the Revolutionary War was fought in this spot; today, the small park offers visitors a half-mile stretch of beach with wonderful views, and a chance to see the remnants of the once mighty fort. Dogs are welcome but must be on a leash.

Freetown Fall River State Forest, Slab Bridge Rd., Assonet (508-644-5522). Pass the day-use area's picnic tables and restrooms, and wander along more than 50 miles of trails and dirt roads at this oasis just outside the city of Fall River. The farm is especially popular with those who like to go the distance, such as mountain bikers, snowmobilers, and horseback riders, though dog walkers will feel welcome as well.

Friends of the Plymouth Pound, Plymouth. This nonprofit organization holds fun fund-raising events each year to benefit homeless animals in the South Shore area. Visitors are always welcome at the group's annual **Memorial Weekend Carnival** at the Armstrong Skating Arena in Plymouth and the yearly **Pet Walk,** usually held on the first Saturday in September at Morton Park in Plymouth. For more information, call 508-224-6651 or visit www.friendsplymouthpound.org.

Horseneck Beach State Reservation, Rte. 88, Westport Point (508-636-8817; 508-636-8816). When you see the stretches of beach and salt marshes at Horseneck, you'll understand why it's one of the most popular parks in Massachusetts—especially in summer. Though pets are not allowed on the beach itself, they are welcome at the campground (see "Accommodations—Campgrounds"), on rocky outcrops, and on trails.

Lloyd Center for Environmental Studies, 430 Potomska Rd., South Dartmouth (508-990-0505; www.lloydcenter.org). Wander along the **Chaypee Woods Trail,** the **Osprey Point Trail,** the **Hardscrabble Farm Loop,** or other paths at this research and environmental center. "Our outdoor property of 55 acres of coastal estuary and upland habitat and its trails are open for free, dawn to dusk, 365 days a year," explains Geoffrey Garth, public affairs coordinator for the center. "We do allow pets to come along with their owners as long as they stay on a leash."

Massasoit State Park, 1371 Middleboro Ave., East Taunton (508-822-7405). This park is a popular gathering place for local dogs and their owners, who enjoy hiking, biking, cross-country skiing, and romping on the scenic trails—if you arrive in fall, be sure to look for the bright cranberry bogs. The park also offers a campground (see "Accommodations—Campgrounds"), horseback riding, picnic areas, and opportunities for nonmotorized boating.

Myles Standish Monument State Reservation, Crescent St., Duxbury (508-866-2580). This wonderful picnic spot (tables are available) has wide views of the coastline's beaches, harbors, and lighthouses; a 14-foot statue of Captain Myles Standish of the original Plymouth Colony; and walking paths through the forest.

Myles Standish State Forest, 194 Cranberry Rd., South Carver

(508-866-2526). Visitors can camp overnight at Myles Standish (see "Accommodations—Campgrounds") or just explore for the day to enjoy forest scenery, picnics, boating, and swimming at any of the park's 16 ponds. Separate biking, hiking, and horse-riding trails ensure something for nearly everyone.

New England Fast Ferry, Union Street, State Pier Ferry Terminal, New Bedford (617-748-1428); adult one-way $38; child one-way $22. Your favorite pooch is welcome to join you on the quick and convenient trip between New Bedford and Martha's Vineyard, provided she stays on a leash and off the seats. The trip takes about an hour, during which you can enjoy a snack bar serving snacks, drinks, and even breakfast.

New Bedford Whaling National Historical Park. Visitor Information Center: 33 William St., New Bedford (508-996-4095). Spread throughout 13 blocks in the restored historic district, this park enables visitors to stroll through the city's renowned whaling past. Among the notable points of interest are the **Seamen's Bethel** (which Herman Melville called the Whaleman's Chapel in *Moby-Dick*), **Waterfront Park,** and the hardy **schooner *Ernestina*.** As you walk the cobblestone streets, you'll also pass by eateries, shops, and other diversions. Free walking tours are offered in July and August; check with Visitor Center staff for the updated schedules.

Pilgrim Memorial State Park, Water St., Plymouth (508-747-5360). You and your pooch can catch a glimpse of the *Mayflower II* at the State Pier and Plymouth Rock, that famous glacial boulder, from this small shady green with benches, picnic tables, a gift shop, and public restrooms.

Plymouth Breakwater, Plymouth. This long wall of stone makes for a fun and scenic jaunt: Walk out to sea and turn back to see the *Mayflower II* and the downtown area. Start the journey at the pretty bridge located at the entrance to the Leo F. DeMarsh Boat Ramp.

Scituate Light, Cedar Point, Scituate Harbor. This is a popular spot with kite fliers, sightseers, and local residents looking for a peaceful respite. The 50-foot bright white tower, constructed in 1811, is made of granite and brick and is managed today by the **Scituate Historical Society** (781-545-1083). Just around the corner from the light you'll find a picturesque downtown area with restaurants, antiques shops, boutiques, and plenty of boats bobbing in the harbor.

Village Landing Marketplace, 170 Water St., Plymouth (508-746-3493; www.villagelandingmarketplace.com). Do some window-shopping at this visitor's village with cobblestone streets, boutiques, bakeries, ice-cream stands, and a view of the harbor. The specialty shops and restaurants here are all locally owned. Be sure to stop in at Four Paws Pet Boutique (see "Hot Spots for Spot").

© BAEVSKIY DMITRY/SHUTTERSTOCK.COM

Walk for Animals, Sharon. The **Neponset Valley Humane Society** in Norwood holds this fund-raising event each year. Complete with prizes, entertainment, and refreshments, it's usually held on the Sunday after Mother's Day at Borderland State Park in Sharon; for updated information, call the society at 781-769-1900 or visit www.neponsethumane.org.

Wompatuck State Park, Union St., Hingham (781-749-7160; 781-749-7161). This 3,500-acre park has a boat ramp and miles of trails for biking, hiking, cross-country skiing, and horseback riding. One of Wompatuck's best-known landmarks is the **Mount Blue Spring,** a source of fresh water. Dogs must be on a leash and cannot swim in the reservoir. To reach the park, follow the signs from Route 228.

QUICK BITES

Barnacle Bill's Seafood, 3126 Cranberry Hwy., Wareham (508-743-5095). Dogs like fish too: You can order both of your favorite seafood meals or sandwiches and enjoy them out on Barnacle Bill's picnic tables. Try the fried green pepper rings and the rich clam chowder.

Café Arpeggio, 139 S. Main St., **Fall River** (508-679-3333); and 800 Purchase St., **New Bedford** (508-999-2233; www.cafearpeggio.com). Veggie burgers, tuna salad, turkey melts, bagels, PB&J, and homemade ice cream are all on the menu at both South Shore Café Arpeggio locations. The Fall River site also has several sidewalk tables. For more information on the Café Arpeggio location in South Boston, see "Greater Boston."

Cape Cod Pizza, 979 Main St., Brockton (508-583-9420; www.capecodcafepizza.com). This dine-in and take-out restaurant specializes in gourmet pizzas. Choose from traditional favorites and more exotic toppings, including tomato and feta, Tex-Mex, buffalo chicken, Greek sausage, and roasted red pepper.

Hingham Lobster Pound, 4 Broad Cove Rd., Hingham (781-749-1984; www.hinghamlobster.com). This is a take-out-only kind of place, offering lobster, children's meals, fried seafood, sandwiches, onion rings, coleslaw, and other seaside-style favorites.

Jamie's Grille & Pub, 360 Gannett Rd., North Scituate Village (781-545-6000; www.jamiespub.com). Jamie's has been family-owned and operated for more than 40 years. Every item on its extensive menu is available for takeout, from nachos and wings to steaks, seafood, pizza, club sandwiches, and burgers. Try the Spicy Meaty Chili, Alpine Burger, London broil, Seafood Medley, or Junior Fisherman's Platter.

Lobster Hut, 25 Town Wharf, Plymouth (508-746-2270; www.lobsterhutplymouth.com). Leashed, well-behaved dogs are welcome on the outdoor patio at Lobster Hut. Order a fried seafood plate, burger, lobster, or chicken fingers from the indoor window and then enjoy your meal while overlooking the water. Locals recommend the seafood rolls, lobster bisque, and fried clams.

New York Bagel, 1572 President Ave., **Fall River** (508-677-4767); and 272 State Rd., **North Dartmouth** (508-990-3350; www.newyorkbagel.com). New York Bagel's two locations offer sandwiches on your choice of fresh-baked bread, rolls, or bagel varieties such as whole wheat, garlic, rye, sun-dried tomato, blueberry, and salsa. You can also choose from more than six varieties of cream cheese.

Pilgrim Path Café and Eatery, S. Park Ave., Plymouth (508-746-6483). This casual eatery serves breakfast, specialty sandwiches, calzones, burgers, soups, pasta, homemade breads, muffins, and desserts; you'll find a few outdoor tables with a view of the *Mayflower II* and the beach. Stuck in your hotel room? Pilgrim Path also delivers.

HOT SPOTS FOR SPOT

Belmont Pet Shop, 17 Flett Rd., Belmont (508-230-3037; www.belmontpetshop.com). Pick up all the basics for your cat, dog, gerbil, or other companion animal at Belmont Pet, which stocks foods and supplies from companies such as Rio Vista, Lupine Pet, and Zoo Med. Serving the area for more than 60 years, this locally-owned boutique also offers grooming and boarding services.

Bite Me! Biscuits, 396 W. Chestnut St., Brockton (508-930-7747). After one visit, this all-natural doggie bakery will no doubt become your canine's favorite South Shore stop. Treats include Dog House Cookies with carob chips, Gingerbread Mailmen, Bonanza Bones, and Lollipups. A line of Bite Me! apparel is also available for animal fans.

Canine College, White Rock Spring Rd., Holbrook (781-

767-3908; info@caninecollege .net; www.caninecollege.net). Whether your dog needs an advanced degree or maybe just a review course in Obedience 101, the Canine College probably has a class to fit your needs. In addition to its training programs, the Canine College also offers overnight boarding, doggie day care, and complete grooming services.

Down to Earth, 751 Kempton St., New Bedford (508-996-1995). Down to Earth is a natural-food store for pets as well as people; the shop specializes in holistic foods, supplements, and all-natural pet products.

Four Paws Pet Boutique & Bakery, 170 Water St., Village Landing Marketplace, Plymouth (508-747-7297; www.fourpaws petboutique.com). Stop by for a sweet treat for your pooch or shop for food, accessories, toys, and New England outfits at this fun shop in Village Landing Marketplace.

Healthy Animal, 808 Washington St. (Rte. 53), Pembroke (781-826-9760; www .thehealthyanimal.com). This health-food store caters to the four-legged members of your family with all-natural and organic products. Shoppers will find nutritional supplements, herbal remedies, pet foods, and fun toys and accessories.

Homeward Bound, 1508 Sassaquin Ave., New Bedford (508-264-0734; 508-998-7557; amyhoubre@yahoo.com; www .homewardboundpetcare.com). Amy Houbre, a veterinary technician, has run this pet-care business for more than a decade. She provides dog-walking and pet-sitting services. Fully insured and bonded, she'll be happy to keep an eye on your favorite canine or feline while you're visiting the area. Homeward Bound is a member of the South New England Professional Pet Sitters Association.

Land of Pawz, 204 Bridge St. (Rte. 3A), North Weymouth (781-335-4960; 1-866-333-PAWZ; landofpawz@aol.com; www .landofpawz.com). If you and your dog need it, Land of Pawz probably offers it. The wide range of services here include doggie day care, grooming, "sleepovers" (aka overnight care), in-home pet-sitting, dog walking, obedience training, pet transportation services, and even retail sales of holistic pet food. Owner Tom Fleming is the Wizard of Pawz!

Patnaude's Aquarium and Pet Super Store, 1193 Ashley Blvd., New Bedford (508-995-4344; 1-800-927-3872). This is a large store with lots of choices in pet food, toys, treats, accessories, cages and kennels, and doghouses. Originally specializing only in aquarium supplies and fish, the store has since branched out to include everyone's favorite land animals as well.

Pawsitively Natural, 10 Marshfield Ave., P.O. Box 421, Humarock 02047 (781-837-0850; www.pawsitivelynatural.net). Located across from the post office in tiny Humarock, this pet-centered shop offers nutritional supplements, all-natural chews, flea collars, cookies and treats for diabetic pets, elevated feeders, doggie flotation devices, pet sunscreen, bandanas, and lots of gift ideas—including Red Sox canine gear of all kinds.

South Shore Pet Nannies, P.O. Box 682, Hingham 02043 (781-749-HELP; 617-413-3017; info@thepetnanny.com; www.thepetnanny.com). Animal-sitting, dog-walking, playgroups, pooper-scooper services: The South Shore Pet Nannies do it all. Owner Nancy Labriola serves the communities of Hingham, Cohasset, Weymouth, Hull, and Scituate.

Village Groomer and Pet Supply, 2245 Providence Hwy., Walpole (508-668-9516; 1-800-439-PETS; www.villagegroomer.net). Open Monday through Saturday, this one-stop shop for pets offers nail trims, ear cleaning, tooth care, show trims, medicated baths, and a variety of other grooming services. You'll also find a gift shop stocked with items for pets and their people.

ANIMAL SHELTERS AND HUMANE SOCIETIES

All Paws Rescue, P.O. Box 569, Accord 02018 (617-770-3814; www.allpawsrescue.org)

Carver Animal Shelter, 67 N. Main St., P.O. Box 232, Carver 02330 (508-866-3444)

Friends of the Plymouth Pound, Braintree, Manomet, and Hyannis (508-224-6651; www.friendsplymouthpound.org)

Friends of the Scituate Animal Shelter, P.O. Box 823, Scituate 02066 (781-545-8703)

Mansfield Animal Shelter, 175 Fruit St., Mansfield (508-261-7339; www.mansfieldshelter.org)

Metro South Animal Care and Adoption Center (MSPCA), 1300 W. Elm St. Ext., Brockton (508-586-2053; www.mspca.org)

Milford Humane Society, P.O. Box 171, Medway 02053 (508-473-7008; www.milfordhumane.org)

Neponset Valley Humane Society, P.O. Box 544, Norwood 02062 (781-769-1900; www.neponsethumane.org)

North Attleborough Animal Shelter, Cedar Rd., North Attleborough (508-699-0128; www.nattleboro.com/animal-control-shelter)

Pine Ridge Animal Center, 55 Anna's Place at 238 Pine St., Dedham (781-326-0729; www.arlboston.org)

Standish Humane Society, P.O. Box 634, Duxbury 02331 (781-834-4663; www.standishhumane.org)

Taunton Animal Shelter, 821 W. Water St., Taunton (508-822-1463; www.tauntonshelter.petfinder.com)

IN CASE OF EMERGENCY

Brockton Animal Hospital, 386 Belmont St., Brockton (508-588-4142)

Buttonwood Pet Hospital, 922 Kempton St., New Bedford (508-996-3159)

Court Street Animal Hospital, 136 Court St., Plymouth (508-747-0774)

Old Derby Animal Clinic, 40 Recreation Park Dr., Hingham (781-749-2800)

North Plymouth Animal Hospital, 345 Court St., Plymouth (508-746-4232)

Roberts Animal Hospital, 516 Washington St., Hanover (781-826-2306)

Tufts Veterinary Emergency Services, 525 SouthSt., Walpole (508-668-5454)

Wessels Animal Hospital, 96 Summer St., Taunton (508-822-2981)

© A KATZ/SHUTTERSTOCK.COM

Cape Cod and the Islands

New Englanders love their Cape and its two bucolic islands, Nantucket and Martha's Vineyard, with a ferocious loyalty. Sure, they're crowded. Sure, they're pricey. But if you're looking for a picture-postcard view of the quintessential New England seashore, this is where you'll find it.

The Cape's many towns have diverse personalities, from the miniature golf, arcades, and campgrounds of the upper and mid-Cape to genteel, quieter spots near the bend of the "elbow." At the tip, the art colony of Provincetown (a very pet-friendly town) attracts visitors with an open mind and a sense of adventure. In Woods Hole, scientists from around the world delve into the latest deepwater discoveries at the Woods Hole Oceanographic Institution. This is also the spot where most people catch a ferry to Martha's Vineyard, a jovial, tourist-friendly island with breathtaking beaches, harbors, and architecture. Nantucket is a bit smaller and farther away from the mainland and, as a result, enjoys a slightly more escapist ambience.

All three areas burst at the seams during the summer season; pet owners are often better off visiting in spring or fall, when more accommodations allow animals and the sidewalks have a bit more room for roaming. The beach rules vary from town to town, but in general your pooch will probably not be allowed at all between 8 AM and 6 PM on most town beaches in summer. But take heart: Leashed dogs are allowed on most beaches at the Cape Cod National Seashore (see "Out and About"). And you'll have plenty of luck at dinnertime—Cape Cod and both islands have an abundance of restaurants with outdoor seating areas offering lobstah, chowdah, and other seafood delights. You'll also find numerous kennels and pet-sitters, opportunities for getting out into the open ocean, and of course spectacular views around every corner.

ACCOMMODATIONS

Hotels, Motels, Inns, and Bed & Breakfasts

Barnstable

Lamb and Lion Inn, Rte. 6A, Barnstable (508-362-6823; 1-800-909-6923; info@lambandlion.com; www.lambandlion.com); $179–259 per night. Laid-back luxury is the goal at the Lamb and Lion, where the amenities include a swimming pool, a hot tub, fireplaces, and three resident Yorkies to keep an eye on things. This award-winning B&B has received accolades from CNN and *Yankee* magazine as the best pet-friendly inn in New England. Guest rooms have private entrances and vary in size and style, and many have fireplaces. Pets weighing less than 25 pounds during the summer season and 40 pounds in the off-season are welcome for an additional $25 per pet, per night, up to a maximum of $100.

Buzzards Bay

Bay Motor Inn, 223 Main St., Buzzards Bay (508-759-3989; baymotorinn@yahoo.com; www.baymotorinn.com); $66–129 per night. Pets are welcome for an additional $10 per night at Bay Motor Inn, located along the edge of the Cape Cod Canal. There are 7 miles of hiking trails within walking distance, and the inn offers cable television, free coffee and local calls, and air-conditioning. The accommodations include standard rooms, efficiencies, and cottages. Pets cannot be left unattended at any time.

Fox Run Bed & Breakfast, 171 Puritan Rd., Buzzards Bay (508-759-1458; foxrun@capecod.net; www.foxrunbandb.com); $85–135 per night. Certified with the National Wildlife Federation's Backyard Habitat Program, Fox Run B&B is surrounded by wetlands, cranberry bogs, and plenty of great bird-watching spots. The three guest rooms are decorated with turn-of-the-20th-century, French Provincial, and Old Cape

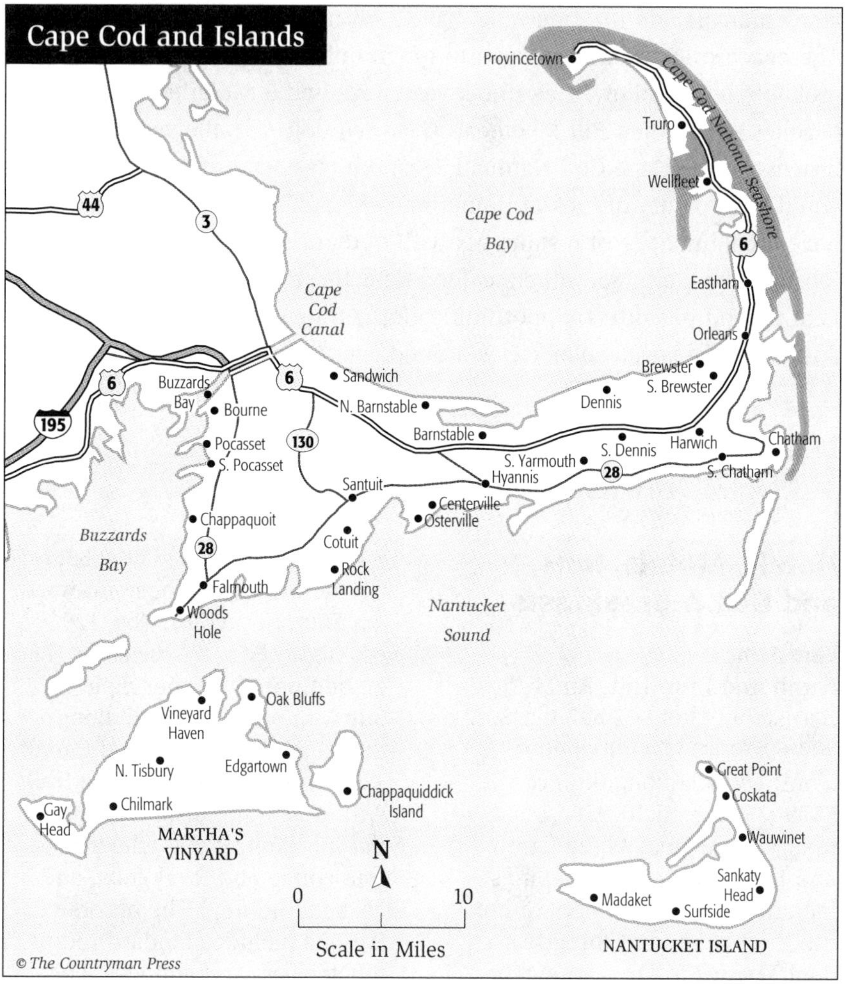

Cod themes. Pets weighing less than 30 pounds are welcome during the off-season (Oct. 15–May 1) and will get a warm greeting from the resident Bichon Poodle mix, Lilly.

Centerville

Centerville Corners Inn, 1338 Craigville Beach Rd., Centerville (508-775-7223; info@centerville corners.com; www.centerville corners.com); $60–180 per night. For an extra $10 per night and prior approval, your pet is welcome to join you at this cozy motor inn located in the small village of Centerville. Amenities include an indoor heated pool and a sauna, free continental breakfasts each morning, cable television, air-conditioning, and in-room refrigerators. Efficiency units are also available. Dogs must be leashed; the motel's pet policy limits its welcome to dogs weighing less than 60 pounds.

East Falmouth

Green Harbor Waterfront Lodging, 134 Acapesket Rd., East Falmouth (508-548-4747; 1-800-548-5556; www.gogreen harbor.com); $88–300 per night. Located on an ocean inlet, Green Harbor Waterfront Lodging has lots of family-friendly amenities, including a children's pool, a heated outdoor swimming pool, a barbecue area with grills, free use of rowboats and paddleboats, and a private beach with a ramp and a dock. Accommodations options include waterfront rooms (some with kitchens), beachside studios, and a three-bedroom cottage. Dogs are welcome for an extra $10 per stay (not per night), as long as they are walked on a leash, picked-up after, and not left alone in the rooms.

Eastham

Cottage Grove, 1975 Rte. 6, P.O. Box 821, Eastham 02642 (508-255-0500; 1-877-521-5522; www .grovecape.com); $100–240 per night or $650–1,550 per week. Cottage Grove is a unique, pet-friendly accommodation on the outer Cape, located about 1½ miles from the main entrance to Cape Cod National Seashore. Each cottage has heat and air-conditioning, cable television, rustic surroundings, and supplied linens. "We are all about community and experience here, and fully believe that people should be able to vacation with their pets," explains owner Greg Wolfe.

Inn at the Oaks, 3085 County Rd. (Rte. 6), Eastham (508-255-1886; 1-877-255-1886; stay@ innattheoaks.com; www.innatthe oaks.com); $175–305 per night. The Inn at the Oaks offers full country breakfasts each morning, concierge services, a playground, a poolroom, massage and other spa services, and a location that's close to restaurants, shops, museums, beaches, and other recreational activities. Well-behaved pets are permitted in the 1st Mate's Suites ($175–235 per night) for an extra $25 per stay (not per night).

East Sandwich

Earl of Sandwich Motel, 378 Rte. 6A (Old King's Hwy.), East Sandwich (508-888-1415; 1-800-442-EARL; www.earlofsandwich .com); $75–149 per night. Set around a small duck pond and surrounded by lawns and flower beds, the Earl of Sandwich Motel

Cape Cod Beach Dog

Want to go whale watching with your BFF? Looking for dog-friendly beaches and campgrounds? Get the inside scoop from local dog lovers at www.capebeachdog.com on the best accommodations, pet-friendly restaurants, and activities for you and your pooch.

offers 24 individually decorated rooms (some with canopy beds), free continental breakfasts, an outdoor swimming pool, air-conditioning, and cable television. Pets are allowed in 12 of the 24 rooms; advance notice is required.

Wingscorton Farm Inn, 11 Wing Blvd., East Sandwich (508-888-0534); $175 per night. Your pet will fit right into the menagerie at Wingscorton, a working farm with sheep, goats, chickens, geese, and other animals. Built in 1758, this historic home offers a library, a dining area, guest rooms, and a carriage-house apartment, all furnished with antiques. Full country breakfasts include specialties such as rhubarb pie, fruit turnovers, fresh eggs, and a variety of juices. Rooms have four-poster beds and fireplaces, along with modern touches like television and full, private baths. Well-behaved children and companion animals are welcome.

Falmouth

The Beach Rose Inn Bed & Breakfast, 17 Chase Rd., Falmouth (508-540-5706; 1-800-498-5706; www.thebeachroseinn.com); $185–250 per night or cottages for $265 per night or $1,590 per week. Listed on the National Register of Historic Places, this cozy 1863 inn is decorated with antiques, quilts, period reproductions, canopy beds, and other quaint touches. Dogs are welcome in the carriage house and cottage with prior approval. The rates include a full breakfast and afternoon snacks. You'll pay an additional $20 per night pet fee.

Falmouth Inn, 824 Main St. (Rte. 28), Falmouth (508-540-2500; 1-800-255-4157; www.falmouthinn.com); $65–120 per night. Pets are allowed at the Falmouth Inn, an accommodation with a heated indoor/outdoor swimming pool in a building that has a retractable roof. The inn also offers cable television with premium movie channels, an outdoor courtyard, a game room, and a restaurant and lounge. Guests also enjoy preferred tee times at the nearby Falmouth Country Club golf course.

Hyannis

Cascade Motor Lodge, 201 Main St., Hyannis (508-775-9717; www.cascademotorlodge.com); $48–165 per night. Choose from standard rooms and efficiencies at this Hyannis motel featuring full baths, air-conditioning, cable television and VCRs, smoking and nonsmoking rooms, and kitchenettes. You can also rent movies and bicycles at the main office. Well-behaved dogs are welcome.

Comfort Inn Hyannis, 1470 Rte. 132, Hyannis (508-771-4804);

A COZY GUEST ROOM AT WINGSCORTON FARM INN IN EAST SANDWICH

$79–189 per night. This centrally located Comfort Inn offers all the most popular amenities, including air-conditioning, free continental breakfasts, premium movie channels, an indoor swimming pool with a hot tub and sauna, a fitness center, and Nintendo for the kids. Pets are welcome in some of the 104 rooms.

Hyannis Port

Marston Family B&B, 70 Marston Ave., P.O. Box 458, Hyannis Port 02647 (508-775-3334); $195–325 per night. Captain Marcus and Lynette Sherman, the innkeepers at this cozy B&B, also host sailing excursions on their 34-foot sailboat, the catboat *Eventide.* (Guests can take advantage of a free ride on the boat.) Their B&B was built in 1786 and has four fireplaces, a screened-in porch, and an outside shower. Children and pets are always welcome; animal owners pay an extra $10 per night, per pet. Dogs must be leashed, treated with anti-flea medications, and house-trained. Two friendly beagles, Riley and Clover, will give you and your pup a warm welcome.

Simmons Homestead Inn, 288 Scudder Ave., Hyannis Port (508-778-4999; 1-800-637-1649; simmonshomestead@aol.com; www.simmonshomesteadinn.com); $130–250 per night. Built in the early 1800s, this recently renovated inn features animal-themed rooms, full breakfasts each morning, wine in the evenings, a barn housing the owner's collection of classic red sports cars, and a relaxed, hospitable atmosphere. All rooms have private baths. Only dogs are welcome, with a one-time charge of $25, though there is a room called the Cat Suite. If your pup tends to chase or otherwise hassle cats, use caution: The innkeeper has 26 felines living here!

Martha's Vineyard

Brady's Bed & Breakfast, 10 Canonicus Ave., Oak Bluffs, Martha's Vineyard (508-693-9137; 1-888-693-9137; www.sunsol.com/bradys); $76–188 per night. The resident cocker spaniel at Brady's will probably greet you when you arrive. This relaxed and quaint seaside B&B has a huge porch facing the ocean, Downeast-style furnishings, upscale bedding, and a weathered-shingle exterior. Well-behaved, well-traveled dogs (sorry, no cats) are welcome without extra fees: "I only charge one bottle of Absolut," says innkeeper E. Brady Aikens.

Vineyard Square Hotel & Suites, P.O. Box 68, Edgartown, Martha's Vineyard 02539 (508-627-4711; 1-800-627-4701; www.vineyardsquarehotel.com); $195–595 per night. Formerly known as The Colonial Inn, a tradition on Martha's Vineyard since 1911, the Vineyard Square Hotel has a great location on the harbor and is within walking distance to all of Edgartown's shops, restaurants, and other attractions. All of the rooms and suites have cable television, robes, hair dryers, and telephones; some also have fireplaces, harbor views, and mini refrigerators. Two of the suites are designated as pet-friendly.

Duck Inn, 10 Duck Pond Way, Aquinnah (Gay Head), Martha's Vineyard (508-645-9018; www.duckinnonmv.com); $155–295 per night. Pets are welcome in one room at this cozy farm and B&B originally designed by a whaler. Gourmet breakfasts include specialties such as crêpes, fresh eggs, and fruit; the house features private baths in some rooms, fireplaces, a hot tub, and peaceful views. The designated pet room has a private entrance.

Island Inn, 30 Island Inn Rd., Oak Bluffs, Martha's Vineyard (508-693-2002; 1-800-462-0269; www.islandinn.com); $145–355 per night. You can bring your pet along at the Island Inn during every month except July and August. Accommodations include a studio, one- and two-bedroom suites, a condo suite, a town house, and a cottage. The inn also has an outdoor freshwater pool, tennis courts, a barbecue and picnic area, a playground, and more than 7 acres to explore.

Marni's House, Vineyard Haven, Martha's Vineyard (508-696-6198; marnivh@vineyard.net); Treehouse Room $180 per night. Located within walking distance to the ferry, this casual B&B is located next to a goldfish pond and across the street from the 80-acre West Chop Woods conservation area. Daily continental breakfasts include homemade breads. Dogs are permitted in the Treehouse Room for an extra $15 per night.

Martha's Vineyard Surfside Motel, P.O. Box 2507, Oak Bluffs, Martha's Vineyard 02557 (508-693-2500; 1-800-537-3007; reservations@mvsurfside.com; www.mvsurfside.com); $95–370 per night. "We're one of the few lodging establishments on the island that welcomes pets, and it almost never comes back to bite us!" jokes Bob Emerson, Surfside's manager. The motel offers standard rooms as well as suites; the motel is located steps from the ferry dock, the historic merry-go-round, and lots of shops and restaurants. Pets must stay on a leash on the property and can't be left alone in the rooms; pet owners pay an extra $15 per night. At check-in, guests with pets receive a helpful brochure listing local pet shops and recreational areas where dogs are allowed, and there are no size restrictions.

The Tivoli Inn, 125 Circuit Ave., Oak Bluffs, Martha's Vineyard (508-693-7928; Tivoli@capecod.net; www.tivoliinn.com); $95–255 per night. This quaint gingerbread house inn is located within walking distance to shops, restaurants, the beach, hiking trails, and more. Visitors can enjoy a wraparound porch, six individually decorated guest rooms, a complimentary continental breakfast, and the company of Saki, the "inn dog." Doggie guests are welcome for an additional $25 per stay (not per night); if your dog is inclined to bark, the innkeepers

THE POOCH-FRIENDLY MARTHA'S VINEYARD SURFSIDE MOTEL HAS A CONVENIENT LOCATION IN DOWNTOWN OAK BLUFFS.

ask that you don't leave her alone in the room.

The Victorian Inn, 24 S. Water St., Edgartown, Martha's Vineyard (508-627-4784; victorianinn@thevic.com; www.thevic.com); $260–425 per night. Located in a former whaling captain's home, the Victorian Inn offers daily gourmet breakfasts, an English garden, antique furnishings, harbor and garden views, and balconies and decks. Dogs are welcome during the off-season (October through May) for an extra $25 per stay (not per night). Dogs must be crated if left alone in the room and should be leashed in common areas.

Nantucket

The Beachside at Nantucket, 30 N. Beach St., Nantucket (508-228-2241; www.thebeachside.com); $35–415 per night. The 52 rooms in the Cliffside Pet Wing are pet-friendly at the Beachside, a hotel offering an outdoor swimming pool, a meeting room, air-conditioning, and complimentary continental breakfasts. All rooms have cable television, wireless Internet access, and small refrigerators; some also have private verandas. The hotel is located within walking distance to Jetties Beach and Main Street. There is a $65 per-night pet fee, part of which is donated to the Nantucket Safe Harbor for Animals.

Brass Lantern Inn, 11 N. Water St., Nantucket (508-228-4064; 1-800-377-6609; info@brasslanternnantucket.com; www.brasslanternnantucket.com); $219–385 per night. Located within walking distance of Nantucket Harbor, the Brass Lantern Inn offers 17 individually decorated guest rooms with private bathrooms, cable television, robes, air-conditioning, expanded continental breakfasts, and free wireless Internet access. Shops, restaurants, and beaches are just a few blocks away. For an extra $20 per night, dogs are permitted in designated rooms with prior approval. "Nantucket is a very dog-friendly island!" says proprietor Michelle Langlois. Pets receive a warm welcome with a bed and bowls, a beach towel, and toys and treats.

Le Languedoc Inn & Bistro, 3 Hussey St., Nantucket (508-228-4298; 1-800-244-4298; languedoc@nantucket.net; www.lelanguedoc.com); $55–250 per night. Pets are permitted with prior approval at this guesthouse located on a residential street. Private and semiprivate baths are available, as are a patio and plenty of space for bicycles. (Parking permits are available upon request.) Beaches, shops, and restaurants are all located within walking distance. Call for details about their pet policy.

North Truro

Outer Reach Resort, Rte. 6, North Truro (1-800-942-5388; www.outerreachresort.com). $69–174 per night. Outer Reach is proud to be pet-friendly and welcomes your animal for an additional $15 per night. The large motel-style resort is located on 12 acres with views of Cape Cod Bay. Choose from waterfront- and park-view rooms, all with air-conditioning. There are also plenty of outdoor picnic areas and decks.

Orleans

Orleans Waterfront Inn, 3 Old Country Rd., Orleans (508-255-2222; info@orleansinn.com; www.orleansinn.com); $250–500 per night. (Although the inn's official address is 3 Old Country Rd., it can be more easily found at 21 Route 6A.) A former sea captain's estate, the Orleans Inn has a rich history as well as modern touches such as private bathrooms, cable television, and a guest kitchen. The 11 rooms are individually decorated with quilts and new furniture; the waterfront suites also have living areas with pullout couches. Pets are welcome without restrictions.

Skaket Beach Motel, 203 Cranberry Hwy. (Rte. 6A), Orleans (508-255-1020; 1-800-835-0298; skaket@verizon.net; www.skaketbeachmotel.com); $67–521 per night. Pets are welcome here during the off-season for an additional $10 per night. Guests can choose from standard and deluxe rooms or apartments; some are poolside.

THE ORLEANS INN IN ORLEANS WELCOMES FOUR-LEGGED GUESTS. (PHOTO COURTESY OF ORLEANS INN)

All rooms have cable television with premium movie channels, air-conditioning, and refrigerators. The motel also recently added two- and three-room suites to its accommodations choices.

Provincetown

Atlantic Light Inn, 11 Pearl St., Provincetown (508-487-0302; 1-800-761-1016; reservations@atlanticlightinn.com; www.atlanticlightinn.com); $99–250 per night. The Black Pearl Inn (formerly known as Ireland House) is located near the center of town and offers private baths, air-conditioning, off-street parking, daily continental breakfasts, and a pet-friendly attitude. Beaches, shops, restaurants, and other attractions are located within walking distance. The innkeepers speak English, German, Spanish—and, of course, dog.

Breakwater Motel, Motor Inn, and Apartments, 716 Commercial St., Provincetown (508-487-1134; 1-800-487-1134; www.breakwatermotel.com); motel and motor inn $65–200 per night; call for weekly rates on apartments. These three separate accommodations are all located near each other in Provincetown; the 11 apartments each have a kitchen, air-conditioning, and cable television. The motel and motor inn are located across from the harbor and offer some waterfront rooms. "Small" pets (call to see if yours qualifies) are welcome but can't be left unattended.

Cape Colony Inn, 280 Bradford St., Provincetown (508-487-1755; www.capecolonyinn.com); $79–199 per night. This newly renovated inn has 51 rooms and welcomes pets of any size for an additional $25 per day. On their Web site, there are directions to the local dog park, as well as information on Provincetown's pet-friendly beaches (some even allow off-leash play). A continental breakfast is included in the room rate, and the grounds offer plenty of space for you and your furry friend to roam.

Gabriel's Apartments and Guest Rooms, 104 Bradford St., Provincetown (508-487-3232; 1-800-9MY-ANGEL; gabrielsma@aol.com; www.gabriels.com); $125–500 per night. From the moment you arrive at the well-landscaped courtyard at Gabriel's, you know you're visiting someplace out of the ordinary. Each of the apartments and guest rooms is named for a notable woman, including Emily Dickinson, Dian Fossey, and Amelia Earhart. Continental vegetarian breakfasts often include blueberry pancakes, oatmeal, fruit salad, and bagels; you'll also find a hot tub, outdoor sundecks, Internet access, individually decorated rooms, and private baths. Your pets will be welcomed by furry residents Mr. Pippin and Miss Potter, and Gabriel's has bowls, waste bags, and even loaner leashes for your use. Bas-Relief Park is next door for long walks.

Officers Quarters, 166 Commercial St., Provincetown (508-487-1850; 1-800-400-2278; www.officersquarters.org); $100–250 per night. Officers Quarters offers six individually decorated guest rooms, daily continental breakfasts, air-conditioning, cable television, wireless Internet access, a hot tub, and in-room telephones and refrigerators. Commercial Street is the hub of all the action in P-Town. Dogs are welcome with prior approval for an extra $35 per night.

Prince Albert Guest House, Commercial St., Provincetown (508-487-1850; 1-800-400-2278; www.princealbertguesthouse.com); $125–350 per night. Co-managed with the Officers Quarters accommodations (see listing above), this historic guesthouse provides its visitors with daily continental breakfasts, maid service, cable television, air-conditioning, telephones, refrigerators, and a hot tub. With prior approval from management, your dog is a welcome guest for an extra $35 per night.

Surfside Hotel & Suites, 543 Commercial St., Provincetown (508-487-1726; 1-800-421-1726; surfsideinnptown@aol.com; www.surfsideinn.cc); call for rate information. This pet-friendly hotel has a private beach, free deluxe continental breakfast each morning, an outdoor swimming pool, a lounge, wireless Internet access, and a location that's close to bike trails, beaches, shopping, and restaurants. "We understand that your dog is a significant part of the family," says Surfside management—dogs are welcome in designated rooms.

White Wind Inn, 174 Commercial St., Provincetown (508-487-1526; 1-888-449-WIND; www.whitewindinn.com); $85–275 per night. Well-behaved pooches are welcome in designated rooms at the White Wind Inn, where guests will find a roomy porch, expanded daily continental breakfasts, a private bathroom for every guest room, air-conditioning, in-room refrigerators, a video library, antiques, stained glass, and unique artwork. Dogs must be quiet, leashed, and steer clear of the common areas and the furniture. The pet-friendly rooms have outside entrances.

Sandwich

Sandwich Lodge & Resort, 54 Rte. 6A, Sandwich (508-888-2275; 1-800-282-5353; sandwichlodge@hotmail.com; www.sandwichlodge.com); $99–240 per night. Guests at the Sandwich Lodge can enjoy an indoor/outdoor heated pool, nice views, and free continental breakfasts. Pets are allowed in the motel-style standard rooms; each room has a private entrance and direct access to a large field. Animal owners pay an additional $15 per night, with a maximum of two pets per room. Note that pets are not allowed on the local beaches from 5/15 to 9/15.

South Harwich

Stone Horse Motel, 872 Main St., South Harwich (508-430-2220; info@stonehorsemotel.com); $139–249 per night. The sign hanging in front of this cute motel tells passersby about its pet-friendly policies; companion animals are welcome in Stone Horse rooms. Accommodations include standard double rooms, double rooms with kitchenettes, and suites with kitchenettes. The motel sits on 3 acres with a heated swimming pool. You'll pay a one-time fee of $15 to bring your pup along.

South Yarmouth

Brentwood Motor Inn, 961 Main St., South Yarmouth (1-800-328-8812; www.brentwoodcapecod.com); $149–339 per night. Choose from town houses, cottages, and motel rooms at this versatile facility, where the amenities include an indoor swimming pool, a hot tub and sauna, a lounge area, and a picnic area with barbecue grills. Dogs are allowed for an additional $10 per night.

Clarion Inn Cape Cod, 1199 Rte. 28, South Yarmouth (508-394-7600; 1-800-527-0359; www.choicehotels.com); $149–199 per night. A member of the Choice Hotel Group, this Clarion won a Gold Award for excellence in 2012. The hotel boasts an indoor pool and fitness center, and pets are welcome for an additional $10 per night, per pet.

Ambassador Inn & Suites, 1314 Rte. 28, South Yarmouth (508-394-4000; www.goambassador inn.com); $120–169 per night. Located just down the road from Cape Cod Community College, this Ambassador Inn (formerly a Quality Inn) offers a swimming pool, free high-speed Internet access, cable television with premium movie channels, alarm clocks, and in-room hair dryers, coffeemakers, irons, and ironing boards. Dogs are welcome with prior approval.

West Yarmouth

Econo Lodge West Yarmouth, 59 Main St., West Yarmouth (508-771-0699; www.choice hotels.com); $59–99 per night. This Econo Lodge offers its guests free continental breakfasts each morning, an indoor heated swimming pool, a game room, and a location that's close to beaches, shopping, restaurants, boat cruises, and Cape Cod Community College. Guest pets are welcome for an additional $10 per night and a $50 security deposit.

Yarmouth Port

Colonial House Inn, Rte. 6A, 277 Main St., Yarmouth Port (508-362-4348; info@colonialhouse capecod.com; www.colonial housecapecod.com); $120–160 per night. The rates at this circa-1820s inn include breakfast as well as dinner; the menu is à la carte, with your choice of up to 14 entrées. The antiques-filled guest rooms in the main house and restored carriage house all have pleasant views and share access to the indoor swimming pool. Dogs are welcome in designated guest rooms for an additional $10 per pet, per night.

Campgrounds

Bourne

Bay View Campground, 260 MacArthur Blvd., Bourne (508-759-7610; www.bayview campground.com); $46–58 per night. In addition to the usual campground amenities such as restrooms, showers, and a camp store, campers at Bay View will also find an ice-cream parlor, Internet access, three swimming pools, two playgrounds, a baseball field, and a tennis court. Dogs are allowed on a leash, as long as owners clean up after them and don't leave them alone at the site.

Bourne Scenic Park, 370 Scenic Hwy., Bourne (508-759-7873; scenicpark@capecod.net; www .bournescenicpark.com); $34–50 per night. This RV-friendly campground features a picnic area, hot showers, a saltwater swimming pool, paved roads, canal fishing, a tenting area, playgrounds, a camp store, scheduled family activities, and a game room. Quiet pets are welcome, but owners must keep them on a leash and clean up after them.

Brewster

Nickerson State Park Campground, Rte. 6A, Brewster (508-896-3491); $15 per night Massachusetts residents; $17 per night out-of-state residents. Choose from more than 400 campsites at this 1,900-acre forested campground in a park with enough recreational opportunities to satisfy all the adults and children in your clan (see "Out and About"). The campground has restrooms, hot showers, picnic tables, a dump station, tent sites, and RV sites (no hookups).

Shady Knoll Campground, 1709 Rte. 6A, Brewster (508-896-3002; www.shadyknoll.com); $26–55 per night. Campers at Shady Knoll will find modern restrooms with hot showers, wireless high-speed Internet access, laundry facilities, movie nights, a camp store, a game room, a lounge, and a playground. Dogs are permitted for an extra $4 per night.

Sweetwater Forest Family Camping Resort, Rte. 124, Brewster (508-896-3773; sweeth2orv@aol.com; www.sweetwaterforest.com); $29–46 per night. Well-behaved pets are welcome for an extra $1 per night at this peaceful family campground; the staff even offers boarding services in case you need someone else to look after your furry friend for a while. Campground amenities include separate tenting and RV areas, 60 acres of woods and lakefront scenery, recreation for the kids, and hot showers.

Buzzards Bay

Scusset Beach State Reservation Campground, 140 Scusset Beach Rd., Buzzards Bay (508-888-0859); $15 per night Massachusetts residents; $17 per night out-of-state residents. Most of the 103 sites at this campground have hookups; campers will also find flush toilets, showers, and a dumping station. Tent camping is offered from May to Columbus Day, though RV camping is available year-round. Scusset Beach also offers Safari Camping for RV clubs. (For more information on the park, see "Out and About.")

East Falmouth

Cape Cod Camp Resort, 176 Thomas Landers Rd., East Falmouth (508-548-1458; www.capecampresort.com); $34–53 per night. Campers at this East Falmouth facility can rent boats or tepees, relax in the teen game room, shop in the camp store, splash in the swimming pool, and romp at the playground. Choose from 200 wooded and open sites for tents and RVs. Pet owners pay an additional fee of $6 per night in season and $3 per night off-season.

Falmouth

Washburn Island Camping, Waquoit Bay National Estuarine Research Reserve, Falmouth (508-457-0495; 1-877-1-CAMP-MASS; www.waquoitbayreserve.org); $8 per night Massachusetts residents; $10 per night out-of-state residents. Those looking for an out-of-the-ordinary experience won't mind the extra effort it takes to reserve a spot and reach this secluded campground. First, you'll need to secure a permit; then you'll need your own boat to reach one of the seven sites (there's no ferry). You'll also have to learn to avoid the deer ticks and poison ivy, which are both plentiful. Dogs must be on a leash and are not permitted in beach areas. (See "Out and About" for information on the reserve.) There's also a reservation fee and no pets are allowed on the beach.

Sandwich

Dunroamin' RV Resort, 5 John Ewer Rd., Sandwich (508-477-0541; www.dunroamintrailer park.com); $35 per night or $240 per week. No tent camping is allowed at this facility, which caters strictly to RVs. Pets are welcome without extra fees, though owners must keep them on a leash and show proof of vaccination. Amenities include full hookups and a picnic table at each site, laundry facilities, a playground, and planned activities in summer.

Peters Pond Campground, 185 Cotuit Rd., Sandwich (508-477-1775; info@peterspond.com; www.sunrvresorts.com); $35–69 per night or $195–435 per week. Leashed pets are allowed at this large campground only from mid-April to July 1, and from Labor Day to mid-October, though a limited number of campers in self-contained vehicles are allowed to bring pets during the summer months. Amenities include a camp store, restrooms, two beaches, two playgrounds, and walking trails.

Shawme-Crowell State Forest Campground, Rte. 130, Sandwich (508-888-0351); $15 per night Massachusetts residents; $17 per night out-of-state residents. Camping is the draw at this popular 700-acre reserve (see "Out and About" for more information about the forest). The campground has nearly 300 sites for tents and RVs, along with restrooms, showers, and picnic tables. Pets are welcome, but as in all state parks they must be leashed, and owners must clean up after them. Starting in 2005, this park also offers yurts—cabin-like camping structures with canvas sides.

Homes, Cottages, and Cabins for Rent

Martha's Vineyard

For vacation rentals in Martha's Vineyard, check these local Web sites, and use the pet-friendly search option:

www.mvol.com

www.mvy.com

www.vineyardvacationhomes.com

Nantucket

For vacation rentals in Nantucket, check these local Web sites:

www.nantucket.net

www.islandpropertiesre.com

www.themaurypeople.com

www.nantucketdreams.com

www.jpfco.com

www.greatpointproperties.com

www.thecottagesnantucket.com

Provincetown

Labrador Landing, 47 Commercial St., Provincetown (917-597-1500; labradorlanding@ mac.com; www.labradorlanding

.com); $1,500–2,500 per week. With a name like Labrador Landing, they'd have to allow pets. Popeye and Brutus, the resident Chihuahuas, will be on hand to welcome you and your four-legged friends to these two luxury waterfront accommodations—a boathouse cottage and a two-story cottage. Pet owners pay a $100 refundable deposit in addition to the standard security deposit.

South Orleans

Ocean Bay View Lodge Cottages, 116 Portanimicut Rd., South Orleans (508-255-3344; www.oceanbayview.com); $500–975 per week. These nine housekeeping cottages are spread throughout 20 acres on Little Pleasant Bay. They vary in size, are fully furnished with kitchens and living rooms, and share access to a private beach, a salt marsh, a playing field, and two boats. Well-behaved dogs and cats are welcome to join their owners.

OUT AND ABOUT

Animal Friends Summer Camp, 96 Megansett Rd., Cataumet (617-226-5670; www.arlboston.org). Unfortunately, this kids and animals camp has closed due to lack of funding, but there is a petition to reopen it, so check the Web site for details or to donate.

Ara's Tours, Nantucket (508-228-1951; ara@arastours.com; www.arastours.com). "Lap pets" are welcome to join their owners on a tour of Nantucket's lighthouses, historic streets, and architecture with local photographer and naturalist Ara Charder. Trips in the air-conditioned vehicle last for about 90 minutes; private charters are also available. "We stop for photographs!" Ara says.

Beebe Woods, Falmouth. This is a great spot for peaceful walks through the woods; you'll almost always bump into other pooches along the trails. From the village Green, take Palmer Avenue to Depot Avenue; follow Depot all the way to the end for parking at the Cape Cod Conservatory and Highfield Theatre. (For a trail map, visit the nearby chamber of commerce on Main Street, call 508-548-8500, or contact info@falmouthcapecod.com).

Black Dog General Store, 3, 5, and 11B Water St., **Vineyard Haven, Martha's Vineyard** (508-693-9223; 1-800-626-1991; www.theblackdog.com). When thinking of the Vineyard, many people call to mind the ubiquitous Black Dog silhouette logo of this wildly popular tavern, bakery, and store, and this is the original location of the 19-store chain. Inside, you can find T-shirts, mugs, socks, golf balls, hats, and nearly everything else emblazoned with the dark pooch's picture. You can also browse dog bowls, biscuits, backpacks, and other good stuff for your four-legged companions. The Black Dog donates a portion of its profits to the National Education for Assistance Dog Service (NEADS). Other locations include: 11 S. Summer St., **Edgartown, Martha's Vineyard** (508-627-3360); 37 Circuit Ave., **Oak Bluffs, Martha's Vineyard** (508-696-9826); and 214 Main St., **Falmouth** (508-495-6000).

Cape Air, Barnstable Municipal Airport, 660 Barnstable Rd., Hyannis (508-771-6944; 1-800-227-3247; www.capeair.com). Don't want to wait in traffic on the Bourne Bridge? No problem. Cape Air welcomes passengers who want to fly in and out of Boston, Providence, New Bedford, Provincetown, Hyannis, Martha's Vineyard, and Nantucket. Dogs are welcome on all flights: Crates and/or extra fees are required in some cases, depending on the route. Visit the Web site for complete route schedules and reservation information.

Cape Cod Light, Light House Rd., North Truro. You'll see the signs on Route 6 for this historic lighthouse. It was moved back from the eroding cliff in recent years, leaving a scenic boardwalk from the light to the edge of the ocean. The lighthouse grounds are surrounded by the Highland Golf Links, one of the East Coast's oldest courses. Pets are allowed on the grounds but not in the gift shop.

Cape Cod National Seashore: Province Lands Visitor Center, Provincetown (508-487-1256); **Salt Pond Visitor Center,** Eastham (508-255-3421). This 43,000-acre national park comprises much of the outer reaches of the Cape. Renowned for its beaches and dune landscape, the preserve is home to many endangered and threatened wildlife species, historic buildings, picnic areas, and photogenic overlooks. The rules for pets here are the opposite of those found in many other parks: Pets are welcome on beaches (except those staffed by a lifeguard) but are not allowed on trails. Dogs must be on a 6-foot leash at all times. The Province Lands Visitor Center is located on Race Point Road off Route 6 in Provincetown; the Salt Pond Visitor Center is located at the corner of Nauset Road and Route 6 in Eastham. Both centers can provide maps, orientation, and ranger-guided activities, and staff members are available to answer questions.

Dolphin Fleet Whale Watch, Standish St., Provincetown (508-240-3636; 1-800-826-9300; www.whalewatch.com). Well-behaved pets are welcome aboard the Dolphin Fleet's whale-watching trips in Cape Cod Bay. Each trip is led by a naturalist from the Center for Coastal Studies, and an onboard galley provides food and drinks. Tickets are available at the company's Web site.

Hy-Line Cruises, Ocean Street Dock, Hyannis (508-778-2600; 1-800-492-8082; hylinecruises.com). Pets are permitted aboard Hy-Line cruise vessels to join the fun on ferry trips to Nantucket

Pets and P-Town

Provincetown may be the most pet-friendly resort area in the state, and if you want to romp in the surf and dig in the sand with your dog, this is the place. All of the beaches are pet friendly and many have off-leash hours where you can let your pooch run to his heart's content. The Pilgrim Bark Park (www.provincetowndogpark.org) is also a great place to play: local artists have donated sculptures to decorate the small and large dog enclosures. For more pet-friendly things to do in Provincetown, visit www.provincetowntourismoffice.org.

and Martha's Vineyard, except in the First Class Lounge area of the seasonal Nantucket ferry. There are no extra fees for dogs, but they must be leashed and stay off the furniture.

Magellan Sportfishing Charters, Rte. 28, Harwich Port (508-237-9823; 1-800-848-TUNA; ccs5@verizon.net; www.capecodsportsmen.com). Well-behaved pets are welcome on full- or half-day charters in search of porgies, striped bass, bluefish, or bluefin tuna. The boat accommodates a maximum of six people; the average price is about $150 per hour.

Nantucket Airlines, Barnstable Municipal Airport, 660 Barnstable Rd., North Ramp, **Hyannis** (508-771-6944; 1-866-227-3247); on **Nantucket** (508-228-6234; www.nantucketairlines.com). You can bring your pet along for the scenic flight to or from Nantucket as long as you give the airlines advance notice. Rover flies for free.

Nickerson State Park, Rte. 6A, Brewster (508-896-3491). You can camp overnight at Nickerson (see "Accommodations—Campgrounds") or just spend the day. On-site, you'll find an 8-mile-long bicycle path, hiking trails, trout-stocked fishing ponds, picnic areas, horseback-riding and cross-country skiing trails, boat launches, and handicapped-accessible facilities. Dogs must be on a leash at all times.

Scusset Beach State Reservation, 140 Scusset Beach Rd., Buzzards Bay (508-888-0859). Fishermen frequent this 380-acre park on the Cape Cod Canal. The park's attractions include a campground (see "Accommodations—Campgrounds"), a fishing pier, picnic areas, biking and hiking trails, and plenty of spots to stop and enjoy the views. Dogs must be on a leash and are not allowed on the 1½-mile-long stretch of beach.

Shawme-Crowell State Forest, Rte. 130, Sandwich (508-888-0351). Horseback riders love this 700-acre patch of reserved land located near the entrance to Cape Cod. The park has more than 15 miles of trails that meander through the woods—often used by cross-country skiers in the wintertime. You'll also find picnic and barbecue areas and an on-site campground (see "Accommodations—Campgrounds").

Steamship Authority Ferries, Rte. 28, **Woods Hole** (508-548-3788; www1.steamshipauthority.com); South Street Dock, **Hyannis** (508-771-4000); $8–16 per adult, one-way; $68–175 per vehicle, one-way. Steamship ferries are the most popular choice for journeys to and from Cape Cod (Woods Hole) and Martha's Vineyard; you can also use them for travel between Hyannis and Nantucket. Crated or leashed pets are welcome without extra fees. Reservations are necessary for vehicles, but not for passengers. Parking can be tricky; in Woods Hole, be prepared to park several miles away in one of the Steamship Authority's lots and ride the shuttle bus to the ferry dock.

Stephen Huneck Gallery, 15 Old South Wharf, Nantucket (508-325-7100; www.dogmt.com). The late artist Stephen Huneck believed in the spiritual connection between dogs and their humans, and wanted to celebrate that at his Dog Mountain Chapel. His work is displayed in a gallery there, although currently volunteers are renovating the property and trying to raise funds to keep both the gallery and chapel open to the public. Check the Web site for current information or to donate. Huneck was also the author of the popular series of children's books featuring his black Lab, Sally.

Walk for Animals, Cape Cod Animal Care and Adoption Center, Massachusetts Society for the Prevention of Cruelty to Animals (MSPCA), 1577 Falmouth Rd., Centerville (508-775-0940; www.mspca.org). This annual walk (2005 marked the eighth) raises much-needed funds for the MSPCA's Cape Cod location, which helps to find new families for homeless pets. Participating dogs receive a bandana, while their human companions walk in a new T-shirt. On average, about 250 people show up for the event each year. Visit the Web site for this year's date and location.

Waquoit Bay National Estuarine Research Reserve, Rte. 28, Falmouth (508-457-0495; www.waquoitbayreserve.org). Pets are welcome on a leash at this impressive 2,500-acre preserve, though owners are advised to take extra precautions against deer ticks—a growing problem in the area. Also, as this is a wildlife preserve with an abundance of hatchlings, dogs are not allowed on or near the beach. You can camp at the **Washburn Island** sites (see "Accommodations—Campgrounds") or explore **South Cape Beach State Park, Waquoit Bay,** numerous ponds, and the **Quashnet River Property.** Start at the headquarters on Route 28 for maps and other information.

Wellfleet Drive-In Theatre, Rte. 6, Wellfleet (508-349-7176; wellfleetcinemas@hotmail.com; www.wellfleetcinemas.com). Open late April through early October. Bring your pup along in the backseat and take in new releases and double features at this old-fashioned drive-in movie theater. There's also a snack bar and playground on-site. Campers and oversized vehicles (defined as SUVs, minivans, and pickup trucks) are welcome but must park in a designated area so as not to obscure others' views.

QUICK BITES

Cape Cod

Ay! Caramba Café, 703 Main St., Harwich (508-432-9800; www.aycarambacafe.com). This Mexican restaurant serves south-of-the-border favorites such as burritos, enchiladas, shrimp Diablo, flautas, carne asada, and chips with salsa. Diners can relax at the outdoor tables or order from the extensive take-out menu.

Bookstore & Restaurant, 50 Kendrick Ave., P.O. Box 1434, Wellfleet 02667 (508-349-3154; www.wellfleetoyster.com). Charlie and Bedford are the resident pooches at this bookshop and eatery; you'll probably run into other four-legged friends while you're browsing the stacks and enjoying a meal at the outdoor café tables. Diners can choose from homemade soups, oysters Rockefeller, fried clams, Greek salad, native scrod, and much more.

Box Lunch, various locations, Cape Cod (www.boxlunch.com). You can find a Box Lunch on Rte. 6 in **North Eastham** (508-255-0799), at the Patriot Square Mall in **South Dennis** (508-394-2202), 781 Main St. in **Falmouth** (508-457-7657), at the original location on 50 Briar Ln. in **Wellfleet** (508-349-2178), and at four other locations throughout the Cape, including Provincetown, Truro, and Hyannis. The local chain specializes in "rollwiches," travel-friendly wraps made with any combination of chicken, turkey, ham, roast beef, and vegetables you can dream up. Visit the Web site for information on all the locations.

Bubala's by the Bay, 185 Commercial St., Provincetown (508-487-0773; www.bubalas.com). At Bubala's, you can choose from sandwiches and salads at lunchtime and upscale entrées at dinner. Recommended by local innkeepers, it has a great location and plenty of outdoor seating by the sidewalk.

Carbo's Bar and Grill, 681 Falmouth Rd., Mashpee (508-477-5238). Located in a shopping center, this casual restaurant has outdoor patio seating with umbrellas and serves pizza and grill favorites.

Chapin's Restaurant, 85 Taunton Ave., Dennis (608-385-7000; www.chapinsrestaurant.com). Open year-round, Chapin's has a "beach casual" theme and a menu that includes choices like Cobb salad, lobster pie, prime rib, fried calamari, fried shrimp, chicken parmigiana, and tuna sandwiches. Outdoor seating and takeout are both available.

Cottage Street Bakery, 5 Cottage St., Orleans (508-255-2821; www.cottagestreetbakery.com). This quaint bakery has a few outdoor tables and a wide selection of ever-changing, freshly baked products. Expect to find treats such as chocolate velvet cheesecake, carrot-raisin muffins, blueberry scones, cheese danish, sticky buns, apple coffee cake, and peanut-butter cookies.

Dockside Ribs n' Lobster, 110 School St., Hyannis (508-778-1880; info@docksidehyannis.com; www.thedocksidehyannis.com). Located next to the Steamship Authority, within walking distance from downtown, this happenin' restaurant offers a take-out window as well as an outdoor dining area where you can enjoy views of the harbor. Clam chowder, lobster ravioli, fried seafood, honey-barbecue chicken, and french dip sandwiches are all on the menu, as well as bar favorites like wings and nachos.

Emack and Bolio's Ice Cream, Rte. 6A, 82 Cranberry Hwy., Oracle Square, **Orleans** (508-255-5844; www.emackandbolios.com). There's lots of outdoor seating at this shop serving gourmet ice cream, smoothies, and espresso. Emack and Bolio's has two other Cape locations with outdoor seating: 117 Main St., **Wellfleet** (508-349-2210); and 2 Kent Pl., **Chatham** (508-945-5506), and a total of 11 locations statewide.

Governor Bradford Restaurant, 312 Commercial St., Provincetown (508-487-2781). Sit at one of the many outdoor tables at this bustling downtown restaurant and choose from wings, steamers, sandwich plates, salads, and fried seafood platters.

Hearth 'n Kettle Restaurants, 874 Main St., **Falmouth** (508-548-6111; www.hearthnkettle.com); Rte. 132 and Bearse's Way, **Hyannis** (508-771-3000); 1196 Main St., **South Yarmouth** (508-394-2252); and Rte. 6A at West Rd., **Orleans** (508-240-0111). Although none of the Cape Cod Hearth 'n Kettle locations has outdoor seating, they all welcome pet owners to order any item on the menu as takeout. Sandwiches, salads, appetizers, desserts, and fresh seafood are all available.

Kream 'n Kone, 961 Rte. 28 (corner of Rtes. 28 and 134), West Dennis (508-394-0808). This may sound like an ice cream stand, but this casual, walk-up-to-the-counter spot serves up everything you might want for a quick lunch or snack, including fried seafood, tuna rolls, hot dogs, onion rings, homemade clam chowder, and ice cream. Locals rave about the fried clams.

Landfall Restaurant, Luscombe Ave., Woods Hole (508-548-1758). After a long ferry ride or a trip down the bike path, relax outside at this scenic harbor-front restaurant constructed of reclaimed wood from shipwrecks and old buildings. Menu items include lobster, clam chowder, swordfish, fried clams, steamers, and scallops, and there's a full bar.

Marley's of Chatham, 1077 Main St., Chatham (508-945-1700). The cat on the sign will lead you to this restaurant with an outdoor patio, serving chicken, seafood, steaks, and vegetarian dishes, and a dog lover's favorite, mozarella paws. Try the baked stuffed quahog, Debbie's Homemade Chicken Potpie, and lobster crêpes. If you can't stay, takeout is also available.

Seafood Sam's, various locations, Cape Cod (www.seafoodsams.com). Located on Coast Guard Rd. in **Sandwich** (508-888-4629), and on Rte. 28 in **Harwichport** (508-432-1422), **Falmouth** (508-540-7877), and **South Yarmouth** (508-394-3504), this local chain serves broiled and fried fish, along with other treats. Outdoor tables are available at the South Yarmouth and Harwichport locations; takeout is available (and very popular) at all four spots.

Skipper Restaurant, 152 South Shore Dr., South Yarmouth (508-394-7406; www.skipperrestaurant.com). The Skipper earned the title of "Cape's Best Chowder" at the 2004 Cape Cod Chowder Festival and continues to win awards at chowder competitions throughout the state; at this Gilligan's Island-inspired eatery (listen to their theme song on the Web site, if you dare), try some of the white gold yourself, along with lobster rolls, BLT sandwiches, chicken tenders, Caesar salad, clams casino, and kids' menu items. Everything on the menu is available for takeout, and seating is available on the outdoor deck.

Spanky's Clam Shack and Seaside Saloon, 138 Ocean St., Hyannis (508-771-2770; www.spankysclamshack.com). You'll find outdoor seating and a take-out service at Spanky's, a casual waterfront restaurant serving "wicked good" shrimp, scallops, breakfast foods, onion rings, chowder, salads, sandwiches, and of course clams. Dogs are welcome to sit in the area adjacent to the patio tables.

Martha's Vineyard

The Bite, 29 Basin Rd., Menemsha, Martha's Vineyard (508-645-9239). Order chicken wings, potato salad, french fries, clam rolls, and fried seafood platters at the take-out window at this ultracasual, fun restaurant with outdoor tables. The Bite is open seasonally from late May to October.

Black Dog Bakery Café General Store, 509 State Rd., Vineyard Haven, Martha's Vineyard

(508-696-8190; 1-800-626-1991; www.theblackdog.com). Pick yourself up a T-shirt while you grab a quick bite to eat from this famous bakery and store (see "Out and About" for more about The Black Dog). Relax at the comfy bench out front while you munch on chocolate-chip cookies, pumpkin muffins, ham-and-cheese croissants, and other treats. **The Black Dog Tavern,** Martha's Vineyard's most famous restaurant, is located right around the corner; they don't have outdoor seating, but it's worth a peek anyway.

Bongo, 15 Main St., Vineyard Haven, Martha's Vineyard (508-693-1347). For more than five years, this sidewalk café and bakery has been serving sandwiches, coffee, homemade breads, and other easy-to-carry items and prepared foods to locals as well as visitors. Everything on the menu is available for takeout, including breakfast sandwiches, cheeseburgers, Greek salads, and grilled chicken wraps.

Giordano's Restaurant, 18 Lake Ave., Oak Bluffs, Martha's Vineyard (508-693-0184; www.giosmv.com). This family-owned restaurant is consistently voted the "Best of the Vineyard" and is now run by the fourth generation of Giordanos. The pizza take-out window at Giordano's can be a dog lover's best friend. Order just a slice or a whole pie and enjoy your bounty at the nearby waterfront park or on one of the restaurant's picnic tables (around the side of the building).

Ice Cream and Candy Bazaar, 5 Dock St., Edgartown, Martha's Vineyard (508-627-8735). The kids will love the sweet treats and creamy ice-cream flavors at this casual spot that's open seasonally; Rover will appreciate the outdoor seating.

Mad Martha's, 23 Lake Ave., **Oak Bluffs** (508-693-8349); 12 Circuit Ave., **Oak Bluffs** (508-693-9151); 20 Union St., **Vineyard Haven** (508-693-5885); and 7 N. Water St., **Edgartown** (508-627-8761), all on Martha's Vineyard. Homemade ice cream is the specialty at this Martha's Vineyard original with four island locations. You won't find outdoor tables, but you can enjoy your cone while you walk around and explore the sights with Fido by your side.

Nantucket

Bartlett's Ocean View Farm Market Kitchen, 33 Bartlett Farm Rd., Nantucket (508-228-9403; www.bartlettsfarm.com). Grab a sandwich or meal on your way to the beach or a picnic. Bartlett's offers many vegetarian selections along with salads, breakfast treats, and desserts. You can even visit the Web site to learn about the soup of the day. This is one of Massachusetts' oldest and largest family-owned farms.

Dune Nantucket, 20 Broad St., Nantucket (508-228-4622; www.dunenantucket.com). Formerly known as Cioppino's Restaurant, Dune has undergone a total sci-fi makeover inspired by the Frank Herbert classic, but don't worry, the menu doesn't include sandworms. The modern and chic décor does use shades of sand color to create a restful, urban vibe, and the menu offers contemporary versions of New England's bounty, including salmon sashimi and lobster, avocado, and corn salad.

Nantucket Cookie Company, Steamboat Wharf, Nantucket (508-228-7732; www.nantucket cookiecompany.net). The motto here is "small batch from scratch," and the Nantucket storefront of this cookie bakery is open from mid-April to December; you can also order your fresh-baked treats from the Web site year-round. Specialties include chocolate-orange, iced lemon, snickerdoodle, walnut chocolate chunk, and oatmeal-cranberry cookies.

HOT SPOTS FOR SPOT

Cape Cod

Cloverleaf Kennel–Cape Cod, 558 Carriage Shop Rd., East Falmouth (508-540-PETS; pet boarding@cloverleafkennel.com). The staff at this boarding and grooming facility give each dog several walks each day and board cats in a separate second-floor space. The kennel is heated and air-conditioned. You'll need proof of vaccination before boarding a pet, and reservations are strongly recommended.

Cohasset Kennel, 235 Cedar St., Cohasset (781-383-1475; info@ cohassetkennel.com; www .cohassetkennel.com). Your dog can enjoy plenty of relaxation and privacy in Cohasset Kennel's indoor/outdoor runs; the facility also offers an agility course, daily playgroups, heat and air-conditioning, small swimming pools, and a separate area for cats. Overnight boarding and doggie day care are both available. Wendy Oleksiak, RN, and a staff of 11 keep the staff-to-client ratio low.

Derbyfield Kennel, 556 Depot St., North Harwich (508-432-2510; www.derbyfieldkennel .com). Recommended by locals, this family-run boarding facility has piped-in music for the animals, indoor and outdoor runs, a separate cattery, heat in winter, limited pickup service, and nightly treats. The kennel is open year-round.

Howl-a-Day Inn, 12 Industrial Park Rd., West Yarmouth (508-790-4695; www.howladayinn capecod.com). You can guess by the name that this creative doggie day care and boarding kennel loves their clientele. Pets are supervised closely, even 24-7 while staying overnight.

KC's Animal Resort, 79 Shank Painter Rd., Provincetown (508-487-7900; www.kcskennel provincetown.com). Located beside a veterinary clinic, KC's offers 22 private kennels, heated floors and air-conditioning, outdoor runs, and a play yard.

THE GOOD DOG GOODS PET-SPECIALTY STORE IS A HAPPENIN' SPOT FOR CANINES ON MARTHA'S VINEYARD.

Your pet can also get a complete grooming—including a bath, ear cleaning, and nail clipping—during her stay. Rates range from $13–15 per night (off-season) and $20–30 per night (in-season). Day care is available for $15–25 per day, including play sessions.

Nauset Kennels, 2685 Nauset Rd., North Eastham (508-255-0081; www.nausetpetservices.com). Nauset offers doggie day care as well as overnight boarding. The facility has several play yards, heat and air-conditioning, personal playtimes, one-on-one walks, and a separate boarding area for cats.

Pilgrim Dog Park, Provincetown (www.provincetowndogpark.com). If Rover needs an off-leash run, head to Pilgrim Park. There are enclosures for both large and small dogs, decorated with quirky sculptures donated by local artists.

Paws and Whiskers, 256 Commercial St., Provincetown (508-487-3441). This "dog bakery and pawticulars" shop sells everything from gourmet, fresh-baked treats to toys, collars, leashes, hats, and bowls. This is the place to come if you're looking for a doggie backpack, paw-shaped Christmas stocking, red bandana, or even a doggie life jacket for your sightseeing trip on the boat.

Martha's Vineyard

Good Dog Goods, 79 Circuit Ave., **Oak Bluffs,** Martha's Vineyard (508-696-7100; www.gooddoggoods.com). Owner Kerry Scott calls her shop "a celebration of dogs"; your pup is welcome to join you inside as you browse the wide selection of items designed especially for dogs and their owners. The shop also has locations at Main Street in **Vineyard Haven** and Winter Street in **Edgartown.,** **Nantucket**

Cold Noses, The Courtyard at Straight Wharf, Nantucket (508-228-KISS). This fun boutique sells dog and cat toys; nautical- and Nantucket-themed collars, leashes, and tags; breed-specific gift items; T-shirts; tote bags; Christmas tree ornaments; books; and more.

Geronimo's of Nantucket, 119 Pleasant St., Nantucket (508-228-3731; www.geronimos.com). Stop by Geronimo's for a doggie-themed shopping experience. You can browse an eclectic collection of ceramic bowls, pet beds, treats, toys, leashes, collars, and animal-related gift ideas such as tote bags, T-shirts, and hats. You can also order your pet necessities online at the store's Web site.

MSPCA Angell Animal Medical Center–Nantucket, 21 Crooked Ln., Nantucket (508-228-1491). In addition to caring for local domestic and wild animals, the Nantucket MSPCA (Massachusetts Society for the Prevention of Cruelty to Animals) can also board and groom your pet in its newly built facility during your visit to the island. Staffed with volunteers and veterinarians, the society also offers humane education, wildlife rehabilitation, and homeless-animal adoption programs.

THE MSPCA ANGELL ANIMAL MEDICAL CENTER IN NANTUCKET OFFERS GROOMING, BOARDING, AND EMERGENCY MEDICAL CARE FOR LOCAL AND VISITING CANINES. (PHOTO COURTESY OF MSPCA)

Sandy Paws of Nantucket, 20 Centre St., Nantucket (508-228-0708). Sandy Paws is a high-end pet boutique offering something for every animal (and animal lover) out there. For four-legged shoppers, the store has fresh doggie treats, toys, chewies, clothing, and other accessories. Their two-legged companions, meanwhile, can enjoy browsing the selection of stationery, hats, accessories for the house, and books.

ANIMAL SHELTERS AND HUMANE SOCIETIES

Animal Rescue League of Boston, Cape Cod Branch, 3981 Main St. (Rte. 6A), East Brewster (508-255-1030; www.arlboston.org)

Cape Cod Animal Care and Adoption Center (MSPCA), 1577 Falmouth Rd., Centerville (508-775-0940; www.mspca.org)

Cape-Marine Animal Rescue, 1 Village Dr., Brewster (508-896-3328)

Martha's Vineyard Animal Care and Adoption Center (MSPCA), 276 Vineyard Haven Rd., P.O. Box 2097, Edgartown 02539 (508-627-8662; www.mspca.org)

Nantucket Animal Care and Adoption Center (MSPCA), 21 Crooked Ln., Nantucket (508-228-1491; www.mspca.org)

IN CASE OF EMERGENCY

Animal Health Care Associates, 20 Airport Rd., West Tisbury, Martha's Vineyard (508-693-6515)

Barnstable Animal Hospital, 157 Airport Rd., Hyannis (508-778-6555)

Brewster Veterinary Hospital, 56 Underpass Rd., Brewster (508-896-2540)

Cape Cod Animal Hospital, 1415 Osterville Rd., West Barnstable (508-428-6393)

Herring Cove Animal Clinic, 79 Shank Painter Rd., Provincetown (508-487-6449)

Pleasant Bay Animal Hospital, Rte. 137 and Queen Ann Rd., Harwich (508-432-5500)

Sandwich Animal Hospital, 492 Rte. 6A, East Sandwich (508-888-2774)

South Cape Veterinary Clinic, 435 Waquoit Hwy., Waquoit Village (508-457-7771)

Vineyard Veterinary Clinic, 276 Vineyard Haven Rd., Edgartown, Martha's Vineyard (508-627-5292)

THE HISTORIC PUBLICK HOUSE IN STURBRIDGE WELCOMES PETS IN ITS COUNTRY-MOTEL ANNEX.

Central Massachusetts

For travelers planning a trip to New England, central Massachusetts may not be high on the to-see list: Some say it lacks the glamour of the seacoast and the lure of covered-bridge landscapes in places like Vermont and New Hampshire. But pet owners will find the area awash with things to do and places to go, including apple orchards, parks, mountains, winding back roads, and city streets. Whether you're hoping to spend a week at a lakefront campground, paddle a canoe, or simply take a nice drive to look at the changing leaves, this often-overlooked section of the state can provide a peaceful escape in an otherwise crowded commonwealth.

Unfortunately, the region is not as accommodating to animal lovers as it used to be. The living-history museum and popular tourist attraction Old Sturbridge Village recently reversed its pet-friendly policies—dogs are no longer allowed to accompany their owners through the museum's many outdoor exhibits and displays. It's always worthwhile to double-check current policies before making reservations and most pet-friendly hotels and inns require pet reservations. Travelers should also note that the most noteworthy natural feature of central Massachusetts, the enormous Quabbin Reservoir, is a public water supply and therefore off-limits to pets.

ACCOMMODATIONS

Hotels, Motels, Inns, and Bed & Breakfasts

Auburn

La Quinta Inn & Suites, 444 Southbridge St., Auburn (508-832-7000; www.lq.com); $79–129 per night. Guests at La Quinta enjoy free continental breakfasts, newspapers, and local calls, along with interior corridors, voice mail, express check-out services, and cable television with premium movie channels and pay-per-view films. Children under 18 stay free, and pets are welcome without extra fees.

Barre

Jenkins Inn, 7 West St., Barre (978-355-6444; 1-800-378-7373; jenkinsinn@juno.com; www.jenkinsinn.com); $160–185 per night. Listed on the National Register of Historic Homes, this Gothic Revival inn offers private bathrooms, full breakfasts on bone china, air-conditioning, parking, satellite television, Internet access, and in-room telephones. Dogs (sorry, no cats) are welcome at Jenkins Inn for an additional $10 per night, which is donated to a local shelter, provided they are not left alone in the rooms.

Fitchburg

Holiday Inn Royal Plaza Hotel, 150 Royal Plaza Dr., Fitchburg (978-342-7100; 1-866-460-7456; www.ihg.com); $94–169 per night. Pets are allowed at the Royal Plaza for an additional $10 per night and a $50 refundable security deposit. Amenities include a swimming pool and water park, a restaurant and lounge, a fitness center, laundry facilities, volleyball and basketball courts, cable television, a 24-hour front desk, and room service. When it's time to walk the dog, you'll have 44 acres to explore. The self-described "pet-friendly hotel" offers Hot Dog Rates and a check-in package that includes a rawhide chew toy and pooper-scooper bags. This is a popular spot for dog shows in the area.

Framingham

Motel 6 Framingham, 1668 Worcester Rd., Framingham (508-620-0500; www.motel6.com); $54–79 and higher per night. Pets are allowed at all Motel 6 locations; the Framingham site offers cable television with premium movie channels, laundry facilities, elevators, free morning coffee, and a location that's convenient to restaurants and shopping. Kids under the age of 17 stay free with their parents. One well-behaved dog is permitted per guest room.

Red Roof Inn Framingham, 650 Cochituate Rd., Framingham (508-872-4499; 1-800-RED-ROOF; www.redroof.com); $61–93 per night. Amenities include cable television, free newspapers, alarm clocks, a 24-hour front desk, express check-out services, free local calls, modem lines, and plenty of parking. Framingham is home to hundreds of independent

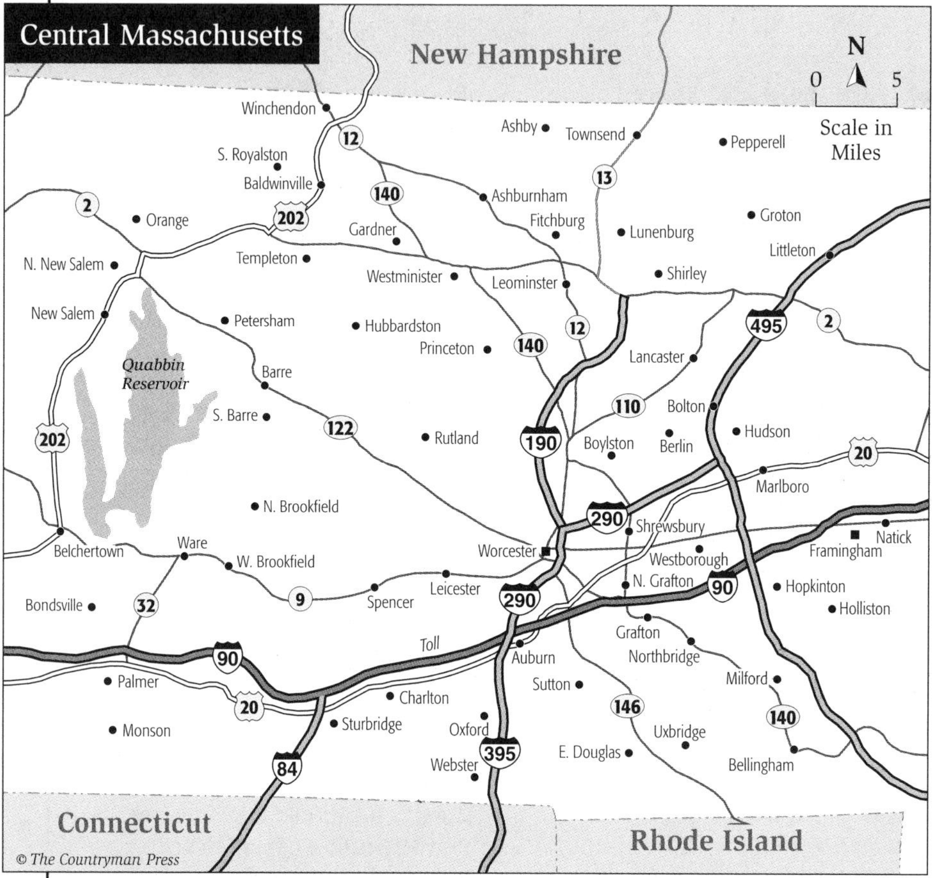

and chain stores, restaurants, businesses, and a hospital. Pets are welcome without extra fees. "We are strictly enforcing the policy of one animal per room," says the motel manager.

Residence Inn by Marriott Boston Framingham, 400 Staples Dr., Framingham (508-370-0001; 1-800-627-7468; www.marriott.com); $129–179 per night. Stay long- or short-term at the Residence Inn, where suites take the place of traditional hotel rooms. At the Framingham location, guests can take advantage of free newspapers, a swimming pool, a fitness center, laundry facilities, studios, and one- and two-bedroom suites. Pet owners pay a one-time $100 nonrefundable fee.

Holland

Restful Paws Pet Friendly Bed & Breakfast, 70 Allen Hill Rd., P.O. Box 3, Holland 01521 (413-245-7792; info@restfulpaws.com; www.restfulpaws.com); $174 per night. Barbara and Raymond Korny started their B&B with a simple premise in mind: Pets are part of the family, too. Four-legged guests will find themselves pampered with beanbag beds, doggie towels, water and food bowls, cleanup supplies (for accidents), walking trails, and toys and chews in the gathering room (dogs must be at least 7 months old). Two-legged visitors, meanwhile, can enjoy a gazebo, air purifiers, clothes steamers, coffeemakers, breakfast nooks, daily continental breakfasts, and four individually decorated guest rooms. Rosie, the resident Canine Hostess, will happily provide canine companionship for visitors who happen to be traveling without their pets in tow. This is one of those rare places where dog lovers can truly feel at home.

Leominster

Motel 6 Leominster, 48 Commercial St., Leominster (978-537-8161); $49–79 per night. Located about 5 miles from Fitchburg, the Leominster Motel 6 amenities include an outdoor swimming pool, a restaurant, nonsmoking rooms, laundry facilities, free morning coffee, and premium movie channels. Well-behaved pets are welcome without extra fees.

RESIDENT POOCH ROSIE INSPECTS THE WALKING TRAILS AT THE RESTFUL PAWS PET FRIENDLY B&B IN HOLLAND. (PHOTO COURTESY OF RESTFUL PAWS PET FRIENDLY BED & BREAKFAST, INC.)

Orange

Executive Inn, 110 Daniel Shays Hwy., Orange (978-544-8864); $50–85 per night. This motel, located near three fishing lakes and a driving range, offers 28 remodeled rooms and free continental breakfasts. The Mohawk Trail is about 10 miles away. Pets are welcome guests for an extra $7 per night.

Travel Inn, 180 Daniel Shays Hwy., Orange (978-544-2986; www.travelinnorange.com); $59–89 per night. Pets are welcome for an additional $5 per night at this motel with a 24-hour front desk, free continental breakfasts, cable television with premium movie channels, alarm clocks, nonsmoking rooms, and free local calls. Refrigerators and microwaves are available upon request.

Southborough

Red Roof Inn Boston Southborough, 367 Turnpike Rd., Southborough (508-481-3904; 1-800-RED-ROOF; www.redroof.com); $59–75 per night. At this Red Roof Inn location, guests can enjoy cable television, express check-out services, a 24-hour front desk, free newspapers, free local calls, voice mail, and coffee and newspapers in the lobby. One pet per room is welcome without extra charges.

Southbridge

Vienna Restaurant & Historic

Inn, 14 South St., Southbridge (508-764-0700; 1-866-2-VIENNA; thevienna@charter.net; www.thevienna.com); $145–165 per night. This historic 1812 inn is on the National Register of Historic Places. "We have had several dog friends stay with us in the past," says proprietor Lisa Krach. "We have walking trails galore in our immediate area, as well as the Westville Dam Conservation Area for picnics right down the street." The inn offers five guest rooms, an Olympic-size swimming pool, a rock-climbing wall, a sauna, and a restaurant that features authentic Viennese and German cuisine. One dog per room is allowed for an additional $25 per night.

Sturbridge

Days Inn Sturbridge, 400 Rte. 15, Sturbridge (508-347-1978; 1-800-225-3297; www.wyndham.com); $85–149 per night. Set in the woods, this Days Inn is located about a mile from Old Sturbridge Village and offers a swimming pool, free daily continental breakfasts, cable television with premium movie channels, express check-out services, and in-room coffeemakers, alarm clocks, refrigerators, and Internet access. Pets are allowed for an additional $10 per night.

Green Acres Motel, 2 Shepard Rd., Sturbridge (508-347-3496); $69–149 per night. With 16 rooms, this Sturbridge motel has a quiet location, a swimming pool, in-room refrigerators, nonsmoking rooms, and cable television. Pets are welcome for $5–8 per night, depending on the season.

Publick House Historic Inn & Country Motor Lodge, 277 Main St., on the common, Rte. 131, Sturbridge (508-347-3313; 1-800-PUBLICK; info@publickhouse.com; www.publickhouse.com); $117–139 per night. The country lodge motel buildings are located just up the hill from the historic Public House Inn & Tavern built in 1771; a walkway connects the two areas. Though pets are not allowed in the main inn, they are welcome in motor-lodge rooms for an additional $10 per night. Each room has a balcony, cable television, and shared access to a swimming pool.

Thomas Henry Hearthstone Inn, 453 Main St., Sturbridge (1-888-781-7775; thhearth@aol.com); $129–379 per night. Built by the current owners, this elegant country inn has homey touches, like in-room whirlpools, as well as modern conveniences. The Great Hall Dining Room serves breakfast and dinner; tea, wine, and brandy are served in front of the fireplaces. Pets are welcome with prior approval; management prefers that you use a crate.

Sturbridge Host Hotel and Conference Center, 366 Main St, Sturbridge (508-347-7393; 1-800-582-3232; www.sturbridgehosthotel.com); $112–204 per night. This 232-room resort hotel looks like a country lodge with a huge fieldstone fireplace and exposed beams in the lobby, filled with comfy sofas for lounging. Pets are welcome for an additional $25 per night with no weight restrictions, and you can take them on scenic walks along Cedar Lake. The resort offers massage and spa services, plus an indoor pool, fitness center, and game room, with two on-site restaurants: The Oxhead Tavern offers outdoor seating in good weather, and the Greenhouse Restaurant serves up a huge country breakfast buffet. Check the special packages on the Web site that include breakfast or add-on activities.

Sudbury

Arabian Horse Inn Bed & Breakfast, 277 Old Sudbury Rd., Sudbury (978-443-7400; 1-800-ARABIAN; info@arabianhorseinn.com; www.arabianhorseinn.com); $169–319 per night. Not only are dogs welcome at this 1880 lavish estate, but there's also "room at the inn" for your horse in Arabian's stables, and the rooms are named after the resident horses. The 1880 Victorian and its grounds are also home to cats, geese, and chickens. Innkeepers Joan and Rick Beers allow animals in the on-site one-bedroom cottage; it has two floors, a king-size bed, a kitchenette, a living-room area, a private garden, a hot tub, and views of the horse pastures. Guests also enjoy the walking trail that winds around the farm. You'll get a full breakfast and as many carrots as you want for feeding the horses.

Westborough

Residence Inn by Marriott Boston Westborough, 25 Connector Rd., Westborough (508-366-7700; www.marriott.com); $139–189 per night. The Westborough Residence Inn offers a swimming pool, laundry services, a fitness center, free morning newspapers and daily hot breakfasts, cable television with premium movie channels, and a 24-hour front desk. Like all Residence Inns, the hotel caters to long-term stays. Pet owners pay a one-time nonrefundable fee of $100.

Westford

Residence Inn by Marriott Boston-Westford, 7 Lan Dr., Westford (978-392-1407; 1-800-331-3131; www.marriott.com); $99–199 per night. This Residence Inn location has a fitness center, a swimming pool, meeting rooms, laundry services, and in-room Internet access. (A great Chinese restaurant and a gourmet coffee shop are also located within walking distance.) The suites have separate sleeping and living areas and kitchens. Animal owners pay an extra $100 nonrefundable fee for their furry friends.

Worcester

Holiday Inn Worcester, 500 Lincoln St., Worcester (508-852-4000; www.ihg.com); $99–219 per night. This fairly new, full-service hotel offers an indoor swimming pool and a sauna; a concierge desk; in-room hair dryers, irons, and coffeemakers; wake-up and turn-down services; room service; a fitness center; and a lounge. Free airport shuttles are also available. Pets are welcome for an extra $25 per night.

Campgrounds

Ashby

Willard Brook State Forest Campground, Rte. 119, Ashby and Townsend (978-597-8802); $12 per night Massachusetts residents; $14 per night out-of-state residents. There are 21 campsites at this state forest campground, complete with picnic tables, fire pits, and flush toilets (but no showers). Open Memorial Day through Labor Day only, the campground offers opportunities for fishing, swimming, hiking, and picnicking. (For more information on Willard Brook, see "Out and About.") Proof of vaccinations is required for pets.

Baldwinville

Otter River State Forest Campground, New Winchendon Rd., Baldwinville (978-939-8962); $12 per night Massachusetts residents; $14 per night out-of-state residents. In addition to 78 traditional campsites for tents and RVs, Otter River also has four yurt camping sites and three group camping areas that can each accommodate up to 15 people. Other amenities include hiking trails, picnic tables, fire pits, and restrooms with showers. (See "Out and About" for more state forest information.)

Monson

Sunsetview Farm Camping Area, 57 Town Farm Rd., Monson (413-267-9269; camp@sunsetview.com; www.sunsetview.com); $36–46 per night. Wagon rides, bingo games, classic-car shows, and guided nature walks are just some of the activities at Sunsetview, where tenters and RVers can enjoy a swimming pool, restrooms with showers, game courts, and a snack bar. Quiet, leashed family pets are welcome as long as their owners clean up after them. There is a limit of two dogs per site.

Oakham

Pine Acres Family Camping Resort, 203 Bechan Rd., Oakham (508-882-9509; 1-866-571-6048; camp@pineacresresort.com; www.pineacresresort.com); $38–50 per night. Tucked-away tent sites and full-hookup RV sites are available at Pine Acres, a lakefront campground with three beaches, a swimming pool, a "kids splash zone," an adult spa, cabin rentals, boat docks and launching areas, a playground, restrooms with showers, a camp store, laundry facilities, and trails for hiking and biking. Pets are welcome for an extra fee of $2 per pet, per night.

Phillipston

Lamb City Campground, 85 Royalston Rd., Phillipston (978-249-2049; 1-800-292-LAMB; lambcity@tiac.net; www.lambcity.com); $24–43 per night or $150–240 per week. Tent and RV campers at Lamb City can make use of a camp store, free Wi-Fi, lake views, swimming pools, and hayrides. Nicki, the resident pooch, will welcome you as you arrive. The Blake family welcomes friendly dogs at their campground, provided their owners can show proof of vaccination and don't leave their dogs alone at the site. Certain breeds are restricted; call or visit the Web site for details.

Sturbridge

Jellystone Park Sturbridge, River Rd., Sturbridge (508-347-9570; rsmith@jellystonesturbridge.com; www.jellystonesturbridge.com); $33–71 per night. With its live bands, two swimming pools, a hot tub, a waterslide, a snack shop, miniature golf, a video arcade, and two playgrounds, this campground located near Old Sturbridge Village offers families plenty to do. Dogs are welcome, but must be on a leash at all times and are not permitted in cabin rentals.

Wells State Park Campground, Rte. 49, Sturbridge (508-347-9257); $12 per night Massachusetts residents; $14 per night out-of-state residents. The 60 campsites at this state park have fire pits and picnic tables, and share access to a dumping station and restrooms with hot showers. Popular park activities (see "Out and About") include hiking, swimming, canoeing, and fishing. Bring proof of vaccinations.

Webster

Webster Sturbridge Family Camp, 106 Douglas Rd., Webster (508-943-1895; www.webstercamp.com); call for rate information. Formerly known as the Webster-Sturbridge KOA, this campground has a swimming pool and 150 sites with an emphasis on recreational vehicles, as well as a special pet-walking trail. Leashed dogs are permitted with the exception of certain breeds, including pit bulls and rottweilers. The campground is located about 10 miles outside Worcester.

West Townsend

Pearl Hill State Park Campground, New Fitchburg Rd., West Townsend (978-597-8802; 978-597-2850); $12 per night Massachusetts residents; $14 per night out-of-state residents. The 51 tent and RV campsites at this 1,000-acre park (see "Out and About") each have fire pits and picnic tables, and access to freshwater spigots and restrooms with showers. The campground, like the park itself, is open to the public only seasonally. Proof of vaccinations is required, and leashes must be used.

Winchendon

Lake Dennison State Recreation Area Campground, Rte. 202, Winchendon (978-297-1609; 1-877-422-6762); $12 per night Massachusetts residents; $14 per night out-of-state residents. The campground at this large state reservation has 151 campsites, fire pits, picnic tables, a dumping station, and restrooms with showers. The lake offers swimming and nonmotorized boating activities; nearby trails and picnic tables provide a peaceful escape. (For more information on the recreation area, see "Out and About.") Proof of a rabies vaccination is required at check-in.

OUT AND ABOUT

Annual Walk-A-Thon, MetroWest Humane Society. The whole family, including the four-legged members, is invited to this yearly festival fund-raiser for the MetroWest Humane Society. Expect to find face painting, pet photo contests, agility competitions, training demonstrations, and even a Dunk the Docs game featuring local veterinarians. For more information, visit www.metrowesthumanesociety.org; write to mwhspaw@yahoo.com; write to or visit the society at 30 Pond St. (Rte. 126), Ashland, MA 01721; or call 508-875-3776.

Arrowhead Acres, 92 Aldrich St. (Rte. 98), Uxbridge (508-278-5017). Though officially a Christmas-tree farm, Arrowhead Acres offers family activities year-round on its 73 acres. Visitors can enjoy hayrides, a petting farm, horseshoe pits, a swimming pool, badminton and shuffleboard courts, a large pavilion for group outings, a pumpkin patch, and of course Christmas-tree tagging in winter. Pet owners are asked to clean up after their animals and keep them on leashes.

Berlin Orchards, 200 Central St. (Rte. 62), Berlin (978-838-2400; www.berlinfarms.com). Dogs on a leash are welcome in the outdoor areas at this large 35-acre orchard, farmer's market, and gift shop located along Route 62. Come for apple and pumpkin picking in fall, maple sugaring in spring, and special events throughout the year. The farm also has animals, an ice-cream take-out window, a cider mill, pony rides, and guided tours.

Coggshall Park, 244 Mount Elam St., Fitchburg (978-343-9892; www.coggshallpark.org). This beautiful 200-acre city park has extensive hiking trails, a scenic pond, and a gazebo that's a popular spot for wedding-day photos. Leashed dogs are welcome, though they're not allowed on the perimeter of the pond or in the playground.

Fruitlands Museum, 102 Prospect Hill Rd., Harvard (978-456-3924; www.fruitlands.org). Leashed pets are welcome at Fruitlands, an outdoor museum of art and history with miles of nature trails, four galleries, a store, a restaurant, historic homes, and changing exhibits on Native Americans, Shakers, and other early inhabitants of the area. Animal owners are asked to clean up messes and to not leave their pets alone in parked cars or tied up on the property.

Hyland Orchard and Brewery, 199 Arnold Rd., Sturbridge (508-347-7500; 1-877-HYLANDS; www.hylandorchard.com). "Hyland's a very pet-friendly place!" says Business Manager Beth Damon. "Our only restriction is that pets not be left in vehicles during the warm months and that they are leashed when on our property." Activities include apple picking in the orchard, picnicking in the recreation area, watching maple-sugaring demonstrations, and joining in at the Peach Festival and haunted-orchard rides.

Lake Dennison State Recreation Area, Rte. 202, Winchendon (978-939-8962). In addition to campsites (see "Accommodations—Campgrounds"), this park also offers a boat ramp; a beach; trails for hiking, horseback riding, and cross-country skiing; and picnic areas with barbecue grills. Of the 10,000 acres managed by the Army Corps of Engineers as a flood-control project, about 4,000 acres are available for public use. Leashed dogs are welcome but are not allowed on the beach.

Otter River State Forest, New Winchendon Rd., Baldwinville (978-939-8962). You can stop by for the afternoon or stay overnight in the campground (see "Accommodations—Campgrounds") at this 12,000-acre park located near the New Hampshire border. Visitors will find a baseball field, picnic areas with shelters and barbecue grills, and trails for hiking, biking, and cross-country skiing. Dogs must be on a leash.

Paws in the Park, Framingham. **Save a Dog,** a Framingham-based animal rescue organization, hosts this annual dog-walk fund-raiser each year, usually on a Saturday in June. Local and visiting pet lovers are welcome to attend. In addition to the walk, there are dog contests, games, food, and obedience demonstrations. For more information, contact Save a Dog at P.O. Box 1108, Framingham, MA 01701, or at saveadog@saveadog.org or www.saveadog.org.

Pearl Hill State Park, New Fitchburg Rd., West Townsend (978-597-8802; 978-597-2850). Open seasonally from Memorial Day to Labor Day, this 1,000-acre park has a 5-acre pond, a campground (see "Accommodations—Campgrounds"), a beach, picnic areas with barbecue grills and shelters, and trails where hiking and cross-country skiing are permitted. Dogs must be on a leash and are not allowed on the beach.

Pet Rock Fest (www.petrockfest.org). This annual festival is cosponsored by several local animal-welfare organizations, including the **Sterling Animal Shelter** (17 Laurelwood Rd., Sterling; 978-422-8585; www.sterlingshelter.org). Thousands of people typically show up for the fun-filled day that includes raffles and lottery prizes, silly contests for dogs and cats, refreshments, music, and more. For more information, visit the Sterling Animal Shelter's Web site.

Walk 'N Wag, Sturbridge. Held each autumn at a nearby location (such as the Spencer Fairgrounds in Spencer), this fun dog-walking event is a fund-raiser for the **Second Chance Animal Shelter** in East Brookfield. Out-of-towners are more than welcome to attend; for more information on this year's dates and times, visit www.secondchanceanimals.org or call the shelter at 508-867-5525.

Wells State Park, Rte. 49, Sturbridge (508-347-9257). There are 10 miles of trails in this 1,400-acre park; you can use them for horseback riding, hiking, dog walking, cross-country skiing, or mountain biking. Wells also has a campground (see "Accommodations—Campgrounds"), a beach, picnic areas, and a boat ramp and launch area for motorized and nonmotorized vessels. Dogs must be leashed and are not allowed on the beach.

Willard Brook State Forest, Rte. 119, Ashby and Townsend (978-597-8802). Located just across the road (Route 119) from **Pearl Hill State Park** (see above listing), this somewhat larger park has more than 2,000 acres; a campground (see "Accommodations—Campgrounds"); myriad trails with permitted uses such as cross-country skiing, hiking, biking, and horseback riding; picnic areas with barbecue grills; and boating and fishing opportunities. Dogs must be on a leash.

QUICK BITES

Bagel Time USA, 194B Park Ave., Worcester (508-798-0440; www.bageltimeusa.com). This friendly city stop offers baker's dozens along with deli and roll-up sandwiches, fresh-brewed coffees, and cool smoothies. Specialty sandwiches include the Hungry Pilgrim (turkey, stuffing, and cranberry sauce) and the Western Omelet (eggs, bacon, cheddar, and lox).

Barber's Crossing, 175 Leominster Rd., **Sterling** (978-422-8438); 861 Main St., Leicester (508-892-7575; www.barbersrestaurant.com). Most people enjoy their Barber's meal inside the Colonial-themed dining rooms, but those with a pooch in tow can order lunch and dinner to go. Menu items include sandwiches, burgers, poultry, steaks, seafood, salads, and dessert.

The Bistro, 57 E. Main St., **Westborough** (508-836-3889); and 895 Southbridge St., **Auburn** (508-832-3113; www.bistro57.com). Bagels, muffins, pastry, three-egg omelets, vegetarian dishes, sandwiches, wraps, and salads are all on the take-out menu at this restaurant's two Central Massachusetts locations. Delivery is available, too.

Dean Park Family Restaurant, 745 Main St., Shrewsbury (508-842-2525). Takeout is available at Dean Park—you can even look at the full menu and place your order online. Choices include pizza, subs, fried seafood, pasta, breakfast (on weekends), garlic bread, specialty sandwiches, taco salad, calzones, soups, and a kids' menu.

Farm at Baptist Common, 342 Baldwinville Rd., Templeton (978-939-8146). When you concentrate on one thing, you're bound to do it well. The farm offers more than 32 flavors of its well-known fudge for an after-dinner (or after-anything) treat.

Herd Rock Calfe and Moo Moo's Ice Cream, Davis Farmland, 145 Redstone Hill, Sterling (978-422-MOOO; www.davisfarmland.com). On a hot day, take a break for "super premium" ice cream or snacks like pizza, chicken fingers, and hot dogs—the child-friendly café even has baby food on hand. Davis Farmland also has animals, play areas for kids, and special events. This is a popular place for u-pick-em fruits in season, and kids love the Mega Maze and Discovery Farm.

Howard's Drive-In, 121 E. Main St. (Rte. 9), West Brookfield (508-867-6504). Walk up to Howard's window and order fisherman's platters, seafood samplers, lobster rolls, tuna sandwiches, burgers, frappes, floats, and ice-cream sundaes.

Meadowbrook Orchards Farm Stand and Bakery, 209 Chase Hill Rd., Sterling (978-365-7617; www.meadowbrookorchards.com). Choose from sweets and fresh-baked treats or more substantial lunch meals like sandwiches and soups at this country farm stand. You can also pick up frozen ready-to-heat-and-eat meals on your way out.

Nancy Chang, 372 Chandler St., Worcester (508-752-8899; www.nancychang.com). With an emphasis on healthy ingredients, such as brown rice, olive and soybean oils, and herbs, Nancy Chang restaurant offers Chinese food for takeout, delivery, or eat-in service. Menu items include stir-fried Maine cod, steamed mixed vegetables, and Chinese broccoli in oyster sauce.

HOT SPOTS FOR SPOT

Barking Lot, 71 W. Main St., Hopkinton (508-435-6633). Take your pooch for a bath or pick up food, toys, treats, and other animal-friendly items at this grooming and pet-supply facility.

Best Friends Pet Care, 10 Fountain St., Ashland (508-881-3441); and 150 Boston Post Rd., Sudbury (978-443-2351; www.bestfriendspetcare.com). The Sudbury and Ashland (also known as The Pet Quarters) locations of Best Friends offer the company's usual pet-care options such as overnight boarding, doggie (and kitty) day care, and optional playtimes ($5 each). Pets must be up-to-date on all vaccinations.

Clip and Dip Dog Grooming, 19 Pond St., Natick (508-653-7425; www.clipanddipma.com). All breeds of canines are welcome at Clip and Dip, which has been offering baths, cuts, flea dips, hot-oil treatments, and other services for more than 12 years.

"I'm Animal Friendly" License Plates

You'll be able to spot fellow animal lovers on the road from their Massachusetts license plate that proudly advertise their feelings. The plates support the spay/neuter grant program of the Massachusetts Animal Coalition (www.massanimal coalition.org).

You'll need to make an appointment before stopping by.

Doggie Den, 14 Blake St., Northboro (508-393-6970; www .thedoggieden.net). Canine massage, doggie day care, all-breed grooming, behavioral consultations, obedience training, and handling classes are all available at this Northboro facility. An on-site boutique carries gourmet dog foods, treats, collars, leashes, and other pet-care items. Daycare rates range from $20–28 per day, depending on the dog's size.

Em's Critter Sitters, 10 Latisquama Rd., Southboro (508-321-2287; thecrittersitters@ hotmail.com). Critter Sitters' owner Emmie L. Himmelman will happily keep your pet busy for a few hours if you can't be there; she serves **Framingham, Southboro, Natick, Wellesley, Westboro,** and other nearby towns and has provided pet care for cats, dogs, geckos, hamsters, and ferrets. The charge is $17 per visit or $45 for overnight care.

Especially for Pets, 67C Main St., Medway (508-533-0275); 81 Union Ave., **Sudbury** (978-443-7682); and 153 Turnpike Rd., **Westborough** (508-366-9696; www.especiallyforpets.com). This Massachusetts-based chain of pet-supply stores has six locations in the area (see "Greater Boston" or their Web site for more listings). Each store offers nearly everything your pup might want or need, including tons of toys, fresh biscuits, shampoos, training equipment, and pet-food brands such as Pinnacle, Eukanuba, Iams, Wellness, Science Diet, and California Natural.

Gemini Dog Training & Daycare, 53-B Ayer Rd., Littleton (978-486-9922; www.geminidogs.com). At Gemini's doggie day-care facilities, your pup can play with new friends in an outdoor fenced-in area, curl up for naps, munch on snacks, and take "bathroom breaks," all under the supervision of an attentive staff. Reservations are required, although Gemini can often accommodate last-minute requests. Proof of vaccine history is required.

Harvard Kennels, 259 Ayer Rd., Harvard (978-772-4242; donna@harvardkennels.com; www.harvardkennels.com). Reservations are required at this popular kennel located about halfway between Worcester and Lowell. Services include doggie day care, dog and cat boarding, grooming, and pickup and delivery.

Kathy's Pet Sitting, Fitchburg region (978-343-3134; www.kathyspetsitting.com). Used frequently by guests at the Best Western Royal Plaza in Fitchburg (see "Accommodations"), this pet-sitting service can provide walks, cuddles, fresh water and food, medications, and whatever else you might need. Business owner Kathy Goguen serves pet lovers in the areas of Fitchburg, Leominster, and Lunenburg.

Pawsitively Pets, 418 Wattaquadock Hill Rd., Bolton (978-779-9977; www.pawsitivelypets.net). If you're looking for short-term care for your favorite pup, Pawsitively Pets is happy to oblige with doggie day-care services as well as overnight boarding. The business also offers baths, cuts, nail clipping, and other grooming services for dogs as well as cats.

Pet Barn, 785 Main St., Holden (508-829-8200; www.elliespetbarn.com). This small family-operated business has a holistic approach to pet care; the Pet Barn carries gourmet and name-brand foods, homeopathic remedies, herbal supplements, toys, chewies, and other supplies. Special orders are welcome.

Pet Source, 141 Boston Post Rd., **Marlborough** (508-229-7792); and 117 Great Rd., **Stow** (978-897-9599; www.petsource.biz). Pet Source is a locally owned and operated chain that offers grooming services, training classes, and retail stores selling treats, toys, accessories, and pet-food brands like Iams, Solid Gold, Innova, Pro Plan, Triumph, and Wellness. The company also manages two more stores in **Lexington** and **Concord** (see "North Shore and Suburbs"). See their Web site for all 10 locations.

Pet World, 1262 Worcester Rd., Natick (508-653-9221; www.petworldnatick.com). This large, well-stocked store carries treats, food, and accessories for dogs, cats, birds, and small animals. It's also the home of **Kitty City,** a shelter for homeless cats in the Greater Framingham area. If you can't find what you're looking for, special orders are welcomed.

ANIMAL SHELTERS AND HUMANE SOCIETIES

All Dog Rescue, P.O. Box 2072, Stow 01775 (617-507-9193; www.alldogrescue.org)

Animal Shelter, Inc., 17 Laurelwood Rd., Sterling (978-422-8585; www.sterlingshelter.org)

Baypath Humane Society, 5 Rafferty Rd., Hopkinton (508-435-6938; www.baypathhumane.org)

Buddy Dog Humane Society, 151 Boston Post Rd. (Rte. 20), Sudbury (978-443-6990; www.buddydoghs.com)

Massachusetts Animal Coalition, P.O. Box 766, Westborough 01581 (978-779-9880; www.massanimalcoalition.org)

MetroWest Humane Society, 30 Pond St. (Rte. 126), Ashland (508-875-3776; www.metrowesthumanesociety.org)

Save A Dog, Inc., P.O. Box 1108, Framingham 01701 (508-877-1407); 604 Boston Post Rd., Sudbury (978-443-7283; www.saveadog.org)

Second Chance Animal Shelter, 111 Young Rd., P.O. Box 136, East Brookfield 01515 (508-867-5525; www.secondchanceanimals.org)

Second Chance Fund for Animal Welfare, P.O. Box 118, Bolton 01740 (978-779-8287; www.secondchancefund.org)

Volunteer Humane Society, 505 Center Bridge Rd., Lancaster (978-365-9470; www.vhscats.org)

World Society for the Protection of Animals (advocacy group)

34 Deloss St., Framingham (508-879-8350; www.wspa-usa.org)

IN CASE OF EMERGENCY

Adams Animal Hospital, 1287 S. Main St., Athol (978-249-7967)

Littleton Animal Hospital, 29 King St., Littleton (978-486-3101)

Marlboro Animal Hospital, 441 Lakeside Ave., Marlboro (508-485-1664)

Metrowest Veterinary Associates, 207 E. Main St., Milford (508-478-7300)

Quabbin Animal Hospital, 180 Ware Rd., Belchertown (413-323-7203)

Slade Veterinary Hospital, 334 Concord St., Framingham (508-875-7086)

Sturbridge Veterinary Hospital, 6 Cedar St., Sturbridge (508-347-7374)

Twin City Animal Hospital, 869 South St., Fitchburg (978-343-3049)

Wellesley-Natick Veterinary, 359 Worcester Rd., Natick (508-653-3420)

Westside Animal Clinic, 546 Mill St., Worcester (508-756-4411)

THE WHITCOMB SUMMIT MOTEL IN THE BERKSHIRES HAS WONDERFUL VIEWS AND A DOG-FRIENDLY ATMOSPHERE. (PHOTO COURTESY OF WHITCOMB SUMMIT MOTEL)

Western Massachusetts

Unfortunately, many of the things that western Massachusetts is famous for, including Tanglewood, the Eastern States Exposition (Big E), the Norman Rockwell Museum, and the Yankee Candle Company factory, are off-limits to animals. On the bright side, however, this beautiful and culturally rich region is also blanketed with vast, dog-friendly state parks and forest preserves—more than any other region in the state, this is a naturalist's heaven.

It's also one of New England's most popular destinations for those looking to get a peek at the changing autumn leaves. From the renowned Mohawk Trail to Routes 7 and 41 and every byway in between, this end of the state has scenic vistas to rival those in the better-known Vermont to the north. Stockbridge draws music, dance, and theater fans from around the country with its many festivals and shows, and the Amherst-Northampton area, otherwise known as the Five College Region, holds its own with busy downtown shopping areas, brewpubs, and intellectual discourse. Your pup may have to wander on the edges of all that culture, but once he sees the mountains, waterfalls, hiking trails, and shady parks around every corner, he probably won't mind.

ACCOMMODATIONS

Hotels, Motels, Inns, and Bed & Breakfasts

Amherst

Lord Jeffery Inn, 30 Boltwood Ave., Amherst (413-256-8200; 1-800-742-0358; reservation@lordjefferyinn.com; www.lordjefferyinn.com); $195–275 per night. A popular setting for weddings and other special events, this historic inn and tavern offers 40 guest rooms as well as eight suites, which have attached sitting rooms and sofa beds. Traditional Colonial décor is combined with special touches like an outdoor fireplace on the patio for enjoying crisp fall nights. The inn, located on the common of Amherst College, is close to three other colleges and the University of Massachusetts, as well as bike trails and shopping. Pets are allowed in designated rooms for an additional $15 per night.

University Lodge, 345 N. Pleasant St., Amherst (413-256-8111; 1-800-582-2929); $79–139 per night. Located close to Amherst College, the University of Massachusetts, and downtown Amherst's shops and restaurants, the University Lodge has 20 rooms (each with two double beds), cable television, and in-room coffeemakers. The lodge has only one pet-friendly room, and there are no additional fees. However, the Hampshire Hospitality Group owns six additional hotels in the area, including a Clarion, Courtyard by Marriott, and Econo Lodge, so if the University Lodge is not available, you can check pet policies and availability at www.hampshirehospitality.com.

Bernardston

Windmill Motel, Rte. 10, Bernardston (413-648-9152); $48–61 per night. Choose from single or double rooms (one bed or two) at this clean 16-unit motel located close to the interstate and the Northfield Mount Hermon School campus. Breakfast is served on weekends in an on-site cafeteria. Dogs are welcome without extra fees.

Chicopee

Econo Lodge, 357 Burnett Rd., Chicopee (413-592-9101; www.choicehotels.com); $59–99 per night. For an extra $10 per night, pets are welcome guests at this Baymont Inn & Suites featuring an outdoor swimming pool, a playground, express check-out services, and in-room hair dryers, microwaves, refrigerators, alarm clocks, irons, and ironing boards. The hotel was formerly known as the Baymont Inn & Suites.

Motel 6 Springfield-Chicopee, 36 Burnett Rd., Chicopee (413-592-5141; www.motel6.com); $49–69 per night. Like all Motel 6 locations, this one welcomes pets without extra charges. Guest amenities include laundry facilities, cable television with premium movie channels, free local calls, and free morning coffee. Kids stay free with their parents.

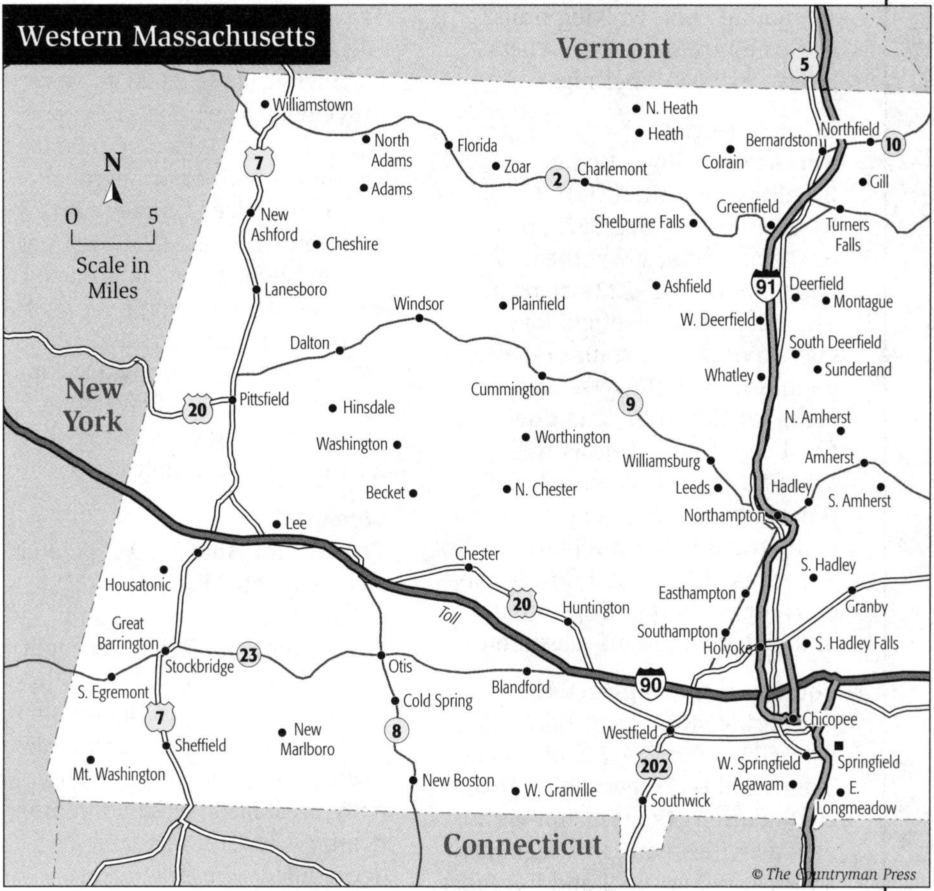

One well-behaved dog is permitted per room.

Quality Inn Chicopee, 463 Memorial Dr., Chicopee (413-592-6171; www.choicehotels.com); $59–99 per night. Formerly a Super 8, the Quality Inn is located just off I-90 and has 106 rooms with traditional décor, a heated swimming pool, a fitness center, cable television, and smoking and nonsmoking rooms. Pets are welcome for an additional $15 per stay (not per night), with a two pet per room maximum.

Florida

Whitcomb Summit Retreat, 229 Mohawk Trail, Florida (413-664-0007; www.whitcombsummit retreat.net); cabins, $69–149 per night. A new owner took over this retreat in 2013 and turned its motel, cabins, and restaurant into a peaceful mountaintop getaway. Pets are allowed in the cabins, but not in the main motel building, at this strategically located motel on 19 acres overlooking the Mohawk Trail. Each cabin can accommodate up to six people with private baths, a 100-mile three-state view, and access to a swimming pool, walking trails, and campfire sites. Pet owners pay an extra $10 per night.

Great Barrington

The Acorn's Hope Bed & Breakfast, 85 Alford Rd., Great Barrington (413-528-2573; acornbb@gmail.com; www.theacornshope.com); $145–222 per night. The Acorn's Hope offers four guest rooms with country décor, antiques, fresh flowers, bathrobes, thick towels, and down-filled comforters. Guests will also find panoramic views, daily breakfasts in the dining room, a living room with a fireplace, and 1½ acres of lawn and flower gardens for exploring. Dogs are permitted during the off-season only.

Comfort Inn & Suites, 249 Stockbridge Rd., Great Barrington (413-644-3200; www.choicehotels.com); $149–179 per night. This is a luxurious Comfort Inn with a new activities wing that includes a heated indoor pool and hot tub, fitness center, and game room. Some suites have Jacuzzis, and all rooms include a free breakfast. Check the specials and packages section for valuable deals on ski weekends. Pets are welcome with no additional fees.

Thornewood Inn, 453 Stockbridge Rd., Great Barrington (413-528-3828; 1-800-854-1008; www.thornewoodinn.com); $145–295 per night. Home also to The Point Restaurant, this elegant inn has lovely gardens and an outdoor pool in addition to cozy indoor common rooms. One well-behaved dog is welcome with no additional fee.

Travelodge Great Barrington, 400 Stockbridge Rd., Great Barrington (413-528-2340; www.travelodge.com); $89–199 per night. Pets are welcome in smoking rooms with prior approval at this Travelodge, a motel with 23 traditional rooms and two larger one-bedroom suites, landscaped grounds, a swimming pool, and in-room coffeemakers and refrigerators. Pet owners pay an extra $10 per night. The Travelodge was formerly known as the Barrington Court Motel.

Greenfield

The Brandt House, 29 Highland Ave., Greenfield (413-774-3329; 1-800-235-3329; www.brandthouse.com); $105–275 per night. This 16-room Colonial estate has wraparound porches, mountain views, gardens, fireplaces, large lawns, 3½ acres for exploring, daily breakfasts, air-conditioning, nearby wooded trails, and a décor filled with original artwork and antiques. With prior approval, well-behaved dogs are welcome for an extra $25 per night, but be sure to reserve a spot early as the house can only accommodate two canine visitors at a time.

Hadley

Howard Johnson Inn, 401 Russell St., Hadley (413-586-0114; www.hojo.com); $79–149 per night. Guests at this HoJo Inn will find cable television with premium movie channels, an outdoor swimming pool, free newspapers, a 24-hour front desk, alarm clocks, meeting/business rooms, and free high-speed

Internet access in the lobby. Pets are allowed in designated smoking rooms only for an additional $20 per night.

Lee

Devonfield Bed & Breakfast, 85 Stockbridge Rd., Lee (413-243-3298; 1-800-664-0880; innkeeper@devonfield.com; www.devonfield.com); cottage, $230–350 per night. Guests' pets are permitted in the Queen Wilhelmina Cottage at Devonfield B&B, where guests enjoy full country breakfasts each day, handmade quilts, private baths, and air-conditioning. The cottage has a wood-burning fireplace, a king-size bed, a whirlpool bath, a full kitchen, and sliding doors that lead to a deck.

Lenox

Birchwood Inn, 7 Hubbard St., Lenox (413-637-2600; innkeeper@birchwood-inn.com; www.birchwood-inn.com); $219–369 per night. This beautiful white inn is nestled in the trees. Your dog is welcome here, too, for an extra $25 per night. The inn offers deluxe rooms, moderate rooms, and mini suites, along with fireplaces, feather beds, antiques, quilts, and a secluded atmosphere. A gourmet breakfast is included in the room rate, and a sumptuous afternoon tea is available for an additional charge.

Stonover Farm, 169 Under Mountain Rd., Lenox (413-637-9100; stonoverfarm@aol.com; www.stonoverfarm.com); $335–575 per night. This luxury B&B is located within walking distance of Tanglewood. In addition to its great location, the accommodation also offers premium mattresses, voice mail, high-speed Internet access, bathrobes, full daily breakfasts, afternoon wine and cheese receptions, and suites with sitting rooms, bedrooms, and bathrooms. Pets are welcome in the Rock Cottage.

Walker House, 64 Walker St., Lenox (413-637-1271; 1-800-235-3098; www.walkerhouse.com); $100–220 per night. "We have cats and always hated to think of leaving them in a kennel, so we understand when pet lovers want to bring their animals along," says Walker House owner Peggy Houdek. The well-landscaped, 202-year-old historic inn has a relaxing porch with rockers, antiques-filled décor, eight guest rooms named for composers, and full country breakfasts. Pets (no cat chasers, please!) must be housebroken and quiet, and there's an additional $10 per-night fee. While you're there, say hello to the resident felines, Hansel, Hazel, and Beanie Alexander.

Sheffield

Birch Hill Bed & Breakfast, 254 S. Undermountain Rd., Sheffield (413-229-2143; 1-800-359-3969; info@birchhillbb; www.birchhillbb.com); $160–225 per night. The Birch Hill home dates back to the era of the American Revolution. In addition to seven guest rooms with private baths, the inn also has a gathering room with antiques, a swimming pool, and resident greyhounds. Your pet is also welcome provided he or she stays on a leash, stays out of the gardens, and is not left unattended.

Race Brook Lodge, Rte. 41, Sheffield (413-229-9019; 1-888-RB-LODGE; www.rblodge.com); $95–275 per night. This post-and-beam lodge fits right into the western Massachusetts landscape with a gathering barn, cathedral ceilings, a wine bar, hardwood floors, a tavern/restaurant, and warm "chintz-free" guest rooms. The designated pet-friendly rooms are all on the first floor and have private entrances; animal owners pay an additional $25 per stay (not per night). There are no televisions or phones in the rooms, but you do get free Wi-Fi.

Staveleigh House, 59 Main St., Sheffield (413-229-2129; 1-800-980-2129; innkeeper@staveleigh.com; www.staveleigh.com); $149–195 per night. This elegant inn is not the type of place where you'd expect to find a "pets welcome" attitude. Luckily for us, two-and four-legged guests are all welcome to enjoy the Staveleigh House's amenities, including plush bathrobes, a breakfast of freshly baked breads, homemade jam, and other treats; Oriental carpets; fireplaces; and a relaxing library. All the western Massachusetts cultural and natural attractions are close by. Well-behaved, well-traveled dogs are welcome in one designated room for an extra $25 per night, and they'll receive a welcome toy from the resident canines.

South Deerfield

Deerfield Inn, 81 Old Main St., Deerfield (413-774-5587; www.deerfieldinn.com); $185–380 per night. This award-winning luxury B&B welcomes small- to medium-size dogs in two of its finest rooms with a one-time $35 fee per stay. A hearty country breakfast is included in the room rate and the Inn's Champney's Restaurant & Tavern is open for lunch and dinner daily. The innkeepers recommend taking your BFF (best furry friend) for a hike on the nearby Canalside Trail.

Red Roof Inn South Deerfield, 9 Greenfield Rd., South Deerfield (413-665-7161); $69–112 per night. This Red Roof Inn location offers clean and simple guest rooms, free morning newspapers, a swimming pool, alarm clocks, cable television, laundry facilities, and a 24-hour front desk. Pets are welcome without extra charges.

Springfield

Sheraton Springfield Monarch Place, 1 Monarch Pl., Springfield (413-781-1010; www.starwoodhotels.com); $119–290 per night. Springfield's largest hotel is in the heart of the city, with stunning views of the river, and is close to the Basketball Hall of Fame and Six Flags New England. With 325 rooms, plus an indoor pool, fitness center, and racquetball courts, the Sheraton welcomes dogs up to 50 pounds with no additional fee.

Stockbridge

Pleasant Valley Motel, Rte. 102, Stockbridge (413-232-8511); $59–

149 per night. Pets are welcome for an additional $10 per night at Pleasant Valley, a 16-room motel with a swimming pool, cable television, in-room microwaves and refrigerators, and smoking and nonsmoking rooms. During the high season, guests can also enjoy free continental breakfasts. The motel is just off the Massachusetts Turnpike for an easy stopover.

West Springfield

Knights Inn West Springfield, 1557 Riverdale St., West Springfield (413-737-9047; www.knightsinn.com); $50–79 per night. Pets up to 20 pounds are welcome guests for an additional $10 per night, per pet (maximum two pets per room) at this Knights Inn, which offers free local calls, a swimming pool, a restaurant, cable television, free parking, hair dryers, and smoking and nonsmoking rooms.

Red Roof Inn West Springfield, 1254 Riverdale St., West Springfield (413-731-1010; www.redroof.com); $55–75 per night. There are no extra fees for animals at this Red Roof Inn, where the amenities include premium movie channels, exterior corridors, free local calls, photocopying and fax services, snack machines, and alarm clocks. One well-behaved pup is permitted per room.

Residence Inn by Marriott West Springfield, 64 Border Way, West Springfield (413-732-9543; www.marriott.com); $139–209 per night. Designed for long-term stays, this Residence Inn has studios and one- and two-bedroom suites with kitchens and separate living and sleeping areas. The West Springfield location also offers a fitness center, daily continental breakfasts, cable television with premium movie channels, and a swimming pool. Pet owners pay a one-time $100 "sanitation fee."

West Stockbridge

Shaker Mill Inn, 2 Oak St., Village Center, West Stockbridge (413-232-4600; 1-877-385-2484; info@shakermillinn.com; www.shakermillinn.com); $129–289 per night. Guest pets are welcome at the Shaker Mill Inn, a one-of-a-kind accommodation that originally served as a stagecoach stop in 1800s. Visitors will find oversized rooms and suites with cable television and air-conditioning; some also have extras like floor-to-ceiling fireplaces, semiprivate decks, kitchenettes, and barnboard paneling. Tanglewood, the Norman Rockwell Museum, and other attractions are close by. Pet owners will pay an additional $15 per stay.

Williamstown

Cozy Corner Motel, 284 Sand Springs Rd., Williamstown (413-458-8006; www.cozycornermotel.com); $59–135 per night. Guests at this 12-room motel enjoy clean, simple rooms, cable television, in-room refrigerators, and free continental breakfasts each morning. A VCR is also available upon request. Pet owners pay an extra $10 per night and sign a pet-policy agreement upon check-in.

Jericho Valley Inn, 2541 Hancock Rd., Williamstown (413-458-9511; 1-800-JERICHO; jvinn@bcn.net; www.jerichovalleyinn.com); cottages, $89–238 per night. Pets are welcome in the cottages at this friendly and clean inn, which also offers standard motel rooms and suites. Tucked away near two ski resorts and two golf courses, Jericho Valley has a scenic hilltop location, complimentary breakfasts, air-conditioning, an outdoor swimming pool, and cable television. The cottages are roomy and bright with fireplaces, kitchenettes, full bathrooms, and separate bedrooms and living rooms. The surrounding forests and lawns provide plenty of room for roaming.

A SECLUDED RENTAL CABIN AT THE JERICHO VALLEY INN IN WILLIAMSTOWN

Campgrounds

Charlemont

Mohawk Trail State Forest Campground, Rte. 2, Charlemont (413-339-5504); $12 per night Massachusetts residents; $14 per night out-of-state residents. Campers at Mohawk Trail's 56 sites have access to restrooms with showers, picnic tables, fire pits, and camping cabins (each can accommodate 3 to 4 people); group camping sites (up to 50 people) are also available. Open seasonally, the park offers guided family programs, trails, and boating (see "Out and About"). Dogs must be leashed at all times.

East Brimfield

Quinebaug Cove Campground, 49 East Brimfield–Holland Rd., East Brimfield (413-245-9525; info@quinebaugcove.com; www.quinebaugcove.com); $35–50 per night. Campers at Quinebaug enjoy scheduled activities like hayrides, fishing derbies, boat races, and bingo nights, in addition to an Olympic-size swimming pool, a boat ramp, a recreation center, and a camp store. Pet owners must clean up messes, show proof of vaccination, and cannot leave their animals unattended.

East Otis

Tolland State Forest Campground, 410 Tolland Rd., P.O. Box 342, East Otis 01029 (413-269-6002); $12 per night Massachusetts residents; $14 per night out-of-state residents. You can camp right at the water's edge at Tolland State Forest, a park that is located alongside a 1,000-acre reservoir (see "Out and About"). The campground itself is situated on a peninsula and has 92 campsites, restrooms with showers, picnic tables, fire pits, and a dumping station. This one fills up quickly; make your reservations early. Proof of vaccinations and leashes are required for dogs.

Gill

Barton Cove Campground, Rte. 2, Gill (413-863-9300); $18 per night. Located on a peninsula at the **Northfield Mountain Recreation and Environmental Center** (see "Out and About"), this campground is owned by Northeast Utilities and offers rustic tent camping (sorry, no RVs) with picnic tables, fire pits, and hibachis. Nearby, you'll find trails through the woods, opportunities to view bald eagles, a boat ramp, and a dinosaur-quarry archaeological area. Leashed dogs are welcome.

Goshen

DAR State Forest Campground, Rte. 112, Goshen (413-268-7098; 1-877-422-6762); $12 per night Massachusetts residents; $14 per night out-of-state residents. Popular as a day-use area (see "Out and About"), this state forest also offers 51 campsites and one group site from Memorial Day to Columbus Day for those who would like to stay overnight. The campground has restrooms with showers, picnic tables, hiking trails, and beaches.

Granville

Prospect Mountain Campground, 1349 Main Rd. (Rte. 57), Granville (413-357-6494; 1-888-550-4PMC; www.prospectmtncampground.com); $25–42 per night tent sites and $50–90 cabins. Though dogs are not allowed in the tepees or rental trailers at Prospect Mountain, they are welcome at tent and RV sites, as well as some cabins, provided they stay on a leash and their owners pick up after them. There is an additional pet fee of $10 per night for cabins with kitchens and baths and $10 per stay for cabins with no facilities. Campground amenities include two ponds, Internet access, playing fields, a playground, a pavilion, a swimming pool, a nature trail, and restrooms.

Lanesboro

Mount Greylock State Reservation Campground, Rte. 7, Lanesboro (413-499-4262);

Beware of Bears

This region is black bear country. When camping, be sure to secure your food supply and if you do see a bear, do not attempt to chase it off by throwing rocks or yelling at it. Take your pet and get to a safe place within your vehicle or cabin.

$5 per night Massachusetts residents; $6 per night out-of-state residents. This fairly small rustic campground is quiet and remote with 31 reservable sites, 4 "walk-in" sites, 5 group sites, outhouses, picnic tables, and fire pits. The Appalachian Trail runs through this notable park (see "Out and About"), where hiking, hunting, and cross-country skiing are allowed. Visitors should note that starting in 2005, most state campgrounds also began charging a one-time "transaction fee" for reservations (usually $8–10) in addition to the nightly rates. Dogs must be leashed and have proof of vaccinations.

Lee

October Mountain State Forest Campground, Woodland Rd., Lee (413-243-1778); $12 per night Massachusetts residents; $14 per night out-of-state residents. The 46 sunny sites at this campground have picnic tables and fire pits and share access to restrooms with showers; some sites are wheelchair accessible. Five group sites can accommodate up to 25 people each. Campers will no doubt enjoy roaming the park (see "Out and About") and relaxing at the picnic areas and on the trails. Rabies vaccination records are required, as are leashes.

Monterey

Beartown State Forest Campground, 69 Blue Hill Rd., Monterey (413-528-0904); $12 per night Massachusetts residents; $14 per night out-of-state residents. This rough-it campground has just 12 sites, picnic tables, fire pits, and plenty of peace and quiet. Campers can also enjoy boating, swimming, fishing, hiking, and more at this huge, wild park (see "Out and About") located in the southwest corner of the state.

North Adams

Savoy Mountain State Forest Campground, 260 Central Shaft Rd., North Adams–Florida (413-663-8469; 413-664-9567); $12 per night Massachusetts residents; $14 per night out-of-state residents. The 45 campsites at Savoy Mountain are nestled in a former orchard. Pets on a leash are permitted, as long as you bring proof of vaccinations. Campers can take advantage of flush toilets, picnic tables, and fire pits along with nearby hiking trails, boat-launch areas, ponds, and waterfalls. (See "Out and About" for more park information.)

Pittsfield

Pittsfield State Forest Campground, Cascade St., Pittsfield (413-442-8992); $12 per night Massachusetts residents; $14 per night out-of-state residents. Picnic tables, flush toilets, and fire pits are available at this state forest campground near the New York border. In addition to the 30 sites, the preserve (see "Out and About") also provides opportunities for boating, hiking, bird-watching, and swimming. Be sure to bring proof of vaccinations.

Windsor

Windsor State Forest Campground, River Rd., Windsor (413-684-0948); $12 per night Massachusetts residents; $14 per night out-of-state residents. Pets are permitted at Windsor State Forest with leashes and proof of vaccinations. Campers here have access to 24 individual sites, as well as 1 group camping site that can accommodate up to 25 people. Facilities include outhouses, picnic tables, and fire pits. Walking trails and waterfalls are nearby. (See "Out and About" for more park information.)

Homes, Cottages, and Cabins for Rent

For vacation rentals, check the Western Massachusetts Craigslist, local chamber of commerce, tourism Web sites, or this local realtor:

www.berkshirecountryhomes realestate.com

OUT AND ABOUT

Beartown State Forest, 69 Blue Hill Rd., Monterey (413-528-0904). Extremely popular with cross-country skiers, Beartown has 12,000 acres and plenty of trails for those who prefer to travel on skis, snowmobiles, horses, bikes, or their own two feet. There's also a campground on-site (see "Accommodations—Campgrounds"), along with a boat ramp, a beach, a 35-acre pond, picnic areas, and restrooms. Pets must be leashed and are not allowed at the beach.

Bridge of Flowers, 22 Water St., Shelburne Falls (www.bridgeof flowersmass.org). Come spring and summer, local gardening enthusiasts cover this early-1900s trolley bridge with an astounding array of flowers in bloom. Located just off Route 2 (the Mohawk Trail), it's a great stop for a picture.

DAR State Forest, Rte. 112, Goshen (413-268-7098). This 1,700-acre forest preserve includes trails for horseback riding, hiking, biking, and cross-country skiing, along with Upper and Lower Highland lakes, where nonmotorized boating is allowed. There are also several shaded picnic areas with great views. Dogs must be on a leash and are not allowed at the beach. (See "Accommodations—Campgrounds" for campground information.)

Downtown Northampton. This is where it's all happening in Northampton, otherwise known as NoHo—home to college students, artists, and a thriving cultural scene. The downtown area is centered along Main Street, which is lined with cafés, bookstores, clothing shops, and park benches that are perfectly suited for people-watching.

Dr. Seuss National Memorial, State and Chestnut streets, Springfield (www.catinthehat

.org/memorial.htm). Surrounded by museums at the Quadrangle, this sculpture garden celebrates a hometown hero (Theodor Seuss Geisel, aka Dr. Seuss, was born in Springfield) on a peaceful and shady green. The fanciful bronze sculptures include a 14-foot *Horton the Elephant* and a tower of 10 turtles from Seuss's book *Yertle the Turtle.*

Historic Deerfield, Rtes. 5 and 10, Deerfield (413-774-5581; www.historic-deerfield.org). This 330-year-old village is home to preserved and restored 18th- and 19th-century homes and buildings, offering a snapshot of what life may have looked like in early rural New England. Though pets are not allowed in the historic buildings or museums, the public street is a wonderful place to stroll, admire the architecture, and imagine a former period in our nation's history.

Look Memorial Park, 300 N. Main St., Florence (413-584-5457; www.lookpark.org). There's a lot going on at this 157-acre park, which boasts picnic areas, special events like crafts fairs and Easter egg hunts, a steamer railroad, a lake and pedal boats, tennis courts, a water-spray park, and walking paths. Dogs are permitted on a leash as long as their owners clean up after them. The entry fee is $2–10 per vehicle (depending on the day and the number of people in the car), and there are extra charges for some of the attractions once you're inside the park.

Mohawk Trail. Locals call it the Highway of History; visitors know it as one of the best leaf-peeping roads in all of New England. The Mohawk Trail is the stretch of Route 2 in northwestern Massachusetts between Williamstown and Orange. Most people try to make stops at the **Mount Greylock** and **Whitcomb** summits, the **Bridge of Flowers** in Shelburne Falls, the **Bissell Covered Bridge** in Charlemont, and the famous **hairpin turn** (use caution: it really is sharp) in North Adams.

Mount Greylock State Reservation, Rte. 7, Lanesboro (413-499-4262). In the northwestern corner of the state, Mount Greylock is not only the highest peak in Massachusetts (at 3,491 feet) but also its first official state park. You can drive or hike to the summit. There are also 45 miles of trails and a campground on-site (see "Accommodations—Campgrounds"). Dogs are welcome on a leash.

Natural Bridge State Park, Rte. 8, North Adams (413-663-6312). Bring your camera to this unusual state park, which is home to the only marble dam in North America. The "natural bridge" of its name refers to a marble arch that has been worn down over the centuries by water rushing through the gorge below. Once privately owned, the land became a state preserve in the mid-1980s.

Northfield Mountain Recreation and Environmental Center.

Visitors Center: 99 Millers Falls Rd. (Rte. 63), Northfield (1-800-859-2960). Owned and managed by Northeast Utilities, this huge swath of green along the Connecticut River has 26 miles of trails, a campground (see **Barton Cove** under "Accommodations—Campgrounds"), guided walks, and family nature programs. The area is popular with horseback riders, mountain bikers, and hikers. You can get maps and other information at the visitors center; dogs must be on a leash.

Norwottuck Rail Trail, Connecticut River Greenway State Park, Warren Wright Rd., Amherst-Belchertown (413-586-8706). Dogs are welcome on a 6-foot leash on this 10-mile-long paved trail, a former railroad line. Use caution with your pooch, as the trail is populated by fast-moving bicyclists, runners, in-line skaters, and cross-country skiers.

October Mountain State Forest, Woodland Rd., Lee (413-243-1778). This is the largest state forest in Massachusetts; visitors will find more than 16,000 acres with a campground (see "Accommodations—Campgrounds"); a section of the **Appalachian Trail** and other trails for hiking, cross-country skiing, and mountain biking; the renowned and scenic **Schermerhorn Gorge;** and plenty of wildlife-viewing opportunities. Leashed pets are welcome.

PawsFest. Get out of the house (or hotel) and join the locals at this annual June celebration designed to raise funds for the Dakin Animal Shelter. The festivities include canine games, bobbing for hot dogs, doggie "good citizen" testing, raffles, prizes, refreshments, and more. For details about this year's date and location, visit www.dpvhs.org, write to info@dakinshelter.org, or call 413-548-9898.

Pittsfield State Forest, Cascade St., Pittsfield (413-442-8992). A 13,000-acre preserve, Pittsfield State Forest attracts nature lovers with its 30 miles of trails (mountain biking, horseback riding, hiking, and cross-country skiing are all approved uses), **Berry Mountain's** scenic vistas, picnic areas, the famous **Balance Rock** geological phenomenon, waterfalls, and abundant wildlife. Dogs must be leashed and are not allowed on the beach.

Savoy Mountain and Mohawk Trail State Forests, Rte. 2, North Adams and Charlemont (413-664-9567; 413-339-5504). Located right next to each other along the Mohawk Trail (Route 2), these two forest preserves comprise a total of 23,000 acres and offer campgrounds (see "Accommodations—Campgrounds") and opportunities for canoeing, hiking, hunting, picnicking, swimming, horseback riding, and mountain biking.

Stanley Park, 400 Western Ave., Westfield (413-568-9312; www.stanleypark.org). Stanley Park's 300 acres include miles of walking trails, a pond, a playground, and a picnic area with barbecue grills. Dogs on a leash are welcome but are not allowed in the rose garden area.

Storrowton Village Museum, 1305 Memorial Ave., West Springfield (413-205-5051; www.thebige.com/sv). Located on the grounds of the Big E state fair, this village is made up of nine 19th-century buildings that were gathered here and assembled around a shady green. Though pets are not allowed on the grounds or inside the buildings during the September fair, you can still stroll by to look at exteriors of the meetinghouse, blacksmith shop, farmhouse, and other buildings during the rest of the year.

Summer Arts and Crafts in Stockbridge Show. This annual outdoor show, typically held in August, has been running for over 20 years and features artisans from all over New England. The dates and location vary from year to year; for more information, contact the Stockbridge Chamber of Commerce at 413-298-5200 or write to info@stockbridgechamber.org.

Tolland State Forest, 410 Tolland Rd., P.O. Box 342, East Otis 01029 (413-269-6002). This isn't the largest of the state parks in western Massachusetts, but it is one of the most interesting. Located along the **Otis Reservoir,** the preserve has great water views; long and leisurely trails for hiking, biking, and cross-country skiing; a campground (see "Accommodations—Campgrounds"); and a boat launch. Dogs are not allowed on the beach and must stay on a leash.

Walk for Animals Western New England, Springfield. This annual fund-raiser is organized by the Springfield branch of the **Massachusetts Society for the Prevention of Cruelty to Animals** (MSPCA); it's usually held in downtown Springfield on a Sunday in fall and has attracted as many as 500 animal lovers and their pets. Another popular yearly event is the society's **Happy Endings Winter Gala,** which takes place every January and includes dinner, dancing, and a silent auction. For up-to-date information on this year's times and locations, call 413-736-2992, visit the society at 171 Union St. in Springfield, or visit their Web site at www.mspca.org.

Windsor State Forest, River Rd., Windsor (413-684-0948). This 1,700-acre preserve is frequented by fishermen, hunters, hikers, bird-watchers, horseback riders, snowmobilers, and cross-country skiers. The park's most famous feature is the 80-foot-high waterfall at **Windsor Jambs Gorge.** The forest also has a campground (see "Accommodations—Campgrounds"), picnic areas, and restrooms.

QUICK BITES

Antonio's, 31 N. Pleasant St., Amherst (413-253-0808; www.antoniospizza.com). Every local college student knows about this downtown pizza haven, where you can get a slice of cheese pizza, or ham and pineapple, veggie, pepperoni, or lots of other traditional and adventurous combinations. Enjoy your slice with Fluffy on one of the benches that line bustling North Pleasant Street.

Atkins Farms Country Market, Rte. 116 and Bay Rd., South Amherst (413-253-9528; 1-800-594-9537; www.atkinsfarms.com). Stop in for lunch at the Atkins Farms deli or snack bar and stay for apple picking. At the **Orchard Run Ice Cream Shop,** your pup can even get a Dog Dish of vanilla ice cream topped with a bone. Cheese, fudge, cider, baked goods, and coffee are just some of the other items for sale at this old-fashioned market. Be sure to try the apple cider donuts! In addition, Atkins Farms hosts a dog parade each year to benefit the local Dakin Shelter. "Last year we had 65 dogs!" says staffer Jen Adams. The event is usually held in spring; call for this year's schedule.

Barrington Brewery, 420 Stockbridge Rd., Great Barrington (413-528-8282; www.barringtonbrewery.net). In addition to homemade beers, the Barrington Brewery also offers an outdoor dining area with casual, family-friendly American fare. Diners can choose from Super Sandwiches, soups, burgers, sausages, sweet potato fries, chili, chicken wings, and much more.

The Black Sheep, 79 Main St., Amherst (413-253-3442; www.blacksheepdeli.com). Pick up a fat sandwich for you and your pup at this Pioneer Valley deli and bakery specializing in bag lunches, pastries, salads, and sandwiches like the New Yorker with salmon and cream cheese, The European with Black Forest ham, or the Carnivore with roast beef. There are several vegetarian options as well, and don't leave without a gourmet treat from the bakery.

Catherine's Chocolate Shop, 260 Stockbridge Rd., Great Barrington (1-800-345-6052; www.catherineschocolates.net). Got a hankering for a chocolate-dipped strawberry? Stop at Catherine's for homemade confections made with the main ingredient that's everyone's favorite guilty pleasure.

Coolidge Park Café, 36 King St., Northampton (413-584-3100; www.hotelnorthampton.com). Located at the Hotel Northampton, this café serves appetizers, burgers, salads, steaks, roasted turkey, lobster ravioli, grilled fish, sandwiches, pasta, and other entrées and "lite fare" at indoor and outdoor dining areas.

Glendale River Grille, Rte. 183, Glendale (413-298-4711). In addition to its main restaurant, Glendale also specializes in boxed lunches to go, featuring salads, fresh bread, sandwiches, and soups. Each lunch comes with springwater, fresh fruit, and dessert.

Gus and Paul's, 1209 Summer Ave., Springfield (413-782-5710, bakery; 413-782-6629, deli; www.gusandpauls.net). This combination deli and bakery serves breakfast, lunch, and dinner, and specializes in New York–style sandwiches and fresh-baked desserts. Outdoor patio dining is available seasonally.

Samel's Deli, 115 Elm St., Pittsfield (413-442-5927; www.samelsdeli.com). Samel's offers "overstuffed" sandwiches, like tuna melts, reubens, and specialty concoctions, along with veggie burgers, salads, fried seafood platters, and roll-ups.

Shelburne Falls Coffee Roasters, 1207 Mohawk Trail, Shelburne (413-624-0116; www.ibuycoffee.com). After you sneak a peek at the Bridge of Flowers, stop in here for java, soup, sandwiches, fresh-baked pastries, and smoothies—all available to go. They also have locations in Northampton, Hadley, Greenfield, and Easthampton.

State Street Deli, Fruit Store, Wines and Spirits, 51 State St., Northampton (413-584-2301; www.statestreetfruit.com). This casual shop has a deli counter and a few sidewalk tables; you'll also find fruit baskets, imported goodies, and free wine tastings every Friday night.

Tom's, 37 State Rd., Whately (413-665-2931). Tom's is a walk-up-to-the-window place with picnic tables—perfect digs for you and your dog. Speaking of dogs, that's the main menu item here, along with french fries, burgers, cold drinks, and other basics.

HOT SPOTS FOR SPOT

All Caring Animal Center, 440 Stockbridge Rd., Great Barrington (413-528-8020). Pet-centered acupuncture, nutritional counseling, chiropractic, homeopathy, and herbal therapy are some of the holistic services offered at this pet-care center, which also provides mainstream veterinary services and boarding.

Animal Crackers Unlimited, 442 Stockbridge Rd., Great Barrington (413-528-1144). Animal Crackers Unlimited is an upscale pet boutique offering gifts and supplies for animals and animal lovers alike. Shoppers will find vitamins and nutritional supplements, doggie toys and treats, and food—including raw-food brands.

ForAnimals, 44 W. Mountain Rd., Lenox (413-445-8843; www.trainingforanimals.com). In addition to group and private training and obedience classes, ForAnimals also offers pet-sitting and "home-style" overnight boarding. Programs include obedience, agility, Tellington TTouch, and "difficult dog" training.

Good Dog, 18 Center St., Northampton (413-586-5242; www.gooddogonline.com). Browse a fun selection of pet gifts and supplies, including mugs, leashes, collars, wall hangings, biscuit jars, and T-shirts, at this downtown shop. While you're there, say hello to the resident Sales Dog, Kayla.

Mount Tom Boarding Kennel and Grooming Salon, 320 Easthampton Rd., Holyoke (413-533-0217-; 413-533-0217). Mount Tom's two main services for pet owners are located at Holyoke Animal Hospital and include overnight boarding in a kennel facility and complete grooming for all breeds of dogs and cats, including cuts and flea baths. Call for an appointment.

Precious Paws, P.O. Box 4, Northampton 01061 (413-585-WOOF; www.precious-paws.com). In the first edition of *Dog-Friendly New England,* Precious Paws was a downtown store; this time around, the part-retail, part-nonprofit organization is located primarily in cyberspace. Founder Elizabeth Frechette is a dog lover and breast cancer survivor who sells doggie-related products to benefit two of the causes closest to her heart: breast cancer research and animal-welfare charities. Based in Northampton, the online store offers infant onesies, children's rompers, towels, and adult clothing emblazoned with her unique black lab/pink ribbon logo. Individual and wholesale orders are available.

ANIMAL SHELTERS AND HUMANE SOCIETIES

A Place for Us (foster care), South Egremont (413-528-9581)

Berkshire Humane Society, 214 Barker Rd., Pittsfield (413-447-7878; www.berkshirehumane.org)

Bosler Humane Society, P.O. Box 12, Baldwinville 01436 (978-939-7316; www.boslerhs.org)

Dakin Animal Shelter, 163 Montague Rd., Leverett (413-548-9898; www.dpvhs.org)

Dog Adoption Network, 1367 Parker St., Springfield (413-783-2642)

Eleanor Sonsini Animal Shelter, Downing Industrial Park, Pittsfield (413-448-9800; www.pittsfieldanimals.org)

F.A.C.E.S. Dog Rescue and Adoption, P.O. Box 704, West Springfield 01090 (413-783-3078; faces.inc@comcast.net)

Massachusetts Pound Puppy Adoption, Becket Animal Control, 557 Main St., Becket (413-623-8934, ext. 56)

P.A.W.S. of Granby, P.O. Box 472, Granby 01033 (413-323-8310)

Pioneer Valley Humane Society, 155 French King Hwy., Greenfield (413-773-3148)

T. J. O'Connor Dog Pound, 627 CottageSt., Springfield (413-781-1484)

Western New England Animal Care and Adoption Center (MSPCA), 171 Union St., Springfield (413-736-2992; www.mspca.org)

IN CASE OF EMERGENCY

All Caring Animal Center, 440 Stockbridge Rd., Great Barrington (413-528-8020)

Berkshire Veterinary Hospital, 730 Crane Ave., Pittsfield (413-499-2820)

Greylock Animal Hospital, 1028 State Rd., North Adams (413-663-5365)

Northampton Veterinary Clinic, 227 South St., Northampton (413-584-6309)

Pioneer Valley Veterinary Hospital, 571 Bernardston Rd., Greenfield (413-773-7511)

Spruce Hill Veterinary Clinic, 4 Plumtree Rd., Springfield (413-782-3183)

Valley Veterinary Hospital, 320 Russell St., Hadley (413-584-1223)

Valley Veterinary Services, 920 Pleasant St., Lee (413-243-2414)

Vermont 4

THE SCOTT BRIDGE IN TOWNSHEND IS THE LONGEST COVERED BRIDGE IN VERMONT.

Southern Vermont

Although southern Vermont is famous for its Green Mountains, the color many people associate with the area is white, white, white. This region is a haven for skiers, offering steep mountain resorts like Stratton, Mount Snow, Haystack, and Okemo as well as hundreds of miles of quiet cross-country trails. In the autumn, of course, visitors come in search of fiery colors, and they're never disappointed with the show.

Vermont's official vacation guide (www.VisitVT.com) opens with a feature called Doggone Good Time, packed with pet-friendly activities and attractions for both two-legged and four-legged visitors. During the winter ski season, visitors with pets may want to look at the more upscale hotels and resorts that offer pet-sitting and dog-walking services, as these are difficult to find in smaller towns or at small inns and motels. Canine lovers may be better off waiting until spring or summer, considered the off-season in southern Vermont, when you can spend your days *with* your dog at a state park, hiking trail, covered bridge, campground, mountain peak, or quaint town green. You'll find all these and more in this picturesque "welcome center" of the Green Mountain State.

ACCOMMODATIONS

Hotels, Motels, Inns, and Bed & Breakfasts

Arcady at the Sunderland Lodge, 6249 Rte. 7A, Arlington (802-362-1176; www.arcadyvt.com); $78–130 per night. Offering a full hot breakfast as part of the room rate, the Arcady welcomes pets for an additional $10 per day. Located on 16 acres of pastoral rolling hills and woodlands, there's plenty of room for your pal to run. Comfortable rooms and an old-fashioned cedar hot tub heated by a wood stove make this a great value.

Inn on Covered Bridge Green, 3587 River Rd., Arlington (802-375-9489; 1-800-726-9480; www.coveredbridgegreen.com); $175–225 per night. The former home of quintessential American artist Norman Rockwell, the Inn on Covered Bridge Green offers upscale Colonial décor and bountiful breakfasts. All rooms have gas fireplaces and spa tubs, or you can choose the Norman Rockwell two-bedroom studio cottage or the Honeymoon Cottage. Pets are welcome with prior approval.

Valhalla Motel, Rte. 7A, Arlington (802-375-2212; 1-888-258-2212; stay@valhallamotel.com; www.valhallamotel.com); $50–90 per night. The 12 recently renovated guest rooms at Valhalla have free Wi-Fi, air-conditioning, cable television, phones, refrigerators, and private baths. Guests can also splash around in an outdoor swimming pool. Pets are welcome for no additional fee.

Bennington

Bennington Motor Inn, 143 W. Main St., Bennington (802-442-5479; 1-800-359-9900; www.bennington-motorinn.com); $78–179 per night. Pets are allowed in designated smoking rooms at the Bennington Motor Inn for an additional $10 per night. The inn has 16 guest rooms, cable television with premium movie channels, air-conditioning, coffeemakers, hairdryers, and refrigerators, and is conveniently located close to shops, restaurants, and cross-country skiing trails.

Knotty Pine Motel, 130 Northside Dr., Bennington (802-442-5487; kpine@sover.net; www.knottypinemotel.com); $62–99 per night. "I'd say 99 percent of pet owners have been great guests," says Knotty Pine proprietor Thomas C. Bluto. He welcomes animals, provided their owners are willing to follow the motel's posted rules of "petiquette." Guests can enjoy a swimming pool, air-conditioning, cable television, in-room coffeemakers and refrigerators, and some efficiency units.

Brattleboro

Econo Lodge Brattleboro, 515 Canal St., Brattleboro (802-254-2360; www.choicehotels.com); $59–129 per night. For an extra $15 per pet, per night, dogs up to 50 pounds are welcome

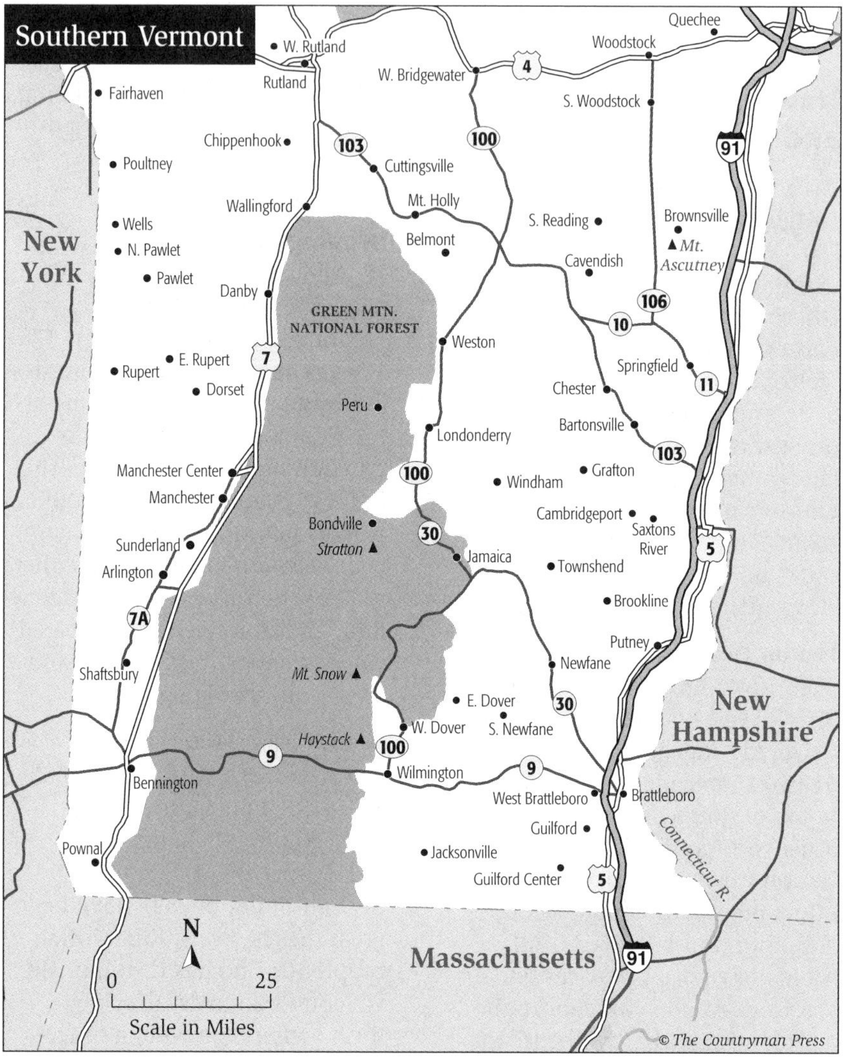

at this Econo Lodge with free continental breakfasts, in-room coffeemakers, a wake-up service, an outdoor swimming pool, cable television, refrigerators, photocopying and fax services, and alarm clocks. Advance notice is required for doggie guests.

Motel 6 Brattleboro, 1254 Putney Rd., Brattleboro (802-254-6007; www.motel6.com); $59–79 per night. This Motel 6 offers cable television with premium movie channels, smoking and nonsmoking rooms, free morning coffee, free local calls, large-vehicle/truck parking, telephones, and a "kids stay free" program. One well-behaved pet is permitted per room.

Brownsville

Pond House Inn Bed &

Breakfast, Bible Hill Rd., Brownsville (802-332-6526; pondhouseinn@yahoo.com; www.pondhouseinn.com); $150 per couple, per night. The Pond House's three guest rooms are secluded on a 10-acre farm with cozy touches like imported soap, queen-size beds, fresh flowers, tile and marble baths, and gourmet breakfasts. Outside, you can relax in the garden or go swimming in the spring-fed pond. "Polite" dogs and horses are welcome for an additional $10 per night. The Pond House also occasionally offers "puppy weekends" with special events and trips for dogs and their owners.

Chester

Motel in the Meadow, 936 Rte. 11 W., Chester (802-875-2626; motel@motelinthemeadow.com; www.motelinthemeadow.com); $70–110 per night. The Motel in the Meadow offers a gift shop and individually decorated guest rooms with names like the Teddy Bear Room, the Lighthouse Room, the Lodge Room, the Maple Room, and the Farm Room. Your dog is welcome with advance notice, provided you agree to clean up any messes and not leave your pooch unattended at any time.

Old Town Farm Inn, 665 Rte. 10, Chester (802-875-2346; 1-888-232-1089; oldtownfarm@otfi.com; www.otfi.com); $89–150 per night. This 1861 B&B has an out-of-the-way location, a common room with a stone floor, individually decorated guest rooms, daily country breakfasts, and dinners featuring traditional Japanese cuisine. Quiet dogs are permitted in designated rooms; owners are asked to use leashes, clean up after their animals, and use a crate if leaving the dog unattended in the room.

Londonderry

Frog's Leap Inn, 107 Rte. 100, Londonderry (802-824-3019; 1-877-FROGSLEAP; www.frogsleapinn.com); $99–150 per night. Charlie and Angel (the dogs) and Sammy (the cat), along with innkeepers Kraig and Dorenna Hart, enjoy welcoming four-legged visitors to their country inn. The expansive grounds boast 32 acres with hiking and cross-country ski trails, a swimming pool, a tennis court, picnic areas, and relaxing gardens. The guest rooms have handmade quilts and private baths.

Ludlow

Andrie Rose Inn, 13 Pleasant St., Ludlow (802-228-4846; 800-223-4846; www.andrieroseinn.com); $99–330 per night. This award-winning chef-owned inn welcomes pets of any size with no additional fees in three of their rooms: Dreamweaver, Sapphire, and Heaven's Gate. Located on a quiet side street in Ludlow Village, the inn includes a sumptuous breakfast in the room rate and is within walking distance of shops and historic sites.

Combes Family Inn Bed & Breakfast, 953 E. Lake Rd., Ludlow (802-228-8799; 1-800-822-8799; info@combesfamilyinn.com; www.combesfamilyinn.com); $75–186 per night. Well-behaved pets are welcome in five rooms at the Combes Family Inn. Each room has pine furniture, air-conditioning, a view of Okemo Mountain, and access to a shared sunporch. The main inn building has a gathering room with a fireplace, a television room, and a dining room, where guests enjoy a full country breakfast each morning.

Timber Inn Motel, Rte. 103, Ludlow (802-228-8666; timberinn@tds.net; www.timberinnmotel.com); $99–199 per night. For an extra $10 per night, dogs (sorry, no cats) are allowed at the Timber Inn, and there's even a space on the Web site booking page to reserve your dog's place. The recently renovated motel is close to the Okemo Mountain ski area and offers knotty-pine guest rooms with one or two bedrooms, an apartment with an outdoor deck, a hot tub, a sauna and an outdoor heated pool, cable television with premium movie channels, and a playground.

Manchester

Econo Lodge Manchester, 2187 Depot St., Manchester (802-362-3333; www.choicehotels.com); $84–109 per night. Up to two pets per room are allowed at the Econo Lodge for an additional $15 per night, per pet.

Manchester View Fine Lodging Hotel, 77 High Meadow Way, Manchester Center (802-362-2739; www.manchesterview.com); $85–300 per night. This AAA three-diamond country inn sits high on a hill in the Green Mountains, minutes from the popular ski areas at Bromley, Stratton, and Magic. The cozy rooms feature elegant touches, including four-poster beds and Jacuzzi soaking tubs. Pets under 20 pounds are welcome with advance approval and an additional fee of $20 per night.

Marlboro

Colonel Williams Inn, Rte. 9, P.O. Box 276, Marlboro 05344 (802-257-1093; info@colonelwilliamsinn.com; www.colonelwilliamsinn.com); carriage house, $100–210 per night. Built in 1769, this historic B&B is a favorite for weddings, civil unions, and weekend getaways. For an additional fee of $25 per stay (not per night), pets are welcome in the efficiency apartments located in the inn's Carriage House building. The rates include a full breakfast.

Mount Snow

Red Oak Inn, 45 Rte. 100, Mount Snow (802-464-8817; 1-866-5-REDOAK; info@redoakinn.com; www.redoakinn.com); $95–194 per night. Guests at the Red Oak inn will find a heated outdoor swimming pool, a hot tub, flower gardens, a dining room serving breakfast, a deck, a tavern, pool tables, and a television lounge. Skiing is right down the road. Pets up to 80 pounds are welcome in designated rooms with a one-time fee of $30; these rooms have direct access to the outdoors. Dogs cannot be left alone in the rooms at any time.

Peru

Johnny Seesaw's, 3574 Rte. 11, Peru (802-824-5533; 1-800-424-

© BAEVSKIY DMITRY/SHUTTERSTOCK.COM

CSAW; jseesaws@sovernet.com; www.jseesaw.com); $90–200 per person, per night. This rustic log lodge is located on 9 secluded acres and has two canine ambassadors, Maxwell and Merlin. Accommodations include lodge rooms, two-room suites, and two-bedroom, two-bathroom cottages with living rooms and fireplaces. Close to Bromley, Stratton, and Manchester, the lodge also has a tennis court, an Olympic-size swimming pool, and a full-service restaurant. Pets are welcome for an extra $10 per night. The rates include a full breakfast.

Putney

Camp Gone to the Dogs, Putney (1-888-DOG-DAZE; www.campgonetothedogs.com); summer sessions, $1,075–1,550 per week with housing. Designed by and for dog lovers, this one-of-a-kind camp is an accommodation and activity center all rolled up into one. Attendees stay in dorms with single, double, or triple rooms; cabins; or Marlboro North, a former private hotel. Some rooms share baths. For more information about the camp's programs here in Putney, see "Out and About." (You can also attend two fall camp sessions in Stowe; see "Out and About" in "Northern Vermont.")

Hickory Ridge House, 53 Hickory Ridge Rd., S. Putney (802-387-5709; 1-800-380-9218; www.hickoryridgehouse.com); $155–285 per night. Listed on the National Register of Historic Places, this 1808 inn has eight guest rooms with modern amenities including free Wi-Fi and cable television. A gourmet

ZORRO OUTRUNS THE COMPETITION AT AN AGILITY TRIAL AT CAMP GONE TO THE DOGS IN PUTNEY. (PHOTO BY STEVE SURFMAN)

breakfast is included in the room rate, and pets are welcome with prior approval.

Putney Inn, Depot Rd., Putney (802-387-5517; 1-800-653-5517; www.putneyinn.com); $98–188 per night. For an extra $10 per night, your pet is allowed in any of the 25 rooms at the Putney Inn—although the innkeepers recommend first-floor rooms as the most convenient for animal owners. Each room has a private bath, private entrances, and period furnishings, including four-poster beds. The inn is perhaps best known for its gourmet dining room, and the room rate includes a full country breakfast.

Shaftsbury

Serenity Motel, 4379 Rte. 7A, Shaftsbury (802-442-6490; 1-800-644-6490; motel@hotmail.com; www.serenitymotel.com); $65–95 per night. Animals are welcome without extra charges at Serenity, where each neatly painted yellow-and-blue cottage unit has a telephone, a covered porch, air-conditioning, a refrigerator, and a coffeemaker. Some of the units are adjoining to accommodate groups. Shaftsbury State Park and the Battenkill River are both nearby.

Springfield

Holiday Inn Express Springfield, 818 Charlestown Rd., Springfield (802-885-4516; 1-800-465-4329; www.ihg.com); $129–179 per night. Located about 20 minutes from the Okemo and Ascutney ski areas, this Holiday Inn Express welcomes pets in designated rooms with a one-time $25 fee. The hotel has 88 guest rooms, a restaurant, laundry facilities, air-conditioning, extended-stay suites with kitchenettes, a fitness center, and an indoor swimming pool.

West Dover

Gray Ghost Inn, Rte. 100 N., West Dover (802-464-2474); $79–305 per night. Loki, the resident pooch, will greet you and your pet when you arrive at this cozy inn with 26 guest rooms, private baths, a gathering room with a fireplace, a game room, an outdoor swimming pool and a hot tub. Pets are welcome during summer and fall only. There are no extra fees for animal guests, although they cannot be left unattended in the guest rooms at any time.

Snow Goose Inn at Mount Snow, Rte. 100, West Dover (802-464-3984; 888-604-7964; stay@snowgooseinn.com; www.snowgooseinn.com); $150–250 per night. Two of the Snow Goose Inn's rooms are designated as dog- and cat-friendly: They have direct access to the outdoors and, like all rooms at the inn, have private baths. Guests and their pups can also take advantage of 3 acres of woods, trails, and gardens; full country breakfasts; and complimentary wine and snacks in the evening. Pets should be leashed, well behaved, and not left unattended at any time.

Weston

Inn at Weston, 630 Main St., Weston (802-824-6789; www.innweston.com); $185–305 per night. This gorgeous country inn wins awards frequently for its upscale restaurant, a dining destination in Southern Vermont. Country chic décor is complemented by modern amenities like whirlpool tubs and saunas, and pets are welcome for an additional $20 per night. Resident canine concierge, Lexi the Golden Retriever, loves to socialize. In addition to breakfast, the inn serves a formal tea in the afternoons and offers live piano music in the candle-lit dining room (reservations recommended). Innkeepers Bob and Linda will be happy to direct you to the many pet-friendly attractions in the area.

The Colonial House, 287 Rte. 100, Weston (802-824-6286; 1-800-639-5033; www.cohoinn.com); $50–130 per night. This old fashioned B&B and motel welcomes pets in the rooms for an additional $10 per night. You'll get what's billed as "Vermont's Best Breakfast," in addition to home-baked cookies and coffee or lemonade in the afternoons. Grandma Miller's Pies and Cakes make the human goodies and also bake doggie treats, available for $1 each.

Wilmington

Inn at Quail Run, 106 Smith Rd., Wilmington (802-464-3362; 1-800-343-7227; meiling@m3realty.com; www.theinnatquailrun.com); $100–210 per night. "We are indeed a happy pet-friendly inn, and happen to enjoy our pet guests and their owners a bit more than the others!" says enthusiastic innkeeper and dog owner Lorin Streim. Your pooch can munch complimentary doggie biscuits and run free on 15 acres

Vermont's Covered Bridges

Vermont is known for its 106 preserved covered bridges, a historic part of this beautiful state's landscape for over a century. A few of the most popular bridges include:

Hammond Covered Bridge: In 1927, the 139-foot bridge floated down the creek during the flood and was towed back to its original site on a barge made of empty barrels. Talk about New England ingenuity! (Rte. 7 Florence-Pittsford)

Baltimore Covered Bridge: This small lattice truss bridge with arched portals was originally located in North Springfield, but was moved in 1970 to its current location near the Eureka Schoolhouse. (Rte. 11 east of Springfield)

Scott Covered Bridge: This bridge spans the West River and is built in sections using two different kinds of trusses. (Rte. 30 Townshend)

Shoreham Covered Railroad Bridge: Built for the Rutland Railroad, the Shoreham Bridge spans the Lemon Fair River. (Rte. 22 A, 3 miles off near Shoreham)

Fisher Covered Bridge: This railway bridge across the Lamoille River has a full-length cupola to vent steam and smoke from locomotives. (Rte. 15 Wolcott)

www.HistoricVermont.org

of property, while you can enjoy gourmet breakfasts and large rooms, including the Ilene, the Charlotte, and the Olivia, with bright décor, air-conditioning, and designer linens. Dog owners pay an extra $15 per night. The inn even offers doggie day-care services upon request.

Campgrounds

Ascutney

Wilgus State Park Campground, Rte. 5, Ascutney (802-675-5422; 1-800-409-7579); $16–37 per night. Get your feet wet at this small state campground located next to the Connecticut River. You'll find 25 sites, a restroom with showers, a group camping area, a playground, and a picnic area. Pets are welcome, as long as they stay on a leash and have proof of vaccination.

Bennington

Greenwood Lodge and Campsites, 311 Greenwood Dr., Bennington (802-442-2547; camp greenwood@aol.com; www.campvermont.com/greenwood); call for rate information. Choose from hostel rooms or 40 wooded campsites at Greenwood, which offers 120 acres, three ponds, a recreation room, restrooms with showers, a playing field, and a volleyball court. "Quiet, good-natured pets" are welcome as long as their owners bring proof of vaccination and don't leave them unattended.

Woodford State Park Campground, 142 State Park Rd., Bennington (802-447-7169; 1-800-409-7579); $16–23 per night. Offering one of southern Vermont's larger state campgrounds, Woodford State Park has more than 80 wooded sites for tents and trailers, in addition to 20 lean-to sites. Campers also have access to restrooms with showers and a dumping station. Don't forget a leash and proof of vaccinations for your pet—you'll need them.

Brattleboro

Fort Dummer State Park Campground, 434 Old Guilford Rd., Brattleboro (802-254-2610; 1-800-409-7579); $14–21 per night. Campers at Fort Dummer can experience a bit of history (see "Out and About") as well as fun in the outdoors. The campground offers 51 sites for tents, 10 sites with lean-tos, two restrooms with showers, a dumping station, hiking trails, lawn areas, and a playground. RV owners should note that there are no hookups, and pet owners must show proof of vaccinations.

Dummerston

Hidden Acres Campground, 792 Rte. 5, Dummerston (802-254-2098; www.hiddenacresvt.net); $28–40 per night. All of the 40 sites at this campground have a picnic table and a fire pit; other amenities include restrooms with showers, hiking trails, an 18-hole miniature golf course, a swimming pool, a camp store, playing fields, a game room, and laundry facilities. Pets must be leashed, and certain breeds are not allowed; call for details.

East Dummerston

Brattleboro North KOA, 1238 Rte. 5, East Dummerston (802-254-5908; 1-800-562-5909; www.koa.com); $35–40 per night. Campers at this KOA can enjoy a swimming pool, pull-through sites with hookups, a gift shop, and recreation areas. Attractions like Santa's Land, miniature golf, and Putney Village are nearby. Quiet, well-behaved pets are welcome at campsites but not in Kamping Kabins.

Jamaica

Jamaica State Park Campground, 285 Salmon Hole Ln., Jamaica (802-874-4600; 1-800-409-7579); $16–37 per night. Two restrooms with showers, 43 campsites, 18 lean-to sites, a picnic area, and a nature center are among the man-made attractions at this campground located in a state park (see "Out and About" for more park information). Pets are not allowed in picnic areas or other day-use areas, and owners must show proof of vaccinations before entering the park.

Pets in Vermont State Parks

Vermont knows that pets are part of the family and they're allowed at all campgrounds, but not in day-use areas (swimming, concessions, bathrooms, etc.). Dogs must be on a leash 10 feet or less in length and have proof of their rabies vaccination, and of course, pet owners must pick up after their pets. There is an extra per-night fee for camping pets (see the specific campground Web site), and some parks have designated pet-friendly sections. Pets are not allowed on beaches or in cabins, except in Cabin A at Lake Carmi, and are also not allowed in picnic areas or pavilions. Visit www.vtstateparks.com/htm/pets.htm.

Winhall Brook Campground at Ball Mountain Lake, 25 Ball Mountain Ln., Jamaica (802-874-4881; 1-877-444-6777); $16–37 per night. This U.S. Army Corps of Engineers property has a day-use area (see Ball Mountain Lake under "Out and About") as well as a campground with 88 tent and pop-up trailer sites and 23 RV sites with hookups. Campers can also use restrooms with showers, a dumping station, playgrounds, and nearby hiking trails.

Newfane

Kenolie Village Campground, 16 Kenolie Campground Rd., Newfane (802-365-7671; www.kenolievillagecampground.com); $20–26 per night. This large family campground has 150 wooded and sunny sites, restrooms with showers, laundry facilities, a camp store, scheduled activities, and a nearby river for fishing, boating, and swimming. Pets are welcome without extra fees, though owners are expected to clean up after them. Kenolie village is open in spring, summer, and fall.

Plymouth

Calvin Coolidge State Park Campground, 855 Coolidge State Park Rd., Plymouth (802-672-3612; 1-800-409-7579); $16–37 per night. This historically significant park (see "Out and About") also abounds with outdoor adventurers; the on-site campground has more than 50 sites, five restrooms with showers, a playground, a dumping station, numerous hiking trails, and secluded "wilderness" camping areas. There are no RV hookups, and pet owners must show proof of vaccination and pay an extra $1 per night.

Pownal

Pine Hollow Campground, RR 1, Pownal (802-823-5569; www.pinehollowcamping.com); $30–37 per night. Leashed, quiet pets are welcome at Pine Hollow, where you'll find 60 sunny and wooded sites for tents and RVs, a group camping area, catch-and-release fishing, bathrooms with showers, hiking and biking trails, a pond, horseshoe pits, and shuffleboard courts.

Townshend

Townshend State Park Campground, 2755 State Forest Rd., Townshend (802-365-7500; 1-800-409-7579; www.vtstateparks.com); $13–22 per night. You'll need a leash and proof of rabies vaccinations to bring your pet along to this popular campground, which offers 30 tent and RV sites, four lean-to sites, bathrooms with showers, hiking trails, a recycling area and Dumpster, firewood, and a picnic area.

Wilmington

Molly Stark State Park Campground, 705 Rte. 9 E., Wilmington (802-464-5460; 1-800-409-7579); $16–37 per night. Tent and trailer campers will feel right at home at this small, quiet campground, where amenities include 23 standard and 11 lean-to sites, restrooms, a playground, and a picnic pavilion. Some hiking trails into the state park (see "Out and About" for more information) begin at the campground. Bring a leash and proof of vaccinations for your pet.

Windsor

Ascutney State Park Campground, 1826 Back Mountain, Windsor (802-674-2060; 1-800-409-7579); $16–37 per night. Hang gliders arriving at Ascutney in search of the park's well-known launch spot at Brownsville Rock might want to consider staying the night at the on-site campground; overnight campers can choose from 39 wooded standard sites in addition to 10 lean-to sites, a dumping station, and restrooms with showers. Bring proof of vaccination for your pet; dogs must be leashed at all times.

Homes, Cottages, and Cabins for Rent

South Londonderry

Farmhouse rental, South Londonderry (732-842-1218; nick@lanirock.com; www.vermontfarmhouse.com); $200–700 per night. Nick Adamson, the owner of this pond-front farmhouse, travels with his two German shepherds and welcomes your pet to his rental. "If only some of the people guests would behave as well as the guest dogs," he jokes. The historic home is surrounded by 80 acres of land with three ponds and offers two fireplaces, a sauna, and satellite television.

To find other Vermont vacation rentals, check the local Craigslist, the nearest chamber of commerce, or visit some of these vacation rental Web sites:

www.vermontlakerental.com

www.vermontrentals.com

www.vermontproperty.com

www.vermontservices.com

www.homeaway.com

OUT AND ABOUT

Ball Mountain Lake, 88 Ball Mountain Ln., Jamaica (802-874-4881). Managed by the U.S. Army Corps of Engineers, this dam and lake recreation area hosts about 175,000 visitors each year; hikers, boaters, and day-trippers enjoy mountain views while photographing wildlife, sitting down for a picnic, or walking the dog. The access road is open seasonally. Whitewater rafters congregate near the dam each spring for the annual planned water release for boaters. There's also an on-site campground (see **Winhall Brook Campground** under "Accommodations—Campgrounds").

Calvin Coolidge State Forest and Park, 855 Coolidge State Park Rd., Plymouth (802-672-3612; 1-800-299-3071). This vast protected forest is made up of more than 16,000 acres in seven towns along scenic Route 100; the 500-acre state park is tucked within it. The park is frequented by overnight campers (see "Accommodations—Campgrounds"), hikers, gold panners, and history buffs who want to check out 19 log cabin lean-tos from the original Calvin Coolidge homestead.

Camp Gone to the Dogs, Putney (1-888-DOG-DAZE; www.campgonetothedogs.com); summer sessions, $1,000–1,150 per week with housing or $900 per week without housing. "Campers" at this unique program can stay on-site (see "Accommodations—Hotels, Motels, Inns, and Bed & Breakfasts") or off: Either way, they're sure to have a tail-waggin' good time. Created by animal lover Honey Loring, Camp Gone to the Dogs is just that: a canine-centered place where you and your pup can take part in seemingly boundless activities or just loll around on the lawn with other like-minded visitors. The rates include meals, classes, lectures, and group activities, including obedience, agility, breed handling, herding, fly ball, Frisbee, doggie costume parties, arts and crafts, and all varieties of "just for fun" contests. A summer session is held in Marlboro, though you can also attend two fall sessions in Stowe (see "Out and About" in "Northern Vermont"). Sit, stay!

Downtown Brattleboro. Like many college towns, this one offers plenty of clothing shops, restaurants, bookstores, pharmacies, bakeries, and downtown sidewalk benches. A nearby pretty park provides a shady spot to take a rest from all that people- and dog-watching.

Fort Dummer State Park, 434 Old Guilford Rd., Brattleboro (802-254-2610; 1-800-299-3071). Fairly small as far as state parks go, this 217-acre historical spot commemorates one of Vermont's earliest settlements. The trails are heavily wooded and populated by deer, grouse, and other native wildlife species. There's also a campground on-site (see "Accommodations—Campgrounds"). Dogs must be leashed but are otherwise welcome.

Green Mountain National Forest. Look at any map of southern Vermont, and you'll notice an enormous swath of green running right down the middle: This vast wilderness is home to ski mountains, hundreds of miles of trails, including the **Long Trail** (see listing on next page) and the **Appalachian Trail,** steep cliffs, majestic views, endangered wildlife, and enough autumn color to take your breath away. There are limitless opportunities for adventure—far more than we could ever fit here. Some of the most popular hiking and walking trails include the **Green Mountain Trail,** a fairly tough 6-mile loop that starts at the Big Branch Picnic Area on Forest Road 10 in Danby; the **Griffith Lake Trail,** a level 4-mile trip off Forest Road 58 in Peru that's popular with snowmobilers and cross-country skiers; the **Hapgood Pond Trail,** an easy 0.8-mile-long nature walk located off Forest Highway 3 just north of Peru; and the **White Rocks/Ice Beds Trail,** a fairly easy walk to fascinating geological features that begins on Route 140 East, just past Wallingford Four Corners. For information, more trail descriptions, directions, and maps, contact the Manchester Ranger District in Manchester Center at 802-362-2307, visit the Green Mountain National Forest Headquarters on 231 North Main Street in Rutland, or visit www.fs.usda.gov/r9.

Jamaica State Park, 285 Salmon Hole Ln., Jamaica (802-874-4600; 1-800-299-3071). This 756-acre park is a favorite among fishermen, who enjoy throwing their line at the **West River.** Hikers and cross-country skiers come for the winding trails, and kayakers and canoeists arrive in April and September to take advantage of the water release from the **Ball Mountain Dam.** Your pup is welcome to come with you for the day or stay overnight at the campground (see "Accommodations—Campgrounds"), as long as he's on a leash.

Long Trail. More than 270 miles long, this renowned and rugged trail stretches from Canada to Massachusetts, passing directly through the Green Mountains of Vermont. The southern part of the trail is considered to be the least difficult, though it is still challenging and recommended for experienced hikers and backpackers. (This is also the part of the state where the Long Trail meets the **Appalachian Trail** for about 100 miles.) You can find a shelter about every 6 miles along the way; in southern Vermont, the two largest are at **Stratton Pond** and **Spruce Peak.** Access the start of the trail in North Adams, Massachusetts, or Williamstown, Massachusetts, or jump in at popular spots such as the **Bromley Mountain** and **Spruce Peak trails,** starting 5 miles east of Manchester Center on Routes 11

THE WINDHAM COUNTY COURTHOUSE AND TOWN GREEN IN NEWFANE

and 30; the busy **Stratton Pond Trail,** located off Kelley Stand Road in Stratton; or the **Homer Stone Brook Trail,** located off Homer Stone Road in South Wallingford. For more information, maps, hiking tips, and directions, contact the Green Mountain Club at 802-244-7037 or visit www.greenmountainclub.org.

Lowell Lake State Park, 1756 Little Pond Rd., Londonderry (802-824-4035; 1-800-299-3071). The main attraction here is the **Lowell Lake Trail,** a meandering 3½-mile-long loop that wraps all the way around the lake. There aren't many steep spots, so it's ideal for pooches looking for an afternoon trot. Parking is available at the Lowell Lake Road boat launch.

Mayfest, downtown Bennington (www.bennington.com). Held each year on Memorial Day weekend, this downtown festival attracts arts, crafts, and food vendors from around New England. Wander the closed-off streets to browse pottery, paintings, woodcrafts, jewelry, and other one-of-a-kind creations.

Molly Stark State Park, 705 Rte. 9 E., Wilmington (802-464-5460; 1-800-299-3071). Located about halfway between Brattleboro and Bennington along Route 9 (otherwise known as the Molly Stark Trail), this park is home to hiking and biking trails, large fields, a campground (see "Accommodations—Campgrounds"), and **Mount Olga,** where a still-standing oak fire tower affords wonderful views. Dogs must be on a leash and are not allowed in picnic areas.

Newfane Town Center and Green, Rte. 30, Newfane. Newfane is home to the well-known **Windham County**

Courthouse, the **Village Union Hall,** and other historic buildings clustered around a picture-perfect green; it's a wonderful spot to stretch your legs and let Rover sniff around the scenery. If you pass by at mealtime, the market across the street from the courthouse offers the ingredients for a picnic (see **Newfane Market and Newfane Country Store** under "Quick Bites").

Northshire Bookstore, 4869 Main St., Manchester Center (802-362-3565; www.northshire.com). "We do allow dogs to browse the store," says Northshire's Liz Barnum. "As a matter of fact, we usually keep a box of dog treats behind the desk!" The family-owned shop has been serving book lovers for more than 30 years, offering a wide selection of topics such as cooking, mystery, humor, architecture, nutrition, music, travel, sports, local interest, science fiction, gardening, and much more.

Scott Bridge, Rte. 30, Townshend. In a landscape filled with quaint covered bridges, this one stands out from the rest: The Scott is the longest covered bridge in Vermont, with both Town lattice and kingpost trusses still holding it together. The 276-foot-long bridge has seen better days (repairs and replacement boards are obvious), but the hardy old girl still makes for a fun and adventurous on-foot crossing.

Summer Concerts on the Green, town green, Rte. 7A, Manchester. From blues to classical and rock, these warm-weather musical concerts usually take place on Friday night from 6:30 to 8. Admission is free. Bring a blanket or a lawn chair, and make sure your pooch isn't the howling type before settling in. For updated schedules, call the Manchester and the Mountains Chamber of Commerce at 1-800-362-4144 or visit their Web site at www.visitmanchestervt.com/arts.

Townshend State Park, 2755 State Forest Rd., Townshend (802-365-7500; 1-800-299-3071). Perhaps best known for its hiking trails that lead to the peak of **Bald Mountain,** this park also attracts visitors with its waterfalls, small pools, picnic areas, scenic views, and wildlife-viewing opportunities. In summer, overnighters also flock to the campground (see "Accommodations—Campgrounds"). Dogs are not allowed in day-use areas and must be leashed.

Wilgus State Park and **Ascutney State Park,** Ascutney (1-800-299-3071). Both located in and around the town of Ascutney near the New Hampshire border, these two state parks offer campgrounds (see "Accommodations—Campgrounds"), picnic areas, scenic views, and hiking and biking trails. Wilgus, located off Route 5, straddles the **Connecticut River** and is especially popular among canoeists; Ascutney, located on Route 44A in Windsor, offers challenging and steep hiking routes, such as the **Summit Road.**

Woodford State Park, 142 State Park Rd., Bennington (802-447-7169; 1-800-658-1622). Located within the **Green Mountain National Forest** along Route 8, 400-acre Woodford State Park is located at a 2,400-foot-high mountain plateau and houses a campground (see "Accommodations—Campgrounds"), a beach, a picnic area, public restrooms, and walking and hiking trails. You can also rent a canoe, paddleboat, or rowboat for use on the surrounding **Adams Reservoir.** Pets must be leashed and are not allowed in picnic areas.

Yankee Dog, Bowser Publications, P.O. Box 144, Jacksonville 05342. This free quarterly newspaper ("all the news that's fit to sniff") is published locally and distributed throughout New England. *Yankee Dog*'s publisher, Debra Theriault, is a great source for southern Vermont–New Hampshire doggie information; for more details or to subscribe, call 802-368-7660 or e-mail Theriault at bowser@sover.net.

QUICK BITES

Al Ducci's Italian Pantry, Elm St., Manchester (802-362-4449). No drooling, please: Dogs get special attention at Al Ducci's, including water bowls and fresh treats. You can order any of the eatery's pasta meals, sandwiches, fresh bread, and baked goods to go and wash them down with coffee, a cold drink, an espresso, or a cappuccino.

Apple Barn and Country Bake Shop, 604 Rte. 7, South Bennington (802-447-7780; 1-888-8-APPLES; www.theapplebarn.com). In addition to the 30 varieties of apples grown in the on-site orchards, the Apple Barn also serves up homemade jellies and jams, maple syrup, classic Vermont cheddar, sweet baked treats, and cold drinks. The Apple Barn's bakery products and agri-tourism programs have made it somewhat famous in these parts: The shop has been featured on The Travel Channel, The Food Network, and *Good Morning America.*

Baba-À-Louis Bakery, 92 Rte. 11, P.O. Box 41, Chester 05143 (802-875-4666; www.babalouisbakery.com). Settle in on the stone wall and enjoy a few of this gourmet bakery's delicious treats. You can expect to find sinful options such as mint brownies, sticky buns, organic granola, cream-cheese brownies, blueberry squares, and French bread. There are no outdoor tables, but everything is available for takeout.

Chelsea Royal Diner, 487 Marlboro Rd., West Brattleboro (802-254-8399; www.chelsearoyaldiner.com). Order your sandwich or meal at the take-out window at this authentic Worcester Diner and eat at one of the many picnic tables. The restaurant has earned a local "Best Breakfast" rating for 10 years in a row. But your pooch will be most interested in a Doggie Vanilla Creamie and a run in the adjacent large field. In the warm months, you'll also find an on-site ice-cream stand.

Curtis's Barbecue, Rte. 5, Putney (802-387-5474; www.curtisbbqvt.com). Takeout and outdoor picnic tables are available at Curtis's, an old-fashioned BBQ joint with smoky grills and heaping portions of chicken, ribs, baked beans, and baked potatoes. The atmosphere is more "picnic" than "restaurant," which suits most visitors just fine. Because it's primarily an outdoor spot, Curtis's open season runs from April to October.

Dot's, 3 West St., Wilmington (802-464-7284; www.dotsofvermont.com). Damaged in Tropical Storm Irene in 2011, Dot's was raising funds to rebuild at the time of this writing. Check their Web site for updates. When they do reopen, try the specialty of the house, fruit pancakes. Everything on the menu is available for takeout.

Frankie's Pizzeria, 14 Harmony Pl., Brattleboro (802-254-2420). Staying in Brattleboro with dog in tow? You're in luck—Frankie's delivers, and the pizza dough is thick and chewy. You can also order a pizza, pasta dinner, or salad as takeout.

Green Mountain Smokehouse, 341 Rte. 5, Windsor (802-674-6653). This take-out meat shop offers more than 10 varieties of homemade sausage, as well as steaks, chicken, bacon, turkey, and other meats, all packaged to go. But Fido will be especially interested in the bucket of dog bones for sale.

Jamaica Coffee House, 3863 Rte. 30, Jamaica (802-874-4643). This eclectic shop serves baked treats, lunch, java, espresso, cappuccino, and ice cream. You can relax with your refreshments at one of the tables out on the porch, or browse the shop's vintage clothing, books, and rare vinyl records. Jamaica State Park is a short five-minute walk away.

Newfane Country Store, 598 Rte. 30, Newfane; Country Store (802-365-7916; www.newfanecountrystore.com). Across from the picturesque green and Windham County Courthouse, this iconic store sells deli sandwiches, baked goods, cold drinks, and convenience items, as well as fudge, candy, gifts, and other fun treats. Be sure to check out the beautiful quilts.

The Vermont Country Store, 657 Main St., Weston (802-824-3184; www.vermontcountrystore.com). The red barn-like Vermont Country Store in Weston is a trip down memory lane, packed with penny candy and nostalgic treats, as well as Vermont maple syrup, local crafts, clothing, and just about everything but the kitchen sink. The Weston store is across from the Village Green, and there is also a location in Rockingham (802-463-2224).

HOT SPOTS FOR SPOT

Handsome Hound, 1868 Harwood Hill, Historic 7A, Bennington (802-442-2333). If your handsome hound needs something (including a bath to make him even more handsome), he'll most likely find it here. The store hosts pet-adoption days, professional pet photography sessions, doggie day-care services and grooming appointments, and a gift shop. You can also use the Web site to order treats, supplements, shampoos, books, and other products.

Knapp's Pets, Hobbies, and Music, 4447 Main St., Bennington (802-442-6252). If you're a guitar-playing, model-train-collecting dog lover (or even if you're just a dog lover), you'll enjoy this store. In the pet section, you'll find a variety of foods, leashes, treats, toys, collars, and other necessities.

One Stop Country Pet Supply, 648 Putney Rd., Brattleboro (802-257-3700; www.onestop countrypet.com). From standard supplies like food and leashes to hard-to-find items like doggie life jackets, animal first-aid kits, and temporary ID tags (a must for on-the-road pets), this Brattleboro shop stocks all the necessities and luxuries you might need while traveling.

Petcetera, 609 Depot St. (Rtes. 11 and 30), Manchester Center (802-362-5447). Located in historic Manchester Center, this fun shop stocks treats and chewies, leashes, collars, food, toys, breath fresheners, and pet-themed stationery and gifts. Training and grooming are also offered. It's sure to be one of your dog's favorite stops.

Puppy Acres Boarding Kennels, 930 Lee Rd., Guilford (802-254-5496). This family-owned and -operated kennel offers overnight boarding on 110 acres of property. There's room for up to 80 dogs, and each pooch has 60 square feet of space to use, including an indoor tiled space and a covered outdoor run. Cats stay in a separate boarding area. Food is included unless you'd prefer to bring your own.

Wundrland Pet Lodge, junction of Rtes. 7 and 103, 27 Squires Rd., North Clarendon (802-773-8011). "We're like a play camp for dogs," says Wundrland owner Nancee Schaffner. "We supervise play with other dogs throughout the day." Early reservations are a must: The kennel usually fills up three months in advance of holidays and popular ski weekends. Rates may vary by season.

ANIMAL SHELTERS AND HUMANE SOCIETIES

Humane Society of the United States: New England Regional Office, P.O. Box 619, Jacksonville 05342 (802-368-2790; www.humanesociety.org)

Jacksonville Humane Society, Rte. 112, Jacksonville (802-368-2790)

Luckydog Animal Control Adoption Program, Maple Hill Rd., P.O. Box 71, Arlington 05250 (802-375-6121)

Morse Rescue Farm, 270 Parker Rd., East Wallingford (802-259-2272)

Second Chance Animal Center, 6779 VT Rte. 7A, Shaftsbury (802-375-0249; www.2ndchanceanimalcenter.org)

Springfield Humane Society, 399 Skitchewaug Trail, Springfield (802-885-3997; www.spfldhumane.org)

TARPS (The Animal Rescue and Protection Society), 1758 Rte. 103 S., Chester (802-875-7777)

Vermont Large Animal Rescue, P.O. Box 1160, Chester 05143 (802-875-4889)

Windham County Humane Society, 916 W. River Rd., Brattleboro (802-254-2232; www.wchs4pets.org)

IN CASE OF EMERGENCY

Arlington Animal Hospital, 3195 Rte. 7A, Arlington (802-375-9491)

Deerfield Valley Veterinary, 85 Rte. 100, West Dover (802-464-0641)

Green Mountain Veterinary Hospital, 48 Treat Hill Rd., Manchester Center (802-362-2620)

Mount Anthony Veterinary Hospital, 832 West Rd., Bennington (802-442-4324)

Poultney Veterinary Services, 330 E. Main St., Poultney (802-287-9292)

Springfield Animal Hospital, 346 River St., Springfield (802-885-2505)

Townshend Animal Clinic, 710 Rte. 30, Townshend (802-365-9663)

Windham Veterinary Clinic , 687 Putney Rd., Brattleboro (802-254-9412)

THE PAW HOUSE INN, A DOG-CENTERED B&B IN WEST RUTLAND

Central Vermont

When pet owners take to the outdoors, many head first to state parks—often the only places where you can relax with a picnic, a great view, and your pooch by your side. But visitors may be surprised to learn that Vermont state parks, like those in many other states, do not allow companion animals into day-use areas, including swimming pools, concession stands, and picnic areas. Leashed pets are allowed on hiking trails and in state campgrounds; still, this bit of bad news can throw a wrench into your plans, especially if you had hoped to spend your day hovering over a barbecue grill in the great outdoors. Pets are welcome at state campgrounds in tents, but not in the cottages and cabins. You must provide proof of rabies vaccination (bring your certificate, not just your tag) at all state campgrounds. For a complete list of pet regulations, visit www.vtstateparks.com/htm/pets.htm.

But central Vermont, luckily, offers much more than state parks. The town of Woodstock, often called "the prettiest little village in America," seduces photographers and antiquers with its small-town charm. To the west, Rutland is a surprisingly pet-friendly small city, even offering a B&B designed especially for dogs and their owners. The college town of Middlebury is welcoming and surrounded by picture-perfect farmland (the poet Robert Frost once called the area home; see "Out and About"). Then, of course, there are all those beautiful Green Mountains, charming visitors with their scenic vistas, ski resorts, challenging hiking trails, and hidden waterways. The best way to see it all is to get lost: Roll down the window, throw away the map, and see where all those intriguing back roads can take you.

ACCOMMODATIONS

Hotels, Motels, Inns, and Bed & Breakfasts

Barre

Knoll Motel, 1015 N. Main St., Barre (802-479-5856; knollmotel@charter.net); $60–120 per night. "All small dogs" (call to see if yours qualifies) are allowed to stay at this motel, which recently celebrated its 54th anniversary. The rooms have one queen-size bed or two double beds, full-size sleeper sofas, irons and ironing boards, microwaves, refrigerators, and cable television. One family suite is also available, and guests can enjoy splashing around in two swimming pools.

Brandon

Inn on Park Street, 69 Park St., Brandon (802-247-3843; 1-800-394-7239; innkeeper@theinnonparkstreet.com; www.theinnonparkstreet.com); $125–185 per night. The Inn on Park Street is an elegant accommodation offering four-poster beds, down comforters, French doors, antiques, sitting areas, pedestal sinks, daily breakfasts, and other extras. All six rooms can be reserved for groups. Dogs are permitted in one of the inn's rooms, the Bonnie Carol Room, for an extra $30 per stay (not per night).

Lilac Inn, 53 Park St., Brandon (802-247-5463; 1-800-221-0720; innkeeper@lilacinn.com; www.lilacinn.com); $150–335 per night. One of the grandest Vermont accommodations to allow pets, the Lilac Inn is a fully restored, early-1900s mansion with wide lawns, gardens and fountains, and large, individually decorated rooms and suites: The Bridal Suite is the most requested. Pets are welcome in designated rooms with prior approval for an additional $35 per stay, and resident canines, Moose and Brady, will give you a five-woof welcome.

Maple Grove Dining Room and Cottages, 1246 Franklin St., Brandon (802-247-6644; info@maplegrovecottages.com); $89–149 per night. Built by the Ethan Allan Furniture Company, Maple Grove (also called Cozy Cottages) is also home to the Otter Valley Winery and the Chowder House Restaurant. Dogs are permitted in some of the rental cottages at Maple Grove for an extra $10 per

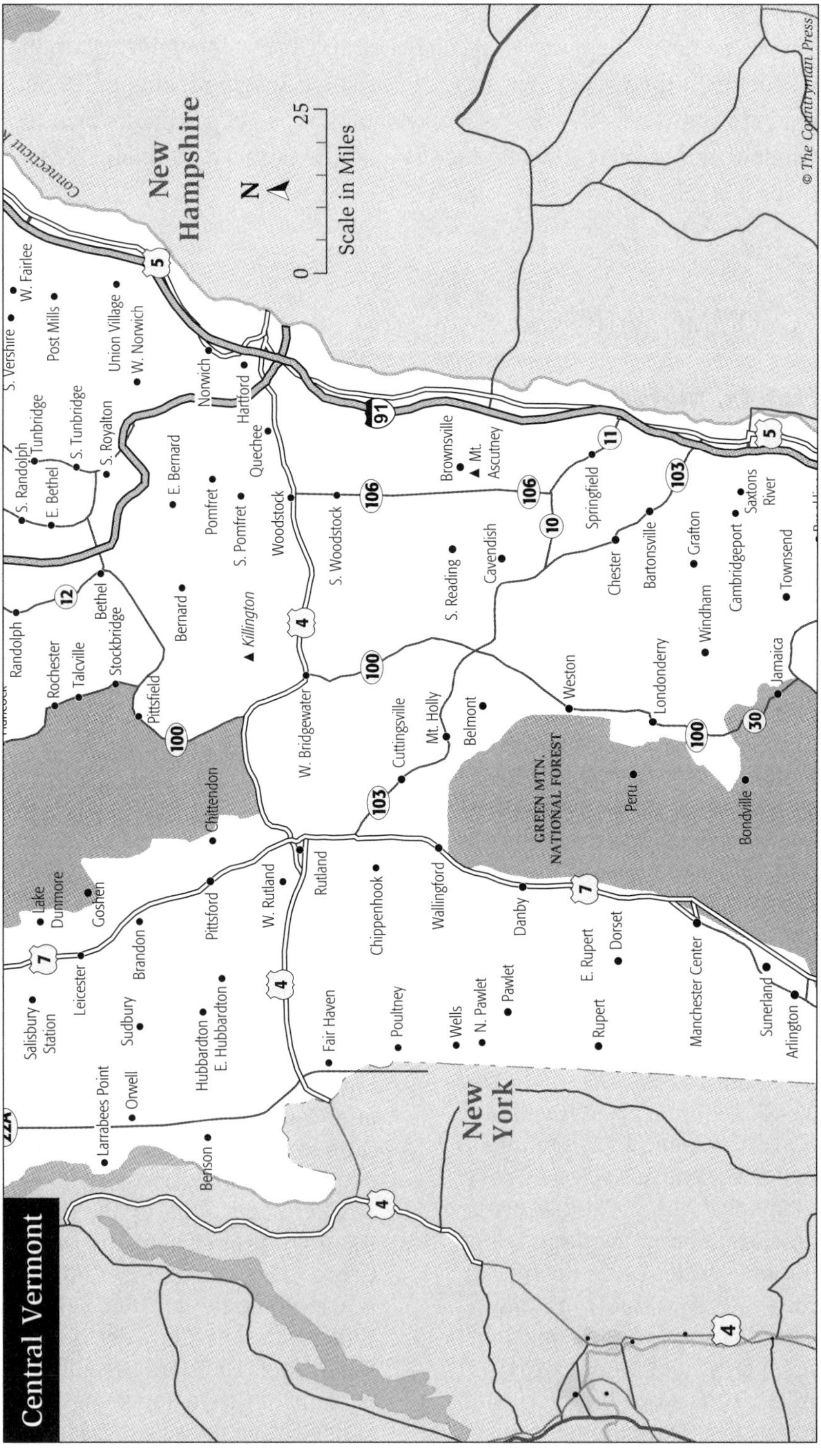
Central Vermont
New Hampshire
New York
Connecticut R.
N
Scale in Miles
0
25
GREEN MTN. NATIONAL FOREST
Killington
Mt. Ascutney
S. Vershire
W. Fairlee
Post Mills
Union Village
W. Norwich
Norwich
Hartford
Quechee
S. Randolph
Tunbridge
S. Tunbridge
S. Royalton
E. Bethel
E. Bernard
Pomfret
S. Pomfret
Woodstock
S. Woodstock
Brownsville
Randolph
Rochester
Talcville
Bethel
Stockbridge
Pittsfield
Bernard
S. Reading
Cavendish
Springfield
Chester
Bartonsville
Grafton
Saxtons River
Cambridgeport
Townsend
Windham
Londonderry
Jamaica
Weston
Belmont
Mt. Holly
Cuttingsville
W. Bridgewater
Chittendon
Lake Dunmore
Goshen
Brandon
Pittsford
W. Rutland
Rutland
Chippenhook
Wallingford
Danby
Peru
Bondville
E. Rupert
Dorset
Manchester Center
Sunderland
Arlington
Salisbury Station
Leicester
Sudbury
Hubbardton
E. Hubbardton
Fair Haven
Poultney
Wells
N. Pawlet
Pawlet
Rupert
Larrabees Point
Orwell
Benson
© The Countryman Press

night, with a maximum of two pets per cottage. Each housekeeping cottage has a private bath, television, and coffeemaker; guests can also enjoy daily continental breakfasts, a miniature golf course, an outdoor swimming pool, and an on-site restaurant. Dogs have plenty of room to roam on the 15-acre tract.

Bridgewater Corners

Corners Inn Restaurant, 52 Upper Rd., Bridgewater Corners (802-396-0036; 1-877-672-9968; www.zcornersinn.com); $65–165 per night. This B&B and restaurant offers five guest rooms, a warm country décor, a dining room and a deck with outdoor seating, and a location that's close to Killington, Okemo, Woodstock, and snowmobile trails. Children are always welcome, and dogs are permitted in one room for an extra $10 per night. Owners are asked not to leave the dog unattended.

Bridport

Champlain Valley Alpacas and Farmstay, 152 Merino Ln., Bridport (802-758-3276; alpaca @wcvt.com; www.champlain valleyalpacas.org); $150 per night. Bring your horse, dog, or other animal along to this tranquil accommodation, one of the oldest Huacaya alpaca farms in Vermont, where you can get an up-close look at a working farm. Hiking and biking trails are nearby, and guests are welcome to participate in the day-to-day workings of the farm as well. Call for pricing to rent the large farmhouse.

Bristol

Firefly Bed & Breakfast, 80 Bull Run Rd., Bristol (802-453-2223; info@fireflybb.com; www.firefly bb.com); $85–130 per night. Bring your horse or well-behaved small- to medium-size pet (dogs up to the size of a Lab are welcome without extra fees) to Firefly, where you'll enjoy full country breakfasts, hiking trails, free Wi-Fi, a pond, and a swimming pool. The three guest rooms have quilts and king-size or double beds; two share a bath and one has a private bath. Doggie guests must have prior approval from the innkeepers, and owners are required to pay a refundable $50 security deposit.

Fairlee

Silver Maple Lodge and Cottages, 520 Rte. 5 S., Fairlee (802-333-4326; 1-800-666-1946; smlodge@localnet.com; www .silvermaplelodge.com); $95–119 per night. Your well-behaved pet is welcome in the Silver Maple Lodge's seven cottage rooms. All have knotty-pine walls and floors, and some have fireplaces, kitchenettes, and sleep sofas. Guests enjoy free continental breakfasts (don't miss the homemade cinnamon rolls!), picnic tables, and a wraparound screened-in porch. (The innkeepers also offer hot-air ballooning/ accommodation packages.)

Killington

Butternut on the Mountain, 63 Weathervane Rd., Killington (802-422-2000); $99–160 per night. This friendly motor inn has 17 guest rooms, airport shuttles, cable television with in-room movies, an indoor swimming pool, a restaurant, and a lounge and laundry facilities. Pets are allowed in designated rooms in summer and fall only; a pet fee may apply if the animal causes any damage. Dogs cannot be left alone in the rooms at any time.

Cascades Lodge, 58 Old Mill Rd., Killington (802-422-3731; 1-800-345-0113; www.cascadeslodge.com); $115–299 per night. This lodge opens in late summer for fall foliage and ski season. Pets are welcome at Cascades with prior approval; pet owners pay an additional fee of $50 per night for one dog for the first two nights and $25 per night for additional nights. The full-service lodge has a fitness center, an indoor swimming pool, a sauna, a restaurant and pub, and mountain-view rooms and suites. Killington's hiking and skiing trails are a short walk or shuttle ride away. Dogs are permitted only in first-floor rooms and should enter and exit via the back door and first-floor hallways.

Cortina Inn & Resort, 103 Rte. 4, Killington (802-772-7118; 1-800-451-6108; cortina1@aol.com; www.cortinainn.com); $99–199 per night. Located on 32 landscaped acres, the recently renovated Cortina Inn has a pond, tennis courts, an indoor swimming pool, 57 rooms and seven deluxe suites, two restaurants, a fitness center, a tavern, a game room, public areas with fireplaces, and two reading rooms. Pets are welcome for an additional $10 per night, provided owners adhere to pet-policy rules they'll receive at check-in.

Inn at Long Trail, Rte. 4, Killington (1-800-325-2540; ilt@vermontel.net; www.innatlongtrail.com); fireplace suites, $119–270 per night. The designated pet rooms at this rustic inn are the two-room fireplace suites with private entrances; the inn also offers a redwood hot tub, a gathering room with a fieldstone fireplace, hardwood floors, and Adirondack-style furnishings. Relax over a pint at McGrath's Irish Pub, the on-site restaurant. Pets must be quiet, leashed, and crated if left alone in a suite. One dog is permitted per room for an extra $10 per night.

Lincoln

The Old Hotel, 233 E. River Rd., Lincoln (802-453-2567; oldhotel@surfglobal.net; www.oldhotel.net); $85–165 per night. Well-behaved "four-footed furry family members" are welcome at The Old Hotel, a B&B dating back to 1840, located in a small Vermont village. The accommodation offers a spacious front porch, a backyard, and a location that's close to hiking trails, rivers, boutiques and gift stores, restaurants, downhill skiing, and cross-country skiing. "We love to have people bring their pets," says Matthew, manager of The Old Hotel. "We just like to know ahead of time if possible." For a large family gathering, you can rent the entire B&B as your vacation house for $2,500–5,000 a week.

Mendon

Econo Lodge Killington Area, 51 Rte. 4, Mendon (802-773-6644; 1-800-992-9067; www.choicehotels.com); $50–150 per night. The 30 guest rooms and efficiencies at this Econo Lodge have cable television, premium movie channels, and air-conditioning; guests can also take advantage of free continental breakfasts, two lounges with fireplaces, a reading loft with almost 1,000 books, a swimming pool and hot tub, picnic areas, and a game room. Pets are allowed for an extra $10 per stay (not per night). Dogs should not be left unattended in the rooms.

Red Clover Inn Restaurant & Tavern, 7 Woodward Rd., US Rte. 4, Mendon (802-775-2290; 1-800-752-0571; innkeepers@redcloverinn.com; www.redcloverinn.com); Carriage House, $160–340 per night. Located near Killington, the Red Clover Inn is a B&B with 14 country-style guest rooms, mountain views, full country breakfasts each morning, and candlelit dinners served every Thursday through Sunday (daily during foliage season and holiday periods). Dogs up to 40 pounds are welcome in certain Carriage House rooms for an extra $15.99 per night. This is a popular après-ski gathering spot.

Middlebury

Middlebury Inn, 14 Court House Sq., Middlebury (802-388-4961; 1-800-842-4666; midinnvt@sover.net; www.middleburyinn.com); $139–242 per night. Pets are welcome in the Contemporary Motel rooms at Middlebury Inn at no extra charge. This historic inn is located across from the town green and offers four levels of accommodations; the motel rooms have air-conditioning, free local calls, cable television, private bathrooms, pullout sofa beds, and in-room coffeemakers. The hotel staff will be happy to point you in the direction of nearby walking trails for you and your pup.

Plymouth

The Salt Ash Inn, 4758 Rte. 100A, Plymouth (802-672-3223; 1-800-725-8274; www.saltashinnvt.com); $94–300 per night. Located in the hometown of Calvin Coolidge, the Salt Ash Inn provides its guests with 17 individually decorated rooms, common areas, an outdoor swimming pool, a hot tub, daily breakfasts, a pub and fireplace lounge, and a rock garden with flowers. Dogs are welcome in five of the inn's rooms for an extra $10 per night. One large pet or two small pets are permitted per room. Check out the special Ski & Stay packages during the winter.

Quechee

Quality Inn at Quechee Gorge, 5817 Woodstock Rd., Quechee (802-295-7600; 1-800-228-5151; www.choicehotels.com); $89–169 per night. For an extra $10 per stay (not per night), your pet is welcome to join you at this Quality Inn, which features a swimming pool, cable television with in-room movies, free Wi-Fi, complimentary breakfast, a restaurant, laundry facilities, fax and photocopying services, and hair dryers and ironing boards. Outside, you'll find a jogging track and a picnic area with tables.

Randolph

Three Stallion Inn, 665 Stick Farm Rd., Randolph (802-728-5575; 1-800-424-5575; info@threestallioninn.com; www.3stallioninn.com); $125–195 per night. Guests at Three Stallion will find a wide range of modern amenities in this 150-year-old property, including a lap pool, a sauna, a hot tub, a fitness center, a restaurant and lounge, individually decorated guest rooms, conference facilities, child-friendly activities, and a traditional country-inn atmosphere. A complimentary continental breakfast is included in the room rate. Dogs are welcome in designated rooms for an additional $20 per pet, per night.

Rutland

Harvest Moon Bed & Breakfast, 1659 N. Grove St., Rutland (802-773-0889; llpink@sover.net; www.harvestmoon.com); $105–130 per night. The two guest rooms at this 1835 farmhouse each have a private bath, antiques, comfortable country furnishings, vintage wallpaper, quilts, and views of the nearby mountains, farmland, and sugarhouse. Gathering areas include a parlor and dining room. Well-behaved, housebroken pets are welcome for an additional fee of $10 per pet, per night.

Holiday Inn Rutland–Killington, 476 Rte. 7 S., Rutland (802-775-1911; www.ihg.com); $89–199 per night. You'll find a swimming pool, in-room movies, and room service at this Holiday Inn, where pets are welcome for an additional fee of $10 per night, per pet. Other amenities include laundry facilities, a restaurant and lounge, air-conditioning, cable television, a sauna, and free airport shuttles. All rooms have refrigerators and microwaves.

Red Roof Inn Rutland-Killington, 401 Rte. 7 S., Rutland (802-775-4303; www.redroof.com); $71–99 per night. Formerly known as the Howard Johnson Rutland, this Red Roof Inn has an indoor heated swimming pool and a sauna; complimentary breakfasts, coffee, and newspapers; laundry facilities; alarm clocks; smoking and nonsmoking rooms; and voice mail. One well-behaved dog is welcome per room without extra fees.

Vergennes

Basin Harbor Club, 4800 Basin Harbor Rd., Vergennes (802-475-2311; www.basinharbor.com); $160–672 per night. Pets are welcome with prior approval at the Basin Harbor Club on Lake Champlain, a historic accommodation with cottages and guest rooms spread throughout the 700-acre property. Guests can enjoy a beach, day-care services, a gift shop, meeting rooms, restaurants, water sports, children's activities, a golf course, a fitness center, and views of the water and the hills. A member of Historic Hotels of America, Basin

Harbor even has a swimming area on Fanny's Beach just for canine visitors, as well homemade Vermont dog biscuits and clean-up mitts with an additional fee of $10 per night, per pet. If you really want to pamper your pal, get the Basin Harbor Club Pet Package, which includes a custom collar and leash, a dog bed with the BHC logo, and a 2-hour private dog walk.

Waitsfield

The Garrison, Rte. 17, Waitsfield (802-496-2352; 1-800-766-7829; www.garrisoncondos.com); $70–260 per night. This unique accommodation offers motel-style rooms or entire condominiums for rent, varying in size from one to four bedrooms with room for 1 to 12 people. Guests in any unit can enjoy the swimming pool, a common area with a game room, a fitness center, and laundry facilities. Well-behaved, quiet dogs are welcome for an additional $10 per night. Call for pricing on condominium units.

Hyde Away Inn, 1428 Millbrook Rd. (Rte. 17), Waitsfield (802-496-2322; 1-800-777-HYDE; hydeaway@madriver.com; www.hydeawayinn.com); $89–179 per night. The Hyde Away has a laid-back, bustling atmosphere with après-ski fun, a casual restaurant, and free breakfasts each morning. The rooms vary in size and style and can each accommodate one to five people. Pets are welcome in the rooms that have private entrances for an additional $10 per night.

Millbrook Inn, 533 Mill Brook Rd., Waitsfield (802-496-2405; 1-800-477-2809; millbrkinn@aol.com; www.millbrookinn.com); $120–150 per night. Dogs are enthusiastically welcomed at this cozy inn with a large backyard—no barkers, please. Each of the seven guest rooms has a private bath and handmade quilt; other amenities include living rooms, a fireplace, an on-site restaurant, and nearby skiing and hiking trails. Dogs cannot be left alone in the rooms, but you'll be able to enjoy breakfast with them on the patio; the innkeepers are happy to recommend local dog-sitters, and the veterinary office next door offers boarding and day care, as well. There is never an extra charge for canine guests. Riley, the resident canine who was saved from a high-kill shelter, loves cross-country skiing.

Weathertop Mountain Inn, 755 Mill Brook Rd. (Rte. 17), Waitsfield (802-496-4909; 1-800-800-3625; www.weathertopmountaininn.com); $119–289 per night. The Weathertop Mountain Inn stands out from the crowd by offering an atypical Vermont inn experience, including eclectic dinners, contemporary décor with Asian art, post-and-beam architecture, a game room, a hot tub, and a sauna. The resident cats, Harley and Slim, will welcome your well-behaved pooch without extra charges, as long as you don't leave your animal alone in the room. The staff can even provide suggestions for doggie day care in the area.

Warren

Golden Lion Riverside Inn, 731 Rte. 100, Warren (802-496-3084; 1-888-867-4491; gldnlion@madriver.com; www.goldenlionriversideinn.com); $96–189 per night. Pets are welcome in some rooms at the Golden Lion for an extra $5 per night; the property has an outside pen with a doghouse and a nearby beach where pets can swim. The modern motel rooms have cable television and telephones, and guests can also enjoy free breakfasts and an outdoor hot tub. Dogs must be crated when left alone in rooms.

Powderhound at Sugarbush, 203 Powderhound Rd., Warren (802-496-5100; 1-800-548-4022; phound@madriver.com; www.powderhoundcondos.com); $159–219 per night. Dogs, cats, rabbits, and even gerbils have stayed at this Mad River Valley lodging, whose name and skiing-doggie logo reveal its pet-friendly nature. The condo lodgings, located behind the historic farmhouse, offer two-room suites, a swimming pool and hot tub, the Doghouse Pub (open only during the winter), and woods and fields for exploring. Dog owners pay an extra $5 per night.

West Rutland

Paw House Inn, 1376 Clarendon Ave., West Rutland (802-558-2661; 1-866-PAW-HOUSE; info@pawhouseinn.com; www.pawhouseinn.com); $135–155 per night. Every traveling dog owner should make a point of visiting this unique B&B at least once. Conceived, designed, and managed exclusively for pooches and their people, the Paw House has human *and* dog bedding in each room, personalized doggie treats upon arrival, and an on-site kennel—known as Mario's Playhouse—where your mutt has her own spot for relaxing while you ski, shop, dine, or catch a movie. You'll also find an exercise area in the backyard, a nearby walking path, full breakfasts each morning, and comfortable common rooms where you can socialize with other two- and four-legged visitors. Rates include up to two dogs (call if you have more than two, as there's a small additional fee).

Woodstock

Braeside Motel, 908 Woodstock Rd., P.O. Box 411, Woodstock 05091 (802-457-1366; info@braesidemotel.com; www.braesidemotel.com); $98–128 per night. Each room at the Braeside Motel has a private entrance, a full bath, a television, a telephone, a refrigerator, and air-conditioning. Guests also have use of an outdoor swimming pool. The motel is located in a quiet area, about 1 mile from downtown Woodstock. Pets are permitted with advance notice for an additional $10 per night.

Kedron Valley Inn, 4778 South Rd., South Woodstock (802-457-1473; 1-800-836-1193; www.kedronvalleyinn.com); $129–359 per night. This historic 25-room inn dates back to 1828, and the oldest building on the 11-acre property, called The Tavern, was originally a store for grist mill workers. Pets are welcome in the log lodge rooms for an additional $15 per night with no weight or breed restrictions. The Kedron Valley Inn is also a dining destination, winning the Wine Spectator award for excellence for its seasonal American cuisine and thoughtful wine list.

Campgrounds

Addison

DAR State Park Campground, 6750 Rte. 17, Addison (802-759-2354; 1-800-409-7579); $16–37 per night. Named for the Daughters of the American Revolution, the organization that donated the park's land, DAR has a designated dog-walk trail, 70 sites for RVs and tents (including 24 lean-tos), and restrooms with showers. This was also the filming site for the movie *What Lies Beneath*. Animals are not allowed in the day-use areas. Bring proof of vaccination.

Fair Haven

Bomoseen State Park Campground, 22 Cedar Mountain Rd., Fair Haven (802-265-4242; 1-800-409-7579); $16–37 per night. This seasonal waterfront campground, popular for picnics and boating, is located beside Lake Bomoseen (see "Out and About" for more park information). Campers can choose from 66 shady or sunny campsites, each with a picnic table and fire pit, and access to restrooms with showers. Pet owners must bring proof of vaccination and use a leash no longer than 10 feet. Dogs are not permitted in any day-use areas.

Gaysville

White River Valley Camping, Rte. 107, P.O. Box 106, Gaysville 05746 (802-234-6780); $22 per night base charge. The White River offers plenty of opportunities for recreation at this family campground; you can rent inner tubes, swim, fish, and boat. On-site, you'll also find a camp store, 100 sites for tents and RVs, 21 acres of woods, basketball and volleyball courts, a playground, and a recreation room. Owners must leash dogs, clean up after them, and follow the campground's other rules of "petiquette."

Hubbardton

Half Moon State Park Campground, 1621 Black Pond Rd., Hubbardton (802-273-2848; 1-800-409-7579); $16–37 per night. Located near the Bomoseen State Park Campground in Bomoseen State Forest (see above listing and "Out and About"), this campground focuses on tent camping with 59 quiet and shady sites. A playground, walking trails, and restrooms with showers are also available. Dog owners must show vet records as proof of vaccination and cannot allow pets in day-use areas.

Leicester

Country Village Campground, 40 Rte. 7, Leicester (802-247-3333; www.countryvillagecampground.com); $22–32 per night. This pet-friendly campground,

© JOOP SNIJDER PHOTOGRAPHY/SHUTTERSTOCK.COM

located about 3 miles north of Brandon, has a dog-walk area, a camp store, and wooded and sunny sites with picnic tables and fire pits. Leashed, quiet dogs are welcome, provided their owners have proof of rabies vaccination and clean up after them.

Salisbury

Branbury State Park Campground, 3570 Lake Dunmore Rd. (Rte. 53), Salisbury (802-247-5925; 1-800-409-7579); $16–37 per night. This state park campground has more than 30 sites, although dogs are permitted in only one section (comprised of about 20 sites). Amenities include restrooms with showers, picnic tables and fire pits, woods and open fields, hiking trails, and mountain streams. Animal owners must use a leash and show vet records as proof of vaccination. Pets are not allowed in the day-use picnic and swimming areas.

Kampersville Lake Dunmore, Lake Dunmore Rd., Salisbury (802-352-4501; 1-877-250-2568; e-mail@kampersville.com; www.kampersville.com); $29–47 per night. Tenters and RVers will find scheduled family activities, 200 campsites, a miniature golf course, two swimming pools, a recreation hall, boat rentals, restrooms with showers, and a camp store at this large, active campground. Pets are welcome on a leash as long as their owners clean up after them and show proof of vaccination. The campground has a limit of two pets per site.

Vergennes

Button Bay State Park Campground, 5 Button Bay State Park Rd., Vergennes (802-475-2377; 1-800-409-7579); $16–37 per night. This former farmland area is now a 253-acre park with 73 campsites for RVs and tents. Campers can use restrooms with showers, a dumping station, picnic tables, a swimming pool, and a playground, and they can rent boats. Dogs are not allowed in the day-use areas, but they are welcome on a leash on nature trails. Don't forget proof of vaccination and a leash no longer than 10 feet.

White River Junction

Quechee State Park Campground, 190 Dewey Mills Rd., White River Junction (802-295-2990; 1-800-409-7579); $16–37 per night. Your dog is permitted at Quechee as long as you use a leash, bring proof of vaccinations, and don't allow your pup into any day-use areas. Managed by the U.S. Army Corps of Engineers, this campground has 47 sites for tents, pop-up trailers, and RVs (no hookups); restrooms with showers; a dumping station; a playground; and a playing field. Quechee Gorge and the North Hartland Flood Control Dam are nearby.

Williamstown

Limehurst Lake Campground, 4104 Rte. 14, Williamstown (802-433-6662; 1-800-242-9876; www.limehurstlake.com); $25–37 per night. Most breeds (call to see if yours qualifies) are welcome at Limehurst, a family campground with a private lake, primitive tent sites, RV sites with hookups, lean-tos, and cottages. Campers can also enjoy a beach, rental boats, a playground, scheduled activities, and a camp store. Owners are asked to leash their pets and clean up after them.

Homes, Cottages, and Cabins for Rent

For vacation rentals, check the local Craigslist ads, or these Web sites:

www.thekillingtongroup.com

www.killingtonholidayrentals.com

www.vermontproperty.com

OUT AND ABOUT

Art in the Park Foliage Festival, Main Street Park, Rutland. This fall-color spectacular takes place each October. It has been attracting visitors for more than 40 years with more than 60 artisans and food vendors, in addition to music, and children's activities. For more information, call 802-775-0356 or e-mail info@chaffeeartcenter.org.

Barre Bike Path, South Barre. You can access this 1-mile-long paved pathway at Fairview Street, Bridge Street, or Parkside Terrace in South Barre. Dogs are welcome on a leash.

Bomoseen State Forest, 22 Cedar Mountain Rd., Fair Haven (802-265-4242; 1-800-658-1622). With more than 2,800 acres, this state forest contains the smaller **Bomoseen State Park,** myriad hiking trails, boat rentals, a beach, many quiet corners, and wildlife-viewing opportunities. Dogs are not allowed in day-use areas but are allowed in the campground (see "Accommodations—Campgrounds").

Branbury State Park, 3570 Lake Dunmore Rd., Salisbury (802-247-5925; 1-800-658-1622). Pets are not allowed in the most popular section of this state park, a wide grassy area with lake access and picnic areas. But ask the rangers for directions to the hiking areas around the corner and you'll find yourself in the company of other dog walkers, horseback riders, and nature lovers enjoying the smooth, quiet trails to scenic vistas. Pets are also allowed in the park's campground (see "Accommodations—Campgrounds").

Chimney Point State Historic Site, Rtes. 125 and 17, Lake

Champlain Bridge, Addison (802-759-2412; www.accd.vermont.gov). This former Native American camping area beside Lake Champlain became a regional trade center in 1,000 B.C. and continued in that role well into the 1600s. Today, the site commemorates that period as well as the 1700s-era French settlements and fort in what is now known as Chimney Point. Dogs are welcome on a leash but are not allowed in the visitor center.

Dead Creek Wildlife Management Area, Rte. 17, Addison. Migratory birds, including geese, red-winged blackbirds, owls, and hawks, are plentiful in this 2,800-acre refuge during spring and fall. For a great view, bring your binoculars to the sheltered viewing area along Route 17 on the drive from Vergennes to Addison; the shelter even provides pictures and descriptions of the birds you're likely to see.

Dog Days of Summer. The Central Vermont Humane Society hosts this unusual annual fundraiser in late August. For one day, the Montpelier Recreation Department opens its swimming pool to four-legged swimmers—around 100 of them, on average. Guests pay an admission fee that helps the society care for homeless pets. The humane society also hosts the **Canines and Company Festival** in September, a benefit auction in November, and a **Walk-A-Thon** in May. For more information about any of the events, visit www.cvhumane.com, call 802-476-3811, or write to P.O. Box 687, Montpelier, VT 05601.

Green Mountain National Forest. The pride of Vermont, the Green Mountain National Forest makes up a huge section of the southern part of the state and continues up into central Vermont with ponds, trails, flora and fauna, primitive campsites, and majestic, untouched forestland. Try one of the following hikes: the **Abbey Pond Trail,** a 2-mile-long route with a waterfall and secluded pond, located about 5 miles north of Middlebury; the **Mount Horrid/Great Cliff Trail,** a fairly steep slope to a lookout point, starting at Route 73 at Brandon Gap; or the **Lincoln Gap West Vista Trail,** a short and easy walk to great views with parking located at Lincoln Gap Road. There are many more: For further description and directions, visit the Green Mountain National Forest Headquarters on 231 North Main Street in Rutland, call 802-747-6700, or visit www.fs.usda.gov/r9.

Kingsland Bay State Park, 787 Kingsland Bay State Park Rd., Ferrisburgh (802-877-3445; 1-800-658-1622). This relatively new state park is the former site of a girls' camp; today it encompasses 265 undeveloped acres with walking and hiking paths beside Lake Champlain. It's a popular area for picnics and boating.

Long Trail. This famous Canada-to-Massachusetts trail passes through the entire state of Vermont and is the oldest long-distance hiking trail in

America. Those who hike the whole trail are called End to Enders. For those who just want to explore a section, the central Vermont portion provides some of the most challenging terrain. Among the best-known sites are the **Camel's Hump** (elevation: 4,083 feet), **Mount Abraham** (elevation: 4,000 feet), and **Skylight Pond. Skyline Lodge** is the largest shelter; others are spaced every 6 to 8 or so miles. For more information, maps, and trail descriptions, contact the **Green Mountain Club** at 802-244-7037 or visit www.greenmountainclub.org.

Mad River Greenway, Waitsfield. This 4-mile-long thin trail is popular with locals; you can hop on just off Route 100 at Tremblay Road or Meadow Road. Dogs must be well behaved and leashed.

Not annual event any longer- **Quechee.** This small, picturesque town is home to a number of central Vermont's most popular attractions, including **Quechee Gorge** (aka the Grand Canyon of New England), the Quechee Gorge village shopping area (www.quecheegorge.com), and the annual **Quechee Balloon Festival,** held each June. Danforth Pewter and the Toy & Train Museum are popular attractions in the village area. The 600-acre **Quechee State Park** is located in nearby White River Junction at 190 Dewey Mills Road. For more park information, call 802-295-2990 or 1-800-299-3071. For more information on

© GORILLAIMAGES/SHUTTERSTOCK.COM

Quechee events and attractions, call the chamber of commerce at 802-295-7900.

Robert Frost Wayside Area and Trail, Rte. 125, Ripton (802-388-4362). Talk about poetic: This wonderful spot, located near Middlebury College's Bread Loaf campus, has a picnic area and short walking trail lined with mounted plaques bearing excerpts from some of Robert Frost's noted poems. The famous writer once lived in a cabin on the grounds. The 1.2-mile loop is the perfect length for a walk with your best friend.

Rock of Ages Quarries, 773 Graniteville Rd., Graniteville (Barre) (802-476-3119; www.rockofages.com). Leashed pets are welcome in the shop and on the grounds at Rock of Ages, a 50-acre, 600-foot-deep working quarry with amazing views of the trenches and massive slabs of granite as they are cut and removed. On hot days, the staff are sometimes also willing to watch your pup in the air-conditioned office while you explore the grounds. Pets are not allowed on the bus tours.

Scenic Drives. Dirt roads outnumber their paved counterparts in Vermont, and visitors often agree that the best way to explore the state is to wander with no particular destination in mind. For some ideal starting places for a journey, try these: **Route 5** along the Vermont border through the towns of Newbury, Wells River, and Ryegate; **Route 4** from Rutland to Woodstock; **Route 100,** alongside Green Mountain National Forest, from Killington to Waitsfield; and **Route 125** from Middlebury to Chimney Point.

Union Village Dam and Recreation Area, entrances in Union Village and Thetford Center. Like the Ball Mountain Lake recreation area (see "Southern Vermont"), this is a U.S. Army Corps of Engineers property offering ample opportunities for fishing trips, picnics, and hikes. The site encompasses about 6 miles of fish-stocked river, as well as picnic tables, and barbecue grills. Pets are welcome.

QUICK BITES

Bridge Restaurant, 17 Rte. 17 W., Chimney Point (802-759-2152; www.thebridgerestaurantvt.com). Located next to the Champlain Bridge to New York and the Chimney Point State Historic Site, this family restaurant serves simple, tasty meals and offers lots of outdoor seating.

FH Gillingham & Sons General Store, 16 Elm St., Woodstock (1-800-344-6668; www.gillinghams.com). This popular general store has been serving Woodstock residents and visitors for more than 100 years. This is the place to come for genuine specialty foods from Vermont, including maple syrup, cheddar, smoked meats, cookies, jams and jellies, seasonings, mustard, cranberry sauce, and more.

Kampersville Deli and Ice Cream Parlor, 1457 Lake Dunmore Rd., Salisbury (802-352-4501; 1-877-250-2568). Part of the Lake Dunmore Kampersville campground (see "Accommodations—Campgrounds") and right around the corner from **Branbury State Park** (see "Out and About") and myriad boating opportunities on Lake Dunmore, this snack bar has take-out service offering your favorite summertime treats.

La Brioche Bakery and Café, 89 Main St., Montpelier (802-229-0443; www.neci.edu/labrioche). This locally renowned eatery serves gourmet sandwiches and pastries indoors, on the patio, or for takeout. Choose from soups, fresh-baked breads with meats and cheeses, scones, cinnamon buns, croissants, muffins, and more. La Brioche is one of the New England Culinary Institute's renowned restaurants.

New Village Snack Bar, 389 West St., Rutland (802-775-2717; www.villagesnackbarvt.com). Order at the window and eat outside at the picnic tables at this casual restaurant serving burgers, french fries and onion rings, seafood, chicken sandwiches, and ice cream.

Pizza Jerks, 1307 Killington Rd., Killington (802-422-4111; www.pizzajerks.com). At this New York–style pizzeria, you can eat in, order a slice or a whole pie to go, or bring home an uncooked pizza to bake in your own oven. In addition to specialties like the Heart Stopper (double cheese, double sausage, and double pepperoni), the "jerks" also cook up calzones, strombolis, and subs.

White Cottage, Rte. 4, Woodstock (802-457-3455). This drive-in-style eatery has been rebuilt since Tropical Storm Irene in 2011, and it's back now, better than ever. With benches and picnic tables outside, it's a great pit stop with your pooch. The menu includes favorite standbys like burgers, hot dogs, banana splits, sandwiches, soups, and fried clams.

Woodstock Farmer's Market, 979 W. Woodstock Rd., Woodstock (802-457-3658; www.woodstockfarmersmarket.com). Stop in at this produce, meat, and seafood market for fresh sandwiches to go. In-house specialties include Ann's California Roll-Up (turkey with cheese, tomatoes, avocado, and pesto-mayo) and the vegetarian Quechee Gorge (cheese and tomato with mustard, served grilled on roasted garlic–parmesan bread). *Vermont* magazine recently distinguished the shop as offering the "Best Sandwich in Vermont."

HOT SPOTS FOR SPOT

4 Dogs and a Wish, 1 Frog Hollow Alley, Middlebury (802-382-9474). You don't need four dogs (one will do) to visit this canine-centered shop offering a host of goodies for you and your furry friend. This "store for eccentric people and their pets" is stocked with items like T-shirts, greeting cards, toys, chews, leashes, bowls, books, and more.

Catamount Pet Supply, 296 Rte. 4 E., Rutland (802-773-7642). Owned and run by veterinarians, this pet shop specializes in offering all-natural foods without by-products or fillers. In addition to foods and treats, the store stocks toys, crates, and other supplies for dogs, cats, and small animals. Grooming is also available.

Diamond Brook Kennel and Pet Country Club, 4597 Rte. 30,

Brandon (802-273-2941; www.diamondbrook.com). Your four-legged friend will get top-of-the-line treatment at Diamond Brook, where the trainers provide obedience classes, supplies, grooming, and boarding. The inside/outside runs are roomy: 56 to 90 square feet for each animal. Complete grooming services are also available; rates vary according to size and services.

Downtown Pet & Aquarium, 25 Center St., Rutland (802-773-4941). This shop focuses on all kinds of pets, from dogs to fish and everything in between. You'll be able to find food, chewies, and other basics for your favorite traveling pooch.

Falls General Store, Rte. 12, Northfield Falls (802-485-8044). Though this shop doesn't specialize exclusively in pet supplies, it is a fun and interesting place to pick up dog food and treats. The large pet section has toys, food, and goodies for dogs, cats, rabbits, gerbils, and other animal friends. While you're there for Rover, you can also grab a fishing license, sandwich, slice of pizza, or a Vermont souvenir for yourself.

Lucky Dog Day Care and Boarding Facility, 60 Pike Hill Rd., Warren (802-496-5944; www.luckydogdaycare.us). There are no cages or kennels at Lucky Dog: just an acre of land, a playroom, and a deck where the dogs romp and play together while their "parents" are off skiing, vacationing, or sightseeing. Pickup and delivery of your pooch is included in the rates, which range from $20 to $30 per day.

Middlebury Boarding and Grooming Kennel, 2819 South St. Ext., Middlebury (802-388-9643; 1-866-388-9643; mbgk@sover.net; www.middleburykennel.com). You can make reservations online for this Middlebury kennel offering overnight boarding for dogs and cats, doggie day care, and grooming for all sizes and breeds. Obedience classes and agility training are also available.

Pet Deli, 1284 Rte. 302, Berlin Suite #8, Barre (802-479-4307). Also known as **All About Pets,** this animal-supply store specializes in high-quality foods and nutritional supplements for all types of companion animals. Your furry friend will appreciate the wide selection of rawhide bones and smoked products at the Doggie Deli counter, not to mention the bulk biscuit bar full of treats.

ANIMAL SHELTERS AND HUMANE SOCIETIES

Addison County Humane Society, 236 Boardman St., Middlebury (802-388-1100; www.homewardboundanimals.org)

Central Vermont Humane Society, 1589 VT 14, Montpelier (802-476-3811; www.cvhumane.com)

Green Mountain Humane Society, 43 N. Main St., White River Junction (802-296-7297)

Lucy Mackenzie Humane Society, 4832 VT 44, Windsor (802-484-5829; www.lucymac.org)

Rutland County Humane Society, 765 Stevens Rd., P.O. Box 558, Pittsford 05763 (802-483-6700; www.rchsvt.org)

Spring Hill Horse Rescue, 175 Middle Rd., Clarendon (802-775-1098; www.springhillrescue.com)

Vermont Humane Federation (advocacy group), 311 Waterbury St., North Clarendon (802-244-5895; www.vermonthumane.org)

Vermont Volunteer Services for Animals, P.O. Box 100, Bridgewater 05034 (802-672-5302)

IN CASE OF EMERGENCY

Barre Animal Hospital, 678 S. Barre Rd., Barre (802-476-4151)

Country Animal Hospital, 1533 Rte. 107, Bethel (802-234-5999)

Eastwood Animal Clinic, 298 Rte. 4, Rutland (802-773-7711)

Kedron Valley Veterinary Clinic, 1205 W. Woodstock Rd., Woodstock (802-457-3135)

Middlebury Animal Hospital, 139 Washington St. Ext., Middlebury (802-388-2691)

Onion River Animal Hospital, 36 Three Mile Bridge Rd., Montpelier (802-223-7765)

River Valley Veterinary Hospital, 3890 Rte. 5, Newbury (802-866-5922)

Vergennes Animal Hospital, 20 Main St., Vergennes (802-877-3371)

Veremedy Pet Hospital, 1217 Rte. 12, Woodstock (802-457-2229)

PETS ARE ALWAYS WELCOME AT THE MOUNTAINEER INN IN STOWE. (PHOTO COURTESY OF MOUNTAINEER INN)

Northern Vermont

From dog chapels to canine camps, northern Vermont is a nearly ideal spot for those whose travel plans include a pet. In addition to its many animal-friendly accommodations, the region also boats big-city attractions; sweeping views of water, mountains, and rolling farmland; secluded campgrounds; ski resorts; and enough hiking trails to keep you and Spot busy for days—or weeks.

Most of the activity is centered on the Burlington and Stowe areas: The former is home to the University of Vermont, spectacular Lake Champlain, great restaurants, and a bustling pedestrian mall; the latter plays host to famous festivals and hopping ski resorts. (Skiers will be pleased to find numerous dog-sitting options and pet-friendly lodgings nearby.) Boaters and fishermen can make the most of northern Vermont's seemingly endless waterways. To the northeast, the more rural areas offer perhaps the most accurate glimpse of Old Vermont, from the quaint Lake Willoughby region to the movie-set-like village of Craftsbury Common. Scenic roads (complete with covered bridges, of course) wind through it all, making almost any drive fun in any season. Canadians can count their blessings for the close proximity; for the rest of us in the lower 48, the destination more than justifies the long ride.

ACCOMMODATIONS

Hotels, Motels, Inns, and Bed & Breakfasts

Averill

Quimby Country Lodge and Cottages, 1127 Forest Lake Rd., Averill (802-822-5533; quimbyc@together.net; www.quimbycountry.com); $130–226 per night. Located in the northeast corner of Vermont along the Canadian border, Quimby Country welcomes dogs and cats to its 600-acre lakefront resort. Accommodations include private cottages with kitchens and maid service; in the high season, the rates include three meals each day and planned family activities. Boat and Windsurfer rentals are free.

Barnet

Inn at Maplemont Farm, 2742 Rte. 5, Barnet (802-633-4880; 1-800-230-1617; maplemont-farm@hotmail.com; www.maplemont.com); $90–160 per night. Two enthusiastic Bernese mountain dogs are the bellhops-in-training at this warm and friendly B&B with a wraparound porch and rocking chairs, deluxe breakfasts, farm animals, four guest rooms, antiques, a dining room, and a relaxing common room. The inn's 43 acres have plenty of hills and pastures for exploring, and the nearby Connecticut River provides canoeing and kayaking opportunities. Pets are always welcome without extra fees, provided they are not left alone in the rooms.

Bolton Valley

Black Bear Inn, 4010 Bolton Access Rd., Bolton Valley (802-434-2126; 1-800-395-6335; blkbear@wcvt.com; www.bbonline.com); $89–355 per night. This mountaintop inn sits on 5,000 acres of hiking and ski trails, close to Stowe, Burlington, and Waterbury. For an additional $10 per day, Black Bear Inn guests can make use of an on-site kennel, otherwise known as the **Bone and Biscuit Inn.** The kennel is open seasonally and offers private indoor/outdoor runs for each animal. Human visitors can enjoy fine dining, tennis courts, a swimming pool, and individually decorated guest rooms with private baths. Look for the mountain getaway package, which includes two nights of accommodations, dinner for two, full breakfasts daily, and wine or a cheese plate in your room.

Burlington

Doubletree Hotel Burlington, 1117 Williston Rd., Burlington (802-658-0250; www.hilton.com); $179–247 per night. The staff at this animal-friendly hotel can recommend local pet-sitters and will present you with their pet policies upon arrival. The DoubleTree has an indoor swimming pool, a fitness center, a restaurant and lounge, room service, and cable television with premium movie channels. All rooms include top-notch amenities, including Crabtree & Evelyn bath products and Wolfgang

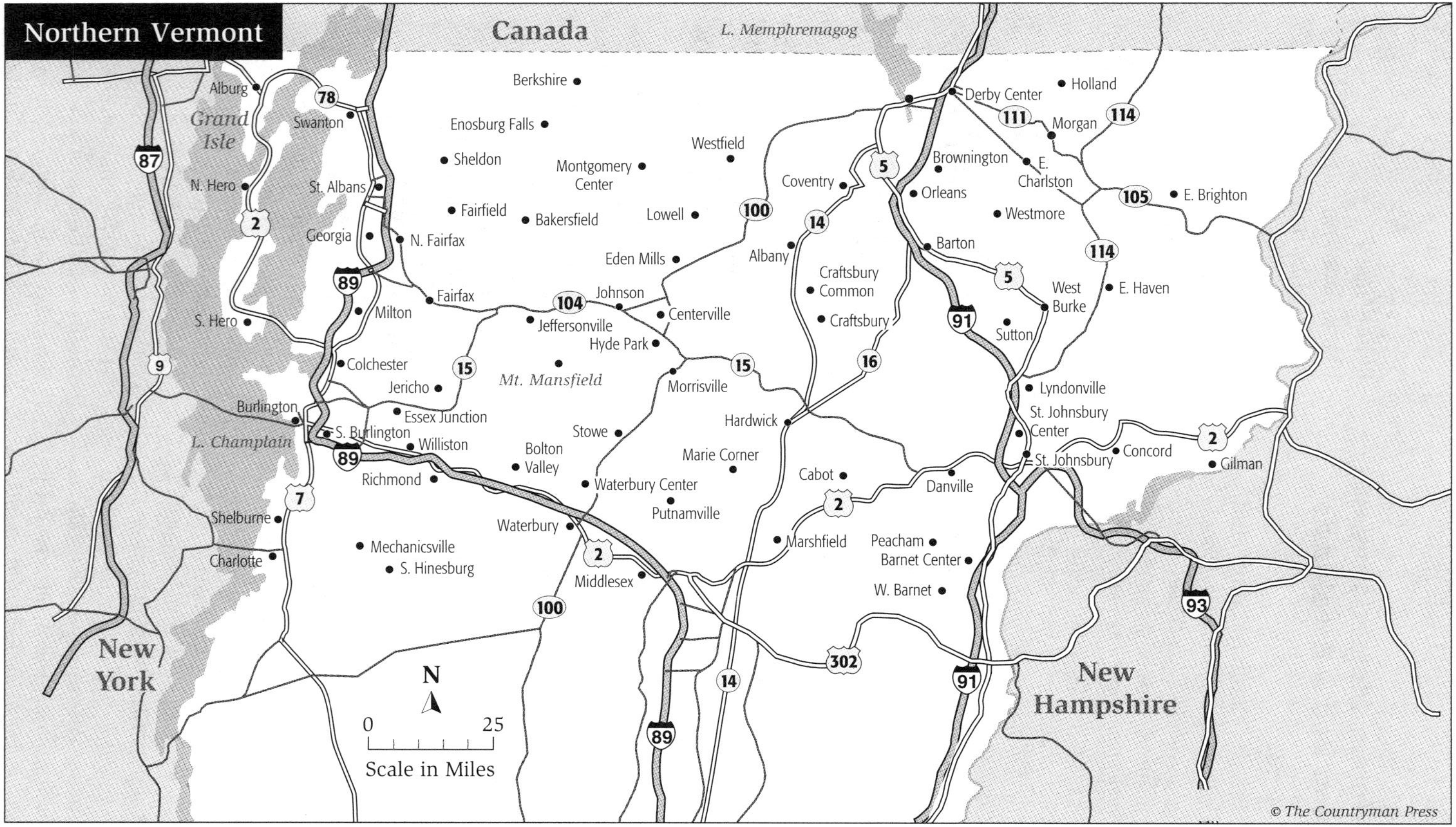
Northern Vermont
Canada
L. Memphremagog
Berkshire
Enosburg Falls
Sheldon
Montgomery Center
Westfield
Fairfield
Bakersfield
Lowell
N. Fairfax
Eden Mills
Fairfax
Johnson
Centerville
Jeffersonville
Hyde Park
Mt. Mansfield
Morrisville
Jericho
Essex Junction
Williston
Stowe
Bolton Valley
Richmond
Waterbury Center
Putnamville
Waterbury
Middlesex
Marie Corner
Hardwick
Mechanicsville
S. Hinesburg
Alburg
Grand Isle
Swanton
N. Hero
St. Albans
Georgia
Milton
S. Hero
Colchester
Burlington
S. Burlington
L. Champlain
Shelburne
Charlotte
New York
Coventry
Albany
Craftsbury Common
Craftsbury
Cabot
Marshfield
Peacham
Barnet Center
W. Barnet
Danville
Derby Center
Holland
Morgan
Brownington
E. Charlston
Orleans
Westmore
E. Brighton
Barton
West Burke
E. Haven
Sutton
Lyndonville
St. Johnsbury Center
St. Johnsbury
Concord
Gilman
New Hampshire
N
0
25
Scale in Miles
87
78
2
9
89
7
15
104
100
14
16
5
91
111
114
105
302
93
© The Countryman Press

Puck coffee. Dogs are permitted with a $75 cleaning fee per stay.

Sheraton Burlington Hotel and Conference Center, 870 Williston Rd., Burlington (802-865-6600; 1-800-325-3535; www.starwoodhotels.com); $199–319 per night. The Sheraton Burlington has a convenient location close to downtown and Lake Champlain, a swimming pool, a restaurant and room service, express check-out services, a fitness center, cable television, a 24-hour front desk, laundry facilities, and a lounge. Pets up to 80 pounds are welcome with no additional fees, provided they are not left alone in rooms. Pet beds and bowls are available at most Sheratons: ask for them when you make your reservation.

Colchester

Days Inn Burlington-Colchester, 124 College Pkwy., Colchester (802-655-0900; www.wyndham.com); $79–149. This Days Inn location offers cable television with premium movie channels, Internet access, an indoor heated swimming pool, laundry facilities, free continental breakfasts each morning, and in-room hair dryers and alarm clocks. Guest pets are permitted in smoking rooms with prior approval.

Hampton Inn Burlington Colchester, 42 Lower Mountain View Dr., Colchester (802-655-6177; www.hilton.com); $159–219 per night. Guests at this Hampton Inn can enjoy a complimentary hot breakfast buffet every morning, free high-speed Internet access, a business center, a swimming pool, a fitness room, laundry facilities, and in-room coffeemakers, hair dryers, irons, and ironing boards. Dogs of any size are welcome without extra fees.

Craftsbury Common

Craftsbury Outdoor Center, 535 Lost Nation Rd., Craftsbury Common (802-586-7767; stay@craftsbury.com; www.craftsbury.com); $235–314 per night. Friendly pets are allowed in two lakeside cabins (B and C) at the Craftsbury Outdoor Center, a fun facility offering activity-filled vacations for those interested in hiking, mountain biking, kayaking, yoga, swimming, sculling, running, and skiing. Pet owners pay a one-time $50 cleaning fee and are asked to keep their animals under control at all times.

Inn on the Common, Rte. 14, 1162 N. Craftsbury Rd., Craftsbury Common (802-586-9619; 1-800-521-2233; www.theinnkeeper.com/bnb/11287); $145–279 per night. Located beside its town's historic common, this 16-room 1700s inn is set on 10 acres with a tennis court, a swimming pool, gardens, and fields. Gourmet breakfasts and dinner are served in the dining room, and the guest rooms are furnished with antiques, woodstoves, fireplaces, and four-poster beds. Dogs are welcome in one of the inn's three buildings for an extra $25 per stay (not per night). "We have been very happy with the pet owners that have come here so far," says the Inn on the Common's

Jim Lamberti. "The Common is right outside the door of our pet-friendly building, offering a great place for dogs to romp." The inn is a member of the Select Registry (www.selectregistry.com).

Eden Mills

Eden Mountain Lodge and Guest House, 1390 Square Rd., Eden Mills (802-635-9070; edenlodge@vtlink.net; www.edenmtnlodge.com); $350–800 for a two-day stay or $500–1,200 per week. "Dogs are number one at this place," says Eden Mountain Lodge owner Jim Blair, a champion musher who provides dog-sledding lessons and trips for interested guests. Choose from the log cabin–style lodge or the cottage. Each is fully furnished, can accommodate up to six people, and has porches and modern kitchens. Eden Mountain Lodge is the home of Ethical Dog Sledding Adventures: check out the Alpha Dog Adventure Tour package.

East Burke

The Inn at Mountain View Farm, 3383 Darling Hill Rd., East Burke (802-626-9924;1-800-572-4509; innmtnview@kingcon.com; www.innmtnview.com); $175–275 per night. The Inn at Mountain View Farm is a 440-acre estate with miles of trails (known as the Kingdom Trails), a restaurant, 14 guest rooms and luxury suites, country antiques, Adirondack chairs, flower gardens, and sweeping views. Dogs are welcome in designated rooms for an extra $50 per night. This very animal-friendly place is also the site of the **Mountain View Farm Animal Sanctuary** for farm animals.

Essex Junction

Homeplace Bed & Breakfast, 90 Old Pump Rd., Essex Junction (802-899-4694; mariot@homeplacebandb.com; www.homeplacebandb.com); $90–115 per night. "I've been extremely lucky so far with guest pets," says Homeplace innkeeper Mariot Huessy. "My dogs love to play with other dogs." The country B&B, nestled in a 100-acre wood, has four guest rooms, books and games, farm animals, European antiques, and full country breakfasts. Dogs are welcome with prior approval for an additional $25 fee, as long as they are not left alone in the rooms.

Fairfax

Inn at Buck Hollow Farm, 2150 Buck Hollow Rd., Fairfax (802-849-2400; 1-800-849-7985 inn@buckhollow.com; www.buckhollow.com); $100–140 per night. Your pets are always welcome with prior notice at Buck Hollow, a gracious and low-key inn where the resident dogs, Isham and Chelsea, and several resident cats will be on hand to show you around. Set on 400 acres of horse fields, forests, lawns, and fields, the farm has an on-site antiques shop, four-poster beds, a swimming pool, a hot tub, and full country breakfasts. (Ask for the Yellow Room, which has a sliding door leading out onto a private porch and the large backyard.)

Jay Peak Resort Area

Phineas Swann, 195 Main St.,

Montgomery Center (802-326-4306; www.phineasswann.com); $139–449 per night. Touted as one of New England's most romantic and luxurious pet-friendly inns, Phineas Swann welcomes canine guests with a rawhide treat upon arrival. You and your pooch are welcome to stay in the most luxurious suites, including the Honeymoon Suite, and the dog-crazy innkeepers provide beds and bowls, as well as dog-walking or pet-sitting services upon request. The inn is located 8 miles from Jay's Peak, so there are plenty of great walks to take with your pal, or you can take a swim with them in the Trout River bordering the property. Ask about the Deluxe Dog Spa package, or in winter, the Pet Perfect Ski Package, both of which include amenities for humans and their animals. Dogs of all sizes and breeds are welcome with a one-time $25 fee per stay, per pet.

Marshfield

Marshfield Inn & Motel, 5630 Rte. 2, Marshfield (802-426-3383; www.marshfieldinn.com); $70–128 per night and higher. The Marshfield Inn & Motel offers two pet-friendly rooms—they even post pictures of guests' dogs on the Web site. Aside from the animal-friendly attitude, the accommodation also offers hiking trails, panoramic views of the surrounding mountains, Adirondack chairs, daily breakfasts, and window boxes with flowers. All rooms are nonsmoking.

North Hero

Shore Acres Inn & Restaurant, Rte. 2, 237 Shore Acres Dr., North Hero (802-372-8722; vtshacres@aol.com; www.shoreacres.com); $114–242 per night. Shore Acres guests have access to boat dockings, tennis courts, a golf course, horseshoe pits, shuffleboard courts, and croquet. Most of the rooms have water views; all have cable television, air

DOGS, HORSES, AND CATS WILL WELCOME YOU AND YOUR PET TO THE INN AT BUCK HOLLOW FARM IN FAIRFAX.

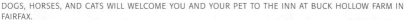

conditioners, and contemporary furnishings. The inn sits directly on Lake Champlain and has 50 acres of land for dogs to explore. Canines are welcome for an extra $15 for one night and $5 each additional night.

Orleans

WilloughVale Inn & Cottages on Lake Willoughby, 793 Rte. 5A, Orleans (802-525-4123; 1-800-253-7302; info@willoughvale.com; www.willoughvale.com); $99–305 per night. The WilloughVale Inn has wonderful water views and 11 individually decorated rooms, including two luxury rooms with fireside hot tubs, four lakefront cottages with decks and private docks, casual seasonal dining in the on-site restaurant, and the Tap Room Bar. This is a place designed for quiet, restful getaways. With prior approval and a pet fee (call for details), one pet weighing less than 50 pounds is welcome in each room or cottage. There is a $30 per night fee for pets, and all room rates include a complimentary continental breakfast.

St. Johnsbury

Fairbanks Inn, 401 Western Ave., St. Johnsbury (802-748-5666; www.stjay.com); $169–189 per night. Dogs of any size (sorry, no cats) are welcome at this small motel for an additional $25 per night. Amenities include 45 guest rooms with balconies, an outdoor swimming pool, laundry facilities, cable television with premium movie channels, air-conditioning, and complimentary continental breakfasts. Animals should not be left unattended in the rooms unless they are crated.

Shelburne

Econo Lodge and Suites, 3164 Shelburne Rd., Shelburne (802-985-3377; 1-800-553-2666; www.choicehotels.com); $79–129 per night. The Econo Lodge provides accommodations for long- and short-term stays with standard rooms and suites offering air-conditioning, cable television, an outdoor swimming pool, laundry facilities, continental breakfasts, in-room movies, a restaurant, a wake-up service, and a picnic area. South Burlington.

Best Western Windjammer Burlington, 1076 Williston Rd., South Burlington (802-863-1125; 1-800-371-1125; www.bestwestern.com); $125–180 per night. Pets are welcome at the Windjammer for an extra fee of $10 per pet, per night ($100 maximum). Amenities at this Best Western hotel include indoor and outdoor swimming pools, a restaurant and pub, free continental breakfasts, a fitness center, a sauna, laundry services, fax and photocopying services, in-room movies, high-speed Internet access, airport shuttles, and cable television with premium movie channels. You may bring up to two pets per room of 80 pounds or less.

La Quinta South Burlington, 1285 Williston Rd., South Burlington (802-865-3400; 1-800-753-3757; www.lq.com); $129–179 per night. Guests at this Comfort Inn can enjoy free wireless Internet access, complimentary deluxe continental breakfast each day, cable television with premium movie channels, an outdoor heated swimming pool, a fitness center, a "kids stay free" program, and a business center. The hotel has a large grassy area for walks.

Stowe

Commodores Inn, 823 S. Main St., Stowe (802-253-7131; 1-800-44-STOWE; www.commodoresinn.com); $98–198 per night. Animals are welcome without restrictions at this full-service, hotel-style inn with king- and queen-size beds, air-conditioning, cable television, a restaurant and lounge, a fitness room, an indoor swimming pool, and two hot tubs. Common areas include a living room with a fireplace and a reading room with board games. Pet guests pay an extra $10 per stay (not per night); the staff is happy to arrange doggie day care.

Golden Eagle Resort, 511 Mountain Rd., Stowe (802-253-4811; www.goldeneagleresort.com); $99–339 per night. Located on 40 acres with Mt. Mansfield in its backyard, the Golden Eagle has its own hiking trails for you and your dog to explore, and is also within walking distance of the Stowe Recreation Path and the local dog lover's favorite Quiet Path (see "Out and About"). Amenities include dog beds, bowls, treats, and personalized waste bags with a one-time $25 fee per stay. Dogs are allowed off-leash on the Golden Eagle trails if they respond to voice control, but must be leashed on the Stowe Recreation path and other public walking areas.

Innsbruck Inn, 4361 Mountain Rd., Stowe (802-253-8582; 1-800-225-8582; www.innsbruckinn.com); $129—229 per night. This Bavarian-style inn located a the base of Vermont's largest peak offers unusual amenities such as a skating rink, paddle-tennis court and an on-site scuba diving school. Guests can choose from superior and standard rooms, suites, efficiency units, and a five-bedroom chalet. Pets are welcome for an additional $15 per night, provided they are not left unattended at any time. You can easily walk to the village or take your pal for a stroll in the 4-acre park.

Mountaineer Inn, 3343 Mountain Rd., Stowe (802-253-7525; www.stowemountaineerinn.com); $99–180 per night. Each room at the Mountaineer Inn has its own deck and shares access to an indoor swimming pool, a large hot tub, a dining room, a lounge, and landscaped grounds along the West Branch River. Guests can choose from basic, standard, and family-style rooms that accommodate up to eight people. Pets are welcome.

Northern Lights Lodge, 4441 Mountain Rd., Stowe (802-253-8541; www.stowelodge.com); $89–148 per night. Dogs and "well-behaved owners" are always welcome in the motel building at Northern Lights for

DOGS CAN RELAX WITH THEIR COMPANIONS IN THE COZY LIVING ROOM OF THE GRÜNBERG HAUS B&B IN WATERBURY. (PHOTO COURTESY OF GRÜNBERG HAUS)

an extra $10 per night. The ski lodge is located in a pine forest and offers indoor and outdoor swimming pools, a hot tub and sauna, movie and game rooms, a breakfast room with a fireplace, cross-country skiing trails, air-conditioning, and complimentary full breakfasts for all guests.

Ten Acres Lodge, 14 Barrows Rd., Stowe (802-253-6838; 1-800-327-7357; tenacres@stowevt.net; www.tenacreslodge.com); Gray Cottage, $225–350 per night. Pets are welcome in the Gray Cottage at Ten Acres Lodge, a converted 1840s farmhouse B&B with a gourmet dining room and lounge, a hot tub, and artwork collections hanging on the walls of the library and gathering rooms. The roomy cottage has two bedrooms, a living room, and a kitchenette.

Topnotch at Stowe Resort and Spa, 4000 Mountain Rd., Stowe (802-253-8585; 1-800-451-8686; info@topnotch-resort.com; www.topnotchresort.com); $300–720 per night. After a multimillion dollar renovation, Topnotch lives up to its name. Tennis, golf, spa treatments, massage, restaurant and bistro dining, cross-country skiing, snowshoeing, hiking, child care, and more are all available at Topnotch, a deluxe accommodation in the mountains. Lodging choices include hotel rooms and townhouse rentals. Your pooch is welcomed with a bed and bowls in your room and canine turndown service at night. Ask about the Rover Reiki massage for a special treat, and the concierge can arrange walks or pet sitters upon request. Pets are welcome in the hotel (but not in the private home rentals) with prior approval. Meal packages are also available.

Waterbury

Grünberg Haus, 94 Pine St. (Rte. 100), Waterbury (802-244-7726; 1-800-800-7760; grunhaus@aol.com; www.grunberghaus.com); $155–185 per night. Though not allowed in the main inn, pets are welcome in the Grünberg Haus cabins for an additional $5 per night. The cabin units, which are open from late May to the end of October, are set in the woods with decks, vaulted ceilings, private bathrooms, queen-size beds, ceiling fans, and woodstoves. Note that there are no televisions in the cabins here, but hiking and cross-country skiing trails wind through the property, so there's plenty for you and your pal to explore.

Williston

Residence Inn Burlington Williston, 35 Hurricane Ln., Williston (802-878-2001; www.marriott.com); $214–269 per night. Guests at this Residence Inn will find daily buffet breakfasts, laundry facilities, a picnic area, an indoor swimming pool, a fitness center, cable television with premium movie channels, fireplaces, VCRs, and suites designed with long-term stays in mind. Your pooch is welcome with a one-time "sanitation fee" of $75.

TownePlace Suites Burlington Williston, 66 Zephyr Rd., Taft Corners, Williston (802-878-5900; www.marriott.com); $159–199 per night. For an extra $75 one-time fee, your pup is a welcome guest at this all-suite facility. The three-story hotel has a picnic area, an indoor children's swimming pool, laundry facilities, a fitness center, cable television, high-speed Internet access, work desks, and voice mail.

Campgrounds

Brownington

Will-O-Wood Campground, 227 Willowood Ln., Brownington (802-525-3575; www.will-o-woodcampground.com); $18–25 per night. Overlooking Lake Willoughby, this family campground has sites for tents and RVs, 100 acres of fields and woods, restrooms with showers, a swimming pool, a camp store, a recreation hall, and laundry facilities. Quiet, leashed pets are welcome, as long as their owners clean up after them and don't leave them unattended.

Burlington

North Beach Camping, 60 Institute Rd., Burlington (802-862-0942; 1-800-571-1198; www.enjoyburlington.com/northbeach); $22–31 per night. Tents, pop-up campers, and RVs will all find a home at this lakefront campground operated by the city of Burlington's Department of Parks and Recreation. Leashed, well-behaved pets are welcome, as long as their owners clean up after them and don't leave them unattended. Campers can enjoy a beach, a snack bar, and bathrooms with showers.

Colchester

Lone Pine Campsites, 52 Sunset View Rd., Colchester (802-878-5447; www.lonepinecampsites.com); $28.50–39.50 per night. This RV campground has 265 sites with hookups, two swimming pools, restrooms with showers, a camp store, miniature golf, laundry facilities, tennis courts, two playgrounds, a video game room, game nights, planned activities, and sports courts. Two pets are permitted per site, as long as they are quiet, leashed, and picked-up after.

Danville

Sugar Ridge RV Village and Campground, 24 Old Stagecoach Rd. (Rte. 2), Danville (802-684-2550; www.sugarridgervpark.com); $31–41 per night or $171–213 per week. Open seasonally, Sugar Ridge is located just west of St. Johnsbury with two heated swimming pools, a miniature golf course, 150 sites for tents and RVs, restrooms with free showers, free Wi-Fi, a snack bar, laundry facilities, a pond, hiking trails, and wagon rides. Most dog breeds (call for more information) are welcome with proof of vaccinations.

Derby

Char-Bo Campgrounds, 347 Hayward Rd., P.O. Box 438, Derby 05829 (802-766-8807; www.char-bo.com); $33–38 per day. This very pet-friendly campground allows dogs on the beach; there are also 150 acres for running and exploring. Campsites at Char-Bo each have views of Lake Salem and the surrounding mountains, and share access to a swimming pool, an on-site pitch-and-putt golf course, picnic and field areas, and horseshoe pits.

Eden Mills

Lakeview Camping Area, 4921 Rte. 100, Eden Mills (802-635-2255; 802-527-1515; elhugh@surfglobal.net; www.lakeviewcampingarea.biz); $35 per night. From owners of tents to pop-up campers and 33-foot RVs, everyone will find a spot at this North Country campground. Most sites have views of Lake Eden; all have picnic tables and fire pits. Guests can also take advantage of beaches, playgrounds, a dumping station, and a gift shop/camp store. Pets are welcome without extra fees.

Enosburg Falls

Lake Carmi State Park Campground, 460 Marsh Farm Rd., Enosburg Falls (802-933-8383; 1-800-409-7579); $16–37 per night. The state's largest campground, Lake Carmi offers 140 sites for tents and RVs (no hookups), 35 lean-to sites, restrooms with showers, a dumping station, rental boats, and walking trails in the state park (see "Out and About" for more park information). Animals are not allowed in day-use areas or on the beach, and dog owners must bring proof of vaccination.

Grand Isle

Grand Isle State Park Campground, 36 East Shore S., Grand Isle (802-372-4300; 1-800-409-7579); $16–25 per night. This lakefront park and campground is the most visited in the state with 120 sites for tents and RVs, and 36 more with lean-tos. Other amenities include restrooms with showers, a boat-launching ramp, boats for rent, a volleyball court, and walking trails. Pets are not allowed in day-use areas or on the beach, and pet owners must bring proof of vaccinations.

Guildhall

Maidstone Lake State Park Campground, 4858 Maidstone Lake Rd., Guildhall (802-676-3930; 1-800-409-7579); $16–37 per night. Pets are welcome to join their owners at this 73-site campground provided they have proof of vaccinations, use a leash no longer than 10 feet, and stay off the beach. Sites for tents, trailers, and RVs (no hookups) are provided, along with flush toilets, showers, a dumping station, and hiking trails. (For more park information, see "Out and About.")

Island Pond

Brighton State Park Campground, 102 State Park Rd., Island Pond (802-723-4360; 1-800-409-7579); $16–37 per night. Looking to get away from it all? There's not much to do at this Northeast Kingdom campground except enjoy the wildlife, forest, water, and peace and quiet. Campers can choose from 63 sites for tents and RVs, and 21 sites with lean-tos. Amenities include restrooms with showers, a dump station, and hiking trails. Dogs are not allowed on the beach, and owners must bring proof of vaccinations and use a leash no longer than 10 feet.

Shelburne

Shelburne Camping Area, 4385 Shelburne Rd. (Rte. 7), Shelburne (802-985-2540; shelbcamp@aol.com; www.shelburnecamping.com); $26–38 per night. Tent campers and RVers will all find sites at the Shelburne Camping Area, which offers a camp store, modern restrooms, a restaurant, and two swimming pools. Dog owners must have proof of vaccinations, use a leash, clean up any messes, and stay with their pets at all times.

South Hero

Camp Skyland on Lake Champlain, 398 South St., South Hero (802-372-4200); www.campskylandvt.com; $26 per night. There are no extra fees for pets at this family campground, but owners are required to use a leash, clean up after their animals, and not leave them unattended at any time. Campers can enjoy boat rentals, restrooms with showers, laundry facilities, a game room, and a lending library. Rustic cabins are also available for rent starting at $425 per week; call for details.

Underhill Center

Underhill State Park Campground, Underhill Center (802-899-3022; 1-800-409-7579); $16–37 per night. Ideal for tent campers looking for a quiet spot, this fairly small campground has 11 sites for tents and 6 sites with lean-tos. A separate camping area with 9 lean-to sites is reserved for groups. The campground has flush toilets and water, but no showers. Dogs must have proof of vaccination and are not allowed in day-use areas. (For more information on the state park, see "Out and About.")

Waterbury

Little River State Park Campground, 3444 Little River Rd., Waterbury (802-244-7103; 1-800-409-7579); $16–37 per night. This large campground set inside Mount Mansfield State Forest offers 81 sites for tenters and RVers (no hookups), along with 20 lean-to sites, restrooms with showers, a playground, a boat launch, boat rentals, and hiking trails. Dogs are not allowed in day-use areas, and pet owners must show proof of vaccination and use a leash.

Rental Agencies

Stowe Country Homes, 541 S. Main St. (Lower Village), Stowe (802-253-8132; 1-800-639-1990; rent@stowecountryrentals.com; www.stowecountryrentals.com). "We have many pet-friendly properties," explains Stowe Country Homesowner Mary Beth Quinn. The agency can help you locate short- and long-term rental apartments, homes, condominiums, and estates throughout the Stowe area. Check the Web site for updated listings and rates.

You can also check these local rental agencies:

www.gostowe.com
www.stoweresorthomes.com
www.stowerealtyrentals.com
www.vermontproperty.com

OUT AND ABOUT

Camp Gone to the Dogs, Stowe (1-888-DOG-DAZE; www.campgonetothedogs.com). Though headquartered in the southern Vermont town of Putney (see "Accommodations—Hotels, Motels, Inns, and Bed & Breakfasts" in "Southern Vermont"), this pooch-centered camp holds its two fall sessions in Stowe. Campers and their dogs can stay on-site or at local hotels, and enjoy all meals and activities included in the camp rates, which range from $1,000–1,550 per week. Participants can spend their time relaxing and throwing a Frisbee around or take part in as many scheduled events and classes as they want. Some of the options include guided walks, grooming demonstrations and workshops, obedience classes, nutrition and training lectures, agility, lure coursing and tracking, skills contests, and costume parties. For more information, inquire with camp director Jeanne Richter.

Church Street Marketplace, Burlington. This outdoor shopping area and gathering place has fountains, food vendors, restaurants with outdoor seating (see "Quick Bites"), and more than 40 clothing boutiques, art galleries, salons, bookshops, and jewelry stores. It's an upbeat place to while away an afternoon window-shopping or people-watching. Parking is available at one of the nearby garages or metered lots.

Dog Mountain, 143 Parks Rd., East St. Johnsbury (802-748-2700; www.dogmt.com). This one-of-a-kind attraction is a must-see for all visiting (and local) dog lovers. The late artist and author Stephen Huneck transformed the hillside of his home into a studio and gallery for his canine-themed, whimsical works, which alone would be interesting enough for most of us. But the highlight of the site is the **Dog Chapel,** a nondenominational house of worship for people and their pets to "celebrate the spiritual bond that people have with their dogs." Friends, fans, and former employees of Dog Mountain are currently raising funds to continue fulfilling Huneck's vision for this moving canine tribute. Visit the Web site for details on how to donate and updates on the progress of the fund-raising.

Kingdom Trails Network. Long valued by mountain bikers, this vast network of trails snakes over mountains, past meadows, and through forests for about 100 miles, offering visitors a chance to experience all the varied terrain the Northeast Kingdom has to offer. Not only bikers but also hikers, snowshoers, and cross-country skiers have taken advantage of the scenic country byways protected and maintained by the **Kingdom Trails Association.** For more information, write to the association at P.O. Box 204, East Burke, VT 05832; call 802-626-0737; e-mail info@kingdomtrails.org; or visit www.kingdomtrails.com.

Lake Carmi State Park, 460 Marsh Farm Rd., Enosburg Falls (802-933-8383; 1-800-252-2363). A great spot for boating, this 7½-mile-long lake is more than 30 feet deep in some spots and is home to walleyes and northern pike. Roads leading to the campground (see "Accommodations—Campgrounds") cut through scenic bogs, forests, and wetlands: Bird-watchers, bring your binoculars. Dogs must stay off the beach and out of day-use areas.

Lake Champlain Ferries. Headquarters: King Street Dock, Burlington (802-864-9804; lct@ferries.com; www.ferries.com). Leashed or crated pets are allowed on board Lake Champlain transportation Company's ferries, which run on three main routes: Burlington, Vermont, to Port Kent, New York; Grand Isle, Vermont, to Plattsburgh, New York; and Charlotte, Vermont, to Essex, New York.

Long Trail. Created and maintained by the **Green Mountain Club** (GMC), this Canada-to-Massachusetts trail winds its way throughout Vermont and is the oldest long-distance hiking trail in the United States. In the northern part of the state, the GMC recommends the hike past **Lake Willoughby** and **Mount Hor;** the **Babcock Trail** and **Big Muddy Pond** area near Belvidere Center; and the **Lake Mansfield Trail** in the Stowe area. For more hiking ideas and maps, call 802-244-7037 or visit www.greenmountainclub.org.

Maidstone Lake State Park, 4858 Maidstone Lake Rd., Guildhall (802-676-3930; 1-800-658-6934). One of the wildest parks in Vermont, Maidstone provides visitors with plenty of opportunities for hiking, boating, fishing, and swimming. Wildlife-watchers will want to keep an eye out for endangered loons, which rear their chicks in deep Maidstone Lake. Dogs are not allowed in day-use areas or on the beach.

Mutt Strutt, Stowe. An annual fund-raising event organized by the **North Country Animal League,** the Mutt Strutt usually takes place in Stowe in July and includes crazy costume contests, pet-supply vendors, entertainment, and children's activities. All dogs, of course, are welcome to attend. For updated information on this year's date and location, call the league at 802-888-5065 (ext. 117), stop by the shelter on Route 100 in Morrisville, or visit www.ncal.com.

St. Albans Drive-In Theatre, Rte. 7, 429 Swanton Rd., St. Albans (802-524-7725; www.stalbansdrivein.com). One of New England's few remaining drive-ins, St. Albans Theatre provides a bit of Hollywood in northern Vermont. Your pooch might be hoping for *Snow Dogs* or *101 Dalmations,* but we can't promise anything.

Scenic Drives. So many lovely roads, so little time . . . For starters, try **Route 2** through Grand Isle and Lake Champlain; **Route 5** from Barton to West Burke; **Route 105** from Newport to Island Pond; and **Route 100** through Stowe and Morrisville.

Stoweflake Hot Air Balloon Festival, Stowe. One of Vermont's most popular annual events, this Stowe festival draws thousands of spectators to its colorful show of hot-air balloons rising into the summer sky. For updated dates and times, call 802-253-2232 or visit www.stoweflake.com.

Stowe Recreational Path, Stowe. This much-loved, 5.3-mile-long path is frequented year-round by bikers, walkers, joggers, cross-country skiers, in-line skaters, and anyone else looking for breath of fresh air. With wonderful mountain views, the trail winds through woods, open areas, and the shops at Stowe Village. Dogs are welcome on a leash. Local dog lovers also enjoy the shorter Quiet Path loop.

Underhill State Park, Underhill Center (802-899-3022; 1-800-

252-2363). This park is best known for its hiking trails that climb the challenging **Mount Mansfield.** You can climb all the way to the top or take more leisurely loops; the famous **Long Trail** (see previous page) passes through here, as well. Dogs are not allowed in day-use areas. If you plan to stay a while, consider the on-site campground (see "Accommodations—Campgrounds").

Vermont City Marathon, Burlington. Get your paper cups of water ready for this huge annual event drawing runners from around the world. The 26.2-mile-long race is sponsored by KeyBank and takes place in downtown Burlington each May. For more information, call 802-863-8412 or visit www.vermontcitymarathon.org.

Waterfront Boat Rentals, Perkins Pier, Maple St., Burlington (802-864-4858; 1-877-964-4858). Set out onto Lake Champlain with a rowboat, kayak, canoe, skiff, or Boston Whaler: All are available for rent at this full-service facility. Rates range $10–75 per hour, $30–195 for four-hour trips, and $35–225 for eight-hour trips.

QUICK BITES

Apple Farm Market, Rte. 2, South Hero (802-372-6611). Take a break for an ice cream, snack, or meal at the Apple Farm Market's outdoor picnic tables, or stop in for fresh Vermont-made food and products.

Northeast Kingdom Country Store, 466 VT 114, East Burke (802-626-4611; www.nekcountrystore.com). Formerly known as Bailey's & Burke, this adorable and authentic country store has been open to the public since 1897; today, the shop carries baskets, wine, Vermont cheeses, handcrafted items like mittens and hats, fudge, and lots of souvenirs and gift ideas. You'll also find a café inside, serving up satisfying country breakfasts, lunches, and dinners.

B&W Snack Bar, Rte. 5, Orleans (802-754-8579). B&W offers affordable finger foods, sandwiches, seafood, burgers, and other roadside snacks; grab a meal to go and hit the road or relax at the outdoor seats.

Church Street Marketplace, Burlington (www.churchstreetmarketplace.com). If you're going to be in the Burlington area, this is the place to go for food and fun with your pooch. The marketplace is lined with more than 26 food vendors and outdoor restaurants, as well as several unique gift shops and boutiques. Park in one of the nearby garages or metered lots.

Pub Outback, 482 Rte. 114, East Burke (802-626-1188). Pet owners often take advantage of the outdoor seating area at this casual, friendly restaurant; menu

Vermont Souvenirs for Dogs

For a "made in Vermont" souvenir for your pal, pick up a fleece dog coat made by the VT Fleece Company (available at a Vermont Country Store location or online at www.vermontcountrystore.com) or a buffalo plaid wool winter coat from Johnson Woolen Mills (www.johnsonwoolenmills.com).

selections include "fajita pitas"; Texas, Mexican, and veggie burgers; steaks, chicken, and seafood dishes; and special kids' meals.

Rusty Nail Bar & Grille, 1190 Mountain Rd., Stowe (802-253-6245). Everything on the Rusty Nail menu is available for takeout; the restaurant also has a seasonal deck and patio tables where well-behaved dogs are welcome. But the Rusty Nail's coolest feature doesn't appear until winter: Just before Christmas, the Ice Bar is built (yes, out of ice) and opened to the public for a unique and chilly good time.

Warner's Snack Bar, Rte. 7, St. Albans (802-527-2377). This ultracasual spot offers fried foods, sandwiches, cold drinks, and other nourishment for hungry travelers: Enjoy your meal with your pet at the outdoor picnic tables.

HOT SPOTS FOR SPOT

Animal Crackers, 430 Shelburne Rd., Burlington (802-864-7814). Open since 1995, this shop was designed for companion creatures and their two-legged friends. The store offers everything from grooming, pet-sitting, and pet-transportation services to a retail shop selling food and supplies.

Gulliver's Doggie Daycare, 59 Industrial Ave., Williston (802-860-1144; pat@doggiedaycare.com; www.doggiedaycare.com). This active and interactive facility has four play yards, climbing and playground equipment, wading pools, and grooming facilities. Dogs play together and socialize with staffers while their owners are out and about. Doggie day care and overnight boarding are both available.

Dogs Etc. Grooming and Pet Care, 782 S. Main St., Stowe (802-253-2547). This grooming shop offers cuts, clips, and shampoos along with a doggie day-care service ($2 per hour), a small retail shop selling food and supplies, and a self-service dog wash area where you can scrub your pooch yourself and leave the mess behind.

Johnson Farm and Garden, 1442 Rte. 15, Johnson (802-888-7282). As one of the biggest pet-supply stores in the region, this shop sells food and supplies for companion and farm animals along with plants, yard tools, and other outdoor necessities.

Oasis Pet Resort, 567 Sias Ave., Newport (802-334-7005; info@oasispetresort.com; www.oasispetresort.com). This oasis in Vermont is a boarding and grooming facility offering overnight care, doggie day care, baths, cuts, nail clipping, and other services. Dogs who are overnight or day-care guests will enjoy walks, playtimes, exercise, and lots of attention from the staff members. Oasis also runs a retail store selling premium foods, pet beds, tote bags, balls, treats, hats, mugs, and other pet-focused merchandise.

Pampered Pet Grooming & Supply, 1127 North Ave #14, Burlington (802-862-5334; www.pamperedpetvt.com). If your dog needs a day of beauty, the Pampered Pet offers full grooming services for all breeds. They also carry several lines of natural dog food in case you run out.

The Pet Advantage, The Blue Mall, 350 Dorset St., South Burlington (802-860-1714; petadv@sover.net; www.thepetadvantage.com). This retail pet shop wants you to "think outside the cage," offering mainly a good selection of aquarium supplies and fish. But dog lovers can also find necessities here, including pet-food brands like Canidae, PRO PAC, and Natural Choice.

Pet Deli, All About Pets, 1284 Rte. 302, Suite 8, Barre (802-479-4307). The Pet Deli is a "premium food shopping center" offering nutritional and recreational supplies for your dog, cat, fish, gerbil, or other pet. Shoppers will find brands such as Wellness, Nature's Recipe, California Natural, and Royal Canin, along with squeaky toys, shampoos, biscuits, and other treats.

Pet Food Warehouse, 2455 Shelburne Rd., **Shelburne** (802-985-3302; www.pfwvt.com); and 2500 Williston Rd., **South Burlington** (802-862-5514; www.pfwvt.com). These two locally owned shops sell biscuits, rawhides, dog and cat beds, animal coats and sweaters, kennels and crates, grooming supplies, cat litter, bird food, magazines and books, and more than 25 brands of pet food. The South Burlington location also offers a Pet Wash Express service, in which owners wash their own pets in the store's tubs.

ANIMAL SHELTERS AND HUMANE SOCIETIES

Animal Rescue of the Kingdom, 360 Lackey Rd., Holland (802-334-6776)

Caledonia Animal Rescue, P.O. Box 4054, St. Johnsbury 05819 (802-623-2799)

Elizabeth Brown Humane Society, P.O. Box 6, St. Johnsbury 05819 (802-748-4281)

Franklin County Humane Society, 30 Sunset Meadows, Bellevue Mountain, St. Albans (802-524-9650)

Frontier Animal Society of Vermont, 4473 Barton–Orleans Rd., Orleans (802-754-2228)

Green Mountain Animal Defenders, P.O. Box 4577, Burlington 05406 (802-878-2230)

Humane Society of Chittenden County, 142 Kindness Ct., South Burlington (802-862-0135; www.chittendenhumane.org)

Humane Society of Greater Burlington, 633 Queen City Park Rd., South Burlington (802-862-0135)

North Country Animal League, 3524 Laporte Rd., Morrisville (802-888-5065; www.ncal.com)

IN CASE OF EMERGENCY

Brown Animal Hospital, 8 Calkins Ct., South Burlington (802-862-6471)

Companion Animal Care, 54 Western Ave., St. Johnsbury (802-748-2855)

Green Mountain Animal Hospital, 1372 North Ave., Burlington (802-658-3739)

Lamoille Valley Veterinary Services, 278 Rte. 15, Hyde Park (802-888-7911)

Newport Veterinary Hospital, 218 Rte. 105, Newport (802-334-2655)

Orleans Veterinary Services, Brownington Rd., Orleans (802-754-6625)

Stowe Veterinary Clinic, 300 Stagecoach Rd., Stowe (802-253-6800)

Tanneberger Veterinary Hospital, 997 Fairfax Rd., St. Albans (802-524-2001)

New Hampshire

5

SAILING IS A POPULAR PASTIME AT NEW HAMPSHIRE'S ELEGANT RESORT WENTWORTH BY THE SEA. (COURTESY OF WENTWORTH BY THE SEA/MARRIOTT)

Southern New Hampshire

Hoping to visit the New Hampshire seashore with your pup? Good luck. This small stretch of coastline, long popular with sunbathers, is about as pet-unfriendly as a place can be. There's a hotel or motel around every corner in the Hampton Beach area, but most innkeepers and motel owners don't allow dogs. In addition, animals are not welcome on the beaches or at the nearby Strawbery Banke outdoor living-history museum and waterfront Prescott Park, both in Portsmouth.

Inland, pet-loving travelers fare slightly better. The Merrimack Valley region, home of the state capital, Concord, and the cities of Nashua and Manchester, does offer a few chain-style accommodations, though this isn't a popular area for tourism. Your best bet for a vacation is the Monadnock region, located in the southwest corner of the state, which offers the vast majority of the area's animal-friendly lodgings. Many of those that do swing open their doors (and doggie doors) to you and your four-legged friends boast homey atmospheres in country settings, friendly innkeepers, and antique architecture. And once you've found a place to stay, you and Rover can set out for mountain hiking, canoeing, covered-bridge crossing, leaf-peeping, and other outdoorsy pursuits. Day trips across the border to Vermont are also popular with visitors to this quiet corner of New Hampshire.

ACCOMMODATIONS

Hotels, Motels, Inns, and Bed & Breakfasts

Bedford

Quality Inn & Wayfarer Conference Center, 121 S. River Rd., Bedford (603-622-3766; 1-877-851-6763; www.choicehotels.com); $99–179 per night. Located at the historic site of John Goffe's Mill, this Quality Inn (formerly known as the Wayfarer Inn) has 194 guest rooms with in-room coffeemakers, irons, and hair dryers. Other inn amenities include a covered bridge, a pond, waterfalls, daily breakfasts, indoor and outdoor swimming pools, a fitness center, and a restaurant and lounge. Pets are welcome for an extra $25 per night.

Chesterfield

Chesterfield Inn, Rte. 9, Chesterfield (603-256-3211; 1-800-365-5515; info@chsterfieldinn.com; www.chesterfieldinn.com); $150–269 per night. This upscale country inn offers whirlpool baths, private decks and terraces, fireplaces, landscaped grounds with gardens, scenic views, refrigerators, air-conditioning, and full gourmet breakfasts made with herbs from the garden and local produce. Pets are welcome in 6 of the inn's 15 guest rooms and have access to the backyard. Add on a pampered pet package that includes toys, treats, and food bowls for an additional $50.

Concord

Best Western Concord, 97 Hall St., Concord (603-228-4300; 1-800-528-1234; www.bestwestern.com); $79–119 per night. For an extra $15 per night (up to $100 maximum), your pet can join you at this Concord hotel with a complimentary breakfast, swimming pool, a fitness center, laundry facilities, free morning newspapers, cable television, and in-room refrigerators, microwaves, wet bars, coffeemakers, and alarm clocks. The weight limit is 80 pounds with two pets per room allowed. Smoking and nonsmoking rooms are available.

Comfort Inn Concord, 71 Hall St., Concord (603-226-4100; www.choicehotels.com); $95–150 per night. Located in the state capital, this Comfort Inn offers an indoor heated swimming pool, a whirlpool, a sauna, a fitness center, cable television and in-room movies, and free daily continental breakfasts. Pets are welcome for an additional $15 per night with a maximum of two pets per room.

Durham

Hickory Pond Inn, 1 Stagecoach Rd., Durham (603-659-2227; 1-800-658-0065; hickorypondinn@aol.com); $89–149 per night. This longtime pet-friendly inn has a relaxed atmosphere, individually decorated guest rooms, cozy gathering rooms, and a greenhouse-style dining room where continental breakfasts are served each morning. The historic building sits next to a large field where there is plenty of room to

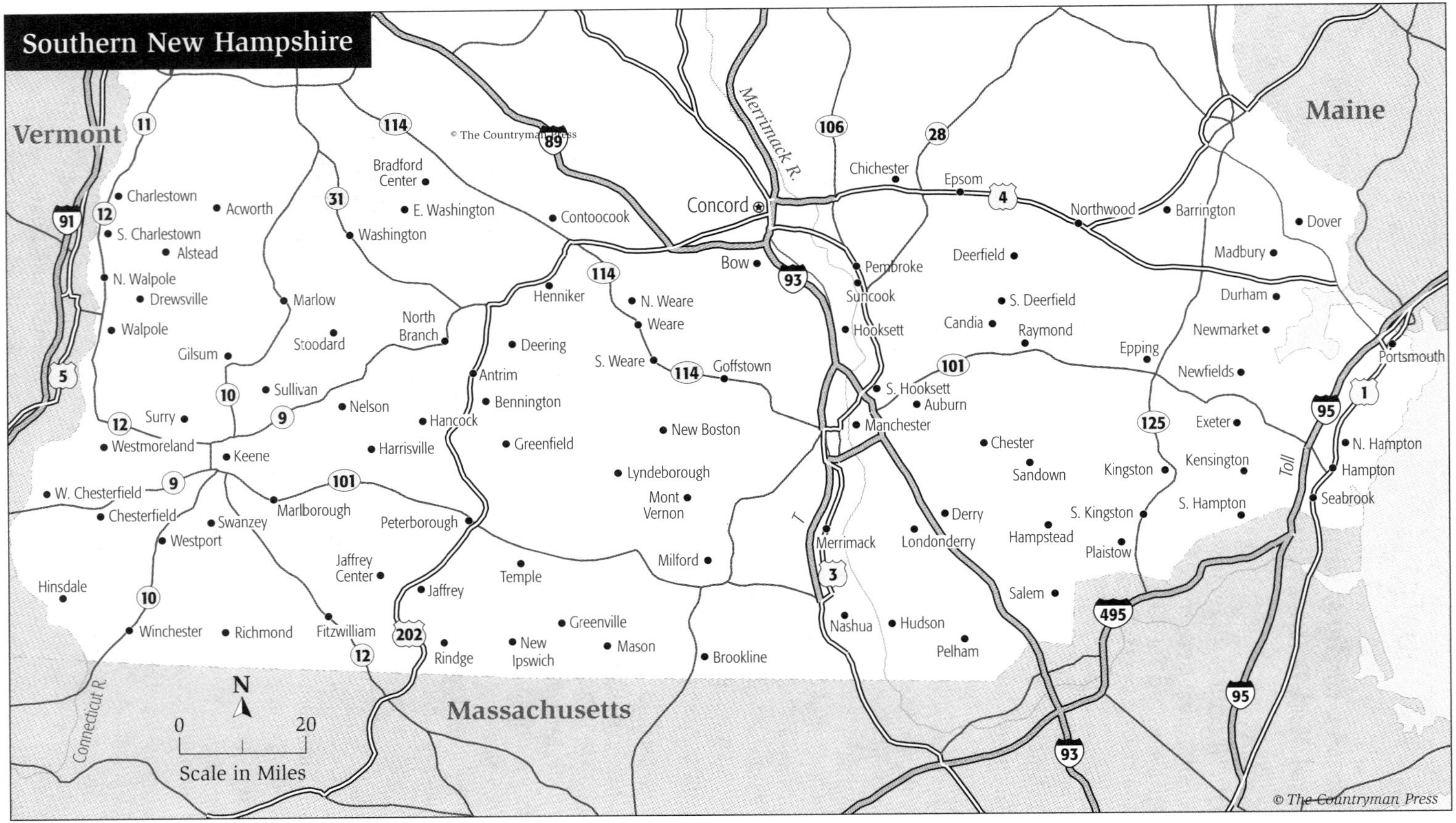
Southern New Hampshire
Vermont
Maine
Massachusetts
Merrimack R.
Connecticut R.
Toll
Concord
Charlestown
S. Charlestown
Alstead
Acworth
N. Walpole
Drewsville
Walpole
Marlow
Gilsum
Stoodard
Sullivan
Surry
Westmoreland
Keene
W. Chesterfield
Chesterfield
Swanzey
Westport
Hinsdale
Winchester
Richmond
Fitzwilliam
Marlborough
Nelson
Harrisville
Hancock
North Branch
Washington
E. Washington
Bradford Center
Contoocook
Henniker
Deering
Antrim
Bennington
Greenfield
Peterborough
Jaffrey Center
Jaffrey
Rindge
Temple
New Ipswich
Greenville
Mason
Milford
Brookline
Mont Vernon
Lyndeborough
New Boston
S. Weare
Weare
N. Weare
Goffstown
Bow
Pembroke
Suncook
Hooksett
S. Hooksett
Auburn
Manchester
Merrimack
Nashua
Hudson
Pelham
Londonderry
Derry
Salem
Chester
Sandown
Hampstead
Plaistow
S. Kingston
Kingston
Candia
Raymond
S. Deerfield
Deerfield
Chichester
Epsom
Northwood
Barrington
Dover
Madbury
Durham
Newmarket
Epping
Newfields
Exeter
Kensington
S. Hampton
Seabrook
Hampton
N. Hampton
Portsmouth
11
12
91
5
10
9
101
202
31
114
89
106
28
4
93
3
101
125
495
95
1
N
0
20
Scale in Miles
© The Countryman Press

walk your dog. Guests can also enjoy free high-speed Internet access, air-conditioning, cable television, and private baths in most rooms. Pets are welcome for an extra $25 per stay (not per night). "We do get a substantial amount of guests with dogs, and we enjoy them all," says owner Jane Sparks.

Francestown

Inn at Crotched Mountain, 534 Mountain Rd., Francestown (603-588-6840; www.innatcrotchedmt.com); $80–150 per night. Children and pets are always welcome at this homey, 13-room country inn, a member of the Select Registry (www.selectregistry.com). The three resident English cocker spaniels will show you around the 1800s home and the property's on-site walking and cross-country skiing trails, flower and vegetable gardens, swimming pool, and tennis courts. Guests will also enjoy the views of the mountain and surrounding valley. Dog owners pay an additional $5 per night, and a full breakfast is included in the room rate.

Hampton

Best Western Inn of Hampton, 815 Lafayette Rd., Hampton (603-780-7234; 1-800-556-4638; www.bestwestern.com); $119–199 per night. Amenities at this coastal hotel include an indoor swimming pool, a complimentary hot breakfast, a hot tub, a fitness center, a restaurant, and a lounge. Guests can choose from standard guest rooms, executive-level rooms, or deluxe suites. Pets are permitted in smoking rooms without extra charges.

Hancock

Hancock Inn, 33 Main St., Hancock (603-525-3318; 1-800-525-1789; innkeeper@hancockinn.com; www.hancockinn.com); $195–270 per night. Dating to 1789, the Hancock Inn is New Hampshire's oldest continuously operating accommodation, and it used to be a cattle driver's stop. Pet guests are welcome in the Drovers Room, a suite on the first floor with a patio, antique furniture, a king-size bed, and a fireplace. Guests also enjoy full country breakfasts, gathering-room parlors, and a tavern.

Keene

Holiday Inn Express Keene, 175 Key Rd., Keene (603-352-7616; 1-888-465-4329; www.ihg.com); $95–249 per night. Pets are allowed in smoking rooms for an extra $25 per night at this Holiday Inn Express, which features a 24-hour front desk, a fitness center, a swimming pool, laundry facilities, "deluxe expanded" continental breakfasts, cable television, and free local calls and morning newspapers.

Manchester

Comfort Inn Manchester, 298 Queens City Ave., Manchester (603-668-2600; 1-800-228-5150; www.choicehotels.com); $92–135 per night. This hotel caters to southern Hew Hampshire travelers with an indoor pool and a sauna; laundry facilities; cable television and VCRs; in-room microwaves, hair dryers, and irons; a newsstand; and free continental breakfasts. Pet owners must stay in smoking rooms and pay with a credit card: The pet fee is $25 per stay with a maximum of two pets per room and a weight limit of 60 pounds. .

Holiday Inn Express Hotel & Suites, 1298 S. Porter St., Manchester (603-669-6800; www.ihg.com); $104–199 per night. Pets are permitted guests at this airport hotel offering free high-speed Internet access, daily buffet breakfasts, 107 guest rooms and suites, an indoor swimming pool and a hot tub, a fitness center, meeting rooms, and laundry facilities. Each room also has a hair dryer, an iron, and an ironing board.

Radisson Hotel Manchester, 700 Elm St., Manchester (603-625-1000; www.radisson.com); $179–204 per night. This Radisson hotel (formerly known as the Center of New Hampshire Holiday Inn) welcomes dogs for an additional $25 per stay (not per night). Guests will find high-speed Internet access, traditional rooms and larger suites, airport shuttles, a swimming pool, a fitness center, voice mail, bottled water, pillow-top beds, and in-room coffeemakers and hair dryers.

TownPlace Suites by Marriott Manchester, 690 Huse Rd., Manchester (603-641-2288; 1-800-627-7468; www.marriott.com); $89–179 per night. Designed for long-term stays, this Marriott facility has studio apartments and one- and two-bedroom suites; all accommodations have full kitchens. Other amenities include a swimming pool, a fitness center, laundry services, free high-speed Internet access, and cable television. Pets are allowed with a one-time nonrefundable fee of $100.

Merrimack

Comfort Inn Merrimack, 242 Daniel Webster Hwy., Merrimack (603-429-4600; 1-800-544-8313; www.choicehotels.com); $69–99 per night. This Days Inn's amenities include in-room coffeemakers and hair dryers, a 24-hour front desk, cable TV, free local calls, laundry facilities, and modem lines in each room. Pets weighing less than 10 pounds are allowed with an extra fee of $25 per night.

Nashua

Holiday Inn Nashua, 9 Northeastern Blvd., Nashua (603-888-1551; www.ihg.com); $109–189 per night. "Small" companion animals (call to see if yours qualifies) are permitted for an extra $25 per stay (not per night) at the Nashua Holiday Inn, where the amenities include an outdoor swimming pool, room service, a fitness center, in-room coffeemakers, a wake-up service, and in-room movies. Air-conditioning, a restaurant, and a lounge are also available.

Red Roof Inn Nashua, 77 Spitbrook Rd., Nashua (603-888-1893; www.redroof.com); $54–69 per night. This economy motel has clean rooms, cable television, laundry facilities, alarm clocks, a 24-hour front desk, in-room modem lines, free newspapers, express check-out services, and free local calls. One dog per room is permitted without extra fees.

Portsmouth

Meadowbrook Inn, Portsmouth Traffic Circle, intersection of Rte. 1 and I-95, Portsmouth (603-436-2700; 1-800-370-2727); $49–129 per night. The Meadowbrook Inn has 120 guest rooms, complimentary daily breakfasts, a lounge, cable television, an outdoor swimming pool, laundry facilities, and meeting rooms. Pets are allowed on a "short-term" basis with a refundable security deposit.

Motel 6 Portsmouth, 3 Gosling Rd., Portsmouth (603-334-6606; www.motel6.com); $52–79 per night. Kids stay for free at this Motel 6, which offers cable television, premium movie channels, laundry facilities, a swimming pool, modem hookups, and a convenient location near downtown shopping and restaurants. One well-behaved pet is welcome per room.

Residence Inn by Marriott Portsmouth, 1 International Dr., Portsmouth (603-436-8880; 1-800-331-3131; www.marriott.com); $159–219 per night. Business travelers are the most frequent guests at Residence Inns, which are designed for long-term stays. The Portsmouth location offers studio apartments and one- and two-bedroom suites, a swimming pool, a 24-hour front desk, a fitness center, and valet laundry services. Pets are allowed with a one-time nonrefundable fee of $100.

New Castle

Wentworth by the Sea, Hotel & Spa, 588 Wentworth Rd., New

ENJOY THE HISTORIC ELEGANCE OF WENTWORTH BY THE SEA ON NEW CASTLE ISLAND. (COURTESY OF WENTWORTH BY THE SEA/MARRIOTT)

TO REALLY "PUT ON THE DOG," RESERVE THE TOWER SUITE AT WENTWORTH BY THE SEA. (COURTESY OF WENTWORTH BY THE SEA/MARRIOTT)

Castle (603-422-7322; 1-866-240-6313; www.wentworth.com); $269–599 per night. Since 1874, this elegant hotel overlooking the Atlantic Ocean has welcomed world leaders, socialites, and celebrities. Renovated by the Marriott Group in 2003, the hotel was named one of the best in the world by *Travel and Leisure* magazine, and it boasts 161 guest rooms and suites, a full-service spa, a marina, and tennis and golf. Pets up to 30 pounds are welcome for an additional $30 per stay and must be leashed at all times; they cannot be left unattended in rooms.

Rindge

Woodbound Inn, 247 Woodbound Rd., Rindge (603-532-8341; 1-800-688-7770; info@woodbound.com; www.woodbound.com); $135–299 per night. Dogs and cats are welcome guests at the Woodbound Inn's waterfront cabins for an additional $15 per night. The one- and two-bedroom cabins are located near the main inn and have picture windows, small decks, Franklin stoves, king-size beds, and daybeds. Guests enjoy complimentary buffet-style breakfasts in the inn's dining rooms and share access to a private sandy beach, a gift shop, the Woodbound Inn's par-3 golf course, and 18 kilometers of hiking and cross-country skiing trails in a country setting.

Salem

Red Roof Inn Salem, 15 Red Roof Ln., Salem (603-898-6422; www.redroof.com); $49–89 per night. Pets are welcome at the Salem Red Roof Inn, which offers express check-out services, cable television, free newspapers and local calls, alarm clocks, and a 24-hour front desk. There are no extra fees for companion animals; one dog per room is permitted.

Surry

The Surry House Bed &

Breakfast, 50 Village Rd., Surry (603-352-2268; innkeepers@thesurryhouse.com); $75–150 per night. Built in 1865, the Surry House is a village farmhouse where guests will find an in-ground swimming pool, a sunroom, a great room, full country breakfasts each morning, cable television, afternoon snacks, flower gardens, and three individually decorated guest rooms. Pets are permitted with prior arrangement.

Temple

Auk's Nest Bed & Breakfast, 204 East Rd., Temple (603-878-3443; auksnest@aol.com); $75–175 per night. This 1700s B&B is located next to 350 protected acres with hiking and cross-country skiing trails. The three guest accommodations, including a newly created three-room suite, overlook gardens and an orchard. The home also has antiques, a screened-in porch, a common room with a fireplace, resident pets, homemade breads and jams, and organic fruits and eggs. Pets are welcome for an extra $5 per night; bring proof of vaccination.

Troy

Inn at East Hill Farm, 460 Monadnock St., Troy (603-242-6495; 1-800-242-6495; info@east-hill-farm.com; www.east-hill-farm.com); $124–150 per adult, per night; $45–99per child, per night. This family-centered resort keeps kids and adults busy with three swimming pools, a sauna, a lake beach, tennis and shuffleboard courts, children's recreation programs, boats, cross-country skiing, horseback riding, and interaction with the on-site farm animals. Leashed dogs are welcome in designated rooms for an extra $10 per dog, per night. The rates include three meals daily.

Wilton Center

Stepping Stones Bed & Breakfast, Bennington Battle Trail, Wilton Center (603-654-

ONE OF SEVERAL LAKEFRONT CABIN RENTALS AT THE WOODBOUND INN IN RINDGE

9048; 1-888-654-9048); $75–85 per night. This 1830s-era restored farmhouse B&B is surrounded by flower gardens, walking paths, and wildlife. Guest rooms are decorated with colors and textures inspired by nature. Breakfasts are served in the sunny garden room. Your leashed dog (sorry, no cats) is welcome to join the dog and cat that already live at Stepping Stones.

Campgrounds

Allenstown

Bear Brook State Park Campground, Rte. 28, Allenstown (603-485-9869); $25 per night. The 98 sites for tents and RVs (no hookups) at this seasonal campground are clustered around Beaver Pond. Camp amenities include laundry facilities, restrooms with showers, and a camp store. Leashed dogs are welcome, but they are not allowed on the beach. (See "Out and About" for more park information.)

Deering

Oxbow Campground, 8 Oxbow Rd., Deering (603-464-5952; office@oxbowcampground.net; www.oxbowcampground.net); $25–34 per night. Along with private sites for tents and RVs, Oxbow has a swimming pond, a beach, a playground, a recreation hall, scheduled family activities, and two camping cabins. Pets should be leashed, quiet, and not left unattended. Although most visiting pets are dogs, the campground has also welcomed parrots and a wide variety of other creatures.

Greenfield

Greenfield State Park Campground, Rte. 136, Greenfield (603-271-3628); $25 per night. Certain sections of this large 257-site campground and park (see "Out and About") are designated for pet owners. Facilities include boat rentals, restrooms with showers, and a camp store. RVs are welcome, though the campground has no

Camping with Pets

The New Hampshire Campground Owner's Association offers a comprehensive guide called *New Hampshire Loves Campers*, which includes pet policies for all of its member campgrounds. Details include the number of pets allowed per campsite, what proof of vaccination/vet record is needed, and what kind of amenities each campground offers. For example, many campgrounds have pet-friendly sections and some, like Chocorua Camping Village, even have their own dog parks. You can order a copy of the guide or download it at www.ucampnh.com/campgroundguide.html.

hookups. Pets must be leashed and are not allowed on the beach.

North Hampton

Shel-Al Campground, 115 Lafayette Rd., North Hampton (603-964-5730; www.shel-al.com); $34–44 per night. Tenters and RVers will both find sites at Shel-Al, a family-run campground located near beaches and other coastline attractions. Campers can also enjoy a playground, shuffleboard courts, a camp store, and restrooms with showers. Leashed pets are welcome, provided their owners clean up after them and don't leave them alone at a site.

Rindge

Woodmore Campground, 21 Woodmore Dr., Rindge (603-899-3362; www.woodmorecampground.com); $35–44 per night. The McLay family runs this waterfront campground located on Lake Contoocook; campers will find a camp store, an adult lounge, a game room, a pavilion area, a swimming pool, a playground, basketball and sand volleyball courts, boat rentals, firewood and propane, and scheduled activities on weekends. Dogs are welcome, but they must be leashed and owners must clean up after them.

West Swanzey

Swanzey Lake Camping Area, 88 East Shore Rd., West Swanzey (603-352-9880; info@swanzeylake.com; www.swanzeylake.com); $28–34 per night or $155–200 per week. "We are pet people and very much enjoy those special members of the family," says Swanzey lake co-owner Jill Amadon. The 88 campsites can accommodate tents as well as RVs. Lake swimming, hanging out at the dock, boating, and shopping at the camp store are popular activities. Dogs are not allowed on the beach or on the lawn; owners are asked to clean up any messes and to not leave their pet unattended at the site.

Homes, Cottages, and Cabins for Rent

Warner

Gossler Camps, 18 Fourth Rd., Warner (603-456-3679; gosslercamps@msn.com); $525–625 per week. Guests have been visiting the Gossler cabins for more than 60 years. They vary in size, but each is fully furnished with a bathroom and a kitchen, and offers views of Tucker Pond. Sailboats, canoes, kayaks, rowboats, and paddleboats are all available to guests. Leashed, quiet dogs are welcome.

OUT AND ABOUT

Abby Fund Yard Sale, Nashua. This annual gathering of shoppers and animal lovers is held each summer to benefit the **Humane Society for Greater Nashua.** Volunteers are always needed to donate items and run booths. For updated information on this year's location and date, contact the society by calling 603-889-BARK, or visit www .hsfn.org.

Annual Pet Step. All leashed and friendly dogs are welcome to attend this yearly fund-raiser for the **Animal Rescue League of New Hampshire.** The festivities include a 1.5-mile dog walk ($10 registration fee), doggie games, agility competitions, Flyball demonstrations, and numerous vendors selling animal-related wares. For more information about this year's event, visit www.rescueleague.org, call 603-472-3647, or write to the shelter at 545 Rte. 101, Bedford, NH 03110.

Ashuelot Covered Bridge, Bolton Rd., Winchester. One of the most-visited covered bridges in New Hampshire, this elaborate and unique crossing was built in 1864. Its bright red roof covers two spans and lattice openings along the 169-foot-long sides.

Bear Brook State Park, Rte. 28, Allenstown (603-485-9874; 603-485-9869). Leashed pets are welcome (though not on the beach) at this 10,000-acre park with a campground (see "Accommodations—Campgrounds") and extensive day-use facilities, including 40 miles of hiking trails for horseback riders, hikers, dog walkers, and mountain bikers. Boat rentals, several fishing ponds, a fitness course, and target and archery ranges are also available.

Canobie Lake Park, 85 N. Policy St., P.O. Box 190, Salem 03079 (I-93 North to Exit 2 in Salem; 603-893-3506; www.canobie.com). It may be hard to believe, but this popular amusement park does in fact welcome well-behaved companion dogs—all breeds except pit bulls and rottweilers—to enjoy the fun with the family. That's not to say that this is a dog-focused place: On a recent trip to the park, Sadie (the canine coauthor of *Dog-Friendly New England*) and her family saw no other dogs at all among the hundreds of visitors. (It's definitely a good idea to call before arriving, just to make sure the policy hasn't changed since the time of this writing.) Also, the setup of an amusement park is not especially convenient for dog owners. If you want to ride the rides, for example, one person will have to stay behind with the pup. Still, it's great to know that vacationers and others with dogs in tow can still enjoy a "day at the park." And funnel cake.

Chesterfield Gorge Natural Area, Rte. 9, Chesterfield (603-239-8153). This relatively small 13-acre park has great views; a walking trail winds past **Wilde Brook** and the impressive **Chesterfield Gorge.** Picnic tables provide nice spots for a rest and a snack. Pets must be on a leash.

Greenfield State Park, Rte. 136, Greenfield (603-547-3497). Hike, boat, fish, bird-watch, or have a picnic at the 400-acre Greenfield State Park, which offers walking trails, ponds,

Pets in New Hampshire State Parks

The policies vary from park to park, but most do allow leashed dogs. However, pets are not allowed in picnic areas, on state beaches, or at historic sites. You can download a complete PDF of regulations at www.nhstateparks.org/explore/visiting/traveling-with-pets.aspx.

wetlands, and forestlands. Pets are allowed in designated areas; watch for signs. The park's best-known feature is its campground (see "Accommodations—Campgrounds" for more information).

Hampton State Pier, off Rte. 1A, Hampton (603-436-1552). If you're in town with your pet and dying for some ocean views, the dogs-allowed pier might be one of your only chances. Located next to the Seabrook Bridge, this popular fishing and boat-launching area is a fun place to hang out and watch the busy harbor activities.

Harbour Trail, Portsmouth. Winding throughout Portsmouth's downtown and historic area, this self-guided tour of the city takes you past the waterfront, quaint backstreets, shops, restaurants, and 17th-, 18th-, and 19th-century homes and churches. Guided tours are available on some weekends, and you can download a free map at www.portsmouthnh.com/harbourtrail. For more information, call 603-610-5518 or visit www.portsmouthnh.com.

Miller State Park, Rte. 101, Peterborough (603-924-3672). You can drive or hike to the 2,290-foot summit of majestic **Pack Monadnock Mountain,** the centerpiece of this popular park that's open daily in warm weather and on weekends in spring and fall. Once you get to the top, there are plenty of well-marked trails of varying lengths for hikers of all abilities. Or just relax and enjoy the summit views and have a picnic at one of the provided tables. (Note: Don't confuse this mountain with the better-known Mount Monadnock down the road, where dogs are not allowed.)

Monadnock Humane Society Adoption and Learning Center, Rte. 10, West Swanzey. With walking trails, agility programs, doggie play areas, and a retail shop (see **Animal Tracks** under "Hot Spots for Spot"), this 74-acre site is a friendly home for local shelter animals and a fun stop for visiting pet owners. The society's annual **Walk for Animals** is its primary fundraiser; usually held in September, the event has something for every cat and dog lover, including talent contests, a sponsored walk, and a Canine Carnival. For more information, visit www.monadnockhumanesociety.org or call 603-352-9011.

Pisgah State Park, Rtes. 119, 63, and 10, Chesterfield and Winchester (603-271-3254). With more than 13,000 acres, this rugged park is New Hampshire's largest. Leashed dogs are welcome to join their owners as they explore forested paths, ponds, wetlands, and marsh ecosystems. Hiking, biking, and fishing are among the most popular activities; motorized vehicles such as snowmobiles and all-terrain vehicles (ATVs) are also allowed.

Portsmouth Dog Park, South Mill Pond, Portsmouth (www.cityofportsmouth.com). Spayed and neutered dogs over four months of age are welcome to romp in this fenced-in, off-leash area with benches, shaded areas, trash cans, and water spigots. Owners are asked to use pooper-scooper bags to clean up any messes. To reach the park, take Pleasant Street from the center of town, then bear right at the park's parking lot. The dog area is located in the center of the park.

Urban Forestry Center, 45 Elwyn Rd., Portsmouth (603-431-6774). This local gem's facilities include a 95-acre forest with self-guided trails, a tree-farm and forestry demonstration area, salt marshes, dense woodlands, and gardens filled with native perennials and annuals. The nature and education center also hosts programs throughout the year to promote the healthy management of New Hampshire's forests and natural resources. Dogs are welcome on a leash; the staff even provides environmentally friendly "mutt mitts" to clean up messes.

QUICK BITES

Barley House, 132 N. Main St., Concord (603-228-6363; www.thebarleyhouse.com). Visiting the State House for business or pleasure? The Barley House is right across the street. You can order lunch or dinner to go from its pub-style menu, with items like firecracker shrimp cocktail, the State House Caesar salad, and smoked pork chops, or grab a burger and a craft brew.

Black Forest Café and Bakery, 212 Rte. 101, Amherst (603-672-0500; www.theblackforestcafe.com). Although this quaint bakery and café does offer an indoor dining room, dog lovers will probably be more interested in the restaurant's Marketplace options: These take-out items include tarragon shrimp salad wraps, barbecue pork sandwiches, hummus and vegetable wraps, soups, and Black Forest chicken salad wraps. Sorry folks . . . no Black Forest cake in sight!

Hermanos Cocina Mexicana, 11 Hills Ave., Concord (603-224-5669; for takeout: 603-228-5788;

www.hermanosmexican.com). Hermanos doesn't have any outdoor seating, but everything on the menu is available for take-out. Make your selection from Mexican specialties like *pollo estufa, taquitos,* Jake's nachos, *pastor de avocado,* and even strawberry burritos for dessert. "We're also happy to provide pet owners with plastic containers full of water for their animals," says Hermanos's Jane Valliere.

Keene Fresh Salad, 44 Main St., Keene (603-357-6677; www.keenefreshsalad.com). Here's a healthy stop for greens, veggies, hot and cold drinks, soups, and a good selection of quick entrées. Selections include greek, chef, chicken Caesar, and club salads. Grab a take-out lunch to enjoy on your hike—or drive—up Pack Monadnock.

Kimball Farm, Rte. 124, Jaffrey (603-532-5765; www.kimballfarm.com). If you passed through the Monadnock region without a visit to Kimball's, you'd be among the minority; this famous ice-cream shop serves its cool treats (more than 40 homemade flavors) from take-out windows with plenty of outdoor picnic tables. Expect a crowd.

L.A. Burdick, 47 Main St., Walpole (603-756-2882; www.burdickchocolate.com). There are a few chairs out in front of L.A. Burdick's, all the better to relax and enjoy your sinful chocolate creations. This café and candy shop has a wide array of yummy choices, including simple cookies, pastries, and chocolates, as well as lunch items like yellowtail tuna and salads.

Main Street restaurants, Durham. Popular with the local college crowd, this strip of coffee shops, bars, and restaurants offers plenty of sidewalk seating in warm weather and take-out meals year-round. Try a slice at **Joe's New York Pizza and Subs** (45 Main St.; 603-868-5300; www.joesnypizza.com) and watch all the local dogs trot by.

Nadeau's Subs, 100 Cahill Ave., **South Side, Manchester** (603-669-SUBS); and 776 Mast Rd., **West Side, Manchester** (603-623-9315; www.nadeausubs.com). Nadeau's offer two locations in Manchester, both serving fat sandwiches, healthy wraps, and a wide variety of salads. The family-run business is perhaps best known for its steak-and-cheese subs, but you'll also find choices like Italian eggplant sandwiches, beef taco wraps, and fried-chicken salad.

Pizza Bella, 178 Rte. 101, Bedford Village Shops, Bedford (603-472-8560; www.pizzabella.net). Pizza Bella offers delivery, take-out, and eat-in dining options for hungry locals and travelers in the Bedford area. In addition to pizza made with fresh dough, the menu choices include ravioli, chicken wings, burgers, chicken parmigiana, antipasto, steak bombs, and cold sandwiches. You can even visit the Web site to view your choices before you call in your order.

HOT SPOTS FOR SPOT

All Dogs Gym & Inn, 505 Sheffield Rd., Manchester (603-669-4644; info@alldogsgym.com; www.alldogsgym.com). No matter what your pet needs might be, All Dogs can probably fill them: The canine-focused center offers myriad training classes, doggie day care with plenty of interaction, overnight boarding with playtimes and optional "luxury suites," agility and other sports classes, and "spa" grooming services.

American K9 Country, 336 Rte. 101, Amherst (603-672-8448; www.americank9country.com). This place has it all for dogs and dog lovers: luxury boarding facilities, doggie day care, a wide array of grooming services, agility and training classes, sheep-herding programs, and even a dog park that's open to the public. Whether you live nearby or you're just passing through, this spot is definitely worth a sniff.

Animal Tracks, Monadnock Humane Society (MHS), Rte. 10, West Swanzey (603-352-9011; www.monadnockhumanesociety.org). Located at the **Monadnock Humane Society's Adoption and Learning Center** (see "Out and About"), this well-stocked retail shop has gift items like mugs and picture frames, along with pet toys, beds, bowls, leashes and collars, and food. All proceeds benefit the animals at the shelter.

Canine Cupboard Gourmet Dog Treats, 102 State St., Portsmouth (603-431-0082; www.caninecupboard.com). This is Portsmouth's original boutique for dogs, located in the historic downtown area. Two-legged and four-legged browsers will find fresh-baked treats such as Muddy Paws, Pupcakes, Peanut Butter Banana Bones, and Homey Cheesecake Chews, in addition to a wide selection of toys, leashes, collars, and gifts for animal lovers. Dogs, of course, are always welcome inside the store.

Concord Agway, 258 Sheep Davis Rd., Concord (603-228-8561; www.osbornesagway.com); and **Hookset Agway,** 343 Londonderry Tpke., Hookset (603-627-6855). Both of these Agway locations stock plenty of pet supplies, including leashes, toys, rawhide chewies, and pet-food brands such as Nutro, Science Diet, Iams, Big Red, and Eukanuba. The newest store is in Winnisquam on Rte. 3 in Belmont.

Granite State Dog Training Center, 90 Rte. 101A, Amherst (603-672-DOGS; www.gsdtc.com). In addition to its extensive training programs, Granite State also offers overnight boarding and doggie day care in heated and air-conditioned indoor/outdoor runs, as well as shampoos, cuts, clips, and other grooming services.

Riverside Canine Center, 48 Bridge St., Nashua (603-889-9800; www.riversidek9.com). Since 1998, Riverside has been providing dogs and dog lovers with services such as doggie day care, canine massage, grooming services, and chiropractic care. But the center is perhaps best known for its wide array of training classes and programs, including agility, obedience, and breed handling.

Rusty's General Store for Animals, 8 Maple St., Hopkinton (603-746-3434). You and your pup can stop by Rusty's for all your food, treat, and supply needs. The store stocks brands such as Timber Wolf Organics, The Wholistic Pet, Artemis, and Katie's Bumpers.

Sendaishi Pet Resort, 355 Straw Rd., Manchester (603-622-9684; www.sendaishi.com). This place sounds more like a summer camp than a kennel: Canine guests can enjoy supervised swimming in two pools, nature trails around a pond and through the woods, a "playschool" program, overnight boarding, doggie day care, grooming, agility classes, and more. Your pet will hardly miss you at all.

Silver Clippers, 9 Broad St., Nashua (603-886-1974; www.silverclippers.com). Licensed with the National Dog Groomer's Association of America, Silver Clippers aims to provide cuts, baths, nail clips, blow-drys, and other services with an extra dose of gentle TLC. Appointments are required.

Woodlawn Pet Resort, 406 Poverty Plains Rd., Warner (603-746-4201; info@woodlawnkennels.com; www.woodlawnkennels.com). Woodlawn offers a variety of services for your four-legged friend, including overnight boarding, doggie day care, playgroups, grooming services, obedience and agility classes, and a small retail shop selling toys, books, training aids, food, and other products.

ANIMAL SHELTERS AND HUMANE SOCIETIES

All Breed Rescue and Adoption, P.O. Box 1861, Seabrook 03874 (603-580-2121)

Animal Allies, P.O. Box 693, Manchester 03105 (603-228-6755)

Animal Placement and Puppy Service, 488 Main St., Sandown (603-887-2228)

Animal Rescue League of New Hampshire, 545 Rte. 101, Bedford (603-472-3647; www.rescueleague.org)

Cocheco Valley Humane Society, 262 County Farm Cross Rd., Dover (603-749-5322; www.cvhsonline.org)

Fast Friends Greyhound Rescue, 14 W. Swanzey Rd., West Swanzey (603-355-1556)

Friends of the Manchester Animal Shelter, 490 Dunbarton Rd., Manchester (603-628-3544)

Greater Derry Humane Society, 57 Lawrence Rd., P.O. Box 142, East Derry 03041 (603-434-1512; www.derryhumanesociety.com)

Humane Society for Greater Nashua, 24 Ferry Rd., Nashua (603-889-BARK; www.hsfn.org)

Manchester Animal Shelter, 490 Dunbarton Rd., Manchester (603-628-3544)

Monadnock Humane Society, 101 W. Swanzey Rd., West Swanzey (603-352-9011; www.monadnockhumanesociety.org)

New Hampshire Animal Rights League (advocacy), P.O. Box 4211, Concord 03302 (603-472-3647; www.nhanimalrights.org)

New Hampshire SPCA, P.O. Box 196, Stratham 03885 (603-772-2921; www.nhspca.org)

Pelham Animal Control, Simpson Mill Rd., Pelham (603-635-2211)

Salem Animal Rescue League, 4 SARL Dr., Salem (603-893-3210; www.sarlnh.org)

IN CASE OF EMERGENCY

Animal Emergency Clinic, 2626 Brown Ave., Manchester (603-666-6677)

Animal Hospital of Nashua, 168 Main Dunstable Rd., Nashua (603-880-3034)

Court Street Veterinary Hospital, 686 Court St., Keene (603-357-2455)

Great Bay Animal Hospital, 31 Newmarket Rd., Durham (603-868-7387)

Henniker Veterinary Hospital, Rte. 114 and Rte. 202, Henniker (603-428-3441)

Jaffrey-Rindge Veterinary Clinic, 109 River St., Jaffrey (603-532-7114)

North Hampton Animal Hospital, 83 Lafayette Rd., North Hampton (603-964-7222)

Russell Animal Hospital, 286 Pleasant St., Concord (603-224-2361)

MULLET TAKES AN AFTERNOON SIESTA ON HIS BALCONY AT THE COPPOERTOPPE INN. (COURTESY OF COPPERTOPPE INN AND RETREAT CENTER)

Central New Hampshire

Lake Winnipesaukee's busy shoreline has attracted New England visitors for years with affordable accommodations, waterslides, video arcades, go-cart tracks, campgrounds, boat rentals, and other family-centered activities and events. Finding a place to stay here is not a problem—unless you're visiting with Rover. "There must be a hundred motels within a mile of us," says one animal-friendly motel owner, "and only one or two allow pets." Still, with that many accommodations to start with, the odds are in your favor of finding at least one "pets allowed" lodging you'll like—and one is all you need. Hotels and motels are not as plentiful in the western reaches, home to renowned Dartmouth College and Lake Sunapee, but this quieter area appeals to those looking to escape the Winnipesaukee crowds.

Activities for pet owners are not plentiful in central New Hampshire. Many of the attractions are indoors, and even most of the outdoor nature centers, boat tours, and town fairs ban companion animals. Also, don't assume that a state park sign is a green light for dogs. Most state parks allow pets (see "Out and About"), and then only on a leash, but pets are not allowed on any state beaches, in picnic areas, or on historic sites. That's not to say there's nothing to do in central New Hampshire with your dog: Scenic drives, canoe trips, quiet walks in the woods, geology lessons, and bustling downtown scenes are plentiful enough to fill up at least one restful and fun vacation in this beautiful region of the state.

ACCOMMODATIONS

Hotels, Motels, Inns, and Bed & Breakfasts

Andover

Owl's Nest Lodge and Conference Center, 22 Camp Marlyn Ln., Andover (603-735-5159; owlsnest@tds.com); cottages, $700 per week; lodge, $60 per person, per weekend. Well-behaved pets are welcome in the Owl's Nest's two cottages, which have private docks, canoes, kitchens, and porches, as well as at the lodge, which is designed to accommodate large groups (up to 50 people) with seven bunk rooms, a dining area, a large kitchen, and a deck. Dogs must be on a leash.

Center Harbor

Lake Shore Motel & Cottages, Rte. 25, 76 Lake Shore Dr., Center Harbor (603-253-6244; www.lakeshoremotelandcottages.com); $110–199. Choose from motel rooms and cottages at this family-oriented accommodation. Each cottage unit has a screened-in porch, a full kitchen, and cable television. The motel building has efficiencies and two- and three-room suites, all with air-conditioning. Well-behaved dogs are welcome as long as their owners clean up after them and don't leave them unattended at any time.

Chocorua

Lazy Dog Inn, Rte. 16, 201

MOLLY LOOKS RELAXED IN HER NAMESAKE ROOM (MOLLY'S MONET ROOM) AT THE LAZY DOG INN IN CHOCORUA. (PHOTO COURTESY OF LAZY DOG INN)

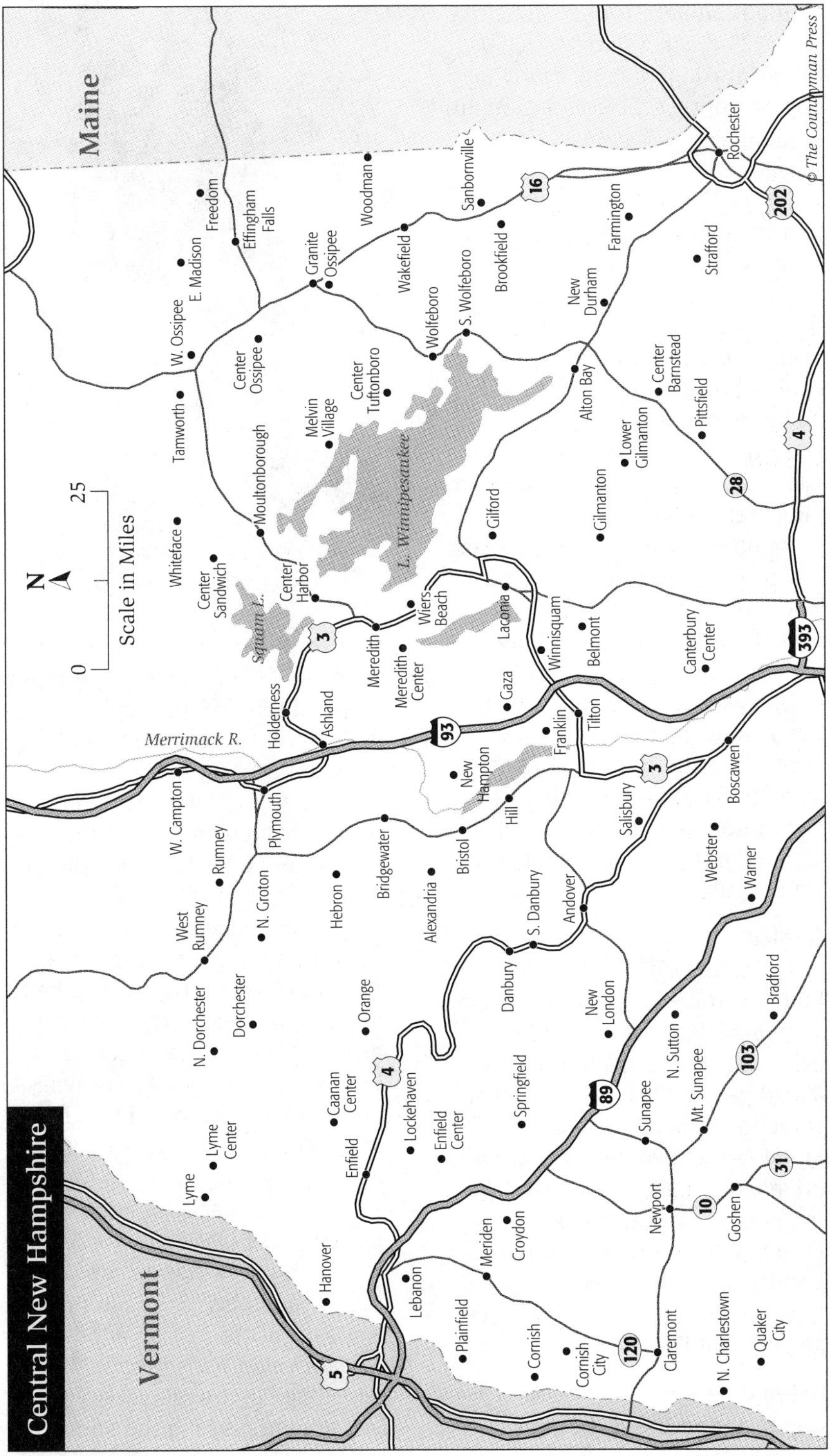
Central New Hampshire
Vermont
Maine
N
0
25
Scale in Miles
Merrimack R.
Squam L.
L. Winnipesaukee
© The Countryman Press
Lyme
Lyme Center
Hanover
Lebanon
Plainfield
Cornish
Cornish City
Meriden
Croydon
Claremont
N. Charlestown
Quaker City
Newport
Goshen
Enfield
Enfield Center
Lockehaven
Caanan Center
Springfield
Sunapee
Mt. Sunapee
N. Sutton
Bradford
New London
Orange
N. Dorchester
Dorchester
West Rumney
N. Groton
Rumney
W. Campton
Plymouth
Hebron
Bridgewater
Alexandria
Bristol
Danbury
S. Danbury
Andover
Webster
Warner
Salisbury
Boscawen
Hill
New Hampton
Franklin
Tilton
Gaza
Ashland
Holderness
Meredith
Meredith Center
Center Harbor
Center Sandwich
Whiteface
Wiers Beach
Laconia
Winnisquam
Belmont
Canterbury Center
Gilford
Gilmanton
Lower Gilmanton
Pittsfield
Center Barnstead
Alton Bay
Moultonborough
Tamworth
Melvin Village
Center Tuftonboro
W. Ossipee
Center Ossipee
E. Madison
Effingham Falls
Freedom
Granite
Ossipee
Wolfeboro
S. Wolfeboro
Wakefield
Woodman
Brookfield
Sanbornville
New Durham
Farmington
Strafford
Rochester
3
4
5
10
16
28
31
89
93
103
120
202
393

White Mountain Hwy., Chocorua (603-323-8350; 1-888-323-8350; info@lazydoginn.com; www.lazydoginn.com); $120–190 per night. Some places *allow* dogs. This place *prefers* them. The inn's motto is "a truly dog friendly bed and breakfast." FDR once stayed here, so it's no surprise to find a "Roosevelt Room." Vacationing dog owners have found a friend at the Lazy Dog Inn, where canine hosts Meghan and Molly will show your pup a howlin' good time with a Doggy Lodge (day-care facility), a fenced-in play area, agility equipment, and a bottomless treat jar in the guest kitchen. The restored farmhouse also has seven individually decorated guest rooms with names like Sit and Stay Awhile Suite, Country Dog Room, and Fetch Me a Quilt Room. As another bonus, the inn has an ideal location for those who want to visit attractions in the central as well as northern regions of New Hampshire.

Franklin

D. K. Motel, 390 N. Main St., Franklin (603-934-3311; saratracy@mymailstation.com); $60–85 per night. For an additional $5–10 per night, your pet is welcome in smoking rooms at D. K. Motel (so named because it offers double and king-size beds). The motel is located at the corner of Route 3A and a dead-end road and has a large fenced-in yard; Max the dog and four parakeets already call D. K. home.

Hebron

CINNAMON, A SLED DOG AT COPPERTOPPE (COURTESY OF COPPERTOPPE INN AND RETREAT CENTER)

Coppertoppe Inn & Retreat Center, 8 Range Rd., Hebron (603-744-3636; www.coppertoppe.com); $179–259 per night. This beautiful resort overlooks Newfound Lake, the deepest lake in the region and one of the cleanest in the world. Coppertoppe loves your "fur-rever" family and offers two special pet packages: the first includes two nights lodging, a full breakfast for two, a dog bed and bowls, treats, toys for Fido, and flowers and treats for his humans, for $343.50; it is available from September through May. The second package offers all of the same amenities for a suite that will accommodate four humans and two dogs, for $456. If you choose a standard room rather than one of the pet packages, expect to pay an additional $15 per night for your pal. Take advantage of a wide variety of water sports during the summer, and if you don't want to leave your dog in the room, enroll him in a training class at the nearby White Mountain College for Pets.

Holderness

The Cottage Place on Squam Lake, 1132 Rte. 3, Holderness (603-968-7116; cottageplace@adelphia.net; www.cottageplaceonsquam.com); $95–285 per night. Dog owners pay an extra $20 per night at The Cottage Place (formerly known as the Black Horse Motor Court.) The cottages vary in size and style; other accommodations options include Cottage Suites and The Lodge. Guests will enjoy a 140-foot sandy lake beach, a boat launch, boat and kayak rentals, a playground, a coffee shop, Internet access, and picnic areas. The cottages are also available for rent by the week.

Laconia

Lake Opechee Inn & Spa, 62 Doris Ray Ct., Laconia (603-524-0111; 1-877-300-LAKE; www.opecheeinn.com); $149–409 per night. This 34-room inn and spa welcomes pets in two of its rooms: One has a king bed, and the other has two queen beds. (The rooms can also be joined for larger parties.) Guests will find hardwood floors, window seats, and in-room fireplaces, refrigerators, and coffeemakers. Other amenities include a full-service day spa, daily continental breakfasts, a gift shop, a fitness center, a game room, a swimming pool, and a hot tub. "We also have special amenities and packages available for owners who would like to spoil their pet a bit," explains the inn's sales and marketing manager Melissa Cota-Robles.

THE LAKE OPECHEE INN & SPA IN LACONIA WELCOMES DOGS IN TWO OF ITS GUEST ROOMS. (PHOTO COURTESY OF LAKE OPECHEE INN & SPA)

CALEB POSES WITH BILL AT THE COPPERTOPPE INN. (COURTESY OF COPPERTOPPE INN AND RETREAT CENTER)

Loudon

Red Roof Inn, 2 Staniels Rd., Loudon (603-225-8399; 1-800-RED-ROOF; www.redroof-loudon.com); $49–102 per night. One "small" pet (call to see if yours qualifies) per room is welcome at this Red Roof Inn, which

THE LAKES REGION OF NEW HAMPSHIRE IS A PERFECT PLACE FOR WATER-LOVING CANINES. (COURTESY OF COPPERTOPPE INN AND RETREAT CENTER)

offers an indoor swimming pool, interior corridors, complimentary continental breakfasts, alarm clocks, and cable television with premium movie channels. Dogs are not permitted in rooms with hot tubs.

Meredith

Inn at Mill Falls, 312 Daniel Webster Hwy, Meredith (603-279-7006; 1-877-203-3577; www.millfalls.com); $359–589 per night during the high season. Part of the Mill Falls at the Lake resort, which includes four inns, two lodges, and two cottages, both the Inn at Mill Falls and Church Landing welcome pets with plush beds, bowls, treats, a toy, and even a throw blanket for the sofa. $10 of the $25 per-night pet fee is donated to the local branch of the New Hampshire Humane Society, and you'll also be required to put a $350 damage deposit on your credit card at check-in, which is totally refundable. Set on 14 acres, the resort includes a lake activity center, 6 restaurants, the Cascade Spa and Salon, and 12 shops in the Historic Mill Falls Marketplace. Check the Web site for specials and package deals.

Town Line Motel, 4 Daniel Webster Hwy., Meredith (603-366-5570); $59–99 per night. "We have pets and we travel, so we know how tough it is to find a place," explains Town Line Motel's Nancy Brown, who manages and cleans the 16-room motel with her husband. Amenities include an outdoor swimming pool, color television, and air-conditioning. Pets are welcome without extra fees.

Mount Sunapee

Mount Sunapee Best Western Sunapee Lake Lodge, 1403 Rte. 103, Mount Sunapee (603-763-2010; 1-800-606-5253; info@sunapeelakelodge.com; www.sunapeelakelodge.com); $131–269 per night. This hotel has a good location for those hoping to explore the Dartmouth–Sunapee Lake region. The lodge's features include a swimming pool, a fitness center, free continental breakfasts, a restaurant and lounge, standard rooms and deluxe suites, cable television, and air-conditioning. Leashed dogs are allowed in designated rooms with advance notice. Pets are welcome for an additional $10 per day, up to $100 maximum, with a weight limit of 80 pounds and up to two pets per room.

Newport

Newport Motel, Rte. 11 and 103, Newport (603-863-1440; 1-800-741-2619; info@newportmotelnh.com); $65–90 per night. For an additional $10 per stay (not per night), your four-legged friend will be a welcome guest at this comfortable 50s-style family-owned motel. Visitors can enjoy coffee, juice, and homemade muffins each morning before they hit the plentiful nearby hiking trails. The motel's most unusual feature is its rates, which don't go up in summer.

Plymouth

Pilgrim Inn & Cottages, 307 Main St. (Rte. 3), Plymouth (603-536-1319; www.pilgriminnlakesregion.com); cottages, $55–145 per night. For an extra $10 per night, you're welcome to bring your pet to the cottages at Pilgrim Inn. Some units have kitchens, and regular rooms receive a complimentary breakfast. The innkeepers can also arrange "golf and stay" packages with three nearby courses, and "ski and stay" packages with Tenney Mountain and Waterville Valley ski areas. Animals must be crated when left alone in cottages.

Rochester

Anchorage Inn, 13 Wadleigh Rd., Rochester (603-332-3350; www.anchorageinns.com); $100–129 per night. Pets are welcome for an additional $15 per night plus a refundable $50 deposit at the Anchorage Inn's Rochester location, which offers a swimming pool, cable television with premium movie channels, air-conditioning, standard rooms, and kitchenette units. You and Spot can roam the property's walking trails and wide lawns, and enjoy its pond during your visit.

Governor's Inn, 78 Wakefield St., Rochester (603-332-0107; info@governorsinn.com; www.governorsinn.com); $99–175 per night. A popular site for weddings, the historic Governor's Inn offers 20 upscale, individually decorated guest rooms with private baths, air-conditioning, cable television, luxurious furnishings, an on-site restaurant, and daily continental breakfasts. Several rooms are set aside for pet owners. There are also two popular restaurants on-site: Spaulding Steak & Ale and the more casual Garage.

Sunapee

Dexter's Inn & Tennis Club, 258 Stagecoach Rd., Sunapee (603-763-5571; 1-800-232-5571; dexters@tds.net; www.dextersnh.com); $125–185 per night. Pets are allowed in some of the 19 guest rooms at Dexter's, an 1800s restored farmhouse with noted gardens, tennis courts, a library, fireplaces, a piano, a game room, a fitness room, lawn games, a swimming pool, a screened-in porch, and gathering rooms. Full country breakfasts are served each morning. You'll have gorgeous views of Mount Kearsage and Mount Sunapee.

Georges Mills Cottages, Sunapee (603-763-2369; info@georgesmillscottages.com; www.georgesmillscottages.com); $110–275 per night. Leashed dogs (sorry, no cats) are welcome in the cottages and town houses at this waterfront family resort between Otter Pond and Lake Sunapee. Some units have screened-in porches and balconies; all have kitchens, living rooms, and dining areas. Guests share access to a beach and docks. Dogs should be with their owners at all times. (The mailing address for the cottages is 1373 Rte. 11, Georges Mills, NH 03751.)

Tamworth

Tamworth Inn, 15 Cleveland Hill Rd., Tamworth (603-323-7721; 1-877-851-6763; tamworthinn@firstbridge.net; www.tamworth.com); $115–300 per night. Dagny, the resident St. Bernard, is the four-legged welcoming committee at the Tamworth Inn, a historic accommodation with antiques, private baths, down comforters, a swimming pool, and daily country breakfasts. Well-behaved pets are welcome for an additional $10 per day, provided they are leashed and not left unattended in the rooms at any time.

Weirs Beach

Channel Waterfront Cottages, 1192 Weirs Blvd. (Rte. 3), Weirs Beach (603-366-4673; www.channelcottages.com); $59–279 per night. These housekeeping cottages overlook a channel leading to Lake Winnipesaukee. The units vary in size and style: Each has cable television, fans, and telephones; some have kitchenettes, screened-in porches, and futon beds. Pets are welcome with advance notice and a $100 refundable fee, provided they are quiet, leashed, and well behaved.

Weirs Beach Cottages and Motel at the Highlands, Rte. 3, Weirs Beach (603-366-4604;

Mt. Washington Valley Goes to the Dogs

The Mt. Washington Valley Chamber of Commerce maintains a list of pet-friendly accommodations (www.mtwashingtonvalley.org), from small inns and motels to luxury resorts. The Mt. Washington National Forest has plenty of trails for hiking, and the region hosts Northern New England's largest pet expo, Bark in the Park, every September.

www.weirsbeachmotelcom); motel, $79–94 per night; cottages, $59–99 per night. The motel rooms and cottage units at Highlands can accommodate one to four people; some have kitchenettes. Shopping, restaurants, waterslides, and boat rentals are all within walking distance, and you can order takeout from the on-site restaurant. Pets are welcome with a $100 refundable security deposit. Expect the nightly rates to be slightly higher during Motorcycle Week.

West Lebanon

A Fireside Inn & Suites, 25 Airport Rd., West Lebanon (603-298-5906; 1-877-258-5900; info@firesideinnwestlebanon.com; www.firesideinnwestlebanon.com); $130–209 per night. Amenities at this full-service hotel include a restaurant, 126 guest rooms, a swimming pool and hot tub, a fitness center, laundry facilities, premium movie channels, free airport shuttles and morning newspapers, alarm clocks, and in-room coffeemakers. Pets are allowed for an extra $10 per night, provided they are not left unattended at any time.

Wolfeboro

The Cottages at Wolfeboro, 54 Center St., P.O. Box 1453, Wolfeboro 03894 (603-569-9999); $89–110 per night. Guests can choose from motel rooms and knotty-pine cottages at Center Street (formerly known as Berry Motel & Cottages). All accommodations have air-conditioning, electric heat, cable television, private baths, and telephones; some have screened-in porches and kitchenettes. Shopping, restaurants, and Lake Winnipesaukee are located within walking distance. Pet owners are asked to clean up after their animals.

Campgrounds

Ashland

Ames Brook Campground, 104 Winona Rd., Ashland (603-968-7998; amesbrook@amesbrook.com; www.amesbrook.com); $36–40 per night. This family campground has sites for tents and RVs, restrooms with showers, a camp store, laundry facilities, a swimming pool, a game room, a playground, and a basketball court. Hiking and biking trails are nearby. Two well-behaved, friendly pets per site are welcome, provided they are leashed at all times.

Yogi Bear's Jellystone Park, 35 Jellystone Park Rd., New Hampton (603-968-9000; www.abcamping.com/jellystonenh); $54–58 per night. What to make of this campground's pet policy? "Pets are permitted, but strongly discouraged." Hmmm. You decide if this is welcome enough for you and Fluffy. (Or if you're desperate enough for a place to park the RV.) The activities at this park include planned family events, swimming, boating, shuffleboard, dances, hayrides, and more.

Gilford

Gunstock Camping, Rte. 11A, 719 Cherry Valley Rd., Gilford (603-293-4341; 1-800-GUNSTOCK; camping@

gunstock.com; www.gunstock.com); $29–47 per night. Campers at Gunstock enjoy a camp store, restrooms with showers, swimming pools, movie nights and other scheduled activities, a propane filling station, and playgrounds. Guests can also take advantage of activities and events throughout the Gunstock ski resort property. Leashed pets are welcome if owners can show proof of vaccination (you must have the certficate, not just tags).

Meredith

Clearwater Campground, 26 Campground Rd., Meredith (603-279-7761; info@clearwatercampground.com; www.clearwatercampground.com); $38–49 per night. Clearwater Campground offers boat rentals, sports courts, a sandy beach, playgrounds, a recreation pavilion, video games, lake fishing, boat slips, modern restrooms, and camper activity nights. Leashed, quiet dogs are permitted, as long as you clean up any messes and steer clear of the beach.

Meredith Woods 4-Season Camping, Rte. 104, 26 Campground Rd., Meredith (603-279-5449; info@meredithwoods.com; www.meredithwoods.com); $35–49 per night. Your leashed, well-behaved pooch is welcome at Meredith Woods, provided you use pooper-scooper bags and control problem barking. Campers at Meredith Woods can enjoy a heated indoor swimming pool, a hot tub, modern restrooms, and a recreation center. Guests here also have full access to the facilities at Clearwater Campground (see listing above), located right across the street. Dogs are not allowed on the beach.

New Hampton

Twin Tamarack Family Camping and RV Resort, 41 Twin TamarackRd., New Hampton (603-279-4387; twintamarack@prodigy.net; www.twintamarackcampground.com); $35–40 per night. Located on the shores of Lake Pemigewasset, this campground offers lots of scheduled activities, a boat launch and boat rentals, sites for tents and RVs, a beach, restrooms with showers, a recreation hall, a swimming pool, and laundry facilities. Quiet, leashed pets are allowed but should not be left unattended at any time.

Newport

Crow's Nest Campground, 529 S. Main St., Newport (603-863-6170; www.crowsnestcampground.com); $30–42 per night. Set along the Sugar River, Crow's Nest has 120 shady and sunny sites with picnic tables, a swimming pool, a miniature golf course, a playground, a fishing pond, a camp store, a recreation hall, laundry facilities, and restrooms with showers. Leashed, well-behaved pets are welcome at campsites but not in rental cabins.

Orford

The Pastures, Rte. 10, Orford (603-353-4759; camp@thepastures.com; www.thepastures.com); $24–30 per night. Leashed dogs are always welcome at

The Pastures, as long as their owners clean up after them. The campground's amenities include 40- to 50-foot-wide sites with picnic tables, a swimming pool, restrooms with showers, boat rentals, volleyball courts, a putting green, and table tennis. Pets are also welcome at all on-site music concerts and festivals, including bluegrass, folk, and acoustic performances.

Washington

Pillsbury State Park Campground, Rte. 31, Washington (603-863-2860; 603-271-3628); $23 per night. Some of the sites at this rustic campground are available for walk-ins; others are offered by reservation only. Open from early May to late November, the campground has primitive sites, pit toilets, canoe rentals, and a playground. One large site is reserved for group youth reservations. For more information on the park, see "Out and About."

Weirs Beach

Weirs Beach Tent & Trailer Park, 198 Endicott St. N., Weirs Beach (603-366-4747; www.weirsonline.com); call for rate information. This campground is located within walking distance to Weirs Beach at Lake Winnipesaukee. Guests will find modern restrooms, a camp store, and 180 sites for tents and RVs. Leashed, quiet dogs are permitted as long they are not left unattended and owners pick up any messes they leave behind.

West Ossipee

Whit's End Campground, 140 Newman Drew Rd., West Ossipee (603-539-6060; whitsendllc@aol.com); $35–41 per night. Whit's End has 130 RV and tent sites spread across 50 acres on the Bearcamp River. Facilities include a heated swimming pool, a hot tub, beaches, a playground, a recreation hall, laundry facilities, modern restrooms, a dump station, and a camp store. Pets are welcome with proof of rabies vaccination.

Homes, Cottages, and Cabins for Rent

For cottages, condos, and vacation home rentals, check the local Craigslist, along with these local real estate rental companies:

www.lakesregion.org
www.lakesregionrentals.com
www.lakesregionrealestate.com
www.preferredrentals.com
www.anchorageatthelake.com

OUT AND ABOUT

Cardigan State Park, Rte. 118, Orange (603-485-2034). Most visitors come to this 5,655-acre park to scale the 3,121-foot peak of mighty Mount Cardigan. Of course, you don't have to go all the way to the top: Picnic areas and shorter (but still scenic) hik-

A DOWNTOWN PARK IN WOLFEBORO OVERLOOKING LAKE WINNIPESAUKEE

ing trails make this park a popular day-trip destination.

Downtown Wolfeboro. In addition to having several restaurants with outdoor seating and take-out ice-cream windows, the downtown area also offers a well-landscaped waterfront park with grassy areas, benches, and peaceful views.

The Fells: John Hay National Wildlife Refuge, Rte. 103A, Newbury (603-763-4789; fells@tds.net; www.thefells.org). Though dogs are not allowed in the gardens at this estate and wildlife preserve, they are welcome to join their owners across the road at the **Sunset Hill** and **Beech Brook trails.** The 4 miles of walking paths take you to the top of the scenic hill and through woodlands. A sign at the trailhead provides a useful trail map for visitors.

Gardner Memorial Wayside Area, Rte. 4A, Wilmont (603-924-5976). This large picnic area is part of the 6,675-acre **Gile State Forest.** Open in spring, summer, and fall, the site has a babbling brook and remnants of a 19th-century mill that once stood on the grounds. Dogs are welcome on a leash.

Laconia Motorcycle Week, Laconia. Suit up your Chihuahua with his best Harley-Davidson bandanna and head to the Laconia area in early June for the longest-running annual bike-rally event in America. Hotels and motels fill up well in advance, so do your planning early.

Lakes Region Humane Society (LRHS) Yard Sale, Tuftonboro. Every Labor Day weekend, the staff and volunteers at this nonprofit animal welfare organization holds a fund-raising yard sale to help the homeless pets in their care, including the Play Fore Pets Golf Tournament and the Dog Days of Summer 5K Run. The society also holds other special events, like sunset cruises and obedience classes, throughout the year. For updated schedules, call LRHS at 603-569-3549, visit www.lrhs.net, or stop by the shelter at 14 Winner's Circle Farm in Tuftonboro.

Madison Boulder Natural Area, Rte. 113, Madison (603-323-2087). This 17-acre area is named for the on-site granite boulder that is an impressive 83 feet long and 23 feet high, and weighs more than 5,000 tons (yes, tons). Thought to have been deposited here from northern New Hampshire by the movement of the glaciers, it is one of the largest such stones, called erratics, in the world. Take in the sight and then relax for a while in the picnic area. Dogs must be leashed.

Meriden Bird Sanctuary, Main St., Meriden. This relatively small 30-acre sanctuary is a popular dog-walking spot with locals. The trails wind through wooded and open areas; dogs are welcome on a leash.

New Hampshire Humane Society (NHHS) Events, Laconia. Pancake breakfasts, triathlons, and ice-cream socials are just some of the special events scheduled each year by the NHHS. If you're going to be in the area, feel free to stop by or lend a hand. For more information on upcoming events, call 603-524-3252, stop by the society's headquarters at 1305 Meredith Center Rd. in Laconia (Tuesday through Saturday), or visit www.nhhumane.org.

Norsk Cross-Country Skiing, 100 Country Club Ln., New London (603-526-4685; info@skinorsk.com). Norsk has been welcoming pooches on a few of its cross-country ski trails for many years. Leashed dogs are welcome on the North Flats, Partridge, Kellom, Sonya, Deer, and Moose trails (8K groomed). The management asks that you read the pet-guidelines page on their Web site before bringing your pup to Norsk. (Note: At the time of this writing, Norsk was considering a relocation; be sure to call for the latest information before planning a visit.)

Pillsbury State Park, Rte. 31, Washington (603-863-2860). Hiking, biking, camping (see "Accommodations—Campgrounds"), canoeing, and wildlife-watching are the main visitor activities at this 2,500-acre state park, where it's not uncommon to see loons, moose, and other native species. In addition to its many local trails, Pillsbury is also home to a stretch of the **Monadnock–Sunapee Greenway,** a 51-mile-long trail that runs between Mount Monadnock and Mount Sunapee.

Rollins State Park, Rte. 103, Warner (603-456-3808). Feeling lazy? You can drive to the scenic upper slopes and picnic area of the park's **Mount Kearsarge** via a 3.5-mile-long road starting at the park entrance. After an energizing picnic, you and Fluffy can hike a half mile to the summit. Either way, the views are impressive.

Scenic Drives. The roads around Lake Winnipesaukee are all fun to drive, including **Route 109, Route 11, Route 3** between Laconia and Holderness, and **Route 25**. Running past Newfound Lake, Route 3 also has pretty views. Toward the west, take a spin on **Route 12A** along the river between Claremont and

Lyme, or on **Route 4** between Boscawen and Danbury. Aside from I-89, there's no fast way to get anywhere in these parts, which is usually a good thing.

Sculptured Rocks Natural Area, between Rte. 3A and Rte. 188, Groton (603-547-3373). Situated on 272 acres along the Cockermouth River, this popular swimming and day-trip spot features interesting geological formations; its rocks have been molded into curves, dips, and odd angles by running water. You can walk through, view the sights from a park bridge, or settle in for a picnic. Use caution when swimming—the water is very cold, and the uneven edges can be dangerous for young children.

Sled Dog Races. Fast dogs heat up the lakes region every January and February. The most popular events are the **Sandwich Notch Sled Dog Race** in Center Sandwich (603-929-3508), the **Tamworth Sprint Race,** the oldest race in the northeast, in Tamworth (603-353-4601), and the **Lakes Region Sled Dog Races** in Laconia (603-524-3064; www.nesdc.org).

Summer Concert Series, Tilton Island Park, Main St. (Rte. 3), Tilton. Bluegrass, swing, rock 'n' roll, barbershop, Dixieland: The musical styles run the gamut at these weekly free concerts, held every Sunday night in July and August. The park is located on a small island in the middle of the Winnipesaukee River, accessed by a footbridge. Bring chairs or blankets. For more information, call 603-286-3000 or e-mail hartwellconcerts@aol.com.

Winslow State Park, Rte. 11, Wilmot (603-526-6168). Located on the opposite side of **Mt. Kearsarge** from **Rollins State Park** (see above listing), Winslow offers the same opportunities for hiking, mountain biking, picnicking, and taking in the views from the mountain's 1,800-foot plateau. The park is named for the Winslow House Hotel, which once stood on the property and was destroyed in a fire.

QUICK BITES

Endeavor Café and Sandwich General Store, 6 Skinner St., Center Sandwich (603-284-9911). Cinnamon-nut toast, calzones, hot and cold sandwiches, tea, and cold drinks are just some of the convenient, easy-travel items you'll find at this café and general store. You can order your ready-to-heat take-out entrées ahead of time and pick them up when you're hungry.

Gilford House of Pizza, 9 Old Lakeshore Rd., Gilford (603-528-7788; www.guilfordhouseofpizza.com). Visitors to the Gunstock Mountain area can call this local pizza favorite for free delivery. Other menu choices include calzones, hot and cold subs and sandwiches, salads, and pasta dinners.

Local Eatery, Victorian Train Station, 17 Veteran's Sq., Laconia (603-527-8007; www.laconialocaleatery.com). Formerly the Black Cat Café, this farm-to-table restaurant lives up to its name, featuring local, organic produce and grass-fed, naturally raised meats and poultry. The menu is based on seasonal availability and changes every two weeks.

Maddie's On the Bay, 11 Dockside St., Wolfeboro (603-569-8888). Maddie's offers grilled sandwiches, fried seafood, and other lunch and dinner choices; order your meal as takeout and relax at the restaurant's waterfront outdoor seating area.

Molly's Restaurant, 43 S. Main St., Hanover (603-643-2570; www.mollysrestaurant.com). This popular downtown restaurant has indoor and outdoor seating and serves wood-fired pizza, burgers, and other traditional lunch and dinner fare to Dartmouth College students and visitors. They also offer both vegetarian and gluten-free selections.

North End Pub, New London Shopping Center, New London (603-526-2875). The take-out menu at the North End Pub includes items such as pizza, subs, burgers, calzones, salads, pasta, chicken wings, nachos, and express lunches.

Old Country Store and Museum, 1011 Whittier Hwy., P.O. Box 186, Moultonborough 03254 (603-476-5750; www.nhcountrystore.com). This old-fashioned store stocks a few items for pet lovers, along with traditional favorites like Boston baked bean pots, cast-iron cookware, kitchen accessories, and decorative items, but hungry passersby will probably most appreciate the shelves filled with Vermont cheeses, maple syrup, candy, and other treats.

Shibley's at the Pier, Rte. 11, The Pier, Alton Bay (603-875-3636; www.shibleysatthepier.com). Shibley's has a walk-up window and offers fast-food treats and, of course, ice cream, as well as indoor seating and a deck. There are a few picnic tables in the parking lot, or you can walk across the street to eat on a bench at the waterfront park.

Waldo Peppers, 187 Weirs Blvd., Weirs Beach (603-366-2150). Takeout and free delivery are both available at Waldo Peppers, a casual and popular spot where hungry visitors can choose from lobster rolls, baby back ribs, calzones, cold subs, burgers, chili, pizza, and ice-cream shakes.

HOT SPOTS FOR SPOT

Ebony Boarding Kennel and Pet Camp, 661 Mayhew Tpke., Plymouth (603-536-4219; www.ebonykennel.com). Ebony provides traditional overnight boarding services ($8–12 per night) with indoor/outdoor runs, heating and air-conditioning, and separate cat quarters. You can also choose special packages, such as Pamper Your Pet ($40), Dogs Day at the Spa ($30), and Inspired Health ($50). In addition, the kennel is home to **Country Dogs Pet Bakery,** which bakes up fresh gourmet doggie treats daily.

Faux Paw, 38 Main St., Meredith (603-279-6675). This upscale pet boutique carries a wide range of stylish fashions, all-natural food, and accessories for your favorite pooch, including designer collars, plush pet beds, and a gourmet treat bakery.

Jeffrey Kropp Pet Care, Canaan (603-523-7875; jeffreykropp1@gmail.com). "I'm a one-person operation, but I try to accommodate people's needs, running the gamut from dog walking to staying overnight at someone's otherwise unoccupied home," explains Jeffrey Kropp, who serves pet owners living in and visiting **Canaan, Lebanon, Grafton, Enfield,** and neighboring towns. Rates vary according to the services requested.

Plymouth Pet and Aquarium, 594 Tenney Mountain Hwy., Plymouth (603-536-3299; www.plymouthpet.com). In addition to stocking food and supplies for cats, dogs, reptiles, birds, small animals, and fish, this store is also home to **Pet Palace Dog and Cat Grooming.** The stocked pet-food brands include Nutro, Wellness, and Canidae.

West Lebanon Supply, 12 Railroad Ave., West Lebanon (603-298-8600; www.westlebanonsupply.com). This feed store offers food and supplies for farm and companion animals, including ID tags, toys, and dog- and cat-food brands such as Iams, Blue Seal, Pro Plan, and Science Diet. If you're too busy to stop by, they'll deliver to neighboring towns.

Windy Hill Kennels, Rte. 107, Gilmanton (603-267-6896). Doggie day care, overnight boarding, grooming, and basic and advanced obedience training are all available at Windy Hill, which also serves as a vocational trade school training students for careers in pet care. The boarding area has indoor/outdoor runs, and each animal receives playtime and basic obedience training each day.

ANIMAL SHELTERS AND HUMANE SOCIETIES

Canine Guardians for Life, P.O. Box 304, Wolfeboro 03894 (www.canineguardiansforlife.org)

Companion Animal Rescue Referral and Education, P.O. Box 417, Canaan 03741 (603-523-9981)

Concord–Merrimack County SPCA, 130 Washington St., Penacook (603-753-6751; www.concordspca.org)

Franklin Animal Shelter, P.O. Box 265, Franklin 03235 (603-934-4132; www.franklinanimalshelter.com)

Lakes Region Humane Society, 11 Old Rte. 28, Ossipee (603-539-1077; www.lrhs.net)

Libby's Haven for Senior Canines, P.O. Box 65, Canterbury 03224 (603-783-9416)

Live and Let Live Farm, 20 Paradise Ln., Chichester (603-798-5615; www.liveandletlivefarm.org)

New Hampshire Humane Society, 1305 Meredith Center Rd., P.O. Box 572, Laconia 03246 (603-524-3252; www.nhhumane.org)

Sullivan County Humane Society, 14 Tremont St., Claremont (603-542-3277; www.sullivancountyhumanesociety.org)

Upper Valley Humane Society, 300 Old Rte. 10, Enfield (603-448-MUTT; www.uvhs.org)

WAG (We Are Animal Guardians), P.O. Box 572, Weare 03281 (603-529-5443; www.wearewag.org)

IN CASE OF EMERGENCY

Claremont Animal Hospital, 446 Charlestown Rd., Claremont (603-543-0117)

Hanover Veterinary Clinic, West Lebanon Rd., Hanover (603-643-3313)

Kindness Animal Hospital, 5 Water Village Rd., Ossipee (603-539-2272)

Lakes Region Veterinary Hospital, 1266 Union Ave., Laconia (603-524-8387)

Milton Veterinary Clinic, 285 White Mountain Hwy., Milton (603-652-9661)

Pleasant Lake Veterinary Hospital, 95 Elkins Rd., Elkins (603-526-6976)

Plymouth Animal Hospital, 42 Smith Bridge Rd., Plymouth (603-536-1213)

Upper Valley Veterinary Services, 7 Slayton St., Lebanon (603-448-3534)

OMNI MOUNT WASHINGTON RESORT, NESTLED IN THE WHITE MOUNTAINS (COURTESY OF OMNI MOUNT WASHINGTON)

Northern New Hampshire

The White Mountain region of the Granite State is especially popular with families, and with good reason: Attractions like Story Land, the Alpine Slide, the Mount Washington Cog Railway, the Fort Splash Waterpark, and Santa's Village, not to mention ski resorts like Attitash, Loon Mountain, and Bretton Woods, provide more than enough diversions for kids and adults alike. The bad news is, pets aren't allowed at most of these man-made attractions (although Story Land does provide kennels). The good news is, you won't have to look far to find fun and interesting nature-made alternatives.

In the Great North Woods, the state parks alone are worth the trip. If you're into camping, hiking, sightseeing, or wildlife-watching, you won't be disappointed in this rustic northern tip of the state. Dramatic gorges, moose-viewing sites, cross-country skiing trails, remote campsites, boat launches, and swimming holes are plentiful. Best of all, almost every North Woods state park welcomes pets, unlike those in many other New Hampshire locations. But you don't have to be outdoorsy to take in the region's beauty; visitors looking for maximum benefit with minimal exertion will find plenty of quick rewards on the Mount Washington Auto Road and historical walking tours, and at roadside waterfalls. Sadly, visitors can no longer enjoy the prominent profile of the Old Man of the Mountain: To the shock and dismay of all New Englanders, that famous 12,000-year-old rock formation collapsed on May 3, 2003.

ACCOMMODATIONS

Hotels, Motels, Inns, and Bed & Breakfasts

Bartlett

Attitash Marketplace Motel, Rte. 302, Bartlett (603-374-2300; 1-800-862-1600; stay@attitashmtvillage.com; www.attitashmarketplace.com); $99–249 per night. Pets are welcome in designated rooms at this motel for an additional $25 per night. Guests can take advantage of cable television, coffeemakers, studios and suites, an indoor swimming pool, a hot tub, tennis courts, a fitness center, playgrounds, a game room, and trails for hiking, mountain biking, and cross-country skiing.

Bartlett Inn, Rte. 302, 1477 White Mountain Hwy.,Bartlett (603-374-2353; 1-800-292-2353; stay@bartlettinn.com; www.bartlettinn.com); $105–195 per night. Dogs are welcome without extra fees in the Bartlett Inn's cottage rooms, provided they are not left unattended. Choose from one-room studios, larger cottages with one or two double beds, and fireplace cottages with kitchenettes and spa tubs. Guests can also enjoy country breakfasts, porch rocking chairs, an outdoor hot tub, a gathering room, nearby hiking and skiing trails, and swimming in the Saco River.

Villager Motel, Rte. 302, Bartlett (603-374-2742; 1-800-334-6988; www.villagermotel.com); $99–129 per night. Accommodations options at the Villager include standard motel units with queen- or king-size beds, efficiency units, chalets, and apartments. Guests can take advantage of a swimming pool, barbecue grills and picnic tables, a playground, and walking trails. Well-behaved, leashed pets are welcome with prior approval for an extra $15 per night.

Bethlehem

Wayside Inn, 3738 Main St. (Rte. 302), Bethlehem (603-869-3364; 1-800-448-9557; info@thewaysideinn.com; www.thewaysideinn.com); $98–188 per night. Pets are welcome in designated motel rooms at Wayside, an 1800s homestead with cross-country skiing and snowmobiling trails, basketball and bocce courts, a beach, river views, a restaurant, and a lounge. All rooms have air-conditioning, cable television, refrigerators, and balconies, and breakfast is included in the rate. Companion animals cannot be left unattended at any time.

Bretton Woods

Omni Mount Washington Resort, 310 Mt. Washington Hotel

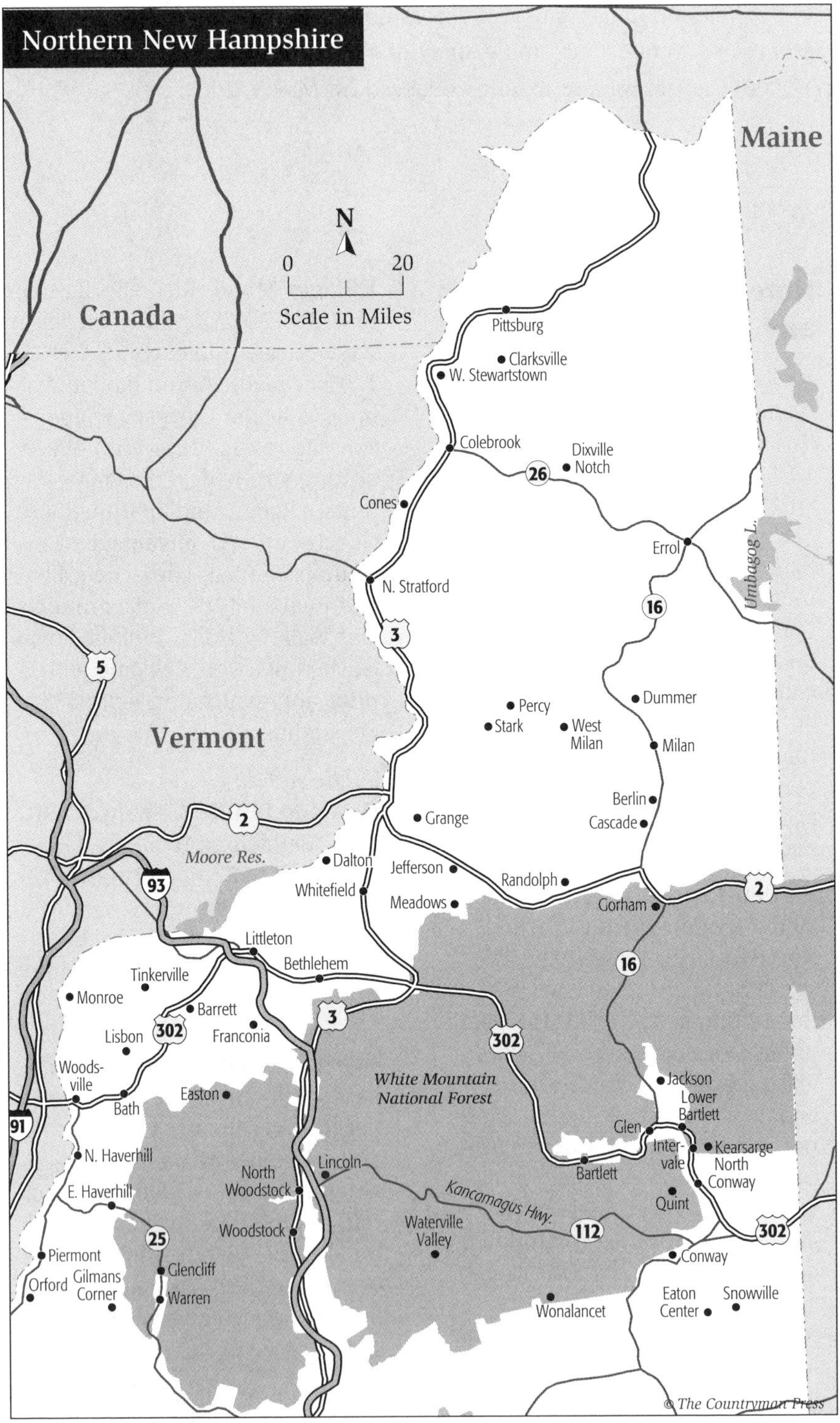
Northern New Hampshire
N
0
20
Scale in Miles
Canada
Maine
Vermont
Pittsburg
Clarksville
W. Stewartstown
Colebrook
Dixville Notch
26
Cones
Errol
Umbagog L.
N. Stratford
16
3
5
Percy
Stark
West Milan
Dummer
Milan
Berlin
Cascade
Grange
2
Moore Res.
Dalton
Jefferson
Randolph
93
Whitefield
Meadows
Gorham
Littleton
Bethlehem
Tinkerville
Monroe
Barrett
Lisbon
302
Franconia
Woods-ville
Bath
Easton
White Mountain National Forest
Jackson
Lower Bartlett
Glen
Inter-vale
Kearsarge
North Conway
Bartlett
91
N. Haverhill
E. Haverhill
North Woodstock
Lincoln
Kancamagus Hwy.
112
Quint
Woodstock
Waterville Valley
25
Piermont
Glencliff
Conway
Orford
Gilmans Corner
Warren
Wonalancet
Eaton Center
Snowville
© The Countryman Press

Rd., Bretton Woods (603-278-1000; www.omnihotels.com); $179–399 per night. Nestled in the White Mountains, the Omni offers a Bow Wow Program for four-legged guests that includes water and food bowls, treats, a squeaky toy, and a map of the property's pet-friendly trails. Your pooch also has his own chef-prepared room-service menu, and hotel bellmen are happy to provide dog-walking services upon request. The nearby Bretton Woods ski area also has pet-friendly trails. The resort boasts a spa, indoor and outdoor pools, horseback riding, tennis, and a top-rated golf course, in addition to fine dining. Pet friendly rooms are in the newly renovated Bretton Arms Inn, a cozy 34-room bed & breakfast adjacent to the hotel. Dogs up to 50 pounds are welcome with a one-time fee of $100 per stay.

OMNI MOUNT WASHINGTON RESORT (COURTESY OF OMNI MOUNT WASHINGTON)

Campton Village

Campton Inn Bed & Breakfast, 383 Owl St., Campton Village (603-726-4449; 1-888-551-0790; camptoninn@aol.com); $75–90 per night. This restored 1830s farmhouse offers five guest rooms with private and shared baths, antique furnishings, a screened-in porch, full country breakfasts, and a location that's close to hiking and biking trails, ski resorts, and a renowned golf course. Well-behaved pets are welcome for an additional charge of $10 per stay (not per night).

Conway

The Foothills Farm, P.O. Box 1368, Conway 03818 (207-935-3799; www.foothillsfarmbedandbreakfast.com); $88–149 per night. For an extra $10 per night, your dog is welcome to join you at the Foothills Farm, a B&B offering antiques, shared and private baths, two separate cottages, a swimming hole for pets and people, riding trails, and even space for your visiting horses in the barn. Full breakfasts are made with fresh produce from the farm's organic gardens.

Sunny Brook Cottages, Rte. 16, Conway (603-447-3922; info@sunnybrookcottages.com; www.sunnybrookcottages.com); $45–130 per night. The 10 cozy cottages at Sunny Brook are open year-round with fireplaces, cable television, linens, kitchens, coffeemakers, covered porches, barbecue grills, and patio furniture. Guests can also swim and fish in the on-site Swift Brook, play at the playground, and hike nearby trails. Leashed dogs are welcome for an extra $10 per stay, as long as owners clean up after them and use a crate when leaving them alone in the cottages. All pets are welcome here; Sunny Brook has hosted ferrets, hamsters, and even rabbits!

Franconia

Gale River Motel and Cottages, 1 Main St. (Rte. 18), Franconia (603-823-5655; 1-800-255-7989; www.galerivermotel.com); $60–220 per night. Gale River offers motel rooms with two double beds, cable television, and air-conditioning, along with two housekeeping cottages that can accommodate five to six people. Most dog breeds are welcome for an extra $10 per night, subject to an "interview" at check-in. You must call ahead for approval to bring your pet.

Lovetts Inn, Rte. 18, 1474 Profile Rd., Franconia (603-823-7761; 1-800-356-3802; innkeepers@lovettsinn.com; www.lovettsinn.com); $125–235 per night. Pets are welcome in some rooms at Lovetts Inn for $30 per stay, a circa-1784 restored home that's listed on the National Register of Historic Places. Accommodations include rooms in the main house and cottages. The guest rooms have private baths, sitting areas, and nice views; the cottages feature fireplaces, private baths, porches, and coffeemakers. A full breakfast is included in the rate.

Westwind Vacation Cottages, 1614 Profile Rd., Franconia (603-823-5532; 1-877-835-3455; info@westwindcottages.com; www.westwindcottages.com); $80–135 per night. Named after local waterfalls like Cascade, Bridal Veil, and Flume, the cottages at Westwind vary in size and style and can accommodate from two to six people. Each has cable television and DVD players, barbecue grills, and picnic tables. Some have full kitchens; others have kitchenettes. There are no extra fees for pets, but they must be leashed when outside.

Gorham

Colonial Fort Inn, 370 Main St., Gorham (603-466-2732; 1-800-470-4224; www.hikersparadise.com); $39–125 per night. "We certainly are pet-friendly," says Colonial Fort proprietor Mary Ann Janicki. "In fact, we believe that people cause more problems than pets do." The motel's rooms have cable television, air-conditioning, refrigerators, and phones; some have whirlpool bathtubs. Guests can also enjoy a swimming pool, a restaurant, and laundry facilities.

Royalty Inn, 130 Main St., Gorham (603-466-3312; 1-800-43-RELAX; innkeeper@royaltyinn.com; www.royaltyinn.com); $59–99 per night. Some of the amenities at the Royalty include indoor and outdoor swimming pools; a hot tub and sauna; a fitness center with stair-climbers, treadmills, a basketball court, and two racquetball courts; a game room; and an on-site restaurant and lounge. Quiet pets are allowed in smoking rooms only for an extra $5 per night.

Top Notch Inn, 265 Main St., Gorham (603-466-5496; 1-800-228-5496; reservations@topnotchinn.com; www.topnotchinn.com); $79–249 per night. Nordi is the official four-legged greeter at Top Notch; he welcomes fellow doggie guests weighing 50 pounds or less in the motel-style rooms (not the country inn–style rooms). The inn offers a swimming pool, a hot tub, and flower gardens. The shops and restaurants of downtown Gorham are within walking distance.

Intervale

Swiss Chalets Village Inn, Old Rte. 16A, Intervale (603-356-2232; 1-800-831-2727; swisschalets@yahoo.com; www.echalets.com); $89–189 per night. This very pet-friendly inn welcomes your animal friends up to 40 pounds (two pets per room) for an additional fee of $15 per pet, per night, and the staff encourages guests to exercise their pets on the 13-acre property. Choose from double, queen, and king rooms and suites with fireplaces and hot tubs. All of the rooms have been recently renovated. Guests can also relax in the swimming pool.

Jackson

River Wood Inn, Rte. 16A, Jackson (603-383-6666; www.riverwoodinn-jackson.com); $85–120 per night. It's no surprise that canines are welcome guests at the Village House, a guest lodging that also serves as the headquarters of Yellow Snow Dog Gear leash and collar manufacturers. Accommodations are available in the main house as well as a backyard annex. Some rooms have kitchenettes, hot tubs, and balconies, and all share access to a swimming pool and hot tub. The inn also has horses, a laid-back atmosphere—you check yourself in and out—and a great location in scenic downtown Jackson.

Jefferson

Applebrook Bed & Breakfast, 110 Meadows Rd. (Rte. 115A), Jefferson (603-586-7713; 1-800-545-6504; info@applebrook.com); $65–150 per night. Perched on a hill overlooking 35 private acres, Applebrook B&B offers White Mountain views, full country breakfasts, and 12 guest rooms with shared and private baths. (Some of these can be combined to form suites for larger groups.) Dogs are welcome for an extra $15 per night; half of that fee is donated to the local humane society's animal shelter.

Josselyn's Getaway Cabins, 306 North Rd., Jefferson (1-800-586-4507; www.josselyns.com); $145 and higher per night. These nine handcrafted log cabins vary in size and style, and each has a theme—from Appalachian to Christmas, Logger's, Workshop, Rainbow, and Moose. Some have air-conditioning, decks, sleeping lofts, separate bedrooms and living areas, and private yards. Dogs are welcome but must be leashed when outside.

Lincoln

Parker's Motel, Rte. 3, Lincoln (603-745-8341; 1-800-766-6835; info@parkersmotel.com; www.parkersmotel.com); $49–179 per night. Parker's Motel offers guests a swimming pool, a hot tub and sauna, free Wi-Fi, a game room, standard motel rooms and larger family rooms, two- and three-bedroom cottages (some with kitchenettes, fireplaces, air-conditioning, and cable television). Pets are allowed in designated rooms and cottages for an additional $10 per night. Most of the units are also available for weekly rentals.

Littleton

Beal House Inn & Restaurant, 2 W. Main St., Littleton (603-444-2661; 1-888-616-BEAL; www.bealhouseinn.com); $79–245 per night. Doggie guests are welcome in three of the suites at Beal House Inn, a romantic accommodation with an on-site restaurant and martini bar, satellite television, hot tubs, air-conditioning, and four-poster beds in some rooms. Dog owners pay an extra $30 per night, per pet and there's a 30 pound weight limit. The rates include a three-course gourmet breakfast for two.

North Conway

Mount Washington Valley Motor Lodge, 1567 White Mountain Hwy., North Conway (603-356-5486; 1-800-634-2383; mtwashingtonvalleyinn@yahoo.com; www.mtwashingtonvalleyinn.com); $122–192 per night. The Mount Washington Valley Inn offers standard guest rooms, family rooms, and corporate-class rooms with king-size beds. Other features include an indoor swimming pool, a hot tub, a game room, and laundry facilities. Pets weighing less than 40 pounds are allowed in designated rooms with a $50 refundable security deposit.

North Conway Mountain Inn, 2114 White Mountain Hwy., North Conway (603-356-2803; 1-800-319-4405; www.northconwaymountaininn.com); $69–159 per night. Dogs are welcome guests at the North Conway Mountain Inn, a two-story motel-style accommodation with exterior corridors, mountain views, cable television, balconies, heat and air-conditioning, and daily maid service.

Oxen Yoke Inn & Motel, 170 Kearsarge St., North Conway (603-356-3177; 877-495-6033; www.theoxenyoke.com); $59–149 per night. For an additional $25 per night, your well-behaved pet is welcome in designated rooms at the Oxen Yoke. Accommodations include B&B-style rooms at the inn, motel units, and cottages. Amenities include cable television, coffeemakers, microwaves, private baths, and a swimming pool. Restaurants, shops, and cafés are within walking distance. Part of the Eastern Slope Inn resort, guests at Oxen Yoke have access to all of the resort's amenities.

Spruce Moose Lodge and Cottages, 207 Seavey St., North Conway (603-356-6239; 1-800-600-6239; www.sprucemooselodge.com); $99–275 per night.

Adult dogs are welcome in the cottages at Spruce Moose for an additional $10 per night, per dog and a $100 security deposit. Choose from the Buckeye (up to four people), the Dakota (up to five people), and the Governor's Bungalow (up to nine people). The lodge also has one designated room where "small" pets are allowed (call to see if yours qualifies). You and your doggie can swim in the river, look for moose tracks, hike some trails, and enjoy any number of other activities.

Stonehurst Manor, Rte. 16, P.O. Box 1937, North Conway 03860 (603-356-3113; 1-800-525-9100; smanor@aol.com; www.stonehurstmanor.com); $146–275 per night. "The Manor loves pets"—and when you check in, they'll prove it with special doggie amenities, including food and water bowls, toys, treats, and a list of the local groomers and other pet-related services. The hotel offers mountain views, a library lounge, and 33 acres to explore. All of the pet-friendly rooms are located on the lower level of the Mountain View Wing. Dog owners pay an extra $25 per night. The rates include a full dinner and breakfast for two people.

Pittsburg

Lopstick Lodge and Cabins, 48 Stewart Young Rd., First Connecticut Lake, Pittsburg (1-800-538-6659; www.cabinsatlopstick.com); $109–279 per night. For an extra $10 per night, well-behaved, quiet pets are welcome in most of the housekeeping cabins at Lopstick. The lodge offers hunting and fishing guide services and cabins of varying sizes and styles; all have porches, full kitchens, and linens and towels; some have hot tubs, fireplaces, and lake and pond views.

Powder Horn Lodge & Cabins, 203 Beach Rd., Pittsburg (1-866-538-6300; sales@powderhorncabins.com; www.powderhorncabins.com); $37–55 per person, per night. Powder Hound's cozy cabins have either two or three bedrooms, kitchens, water views, cable television, microwaves, and coffeemakers. Some also have fireplaces. Dogs are welcome during most of the year for an extra $10 per night, as long as they are not left unattended. Pets are not permitted during snowmobile season, from December 15 to April 15.

Tall Timber Lodge, 609 Beach Rd., First Connecticut Lake, Pittsburg (603-538-6613; 1-800-835-6343; www.talltimber.com); $155–350 per adult, per night. Guests choose from 24 one-, two-, three-, or four-bedroom log cabins at this quiet lakefront resort. All cabins come equipped with woodstoves, kitchens, and linens; some have wraparound decks, living rooms, lake views, cathedral ceilings, and color televisions. Pets are always welcome for an additional $15 per night.

Shelburne

Town and Country Motor Inn, Rte. 2, Shelburne (603-466-3315; 1-800-325-4386; labnon@ncia.net; www.townandcountryinn.com); $99–295 per night. Town and Country is a pet-friendly motor inn offering 160 guest rooms, an indoor swimming pool, a sauna and hot tub, a fitness center, a video arcade, and a steam room. Live entertainment is provided on Saturday night, and the staff can also arrange golf vacation packages. Dogs are welcome in first-floor rooms for an extra $10 per night.

Sugar Hill

Hilltop Inn, 1348 Main St., Sugar Hill (603-823-5695; 1-800-770-5695; info@hilltopinn.com; www.hilltopinn.com); $120–195 per night. Cross-country skiers will enjoy their stay at this historic B&B that dates back to 1895; you don't even have to leave the grounds to access 20 acres of winding Nordic trails. Amenities include guest rooms and suites, antique furnishings, handmade quilts, ceiling fans, flannel sheets, and electric blankets. The two resident pooches, Beemer and Bogie, will show your canine the way to the walking trails and the large fenced-in play area for dogs. Guests with canines pay an extra $10 per night.

Spalding Inn, 199 Mountain View Rd., Whitefield (603-837-9300; www.thespaldinginn.com); cottages, $99–299 per night. Innkeepers Diane and Michael Flinder welcome companion animals in the Spalding Inn's guesthouse cottages for an extra $10 per night. Located on 200 acres of lawns, gardens, and orchards, the inn's cottages have fireplaces, kitchens, living rooms, and separate bedrooms. Rates include a full breakfast each morning; dinner plans are also available.

Woodsville

All Seasons Motel, 36 Smith St., Woodsville (603-747-2418; 1-800-660-0644; www.theallseasonsmotel.com); $60–90 per night. Owned by Dave and Maryanne Robinson, the same couple who run the nearby Nootka Lodge (see listing below), the All Seasons Motel welcomes pets in some rooms. Guests can choose from standard rooms or efficiencies and enjoy a swimming pool, air-conditioning, a playground, and cable television with premium movie channels.

Nootka Lodge, Rtes. 10 and 302, Woodsville (603-747-2418; 1-800-626-9105; manager_info@nootkalodge.com; www.nootkalodge.com); $85–140 per night. This unusual motel has a log cabin design: Rooms on the second floor have cathedral ceilings and balconies; first-floor rooms have interior log walls. Other guest amenities include a swimming pool, a hot tub, a fitness room, and a game room. Pets are welcome in about half of the rooms. (The owners of Nootka Lodge also own the All Seasons Motel in Woodsville; see above listing.)

Campgrounds

Bath

Twin River Campground and Cottages, Rtes. 302 and 112, Bath (603-747-3640; 1-800-811-1040; twinrivercampground@charterInternet.net; www.twinrivernh.com); campsites, $28–39 per night; cottages, $85–105 per night; rustic cabins, $50 per night. Twin River offers campsites for tents and RVs, cottage and cabin rentals, restrooms with showers, a swimming pool, gold panning, hiking trails, a camp store, laundry facilities, a recreation hall, and a playground. Most dog breeds (call for details) are allowed, as long as owners clean up after them. There is no extra charge for animals at campsites; in the cabins and cottages, dog owners will pay an extra $5 per night.

Cambridge

Umbagog Lake State Park Campground, Rte. 26, Cambridge (603-482-7795); campsites, $30–35 per night; cottages, $80 per night. Located in one of New Hampshire's newest state parks, Umbagog's camping area contains 69 sites: 34 in the remote wilderness and 35 at a base camp with hookups. Visitors will also find canoe, kayak, and rowboat rentals; restrooms with showers; a camp store; and laundry facilities. The remote sites can be accessed only by boat. Well-behaved pets are welcome in all locations except the beach.

Campton

Goose Hollow Camp and RV Park, Rte. 49, Campton (603-726-2000; www.nhcampgrounds.com); $35–41 per night. Pets on a leash are welcome guests at Goose Hollow, a campground with 200 sunny and open sites, picnic tables and fire pits, a camp store, a game room, a swimming pool, a half-mile of river frontage, a playground, bingo and bonfire nights, walking trails, laundry facilities, and restrooms with showers. Owners are asked to clean up after their animals.

Errol

Mollidgewock State Park Campground, Rte. 16, Errol (603-482-3373); $23 per night. Tucked inside the Thirteen Mile Woods Scenic Area, this campground has 47 primitive tent sites, most available by reservation only. Water and pit toilets are available. The park is popular with canoeists, kayakers, moose-watchers, and fishermen. Dogs are allowed.

Gorham

Moose Brook State Park Campground, 30 Jimtown Rd. (Rte. 2), Gorham (603-466-3860; 603-271-3628); $25 per night. The 62 sunny and shady sites at Moose Brook vary in size and location, and are available for tents, pop-up campers, and RVs (no hookups). Some are set aside for youth groups, and most are available by reservation only. Leashed pets are welcome. (For more information on the park, see "Out and About.")

Harts Location

Dry River Campground, Crawford Notch State Park, Rte. 302, Harts Location (603-374-2272; 603-271-3628); $23 per night. Dry River is open seasonally, from May to December. Though not allowed in the park itself, leashed pets are welcome in this campground and the Willey House area. The campground has 31 sites (most available only by reservation) and restrooms with showers.

Littleton

Crazy Horse Campground, 788 Hilltop Rd., Littleton (1-800-639-4107; mail@crazyhorsenh.com; www.crazyhorsenh.com); $32–42 per night. Leashed dogs are allowed at all campsites at Crazy Horse, a family campground located on 88 acres beside a lake. The facilities include a swimming pool, restrooms with showers, laundry facilities, a playground, and separate areas for tents and RVs. Scheduled activities include bonfires, make-your-own-sundae nights, and musical entertainment.

North Conway

Saco River Camping Area, Rte. 16, 1550 White Mountain Hwy., North Conway (603-356-3360; www.sacorivercamping area.com); $35–55 per night. Campers at Saco River can enjoy 40-by-40-foot waterfront, wooded and grassy campsites; a swimming pool; laundry facilities; restrooms with showers; canoe and kayak rentals; pony rides; wireless Internet access; and playgrounds. Most dog breeds are welcome (call to see if yours qualifies), except at the beach, pool, and playground areas; there is a limit of two dogs per site.

Pittsburg

Deer Mountain Campground, Rte. 3, Pittsburg (603-538-6965; 603-271-3628); $23 per night. This state-run campground offers 24 rustic sites with picnic tables and fire pits, and is located along the Connecticut River and the Canadian–American border. Most sites are available by reservation only, though a few are left open for walk-ins. Youth groups are encouraged to make reservations. Well-behaved pets are always welcome.

Lake Francis State Park Campground, Rte. 3, Pittsburg (603-538-6965); $25–35 per night. The park is open seasonally, from May to December. Fishermen frequent this quiet campground, which offers sites (some waterfront) for tents and RVs, limited hookups, tent platforms, a boat launch, and a day-use area. Pets are welcome.

Stewartstown

Coleman State Park Campground, 1155 Diamond Pond Rd. (off Rte. 26), Stewartstown (603-2375382); $25 per night. Located at Little Diamond Pond, this campground offers a roughing-it experience with limited facilities. The 30 sites can accommodate tents and RVs, though there are no hookups. A boat launch and plentiful trout make this a popular spot with fishermen; other activities include hiking, mountain biking, cross-country skiing, and snowmobiling.

Warren

Scenic View Campground, 193AA S. Main St., Warren (603-764-9380; info@scenicviewnh .com; www.scenicviewnh.com); $31–44 per night. Animal lovers will appreciate Scenic View's newest service, called Pup Tent, in which staffers walk, feed, and play with your pet (for a fee) while you're out and about. The campground also offers scheduled family activities, a swimming pool, a recreation hall, two playgrounds, hiking trails, restrooms with showers, and a camp store. The campground is also home to Mt. Mooselaukee Mining Company, where kids can hunt for gems and pan for gold.

Woodstock

Broken Branch KOA, Rte. 175, 1000 Eastside Rd., Woodstock (603-745-8008; 1-800-KOA-9736; www.koa.com); $35 per night. This animal-friendly campground has plenty of activities to keep families busy, including a miniature golf course, a playground, hiking trails, a swimming pool, hayrides, a camp store, laundry facilities, and restrooms with showers. Guests can also swim and fish in the nearby river. Pets must be leashed and cannot be left alone; kennel space is available upon request.

Homes, Cottages, and Cabins for Rent

For vacation rentals, check the local Craigslist and chamber of commerce, or try these local rental agencies:

www.nhtourguide.com
www.whitemountains accommodations.com
www.attitashrealty.com

OUT AND ABOUT

Appalachian Mountain Club (AMC) Visitor Center, Rte. 16, Pinkham Notch (603-466-2727). The AMC has been instrumental in establishing, protecting, and maintaining many of New Hampshire's best hiking trails; the organization's Pinkham Notch Visitor Center, also known as the Trading Post, is a popular starting point for many Mount Washington–area hikes, including the **Tuckerman Ravine Trail** (often used by hardy spring skiers) and the northern New Hampshire section of the **Appalachian Trail.** The center offers food, public restrooms, and a supply and gift shop with maps and souvenirs.

Bark in the Park, North Conway. One of New England's largest animal expos, this fund-raiser for the **Conway Area Humane Society** (CAHS) includes obstacle courses, agility demonstrations, pet-supply vendors, costume contests, and more. The event is typically held at North Conway's Schouler Park in September. For more information on this or any of the CAHS's other events (including the annual **Great Critter Caper** and the annual **Par for Paws Golf Tournament**), visit www.conwayshelter.org, e-mail info@conwayshelter.org, call 603-447-5955, or stop by the shelter at 223 East Main Street in Conway.

Bedell Bridge State Park, Rte. 10, Haverhill (603-271-3556). Frequented by fishermen, this state historic site has about 40 acres with walking trails, a picnic area, and a boat launch. It is the former home of the Burrtuss Bridge, a two-span covered bridge that was destroyed by high winds in 1979. Leashed pets are welcome.

Bethlehem Walking Tours, Bethlehem (www.bethlehemwhitemtns.com). These self-guided walking tours take you through Bethlehem's historic and notable areas; maps are available at the visitors center at 2182 Main St. (Rte. 302). **Mystery Lantern Tours** are guided walks during which local experts share the true stories and tall tales of the town's colorful past. For more information on both, call the Bethlehem Heritage Society at 1-888-845-1957 or e-mail info@bethlehemwhitemtns.com.

Glen Ellis Falls, Pinkham Notch. With a well-marked parking area on Route 16 in Pinkham Notch, these impressive 65-foot-high falls are easy to find. A walking path and stairs take you from bottom to top and back. The site has a scenic observation area and tall rock walls.

Great North Woods State Parks. As host to more than 10 large, pet-friendly parks and natural areas, the northernmost region of New Hampshire is an ideal spot for animal-loving outdoorsy types. Try these highlights: **Androscoggin Wayside Park** (Route 16 in Errol) has a trail and picnic area overlooking river rapids; **Beaver Brook Falls Wayside Park** (Route 145 in Colebrook) offers a scenic waterfall and picnic areas; **Dixville Notch State Park** (Route 26 in Dixville) is a popular area with a 5-mile-long trail, a gorge, and waterfalls; **Milan Hill State Park** (Route 16 in Milan) has an auto road to the Milan Hill summit; and **Nansen Wayside Park** (Route 16 in Berlin) attracts boaters, fishermen, and day-trippers. For more information on campgrounds, see "Accommodations—Campgrounds." For maps, directions, and details about these or other state parks, contact the New Hampshire Division of Parks and Recreation at 603-271-3254; or visit www.nhstateparks.org.

Kancamagus Highway. Stretching from Lincoln to Conway, this 34-mile scenic byway passes through mountains, gorges, ponds, and rivers. You'll find ample opportunities to stop along the way for picnics, hikes, and overlooks. On a summer or fall afternoon with the top down, it can't be beat.

Moose Brook State Park, Jimtown Rd. (Rte. 2), Gorham (603-466-3860). Companion animals are welcome at Moose Brook, often used as a starting point for hikes into the Presidential and Crescent mountain ranges. Visitors can fish in the Peabody and the Moose rivers, swim in Moose Brook, camp (see "Accommodations—Campgrounds"), or picnic by

YOU AND ROVER CAN ENJOY TRAILS, PONDS, AND BEAVER DAMS AT THE ROCKS ESTATE IN BETHLEHEM.

the water's edge. Pets must be leashed and well behaved.

Mount Washington Auto Road, Rte. 16, 1 Mt. Washington Auto Road, Gorham (603-466-3988; www.mtwashingtonautoroad.com). Sometimes called the first man-made tourist attraction in the United States, this 8-mile-long road leads drivers 6,288 feet up to the top of New England's highest mountain. The THIS CAR CLIMBED MOUNT WASHINGTON bumper sticker is free, but you'll have to pay $26 per vehicle for the privilege of earning it. Some

Moose Country

Northern New Hampshire has more of the state's 5,000 moose than any other region. Moose spotting is a popular pastime, and Routes 3 and 16 are known locally as "Moose Alley." There's even an annual Moose Festival in Colebrook every August (www.northcountrychamber.org).

hardy souls also choose to hike, bike, cross-country ski, or snowshoe their way to the top.

North Conway Sidewalk Sales, North Conway. Finally, shopping with Spot! Held each Memorial Day weekend at Settler's Green, this sidewalk sale brings the merchandise from 50 big-name outlet stores outdoors. Browse the clothes, shoes, and accessories, and enjoy the demonstrations and entertainment.

Rocks Estate, Rte. 302, 4 Christmas Ln., Bethlehem (603-444-6228; info@therocks.org; www.therocks.org). The estate is located about a half mile from Exit 40 off I-93. Your dog must be on a leash in the parking and picnic areas, but other than that, Rover is welcome to join you leash-free on the trails at this Christmas-tree farm and wildlife sanctuary managed by the **Society for the Protection of New Hampshire Forests.** It's a great, easy walk, complete with history lessons (thanks to descriptive signs along the way), beaver dams, open fields, and shady woodlands.

Story Land, Rte. 16, Glen (603-383-4186; www.storylandnh.com). This enchanting amusement park has been bringing smiles to kids' faces for more than six decades: Most New England residents can recall at least one fun trip—as a kid, a parent, or a grandparent—to enjoy the swan boats, antique cars, and rides like Cinderella's Pumpkin Coach, the Polar Coaster, Flying Fish, Dr. Geyser's Raft Ride, the Buccaneer Pirate Ship, the Huff Puff and Whistle Railroad, and the Crazy Barn. But what, you might be asking, does this have to do with dogs? Canine-loving vacationers with young children will be extremely pleased to learn that Story Land also has kennels on the property—26 of them, in fact, all double-locked and attended-to by park staffers. Granted, the kennels are nothing fancy. But the park will supply plenty of water and treats for your pup while you enjoy a guilt-free day at the park to soak up the sun, fun, and happy memories. Story Land was designed primarily for children between the ages of 2 and 12. The kennels are first-come, first-serve, so plan to get there early.

Wildcat Mountain, Pinkham Notch (1-800-255-6439; www

.skiwildcat.com). "The philosophy here is that while pets are not welcome in so many other places, here they need not stay in the car while you're out having all the fun," says Irene Donnell, communications director for the Wildcat Mountain Ski Area. "Your pet can ride along with you in the gondola and enjoy the bird's-eye scenery too!" Animals are not allowed in the lodge, and owners are asked to clean up after their animals and keep an eye on them. Try the Way of the Wildcat Trail, a self-guided walk with explanatory signs about local history and ecology that leads to Thompson Brook Falls and its swimming hole.

QUICK BITES

Bishop's Ice Cream, 183 Cottage St., Littleton (603-444-6039; www.bishopshomemadeicecream.com). Enjoy your cone, sundae, milkshake, or banana split on the benches out in front of Bishop's, an ice-cream shop serving classic flavors—and a few newfangled ones, too.

Blueberry Muffin, 1769 White Mountain Hwy. (Rte. 16), Conway (603-356-5736; www.blueberrymuffin.com). Outdoor patio seating is available seasonally at the Blueberry Muffin, a casual restaurant at the Yankee Clipper Inn (a pet-friendly motel), serving pancakes, sandwiches, soups, blueberry muffins (of course), and other breakfast and lunch items.

The Brick Store, Rte. 302, P.O. Box 118, Bath 03740 (1-800-964-2074; www.thebrickstore.com). Billed as "the oldest continuously operated general store in the United States," The Brick Store has been serving food and selling sundries since the 1790s. Takeout and outdoor benches are available, which should make it easy for you to enjoy maple brittle, homemade fudge, apple jam, Vermont cheddar, penny candy, and lots of other snacks.

Cold Mountain Café, 2015 Main St., Bethlehem (603-869-2500; www.coldmountaincafe.com). Treat yourself to a freshly made sandwich, baked goodie, or hot or cold drink at this laid-back coffeehouse. Sit on the patio and enjoy soups, quiche, salads, or sandwiches for lunch, or filets and crabcakes for dinner. The café is closed on Sundays.

Trail's End Ice Cream, Rte. 302, Bartlett (603-374-2288). In addition to its homemade ice cream, frozen yogurt, toppings, coffee, and cold drinks, Trail's End also offers a playground and an outdoor seating area with picnic tables and great views of the White Mountains.

Willey House Snack Bar, Dry River Campground, Crawford Notch State Park, Rte. 302, Harts Location (603-374-2272). Located at the beautiful Crawford Notch

State Park, this roadside snack bar offers picnic-table seating for enjoying your quick treats. The Willey House is famous for being the only surviving building in the aftermath of an 1828 landslide.

Zeb's General Store, 2675 White Mountain Hwy., P.O. Box 1915, North Conway 03860 (1-800-676-9294; www.zebs.com). Fill your picnic basket to overflowing at this general store and food shop in North Conway. The "100 percent New England" products include peanut brittle, pretzels, crackers, smoked cheeses, salsa, chip dips, coffee, cocoa, penny candy, jams, honey, caramel corn, and gift baskets.

HOT SPOTS FOR SPOT

Four Your Paws Only, 1821 White Mountain Hwy., North Conway (1-800-327-5957; www.fouryourpawsonly.com). A popular canine hangout for visitors and locals, this fun, well-stocked shop features a Doggie Bakery filled with human-grade pet treats, animal-related décor for house and garden, breed-specific clothing and hats, and plenty of other items for pets and animal lovers. The staff is also active in the community and hosts many pet-related events throughout the year: Check out the "events" page on the Web site for all the up-to-date information. Many of the local hotels and resorts offer discounts for this store, so check with the concierge or front desk.

KC's Meadow Kennel, 224 Martin Meadow Pond Rd., Lancaster (603-788-2637; info@kckennel.com; www.kcsmeadowkennel.com). Specializing in overnight boarding and grooming, KC's offers heated and air-conditioned indoor/outdoor runs and four individual exercise sessions each day for dogs; there are also limited facilities for cats. All pets must have proof of vaccination. Brushing, washing, nail clipping, and ear cleaning are part of the standard grooming services.

Littleton Pet Center and Kennel, 1985 St. Johnsbury Rd., Littleton (603-444-6285; www.littletonpetcenterandkennel.com). This complete pet-care center (aka "pet vacation resort") provides overnight boarding, doggie day care, and all-breed grooming for dogs and cats. You can also stop in to buy premium dog food, leashes, collars, and other supplies.

Vikki's Bed, Bath & Biscuit, 590 E. Main St., Center Conway (603-447-3435). In addition to providing all-pet and all-breed grooming, Vikki's (formerly known as Karla's Grooming and Village Kennels) also offers day care and overnight boarding for dogs and cats. The kennel's small size (20 runs) ensures that each pet gets lots of individual attention. Rates are $15 per day for day care and $13 per night for boarding.

ANIMAL SHELTERS AND HUMANE SOCIETIES

Conway Area Humane Society, 223 E. Main St., P.O. Box 260, Conway 03818 (603-447-5955; www.conwayshelter.org)

Lancaster Humane Society, 564 Martin Meadow Pond Rd., Lancaster (603-788-4500; www.lhsnokill.org)

IN CASE OF EMERGENCY

Colebrook Veterinary Clinic, 180 Main St., Colebrook (603-237-8871)

Lancaster Veterinary Hospital, 329 Main St., Lancaster (603-788-3351)

Landaff Veterinary Clinic, 460 Mill Brook Rd., Landaff (603-838-6687)

North Country Animal Hospital, 2237 W. Side Rd., North Conway (603-356-5538)

Whitefield Animal Hospital, 38 Lancaster Rd., Whitefield (603-837-9611)

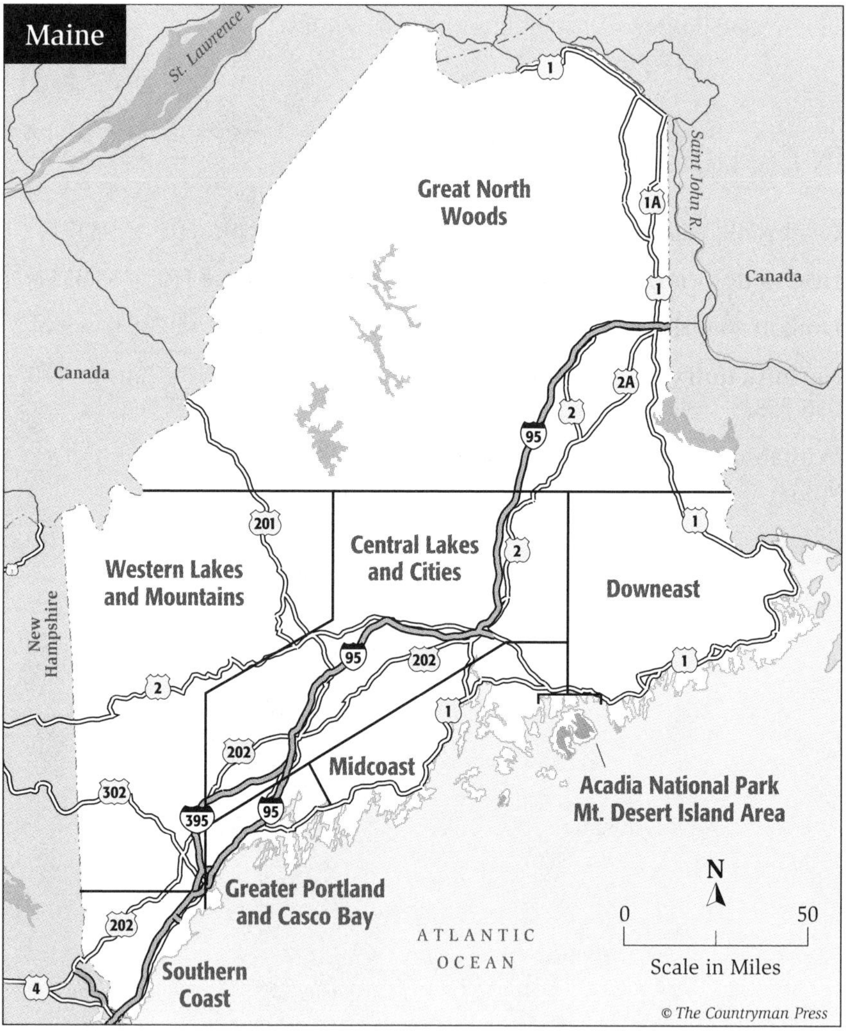

Maine
St. Lawrence R.
Canada
Canada
Saint John R.
Great North Woods
Central Lakes and Cities
Western Lakes and Mountains
Downeast
New Hampshire
Midcoast
Acadia National Park Mt. Desert Island Area
Greater Portland and Casco Bay
Southern Coast
ATLANTIC OCEAN
N
0
50
Scale in Miles
1
1A
1
2A
2
95
201
2
1
95
202
2
1
202
1
302
395
95
202
4
© The Countryman Press

Maine C

THE WELLS BREAKWATER AND BOARDWALK REWARD VISITORS WITH GREAT VIEWS AND SALTWATER SPRAY.

Southern Maine Coast

In a state known for its rocky coast, the southern tip of Maine offers that most unusual of Vacationland's attractions: vast stretches of smooth, sandy beach. Massachusetts city dwellers and suburbanites have long flocked to this region for summer adventures; it is second only to Acadia National Park in visitation in the state. The south coast is a singularly beautiful and welcoming area for almost any type of traveler, but pet owners should be forewarned that they will face some challenges when vacationing here.

While there are many great reasons to visit this region, let's face it—most people come for the beaches. From the famed, lively stretch at Old Orchard to Ogunquit and York's lower-key shores, the beach umbrellas go up in June and stay up until fall. Sadly, however, pets are not invited to the beach party during the high season, at least not during peak times during the day. Many towns along the coast have implemented a "no dogs on the beach" policy from 8 or 9 AM to 5 or 6 PM throughout the entire high season. (Some don't allow dogs at any time of the day in the high season.) However, after September 15, there are few, if any, restrictions on beach play for canines.

In small resort towns like Ogunquit, you'll find plenty of accommodations in locally owned motels, inns, and B&Bs, but the large resorts do not usually accept four-legged visitors.

That said, the situation does seem to be on the upswing for dog owners. This edition of *Dog-Friendly New England* lists a few more hotels, motels, and campgrounds than the last edition did—a good sign for animal lovers. In addition, the southern coast does have noteworthy parks and hiking trails, scenic rivers and lakes, picturesque lighthouses, walkable historic districts, wonderful window-shopping, and of course fabulous seafood. And if you don't mind waiting until after dinner or before breakfast to hit the beach, you can do that, too. Don't let a few challenges discourage you from exploring this unique slice of New England; it may take a little more planning, but once you're strolling Kennebunkport's quaint shopping areas, gazing at York's Nubble Light, cracking open a lobster, or hiking one of the area's expansive state parks with Spot at your side, you'll be glad you made the effort.

ACCOMMODATIONS

Hotels, Motels, Inns, and Bed & Breakfasts

Eliot

Farmstead Bed & Breakfast, 999 Goodwin Rd., Eliot (207-439-5033; 207-748-3145; farmsteadb@aol.com; www.farmstead.qpg.com); $60–96 per night. Dogs, cats, and even cockatoos have stayed at the Farmstead; animals of all stripes are welcome as long as they are never left alone in the rooms. (A note to dog owners: There is a resident cat here, so make sure your pooch stays on a leash at all times.) The B&B bills itself as the perfect blending of historic charm with modern conveniences.

Kennebunk

English Robin Guest House, 99 Western Ave., Kennebunk (207-967-3505); call for rate information. Owner Ann Smith welcomes pets at her family-oriented guesthouse without any extra fees, though she does restrict her four-legged clientele to adult animals only (no puppies or kittens). Two of the units have private entrances; the third, called The Barn, is a converted carriage house with a family room and full kitchen.

The Kennebunk Inn, 45 Main St., Kennebunk (207-985-3351; info@thekennebunkinn.com; www.thekennebunkinn.com); $85–245 per night. Step back

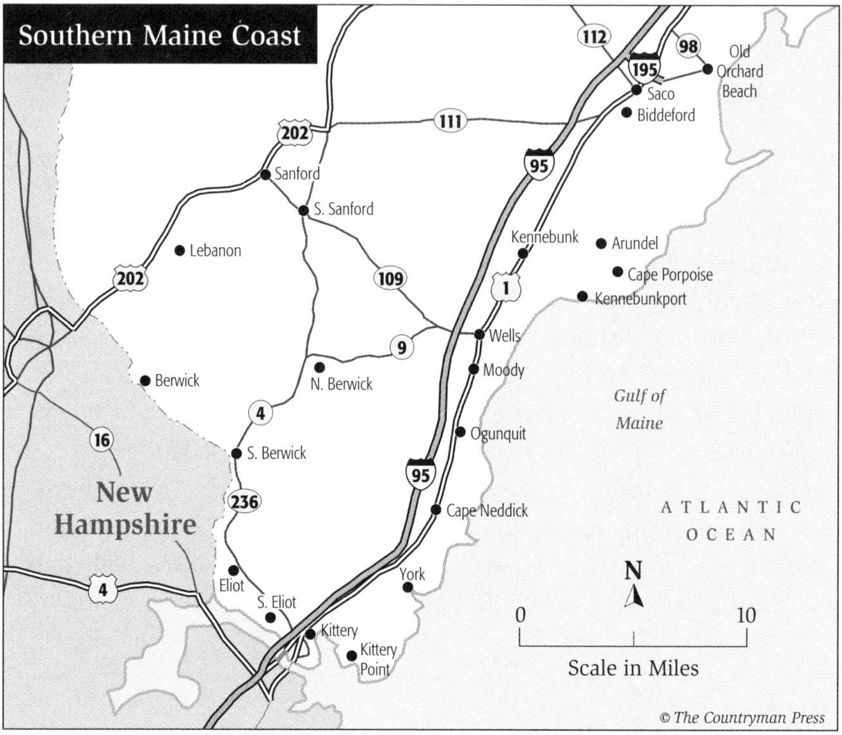

in time at this 200-year-old inn offering New England charm, tasteful period décor, and modern conveniences. Amenities include free Internet access, beach passes, a restaurant and tavern, and cable television. Two rooms on the first floor are designated as pet-friendly: Guests bringing a furry companion will pay an extra $20 one-time fee.

Kennebunkport

The Captain Jefferds Inn, 5 Pearl St., Kennebunkport (207-967-2311; 1-800-839-6844; captjeff@captainjefferdsinn.com; www.captainjefferdsinn.com); $149–399 per night. This charming inn has an equally charming history: The 1804 Federal-style home was built by Captain William Jefferds as a wedding gift for his daughter. The current owners refurbished the inn in 1997 and now offer 15 themed guest rooms. Dogs are permitted with prior approval for an additional $30 per night in the five carriage house rooms that have outdoor access.

The Colony Hotel, 140 Ocean Ave., Kennebunkport (207-967-3331; 1-800-552-2363; reservations@thecolonyhotel.com; www.thecolonyhotel.com); $145–545 per night. The Colony has an impressive façade reminiscent of New England's earliest grand resorts. Expect a luxurious stay: Rooms have period furnishings and verandas that overlook the ocean. Dogs on a leash are allowed on the hotel's private beach and by the pool area, but not in the pool water itself. A "walking area" is provided for pet owners, who pay an extra fee of $30 per night, per pet. The Colony considers itself an "environmentally responsible hotel" and employs forward-thinking programs of waste reduction, water and energy conservation, and material reuse. A full breakfast buffet is included in the room rate.

The Edgewater Inn, 126 Ocean Ave., Kennebunkport (207-967-3315; www.edgewaterinnmaine.com); $149–299 per night. Formerly known as the Green Heron Inn, the Edgewater is owned by dog lovers who have included a "canine travelers" section on their Web site with tips on great walks: the Government Wharf Beach across the street even has waste bags for your pooch. With a key location on famed Ocean Avenue and locally renowned hearty breakfasts, the EdgewaterInn is a wonderful stop for any traveler—but it's especially nice for pet owners. The inn's new owners welcome dogs up to 50 pounds for an additional $35 per night in certain rooms with prior notice, as long as they are not left unattended during their stay.

The Lodge at Turbat's Creek, 7 Turbat's Creek Rd., Kennebunkport (207-967-8700; www.lodgeatturbatscreek.com); $99–299 per night. The lodge, open May through October, bills itself as "unpretentious and comfortable," and offers exterior corridors, colorful landscaping, and 26 clean, well-furnished rooms. Guests enjoy continental breakfasts (delivered daily from a local bakery) and a heated outdoor swimming pool. Well-behaved pets are welcome in four of the lodge rooms for an additional $20 per night.

The Seaside Inn & Cottages, 80 Beach Ave., P.O. Box 631, Kennebunkport 04046 (207-967-4461; 1-866-300-6750; www.kennebunkbeachmaine.com/seasideinn); $1,195–2,295 per week or $3,899–6,995 per month. Though pets aren't allowed in the motor inn, they can stay in some of the Seaside's well-equipped cottages—and best of all, they can join their owners at the site's private, sandy beach. Seaside charges a fee of $50 per pet, per week, but that will be refunded at the end of your stay providing your animal didn't cause any damage or leave a mess.

Shorelands Guest Resort, Rte. 9, 247 Western Ave., Kennebunkport (207-985-4460; 1-800-99-BEACH; info@shorelands.com; www.shorelands.com); $69–249 per night. Shorelands offers motel rooms, two-bedroom apartments, and cottages, along with a swimming pool and hot tub, barbecue areas, a playground, laundry facilities, and bicycles for borrowing. Pet owners pay a fee of $15 per night; animals must stay off the furniture, stay on a leash, and stay in the company of their owners. The resort has designated dog-walking areas located off of the main grounds and is open from mid-April through the second week of Christmas Prelude.

The Yachtsman Lodge and Marina, Ocean Ave., Kennebunkport (207-967-2511; innkeeper@yachtsmanlodge.com; www.yachtsmanlodge.com); $169–329 per night. Each room in this luxury hotel, which overlooks the Kennebunk River, features décor intended to mimic the interior of the yachts that cruise along the Maine seacoast: French doors open to a waterfront patio, and down comforters cover the beds. Guests also enjoy the complimentary use of bikes and canoes, as well as a continental breakfast. Certified as pet friendly with a "Pets Can Stay" seal of approval, four-legged guests are welcome for a fee starting at $25 per night, per pet.

Kittery

Coachman Inn, Rte. 1, Kittery (207-439-4434; 1-800-824-6183; www.coachmaninn.net); $101–199 per night. Just 10 minutes from Cape Neddick, the Coachman Inn is a modern hotel across the street from the Kittery Outlet shops. The Inn welcomes pets for an additional $10 per night, per pet (max two per room), and features free Wi-Fi and HBO, as well as an outdoor pool and lobby lounge area with game tables.

Enchanted Nights Bed & Breakfast, 29 Wentworth St., Kittery (207-439-1489; www.enchantednights.org); $35–250 per night. The owners of this B&B are serious animal lovers—they serve vegetarian breakfasts, own pets themselves, and donate the pet fee ($10–20 per stay, not per night) to the local animal shelter. You won't have to sacrifice any comfort to get this kind of welcome, however; the rooms have whirlpools, fireplaces, air-conditioning, cable television, DVD players, VCRs, feather beds, and antique furniture.

Litson Villas, 127 State Rd., Kittery (207-439-5000; 1-800-8455; info@litsonvillas.com; www.litsonvillas.com); $65–149 per night. Dogs are welcome for overnight stays at Litson Villas, a group of 27 affordable and neatly kept cottages located about 1 mile from the Kittery outlet stores. Each cottage has a porch, cable television, and a full-size refrigerator, stove, and microwave. There are no extra fees for pet owners, but they are asked to "scoop the poop," use a leash, and not leave their pups unattended in the villa.

Ogunquit

Marginal Way House and Motel, P.O. Box 697, Ogunquit 03907 (207-646-8801; info@marginalwayhouse.com; www.marginalwayhouse.com); $49–235 per night. The Marginal Way offers three accommodations options: a hotel, a motel, and efficiency apartments. Guests can enjoy ocean views and a location that's close to shops, galleries, restaurants, and the beach. Dogs are permitted in designated rooms during the off-season (from Labor

Day to June 23) for an extra $10 per night.

Majestic Regency Resort Hotel, 102 Post Rd, Wells (207-646-9601; www.majesticregency.com); $ 49–179 per night. Located right on the Ogunquit–Wells line, this 5-acre family resort welcomes your furry family members under 50 pounds for an additional $10 per night, per pet, up to two per room. With old fashioned amenities including shuffleboard, croquet, and a horseshoe pit, as well as more modern activities like a swimming pool and fitness center, the regency will remind you of vacations gone by. Your room rate includes free Wi-Fi and a complimentary continental breakfast with apple fritters.

The Inn on Shore Road, 38 Shore Rd., Ogunquit (207-646-2181; www.innonshoreroad.com); $119–279 per night. White picket fence, gabled roof, quilts, breakfast nook—this place is about as quaint as it gets. Formerly known as the West Highland Inn, the Inn on Shore Road has retained all the charming elements, including welcoming pets for an additional $30 per stay with a one-pet-per-room rule. Dogs cannot disturb other guests, owners are responsible for cleaning up after their animals, and pets are not allowed on the furniture.

Old Orchard Beach

Alouette Beach Resort, 91 E. Grand Ave., Old Orchard Beach (207-934-4151; 1-800-565-4151; www.alouettebeachresort.com); $69–196 per night. Located on the beach, Alouette offers an indoor swimming pool, laundry facilities, a sundeck, cable television with premium movie channels, high-speed Internet access, and delivery service for breakfast in bed or a pizza munchie attack. Dogs are permitted in certain rooms for an additional $10 per night and a $50 refundable security deposit. And as you may have guessed, there's a French version of the Web site.

Beach Walk Oceanfront Inn, 109 E. Grand Ave., Old Orchard Beach (207-934-2381; 1-877-342-3224; www.beachwalkoceanfrontinn.com); $70–209 per night. Managed by the same family that runs the Alouette Beach Resort (see listing above), this beach motel has a heated freshwater swimming pool and a location that's within a stone's throw of the ocean. With advance notice, your pet is welcome in designated rooms for an extra $10 per night plus a refundable $50 security deposit.

Beau Rivage Motel, 54 E. Grand Ave., Old Orchard Beach (207-934-4668; 1-800-939-4668; brivage@gwi.net; www.beaurivagemotel.com); $45–135 per night. This motel has rooms, apartments, and suites with air-conditioning, cable television, and telephones. Guests can take advantage of a swimming pool, hot tub, sauna, and deck, or walk a block to reach the beach. (Dogs are permitted on the beach during the off-season only.) "Small" dogs (call to see if yours qualifies) are welcome in designated rooms with a $10 per night charge and a $25 nonrefundable security deposit.

Old Colonial Motel, 61 W. Grand Ave., Old Orchard Beach (207-934-9862; oldcol@gwi.net; www.oldcolonialmotel.com); $80–270 per night. Located directly on the beach, this motel has exterior corridors, an outdoor swimming pool, an exercise room with a hot tub and sauna, a video-rental area with more than 800 movies, a snack counter, and beach chairs and umbrellas available for rent. Pets that weigh less than 40 pounds are welcome for an additional $5 per night.

Sandpiper Beachfront Motel, 2 Cleaves St., Old Orchard Beach (207-934-2733; www.sandpiperbeachfrontmotel.com); $65–170 per night. The Sandpiper enjoys a prime location right on Old Orchard Beach. Owners Denis and Daphne Rioux pride themselves on providing "down-home hospitality" and a friendly atmosphere with daily maid service, free coffee, air-conditioning, and kitchenettes. Pets can come along for the fun for an extra $10 per night.

Sea View Motel, 65 W. Grand Ave., Old Orchard Beach (207-934-4180; 1-800-541-8439; www.seaviewgetaway.com); $70–270 per night. Choose from rooms, suites, and studios at this three-story beachfront accommodation with a swimming pool. One pet weighing less than 60 pounds is allowed per room with a $100 cash deposit. Owner Kim Verreault has set aside a special "pet relief" area on the property and asks that animals not be left alone in rooms.

Saco

Hampton Inn Saco–Old Orchard Beach, 48 Industrial Park Rd., Saco (207-282-7222; www.hilton.com); $109–149 per night. This modern chain hotel has in-room coffeemakers, irons, and safe-deposit boxes; an exercise room; a pool; cable television; and a free airport shuttle. It's located in a commercial area about 2 miles from Old Orchard Beach and about 10 minutes from Portland. Pets are welcome with no extra fees.

Rodeway Inn, 21 Ocean Park Rd., Saco (207-282-5589; www.choicehotels.com); $65–159 per night. Stay near all the action at this Saco Rodeway Inn (formerly known as the Classic Motel) offering air-conditioning, an indoor heated swimming pool, free daily continental breakfasts, a picnic area, voice mail, a wake-up service, cable television, and in-room coffeemakers and hair dryers. Pet owners pay an extra $10 per night plus a refundable $50 security deposit.

Wells

Ne'r Beach Motel, 395 Post Rd., Wells (207-646-2636; nerbeach@maine.rr.com; www.nerbeach.com); $59–149 per night. Adult dogs and their owners are always welcome at Ne'r Beach Motel, which is located half a mile from the beach. The motel has a large grassy area for walking dogs; quiet pets are welcome with prior

Maine Parks and Pets

Dogs are not allowed on state park beaches, but are allowed in all state parks and state park campgrounds except Sebago Lake State Park Campground. Pets must be on a leash no longer than 4 feet in length, and you must clean up after your pet. For a complete list of regulations and campgrounds, see www.maine.gov/dacf/parks/camping/reservations/pets.shtml.

notice for $12 per night, on the condition that they stay leashed and are never left alone in a room. Say hello to resident pup Bentley Harrison when you check in. The motel is closed November to March.

New Harbor View Cottages, 1061 Post Rd., Wells (207-646-3356; 1-877-281-9609; cottages@newharborview.com; www.newharborview.com); $85–210 per night. These warmly decorated, fully furnished cottages with pine-board interior walls sit together in a row and share a large lawn. Choose from one or two bedrooms: All have screened-in porches, full-size kitchens and bathrooms, and ceiling fans; linens and towels are provided. Pets are welcome with prior approval for an extra fee of $5 per night.

Seahorse Resort Wells, 1661 Post Rd., P.O. Box 97, Wells 04090 (207-646-5545; www.seahorseresortwellsmaine.com); $69–139 per night. Guests at can choose from motel rooms, efficiencies, and cottages and enjoy an outdoor swimming pool, picnic tables and grills, playground equipment, and vending machines. With advance arrangements, your pet is welcome to join you in designated rooms for an extra $15 per pet, per night. Owners are asked to use a leash, keep their animals off the furniture, and limit the number of pets to two per room.

York

Best Western York Inn, 2 Brickyard Ln., York (207-363-8903; www.bestwestern.com); $99–1499 per night. For an extra $10 per night, your pooch is welcome to join you at the Econo Lodge located near Cape Neddick and all the southern Maine attractions. Other amenities include an indoor swimming pool and free daily continental breakfasts. Guest dogs must weigh 50 pounds or less; the hotel has a limit of two dogs per room.

Campgrounds

Alfred

Walnut Grove Campground, 599 Gore Rd., Alfred (207-324-1207; walnutgrove@adelphia.net; www.walnutgrovecampground.net); $26–30 per night. Walnut Grove provides its guests with an outdoor swimming pool, a playground, sports courts, laundry facilities, a snack bar, a convenience store, and planned activities like barbecues, dances, and Octoberfest celebrations. Leashed pets are welcome; owners should bring proof of vaccinations.

Berwick

Beaver Dam Campground, 551 School St. (Rte. 9), Berwick (207-698-2267; camp@beaverdamcampground.com; www.beaverdamcampground.com); $31–44 per night. Beaver Dam Campground is a very pet-friendly place, welcoming "four-legged family members" along for the fun. Campers will find waterfront and wooded sites, a playground, a sandy beach, a game room, a camp store, a pond, a big-screen movie rooms, rainy-day activities, two fishing docks, and boat rentals. In 2005, the campground also opened its Bark Park dog-run area.

Biddeford

Homestead by the River, 610 New Country Rd., Biddeford (207-282-6445; info@homesteadbytheriver.com; www.homesteadbytheriver.com); $30–37 per night. Spend some time camping at Homestead by the River and you'll find a family-friendly atmosphere with canoe and kayak rentals, a swimming and picnic area on the river, a playground, a game room, a camp store, laundry facilities, and restrooms with showers. Leashed, friendly pets (all breeds except pit bulls) are welcome with advance notice.

Cape Neddick

Dixon's Coastal Maine Campground, 1740 Rte. 1, Cape Neddick (207-363-3626; info@dixonscampground.com; www.dixonscampground.com); $30–44 per night. Dixon's offers wooded and open campsites for tents and RVs, a camp store, a dumping station, a heated swimming pool, and a playground. Quiet pets are permitted, as long as owners use a short leash, don't leave their animals unattended, and clean up any messes.

Kennebunkport

Red Apple Campground, 111 Sinnott Rd., Kennebunkport (207-967-4927; www.redapplecampground.com); $42–56 per night. Red Apple's motto is "Clean, quiet, and relaxing—the way camping should be." The property provides its guests with 140 large sites, paved roads, restrooms with showers, a recreation hall, a playground, a camp store, free high-speed Internet access, a business center, free daily newspapers, and a close-to-the-ocean location. Well-behaved pets are welcome; reservations are recommended.

Lebanon

Heavenlee Acres, 75 Cemetery Rd., Lebanon (207-457-1260; www.heavenleeacres.com); $36–40 per night. Open from May to September, Heavenlee Acres has a swimming pool, a recreation hall, a playground, and lots of planned activities like bingo games, craft classes, ice-cream socials, dances, card games, barbecues, and Fourth of July celebrations. Leashed, quiet pets are permitted, although they are not allowed in the playground or pool areas.

Flat Rock Bridge Family Resort, 21 Flat Rock Bridge Rd., Lebanon (207-339-9465; www.flatrockbridge.com); $40 per night or $118–105 per week for cabin and trailer rentals. Flat Rock features a free 360-foot waterslide, two heated swimming pools, a sandy beach, four hot tubs, miniature golf, sports courts, group activities, a snack bar, a camp store, and many more amenities. Doggie guests are an extra $5 per night, per pet, with a two-dog maximum for nightly rentals; there is no extra pet charge for weekly rentals.

Old Orchard Beach

Hid'n Pines Family Campground, 8 Cascade Rd., P.O. Box 647, Old Orchard Beach 04064 (207-934-2352; hidnpine@maine.rr.com; www.mainefamilycamping.com); $25–47 per night. The long stretch of Old Orchard Beach is located within walking distance from this family campground. Amenities include a heated swimming pool, a playground, a basketball court, modern restrooms with showers, tent and RV sites, Internet access, security gates, a recreation room, and an arcade. Leashed dogs are welcome and can enjoy a designated dog-walking area. Dogs are not allowed in the pool area.

Old Orchard Beach Campground, 27 Ocean Park Rd., Old Orchard Beach (207-934-4477; relax@gocamping.com; www.gocamping.com); $30–40 per night. Visitors to this camping facility will find an outdoor swimming pool, recreation rooms, a playground, athletic fields, a camp store, restrooms with showers, and laundry facilities. Quiet leashed pets are permitted, as long as they are not left alone at the site and owners agree to clean up after them. Certain breeds are restricted; call for details.

Powder Horn Family Camping, Hwy. 98, P.O. Box 366, Old Orchard Beach 04064 (207-934-4733; www.mainecampgrounds.com); $30–57 per night. The pool complex at Powder Horn will keep everyone busy, offering two swimming pools, a children's pool, and two hot tubs. Campers can also enjoy a miniature golf course, three playgrounds, a recreation room, an arcade, and more. Leashed dogs are permitted, as long as they are not left alone at the sites. The campground also provides a designated dog-walking area.

Wagon Wheel Campground & Cabins, 3 Old Orchard Rd., Old Orchard Beach (1-888-886-2477; www.sunrvresorts.com); $29–37 per night. The Wagon Wheel Campground welcomes most breeds of dogs, provided they are leashed, not left alone, and cleaned-up after. Amenities here include a shuttle service to the beach, swimming pools, a camp store, a playground, a recreation hall, a dumping station, laundry facilities, and restrooms with showers.

Wells

Elmere Campground, 525 Post Rd. (Rte. 1), Wells (207-646-5538); $14–20 per night. Located 1 mile from the ocean and halfway between Wells and Ogunquit, this family-friendly campground is an affordable home base for exploring the region. Each site has a fire pit and picnic table; campers also have access to full hookups, hot showers, and flush toilets. Dogs are welcome on a leash at no extra charge.

Gregoire's Campground, 697 Sanford Rd., Wells (207-646-3711; 1-800-639-2442, ext. 620); $25–30 per night. Tents, campers, and trailers will all find a spot to rest at Gregoire's, a 30-acre family-owned campground located just off the Maine Turnpike. A recreation hall, convenience store, and outdoor play equipment are available on-site, and the Wells trolley stops by regularly. Each campsite has a fireplace and picnic table. Dogs must stay on a leash.

Ocean View Cottages and Campground, 84 Harbor Rd., Wells (207-646-3308; www.oceanviewcampground.com); campsites, $32–40 per night; cottages, $750–950 per week. Ocean View has plain-and-simple tent sites, RV hookup sites, and housekeeping cottages. Some of the larger cottages feature full-size kitchens, cable television, wall-to-wall carpets, and air-conditioning. Campers also have use of a swimming pool, tennis courts, a playground, a recreation hall, and a game room. Quiet dogs are welcome, as long as they are not left unattended and are kept on a leash.

York Harbor

Libby's Oceanside Campground, Rte. 1A, 725 York St.,York Harbor (207-363-4171; www.libbysoceancamping.com); $50–92 per night. Pull your RV right up to the beach and watch the waves roll in. With a setting like this, the view is the primary attraction (and the higher-than-average nightly rates show we're willing to pay for it). Sites have water, sewer, and electricity hookups. Pets are welcome but must be leashed and can't be left alone at the campground.

Rental Agency

Rivers by the Sea, 79 Ocean Ave. Ext., York (207-363-3213; 207-363-3230; info@riversbythesea.com; www.riversbythesea.com). This 20-year-old agency helps clients find permanent homes as well as summer and off-season vacation rentals. Of their current 200 listed rental properties, some do allow pets. The homeowners generally charge an additional refundable pet deposit (anywhere from $150 to $500). The agency asks that pet owners clean up after their animals and not leave them alone "for too long" in any of the properties.

OUT AND ABOUT

Animal Welfare Society (AWS), 46 Old Holland Rd., West Kennebunk (207-985-3244; awsedr@cybertours.com; www.animalwelfaresociety.org). Steven Jacobsen, executive director of this animal shelter and welfare society, invites out-of-towners to visit AWS's headquarters, where more than 2 miles of walking paths are available for ambles through the woods and fields. The society also hosts events and gatherings throughout the year, including the annual **Morris Insurance Strut Your Mutt Dog Walk-A-Thon** (usually held the third Sunday in September on Mothers Beach) and the **AWS Craft Show** (usually held the Saturday prior to Labor Day weekend on the Kennebunkport village green).

Architectural Walking Tours, Brick Store Museum, 117 Main St., Kennebunk (207-985-4802; info@brickstoremuseum.org; www.brickstoremuseum.org); $5 per person. Take an informative stroll through **Kennebunk's Summer Street district,** which is on the National Register of Historic Places. Rich in architectural history, the district includes examples of Colonial, Greek Revival, Queen Anne, Italianate, and Federal-style buildings, mostly homes that once belonged to the area's wealthy ship captains and merchants. The tour is led by staffers and volunteers from the Brick Store Museum. The museum also sponsors ArtWalk.

Cape Porpoise, Kennebunkport. After you've visited the region's gift shops and tourist traps, make a point to stop by this working fishing village located about 3 miles east of Dock Square (see listing below). Renowned for its seafood, this is a quiet, picturesque place where locals still work at the trades that Maine is famous for.

Captain Satch and Sons, 793 Morrills Mill Rd., North Berwick (207-475-4705, reservations; 207-475-4676, cell; satch@cybertours.com; www.captainsatch.tripod.com); call for rates. The Captain Satch boats depart twice daily from Wells Harbor for four- and six-hour bass fishing charters. They can accommodate six people per trip and do allow pets as long as no human passengers are uncomfortable with the arrangement. "I enjoy letting guests take their pets along, as I have always had dogs myself and still have many other pets at home, including cats, a horse, and a parrot," says Captain Satch McMahon. Trips range from 2-hour family cruises to 10-hour fishing excursions.

Dock Square, downtown Kennebunkport (www.kennebunkport.org). A maze of art galleries, gift shops, restaurants, and boutiques, Dock Square is the one place every visitor to Kennebunkport wanders through at least once or twice. Traffic can be terrible (and parking even worse), but the place has a charm and lure that few tourists can resist. With a dog in tow, you may have to limit yourself to window-shopping, but you'll nonetheless enjoy meandering through the tree-lined streets and gaping at the former estates (now mostly B&Bs) that watch over the area.

Ferry Beach State Park, 95 Bayview Rd., Saco (207-283-0067; 207-624-6080). With all of the region's beaches and attractions competing for attention, it might be easy to miss this 100-acre, diverse park—but don't. The sweeping terrain includes wetlands, open beaches, dunes, and woods; trails are color-coded and easy to follow. You're likely to see piping plovers, rare black tupelo trees, goldenrod, highbush blueberry bushes, and, unfortunately, poison ivy. Pet owners are expected to clean up after their animals.

Finestkind Scenic Cruises, 70 Perkins Cove, Ogunquit (207-646-5227; captain@finestkindcruises.com; www.finestkindcruises.com); $17–30 per person. Well-behaved pets are welcome to join their owners at Finestkind for a breakfast cruise, a Nubble Lighthouse cruise, a lobstering trip, or an evening cocktail cruise. (The company does reserve the right to deny access to a pet if one of the passengers is allergic to or afraid of animals.) Finestkind's three traditional wooden boats are docked at Perkins Cove; dogs are also welcome on board the company's sailboat.

Fort McClary State Historic Site, Kittery Point Rd. (Rte. 103), Kittery (207-384-5160). Kittery is called the Gateway to Maine, and Fort McClary protected that gateway from intruders for nearly 300 years during the Revolutionary War, the War of 1812, the Civil War, the Spanish-American War, and World War I. Open during the warmer months, the site includes historic structures such as the Blockhouse, the Rifleman's House, and the remains of a barracks building. Dogs must be on a leash.

Ghostly Tours of York, 250 York St., York Village (207-363-0000;); $10 per person. The town of York is made up of three distinct communities, which the locals call "the Yorks": York Beach, York Harbor, and York Village. In the village, the local historical society maintains a complex of seven historic buildings that highlight the town's past. Ghostly Tours' candlelit nighttime walking trips are narrated to give visitors a glimpse at the spookier side of Old York's folklore—and to raise the hairs on the back of your neck.

Lower Village, downtown Kennebunk. This tourist mecca sits across the river from its larger cousin, Dock Square (see above listing). Formerly a bustling hub for sea merchants, today the area is lined with shops and eateries. Boats still travel in and out, though now they're likely to be seeking pleasure, not business.

McDougal Orchards, 201 Hanson's Ridge Rd., Springvale

(207-324-5054; www.mcdougal orchards.com). In fall, your leashed dog is welcome to help you pick your own apples at this expansive orchard; in winter, it doubles as a cross-country ski area. Well-behaved dogs under voice control can join skiers on the trail on weekdays (but not weekends). Visitors are asked to clean up any messes left behind by their companion animals.

Memorial Park, Heath St., Old Orchard Beach. They may not be allowed on Main Street, the beach, or the pier from May to Labor Day, but dogs are welcome to romp leash-free at an exercise area in a corner of this pretty park.

Nubble Light, The Nubble. One of the most photographed sights on the south coast, the 1879 Nubble Light sits with its keeper's Victorian-style cottage on an offshore island but can be viewed from the tip of the Cape Neddick peninsula (Route 1A to Nubble Road).

Ocean Avenue, Kennebunkport. Hop in the car and cruise along this breathtaking strip of road beside the Atlantic. You'll find places to pull off and enjoy the many views, including that of former president George Bush's summer estate, located on its own jetty known as **Walker Point.** Don't worry about missing it—even if the home itself were hard to see (which it's not), the crowds of pointing tourists would inevitably lead your eyes in the right direction.

Rachel Carson National Wildlife Refuge, 321 Port Rd., Wells (207-646-9226). Rachel Carson is the author of *Silent Spring,* a 1962 book that many credit with single-handedly starting the environmental movement in the United States. Today her name lives on at this 7,600-acre refuge spread throughout York and Cumberland counties. Start at the Route 9 headquarters to get maps and orient yourself before setting off to explore the coastal wilderness. Leashed dogs are welcome in designated areas; watch for signs.

Vaughan Woods State Park, 28 Oldsfields Rd., South Berwick (207-384-5160; 207-624-6080). To find the park, take Route 236 to the intersection of Vine Street and Oldsfields Road and watch for the signs. If you're only in southern Maine for a vacation, you probably won't have enough time to explore all 250 acres of this vast, heavily forested park that lies along the Salmon Falls River. The trails wind through seemingly endless tracts of old-growth forest; if you're looking for solitude, this is the place. Dogs must be on a leash.

Wells Breakwater, Wells. Feeling adventurous? Walk all the way out to the end of the rocks at this somewhat hard-to-find jetty and small wildlife preserve. (From Post Road, turn onto Mile Road and drive past the marsh and Billy's Chowder House. Take the next available left and drive to the end of the peninsula until you reach an unmarked parking area.) Dogs on a leash are wel-

THE WIGGLY BRIDGE IS THE SMALLEST SUSPENSION BRIDGE IN THE UNITED STATES.

come as long as owners clean up after them; pooper-scooper bags and trash cans are provided.

Wells Harbor Saturday Night Concerts, Wells Harbor Park, Wells (www.wellstown.org). Surfer tunes, piano recitals, Elvis impersonators, country crooners—you name it, you'll probably find it one Saturday night at Wells's weekly free summer concert series. (Check out www.wellsmaine.com/free-concerts for the latest lineups before your visit, or call the Wells Chamber of Commerce at 207-646-8104.) Pets are welcome to groove along with the music but must be leashed and nondisruptive.

Wells Recreational Area, Rte. 9A, Wells. Dogs on a leash are welcome at this 70-acre site complete with a pond, a picnic area, a baseball diamond, a soccer field, and tennis and basketball courts. It's a great spot for flying a kite or just relaxing away from the tourist crowds. Owners must pick up after their animals.

Whaleback Light, Kittery. Although it sits in Maine waters and is operated by the town of Kittery, the townspeople of nearby Portsmouth, New Hampshire, also claim this well-known lighthouse as a source of local pride. You can catch a glimpse of the historic structure from Fort Foster and other spots along the shoreline, though you'll get your best view from on board a boat sailing in or out of Portsmouth Harbor.

Wiggly Bridge, Old Mill Rd., York. The name is silly, but accurate: The country's smallest suspension bridge really does shimmy and shake when you walk across it. Park on the street and walk down the raised path, across the bridge, and into **Sherman Woods,** a small preserve. It's a fun stop for getting your feet wet, walking, and exploring.

York Harbor Shore Path, York. This mile-long scenic walking path is where you'll find the area's famous "wiggly bridge" (see above listing), a favorite with kids. The trail starts at Lindsay Road and goes, well, over the river and through the woods. It's an easy and fun way to explore York's shoreline.

QUICK BITES

Barnacle Billy's, 70 Perkins Cove, Ogunquit (207-646-5575; www.barnbilly.com). Barnacle Billy's is actually two restaurants sitting side by side at Perkins Cove. "Both have a very informal outside dining area," says Billy himself. "We have many cus-

BOB'S CLAM HUT IN KITTERY IS THE PLACE TO GO FOR FRIED CLAM BASKETS. (COURTESY OF BOB'S CLAM HUT)

tomers who bring their pets to dine outside with them." Diners choose from a varied menu that includes items like lobster, burgers, barbecue chicken, and Billy's famous rum punch.

Bob's Clam Hut, 315 Rte. 1, Kittery (207-439-4233; www.bobsclamhut.com). They call themselves a "corny little clam hut by the side of the road," and that's just about right. Upscale it may not be, but Bob's has been keeping 'em coming to its take-out window and heated indoor restaurant since 1956. Deep-frying, as you might expect, is a specialty, as are baskets with fries and 'slaw.

Capt'n Hook's Fish Market and Takeout, Rte. 1, Wells (207-646-6646; www.captainhookstakeout.com). This fish market and seafood take-out restaurant has a picnic area where you can enjoy traditional lobster dinners as well as sandwiches, lobster rolls, and all kinds of fried seafood. Capt'n Hook's is open seven days a week from May to Labor Day.

The Clam Shack, Dock Street (at the bridge), Kennebunkport (207-967-2560; www.theclamshack.net). You'll smell the delicious deep-fried odor of this always crowded take-out stand while you're waiting in traffic to get into Dock Square (see "Out and About"). Seafood and more seafood is on the menu.

David's Café, 21–23 Shore Rd., Ogunquit (207-646-5206). Open April through October, this casual café has plenty of outdoor seating and serves soup and chowder, lobster bisque, salads, seafood sandwiches and rolls, pasta, chicken, vegetarian entrées, and a rotating list of daily specials. The café is open from April to October. In 2013, chef David Turin opened two new upscale restaurants at the luxury Boathouse Hotel & Marina complex: David's Opus Ten and David's Kennebunkport.

Dockside Café, 127 Ocean Ave., Kennebunkport (207-967-3625). Dockside is perhaps best known for its breakfasts, including plump pancakes and corned-beef hash. Come midday, however, you can enjoy lunch here, too. A few outdoor tables are available, and the restaurant (located behind Schooners Inn) has nice views of the river.

Rapid Ray's, 179 Main St., Saco (207-282-1847; www.rapidrays.biz). Walk up to the take-out counter to order your chili dog, lobster roll, cheeseburger, onion rings, french fries, clam cake, or whatever other kind of greasy good treat you're craving.

Scoop Deck, Eldredge Rd. (at Rte. 1), Wells (207-646-5150; www.scoopdeck.com). Pet owners will appreciate the take-out window at this roadside stop serving steamed hot dogs, ice cream and frozen yogurt, cold drinks, and other summer staples. Nothin' fancy, but oh so good.

HOT SPOTS FOR SPOT

Digs, Divots & Dogs, 311 West St., Biddeford (207-967-5661; www.digsdivotsanddogs.com). This unique store sells gifts for (you guessed it) gardeners, golfers, and dog lovers. Whether you qualify as one of those or as all three, you're sure to find some fun items to suit your fancy.

Dog N' Cat Kennel, 41 Columbus Cir., Lebanon (207-457-2268; www.dogncatkennel.homestead.com). If you're looking for overnight boarding, the Dog N' Cat Kennel offers 10-foot-by-10-foot "doggie hotel rooms" in addition to an "in-home" care option. The kennel also offers doggie day care and drop-off/pick-up services.

Downeast Pet Supply, 41 Western Ave., P.O. Box 3060, Kennebunk 04043 (207-967-8282). Stop at Downeast for all your pet necessities, from pet beds and carriers to treats, toys, and grooming supplies. Stocked pet-food brands include Iams, California Natural, Wysong, Old Mother Hubbard, Solid Gold, and Wellness.

June Bug's Beach House, 16 Shore Rd., Ogunquit (207-646-4000; cooldogs2@earthlink.net; www.junebugsbeachhouse.com). This eclectic shop is named after one of the owners' rescue dogs; it specializes in handcrafted goods made in the USA, including purses, apparel, jewelry, and spa products for people; candles, frames, mirrors, signs, pillows, rugs, pottery, and cast-iron accessories for the home; and collars, scarves, toys, all-natural treats, beds, bowls, and bath products for pets.

Keoke Kennels, 5 Hodgman Ave., Saco (207-282-6574; coblike2002@yahoo.com). For more than 30 years, Mary Plummer has run this overnight boarding facility located about a mile from Old Orchard Beach. Dogs have indoor/outdoor pens with roofs, and cats have large indoor pens. Animals are welcome for long-term boarding or for just one night; grooming is also available. "In the summertime, about 70 percent of the dogs we have here are with their owners on vacation," Plummer says.

Lebel Dog Grooming, 1501 Post Rd., Wells (207-641-2027; www.lebeldoggrooming.8k.com). If your pooch gets socked by a skunk on vacation, never fear: Janette Lebel, owner of this cozy grooming salon, will take care of that smelly problem. She can also do a flea bath, cut, shampoo, earwax flushing, and soothing hot-oil skin treatments. Lebel's shop also carries a variety of pet health-care products like bowls, leashes, collars, and coats.

Meadow Winds Farm, 331 Rte. 103, York (207-439-7800; mwfarm@aol.com). Chuck and Peggy d'Entremont run this facility with their daughter, Katie. Twenty 4-by-13-foot indoor pens provide overnight boarding for dogs, which get out four times a day to romp in an outdoor run or indoor playroom. Cats have a separate area with windows and litter boxes. All the animals get lots of attention throughout their stay. "We treat them the same way we would want our pets to be treated," says Chuck. Rates are generally $25 per night.

Paw-zn-Around, 8 New County Rd., Saco (207-283-6642; info@paw-zn-around.com; www.paw-zn-around.com). At this doggie day-care facility, animals interact with each other in playgroups and romp in kiddie pools in the summertime. Dogs are welcome for half-day ($21) or full-day ($28) stays; owners can also take advantage of obedience training, overnight boarding, handling classes, and grooming. Owner Jeanne Labonte asks only that your dog be up-to-date on standard vaccinations and non-aggressive toward people and other dogs. Credit cards are accepted.

Pet Life, Saco Valley Shopping Center, 4 Scamman St., **Saco** (207-282-2850); and Center for Shopping, 1364 Main St., **Sanford** (207-490-2412; www.petlifestores.com). This pet-supply store's two southern Maine locations are good stops for refills on treats, toys, food, and other basic needs for all furry, feathered, or scaled travelers. For information on the store's other locations in the state, see "Greater Portland and Casco Bay," "Western Lakes and Mountains," and "Central Lakes and Cities." There are nine stores in Maine, as well as locations in Massachusetts and New Hampshire.

Reigning Cats & Dogs, 3 Garden St., **Kennebunk** (207-985-1414); and 913 Post Rd., Rte. 1, **Wells** (207-646-7788; www.rcdpets.com.com). These two animal-centered shops have "anything they want, everything you need." That includes premium pet foods, shampoo, toys, carriers, leashes, nutritional supplements, and "spa" grooming services. The Wells site is located behind Sportshoe Center; the Kennebunk store is located next to the Garden Street Market.

Sweets Pet Supply, 112 York St. (Rte. 1 S.), Kennebunk (207-985-3734). This pet shop specializes in canine treats, according to owner John Kelley. "It's like a candy store for dogs in here," he says. Sweets also sells holistic food and medications, along with supplies for cats, birds, and other small animals. Kelley also does grooming by appointment.

Town 'N' Country Grooming, 1532 Post Rd., Wells (207-646-1533). "I love my job!" says groomer and owner Kathy Levesque, which might explain why she's still at it after 20-plus years. In addition to washing and clipping all breeds of dogs, she also works with quite a few cats, especially the state's famous Maine Coons.

ANIMAL SHELTERS AND HUMANE SOCIETIES

Almost Home Rescue, 66 Pleasant Hill Rd., Hollis (207-727-5013; www.almosthomerescue.net)

Animal Welfare Society, P.O. Box 43, West Kennebunk 04094 (207-985-3244; www.animalwelfaresociety.org)

Another Chance Animal Rescue, P.O. Box 552, 37 Market St., North Berwick 03906 (207-676-9330; www.anotherchanceanimalrescue.org)

Creature Comforts Animal Shelter, 195 State Rd., Kittery (207-439-6674)

Hemlock Hill Farm Sanctuary, RFD 2, Box 474, North Lebanon (207-457-1371)

Lebanon Animal Control Shelter, 32 Little River Rd., Lebanon (207-457-2158)

New England Federation of Humane Societies, c/o AWS, P.O. Box 43, West Kennebunk 04094 (207-985-3244, ext. 107)

Old Orchard Beach Animal Shelter, 136 Saco Ave., Old Orchard Beach (207-934-4911)

Part of the Family Animal Sanctuary, 22 Sunrise Ave., Saco (207-283-0690)

Voice for Animals, P.O. Box 522, York 03909 (207-743-6290; www.voiceforanimals.net)

IN CASE OF EMERGENCY

Animal Medical Associates, 838 Portland Rd., Saco (207-282-5151)

Kennebunk Veterinary Hospital, 149 Fletcher St., Kennebunk (207-985-4277)

Kittery Animal Hospital, 195 State Rd., Kittery (207-439-4158)

Post Road Veterinary Clinic, 746 Post Rd., Wells (207-646-7200)

Scarborough Animal Hospital, 129 Rte. 1, Scarborough (207-883-4412)

Village Veterinary, 11 York St., York (207-351-1530)

York County Veterinary Emergency, Hill Rd., Kennebunkport (207-284-9911)

YOUR DOG CAN RELAX BY THE OCEAN AT THE INN BY THE SEA IN CAPE ELIZABETH. (COURTESY OF INN BY THE SEA)

Greater Portland and Casco Bay

From city streets to country lanes, mountain peaks to rushing rivers, and deep woods to open ocean, the Greater Portland region at times seems like 10 vacation spots all rolled up into one convenient package. One day you might find yourself browsing shops and galleries in the highbrow corners of Old Port; the next, you're outlet hopping in Freeport or hiking a trail on the way back to your waterfront campsite.

And then, of course, there are the islands: So many dot sparkling Casco Bay that they have been termed the Calendar Islands—one for each day of the year. There might not be *quite* that many, but there are certainly more inlets, estuaries, tiny downtowns, and rocky picnic spots than you could ever explore in just a week or two. Fortunately, the local ferry service (see Casco Bay Lines under "Out and About") allows pets on board for visits to many of the isles, and Orrs Island and Bailey Island are connected to the mainland via roadways.

For the most part, animal owners will find this region to be an accommodating place—pet shops and doggie day cares are plentiful, and the region's many state parks allow ample opportunity for four-legged explorations. If you enjoy camping with your dog, you'll find many scenic campgrounds, some with acres of oceanfront and others with their own off-leash dog parks. Greater Portland attracts and welcomes tourists but is not defined by its tourism—perhaps that's what makes it so appealing. Grab the leash and enjoy.

ACCOMMODATIONS

Hotels, Motels, Inns, and Bed & Breakfasts

Bath

Holiday Inn Bath-Brunswick Area, 139 Richardson St., Bath (207-443-9741; www.ihg.com); $109–299 per night. Pets are permitted to stay at this Holiday Inn, which has an outdoor swimming pool, free high-speed Internet access, a hot tub and sauna, laundry facilities, a fitness center, a lounge, a "kids eat free" program, and in-room coffeemakers, hair dryers, irons, and ironing boards.

Inn at Bath, 969 Washington St., Bath (207-443-4294; 1-800-423-0964; innkeeper@innatbath.com; www.innatbath.com); $150–245 per night. Located in Bath's picturesque historic district, the Inn at Bath offers upscale rooms and suites, some of which have whirlpool baths, fireplaces, and outdoor entrances, which are always useful for pet owners. Dogs are permitted with prior approval for an extra $15 per night, but owners must sign a pet-policy form that details the inn's animal-related regulations.

Brunswick

Rodeway Motor Inn, 287 Bath Rd., Brunswick (207-729-6661; www.choicehotels.com); $69–129 per night. "We have a nicely wooded area for walking pets in the back of the property," says Viking owner and animal lover Sue Kelly. "As long as people are considerate about picking up after their pets, we welcome them." All 38 rooms have parking spaces in front of the door, refrigerators, and microwaves. For larger families or groups, there are deluxe efficiencies. The inn also has an outdoor heated pool and picnic area.

Cape Elizabeth

Inn by the Sea, 40 Bowery Beach Rd., Cape Elizabeth (207-799-3134; 1-800-888-4287; info@innbythesea.com; www.innbythesea.com); $229–679 per night. This luxury resort is somewhat renowned among traveling animal owners. The management strives to provide four-footed guests with "the same level of service and excellence that our human guests have come to know and love." Pet-friendly suites have "special dog amenities," and the room-service pet menu (yes, you read that right) includes items such as the Bow Wow Sirloin Burger, frozen peanut better yogurt treats, and homemade biscuits.

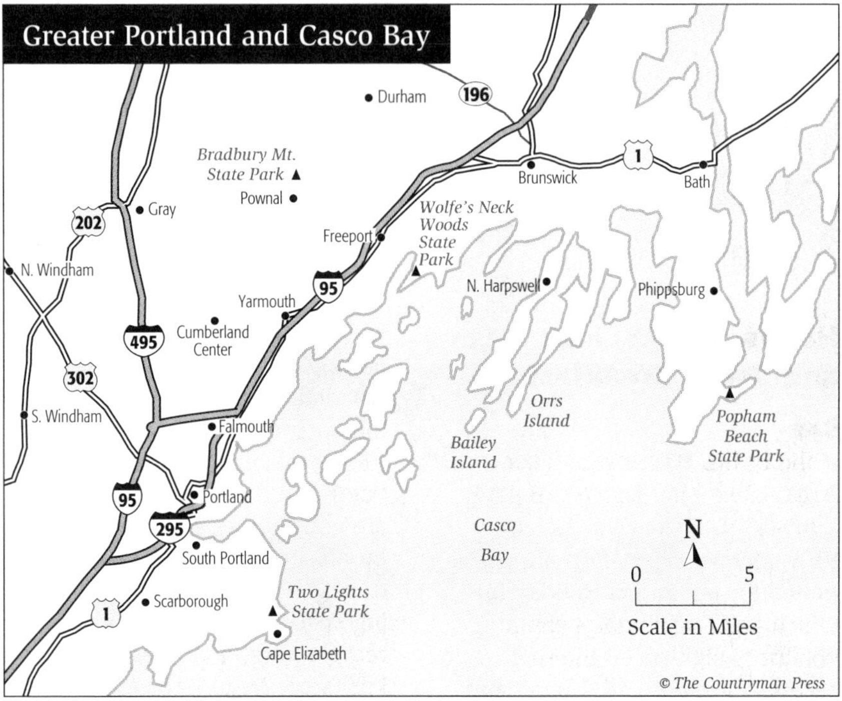

Falmouth

Quaker Tavern Bed & Breakfast, 377 Gray Rd. (Rte. 26 N.), Falmouth (207-797-5540; quakerbb@aol.com; www.quakertavernbb-inn.com); $75–100 per night. Thirteen acres surround this historic B&B; the innkeeper, Donna Little, prefers to walk through them barefoot, and so asks pet owners to always clean up after their animals! Each of the four guest rooms in the building (circa 1780) has a fireplace, feather bed, and private parlor. There are no extra fees for animals, but owners are asked to bring along a pet bed. An organic continental breakfast is included in the rate.

Freeport

Best Western Freeport Inn, Rte. 1, Freeport (207-865-3106; 1-800-99-VALUE; info@freeportinn.com; www.bestwestern.com); $129–179 per night. Your dog will have no trouble finding trouble at this pet-friendly inn; with 25 acres of lawns, a tidal river, and a "pet exercise area," there's plenty of room to get out and about. Some of the 80 rooms have water views, and all have cable television, air-conditioning, and premium movie channels. Pets up to 80 pounds are allowed in designated rooms for an additional $20 per stay, with a maximum of two pets per room; doggie cleanup bags are provided.

Econo Lodge Freeport, 537 Rte. 1, Freeport (207-865-3777; www.choicehotels.com); $99–1294 per night. This Econo Lodge offers free daily continental breakfasts, a picnic area, high-speed Internet access, cable television, free local telephone calls, exterior corridors, and a location that's close to all the area's attractions. Dogs weighing 40 pounds or less are welcome; one pet is permitted per room.

Maine Idyll Motor Court, 1411 Rte. 1, Freeport (207-865-4201; www.freeportusa.com/memberprofile/maine-idyll-motor-court); $61–118 per night. The 20 furnished cottages at this complex have one to three bedrooms, refrigerators, and electric or gas heat; some have fireplaces and kitchenettes. You'll also find two playgrounds, picnic tables, and plenty of woodsy areas for dog walks. Canines are always welcome guests for an additional $3 per night.

Maple Hill Bed & Breakfast, 18 Maple Ave., Freeport (207-865-3730; 1-800-867-0478); $100–160 per night. "Our goal is to be family-friendly, which means welcoming babies, grandparents, parents—and pets," explains Lloyd Lawrence, who runs Maple Hill with his wife, Susie. Pet owners pay an extra fee of $10 per night, per pet, and are asked to keep the animal in a crate if they leave the room. (They have crates available if you forget yours.)

White Cedar Inn, 178 Main St., Freeport (207-865-9099; 1-800-853-1269; info@whitecedarinn.com; www.whitecedarinn.com); $130–175 per night. The White Cedar Inn recently changed hands, but luckily for us the new owners are continuing the inn's dog-friendly legacy. For an extra $20 per night, your pup is welcome to join you in the Bowdoin Room, which has two queen beds, a private bathroom, and a sitting area with a television and gas fireplace. Plastic pooper-scooper bags are provided, and the owners are also happy to recommend local pet-sitters. Dogs must remain in your company at all

PETS ARE WELCOME AT THE ECO-LUXURIOUS INN BY THE SEA.

times, except while you're enjoying breakfast.

Orrs Island

Tower Hill Bed & Breakfast, 1565 Harpswell Islands Rd., Orrs Island (207-833-2311; 1-888-833-2311); $130–160 per night. With brass beds, quilts, private baths, and sitting rooms, the three suites at Tower Hill are warm and welcoming. Harpswell Sound, a forest, and a wildlife-filled marsh are all just a few minutes' walk away. The innkeepers welcome one neutered, small- to medium-size dog per room with prior approval for an extra $20 per night.

Phippsburg

Edgewater Farm Bed & Breakfast, 71 Small Point Rd., Phippsburg (207-389-1322; www.ewfbb.com); $95–225 per night. Organic perennial gardens encircle the lawns at this charming B&B located on a Casco Bay peninsula. "We're very dog-friendly here, and I find that most people's dogs are well behaved and not a problem," says Carol Emerson, who runs Edgewater Farm with her husband, Bill. All six of the guest rooms have private baths, and guests can also take a dip in the indoor heated pool or outdoor hot tub. Pet owners pay an extra $25 per stay (not per night).

Hidden Mountain Cottages, 1659 Main Rd., Phippsburg (207-389-1457; lucrecia@hiddenmtn.com; www.hiddenmtn.com); $70–100 per night or $550–800 per week. These small yellow cottages vary in size and have showers, double beds, refrigerators, and televisions; linens and towels are provided. Pets are welcome without additional fees. An on-site gift shop sells T-shirts, kids' books and activity sets, clothing, jewelry, and handmade crafts. The cottages are open mid-May to mid-October.

Small Point Bed & Breakfast, 312 Small Point Rd., Phippsburg (207-389-1716); $130 per night or $850 per week. Pet owners can stay at Small Point's 1890s carriage house; the renovated structure can comfortably accommodate a couple or a family (up to three children) with a queen-size bed, sitting area, and loft. A Vermont Castings propane stove keeps things cozy, and guests also have a refrigerator, a microwave, a toaster oven, and a coffeemaker. Dogs are welcome (sorry, no cats).

Portland

Best Western Merry Manor Inn, 700 Main St., Portland (207-774-6151; info@merrymanorinn.com; www.bestwestern.com); $99–159 per night. This hotel is set on 5 acres of woods with hiking trails. There are no extra fees for pets, though owners are asked to keep their furry friends quiet and not leave them alone in the rooms. The Merry Manor also has facilities for conferences and banquets, and is a few minutes away from the Old Port district (see "Out and About").

Holiday Inn Portland West, 81 Riverside St., Portland (207-774-5601; www.ihg.com); $79–169 per night. This chain hotel has a

A VIEW FROM THE DOG EXERCISE AREA AT THE PET-FRIENDLY BEST WESTERN FREEPORT INN

garden courtyard, country-style rooms, and a location that's close to the airport and the highway. There are no extra fees for pets, but guests traveling with animals are welcome only in the designated smoking rooms.

Howard Johnson Plaza Hotel, 155 Riverside St., Portland (207-774-5861; info@hojoportland.com; www.hojo.com); $100–169 per night. Pets are welcome at the HoJo Plaza with advance notice and a $50 refundable deposit. Amenities include an indoor swimming pool, a hot tub, a free airport shuttle, two on-site restaurants, and an exercise room. Some rooms have Jacuzzis; all have coffeemakers, irons and ironing boards, and hair dryers.

Inn at St. John, 939 Congress St., Portland (207-773-6481; 1-800-636-9127; theinn@maine.rr.com; www.innatstjohn.com); $129–185 per night. The Inn at St. John has a European, upscale look that complements the cobblestone streets, chic boutiques, and artistic community that surround it. The hotel also offers air-conditioning, free continental breakfasts, bicycle storage, airport pickups, and nonsmoking rooms. Pets are welcome at no extra charge.

Motel 6 Portland, 1 Riverside St., Portland (207-775-0111; www.motel6.com); $59–79 per night. You can expect the standard chain-motel accommodations at this Motel 6, which, like all of the company's locations through the country, accepts one "small" pet per room (call to see if yours qualifies). Expect to take advantage of cable television with premium movie channels, laundry facilities, a "kids stay free" program, and free coffee in the lobby.

Residence Inn Downtown Portland Waterfront, 145 Fore St., Portland (207-761-1660; www.marriott.com); $239–319 per night. Located on the water in the heart of downtown Portland, this Residence Inn has 179 suites, and welcomes pets with a one-time $100 sanitation fee per stay. Portland was named the Best Small Foodie Town, and you'll be in a perfect location to explore the city's diverse offerings. The hotel has an indoor pool, fitness center, restaurant, and lounge.

Scarborough

Pride Motel and Cottages, 677 Rte. 1, Scarborough (207-883-4816; 1-800-424-3350; pjor@prodigy.net; www.pridemotel.com); $80–145 per night. For an extra $5 per night, pet owners are welcome in any of Pride's seven motel rooms or 10 red-and-white-painted cottages. All have free HBO and air-conditioning; some motel rooms have kitchenettes, and all of the cottages have a full-size kitchen. Other amenities include an outdoor swimming pool, a volleyball court, and a recreation room.

South Portland

Econo Lodge South Portland, 80 John Roberts Rd., South Portland (207-772-3838; www.choicehotels.com); $79–109 per night. Hotel services at this Econo Lodge include wireless Internet access, free daily continental breakfasts, cable television, free weekday newspapers, a wake-up service, and in-room coffeemakers, irons, and ironing boards. Dogs weighing less than 40 pounds are permitted for an extra $10 per night, with a maximum of one pet allowed per room.

Portland Marriott at Sable Oaks, 200 Sable Oaks Dr., South Portland (207-871-8000; www.marriott.com); $169–229 per night. For an extra $50 one-time fee, your pooch is a welcome guest at this South Portland Marriott. Visitors can enjoy amenities such as high-speed Internet access, concierge services, meeting rooms, express check-in and check-out services, a restaurant and lounge, room service, free newspapers, laundry facilities, and free local telephone calls.

Campgrounds

Durham

Freeport-Durham KOA, 82 Big Skye Ln., Durham (207-688-4288; www.koa.com); $26–30 per night. This campground has shady and sunny sites, a playground, horseshoe pits, a swimming pool, sports courts, a baseball field, and walking trails. KOA welcomes pets at its campgrounds, provided they are leashed, not aggressive, quiet, and cleaned-up after. Dogs are not permitted in cabins.

Freeport

Cedar Haven Campground, 39 Baker Rd., Freeport (207-865-6254; 1-800-454-3403; www.cedarhavenfamilycampground

.com); $24–50 per night or $150–215 per week. Most of Cedar Haven's 58 campsites are wooded; 10 are reserved for tents, and the rest have hookups for RVs. Amenities include a swimming pond, a game room, a camp store, hot showers, and laundry facilities. Small camping cabins are also available for rent. Pets are welcome but must stay on a leash and off the beach and recreation field.

Desert Dunes of Maine Campground, 95 Desert Rd., Freeport (207-865-6962; info@desertofmaine.com; www.desertofmaine.com); $25–39 per night. Located next to the unusual geographical area known as the Desert of Maine, this family campground has trails, open and shaded sites for tents and RVs, hot showers, picnic tables, volleyball and basketball courts, horseshoe pits, and laundry facilities. There's also a fenced dog park and agility course for off-leash play. Pets must be quiet, on a leash, and accompanied by their owners at all times.

Winslow Memorial Park and Campground, Staples Point Rd., Freeport (207-865-4198); $17–19 per night. Managed by the town of Freeport, this park and campground is set on a Casco Bay peninsula with 100 campsites, a large picnic area, hiking trails, ocean views, a playground, and a boat launch. Dogs are welcome on a leash for a fee of $1 per night, though they are not allowed on the beach, playground, or volleyball court.

Orrs Island

Orr's Island Campground, 44 Bond Point, Orrs Island (207-833-5595; camping@orrsisland.com; www.orrsisland.com); $215–325 per week. Situated on 42 acres in Casco Bay, this family campground has a half-mile-long beach, 70 wooded sites for tents and trailers, a camp store, canoe rentals, laundry facilities, and a recreational field. Dogs are allowed at the beach but must stay on a leash. Owners are asked to accompany their animals at all times; there are no extra fees for pets, but there is a one-dog-per-site limit.

Phippsburg

Meadowbrook Camping Area, 33 Meadowbrook Rd., Phippsburg (207-443-4967; 1-800-370-CAMP; mbcamp@meadowbrookme.com; www.meadowbrookme.com); $24–36 per night. Choose from tent and RV sites at this 42-acre campground, where dogs on a leash are welcome as long as their owners clean up after them. "We have a mile-long nature trail that winds its way through the woods to a 25-acre beaver pond where your pet can swim and exercise," says Meadowbrook's Chris Mixon. "It's a Lab's heaven." Aside from the scenery, amenities include a heated pool, bathrooms, and a recreation hall with a kitchen.

Pownal

Blueberry Pond Campground, 218 Poland Range Rd., Pownal (207-688-4421; 1-877-290-1381; fun@blueberrycampground.com;

www.blueberrycampground.com); $29–39 per night. This campground is located in a quiet inland area, away from the coastline crowds. Tenters and RVers can choose from private, wooded sites or sunny spots. On-site, you'll also find hiking trails, swing sets, hot showers, fire pits and barbecue grills, picnic tables, and a camp store. Dogs must be on a leash and can't be left alone.

Bradbury Mountain State Park Campground, 528 Hallowell Rd., Pownal (207-287-3824; 1-800-332-1501); $11 per night Maine residents; $19 per night out-of-state residents. The camping accommodations at this scenic park (see "Out and About") are mainly designed to accommodate tents and small campers, though there are a few large and extra-large sites for campers up to 35 feet in length. The campground has a play area, a picnic area, handicapped-accessible toilets, showers, hiking trails, and a boat launch. Dogs must be leashed.

Scarborough

Bayley's Camping Resort, 275 Pine Point Rd., Scarborough (207-883-6043; tbayley@gwi.net; www.bayleys-camping.com); $25–65 per night. There's no extra fee for pets at Bayley's, though dogs must be on a leash at all times, can't be left unattended, and are prohibited from certain areas, including the playground, ponds, and pool. Tent campers can set up at Bayley's Acres, an area separate from the RV sites with no hookups; and families can take advantage of an on-site restaurant, a game room, a general store, basketball courts, fishing ponds, and activity fields.

Wassamki Springs, 56 Saco St., Scarborough (207-839-4276; wassamkisprings@aol.com; www.wassamkisprings.com); $25–49 per night or $150–342 per week. With a 1-mile-long stretch of beach, a trout-stocked fishing pond, boat rentals, scavenger hunts, spooky storytelling, and hayrides, there's plenty for families to do at this busy campground. Dogs must be leashed and should accompany their owners at all times. Wassamki allows most breeds of dogs; call to see if yours qualifies.

Homes, Cottages, and Cabins for Rent

To find local vacation rentals, check Craigslist, local real estate rental agencies, or large online agencies, including:

www.mainehuts.org
www.homeaway.com
www.vrbo.com
www.vacationrentals.com
www.cyberrentals.com

Rental Agencies

Ashmore Realty Island Rentals, 20 Welch St., Peaks Island (207-766-2981; rentals@ashmorerealty.com; www.ashmorerealty.com). Ashmore is full of pet-loving rental agents (Cicely the dog is a frequent visitor at the office). Pets are allowed at many of the agency's listed rental properties, though owners usually have to pay a $100 security deposit. Available units range from small summer cottages to full-size, year-round homes, priced from about $550 to $2,600 per week. All are located on Peaks Island in Casco Bay.

Casco Bay Properties, P.O. Box 335, Freeport 04032 (207-865-2092; pam@cascobayproperties.com). Pam Perry is the new owner of this company that specializes in finding short-term accommodations for vacations and corporate stays. Choices range from studio apartments to one-, two- and three-bedroom suites and full-size homes, all fully furnished and equipped. Many rentals are located directly on the ocean.

OUT AND ABOUT

Baxter Woods, Portland. Dogs can run off-leash at this 30-acre park at Forest and Stevens avenues in Portland. Pets must be under voice control but are otherwise welcome to roam the trails and woods alongside their owners.

Bradbury Mountain State Park, 528 Hallowell Rd., Pownal. This inland park comprises about 590 acres of forest, crisscrossed with trails designed for hikers, bikers, snowshoers, cross-country skiers, and, we like to think, dog walkers. (The park also allows horseback riders, so make sure your pooch isn't afraid of his larger animal friends.) Take in the view from the summit, or enjoy the on-site picnic tables, playground, and baseball field.

Casco Bay Lines, Franklin St., Portland (207-774-7871; info@cascobaylines.com; www.cascobaylines.com); passengers, $3.85–11.25; cars, $45–65. Sometimes described as a lifeline for the residents of the Casco Bay islands, this ferry service (the oldest in America) is the chief mode of transport to and from the mainland and **Peaks Island, Little Diamond Island, Great Diamond Island, Diamond Cove, Long Island, Chebeague Island,** and **Cliff Island.** The company also provides scenic cruises and trips (prices vary). Leashed dogs and other pets are welcome on board all Casco Bay vessels for a $4.10 round-trip charge.

Chase Charters, Falmouth (207-767-5611; steve@chasecharters.com.com; www.chasecharters.com); call for daily and weekly rates. This charter company has two sailboats (36 and 40 feet) and one 26-foot powerboat; the skippers can take you to a particular destination or design a trip that will take you past the Maine coast's most spectacular sights. Popular destinations include the **Harraseeket River, Richmond Island, Hog's Island, and Boothbay Harbor.** Owner Pete Stoops says he's never had a dog on board, but pets are welcome as long as owners clean the boat carefully after use.

Crescent Beach State Park, 66 Two Lights Rd., Cape Elizabeth. Pets are not allowed on the beach for which this 243-acre park was named, but they are allowed (on a leash) in the picnic area, playground, coves, and wooded areas, and on the rock ledges and trails. The park is closed to vehicles during the off-season, but visitors are welcome to hike or cross-country ski their way in to enjoy the sights.

Deering Oaks Park, Portland. Located between Deering and Forest avenues, this is Portland's largest park. An amble through the 53 acres will take you past rose gardens, basketball and tennis courts, hiking trails, and a pond (ice-skating is allowed). Dogs are welcome on a leash.

Eastern Promenade, Portland (www.easternpromenade.org). This 4.2-mile-long paved trail runs from India Street to Tukey's Bridge in Portland. It's extremely popular with dog walkers, in-line skaters, and joggers. The views of Casco Bay are great, and the trail is mostly flat, making for a relaxing and scenic outing.

A RESCUED STRAY RELAXES AFTER A GAME OF FETCH AT THE EASTERN PROMENADE IN PORTLAND.

Old Port, Portland. Spend a day wandering through this old-meets-new shopping and arts district in Portland. Stretching from the harbor on up, Old Port is an intriguing mix of bustling docks, umpteen restaurants, gift shops, microbreweries, antiques stores, art galleries, and condominiums. Cars can traverse the cobbled streets, but this place is really made for walking—slowly. Take your time and let it all sink in.

Portland Head Light, 1000 Shore Rd., Cape Elizabeth. As one of Maine's more famous lighthouses, Portland Head attracts more than its share of shutterbugs. The 1791 beauty is located in **Fort Williams Park** (Route 207 to Route 77 to Shore Road). There's a large parking lot on-site; expect to run into tour buses full of admirers. Dogs must be on a leash.

Two Lights State Park, 66 Two Lights Rd., Cape Elizabeth. You won't find a much better spot for a picnic overlooking Casco Bay than Two Lights, named for (you guessed it) two nearby lighthouses—they were the first "twin" lights in the state, both built in 1828. Picnic tables sit on a cliff over the ocean, and the park's 40 acres also include charcoal grills, shoreline trails, and unbeatable views. Dogs must be on a leash.

Window-Shopping in Freeport. When you ask local B&Bs and hotels where they're located, most start by telling you how far they are from L. L. Bean—that might give you some idea of how important shopping is to the residents and visitors of Freeport. There are small boutiques and walkable historic districts here, too, but the big draw is the outlets: more than 125 big-name stores offering bargains, bargains, bargains.

Wolfe's Neck Woods State Park, 425 Wolfe's Neck Rd., Freeport. Interpretive signs guide you along more than 5 miles of trails of this 233-acre park; along the way, you'll pass by quiet wooded areas, estuaries, and the shoreline of the Harraseeket River and Casco Bay. Wolfe's Neck's most famous animal inhabitants are the ospreys that mate and nest nearby. Dogs must be on a leash.

Yarmouth Clam Festival, Yarmouth (www.clamfestival.com). This annual carnival, crafts fair, and seafood extravaganza starts each year on the third Friday in July and lasts for three days. The competition is stiff during the clam-shucking contest, road races, bike races, and canoe and kayak races, and the parade and fireworks always draw a crowd. This is definitely the place to be seen for Yarmouth residents and visitors. Dogs must be on a leash.

QUICK BITES

Bill's Pizza, 177 Commercial St., Portland (207-774-6166). The picnic tables go out and the umbrellas go up in the springtime at Bill's. Dogs on a leash can join their owners for pizza, subs, soups, chili, salads, wine, and ice-cold beer.

Coffee by Design. This Portland-area chain has three shops in the downtown area: 620 Congress St. (207-772-5533; www.coffeebydesign.com), 43 Washington Ave., and 67 India St. (207-879-2233). All three locations have outdoor seating and are pet-friendly. Choose from baked goods and freshly roasted signature coffees, including Tuxedo Mochas, Caramel Cream Lattes, and Peanut Butter Mochas.

Cole Farms, 64 Lewiston Rd., Gray (207-657-4714; info@colefarms.com). This restaurant also has a picnic area, gift-shop area, and playground, and a take-out window serving informal favorites such as burgers and fries, chowder, chicken, baked beans, seafood, sandwiches, and ice cream.

Federal Spice, 225 Federal St., Portland (207-774-6404). In the summertime, pets can sit beside their owners at Federal Spice's outdoor seating area to enjoy multiethnic food specialties, including wraps and quesadillas.

Gilbert's Chowder House, 92 Commercial St., Portland (207-871-5636; www.gilbertschowderhouse.com). Locals consistently rank this plain-and-simple eatery as their favorite spot for chowder. Other choices include lobster, fried clams, soup in bread bowls, and plenty of cold beer. Outdoor deck seating at picnic tables is available.

Harraseeket Lunch & Lobster, Freeport Wharf, Town Landing, Freeport (207-865-3535; www.harraseeketlunchandlobster.com). Head away from the outlets and toward the water to find this ultracasual waterfront restaurant. You'll walk up to the window to order your fried clams, chowder, lobster roll, hot dog, or other yummy snack.

The Lobster Shack Restaurant, 225 Two Lights Rd., Cape Elizabeth (207-799-1677; www.lobstershacktwolights.com). Enjoy your lobster, chowder, stew, fisherman's plate, crabcakes, or other seafood meal at one of the many picnic tables overlooking Portland Harbor and the Atlantic Ocean. The only thing between you and the water is a dramatic, rocky ledge.

HOT SPOTS FOR SPOT

Another Dog Day, 156 Pleasant Hill Rd. #3, Scarborough (207-883-1445). Dying to go whitewater rafting? Or skiing? When your pooch can't come along, this doggie day-care spot will be happy to lend a hand. According to owner Lisa Sands, Another Dog Day has an indoor play area and outdoor fenced-in area to keep the animals active and busy during their stay. They also offer grooming and a "doggie motel," aka overnight boarding.

Brickyard Kennels, 14 Snowhook Trail, North Yarmouth (207-829-5661; www.bykme.com). This kennel specializes in spoiling: Dogs can cuddle up to heated ceramic floors and lambskin bedding, and have all the treats they can eat; cats hang out in three-story kitty condos and scratch to their heart's content on rope-covered posts. Doggie day care ($20) is available, along with overnight lodging ($20 per dog, $18 per cat). Dogs that stay three nights or longer get a complimentary bath, and all animals get plenty of personalized attention.

Doggie Cottage, 35 Bull Run Rd., **Gray** (207-657-7311; www.thedoggiecottage.com). The Doggie Cottage is actually an "all-inclusive pet resort" specializing in doggie day care and overnight stays. The resort is designed to mimic a home-style environment to make the pets more comfortable—there's a living room, a recreation room, six outdoor play areas, and 10 private theme rooms with furniture, color television, music, aromatherapy, and tile floors. "It's fun here," says Sean Kelley, who designed the canine resort with his wife, Jill. "It's more like a dog park than a kennel." Their "turndown service" includes a cookie on the pillow and a hug before bed. The Kelleys recently opened a second location at 81 Holmes Road in **Scarborough** (207-883-1914).

The Fish & Bone, 195 Commerical St., Portland (207-773-5450; www.fetchportland.com). Owner Kathy Palmer, welcomes your canine or feline into her well-stocked pet store that has changed its name, but not the great products it sells."If you're a regular and you come *without* your dog, we usually ask, 'Didn't you forget something?'" Palmer says. In addition to running the shop, she's also working on making Portland more dog-friendly. Merchants who allow dogs into their store are given free dog treats to hand out to canine customers and are included in the Fish & Bone's "Dog-Friendly Portland" listings (available at the store and on the Web site). The store also donates 10 percent of its profits to animal and environmental charities. This is definitely a don't-miss stop when you're in the Portland area.

General Store for Pets, Falmouth Shopping Center, 251 Rte. 1, Falmouth (207-781-4950). The wide selection at this animal-centered General Store includes pet shampoos, rawhide chews, doggie boots, Nylabone treats, pet beds, food and water bowls, collars, leashes, and pet-food brands such as Science Diet, Wellness, Triumph, Eukanuba, and Nutro.

Pet Life, Northgate Shopping Center, 91 Auburn St., Portland (207-797-0779; www.petlifestores.com). This Maine company refuses to sell puppies from puppy mills, instead opting to host regular adoption events with local humane societies. ,Once you've found your Best Friend, you'll find all the food and supplies you need to keep him happy at several locations throughout the state. For more information, see "Southern Maine Coast," "Western Lakes and Mountains," and "Central Lakes and Cities."

Paws Applause, 27 Gorham Rd., Scarborough (207-885-0077; www.pawsapplause.com). This all-natural pet-supply store and grooming salon can provide your pet with a full array of grooming services as well as organic foods, nutritional supplements, biscuits, bones, toys, and much more.

Pet Pantry, 177 Main St., Freeport (207-865-6484; 1-888-772-9392; info@petpantry.com; www.petpantry.com). Half of this 4,000-square-foot store is stocked with supplies for pets—the other half is filled with animal-related items for their owners. Most are breed-specific gifts and sundries, including T-shirts, mugs, jewelry, notepads, and bags. One of the shop's most interesting new items is a "recordable" dog toy—your pup can chew away and hear your voice all day while you're gone.

Pet Quarters, 147 Bath Rd., Brunswick (207-373-0432; www.petquartersne.com). This store is part of a locally owned chain of eight shops. According to the manager, much of Pet Quarters's summer business comes from out-of-town visitors traveling with their animals. You'll find a decent selection of food, supplies, and treats for dogs, cats, and small animals.

Planet Dog Company Store, 211 Marginal Way, Portland (207-347-8606; www.planetdog.com). Planet Dog makes a popular line of doggie toys and accessories that are sold in pet shops throughout the country. The company's headquarters are right here in Portland, however, and the Company Store is "the place to be" for visiting and local pups. Four-legged shoppers will get a scratch behind the ears and a chance to test out some of the merchandise; two-legged visitors can browse through racks of colorful toys, chews, and clothing items.

ANIMAL SHELTERS AND HUMANE SOCIETIES

Animal Refuge League, 449 Stroudwater St., Westbrook (207-854-9771)

Carway Kennels Animal Shelter, 52 Cumberland Rd., North Yarmouth (207-829-6612)

Coastal Humane Society, 30 Range Rd., Brunswick (207-725-5051; www.coastalhumanesociety.org)

Maine Animal Coalition (advocacy), P.O. Box 6683, Portland 04104 (207-773-2215; www.maineanimalcoalition.org)

Maine Friends of Animals, 190 Rte. 1, Falmouth (207-781-2187)

Shelter Friends Rescue, P.O. Box 3, Freeport 04032 (caninerescue@suscom-maine.net)

IN CASE OF EMERGENCY

Animal Emergency Clinic, 352 Warren Ave., Portland (207-878-3121)

Bath-Brunswick Veterinary Association, 257 Bath Rd., Brunswick (207-729-4164)

Falmouth Veterinary Hospital, 174 Rte. 1, Falmouth (207-781-4028)

Forest Avenue Veterinary Hospital, 973 Forest Ave., Portland (207-797-4840)

Portland Veterinary Specialists, 2255 Congress St., Portland (207-780-0271)

Veterinary Centre, 207 Ocean House Rd., Cape Elizabeth (207-799-6952)

PORTER PRESERVE IN BOOTHBAY IS ONE OF THE MANY SCENIC, DOG-FRIENDLY PROPERTIES MANAGED BY THE BOOTHBAY REGION LAND TRUST. (PHOTO COURTESY OF BOOTHBAY REGION LAND TRUST)

Midcoast Maine

Purists say that this is where the real Maine coast begins: From Boothbay Harbor all the way up to the Blue Hill peninsula, you'll find small fishing villages, gracious former ship captains' estates, historic transportation museums, spectacular oceanfront parks, and tiny, inspirational islands. Many Vacationland visitors simply speed through the midcoast area on their way to Acadia. But if you stop to catch your breath, you'll find Searsport, Rockland, Monhegan Island, Castine, and other midcoast spots are more than satisfying destinations in and of themselves.

This is a diverse region in both geography and personality. Throughout the area, simple pleasures combine seamlessly with luxury: clam shacks and fine dining, state parks and manicured lawns, ramshackle thrift shops and upscale art galleries. There are hundreds of midcoast inns, motels, and B&Bs, but not all of them allow pets. Luckily, the innkeepers listed here are friendly and welcoming enough to make up the difference.

ACCOMMODATIONS

Hotels, Motels, Inns, and Bed & Breakfasts

Belfast

Belfast Harbor Inn, 91 Searsport Ave., Belfast (207-338-2740; 1-800-545-8576; stay@belfastharborinn.com; www.belfastharborinn.com); $59–159 per night. Choose from pool-view or ocean-view rooms at this scenic inn situated on 6 acres beside Penobscot Bay. All rooms have either king- or queen-size beds with updated furnishings, and guests can take advantage of a heated outdoor pool. Pet owners pay an extra fee of $10 per pet, per night.

Belhaven Inn Bed & Breakfast, 14 John St., Belfast (207-338-5435; stay@belhaveninn.com; www.belhaveninn.com); $120 per night. Pets are welcome in the efficiency suite of this 1851 Victorian inn; the suite has a kitchen, queen-size bed, daybed sitting area with television, bathroom with skylight, sundeck, and private entrance. You also get a full country breakfast included in the rate. "The entrance opens to a spacious side lawn, perfect for walks," explains innkeeper Anne Bartels. "We have pet bowls for those who forget them, and doggie biscuits for welcoming." Dogs must be vaccinated and leashed, and cannot be left alone in the suite unless crated.

Comfort Inn Ocean's Edge, Rte. 1, 159 Searsport Ave.,Belfast (207-338-2090; 1-800-303-5098; www.choicehotels.com); $120–230 per night. True to its name, this hotel overlooks Penobscot Bay, and each designated pet-friendly room has its own patio that takes in the view and opens out to a 4-acre backyard. Amenities include a heated indoor pool and sauna, a restaurant, laundry machines, free continental breakfasts, free

PET OWNERS CAN EXPLORE 6 WATERFRONT ACRES AT THE BELFAST HARBOR INN. (PHOTO COURTESY OF BELFAST HARBOR INN)

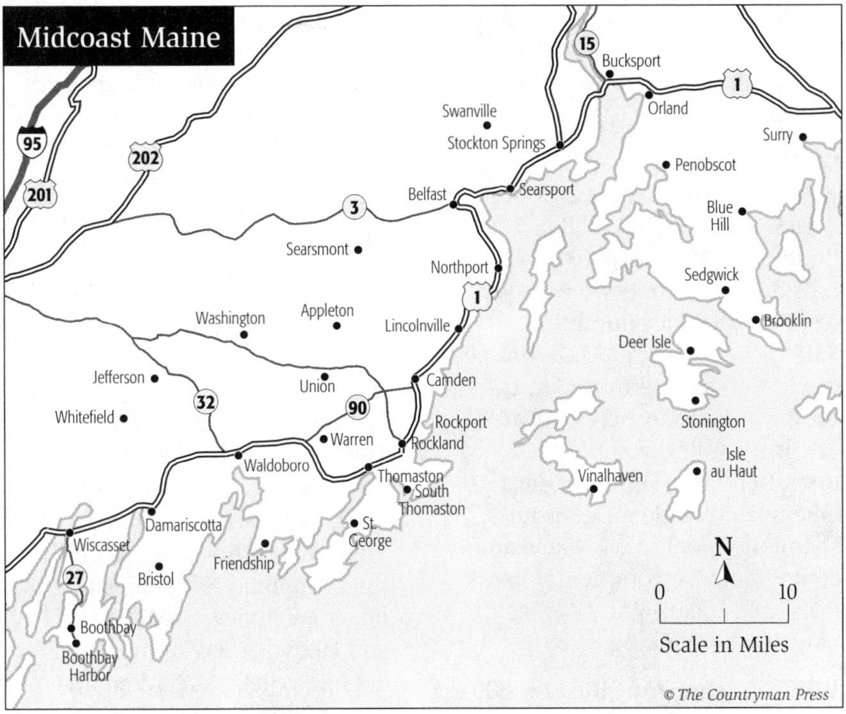

wireless Internet access, and a game room. Dogs are allowed in certain rooms for a fee of $10 per night.

Seascape Motel and Cottages, 202 Searsport Ave., Belfast (207-338-2130; 1-800-477-0786; dogscanstay@seascapemotel.com; www.seascapemotel.com); $84–189 per night. You know a place is pet-friendly when its e-mail address is "dogs can stay"! For an extra $10 per night, dogs up to 25 pounds are welcome in Seascape's cottages (except in the months of July and August), which vary in size and style and offer fully equipped kitchens, cable television, and free local calls. Guests can also enjoy free continental breakfasts, a heated swimming pool, and views of Penobscot Bay. "There's a large area behind the cottages for walking, and scooping is always appreciated," says manager Chris Signorino. "Show us the latest edition of *Dog-Friendly New England* and we'll waive the $10 fee for pets!" Discounts are offered for AKC, AAA, and AARP members.

Blue Hill

Auberge Tenney Hill Guesthouse, 1 Mines Rd., Blue Hill (207-374-2169; raguay@hypernet.com); $95–135 per night. At this historic B&B, built in 1869, guests enjoy fresh pastries from local bakeries every morning on the sunporch, where the hosts also serve tea each afternoon. Daylilies surround the outdoor patio, and the rooms are decorated with antiques in a Victorian style. Pets are permitted with prior approval from the innkeepers.

Boothbay

Hillside Acres Cabins & Motel, Adams Pond Rd., P.O. Box 300, Boothbay 04537 (207-633-3411; hillside@clinic.net; www.ohwy.com/me/h/hiaccamo.htm); $35–75 per week or $372–504 per week. Pets are permitted in the cabins at Hillside Acres, located about 1.5 miles from downtown Boothbay Harbor. Guest amenities include an outdoor swimming pool, cable television, complimentary continental breakfasts, and lots of grassy areas for playing and walking.

White Anchor Inn, Rte. 27, 609 Wicasset Rd., Boothbay (207-633-3788; stay@whiteanchorinnboothbay.com; www.whiteanchorinnboothbay.com); $69–109 per night. The 23 units at the White Anchor have color televisions, heat, and air-conditioning. Animals are welcome in designated pet rooms for an extra $10 per stay (not per night), as long as they remain on a leash while on the property and are not left alone in the rooms. Pet rooms are located on the ground floor, making walks on the 6-acre grounds more convenient.

Boothbay Harbor

Flagship Inn, 200 Townsend Ave., Boothbay Harbor (207-633-5094; 1-800-660-5094; flagship@boothbaylodging.com; www.boothbaylodging.com); $74–238 per night. This clean, friendly place is located next to Pier 1, Boothbay's activities hub. The inn offers large, air-conditioned, motel-style rooms with exterior corridors, free wireless Internet access, a heated outdoor swimming pool, and free coffee and juice each morning in the lobby. The interior of the inn was renovated in 2005. One animal is allowed in each designated pet room for an extra $10 per night.

Brooklin

Lookout Bed & Breakfast, 455 Flye Point Rd., Brooklin (207-359-2188; www.thelookoutinn.biz); $1,022–1,459 per week. This country inn, located on the tip of the Blue Hill peninsula, offers great views of Blue Hill Bay and Herrick's Bay, a meadow, an organic vegetable garden, and a flower garden. Pets are welcome in any of the seven on-site cottages for an extra $40 per week; the one- to four-bedroom cottages all have ocean views, kitchens, and small decks.

Bucksport

Bucksport Motor Inn, 70 Rte. 1, PO Drawer AA, Bucksport (207-469-3111; 1-800-626-9734; bucksprt@aol.com; www.bucksportmotorinn.com); $59–109 per night. The Bucksport Motor Inn offers all nonsmoking rooms, a picnic area, cable television, exterior corridors, and in-room coffeemakers. Leashed pets are permitted in some rooms, but owners are asked to use a leash and not leave their animals unattended at any time. "We more than love to see pets here," say the new owners, Eddie and Val Mason. Winston, the resident golden retriever, will probably be on hand to help you check in.

Camden

Blue Harbor House, 67 Elm St., Camden (207-236-6523; 1-800-248-3196; info@blueharborhouse.com; www.blueharborhouse.com); Captain's Quarters Suite, $145–185 per night. The Blue Harbor House is a quaint village inn with 11 rooms and suites (some with fireplaces, canopy beds, and whirlpools) and a dining room serving breakfast and dinner. Breakfast includes specialties like blueberry pancakes, rum raisin french toast, and potato quiche. Dogs are welcome in the Captain's Quarters Suite.

Camden Harbour Inn, 83 Bayview St., Camden (207-236-4200; 1-800-236-4266; info@camdenharbourinn.com; www.camdenharbourinn.com); $250–575 per night. The Camden Harbour Inn is a four-season accommodation offering 20 guest rooms on three floors; some rooms have fireplaces, decks, and balconies. Other features include flower gardens, antiques, and panoramic harbor views. Guest pets are welcome in some rooms, as long as owners agree to follow the inn's pet policies. Camden Harbour provides plush pet beds, as well as bowls, biscuits, and balls for playing in the huge backyard.

Camden Riverhouse Hotel & Inns, 11 Tannery Ln., Camden (207-236-0500; 1-800-755-7483; info@camdenmaine.com; www.camdenmaine.com); $119–249 per night. For an extra $15 per night, doggie guests are welcome in certain first-floor rooms at Camden Riverhouse, provided they are not left unattended and prior approval has been given. The hotel offers an indoor swimming pool and a hot tub, a fitness center, laundry facilities, and deluxe daily continental breakfasts.

High Tide Inn, Rte. 1, Camden (207-236-3724; 1-800-778-7068; info@hightideinn.com; www.hightideinn.com); $65–260 per night. Pets are allowed in certain designated rooms at this oceanfront accommodation that includes an inn, cottages, and a motel. High Tide's best feature is its location: The only thing between guests and the ocean is a vast expanse of lawn. You'll also find a private beach, library, and large porch where breakfast is served each day.

Castine

Castine Harbor Lodge, 147 Perkins St., P.O. Box 215, Castine 04421 (207-326-4335; 1-866-566-1550; chlodge@verizon.net; www.castineinn.com); $90–245 per night. The innkeepers at this large oceanfront 1893 lodge have one black Lab and cats; they welcome your pet, as well, with a fee of $10 per night. All 16 guest rooms have water views and country-cottage furnishings, including Oriental rugs, private baths, and interesting artifacts. Other amenities include a 350-foot porch and a private dock. It's a great place for dogs who love to play in the water.

SHORELINE CABINS FOR RENT AT THE HARBOUR VILLAGE IN EDGECOMB

Manor Inn, Battle Ave., Castine (207-326-4861; info@manor-inn.com; www.manor-inn.com); $140–275 per night. An impressive, historic home overlooking a large lawn and the open ocean beyond, the Manor Inn offers 14 rooms individually decorated with period furniture and bright touches. A full breakfast that includes pancakes, waffles, and omelets is included in the rate. The innkeepers charge a one-time $25 pet fee but otherwise welcome animals to explore the home and grounds with their owners.

Deer Isle

Pilgrim's Inn, 20 Main St., Deer Isle (207-348-6615; 888-778-7505; innkeeper@pilgrimsinn.com; www.pilgrimsinn.com); $199–229 per night. Pets are allowed in three of the on-site cottages at Pilgrim's Inn: Each of Ginny's Cottages has a living room, a kitchenette, water views, a deck, and a separate bedroom with a queen-size bed. Rugosa Rose Cottage is a two-story cottage with a queen bed, a bathroom, a private deck, and water views.

East Boothbay

Sunset Beach, 727 Ocean Point Rd., East Boothbay (207-633-2800; 1-800-633-3008; res@sunsetbeachmaine.com; www.smugglerscovemotel.com); $99–200 per night. Guests at Sunset Beach, formerly known as Smuggler's Cove Inn, can enjoy a heated outdoor swimming pool, a private sandy beach, rowboats, a fishing pier, free local telephone calls, cable television, ocean views, and 3 acres for exploring. Dogs are welcome in designated rooms for an extra $20 per night and a $50 security deposit.

Edgecomb

Harbour Village & Resort, 7 Island Ln., Edgecomb (207-882-6343; 1-800-437-5503; www.midcoastshvr.com); $208–312 per night. Located on the water next to the village of Wiscasset, the Harbour Village's accommodations include the inn itself, a lodge, and 15 cottages. Formerly known as Sheepscot River Inn, the resort offers boat charters, kayak rentals, a spa, and an indoor pool. Animal owners pay a fee of $10 per night and might just find doggie biscuits at check-in. Weekly discounts are available.

Lincolnville

Pine Grove Cottages, 2076 Atlantic Hwy., Lincolnville (207-236-2929; 1-800-530-5265; pine@tidewater.net; www.pinegrovemaine.com); $100–195 per night. You'll pay an additional $10 per night, per dog (limit two) for guest pets at Pine Grove, which offers efficiency cottages with private decks—some even have ocean views. Amenities include cable television, heat and air-conditioning, telephones, and barbecue grills. The property is comprised of 3 rambling acres and is located about 1 mile from the beach and the ferry.

Penobscot

Brass Fox Bed & Breakfast, 907 Southern Bay Rd., Penobscot (207-326-0575; brassfox@netscape.net); $90–135 per night. Dogs are allowed at the Brass Fox with prior approval, but only during the off-season—defined here as the day after Columbus Day through the Thursday before Memorial Day. The B&B is an 1830s farmhouse that has been recently remodeled with antiques and tin ceilings: Each guest room has a private bathroom and access to the deck.

Rockland

Navigator Motor Inn, 520 Main St., Rockland (207-594-2131; 1-800-545-8026; navigator@hotmail.com; www.navigatorinn.com); $79–169 per night. Located across the street from the Maine State Ferry Terminal, the Navigator has 81 rooms and five suites, all with refrigerators. There's also a restaurant on-site. No pets are allowed in the suites, but they are welcome in the rooms on the condition that they're not left alone at any time.

Trade Winds Motor Inn, 2 Park Dr., Rockland (207-596-6661; 1-800-834-3130; twmi@midcoast.com; www.tradewindsmaine.com); $64–184 per night. Although not permitted in the suites, dogs are welcome in any of the 138 rooms at the Trade Winds; many have balconies and views of the Rockland Breakwater Lighthouse and Rockland Harbor. The in-town location is within walking distance of shops, restaurants, and museums. Animals must be accompanied by their owners at all times. The rate includes a continental breakfast.

Rockport

Oakland Seashore Cottages and Motel, 50 Dearborn Ln., Rockport (207-594-8104; www.oaklandseashorecabins.com); $70–140 per night or $460–875 per week. The small cabins and motel at Oakland Seashore are surrounded by a 75-acre forest and front a private beach. Accommodations are simple and clean with full bathrooms and maid service; some have kitchenettes. In an effort to maintain the "peace and quiet," no telephones or televisions are provided. Quiet, well-behaved pets are welcome for $30 per stay.

Searsport

Homeport Inn, 121 E. Main St., Searsport (207-548-2259; hport inn@acadia.net; www.homeport historicinn.com); $750–1000 per week. Though not allowed in the historic inn building, pets are welcome in Homeport's Victorian Cottages. Each has two bedrooms with full and twin beds, a kitchen, heat, and supplied linens; they share access to the property's large lawns, gardens, and ocean views. The cottages rent by the week only. The inn is also home to the Mermaid Restaurant & Pub.

Inn Britannia, 132 W. Main St., Searsport (207-548-2007; 1-866-INN-BRIT; info@inn britannia.com); $100–160 per night. This historic inn underwent a complete renovation in 2002; well-behaved dogs that weigh less than 50 pounds are allowed in the London Room, which has a private entrance and can accommodate up to three people. Guests enjoy ocean views, afternoon tea, and walks on the property's 5 acres.

Spruce Head

Craignair Inn, 5 Third St., Spruce Head (207-594-7644; 1-800-320-9997; innkeeper@ craignair.com; www.craignair .com); $150–170 per night. This 1928 restored home offers 21 guest rooms (14 with private baths) decorated with antique furniture and quilts; many have ocean views. Downstairs, guests relax in the parlor, library, and dining room. With prior approval, dogs are allowed in about half of the rooms for a fee of $10 per night.

Stonington

Boyce's Motel, 44 Main St., Stonington (1-800-224-2421; www.boycesmotel.com); $69–130 per night. This motel has a great location overlooking Stonington Harbor and is a short walk from the shops and restaurants of the village. For an extra $10 per night, dogs are welcome in designated rooms, apartments, and efficiencies but should not be left alone on-site. The apartments have sundecks, and all rooms have heat, cable television, and in-room coffeemakers.

Tenants Harbor

East Wind Inn, 21 Mechanic St., Tenants Harbor (207-372-6366; 1-800-241-VIEW; info@eastwind inn.com; www.eastwindinn .com); rooms and suites, $148–220 per night. Gent, the resident black Lab, enjoys having canine guests with prior notice at the East Wind for a fee of $15 per visit; innkeeper Tim Watts just asks that your dog be well socialized and friendly. All of the inn's buildings offer sweeping views and antique furnishings. The inn also has a wharf restaurant with outdoor seating, where dogs are allowed (see Chandlery Grill under "Quick Bites"). All in all, a very pet-friendly place.

West Boothbay Harbor

Beach Cove Hotel & Resort, 48 Lakeview Rd., West Boothbay Harbor (207-633-0353; 1-866-851-0450; stay@beachcovehotel.com; www.beachcovehotel.com); $85–220 per night. Animals are welcome guests at the Beach Cove Hotel, formerly known as the Lakeview Inn, a waterfront inn with a large dock, a swimming pool, a beach, canoes, air-conditioning, cable television, and balcony suites. The on-site restaurant serves hearty American dinners. Shops, nature trails, and the Boothbay Railway Village (see "Out and About") are a short drive away. Dog owners pay an extra $5 per night, per pet.

Spruce Point Inn Resort & Spa, Box 237, Boothbay Harbor (207-633-4152; spi@sprucepointinn.com; www.sprucepointinn.com); $300 per night. This 57-acre seaside resort offers a Paws & Pillows Package that includes deluxe accommodations, a comfy dog bed and bowls, and treats for both the humans and canines in the room. Choose from lodge rooms, cottages, and townhouses, and enjoy sailing, hiking, spa treatments, and fine dining with locally fished, farmed, and grown ingredients. Download the free mobile app for a complete guide to the resort.

Campgrounds

Belfast

Moorings Oceanfront RV Resort, 191 Searsport Ave., Belfast (207-338-6860; mooringscamp@yahoo.com; www.oceanfrontrvcamping.com); $57–67 per night. Located directly on the water, Moorings has great views, 44 sites (some pull-throughs), a dumping station, a private beach, a kayak launch, Internet access, restrooms with showers, a playground area, a volleyball court, free coffee each morning, and scheduled special events. Doggie guests are an extra $1 per night; the campground allows a maximum of two pets per site.

Camden

Camden Hills State Park Campground, 280 Belfast Rd. (Rte. 1), Camden (207-236-3109; 207-236-0849); $15 per night Maine residents; $25 per night out-of-state residents. This fairly remote and scenic campground offers 112 sites, flush toilets, hot showers, and a picnic area in an expansive state park (see "Out and About"). It's an ideal spot for tenters looking for a "true Maine," somewhat wilderness-like experience, yet it is still close to the shops, restaurants, and activities of downtown Camden. Dogs must be leashed at all times.

Damariscotta

Lake Pemaquid Camping, Egypt Rd., P.O. Box 967, Damariscotta 04543 (207-563-5202; www.lakepemaquid.com); $24–44 per night or $145–250 per week. Your dog or cat will be greeted by free pet treats at the camp store at this family-friendly, lakefront campground. Some of the 200 sites are waterfront; all have a fire pit and picnic table and can accommodate a tent, trailer, or RV. Facilities include a large snack bar, a swimming pool, tennis courts, and a beach. Dogs must be on a leash.

Georgetown

Sagadahoc Bay Campground, P.O. Box 171, Georgetown 04548 (207-371-2014; kosalka@midmaine.com; www.sagbaycamping.com); $26–48 per night. Many of the 55 RV and tent sites at this cozy campground are at the water's edge; all tent sites are secluded in the woods, and all RV sites have hookups for water and electric. When the tide goes out, there are miles of hard-packed sand for your dog to run along. The resident poodle, Kampa, will show your dog the ropes.

Lincolnville

Warren Island State Park Campground, P.O. Box 105, Lincolnville 04849 (207-236-3824; 207-236-0849); $14 per night Maine residents; $24 per night out-of-state residents. Talk about seclusion: There's only one way to access this site, and unless you enjoy long swims, you'd better have a boat. Warren Island sits off the coast of Lincolnville in Penobscot Bay. There are no phones, no ferry, and just 10 campsites. Fresh drinking water is provided, along with mooring facilities. Dogs are allowed on a leash.

Nobleboro

Duck Puddle Campground, P.O. Box 176, Nobleboro 04555 (207-563-5608; dcpinfo@midcoast.com; www.duckpuddlecampground.com); $32–60 per night. Leashed, friendly pets are welcome to join the fun at Duck Puddle, a lakefront campground facility with shaded and sunny sites, a camp store, a boat dock and launch, boat and canoe rentals, modern restrooms, and a dumping station. Each site also has a fire pit and a picnic table.

Rockport

Camden Hills Campground, Rte. 90, Rockport (207-236-2498; 1-888-842-0592; www.camdenhillscampgrounds.com); $33–44 per night or $600–1,100 per month. This recently renovated campground can accommodate any size RV and offers full hookups and cable television connections. The site also has a swimming pool and hot tub, along with a camp store, laundry facilities, and restrooms. Two pets are allowed per site as long as their owners pick up after them and keep them on a leash.

Megunticook Campground By the Sea, Rte. 1, Rockport (207-594-2428; 1-800-884-2428; mail@campgroundbythesea.com; www.megunticookcampgrounds.com); $35–45 per night. The woods meet the sea at Megunticook, a campground for RVers and tenters with a heated swimming pool, a bathhouse, laundry facilities, a camp store, lobster bakes, free coffee, a playground, and waterfront gardens. Pets must be on a leash and accompanied by their owners (with cleanup bags) at all times.

Searsport

Searsport Shores Camping Resort, 216 W. Main St., Searsport (207-548-6059; camping@ime.net; www.campocean.com); $34–82 per night. Dogs (one per site) are welcome on the campground's trails and beach as long as they are leashed and quiet, and owners must clean up after them. Guests enjoy planned activities, a private beach, a canoe and kayak launch, hot showers, a playground, and a video arcade. With 40 acres of oceanfront property, Searsport Shores encourages visitors to call and pick out a perfect spot on the phone so you can tell the owners your preferences for sun or shade, privacy, etc.

Southport

Gray Homestead Oceanfront Camping, 21 Homestead Rd., Southport (207-633-4612; www.graysoceancamping.com); $32–50 per night. This waterfront campground offers 40 sites for tents and RVs, oceanfront seasonal RV sites, restrooms with showers, a small beach, laundry facilities, picnic tables and fire pits, a dump station, kayak rentals, and plenty of opportunities for boating and fishing. Two well-behaved pets are permitted per site, provided you use a leash, clean up any messes, and don't leave your dog unattended.

South Thomaston

Lobster Buoy Campsites, 280 Waterman Beach Rd., South Thomaston (207-594-7546; www.campmaine.com); $25–37 per night. You'll want to bring your fishing gear along to this campground on the water, featuring a 400-foot beach, hot showers, and flush toilets (no sewer hookups). All of the 40 sites are located within 150 yards of the ocean; 12 are reserved for tents, and the rest have water and electric hookups. One quiet, leashed dog is allowed per site.

Stonington

Old Quarry Ocean Adventures, Settlement Quarry Rd., Stonington (207-367-8977; 1-877-479-8977; info@oldquarry.com; www.oldquarry.com); $40–60 per night. Water-loving dogs and their companions will get more than just their feet wet at this campground, located on the shore of Webb Cove, which offers 10 tent sites along with a kayak and boating center. Its owners strive to maintain a peaceful, private, and all-natural camping experience—no RVs allowed. Hiking trails connect to the 9-acre site.

Wiscasset

Chewonki Campground, P.O. Box 261, Wiscasset 04578 (207-882-7426; www.chewonkicampground.com); $35–698 per night. Leashed, quiet pets are welcome at Chewonki, a campground where you'll find 50 acres for exploring, 47 sunny and shady campsites, saltwater-filtered swimming pools, views of Montsweag Bay, restrooms with showers, a camp store, a dumping station, a recreation hall, a playground, tennis, canoeing and kayaking, and even an art studio.

Homes, Cottages, and Cabins for Rent

Lincolnville Beach

Beach House Suites, Lincolnville Beach (207-789-5200; info@beachhousesuites.net; www.beachcottageinn.com); $1,015–1,550 per week. These two waterfront suites—one upper, one lower—offer views of Penobscot Bay and are a short walk from the town pier, shops, and eateries. Both units have a full kitchen, cable television, a washer and dryer, linens and towels, and two bedrooms. One pet is allowed per unit, provided he is quiet, housebroken, and not left alone.

Woolwich

Whitney's Wilderness Cabins, 141 Old Stage Rd., Woolwich (207-442-7676; www.home.gwi.net/~awhitney/; awhitney@gwi.net); $35–40 per night or $200–225 per week. Think rustic: If you're looking for a secluded, "roughing it" experience, these small, simple cabins can provide it. Cabin 1 has a double bed and bunk beds; Cabin 2 has two twin beds. Both have a gas stove, television, and "portable potty." A nearby well provides water, and a shower is located on the grounds. The Kennebec River is nearby.

Rental Agencies

Landworks LLC, 389 Muzzy Ridge, Searsmont (207-342-5444; info@landworkswaterfront.com; www.landworkswaterfront.com/cottages.html). Landworks offers a wide range of midcoast rental cottages in various sizes, styles, and price ranges. At the time of this writing, the offerings included properties such as the 100-year-old Fisherman's Cottage in Camden ($1,900 per week), the hilltop Bird's Wing Cottage in Northport ($2,300 per week), the oceanfront Day Lily Cottage in Belfast ($2,300 per week), and the Call of the Loon Cottage on Hobbs Pond ($1,750 per week). Pets are welcome at some properties for an extra $125 per week.

OUT AND ABOUT

Birch Point State Park, Owls Head. This is a scenic, oceanfront parcel of land that overlooks Penobscot Bay and offers a rare, northern Maine sand beach. Dogs are not specifically prohibited from the beach, as they are at many other waterfront parks, though they must be on a leash and owners must clean up after them. Finding the park can be a little tricky: It's located just south of Ash Point along the Mussel Ridge Channel. From Route 73 take North Shore Drive, turn right onto Ash Point Drive, continue past the airport, turn right onto Dublin Road, then turn left onto Ballyhoc Road and look for the STATE PARK sign less than a mile in on the left. The park is also signposted from Route 73 in Owls Head.

© ARENA CREATIVE/SHUTTERSTOCK.COM

Boothbay Railway Village, Rte. 27, Boothbay (207-633-4727; staff@railwayvillage.org; www.railwayvillage.org); $8 adults, $4 children. This is a great stop for history buffs: The 30-acre museum has 60 antique cars and farm vehicles and a nostalgic steam-train ride. In addition, an on-site outdoor village features historic structures, including the 1847 Town Hall, the 1923 Spruce Point Chapel, and a one-room schoolhouse, along with live demonstrations and a village green. Pets on a leash are permitted as long as their owners pick up after them.

Boothbay Region Land Trust. Headquarters: 1 Oak St., Boothbay Harbor (207-633-4818). The 27 miles of hiking trails that comprise the trust are spread throughout Boothbay, Boothbay Harbor, Edgecomb, and Southport. The trust manages 13 properties, including the 12-acre **Colby Wildlife Preserve** at Salt Marsh Cove; the 94-acre **Linekin Preserve** along the Damariscotta River; the 46-acre **Lobster Cove Meadow,** which stretches from the Damariscotta River to Linekin Bay; and the 19-acre **Porter Preserve** on Barters Island in Boothbay. Trail maps are available at the trust's Boothbay Harbor headquarters. Dogs are welcome in most areas on a leash, as long as their owners pick up after them; canines are not permitted on Damariscove Island, which is a nationally protected bird sanctuary.

Camden Hills State Park, 280 Belfast Rd. (Rte. 1), Camden. Get a bird's-eye view of the midcoast region from atop **Mount Battie,** located within the park (the summit is accessible by auto road or by foot). There are few places to better enjoy the dramatic fall foliage and year-round vistas. Within the 5,000-acre park you'll find 30 miles of trails, more than a few remote spots, the renowned 800-foot **Maiden Cliff,** and a campground (see "Accommodations—Campgrounds").

Damariscotta Lake State Park, 8 State Park Rd., Jefferson. With plenty of opportunities for swimming, fishing, and sunbathing, this 17-acre shoreline spot is especially popular in summer. Indeed, the park is only open between Memorial Day and Labor Day, and parking can be a challenge. Picnic areas with grills, a playground, and flush toilets are also available on-site. Owners must clean up after their leashed pets.

Dodge Point, River Rd., Newcastle. This impressive 500-

acre preserve is located along the Damariscotta River. Keep your eye out for beaver dams and other coastal wildlife. The wooded and waterfront trails are popular in summer for hiking and in winter for cross-country skiing. Dogs must be on a leash.

Heritage Park, end of Main St., Belfast. Pull up a seat at a picnic table and watch the boats go by at this popular grassy area. In addition to the great views, the area also has historic architecture, interesting shops, and a turn-of-the-20th-century feel. Dogs must be on a leash.

Humane Society of Knox County Events, 17 Buttermilk Ln. Ext., Thomaston; P.O. Box 1294, Rockland 04841 (207-594-2200; www.humanesocietyofknox county.org). The society offers visitors and their furry companions plenty of chances to join in at animal-friendly activities and fund-raisers. Among the society's most popular events are: the **Fur 'n' Foliage Pet Walk,** usually held in autumn; the **Art for Animals** silent auction, held the second Sunday in August at Sparrow Framing in Rockland; and the **Blessing of the Animals,** held with the help of a local pastor on the third Saturday of September at the society's shelter facility.

Monhegan Boat Line, P.O. Box 238, Port Clyde 04855 (207-372-8848; Barstow@monheganboat .com). Call for fares. Monhegan is one of Maine's best-known and most-visited islands. Tiny and dramatic, it's especially popular among artists—in summer, you'll trip over an easel no matter where you wander. The Monhegan Boat Line can get you there, and welcomes pets on a leash for an extra $2 round-trip fee. One note of caution: Company representatives say that the deer tick/Lyme disease problem is growing on Monhegan Island and recommends that owners inspect their pets carefully after a visit.

Owls Head Light, Owls Head State Park, West Penobscot Bay, Owls Head. The well-known lighthouse is only 30 feet high—a tiny stature for a Maine light—but the structure sits on a hill that nonetheless leaves it towering nearly 100 feet above the water. The much-painted building stands guard at the entrance to Rockland Harbor.

Reid State Park, Seguinland Rd., Georgetown. Sand dunes and beach grass mark this seashore park, where visitors can enjoy picnic areas with grills and a snack bar. The site also has flush toilets. The natural wonders here include tidal pools, wild roses, and long stretches of beach (keep watch for poison ivy). Because this is an active bird-nesting area, dogs should be kept under close control and on a leash at all times.

Wiscasset, Waterville & Farmington (WW&F) Railway Museum, Sheepscot Station, P.O. Box 242, Alna 04535 (207-882-4193; webmaster@wwfry .org; www.wwfry.org). Vintage-railroad buffs will appreciate this slice of transportation history.

The WW&F, a 2-foot gauge common carrier, stopped operations in 1933; today, a railway museum stands at the site of the original Sheepscot station. Admission is free, and leashed pets are permitted on the grounds but not on the train itself.

QUICK BITES

Boothbay Region Lobstermen's Co-Op Restaurant, 97 Atlantic Ave., Boothbay Harbor (1-800-9961740; www.boothbaylobsterwharf.com). Members of the co-op ship lobster "anywhere, anytime," and also serve up their best catches at this casual lobster pound. Sit outside and dine on seafood dinners and baskets, sandwiches, and snacks like fried zucchini, macaroni salad, chowder, and pie.

Cappy's Chowder House, 1 Main St., Camden (207-236-2254; goodeats@cappyschowder.com; www.cappyschowder.com). "We love pets and have doggie water out all the time," says owner Johanna at Cappy's Chowder, a reasonably priced, well-known local eatery with takeout and outdoor seating. The menu offers seafood, nachos, salads, sandwiches, and bakery treats.

Captain's Fresh Idea, Rte. 1, 3499 Atlantic Hwy., Waldoboro (207-832-4880). Captain's has "wicked good" seafood, lobster rolls, fried clams, and burgers, along with a take-out window, outside tables, and a large yard—perfect for walking Fido after lunch or dinner.

Chandlery Grill, East Wind Inn, Mechanic St., Tenants Harbor (207-372-6366). Located at the **East Wind Inn** (see "Accommodations—Hotels, Motels, Inns, and Bed & Breakfasts"), the Chandlery serves casual lunches and dinners on the wharf; picnic tables and lots of flat, large rocks provide seating. Dogs often accompany their owners here for boiled lobster, seafood rolls, or sandwiches.

Cod End Cookhouse & Fish Market, Commercial St., Tenants Harbor (207-372-6782; www.codend.com). Open seven days a week during the summer, Cod End offers outdoor picnic tables and traditional New England meals made with lobster, haddock, pollock, flounder, sole, clams, mussels, and other sea creatures.

Cook's Crossing Ice Cream Shop, 237 E. Main St., Searsport (207-548-2005). For a fun stop on a hot afternoon, grab a cone at this restored-railroad-station-turned-ice-cream-shop. There's also a gift store on-site and a small deck for lounging. "We also offer a doggie dish with a dog biscuit on top," says a Cook's Crossing staffer. "Dogs love our spot!"

Dunton's Doghouse, Sea St., Boothbay Harbor. No, it's not *that* kind of dog house. But it's the next best thing: This ramshackle place serves no-nonsense favorites from its outdoor takeout window. Choose from clam cakes, chicken nuggets, curly fries, cheeseburgers, haddock sandwiches, mozzarella sticks, grilled ham-and-cheese, cheese dogs, and similar fare.

Fat Boy Drive-In, Rte. 24, Brunswick (207-729-9431). You won't be the only one at Fat Boy to order your meal at the counter and enjoy it while sitting in your car. You can even watch planes take off from the Naval Air Station while you sample your BLT sandwich, burger, onion rings, lobster roll, or fried clams.

Lobster Dock, 49 Atlantic Ave., Boothbay Harbor (207-633-7120; www.thelobsterdock.com). "The only thing better than the view is the food." So goes the slogan of this ultracasual eatery sitting right on the water. Artichoke hearts, crabcakes, shrimp cocktail, clam chowder, home-baked biscuits, lobster, and beer-battered onion rings are all on the menu. (The Web site even provides "how to eat a lobster" instructions.) Outdoor picnic tables are available.

Scarlet Begonias, 16 Station Ave., Brunswick (207-721-0403; www.scarletbegoniasmaine.com). At this new location of an old favorite, you can order hearty soups, garlic bread, salads, sandwiches, pasta, and personal pizzas as takeout. The new place has outdoor seating so you can dine with your well-behaved dog.

Sea Basket Restaurant, Rte. 1, Wiscasset (207-882-6581; www.seabasket.com). Takeout is a specialty here: Call ahead and the Sea Basket will have your order ready when you arrive. You and the kids can choose from staples like peanut butter-and-jelly sandwiches, crabcakes, scallops, chowder, and dinner baskets served with fries, a roll, and tartar sauce. You can find the whole menu online.

Second Read Books and Coffee, 328 Main St., Rockland (207-594-4123; www.rockcitycoffee.com/secondread.htm). This coffee shop and bookstore carries a wide selection of used and new books as well as sandwiches, soups, pastries, and locally roasted coffee. Well-behaved dogs are welcome to pass the time with their owners in the sidewalk seating area.

3 Dog Cafe, 309 Commercial St. (Rte. 1), Rockport (207-230-0955; www.3dogscafe.com). Formerly known as Sweet Sensations, 3 Dog Café is "THE" place to be for dog lovers. Steve Watts, aka the Macaroon Man, is a pastry chef, dog lover, and the owner of this bakery specializing in (you guessed it) macaroons, along with wedding cakes and a host of other tasty treats. "We have an outside deck, and many people bring their dogs in the summer," Steve says. "We're known for our dog biscuits, which we make from scratch."

Young's Lobster Pound, 4 Mitchell Ave., Belfast (207-338-1160; rayyoung@mint.net). With outdoor seating and a separate picnic area, this seafood eatery is an oasis in the desert for hungry pet owners. The friendly staffers serve up lobsters (choose your own), clams, crabmeat, mussels, king crab legs, haddock, halibut, sole, cod, and other delights in a casual setting.

HOT SPOTS FOR SPOT

Animal House, 6 Hopkins Hill Rd., Newcastle (207-563-5595; www.theanimalhouse.net). This "boutique for pets" has a focus on organic and holistic products, including grooming supplies, homeopathic remedies, flea and tick treatments, training aids, collars, food and water bowls, toys, and premium foods such as Wellness, Solid Gold, and Artemis. The shop is located in a hard-to-miss cute yellow house.

Canine Country Club, 387 Atlantic Hwy. (Rte. 1), Northport (207-338-8300; www.caninecountryclub-me.com). This state-of-the-art kennel has 54 runs in a 12,000-square-foot facility; floors have radiant heat, and there's even a doggie septic system to control odors. Most dogs stay overnight, though day care is available upon request if space permits. Grooming and training are also available, and staff play with the dogs throughout the day. Rates are $7–18 per day for day care and $14–28 per night for boarding.

Family Pet Center, 38 Starrett Dr., Belfast (207-338-4480). Located in Reny's Plaza on the corner of Routes 1 and 3, this store stocks Eukanuba, Nutro, Science Diet, and most other popular pet-food brands. You'll also find a full line of leads, collars, doggie sweaters and coats, natural bones, rawhide treats, and toys for all types of pets. The store is open seven days a week.

Hollydachs Pet Center, 246 Main St., Rockland (207-594-2653). This family-owned pet shop houses reptiles, fish, guinea pigs, hamsters, and all other small animals, and sells supplies for cats, dogs, and other pets. In addition to leashes, bowls, and other paraphernalia, you'll also find food brands such as Science Diet, Precise, Triumph, and California Natural.

Paws Wings & Things Kennel, 260 State Rte. 46, Bucksport (207-9021165www.pawswingsandthings.com). Located in a country setting, this cleverly named kennel caters to four-legged guests with indoor/outdoor runs, radiant heated floors, skylights, and large fenced-in play yards where your pup can enjoy plenty of socialization. Overnight boarding, doggie day care, and grooming are all available.

Louis Doe Pet Center, 92 Mills Rd., Newcastle (207-563-3234).

This crowded and homey store sells supplies and food for small animals, birds, cats, dogs, and fish. You'll find all the premium brands of dog and cat foods, along with horse feeds, bowls, leashes, and toys.

ANIMAL SHELTERS AND HUMANE SOCIETIES

Alna Animal Shelter, 21 Ames Rd., Alna (207-882-7421)

Belfast–Waldo County Humane Society, P.O. Box 479, Belfast 04915 (207-338-1403)

Boothbay Region Humane Society, 45 Montgomery Rd., Boothbay Harbor (207-882-9677)

Bucksport Animal Holding Facility, P.O. Drawer X, Bucksport 04416 (207-469-7951)

Camden-Rockport Animal Rescue League, P.O. Box 707, Rockport 04856 (207-236-8702)

Humane Society of Knox County, 65 Dexter St. Ext., Thomaston (207-594-2200; www.humanesocietyofknoxcounty.org)

Lincoln County Animal Shelter, P.O. Box 7, Edgecomb 04556 (207-882-9677)

IN CASE OF EMERGENCY

All Creatures Veterinary Hospital, 881 West St. (Rte. 90), Rockport (207-594-5039)

Belfast Veterinary Hospital, 193 Northport Ave., Belfast (207-338-3260)

Boothbay Animal Hospital, 1033 Wiscasset Rd., Boothbay (207-633-3447)

Maine Coast Veterinary Hospital, 163 South St., Blue Hill (207-374-2385)

PenBay Veterinary Associates, 599 Commercial Street (Rte. 1), Rockport 04856 (207-594-8300)

Searsport Veterinary Hospital, 322 W. Main St., Searsport (207-548-2924)

Union Veterinary Clinic, Rte. 17, Union (207-785-4709)

A WALK AROUND JORDAN POND PROVIDES TYPICALLY BEAUTIFUL ACADIA VIEWS.

Acadia National Park & Mount Desert Island

It's hard to imagine a more dramatically scenic spot than Mount Desert Island. Home to Acadia National Park, the region offers an unusual mix of beaches, mountains, lakes, quaint downtowns, and—perhaps its most famous feature—mile upon mile of rugged, rocky coastline. Pet owners will feel welcome here; dogs are a common sight on park trails and city streets alike, and shopkeepers, passersby, and even the occasional traffic cop often make a point of stopping to scratch your pooch's ears. Whether you and your pet prefer challenging hikes, leisurely strolls, or lazy waterfront lounging, you'll find what you're looking for in this popular Downeast spot. (Tourist tip: The locals pronounce their island's name, true to its French roots, as Dessert.)

Bar Harbor is the most populous and bustling town in the region, serving as willing host to the thousands of tourists who want to be as close as possible to Acadia's main entrance. Despite the annual influx of summer crowds, the town manages, for the most part, to maintain a dignified and unhurried ambience. Those looking for a more isolated vacation experience should opt for lodging on the Quiet Side of the island in

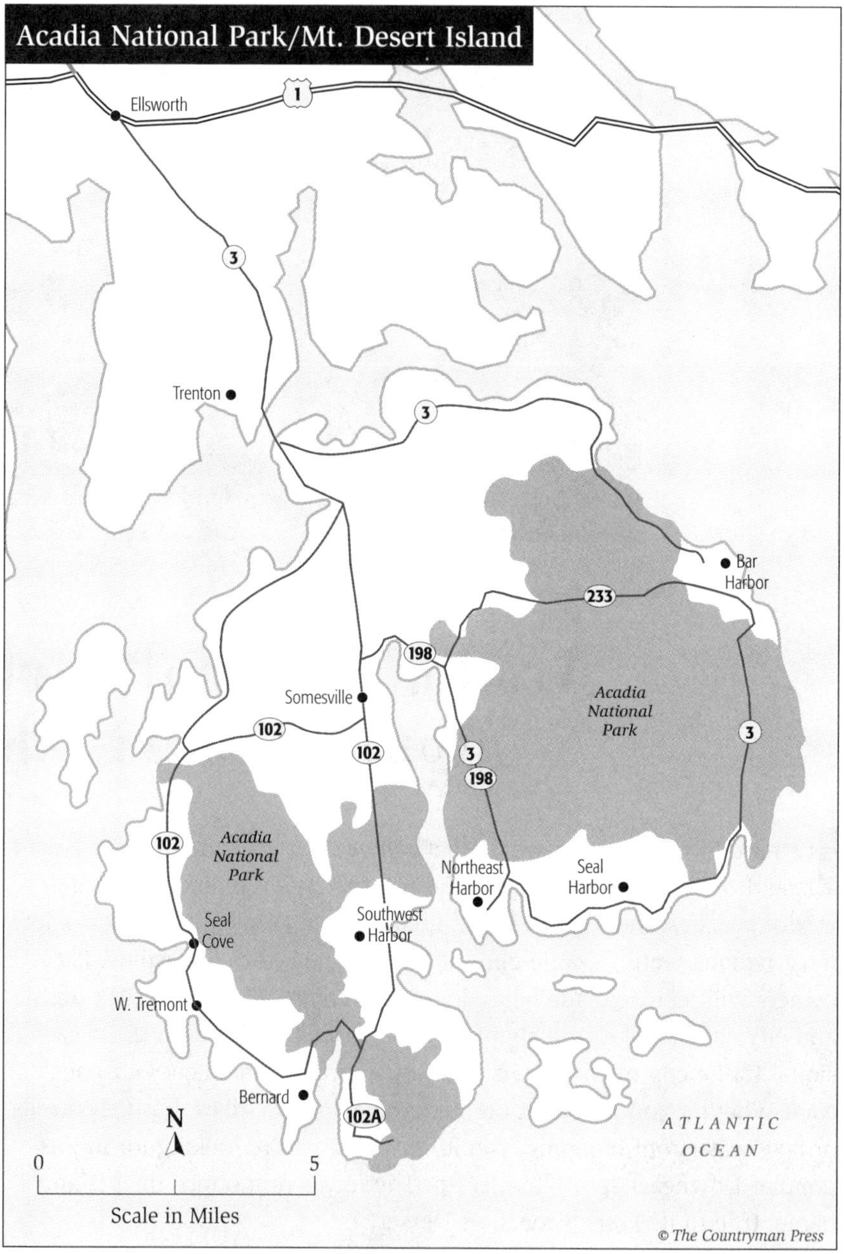

sleepy, lost-in-time towns such as Southwest Harbor, Bass Harbor, Seal Cove, and Somesville. Here you'll find restaurants and shops (though not nearly as many as in Bar Harbor) as well as solitude—even during the high season. The only catch: Acadia's main entrance is a 15- to 35-minute drive away, though many alternate access points and trails are scattered throughout the island's Quiet Side as well. Across the bridge on the mainland, Trenton, Ellsworth, and neighboring towns offer more affordable lodging options and a more commercial atmosphere: Mini-golf courses, strip malls, outlets, RV parks, and motels line Route 3, the main road heading onto the island.

Bar Harbor and its neighboring towns all have leash laws, and local officials ask pet owners to follow the rules of doggie etiquette and to carry pooper-scooper bags at all times. Other than that, the rules are few and the attitude is welcoming. All in all, this shapes up to be one of the most—if not *the* most—dog-friendly spot in all of New England.

ACCOMMODATIONS

Hotels, Motels, Inns, and Bed & Breakfasts

Bar Harbor

Balance Rock Inn, 21 Albert Meadow, Bar Harbor (207-288-2610; 1-800-753-0494; bar harborinns@aol.com; www.balancerockinncom); $155–635per night. With impressive views of Frenchman's Bay, antique furnishings, perennial gardens, and in-room hot tubs, this luxury inn is among Bar Harbor's most elegant. A limited number of pets are allowed as guests at any one time for a $30 per night fee; pet owners are asked to keep their animals off the furniture and not to leave them alone in rooms.

Bar Harbor Inn, Newport Drive, Bar Harbor (207-288-3351; 1-800-248-3351; www.barharborinn.com); $89–385 per night. This full-service resort includes the **Main Inn,** the **Oceanfront Lodge,** and the **Newport Motel.** The New England–style inn, home to the historic **Reading Room Restaurant,** is the most elegant option. Rooms in the lodge each have private balconies with water views, while the motel rooms overlook landscaped grounds. Outdoor seating is available at the restaurant. Dogs weighing less than 25 pounds are welcome in certain rooms for a fee of $25 per pet, per night.

Days Inn Bar Harbor–Frenchman's Bay, 120 Eden St., Bar Harbor (207-288-3321; www.wyndham.com); $101–1189 per night. This Days Inn location offers its guests a 24-hour front desk, Internet access, free newspapers, a swimming pool, free continental breakfasts each morning, cable television, laundry facilities, and in-room alarm clocks and hair dryers. Dogs are permitted in designated rooms for an extra $10 per stay (not per night).

Eden Village Cottages and Motel, Rte. 3, Bar Harbor (207-288-4670; info@edenvillage.com; www.edenvillage.com); motel, $49–114 per night; cottages, $434–704 per week. Eden Village's 25 acres include a pond, a playground, and a picnic area with grills. Each housekeeping cottage is equipped with a kitchenette, a fireplace, and a screened-in porch. Dog owners (sorry, no cats) must clean up messes, keep dogs off the furniture, keep barking to a minimum, and pay a $10 per-night cleaning fee and a $100 refundable deposit.

Gale's Gardens Guesthouse, 7 Daylilly Ln., Bar Harbor (207-288-3273; www.galesgardensguesthouse.com); $695–1,395 per week. Pets are welcome with prior approval at this charming log cabin located 1 mile from the Acadia park entrance and 4 miles from Bar Harbor. The cabin sits on 2 wooded acres off the road with lots of local wildlife, and it features a fully-equipped kitchen, two bedrooms, a cast-iron stove, and a cozy loft for reading or watching television.

Hanscom's Motel & Cottages, 273 Hwy. 3, Bar Harbor (207-288-3744; www.hanscomsmotel.com); $86–120 per night. Pets are welcome at this small, clean motel with both rooms and cottages, located about 2 miles from the park entrance and about 4 miles from town. There's also a nice picnic area with grills so you can have a cookout with your furry friend.

Hutchins Mountain View Cottages, 286 State Hwy. 3, Bar Harbor (207-288-4833; 1-800-775-4833; info@hutchinscottages.com; www.hutchinscottages.com); $48–150 per night. These family-owned and -operated cottages are located 1 mile from the park and 4 miles from downtown Bar Harbor. The cottages are situated on 20 acres of land with views of Cadillac Mountain. Each has a screened-in porch, and some have a living room and fireplace. Rover is welcome to make himself comfortable without extra charges.

Rose Eden Cottages, 864 State Hwy. 3, Bar Harbor (207-288-3038; www.roseeden.com); $49–119 per night. Located on Route 3 about 10 minutes from Bar Harbor, Rose Eden is a pet-friendly place with housekeeping cottages decorated in various Maine themes. Each cottage has cable television, electric heat, and private baths with showers; some also have coffeemakers, microwaves, and refrigerators. A wooded area behind the cottages offers a setting for barbecues, campfires, and playing for the kids. Local canine, Jessie, offers a big woof welcome on the Web site! There is a $10 per night pet fee, but no weight limit.

Ellsworth

Ramada Inn Ellsworth–Acadia National Park, 215 High St., Ellsworth (207-667-9341; www.wyndham.com); $125–175 per night. Pets are allowed at this Ramada Inn location (formerly a Holiday Inn), where you'll find high-speed Internet access, laundry facilities, a sauna and hot tub, indoor tennis courts, cable television with premium movie channels, a 24-hour business center in the lobby, meeting rooms, and an indoor swimming pool. The nightly pet fee is $20 for the first dog and $10 for an additional dog.

Jasper's Motel, High St., Ellsworth (207-667-5318; info@jaspersmaine.com); $69–136 per night. With an attached restaurant, clean rooms, and reasonable rates, this motel appeals to visitors looking for a hassle-free vacation. Jasper's is located about 23 miles from Acadia and features single, double, and cottage-style rooms, some of which are smoke-free. Those traveling with animals pay an extra fee of $10 per night, per pet.

Twilite Motel, Rtes. 1 and 3, Ellsworth (207-667-8165; 1-800-395-5097; info@twilitemotel.com; www.twilitemotel.com); $59–126 per night. Though technically classified as a motel, Twilite has many of the homey touches you'd expect to find at an inn or B&B. Dogs weighing less than 25 pounds are welcome in certain rooms with a fee of $10 per night, per pet. The motel is about 18 miles from Acadia and offers free continental breakfasts, all nonsmoking rooms, wireless Internet access, a gift shop, and cable television.

Acadia Birches Knights Inn, Rte. 1, Ellsworth (207-667-3621; 1-800-435-1287; www.acadiabirchesmotel.com); $69–199 per night. Efficiencies and standard rooms are available at this motel, formerly known as the White Birches Motel, along with a few Presidential Suites that feature whirlpool tubs, wet bars, couches, and 35-inch televisions. The accommodations sit next to the White Birches Golf Course, and there's also a restaurant on-site. Pets are welcome without extra fees.

Southwest Harbor

Harbor View Motel and Cottages, 11 Ocean Way, Southwest Harbor (207-244-5031; 1-800-538-6463; www.harborviewmotelandcottages.com; motel, $55–128 per night; cottages, $400–815 per week. This aptly named motel and cottage complex overlooks bustling Southwest Harbor; if you like the music of clanging boats, this is the spot for you. The seven housekeeping cottages all have picture windows. Dogs are allowed in all of the cottages and some of the motel rooms for an extra $9 per night or $50 per week.

Trenton

Acadia Gateway Motel & Cottages, 329 Bar Harbor Rd., Trenton (207-667-9458; 1-800-833-9515; www.acadiagatewaymotelandcottages.com); cottages, $50–101 per night. "Small pets" (call to see if yours qualifies) are permitted in the cottages at Acadia Gateway. Each cottage has one or two beds, color television, individual climate control, and daily maid service. Microwaves and refrigerators are available upon request.

Campgrounds

Acadia National Park

Acadia National Park Campgrounds (www.acadia.national-park.com). The park has two pet-friendly campgrounds: Blackwoods ($18–20 per night), located 5 miles south of Bar Harbor; and Seawall ($14–20 per night), 4 miles south of Southwest Harbor. Dogs are allowed at both but must be kept on a leash and can't be left alone. Campers can make reservations in advance at Blackwoods (1-800-365-2267), but Seawall operates on a first-come, first-served basis—making it a risky proposition during the busy season from July to September. At both campgrounds, sites are located within a 10-minute walk of the ocean and within a half-mile walk of showers and a camp store. From spring to fall, campers can also make use of restrooms, cold running water, picnic tables, and a dumping station. Utility hookups, however, are not provided. Dogs are not permitted at the park's Isle au Haut Campground.

Bar Harbor

Bar Harbor KOA, 136 County Rd., Bar Harbor (207-288-3520; barharbor@koa.net; www.koa.com); $30–75 per night. Formerly known as Barcadia Campground, this facility has great views of Western Bay, oceanfront and wooded sites for tents and RVs, a game room, a patio, a playground, a private beach, and sports courts. KOA welcomes "four-legged campers" as long as they are not aggressive

ACADIA NATIONAL PARK, LOW TIDE AT HARBOR ISLAND, BAR HARBOR, MAINE (SHARON KENNEDY)

and owners agree to use a leash and clean up any messes.

Bar Harbor Woodlands KOA, 1453 State Hwy. 102, Bar Harbor (207-288-3520; www.koa.com); call for rate information. KOA recently acquired this property, formerly known as the Spruce Valley Campground. The facilities include 100 wooded and sunny sites on 50 acres, a playground, a heated swimming pool, a recreation room, a pond, a camp store, laundry facilities, and a basketball court. Friendly dogs are permitted, as long as they are quiet, leashed, cleaned-up after, and not left unattended.

Hadley's Point Campground, 33 Hadley's Point Rd., Bar Harbor (207-288-4808; www.hadleyspoint.com); $25–37 per night. Leashed pets are welcome at Hadley's Point without any extra fees—though owners are expected to clean up after their animals and not leave them unattended. Each RV and tent site has a fireplace and picnic table; campers can also take advantage of a heated pool, laundry facilities, shuffleboard courts, church services, and plenty of planned activities.

Mount Desert Narrows Camping Resort, Bar Harbor Rd., Bar Harbor (1-877-570-2267; www.rvonthego.com); call for current rates. Campers can settle in for a fun stay at this oceanfront resort featuring nightly live entertainment in summer (including magicians, Elvis impersonators, sing-alongs, crafts, and movies), 25 acres of tenting, complete hookups for RVs, a heated pool, canoe rentals, a camp store, and a playground. Dogs must be quiet, on a leash, and attended-to at all times.

Bass Harbor

Bass Harbor Campground, Rte. 102A, Bass Harbor (207-244-5857; 1-800-327-5857; info@bassharbor.com; www.bassharbor.com); campsites, $22–45 per night; cabins, $400–675 per week. Kids and dogs alike will find plenty to do at this bustling campground featuring 130 sites, a heated pool and hot tub, full hookups, separate tenting areas, hot showers, laundry facilities, a playground, and a gift shop. Owner Mike Clayton has just one request of pet lovers: "You know the jerk who ruins it for everyone else by not taking care of his pets? Well don't bring him!" Well, OK, two more requests: Dogs must be leashed at all times, and owners are asked to clean up any messes.

Quietside Campground, Rte. 102, Bass Harbor (207-244-0566; quietside@acadia.net; www.quietsidecampground.com); campsites, $22–26 per night; cabins, $58–70 per night. While Quietside does have a few large RV sites, they mainly cater to visitors with pop-up campers and smaller RVs; the campground also has tent sites and cabins for rent. Pets are welcome for an extra fee of $1 per pet, per night, but must be quiet and well behaved, and owners are expected to clean up after their animals.

Ellsworth

Patten Pond Camping Resort, 1470 Bucksport Rd. (Rte. 3), Ellsworth (207-667-7600; 1-877-667-7376; www.rvonthego.com); $20–44 per night. With boat rentals, playgrounds, basketball and volleyball courts, a game room, and a camp store, this waterfront resort caters to families. Acadia National Park is about 20 minutes away, and Route 3 is lined with other activities to keep the kids busy. Dogs must be on a leash at all times, and pet owners are required to clean up after their animals.

Mount Desert

Mount Desert Campground, 516 Sound Dr., Somesville, Mount Desert (207-244-3710; mdcg@midmaine.com; www.mountdesertcampground.com); $29–52 per night (off-season). This quiet waterfront campground primarily caters to tenters but does have a few sites available for RVs. Visitors enjoy a view overlooking the northern end of Somes Sound, a boat-launching ramp and canoe rentals, a camp store, and lots of blueberry bushes. Dogs are allowed only during the spring and fall. Pets are not allowed from June 29 to August 30.

Somes Sound View Campground, 86 Hall Quarry Rd., Mount Desert (207-244-3890; www.ssvc.info); $30–60 per night. At this campground you can perch your tent or RV right at the pink granite water's edge. Each site has a fire pit and picnic tables; campers share restrooms, a dumping station, ice and soda machines, and firewood. Take advantage of the nearby water with canoe rentals and a fishing dock. Pets must be vaccinated and remain on a leash throughout your stay.

Southwest Harbor

Smuggler's Den Campground, 28 Main St., Southwest Harbor (207-244-3944; www.smugglersdencampground.com); $26–41 per night. Tucked into the trees on the Quiet Side of Mount Desert Island, Smuggler's Den has a heated pool, a recreation field, and forested and sunny sites to accommodate tenters and RV owners alike. Acadia's Echo Lake is a 20-minute walk away, and many of the park's carriage roads and trails are a short car ride away. One dog per site is welcome.

Trenton

Narrows Too Camping Resort, 1150 Bar Harbor Rd., Trenton (207-667-4300; www.rvonthego.com). This resort offers a waterfront location, a heated pool, basketball and volleyball courts, and an on-site mini-golf course. No need to rough it—you'll also find hot showers, a camp store, and laundry facilities. Dogs must be on a leash and shouldn't be left alone. Rentals range from cabins and cottages to travel trailers; call for current rates.

Homes, Cottages, and Cabins for Rent

Bar Harbor

"Eight Great Places," 127 Lookout Point Rd., Bar Harbor (1-866-202-1227; pauld@acadia.net); $995–1,195 per week. Paul DeVore and Karen Keenney own and rent eight properties on and around Mount Desert Island, each categorized by its intended use: "romantic," "family," or "reunion." They call themselves "pet negotiable," meaning they like to talk to pet owners to match them up with a property that best suits their needs. "For example, multiple pets might be okay in one of the larger houses but inappropriate for the honeymoon suites," Paul says.

Manset

The Mansell House, Shore Rd., Manset (207-244-5625; mansell@downeast.net; www.mooringsinn.com); $95–175 per night. This house has three accommodations for visitors: two efficiency apartments (each with one double bed) and one penthouse apartment. All have decks and great

© ROBERT MANLEY/SHUTTERSTOCK.COM

views of Manset and the Acadia mountain skyline. The penthouse can sleep four. There is no extra fee for pet owners, though animals are not allowed to be left alone in the apartments. Manset is part of Southwest Harbor. The Mansell House is affiliated with the Moorings Inn; for more information, visit the Moorings Inn Web site and click on the "Mansell House" link.

Mount Desert

Acadia Pines Chalets, Mount Desert (207-244-9251; epat@epatfoster.com; www.home.myfairpoint.net/epat3); $650–1,050 per week. Owner E. Pat Foster offers three chalet-style cottages for rent in the Somes Sound area. Spread out on 7 acres near Echo Lake, the cottages are roomy enough for six people and also have living areas with cathedral ceilings, fully equipped kitchens, private decks, and fireplaces. Pets are considered on a case-by-case basis.

Southwest Harbor

Seawall Point, 490 Seawall Rd., Southwest Harbor (207-244-3980; knorberg99@hotmail.com; www.seawallpointcottage.com); $530–575 per week. "We welcome pets because we've never had any problems," say the owners of this cozy cottage near Acadia's seawall and Wonderland Trail. "Pet owners are always considerate." Set on a lawn and surrounded by apple and evergreen trees, the secluded cottage features a screened-in porch, simple country furnishings, one double and one twin bed, a kitchen and dining area, and a barbecue grill.

West Tremont

Parsons' Oceanfront Cottages, HCR 33, West Tremont (207-244-5673; 207-664-4113; www.parsonsoceanfrontcottages.com); $800–1150 per week. The three Parsons rentals share access to a private pebble beach and have water views. An extra fee of $10 per night or $50 per week will give your dog access to the cottages as well, though the smallest, the First Mate's Cabin, is a bit too snug to accommodate you along with your furry friends. The Captain's Cottage is closest to the water, and the Guest House is the largest of the three. No matter which one you choose, the Parsons—who live on-site—will make sure you feel at home.

Rental Agencies

L.S. Robinson Co. Real Estate, 337 Main St., Southwest Harbor (207-244-5563; info@lsrobinson.com; www.lsrobinson.com). Need help finding a dog-friendly rental in the Bar Harbor area? L.S. Robinson's office dogs, Cooper, Emma, and Burlee, are on the case. The agency, which also handles vacation rentals for the Lynam Real Estate Agency in Bar Harbor, helps visitors find homes for rent in every corner of the island. You can search the company's Web site by category, including one that highlights rentals where dogs are considered welcome guests. Some homeowners do charge a pet fee; the exact amount varies from rental to rental.

Maine Island Properties, 1281 Main St., Mount Desert (207-244-4348; info@maineislandproperties.com; www.maineislandproperties.com). This vacation rental agency handles every type of accommodation, from rustic cabins to luxurious oceanfront homes. Several homes will consider doggie guests; there is usually a pet fee of $50–100 per week.

OUT AND ABOUT

Acadia National Park. Few national parks allow pet owners to bring their best friends along for the ride (or hike, as the case may be). Luckily for us, Acadia is the exception. Start your adventure at the **Hull's Cove Visitor Center** to pick up maps and guidebooks, then get oriented with a trip around the famed **Park Loop Road** (the visitors center sells an excellent point-by-point "Motorist Guide to Park Loop Road" for $1.25). With plenty of turnoffs and parking areas, the 27-mile-long road winds its way past Acadia's most prized mountain and ocean views and historic sites.

Once you're ready to leave the car behind, the options for hiking, biking, and gaping are almost limitless. You can scale cliffs on iron rungs and ladders if you want, but hikers with pets in tow tend to stick to shorter, less strenuous byways. Some of the best include: **Ocean Trail** (stretching from Otter Point to Sand Beach; the views from this smooth, narrow dirt path will literally take your breath away); **Jordan Pond Nature Trail** (mostly flat with some rocky areas; smaller dogs may have to be carried in certain spots); and **Wonderland Trail** (bring a picnic lunch—even during the most crowded season, you'll find a rocky ledge or pebble beach all to yourself). You'll also want to stop by **Thunder Hole,** where trapped waves and air in the rocks sometimes make a thundering sound and an impressive display, as well as **Bubble Pond** and **Bubble Pond Bridge.** A 44-mile-long web of historic stone roads, known as the **Carriage Roads,** is especially popular among bicyclists. And few visitors leave Acadia without watching at least one sunset from the top of **Cadillac Mountain:** hardy souls make the hike, but you can also take the easy way out with a beautiful drive up a paved road. Expect a crowd.

All dogs must be on a leash no longer than 6 feet, and pet owners are required to clean up after their animals. Dogs are not allowed on Sand Beach, Echo Lake Beach, or Isle au Haut Campground, or on any ranger-led activities. And when you hear that this is a pet-friendly place, don't just think dogs—you'll probably run into a few sightseeing cats, as well!

Bar Island Crossing, Bar Harbor. From downtown Bar Harbor, follow West Street to Bridge Street and you'll stumble across this sandbar that connects the town to a tiny, forested section of Acadia known as Bar Island. The island is beautiful (and has great views), but the real fun here is the crossing itself. Like a long beach with water on both sides, it harbors hundreds of tide pools perfect for two- and four-footed explorers. Time your visit carefully, however: If you're out on the island once high tide rolls in, you'll find yourself stranded.

Canoeing. You'll find canoe-rental stands alongside main roads throughout the island; rent for a few hours or a few days and explore the inlets and outlets of Long Pond, Somes Sound, or Eagle Lake. As always seems to happen on the island, the view around every corner is more spectacular than the last.

Downeast Windjammer Cruises, Bar Harbor Inn Pier, 27 Main St., Bar Harbor (207-288-4585; 207-546-2927; decruise@midmaine.com; www.downeastwindjammer.com); $27.50–39.50 per person. Crewmember Maggie, a black Labrador, is the most popular sailor on the *Margaret Todd*. Captain Steven F. Pagels welcomes pets and their owners on board Windjammer's vessels for 1½- to 2-hour cruises, 4-hour fishing expeditions, and 1-hour ferry trips from Bar Harbor to Winter Harbor and back. Dogs must be leashed and well behaved, but otherwise are free to enjoy the sea air in their fur. There are no extra charges for canine guests. (For mail correspondence, write to P.O. 28, Cherryfield, ME 04622.)

Hadley Point Beach, Rte. 3, Bar Harbor. Pooches may not be allowed at Acadia's beaches, but this town-owned property allows dogs on the condition that their owners adhere to local leash laws and have pooper-scooper bags handy. The scenic saltwater beach, complete with picnic area, sits along Frenchman's and Thomas bays and is prized by local sailboarders for its strong north wind. After you enjoy a picnic with Spot in the midafternoon sun, you'll probably add this gorgeous spot to your top-10 list, too.

Independence Day Parade, downtown Bar Harbor. Break out the red, white, and blue: This town gets seriously patriotic on the Fourth of July, and nearly everyone—including pets of all shapes and sizes—shows up for the extravaganza. Volunteers from several local animal rescue organizations march in the parade (along with the dogs in their care that need homes), and so many canines attend with their owners that children on floats often throw candy and dog biscuits to the crowd.

Lulu Lobster Boat Ride, 55 West St., Bar Harbor (207-963-2341; 1-866-235-2341info@lululobsterboat.com; www.lululobsterboat.com); $15–25 per person. Hop on a traditional Downeast lobster boat for a slow, scenic tour of Frenchman's Bay, touted in more than 200 reviews on Trip Advisor as the most fun thing to do in Bar Harbor. Captain John L. Nicolai is an animal lover and does allow pets on board with a few restrictions: Because the vessel holds a maximum of 15 passengers, each passenger must be comfortable with the idea of traveling with a pet on board. Also, dog owners are responsible for keeping their pet on a leash and repairing any animal-caused damage.

TWO HAPPY PASSENGERS ENJOY THE RIDE ON THE LULU LOBSTER BOAT IN BAR HARBOR. (PHOTO COURTESY OF LULU LOBSTER BOAT RIDES)

***Sea Princess* Nature Cruises,** Town Marina, Southwest Harbor (207-276-5352; www.barharborcruises.com); $18–28 per person. The *Sea Princess* sets out for morning, afternoon, and sunset cruises each day to take in the wildlife and scenery of Acadia National Park, Somes Sound, Little Cranberry Island, and Bear Island Lighthouse. Children under age four ride for free, and pets can join the fun as long as they're on a leash and friendly to other passengers.

Shore Path, Bar Harbor. This footpath starts near the Bar Harbor Inn and continues for a mile or so along the water, allowing an unusual view of Frenchman's Bay on one side and Bar Harbor's most impressive waterfront homes on the other. It's a perfect spot for a jog, but most prefer to take it a bit slower and soak in all the scenery.

Window-Shopping in Bar Harbor. You can spend the good part of a day perusing the hundreds of in-town shops selling clothing, candy, ice cream, art, sunglasses, maps, Maine blueberry jam, pottery, and nearly every other type of product imaginable. (At Ben and Bill's on Main Street, you can even get a "doggie ice cream" with a biscuit on top.) A small, picturesque park in the center of it all provides shade, and the waterfront is never more than a few blocks away. All in all, it's a fun and relaxing destination when you need a break from all that hiking.

QUICK BITES

Beal's Lobster Pound, 182 Clark Point Rd., Southwest Harbor (207-244-3202; www.bealslobster.com). Dogs are welcome on a leash at this ultracasual, outdoor restaurant. Plan to get down and dirty cracking your lobster, munching corn-on-the-cob with melted butter, and digging into Captain's Galley menu items like fried foods and burgers.

Café 2 and **Eat-A-Pita,** 326 Main St., Southwest Harbor (207-244-4344; www.eatapitasouthwestharbor.com). These two restaurants sit side by side in downtown Southwest Harbor. At Café 2 (formerly known as Chef Marc), diners can choose from a variety of upscale lamb, seafood, pasta, and vegetarian dishes. Eat-A-Pita's casual menu is best known for blueberry pancakes and generously stuffed pita sandwiches and salads. Both offer outdoor seating next to the sidewalk.

China Joy Restaurant, 195 Main St., Bar Harbor (207-288-8666). Sure, you like lobster. But when you're ready for a break from all that seafood, try China Joy for a change of pace. The Asian cuisine here includes all your favorites like wonton soup and chow mein. Outdoor seating and lunch and dinner buffets are also available. And yes, they have lobster, too.

Ellsworth Giant Sub, Rte. 3, Ellsworth (207-667-5585). This is a good, quick stop for lunch: Choose from 60 eat-in or take-out varieties of hot and cold subs and sandwiches. A grassy area with picnic tables is available for relaxing and eating in the sunshine.

Pond House, 1 Park Loop Rd., Acadia National Park, Bar Harbor (207-276-3316). Located within the park, this historic restaurant has outdoor tables sitting high atop a hill overlooking Jordan Pond. (A hiking trail encircles the pond and makes for a great walk before or after your meal; see **Jordan Pond Nature Trail** in **Acadia National Park** under "Out and About.") The menu includes soups, sandwiches, crabcakes, chowder, prime rib, and salads, but most people come for the famous popovers, served with butter and strawberry jam, and the homemade ice cream and lobster stew. The waitstaff have been known to bring water bowls to thirsty four-legged patrons, as well. Your wait time will be shorter (usually 15 minutes or less) if you call ahead.

Maine-ly Delights, 48 Grandville Rd., Bass Harbor (207-244-3656; www.mainelydelights.com). Overlooking the bustling waterfront of Bass Harbor, this take-out spot offers lobster, burgers, hot dogs, and the house specialty: doughboys with ice cream and fresh fruit. Place your order at the take-out window and settle into the outdoor seating area.

Rupununi, 119 Main St., Bar Harbor (207-288-2886; www.rupununi.com). This popular restaurant sits in the heart of the downtown action. If you can get a table on the patio next to the street, you can park your pooch next to you, curbside. ("We will hold tables along the rail for folks with dogs," says one staffer.) While your pup relaxes, you can enjoy menu items like lobster, the Fisherman's Fried Sampler, littleneck clams, burgers (in beef, veggie, and ostrich varieties), baby back ribs, steak, chicken, and apple-crumb pie.

The Seafood Ketch, 47 Shore Rd., Bass Harbor (207-244-7463; www.seafoodketch.com). This welcoming, casual restaurant allows leashed dogs on its deck and lawn seating areas, which overlook Bass Harbor. A full-service bar offers wine, beer, and cordials, and the menu includes fresh seafood (of course) and homemade breads and desserts. Lunch and dinner are served from 11 AM to 9 PM, and daily specials are always offered.

Note: To find additional restaurants in the Bar Harbor area, or to look at complete menus, visit www.barharbormenus.com.

HOT SPOTS FOR SPOT

Acadia Woods Kennel, 31 Greta's Ln., Bar Harbor (207-288-9766; acadiawoods@acadia.net). This kennel prides itself on providing plenty of personal attention to each of its four-legged visitors, including twice-daily walks for dogs. You can leave your pet overnight (each dog has a heated sleeping area and a private, covered outdoor run; cats have two-story "condos"), or drop him off just for the day. For dogs, you'll have to prove he's received rabies, distemper, and parvovirus vaccination. Cat owners must show proof of rabies and distemper protection.

Bark Harbor, 150 Main St., Bar Harbor (207-288-0404; info@barkharbor.com; www.barkharbor.com). Four-footed customers are more than welcome inside this fun store designed with them in mind. Your dog can drool at the all-natural treats in the antique bakery case while you browse a wide selection of designer collars, leashes, books, picture frames, embroidered T-shirts, towels, and "Paw-tery." This is a can't-miss stop for visiting pet lovers; the staffers will even provide a list of nearby restaurants that allow your pet to dine with you outdoors.

ANIMAL SHELTERS AND HUMANE SOCIETIES

Southwest Harbor Animal Shelter, 15 Wood St., P.O. Box 434, Southwest Harbor 04679 (207-244-3749; www.southwestharboranimalwelfare.org)

SPCA of Hancock County, P.O. Box 1008, Mt. Desert 04660 (207-288-0151; www.spcahancockcounty.org)

IN CASE OF EMERGENCY

Acadia Veterinary Hospital, 21 Federal St., Bar Harbor (207-288-5733)

Bucksport Veterinary Hospital, 11 Gross Point Rd., Orland (207-469-3614)

Ellsworth Veterinary Hospital, 381 State St., Ellsworth (207-667-3437)

Maine Coast Veterinary Hospital, 163 South St., Blue Hill (207-374-2385)

Southwest Harbor Veterinary, Seal Cove Rd., Southwest Harbor (207-244-3336)

THE FLOWER-FILLED WALKWAYS AT MICMAC FARM IN MACHIASPORT BECKON TO FOUR-LEGGED TRAVELERS AND THEIR COMPANIONS. (PHOTO COURTESY OF MICMAC FARM GUEST HOUSES AND GARDNER HOUSE)

Downeast Maine

Most coastal Maine visitors never make it past Acadia. If you're among the hardy few who keep driving north, you'll be more than rewarded for your efforts when you enter this pristine and wild corner of the state. The region has many nicknames: Downeast, so called because ships sail downwind from Boston and New York to get here; the Bold Coast, a name that refers, perhaps, to the grit of the locals; and the Sunrise Coast, because the sun touches these shores before any other spot in the country.

Downeast towns are small and genuine—when asked for her street number, one Cherryfield resident reacted with surprise: "We don't have street numbers!" she explained. More than 85 percent of the nation's blueberries are grown here, and many of the locals are involved with that, well, fruitful industry. You'll see the full beauty of the blue splendor if you arrive in late summer (see Blueberry Barrens under "Out and About").

There are fewer accommodations here than there are farther south, along with fewer restaurants and tourist businesses—a blessing for those looking to escape the crowded hotels and T-shirt shops of other vacation areas. For the most part, your pets can romp with you as you explore rocky beaches, wildlife refuges, and lively festivals. You may want to stock up on food and supplies beforehand, however: Compared to other, more populated regions, pet shops are in short supply here.

ACCOMMODATIONS

Hotels, Motels, Inns, and Bed & Breakfasts

Eastport

Motel East, 23A Water St., Eastport (207-853-4747; ; www.themoteleast.com); $90–110 per night. Rooms at this oceanfront motel have views of Passamaquoddy Bay and Campobello Island; most have private balconies, and all have a queen-size bed and full bath (suites and nonsmoking rooms are also available upon request). Pets are welcome for an extra $20 per night.

Todd House Bed & Breakfast, 1 Capon Ave., Todd's Head, Eastport (207-853-2328; www.toddhousemaine.com); $80–110 per night. Pet owners (or any visitor, for that matter) will feel welcome at Todd House, a waterfront B&B. The five guest rooms are adorned with quilts, wooden chests, and Shaker-style furniture; some have private entrances to the large yard out back, ideal for canine romping. Built during the Revolutionary War, the Todd House is on the National Register of Historic Places."I welcome all pets," says innkeeper Ruth McInnis. "I've had everything from owls to tarantulas stay here. I loved the owls!"

Edmunds

Robinson's Cottages, 231 King St., Edmunds (207-726-9546; www.robinsonscottages.com); $455–520 per week. These seven rustic cottages, ranging in size from one to four bedrooms, sit beside the Denny's River. Most have a screened-in porch; all have kitchenettes, outdoor grills, and picnic tables. Linens, towels, and blankets are also provided, and guests can use the canoes and rowboats free of charge. Pets are welcome.

Grand Lake Stream

Canal Side Cabins, P.O. Box 77, Grand Lake Stream 04637 (207-796-2796; canalside@midmaine.com; www.canalsidecabins.com); $44 per night or $360–525 per week in July and August. These informal cabins were designed with families and sportsmen in mind. Each is heated with a furnace or fireplace and has a living room, dining area, kitchen, and full bathroom. The smallest cabins accommodate two people; the largest sleeps seven. Well-behaved pets are welcome for an extra $5 per night.

Hancock Point

Crocker House Country Inn, 967 Point Rd., Hancock Point (207-

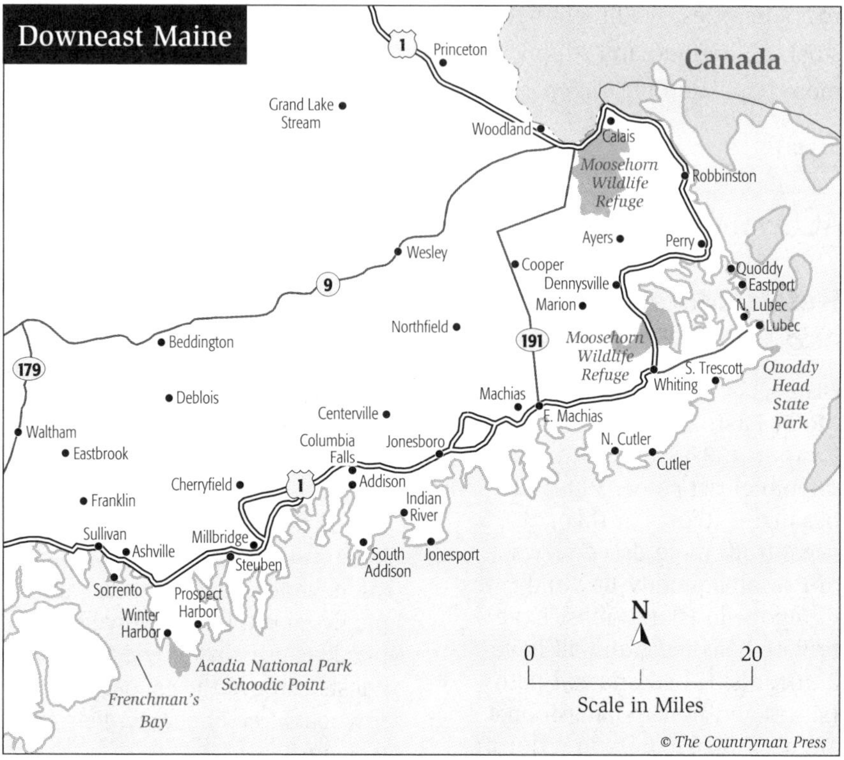

422-68061-877-715-6017; www.crockerhouse.com); $85–165 per night. Tucked away on a quiet peninsula, this 1884 inn is located at the midpoint between Acadia National Park's Cadillac Mountain and Schoodic Point. Pets are not allowed in the dining room, but they are welcome in the 11 guest rooms, each of which has a private bathroom, air-conditioning, Internet access, and a unique décor.

Harrington

Ocean Spray Cottages, RR 1, Box 38, Harrington (207-483-2780; www.oceanspraycottages.com); $90–110 per night or $600–700 per week. These two-bedroom heated cottages are available for rental year-round. Each can accommodate four people and offers a living room, a kitchenette, and window bird feeders. "We have three dogs and love to meet our customers' pets," says owner Cathy Strout. "Our experience has been that anyone who travels with their pets takes really good care of them."

Machias

Machias Motor Inn, Rte. 1, 103 Main St., Machias (207-255-4861; www.machiasmotorinn.com); $94–124 per night. Dogs (sorry, no cats) are welcome guests at the Machias Motor Inn, where you'll find water views, air-conditioning, an on-site restaurant and a banquet facility, and easy accessibility to snowmobile and ATV trails.

Machiasport

Micmac Farm Guest Houses and Gardner House, Rte. 92, 47 Mic Mac Ln., Machiasport (207-255-3008; www.micmacfarm.com); \$80–95 per night or \$495–595 per week. Animals are allowed inside the guest cabins at this cozy, secluded farm. The three cabins and farmhouse are surrounded by 50 acres of forest and meadow; each cabin has two double beds, a full bathroom, knotty-pine walls, a dining area with a kitchenette, and electric heat. The decks have sliding doors and views of the Machias River.

Sorrento

Bass Cove Farm Bed & Breakfast, 312 E. Side Rd., Sorrento (207-422-3564; basscove@downeast.net); \$75–105 per night. This B&B is secluded enough to offer repose but close enough to the sights to be convenient. "We've enjoyed the company of dogs, cats, a rabbit, and a bird," says Bass Cove innkeeper Mary Ann Solet. She asks that pets not be left alone in the rooms for long periods of time; there are no extra pet fees.

Campgrounds

Alexander

Pleasant Lake Camping Area, 371 Davis Rd., Alexander (207-454-7467; pllake@midmaine.com); call for rate information. Just off Route 9 you'll find this family camping area with 120 tent and RV sites (some waterfront), full hookups, picnic tables, and fire rings. There's plenty here to keep the family busy, including basketball courts, hiking trails, a boat ramp, horseshoe pits, a playground, and a camp store. Quiet, well-behaved pets are welcome on a leash.

Danforth

Greenland Cove Campground, East Grand Lake, Danforth (207-448-2863; 207-532-6593; www.mainerec.com/gcc); \$25 per night. Pets on a leash are welcome at this lakeside, rural campground that caters to fishermen and families. On-site, you'll find wooded trails, a sandy beach, waterfront and wooded campsites, water and electric hookups for RVs, boat rentals, a camp store, a heated pool, a game room, and a playground.

Dennysville

Cobscook Bay State Park Campground, RR1, Box 127, Dennysville (207-726-4412); \$14 per night Maine residents; \$19 per night out-of-state residents. The 100 campsites at this state park (see "Out and About") are fairly secluded to provide a rustic camping experience: Some are located right on the water. Amenities include hot showers, shelters, and a picnic area. Cobscook Bay surrounds the park on three sides. Owners are expected to clean up after their pets and keep them on a leash.

Eastport

Seaview Campground, 16 Norwood Rd., Eastport (207-853-

4471; info@eastport.com; www.eastportmaine.com); $14–37 per night or $500–975 per month. This oceanfront campground juts out into Passamaquoddy Bay. Tenters and RV owners can enjoy the beach, dock, boat launch, recreation hall, laundry facilities, showers, and flush toilets, along with a host of planned activities including barbecues, fish frys, and pig roasts. Quiet, leashed pets are welcome but cannot be left alone at a campsite.

Harrington

Sunset Point Campground, 102 Marshville Rd., Harrington (207-483-4412; www.sunsetpointcampground.com); call for rate information. Campers at Sunset Point will find restrooms with showers, 30 sites for tents and RVs (including some pull-throughs), laundry facilities, vending machines, island views, and trailer rentals. Leashed, friendly pets are welcome.

Steuben

Mainayr Campground, 321 Village Rd., Steuben (207-546-3780; info@mainayr.com; www.mainayr.com); $18 per night. Located on 25 acres at the edge of a tidal cove, Mainayr is a quiet campground with 35 sites for tents, campers, and RVs. Families can enjoy a playground, a small beach, laundry facilities, and a camp store; a saltwater tank houses fresh lobsters for campers to cook at their fire pits, located at each site. Well-behaved pets are welcome on a leash.

Homes, Cottages, and Cabins for Rent

Lubec

West Quoddy Rental, 37 Loon Ln., Lubec (207-733-2457; rental@westquoddygifts.com); $650–700 per week. Pets are welcome for an extra $50 per week at this three-bedroom home located within a mile of West Quoddy Head Lighthouse. The home has a view of Lubec Channel, private shore access, a living room, a full kitchen, and satellite television with 50-plus channels. Linens are provided for the queen-, full-, and twin-size beds along with a daybed.

Pembroke

Yellow Birch Farm, 272 Young's Cove Rd., Pembroke (207-726-5807; yellowbirchfarm@acadia.net); $400 per week. Dogs can join the fun at the Yellow Birch's weathered-shingle cottage: "We love to meet other people's dogs," says owner Gretchen Gordon. "And there are lots of super places here for a dog to run: around the farm, at the shore, or on our dirt road." The cottage has one double and two twin beds, a barbecue grill, a toaster, and a coffeemaker.

Sorrento

Downeast Coastal Cottage, near Rte. 1, Sorrento (207-422-3639; 520-803-0243; ruthnski@aol.com); $75 per night or $475 per week. This cozy one-room guesthouse is big enough for two and is located on a private 10-acre farm. Gardeners, take note: The farm's owners raise vegetables for sale, and are willing to offer reduced rates in summer to guests who want to help out with planting, harvesting, and weeding. Flea-free and well-behaved pets are welcome with an extra cleaning fee of $25.

South Princeton

The Hideaway on Pocomoonshine Lake, 29 The Hideaway Ln., South Princeton (207-427-6183); $125 per night or $700 per week. Dogs, cats, and even birds have stayed at these waterfront housekeeping cottages located at the headwaters of the East Machias River. Each rental has a large screened-in porch, a "great room" (living, dining, and kitchen area), a full bathroom, one or two bedrooms, a charcoal grill, a dock, and a rowboat. There are no extra fees for pets.

Whiting

Summer Cottage, c/o Puffin Pines Country Gift Store, Rte. 1, P.O. Box 99, Whiting 04691 (207-733-9782; patsue1046@aol.com; www.patsplacelubecmaine.com); $500–600 per week. Owner Pat McCabe has been renting this cottage and welcoming pets for more than 10 years. Located about 100 feet from Lubec Channel, the cottage accommodates up to four people with two bedrooms, one bathroom, a kitchen/living room area, a TV/VCR, a deck overlooking the channel, a microwave, a coffeemaker, and a barbecue grill. Dogs and cats are welcome.

Rental Agencies

Hearts of Maine Seaside Rental Properties, 5 Ocean Whisper Dr., Addison (207-483-4396; info@heartsofmaine.com; www.heartsofmaine.com). This rental agency is extremely pet-friendly: More than 75 percent of the listed properties allow animals. "We have very few problems with pets at our rentals, and we know that pets are an important

THE DOG-FRIENDLY ROBINSON'S COTTAGES IN EDMUNDS ARE LOCATED BESIDE THE DENNY'S RIVER. (PHOTO COURTESY OF ROBINSON'S COTTAGES)

part of people's families," says Greg Burr, who owns the agency with his wife, Sue. The homes and apartments are located in Castine, Lubec, and everywhere in between—animals must be flea-free and quiet, and owners must pick up after them.

OUT AND ABOUT

Acadia National Park, Schoodic Section. Spread throughout the towns of Gouldsboro and Winter Harbor, this is the only section of Acadia National Park located on the mainland. Much like the Loop Road in the Mount Desert Island section of the park, Acadia's Schoodic region also offers a one-way, scenic "loop" around the peninsula with impressive views of the rocky coastline and wild terrain. This section of the park is relatively small (2,194 acres compared with Mount Desert Island's 30,300 acres), but the crowds are smaller, too—a bonus in these popular parts.

Blueberry Barrens. Washington County produces the majority of the blueberries grown in the United States. Starting in August, the region's barrens are ready for harvest, and the entire landscape in these parts turns, well, blue. To get the best views of this unusual sight, follow **Route 193** from Cherryfield toward Deblois, **Route 1** heading north from Harrington or Jonesboro, or **Route 9** in Wesley.

Blueberry Festival, Centre Street Congregational Church, Centre St., Machias. Usually held during one of the last weekends in August, this Friday-through-Sunday annual fair celebrates the region's blueberry harvest with musical performances, fish frys, parades, more than 100 crafters and artists, and of course blueberry pancake breakfasts.

Bold Coast Trail, SR-191, Cutler. As the largest stretch of undeveloped coastline in the state of Maine, this 4½-mile-long trail holds special appeal for residents and visitors alike. Along the way, you'll pass cliffs, beaches, forests, and sea arches; out at sea, whales, songbirds, and herring may be passing by. Primitive camping is allowed off the main trail. To find the trailhead, drive 1 to 2 miles north of Cutler along SR-191 until you reach the small entrance.

Calais Waterfront Walkway. This wonderful, winding pathway is worth a visit. Part of the former train line of the Calais Railway, it hugs the St. Croix River from the library to Todd and South streets, with benches and picnic tables along the way. The 1-mile-long walkway passes right by the **International Bridge.**

Cherryfield Historic District, Cherryfield–Narraguagus Historical Society, Cherryfield (207-546-7979). A quiet walk through this quaint old section of town will take you past impressive examples of Second Empire, Federal, Greek Revival, Italianate, and Queen Anne architecture—in taverns, shops, and homes. The local historical society publishes a brochure for a self-guided tour that starts at the corner of Main Street and Route 1.

Cobscook Bay State Park, RR 1, Box 127, Dennysville (207-726-4412). Bald eagles, wildflowers, and more than 200 species of birds make their home in this 888-acre park, whose name comes from the Passamaquoddy word for "boiling tides." The trails are especially popular among hikers and cross-country skiers. The park entrance is located about 4 miles south of Dennysville along Route 1. There is also an extensive campground on-site (see "Accommodations—Campgrounds").

Deer Island Ferry, Water Street Terminal, Eastport (506-747-2159; www.eastcoastferriesltd.com); passengers, $3; car and driver, $14. East Coast Ferries Ltd. Operates this service to take travelers to and from Eastport, Maine, and Deer Island, New Brunswick. The tiny island makes for a great day trip, with galleries, shops, villages, lobster pounds, beaches, and whale-watching excursions. Restrained pets are welcome on the ferry, provided their owners clean up after them.

International Festival, Calais. The town of Calais hosts this festival every August with its Canadian friends across the border in St. Stephen, New Brunswick. The weeklong festival typically include parades, horse shows, fireworks, beer and food tents, and crafts fairs. For up-to-date festival information and locations, call the Calais Regional Chamber of Commerce at 207-454-2308.

Moosehorn National Wildlife Refuge, Charlotte Rd., Baring. Moose, wood ducks, eagles, blue herons, barred owls, ruffed grouse—this is wild Maine at its finest. The park has nearly 60 miles of roads and trails available for hiking, bird-watching, and cross-country skiing. Beavers build dams in the 50 lakes and marshes, and woodcocks perform their astounding aerial mating dances each spring. This is a big place with big wildlife (black bears are often seen foraging through the blueberry patches in late summer), so exercise extreme caution with your pets.

Petit Manan National Wildlife Refuge, Pigeon Hill Rd., Steuben. Among the more famous residents of this 3,000-acre preserve are endangered peregrine falcons. You might also spot kestrels, goshawks, puffins, and sandpipers in the marshes, peat bogs, and forests that make up Petit Manan. Much of the park's island property is accessible only by boat, but you can get to Petit Manan Point by car. Two trails—Birch and Shore—leave from the parking area on Pigeon Hill Road.

Robertson Sea Tours, Milbridge Marina, Milbridge (207-546-3883; info@robertsonseatours.com; www.robertsonseatours.com); tours, $20–45 per person; charters, $300 per day. Captain James Robertson welcomes pets aboard his boat for Petit Manan Puffin Cruises, Scenic Island Tours, Island Lobster Cruises, and personalized, private charters. (A seaworthy golden retriever was a guest on a recent voyage.) While at sea, don't be surprised to spot seals, porpoises, blue herons, ospreys, and bald eagles.

Rocky Lake Public Reserve, SR-191, East Machias. More than 11,000 acres of coastline, forests, coves, inlets, and primitive camping sites await visitors to this pristine reserve. Fishermen gather at the **East Machias River, Meadow Brook, Northern Inlet, Rocky Lake, Second Lake,** and other fishing and swimming holes throughout the area; and bird-watchers, hikers, and boaters will find plenty to do here as well. As with all northern Maine and wilderness areas, use caution during hunting season.

West Quoddy Head Light, Quoddy Head State Park, Lubec (207-733-0911; 207-941-4014). This barberpole of a lighthouse has graced innumerable calendars and coffee-table books. Located in Quoddy Head State Park, its 49-foot, red-and-white-striped tower watches over the Bay of Fundy and the town of Lubec. There are other, equally beautiful lighthouses in the Quoddy Loop area, but this is by far the most famous. The 532-acre park is located about 4 miles off Route 189 in Lubec.

QUICK BITES

Crossroads Restaurant, Rte. 1, Pembroke (207-726-5053). Area residents like to linger at this family-style seafood restaurant, attached to a motel of the same name. But there are also plenty of menu items available for take-out, if you want to bring some lunch along with you when you go to see the sights.

Downeast Deli, Rtes. 186 and 195, Prospect Harbor (207-963-2700). You can relax on Downeast Deli's lawn or pack up your picnic basket with New York–style hoagies, soups and chowders, seafood sandwiches, and even pizza. The deli is located 2 miles from the Schoodic section of Acadia National Park.

Eastport Chowder House, 167 Water St., Eastport (207-853-4700). Located at the Deer Island Ferry Landing, this restaurant is open seasonally and recently earned *Yankee* magazine's recommendation for "Best Lobster Roll." It's reasonably priced and has great views of the bay.

Frank's Pizzaria and Deli, 33 Water St., Eastport (207-853-2709). Call ahead and order pizza, sandwiches, subs, calzones, salads, chicken dishes, pasta, and more at this primarily take-out restaurant.

Lobster Crate, Rte. 190, Perry (207-853-6611). This casual seafood restaurant, recommended by the locals, has plenty of picnic tables as well as a take-out window. It's a great "roadside" kind of place with simple, good food.

Polar Treat, Rte. 1, Perry. Help yourself to lunch, frozen yogurt, or ice cream (including three flavors of soft-serve) at this A-frame take-out spot. For Rover, the staff serves up "doggie dishes" of ice cream with a dog bone on top.

Raye's Mustard Mill, 83 Washington St., Eastport (207-853-4451). The Raye family has been producing fine mustards in this area since 1903; today, you can order any of their varieties online or stop by the Pantry Store for mustard sets, gourmet foods, ice cream, hot dogs, kielbasa, and more delicious eats.

Rosie's Hot Dogs, Town Wharf, Eastport. The dogs at this famously popular take-out stand are served with locally ground mustard from Raye's (see listing above). You can also order onion rings, french fries, and chili and eat at the picnic tables overlooking the harbor.

Schoodic Snacks, Main St. (Rte. 186), Winter Harbor (207-963-2296). Oven-baked fries, hamburgers, hot dogs, crab rolls, steamers, and lobster are available at this casual take-out place with picnic tables.

HOT SPOTS FOR SPOT

Amittai Grooming Kennel, Hilltop Ln. (Rte. 193), Cherryfield (207-546-7425). Cynthia Huntington has been a dog groomer for more than 30 years—at one time on the show circuit, and now in homey Cherryfield. Much of her business comes from Downeast visitors and vacationers. She charges about $25 for most visits, and can do shampooing, skin treatments, clipping, and more.

C.P.L. Kennels, Kendall Head Rd., Eastport (207-853-4484). Animal lover Carolyn Lowe boards cats and dogs at her small facility (there are 10 runs available for dogs). She also provides day care for the pets of locals and vacationers. "In a lot of cases, I take care of dogs while their owners are out whale-watching or sightseeing," Lowe explains.

Dogs by Dawn, Rte. 1, Box 2280, East Machias (207-255-3994). Boarding, grooming, and doggie day care (for $1 an hour) are all available at this full-service facility. Grooming services include shampoos and breed-specific clipping, and the building has 17 kennels and seven indoor/outdoor runs.

Pet Pantry, 24 High St., Milbridge (207-546-7941). This well-stocked shop offers dog and cat food, bird supplies, treats, toys, shampoos, and other necessities. The owners also run obedience-training classes in an adjoining room.

ANIMAL SHELTERS AND HUMANE SOCIETIES

The Ark Animal Shelter, P.O. Box 276, Cherryfield 04622 (207-546-3484; www.thearkpets.org)

Pet Society Animal Shelter, P.O. Box 313, Cherryfield 04622 (207-546-3310)

IN CASE OF EMERGENCY

Calais Veterinary Clinic, 234 North St., Calais (207-454-8522)

Four Corners Veterinary Clinic, RR1 Box 3, Columbia Falls 04623 (207-483-4727)

Marquis Veterinary, 307 Main St., Baileyville (207-427-6364)

Milbridge Veterinary Clinic, 1 High St., Milbridge (207-546-7909)

Perry Veterinary Clinic, 1074 Rte. 1, Perry (207-853-0671)

Sunrise County Veterinary Clinic, Stagecoach Rd., East Machias (207-255-8538)

TWO GUESTS OF THE MOOSEHEAD HILLS CABINS IN GREENVILLE TAKE IN THE GREAT NORTH WOODS SCENERY. (PHOTO COURTESY OF MOOSEHEAD HILLS CABINS)

Great North Woods

This is Maine's true wilderness: From vast tracts of forest to majestic lakes and mountains, the Aroostook and northern Katahdin region is not for the faint of heart—or the tourist in search of indoor luxuries. In other parts of the state you hear about moose; here you see them, provided you know where and when to look. The friendly, laid-back local innkeepers and shop owners will be more than happy to share that information, along with anything else you might need to know about their neck of these woods.

This area has many leisure possibilities, including hiking, boating, and leaf-peeping, but most people, it seems, come to northern Maine to hunt. (For that reason, you'll want to use extra caution while exploring the backcountry during open season.) The vast majority of the accommodations here are set up to provide a home base for hunters and fishermen, but snowmobilers, as well, have discovered the region's charms and are becoming a growing force behind the local tourism industry. Much of the land and many of the roads of the North Woods are owned by timber and paper companies; be prepared to pay fees as you drive along.

Another important fact to note before you pack your bags is that dogs are not allowed in Baxter State Park, the 200,000-acre reserve that is the region's jewel and best-known attraction. But if you don't mind missing out on Baxter, numerous other parks, reserved lands, and campgrounds do welcome dogs. Beautiful Moosehead Lake, wildlife-viewing "safaris," and other adventure-filled spots also exist for you and your four-legged friend to explore together.

ACCOMMODATIONS

Hotels, Motels, Inns, and Bed & Breakfasts

Caribou

Caribou Inn & Convention Center, 19 Main St., Caribou (207-498-3733; 1-800-235-0466; www.caribouinn.com); $115–159 per night. This long-standing Caribou favorite has 73 rooms and three executive suites, along with a restaurant serving breakfast, lunch, and dinner; a fitness center, an indoor pool, a sauna and whirlpool; and a lounge with a pool table, televisions, and Friday-night comedy shows. Pets are enthusiastically welcomed.

Russell's Motel, 357 Main St., Caribou (207-498-2567; russellsmotel@maine.rr.com; www.russellsmotel.com); $55–65 per night. This small, simple, and clean motel offers an affordable night's stay in Caribou, and its location beside an established, groomed trail makes it popular with snowmobilers. "We do offer lodging to people with dogs and cats," says owner Donna Murchison. "All I ask is that the pets not bother other people and that the owners clean up after their animals."

Crouseville

Rum Rapids Inn Bed & Breakfast, 26 Rum Rapids Dr., Crouseville (207-455-8096; info@rumrapidsinn.com; www.rumrapidsinn.com); $89 per night and higher. This is the only B&B in Presque Isle; lucky for us, innkeeper Judy Boudman allows pets in one of the quaint rooms. "There is ample room on the grounds for exercising a pet, including nature trails and river walks," Judy explains. She also runs a gourmet restaurant on-site and serves a full Scottish breakfast each morning. Check out the special two-night weekend packages on the Web site.

Eastport

Milliken House B&B, 29 Washington St., Eastport (207-853-2955; 1-888-507-9370; millikenhouse@eastport-inn.com; www.eastport-inn.com); $80–90 per night. The Milliken House B&B is an 1846 Victorian home located a few blocks from the Historic District and waterfront. Guests will find five guest rooms,

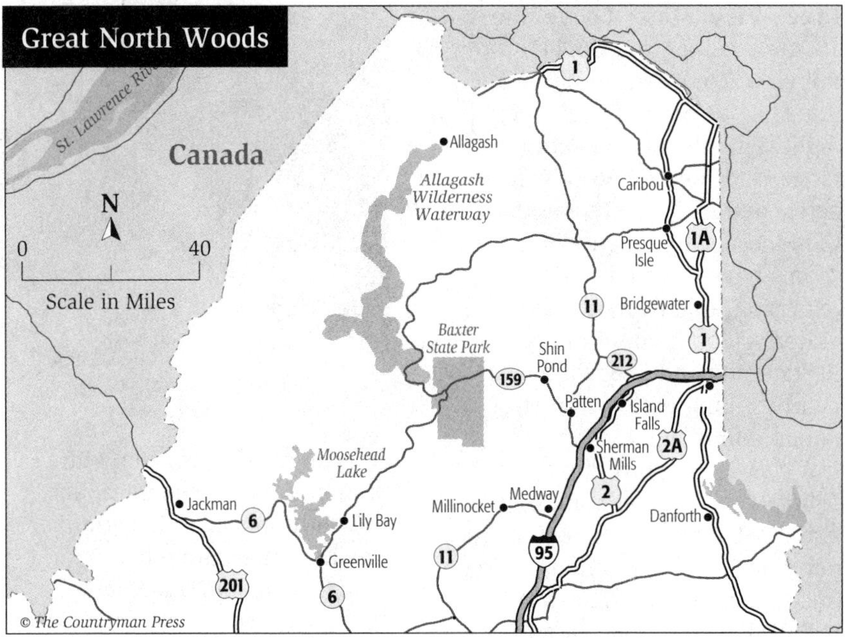

antiques, bedside chocolates, fresh-cut flowers, and full daily breakfasts with specialties like blueberry crêpes, hot buttermilk pancakes with fresh fruit, and quiche Lorraine. Children and well-behaved pets are welcome.

Fort Kent

Northern Door Inn, 356 W. Main St., Fort Kent (207-834-3133; northerndoorinn@fkglobal.com; www.northerndoorinn.com); $76–100 per night. This one-story hotel (also called La Porte Du Nord) was recently remodeled; most rooms have two double beds and standard hotel-style furnishings. Staff are knowledgeable about all of the local events and festivals, and the inn frequently hosts family reunions and other gatherings on-site. Wireless Internet access is also available. Dogs are welcome to stay for an extra $5 per night, per pet. This is a popular spot for snowmobiling.

Greenville

The Black Frog, Pritham Ave., Greenville (207-695-1100; info@theblackfrog.com); $110–130 per night. This informal lodging and restaurant is located at the southernmost tip of Moosehead Lake. The two available suites have views of East Cove and are within walking distance of the busy village. "Our only restrictions for pets are that they be housebroken, not eat the furniture, and not keep us up all night," explains owner Leigh Turner. "And if they'd like to play with our 100-pound Doberman pinscher, all the better." For more information about the Black Frog restaurant, see "Quick Bites."

Kineo View Motor Lodge, Rte. 15, Greenville (207-695-4470; the view@moosehead.net; www.kineoview.com); $99–159 per night. This three-story motor lodge is located on 55 private acres, and each room overlooks the Moosehead Lake region. The rooms have large balconies, color television, microwaves, refrigerators, and air-conditioning. Restaurants and shops are nearby, along with skiing at Squaw Mountain and prime leaf-peeping opportunities in fall. Animals are welcome in designated pet rooms for an extra $10 per night, but they cannot be left unattended at any time. The rate includes a free breakfast and free Wi-Fi.

Leisure Life Resort, P.O. Box 1134, Greenville 04441 (207-695-3737; 1-800-726-2302; www.leisureliferesort.com); $75–87 per night. Animals are welcome for an extra $10 per night at this 36-acre hotel with 17 rooms and efficiencies. Located on the ITS 86 snowmobile trail, the hotel also offers a swimming pool, an on-site driving range, room service, a restaurant and lounge, volleyball and basketball courts, horseshoe pits, and a catch-and-release trout pond.

Greenville Junction

Chalet Moosehead Lakefront Motel, Rte. 15, Greenville Junction (207-695-2950; 1-800-290-3645; www.chaletmooseheadlakefrontmotel.com); $84–140 per night. Every unit in this motel has a picture window and a view of the lake, as well as daily maid

© JERRY SANCHEZ/SHUTTERSTOCK.COM

service, cable television with premium movie channels, and a full bathroom. The larger efficiencies have a separate bedroom, a living room, and a kitchenette. With advance notice, dogs (sorry, no cats) are welcome in some motel rooms and efficiencies for an extra $10 per night, provided they aren't left alone in the room at any time.

Island Falls

Sewall House Yoga Retreat, 1027 Crystal Rd., P.O. Box 254, Island Falls 04747 (646-316-5151; 1-888-235-2395; info@sewallhouse.com; www.sewallhouse.com); $200 per day and higher. This is one of the most unusual accommodations in northern Maine—a B&B with an emphasis on yoga and meditation, set near deep woods and Mattawamkeag Lake. The daily schedule includes a morning and afternoon yoga class; free time for bicycling, journaling, swimming, hiking, and other activities; and breakfast, lunch, and dinner. Pets are welcome; there is a cat already in residence. The rates include yoga classes and vegetarian meals.

Jackman

Allen's Four Seasons Accommodations, 37 Johns St., Jackman (207-668-7683; 1-888-668-0098; www.allensfourseasonsaccomodations.com); $25–101 per night. Allen's offers a wide variety of options when it comes to finding a place to bunk for the night: Guests can choose from a motel, a lodge, a campground, a wilderness park, and a mobile home park. The amenities also include a volleyball court, a fishing pond, and laundry facilities. Canoes, campers, motorboats, lobster pots, and party tents are also available for rent. Dogs are welcome.

Patten

Mt. Chase Lodge, Rte. 159, Upper Shin Pond, Patten (207-528-2183; mtchaselodge@pivot.net; www.mtchaselodge.com); $69–79 per person, American Plan (meals included). For an extra $5 per night (and preapproval from innkeepers Rick and Sara Hill), guests can bring pets along for a stay in one of the lodge's cabins, which can accommodate two to eight people. Cabin guests can cook for themselves or choose a plan that allows them to enjoy family-style meals in the lodging dining room.

Presque Isle

Northern Lights Motel, 72 Houlton Rd., Presque Isle (207-764-4441; motel@northernlightsmotel.com); $79 per night and higher. Each of the 14 units in this comfortable motel is individually decorated with pine-board walls, bright bedspreads, wood furniture, microwaves, and mini refrigerators. Guests will find swings and a gas barbecue grill out on the lawn, and free Internet access and coffee in the lobby. Dogs are always welcome in designated rooms.

Presque Isle Inn & Convention Center, 116 Main St., Presque Isle (207-764-3321; 1-800-533-3971; www.presqueisleinn.com); $95–142 per night. Recently acquired by the owners of the Caribou Inn, this very pet-friendly hotel has 151 newly renovated rooms, indoor corridors, an on-site tavern with a wide-screen television, a pool and sauna, an attached restaurant, meeting rooms, and live entertainment on weekends. There are no extra fees for pets.

Rockwood

Birches Resort, P.O. Box 41, Rockwood 04478 (1-800-825-WILD; wwld@aol.com; www.birches.com); cabins, $144–333 per night; cabin tents and yurts, $25–40 per person, per night. Dogs on a leash are welcome in the cabins, cabin tents, and yurts (but not in the lodge) for an extra fee of $10 per pet, per night. Dogs are also allowed on the on-site cross-country ski trail. The resort serves as a base for Wilderness Expeditions, an adventure tour company that escorts guests on biking, kayaking, floatplane, white-water rafting, ice-fishing, and moose-viewing trips.

Sherman Mills

Katahdin Valley Motel, P.O. Box 412, Sherman Mills 04776 (207-

365-4554; 1-888-500-2418; kvm@pivot.net; www.katahdinvalleymotel.com); $45–95 per night. Just off the highway (Exit 264 off I-95), this motel is neat, affordable, and convenient. Choose from standard rooms and larger apartments with washers/dryers and kitchenettes. Snowmobilers especially appreciate Katahdin Valley's location, right beside the ITS 83 groomed trail. Dogs are welcome for an extra fee of $5 per night.

Weston

First Settler's Lodge, Rte. 1, Weston (207-448-3000; info@firstsettlerslodge.com; www.firstsettlerslodge.com); cabin and cottages, $125–150 per night. Although animals are not allowed in the lodge itself, they are permitted at three lodge-owned private rentals—one cabin and two cottages—located near the Baskahegan and Mattawamkeag rivers. (For the most part, these are used by game hunters in fall.) The lodge can arrange guides and trips for fishing, snowmobiling, and boating, and other activities.

Campgrounds

Abbott Village

Balsam Woods Campground, 112 Pond Rd., Abbott Village (207-876-2731; info@balsamwoods.com; www.balsamwoods.com); $25–65 per night. Campsites and cabins are available at Balsam Woods, which also offers a snack bar (with burgers, fries, and other treats), a lobster pound, a camp store, laundry facilities, and firewood, gas, and propane. Every site has cable television and Wi-Fi capability. "We have always welcomed pets," says owner Jay Eberhard. "We just ask that pets not be left alone to bark or disturb other campers, and owners are required to clean up after their pets." Animals are not allowed in the buildings or pool area.

Greenville

Lily Bay State Park Campground, HC 76, Lily Bay Rd., Greenville (207-695-2700; 207-941-4014); $14 per night Maine residents; $19 per night out-of-state residents. Two separate Lily Bay campgrounds have 91 sites, some of which are right on Moosehead Lake. Campers can enjoy a boat launch, swimming area, beach, and hiking trail along the water. This is a great way to see the lake and its famous Mount Kineo. Dogs are welcome as long as their owners pick up after them.

Moosehead Family Campground, 312 Moosehead Lake Rd. (Rte. 15), Greenville (207-695-2210; www.mooseheadcampground.com); $22–35 per night. Pets on a leash are welcome at this campground, where you'll find shaded and sunny sites for RVs and tents, along with a playground, a game room, a camp store, picnic tables, and free coffee and tea—all within a mile of Moosehead Lake. Animals cannot be left alone at campsites, and owners must pick up after them.

Island Falls

Birch Point Campground & Cottages, 33 Birch Point Ln.,

Island Falls (207-463-2515; endpoint@pivot.net; www.birchpointcampground.com); cottages, $75–95 per night; campground, $27–34 per night. Birch Point has plenty of opportunities for recreation, including swimming, fishing, boating, candlepin bowling, golf, and playing in the playground. Guests can choose from campsites or eight housekeeping cottages, each of which can accommodate two to five people. All pets must be leashed and picked-up after. There is an extra $5 charge for pets staying in the cottages.

Jackman

Jackman Landing, 582 Main St., Jackman (207-668-3301); $25–35 per night. With 25 sites, 16 of them for RVs, Jackman Landing offers canoe rentals and float plane rides, and is close to the whitewater rafting action on the Kennebec.

Loon Echo Family Campground, Rte. 201, Jackman (207-668-4829; loonecho@webtv.net); $20 per night. Loon Echo's owners, Bill and Holly Erven, are true animal lovers—they even raise and train service dogs to help the handicapped. Dogs are welcome at their campground as long as they stay on a leash and aren't left alone at a site. Campers here will find lots of fly-fishing opportunities, a recreation area, vegetable gardens, abundant wildlife, boat docking, and sites for tents and RVs; waterfront camping cabins are also available.

Moose River Campground, 107 Heald Stream Road, Jackman (207-668-3341; camping@mooserivercampground.net); $25–35 per night. Moose River Campground is located on the shores of Attean Lake, about a half mile from the river for which it is named. Campers here enjoy fishing, swimming, boating, and hiking. There are sites for tenters and RVers, along with restrooms, a solar-heated swimming pool, laundry facilities, boat rentals, and a dining room. Pets are welcome, although the owners ask that you use a leash and clean up any messes.

Medway

Katahdin Shadows Campground and Cabins, Rte. 157, Medway (207-746-9349; 1-800-794-5267; katshadcamp@midmaine.com; www.katahdinshadows.com); campsites, $24–36 per night; cabins, $26–88 per night. This is an exceptionally pet-friendly campground; the owners offer pet-sitting for $30 per day. The cabins are old-fashioned log-style (all are heated and some include kitchenettes), and the campground offers boat rentals, a pool, athletic fields, a function hall, a camp store, and free morning coffee. Boat rentals are available nearby.

Millinocket

Allagash Gateway Campsites and Camps, P.O. Box 396, Millinocket 04462 (207-723-9215; info@allagashgateway.com; www.allagashgatewaycamps.com); $15–30 per night. Pets must be leashed and attended-to at all times, but are otherwise welcome at Allagash Gateway for an extra $10 per stay (not per night). The campground on Ripogenus Lake has a boat dock and launch, a camp store selling gas and sundries, wooded and sunny campsites, and a well for drinking water. Each site has a fire pit, picnic table, and trash can.

Hidden Springs Campground, Baxter Park Rd., Millinocket (1-888-685-4488; tentrus@midmaine.com); $20–30 per night. "As pet owners, we know how hard it is to leave the baby home," says Hidden Springs owner Gail Seile. Dogs must be on a leash and not left alone at tent sites, and owners must clean up after them. The campground has miles of bike trails and facilities for tenters and RVers, and is close to shops, restaurants, and grocery stores. (For mail correspondence, write to 224 Central St., Millinocket 04462.)

Jo-Mary Lake Campground, Rte. 11, P.O. Box 329, Millinocket 04462 (207-723-8117; 207-746-5512); call for rate information. Located on the south shore of Jo-Mary Lake, this campground's facilities include a sandy beach, boat and canoe rentals, a playground, a recreation room, a camp store, RV rentals, and a dumping station. Leashed pets are allowed in all areas except the beach.

Mount Chase

Shin Pond Village, 1489 Shin Pond Rd., Mount Chase (207-528-2900; www.shinpond.com); $22–39 per night. A family- and pet-friendly campground, Shin Pond offers tent sites with picnic tables and fire pits, and RV sites with hookups. Lakes, mountains, and forests are close by. The campground also has housekeeping cottages for rent, and a gift shop and country store. Pets are welcome in the cottages for an additional fee of $5 per day.

Presque Isle

Arndt's Aroostook River Lodge and Campground, 95 Parkhurst Siding Rd., Presque Isle (207-764-8677; www.arndtscamp.com); $29–35 per night, $174–210 per week, or $440–540 per month. Though not permitted in the lodge, pets can join their owners in the campground section of this Presque Isle riverfront facility. Secluded and private, Arndt's is also close to shopping, restaurants, a golf course, and bike trails; on-site, campers make use of a recreation hall, laundry facilities, a bike rental shop, and a shower/bathhouse. Dog owners are asked to use a leash and clean up after their animals.

Aroostook State Park Campground, 87 State Park Rd., Presque Isle (207-768-8341; www.mainerec.com/arpark4.asp); $12 per night Maine residents; $15 per night out-of-state residents. With 29 well-spaced sites, this campground can accommodate tents, pop-up campers, and a few RVs. You can launch a boat or catch some rays at Echo Lake. Toilets, shelters, picnic areas, and water spigots are also provided. (See "Out and About" for more park information.)

Fieldstone Cabins and RV Park, 559 Sweden St., Caribou (207-

© A KATZ/SHUTTERSTOCK.COM

551-9319; 1-800-451-5281; www.fieldstonecabins.com); $125 per night or $700–800 per week. Fieldstone's 100-year-old log cabins are homey, clean, and full of country touches like lofts, wooden ladders, front porches, and rustic interiors. Each is equipped with a kitchen, a gas grill, a full bathroom, two bedrooms, two double beds, and a twin bed. The park also has sites for RVs; the cabins are located in Stockholm on Madawaska Lake.

Rockwood

Gray Ghost Camps, Rte. 15, Rockwood (207-534-7362; grayghostcamps@acadia.net; www.grayghostcamps.com); $100–200 per night or $600–1200 per week. Guests at Gray Ghost can take full advantage of Moosehead Lake by paddling a kayak, canoe, or paddleboat—all available free of charge for guests. Motorboats and snowmobiles are available for rent. All cabins are equipped with kitchens and bathrooms. Well-behaved pets are welcome as long as their owners clean up after them.

Seboomook Wilderness Campground, HC 85, Rockwood (207-280-0555; seboomook@starband.net; www.seboomookwildernesscampground.us); $20–30 per night. Animals are welcome at the Adirondack shelters, tent sites, and RV sites with hookups at Seboomook, which is located at the upper end of Moosehead Lake. The site offers a sandy beach, an activity/lawn area, and a camp store. Fishermen and hunters are frequent guests, as are families and cross-country skiers. There are no extra fees for pets.

Sinclair

Waters Edge R.V. Resort Campground, Rte. 162, Lot 334, Sinclair (207-543-5189; 941-793-6280; www.koa.com); $18–22 per night. Waters Edge is now part of the KOA Campground family and subject to the company's pet policy, which usually includes a small per-night pet fee. Call for specific rates and policy details. Full hookups are available, as are regularly scheduled events and activities, a dining room, a grocery and souvenir store, a recreation hall, restrooms, and laundry facilities. Discounts are available for longer stays.

Homes, Cottages, and Cabins for Rent

Eagle Lake

Picture Perfect Cottages, Eagle Lake (207-834-4510; 207-834-4510; briant@sjv.net); $275–470 per week. Each of these three lakefront homes has a screened-in porch and access to about 100 feet of water frontage. Though they vary slightly in size, the Brown Log Cottage, Kamp Kumfort, Ash Brown Camp, and White Cottage all have two bedrooms and a bathroom, along with hot-air heating. Bedding and linens can be provided for an extra charge. Pets are welcome for an additional $25 per week.

Greenville

Moosehead Hills Cabins, 418 Lily Bay Rd., Greenville (207-695-2514; info@mooseheadhills.com; www.mooseheadhills.com); $139–375 per night or $950–2,500 per week. With a canine bell-hop named Scooby Doo, a feline office manager named Tuesday, and a kitty activities director called Dingo, you can tell right away that this is a pet-loving place. These large log cabins have two to three bedrooms, sun-set views over Moosehead Lake, fireplaces, decks or porches, and full baths (three with whirl-pools). "We love animals and we welcome them at our cab-ins," says owner Sally Johnson, who is also happy to arrange guided hiking and snowmobiling trips, in-cabin massages, and moose-viewing "safaris." Pet owners pay an additional fee of $15 per pet, per day.

Moosehead Lake

Moosehead Lake Vacation Home, Moosehead Lake (207-695-8953; www.moosehead.net); $600–900 per week. The owners of this rental are animal owners and lovers, and welcome pets at their two-bedroom, 1½-bath waterfront home. Greenville is about 15 minutes away, and a marina is within short walking distance. Renters also share a private beach and can walk to a nearby hiking trail.

Rockwood

Sundown Cabins, Rtes. 6 and 15, Rockwood (207-534-7357; sundown@prexar.com; www.sundowncabins.com); $80–140 per night or $700–800 per week. These cheery, sunny rentals, which vary in size and style, sit along the edge of Moosehead Lake. Popular with sportsmen as well as families, the cabins accommodate two to eight-plus people and offer heat, kitchens, picture windows, cable tele-vision, outdoor gas grills, and linens. Pets are welcome in each cottage without extra charges.

Rental Agencies

Maine Escapes Cabins, P.O. Box 157, Rockport 04856 (207-691-1101; info@maineescapes.com; www.maineescapes.com); call for rates and pet-friendly cabins. This company manages rentals throughout Maine and has a photo of a pooch rolling on the beach on their home page; dogs are welcome at the cabins for an extra $5 per night. Rates and details vary from site to site. At the time of this writ-ing, the company offered units such as **Kineo Escape Cabin** (an exposed-beam log home at the mouth of the Moose River) and the **Moose River Escape Cabin** (a Northwoods cabin tucked into the woods). Renters are asked to clean up after their pet inside as well as outside, and will be charged for any animal-related damage to the property.

Mooers Realty, 69 North St., Houlton (207-532-6573; mooers realty@mooersrealty.com; www.mooersrealty.com). Though Mooers primarily deals in sales, the agents can also help you find short-term rental housing (usually for a month or more). Some of the homes do allow pets; you can check out the Web site for the latest vacancies. The Realtor typically charges a $100 finder's fee.

Northwoods Camp Rentals, Main St., Greenville (207-695-4623; info@mooseheadrentals.com; www.mooseheadrentals.com). This agency oversees the rental of about 50 homes in the Moosehead Lake area, from basic, rustic cabins to more luxurious accommodations. Many are waterfront, and some of the owners do allow pets. The rental period is typically Saturday to Saturday, though some exceptions can be made for long weekends.

OUT AND ABOUT

Allagash Wilderness Waterway. This 92-mile-long protected area stretches along lakes, rivers, and ponds from the town of Allagash all the way down to the top of Baxter State Park. It is extremely popular with ice fishermen, hikers, and canoe campers (motorboats and personal watercraft are prohibited). The Bureau of Parks and Lands does not recommend the waterway for casual or first-time campers; facilities are primitive and remote, access to roads is limited, and visitors must be fully self-sufficient and prepared to handle emergencies on their own.

Annual Great Big Dog Wash. This yearly event is filled with soapsuds and good intentions as visiting and local dog owners gather to wash their mutts for a good cause. All the funds raised **benefit Precious Paws Rescue and Adoption,** a nonprofit organization based in Van Buren. The festivities are typically held in August, and usually also include a car wash, vaccination clinic, and microchip clinic. For more information about this year's date and location, call 207-868-2828.

Aroostook State Park, 87 State Park Rd., Presque Isle (207-768-8341). This 600-acre park was Maine's first, though it began with only 100 acres and gradually expanded to its current size. Located on the U.S. border with Canada, Aroostook's **Quaggy Jo Mountain and Echo Lake** are popular with Canadians and Americans alike. Visitors also take advantage of groomed cross-country and snowmobiling trails, various marked hiking trails, and bird-watching opportunities. Camping is also available (see "Accommodations—Campgrounds"). Dogs must be on a leash.

Central Aroostook Humane Society "Pause for the Cause" Walk-A-Thon, Presque Isle. Locals and visitors alike are welcome at this annual fund-raising event, usually held in early May or June. Pets and their owners take a 2-mile trek to benefit the humane society, which shelters and adopts out homeless animals. For more information, write to the society at P.O. Box 1115, 26 Cross St., Presque Isle, ME 04769, call 207-764-3441, or visit www.centralaroostook humanesociety.org.

Eagle Lake Public Reserved Land, Eagle Lake (207-827-5936). This is a great access point for fishing, boating, or exploring 23,000 acres of the Eagle and Square lakes area. For access, launch your boat in the town of Eagle Lake or take Route 11 to Sly Brook Road.

Fort Kent State Historic Site, off Rte. 1, Fort Kent. This site's blockhouse stands as evidence of an 1800s conflict between Maine and New Brunswick, Canada. The lumbermen of each area felt entitled to the valuable forests that surrounded the St. John River, and often invaded the other's lands to illegally harvest trees. The border dispute continued even after the fort was built in 1839 as a base for protecting and monitoring Maine forestland. Today you can get a peek at the blockhouse, along with equipment and artifacts from the volatile era.

Gero Island. More than 3,800 acres of public reserve land are available for exploration at this Piscataquis County island and nearby **Chesuncook Village.** The island is located in the middle of **Chesuncook Lake** and is frequented by canoeists, fishermen, and campers.

Island Falls Summerfest, Island Falls. Typically held in late July and early August, this weeklong celebration of summer includes fireworks, concerts, boat races, road races, dance competitions, a crafts fair, a parade, an auction, antique-car shows, and more. For the latest information, call 207-463-3628.

Lily Bay State Park, HC 76, Lily Bay Rd., Greenville (207-695-2700; 207-941-4014). About 9 miles north of Greenville, you'll find this 924-acre park on the eastern shore of **Moosehead Lake.** Fishing, hiking, snowmobiling, boating, and cross-country skiing are among the common activities; camping is also available (see "Accommodations—Campgrounds"). Moose, bear, deer, and many species of birds all live nearby. The cliffs of **Mount Kineo** rise 800 feet over the lake. Pet owners must clean up after their animals.

Maine Potato Blossom Festival, Fort Fairfield (www.fortfairfield.org). This annual celebration is held during the third week in July, when the local potato fields come into bloom. Activities typically include a parade, pageants, arts and crafts, fireworks, and (believe it or not) mashed-potato wrestling contests.

Market Square, Houlton. This is a cute downtown area with shops, eateries, banks, and tree-lined sidewalks. For tourists looking for a break from the wilderness, Houlton is a wonderfully civilized place to wander for a morning or afternoon. Dogs must be on a leash, and owners must pick up after them.

Moose Viewing. The **Greenville area** is rumored to have the largest population of moose in the United States. Get some advice from locals and set out on your own, or ask your innkeeper or campground manager to help you set up a viewing "safari" with local guides. Though hunting has traditionally been the moose-related activity of choice in these parts, shooting these majestic animals with nothing but a camera is quickly growing in popularity.

Patten Lumbermen's Museum, 25 Waters Rd., P.O. Box 300, Patten 04765 (207-528-2650; www.lumbermensmuseum.com). Open seasonally, this nonprofit organization preserves the history of Maine's logging industry with artifacts, equipment, documented personal tales, and other exhibits. The annual **Bean Hole Day** event is held each August, featuring traditional lumbermen's fare like bean-hole beans (baked overnight in the ground), reflector-oven biscuits, and campfire coffee. Well-behaved, leashed dogs are welcome at the museum and its events.

Presque Isle Bike Path, Presque Isle. Stretching for 4 miles along the former C.R. Railroad track bed, this path starts at North Main Street and ends at Riverside Drive. Bikes, of course, are everywhere, but you'll also find joggers, walkers, and parents pushing baby strollers, all out to enjoy the fresh northern Maine air.

Scraggly Lake Public Reserved Land, Scraggly Lake Rd., Penobscot. Pets on a leash are welcome at this 10,000-acre tract of forest located just north of Baxter State Park. With trails, ponds, bogs, lakeshore, marshes, wetlands, and a boat launch, you won't run out of things to do. Due to its remote location, visitors are advised to arrive prepared for first-aid emergencies and to bring plenty of water and food. To access the park, take the Route 159 extension out of Shin Pond to American Thread Road.

QUICK BITES

Auntie M's, 13 Lily Bay Rd., Greenville (207-695-2238). Pets are allowed to join their owners at the outdoor seating area of this family restaurant as long as they don't disturb other diners. Breakfast, lunch, and dinner are served each day, with menu items ranging from homemade soups and desserts to burgers and dogs, and daily specials are offered in addition to the regular menu.

Bishop's Store, 461 Main St., Jackman (207-668-3411; www

.bishopsstore.com). On your way to the trail or the lake? Stop here first for take-out pizza, sandwiches made with fresh bread, other small grocery items, and a lunch counter with a full menu. The store has been in business for more than 50 years.

Black Frog Restaurant, Pritham Ave., Greenville (207-695-1100). Doggie guests are welcome at the Black Frog's lodging facility (see "Accommodations—Hotels, Motels, Inns, and Bed & Breakfasts"). While you're there, take advantage of the on-site restaurant, as well. This is an eatery with a sense of humor and a laid-back style: Diners can choose from "boom logs," aka mozzarella sticks ("works the opposite of prune juice"), Tom's Tragedy (sliced turkey), and The Chicken That Didn't Make It Across the Road sandwich.

Blue Moose Restaurant, Rte. 1, Box 228 (ITS 80), Monticello (207-538-0991). Snowmobilers, leaf-peepers, anglers, and tourists are among the diners you'll find at this log restaurant with a woodstove and home-cooked meals. No outdoor seating is available, so you'll have to order your food to go.

Coffin's General Store, Rte. 11, Portage Lake (207-435-2811). Popular with local sportsmen, this quick-stop store offers pizza and sandwiches, groceries, souvenirs, hunting and fishing licenses, and snowmobile registrations.

Eastport Chowder House, 167

© A KATZ/SHUTTERSTOCK.COM

Water St., Eastport (207-853-4700; 1-888-EASTPORT; www.fis.com/eastport/restaurant.html). Formerly known as the Cannery Restaurant, this local institution serves lobster, smoked salmon, fresh veggies, steaks, and pasta in the dining room or outside on the wharf tables. The staff are also happy to prepare box lunches for picnics or ship lobster anywhere you'd like.

Mai Tai Restaurant, 449 Main St., Presque Isle (207-764-4426). After a day of exploring, stop by Mai Tai for fresh Chinese takeout. You'll find all your favorites, including lo mein, fried rice, sesame chicken, vegetarian specialties, chow mein, dumplings, and shrimp with snow peas.

Rod-n-Reel Café, 44 Pritham Ave., Greenville (207-695-0388). With permission, well-behaved dogs are allowed on the Rod-n-Reel's outdoor deck or the lawn seating area. The restaurant, located across from Moosehead Lake, offers Ray's Famous Prime Rib dinners, burgers, baked and fried seafood, a variety of sandwiches, and a full bar. The atmosphere is casual and cozy.

York's Dairy Bar, North Rd., P.O. Box 5, Houlton 04761 (207-532-6079). Open seasonally, York's serves cool ice-cream treats, along with burgers, fries, onion rings, and other quick meals, from its take-out window. You can relax at the outdoor tables and even walk the dog at a nearby grassy area.

HOT SPOTS FOR SPOT

Home Farm Kennels, 186 Old Washburn Rd., Caribou (207-498-8803). This overnight boarding facility, which started 26 years ago with the slogan "The Inn for Precious Pets," is popular with local animal owners and visitors—especially snowmobilers who are eager to hit the trail. There are 28 indoor/outdoor runs.

Jean's Serendipity, 79 Main St., Houlton (207-532-3567). This store sells a little bit of everything, including pet supplies. Visitors will also find gifts, collectibles, wind chimes, horse tack, and a wide selection of clothing. All-breed dog grooming is available by appointment for $20–50 per dog.

Natalie Voisine Pet Sitting, 322 Katahdin Ave., Millinocket (207-723-5722). "A lot of people are surprised to learn when they show up that dogs aren't allowed in the park," says pet-sitter Natalie Voisine, who often jumps in to save the day. For $20 per day, she'll keep an eye on your pooch in her home while you explore Baxter. "There's no time limit; people can stay out as long as they want," Natalie explains. "I just like dogs, and like to have them around." Her only restriction: She likes to talk with owners beforehand to learn about the dog's breed and temperament. She'll even pick up your dog at the campground or hotel for an extra $10.

ANIMAL SHELTERS AND HUMANE SOCIETIES

Central Aroostook Humane Society, 26 Cross St., Presque Isle (207-764-3441; www.centralaroostookhumanesociety.org)

Critter Hill Rescue, 97 Ashby Rd., Presque Isle (207-472-3662)

Houlton Humane Society, RR1, Box 330H, Houlton 04730 (207-532-2862; www.houltonhumanesociety.org)

Madawaska Animal Holding Facility, 428 Main St., Madawaska (207-728-6356)

Mamaw's Animal Shelter, P.O. Box 165, Blaine 04734 (207-425-2903)

Moose River Animal Shelter, P.O. Box 834, Jackman 04945 (207-668-5761)

P.A.W.S., Rte. 1, Box 1142, Woodland (207-454-8733)

Paws Animal Welfare, RR3, Box 845, St. Francis (207-398-3511)

P.A.W.S. Humane Society, P.O. Box 182, Calais 04619 (207-454-7662)

Peaceable Kingdom, P.O. Box 13, Limestone 04750 (207-722-4043)

Precious Paws Rescue and Adoption, 15 Main St., Van Buren (207-868-2828)

Van Buren Animal Holding Facility, 65 Main St., Van Buren (207-868-3481)

IN CASE OF EMERGENCY

Animal Hospital of Houlton, 48 Court St., Houlton (207-532-4800)

Caribou Veterinary Clinic, 31 Herschel St., Caribou (207-498-3873)

Chester Animal Hospital, Pea Ridge Rd., Lincoln (207-794-3457)

Fort Kent Animal Hospital, 402 Frenchville Rd., Fort Kent (207-834-5077)

Greenville Veterinary Clinic, Pritham Ave., Greenville (207-695-4408)

North Woods Animal Clinic, 153 Main St., East Millinocket (207-746-9052)

Presque Isle Animal Hospital, 79 Mapleton Rd., Presque Isle (207-764-6392)

THE HOLT POND NATURE AREA IN BRIDGTON IS A SECLUDED SPOT WITH BOARDWALKS, WOODS, AND WETLANDS.

Western Lakes and Mountains

Naples, Paris, Mexico, Denmark, Peru, Sweden: The internationally named towns of the Western Lakes and Mountains region hint at its diverse travel offerings, from majestic peaks to cool river valleys. The area's lakes, ski trails, and spectacular foliage keep the tourists coming—and the innkeepers hopping—year-round. For many skiers, Sunday River is *the* downhill resort of the Northeast, and the nearby village of Bethel is its perfect companion. (The region is also home to the Sugarloaf, Saddleback, and Mount Abram resorts.) The southern Sebago Lake region, long popular with families, is full of campgrounds, activities, and lazy-day fun to keep the kids busy. And as for anglers, they'll flock to just about any spot in this waterlogged section of the state.

With so much of the focus on the outdoors, dog owners will find plenty to see and do here with their animals. Unfortunately, despite the numerous lodging options in western Maine, dog owners have fewer accommodation choices here than in many other parts of the state. Still, the inns, motels, campgrounds, and vacation homes that do allow animals are exceptionally friendly and enthusiastic about welcoming you and your pet. They'll give your vacation a good start, and Mother Nature will deliver the rest.

ACCOMMODATIONS

Hotels, Motels, Inns, and Bed & Breakfasts

Andover

Andover Guest House, 28 S. Main St., Andover (207-392-1209; info@andoverguesthouse.com); $40–55 per night. Located in a quaint historic village, the Andover Guest House is a restored 18th-century Colonial with seven guest rooms and a bunk room that can accommodate up to 10 people ($15 per person, per night). Guests can feel free to lounge in the living room, relax on the porch, or use the kitchen 24 hours a day to prepare and eat meals. Pets are welcome.

Bethel

Bethel Inn & Country Club, On the Common, P.O. Box 49, Bethel 04217 (207-824-2175; www.bethelinn.com); $169–249 per person, per night. With a renowned golf course and a location right down the road from the Sunday River ski area, this hotel attracts visitors throughout the year (the rates include greens fees, breakfast, and dinner). Guests can also enjoy an outdoor swimming pool, a dining room and tavern, game rooms for the kids, and cross-country ski clinics. Dogs—sorry, no cats or other pets—are allowed in some rooms for an additional $10 per night. Most of the 158 rooms have fireplaces, and your dog has acres of outdoor space for walks.

Briar Lea Inn & Restaurant, 150 Mayville Rd., Bethel (207-824-4717; 1-877-311-1299; jollydraymanatbriarleainn@yahoo.com); $85–140 per night. Situated just outside the village, this 150-year-old Bethel farmhouse is only a few minutes from Sunday River. The six guest rooms are decorated with antiques. "We've had really good experiences with pets here," says innkeeper Gary Brearley. "For the most part, I find that people who travel with pets take really good care of them." Well-behaved companion animals are welcome for an extra $10 per night but cannot be left alone in the rooms.

Chapman Inn Bed & Breakfast, 2 Church St., Bethel (207-824-2657; info@champmaninn.com; www.chapmaninn.com); $69–139 per night. This antiques-filled inn is one of the oldest buildings in Bethel; inside, you'll find sleigh beds, quilts, two saunas, and a business center. Those seeking a bargain will appreciate the on-site dorm, which offers a semiprivate bunkhouse and recreation hall. Pets are welcome for an extra $10 per day, though they must be crated when left alone.

Sudbury Inn, Main St., Bethel (207-824-2174; 1-800-395-7837; info@sudburyinn.com; www.thesudburyinn.com); $99–219 per night. Relax on the front porch, nap on your canopy bed, dine in the restaurant, or hang out in the

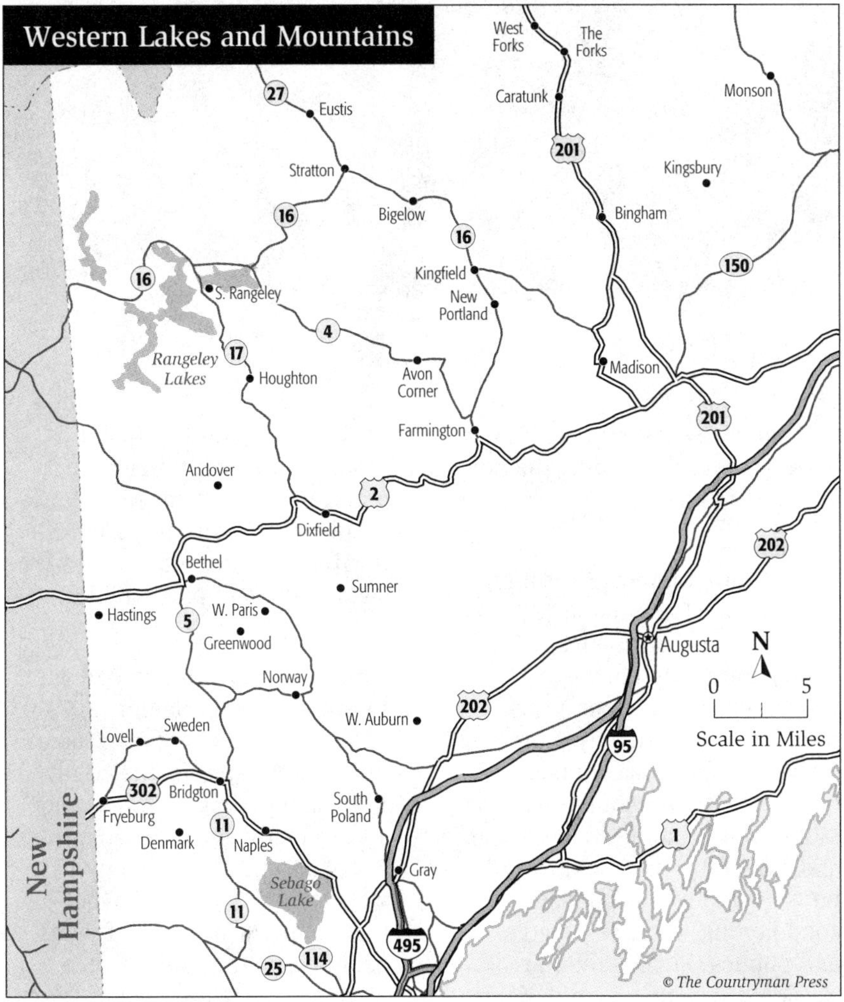

pub at The Suds, as the locals call it. The inn's Main Street location is within walking distance of shops, restaurants, and a small movie theater. Dogs used to be welcome in the Carriage House annex only during the off-season —now they're welcome year-round for an extra $15 per night. Canine visitors will also find a dog run, complimentary welcome biscuits, water bowls, and optional dog-walking services.

Casco

Maplewood Inn & Motel, 549 Roosevelt Trail (Rte. 302), Casco (207-655-5131; info@shindamen.com; www.maplewoodinnandmotel.com); $69–168 per night. Dogs are allowed in the motel section of Maplewood for an extra $15 per night, although owners are asked to keep pets off the furniture and beds. The recently renovated rooms are simple and clean, with wall-mounted televi-

GUESTS AT THE SUDBURY INN IN BETHEL CAN EXPECT TO FIND A DOG RUN AND COMPLIMENTARY DOGGIE BISCUITS AT CHECK-IN. (PHOTO COURTESY OF SUDBURY INN)

sions and air-conditioning. The motel units look out over the outdoor swimming pool.

Farmington

Mount Blue Motel, 454 Wilton Rd. (Rte. 2), Farmington (207-778-6004; mtbluemotel@gwi.net; www.mountbluemotel.com); $48–85 per night. Open year-round, this eco-friendly motel offers affordable accommodations near snowmobile trails and Mount Blue State Park (see "Out and About"). The smoking and nonsmoking rooms have air-conditioning, cable television, and phones. Picnic tables are outside. Dogs are welcome for an additional $7 per stay (not per night), although they cannot be left alone in the rooms.

Kingfield

Herbert Grand Hotel, P.O. Box 67, 246 Main St., Kingfield 04947 (207-265-2000; 1-888-656-9922; innkeeper@herbertgrandhotel.com; www.herbertgrandhotel.com); $79–150 per night. For an extra $25 per stay (not per night), your dog is a welcome guest at the Herbert Grand. The historic hotel dates to 1917 and provides its guests with extra touches like high tin ceilings, a grand piano, oak panels, a lobby fireplace, a restaurant, a large lawn area, Adirondack chairs, swing sets, and picnic tables.

Naples

Augustus Bove House Bed & Breakfast, RR 1, Naples (207-693-6365; augbovehouse@pivot.net; www.naplesmaine.com); $135–250 per night. A dog and a cat already live at Augustus Bove, and they'll be happy to welcome your well-behaved, "small" pet (call to see if yours qualifies) to this B&B located within walking distance of shops and restaurants. Homemade breakfasts typically include pancakes, french toast, apple-walnut syrup, and other goodies. Each room is individually decorated. Pets are welcome in certain rooms for an extra $10 per night, as long as visiting dogs have been given the "kennel cough" vaccine and sleep in a crate or bedding from home.

Rangeley

Rangeley Inn, P.O. Box 160, Rangeley 04970 (207-864-

3341; 1-800-MOMENTS; info@therangeleyinn.com; www.therangeleyinn.com); $84–114 per night. This historic inn has been completely restored with modern conveniences, but still harkens to the past with a tucked-away location, lake vistas, a fireside tavern, antiques, woodstoves, and Adirondack furniture. The inn offers two designated "pet rooms"; pet owners pay an additional $15 per night. Don't be surprised to see brides and grooms celebrating their vows on-site.

Town & Lake Motel and Cottages, 2668 Main St., P.O. Box 47, Rangeley 04970 (207-864-3755; info@rangeleytownandlake.com; www.rangeleytownandlake.com); $85–225 per night. Guests at Town & Lake can choose from motel rooms and two-bedroom cottages; all accommodations have lake views, cable television, and access to free boat slips and a waterfront yard. Some have kitchenettes/kitchens and fireplaces. Pets are welcome in the motel and cottages for an extra $5 per night.

Wilhelm Reich Museum Cabins, Dodge Pond Rd., Rangeley (207-864-3443; wreich@Rangeley.org; www.wilhelmreichtrust.org/cottages.html); $525–675 per week. Two housekeeping cabins, Bunchberry and Tamarack, are available for rent at this museum and nature center commemorating the life and work of scientist Wilhelm Reich. Located on Dodge Pond, the rentals have full kitchens and bathrooms, fireplaces, living rooms, and accommodations for five to eight people. Pets are welcome for an additional $4 per day. Bunchberry is available for rent year-round; Tamarack is available for rent from September 1 to late June.

Raymond

Northern Pines Bed & Breakfast, 31 Big Pine Rd., Raymond (207-935-7624; norpines@pivot.net; www.people.maine.com/norpines); $95–130 per night or $570–780 per week. "We're always happy to have dogs as guests," says Northern Pines innkeeper Marlee Turner. "We charge $5 per dog, and they're free to roam the property and swim in the lake." Guests can enjoy a variety of spa services, including massage, herbal facials, and body wraps (for $60 per service), in addition to more traditional Maine vacation pursuits such as swimming, hiking, and boating. (For mail correspondence, write to P.O. Box 210, Brownfield, ME 04010.)

Wind in Pines on Sebago Lake, Rte. 302 to Fire Ln. 175, Raymond (207-655-4642; wind-in-pines@juno.com; www.wind-in-pines.com); $500–1,400 per week. This "family vacation colony" includes 11 housekeeping cottages and a beach on Sebago Lake. Each cottage is unique and can accommodate from two to eight people. Several have fireplaces, most have screened-in porches, and all have full kitchens. Dogs are permitted for an extra $75 per week; they must be leashed and are not allowed in the beach area.

Rumford

Madison Inn, Rte. 2, Rumford (207-364-7973; 1-800-258-6234; innkeeper@madisoninn.com); $85–150 per night. This motor inn, which bills itself as Fido-Friendly, is open year-round with 60 rooms; all have air-conditioning and cable television, and some have a full kitchen and living room/dining room area. Guests can also use the fitness center, outdoor swimming pool, restaurant and lounge, hiking trails, sauna, and game room. There's also a campground next door (see Madison's Riverside Wilderness Campground under "Campgrounds").

Rumford Point

The Perennial Inn, 141 Jed Martin Rd., Rumford Point (207-369-0309; info@perennialinn.com; www.perennialinn.com); $130–149 per night. Pets are always welcome at the Perennial Inn, where the resident canine Killingworth's Lilly is ready to show your dog the ropes. Pets can even enjoy extras like ceramic bowls, a pet bed or crate, and a treat upon arrival. For its human guests, the inn offers plush bathrobes, down comforters, a pool table, a hot tub, flower gardens, and six guest rooms with sitting areas. Innkeepers Jordan and Darlene Ginsberg also raise Killingworth Labrador retrievers; if you're lucky, you might arrive at the inn in time to visit with a new litter of puppies.

Waterford

Waterford Inne, 258 Chadbourne Rd., Waterford (207-583-4037; www.waterfordinne.com); $125–200 per night. Set on 25 wooded acres, this historic farmhouse offers peace and quiet, flower and vegetable gardens, daily country breakfasts, and four-course dinners. Pewter, antiques, and Americana decorate the guest rooms and main living areas. Well-behaved pets are welcome for an additional $15 per night.

West Paris

Snow Falls Cabins, c/o River Restaurant, Rte. 26 at Snow Falls, West Paris (207-674-3800; www.riverrestaurant.com); $55–75 per night. These seasonal cabins on the Little Androscoggin River, managed by the owners of the nearby River Restaurant (see "Quick Bites"), can accommodate two to four people. Each has a shower, at least one full-size bed, and a kitchenette. Well-behaved pets on a leash are welcome; there's also a dog kennel on-site for guests' use.

Campgrounds

Bethel

Bethel Outdoor Adventure and Campground, 121 Mayville Rd. (Rte. 2), Bethel (207-824-4224; 1-800-533-3607; info@betheloutdooradventure.com; www.betheloutdooradventure.com); $16–25 per night. Located on the Androscoggin River, this camp-

WELL-BEHAVED PUPS ARE WELCOME AT THE WATERFORD INNE, A HISTORIC FARMHOUSE IN WATERFORD WITH 25 ACRES FOR EXPLORING. (PHOTO COURTESY OF WATERFORD INNE)

ground is popular with families and pet owners who like to take canoe trips. "We can tell them about all the islands to stop at on the way," says owner Pattie Parsons. Pets on a leash are welcome as long as their owners clean up after them; in addition, Pattie's sons have started a doggie day-care business on-site (see "Hot Spots for Spot").

Brownfield

River Run Camping and Canoe Rental, Rte. 160, Brownfield (207-452-2500; www.riverruncanoe.com); $10 per person, per night. This secluded 100-acre campground caters to tenters with wooded and waterfront sites as well as private beaches. River Run also specializes in canoe rentals for day trips ($21–35 per day) and provides a shuttle service to Swan's Falls, Lovewell Pond, Walker's Bridge, and other locales. Quiet, leashed dogs are welcome at no extra charge.

Shannon's Saco River Sanctuary, Rte. 160, Brownfield (207-452-2274; info@shannonscamping.com); $27–32 per night. This waterfront campground has sites for tents and RVs alike; full hookups are available. The facilities include a camp store, a playground, a sandy beach, a dock for fishing and boating, a recreation hall, and bathrooms with showers. Quiet, leashed dogs are welcome.

Woodland Acres Campground, 33 Woodland Acres Dr. (Rte. 160), Brownfield (207-935-2529; info@woodlandacres.com.com; www.woodlandacres.com); $34–41 per night. For an extra $5 per stay (not per night), leashed dogs are welcome to join the fun at Woodland Acres, a Saco River campground and canoe-rental service. Campers can choose from wooded or riverfront sites for tents and RVs, and take advantage of the camp store, a playground, and restrooms with hot showers. Pets cannot be left unattended.

Naples

Loon's Haven Family Campground, Rte. 114, Naples (207-693-6881; loonshaven@yahoo.com; www.loonshaven.com); $25–45 per night. With three beaches on Trickey Pond and campsites for tents and RVs, Loon's Haven is especially popular with young families. You can rent rowboats and canoes at the boat ramp; fish for trout, bass, and salmon; hang out on the volleyball and basketball courts; frolic at the playground; or take part in movie nights, dances, bingo games, and other planned activities. Pets are welcome.

Naples Campground, 295 Sebago Rd., Rte. 114, Naples (207-693-5267; info@naplescampground.com; www.naplescampground.com); $25–45 per night. Campers at Naples Campground will find a camp store, three bathhouses with showers, a heated outdoor swimming pool, laundry facilities, two playgrounds, canoe rentals, beach passes to the nearby state park beach, sports courts, two dog-walk and exercise areas, and planned activities. Quiet, leashed pets are permitted in all areas except the pool and playground; owners are asked to clean up after their animals.

North Bridgton

Lakeside Pines Campground, Rte. 117, North Bridgton (207-647-3935); $44–60 per night or $308–625 per week. This campground has 185 sites; some are set in the middle of the action and others are secluded. The shorefront is 3,500 feet long with a beach, two swimming areas, and canoe rentals. Quiet, leashed pets are welcome "for now," although they are not allowed on the beach and must be with their owners at all times.

Oquossoc

Black Brook Cove, P.O. Box 319, Oquossoc 04964 (207-486-3828; info@blackbrookcove.com; www.blackbrookcove.com); $23 per night. Well-behaved pets are welcome at Black Brook Cove, a campground with sites for tents and RV (including some pull-throughs) and ample opportunities for fishing, hiking, kayaking, and boating. The property is located in a cove in Aziscohos Lake and offers docking facilities, a launch area, and boats, canoes, and kayaks for rent. Well-behaved pets are welcome.

Oxford

Two Lakes Camping Area, P.O. Box 206, Oxford 04270 (207-539-4851; twolakes@megalink.net; www.twolakescamping.com); $23–35 per night. The long list of amenities at Two Lakes includes three playgrounds, a camp store, a dock, a boat ramp, a snack bar, modern restrooms, laundry facilities, a pavilion, a dumping station, 50 acres for exploring, and 119 campsites. Dogs aren't allowed on the main beach, but they can enjoy their own designated swimming area. No pets are permitted in cabin or trailer rentals.

Peru

Honey Run Beach and Campground, 456 East Shore Rd., Peru (207-562-4913; hrbc456@earthlink.com; www.honeyruncampground.com); $18–34 per night. Relax on Honey Run's private beach on Worthley Pond, or explore the rest of the campground's 93 acres. The facilities include tent and RV sites, a camp store, boat rentals, restrooms with hot showers, telephones, and laundry facilities. Dogs are welcome, but they must be vaccinated and on a leash.

Poland Spring

Poland Spring Campground, P.O. Box 409, Poland Spring 04274 (207-998-2151; www.polandspringcamp.com); $30–37 per night. Designed with families in mind, Poland Spring Campground offers plenty of diversions, including a heated swimming pool, two playgrounds, a teen hall/game room, sports courts, two recreation halls, a sandy swimming area, a camp store, laundry facilities, restrooms with showers, and lots of planned activities. One dog per site is free; each additional dog is $5 per night.

Rangeley

Rangeley Lake State Park Campground, HC 32, Box 5000, Rangeley (in-season: 207-864-3858; off-season: 207-624-6080); $15 per night Maine residents; $20 per night out-of-state residents. With just 50 sites, this camping retreat located in the midst of Rangeley Lake State Park (see "Out and About") offers a remote outdoor experience. Still, you won't be totally on your own: The campground also has a playground, a picnic area, a boat launch, and bathrooms with hot showers. Leashed dogs are welcome as long as owners pick up after them. The campground is open from May 15 to October 1.

Rumford

Madison's Riverside Wilderness Campground, Rte. 2, Rumford (207-364-7973; 1-800-258-6234; innkeeper@madisoninn.com); $20–35 per night. This campground sits on the Androscoggin River next to the Madison Inn (see "Hotels, Motels, Inns, and Bed & Breakfasts") and can accommodate tents, campers, and RVs. Each site has a picnic table and fire pit, and campers can also enjoy free use of canoes as well as the fitness center, pool, restaurant, and lounge at the inn. Pets on a leash are welcome.

Solon

The Evergreens Campground and Restaurant, Ferry St., Rte. 201A, Solon (207-643-2324; info@evergreenscampground.com; www.evergreenscampground.com); $15 per person, per night. Pets are welcome in the campground, but not the cabins, at this camping facility surrounded by pine, birch, and oak trees. The Evergreens has a restaurant, modern restrooms with showers, tube rentals, canoe rentals, guided tours, ATV trails, and a camp store.

Standish

Sebago Lake Family Campground, 1550 Richville Rd. (Rte. 114), Standish (207-787-3671; www.sebagolakecamping.com); $30–50 per night. In addition to the picnic table, barbecue grill and fire pit found at each site, this family campground also offers a private sandy beach, rowboat rentals, a playground, a camp store and gift shop, seasonal sites, boat moorings, restrooms with showers, and laundry facilities. Leashed dogs are permitted in all areas except the beach.

Steep Falls

Acres of Wildlife Campground, Rte. 113, Steep Falls (207-675-2267; office@acresofwildlife.com; www.acresofwildlife.com); $25–45 per night. For an extra $5 per night, dogs are permitted at campsites but not in rental units or in the inn at Acres of Wildlife, a large private campground located just south of Sebago Lake. Amenities include two eateries, a country store, family activities throughout the season, boat rentals, mini golf, and a playground. Dogs must be on a leash, and owners must clean up after them. For an extra $2–5 per night (depending on the season), your pooch is welcome. Dogs are allowed to swim in the on-site pond but not in the lake.

Waterford

Papoose Pond, 700 Norway Rd. (Rte. 118), Waterford (207-583-4470; thepond@papoosepondcamping.com; www.papoosepondresort.com); $25–54 per night. "We consider our facility very pet-friendly, and many of our guests return each year because of our pet policies," explains General Manager A.R. "Rocky" Cameron. Animals are allowed in many of the campsites and some of the cabins at this waterfront campground, which features a half-mile-long beach, regularly scheduled family activities and entertainment, a café, a recreation hall, and tennis and basketball courts. Pets must be on a leash and are not allowed on the beach.

Weld

Mount Blue State Park Campground, 299 Center Hill Rd., Weld (207-287-3824; 1-800-332-1501); $15 per night Maine residents; $20 per night out-of-state residents. The campground at this 5,000-acre park (see "Out and About") includes 136 sites for tents and trailers, a playground, picnic tables and fire pits, a nature center, bathrooms, showers, and a boat launch. Although your pet isn't allowed on Webb Beach, he is free to wander the trails and other areas of this park as long as he's on a leash.

West Poland

Hemlocks Campground, P.O. Box 58, 35 Larch Dr., West Poland 04291 (207-330-5065; 1-888-998-2384; info@hemlockscampground.com; www.hemlockscamp.com; $25–45 per night. Hemlocks Campground provides its visitors with a General Store, an arcade, and lots of special activities like Mother's Day breakfasts, a children's fishing derby, potluck suppers, and ice-cream socials. Dogs are welcome if they are leashed and quiet; owners are asked to clean up after their animals and bring proof of vaccinations.

Homes, Cottages, and Cabins for Rent

Oquossoc

Moose Lodge, Judkins Road, Oquossoc (207-864-2224; 207-

324-8142; mooselodge@rangeley vacations.com; www.etravelmaine .com/mooselodge); $200 per night or $995–1,295 per week. Well-behaved animals are welcome at this waterfront cottage on Rangeley Lake for an extra $50 per stay (not per night). The house has cathedral ceilings, picture windows, two bedrooms and a pullout couch, a woodstove, a TV/VCR, and a barbecue grill. The property has access to snowmobile and cross-country ski trails, and the lawn opens up to a cove for swimming and boating. (For mail correspondence, write to P.O. Box 519, North Berwick, ME 03906.)

Rangeley

Hunter Cove Cabins, Hunter Cove Rd., Rangeley (207-864-3383; Norway@rangeley.com; www.huntercove.com); $200 per night or $850–1,150 per week. Located directly on Rangeley Lake, these large cabins have extras like rocking chairs, knotty-pine walls and ceilings, woodstoves, and sleeping lofts for the kids. Each cabin also has a living room/dining room area, full kitchen, screened-in porch, picnic table, and barbecue grill. Dogs are welcome for an extra $10 per day, per pet.

Rental Agency

Russell's Lakeside Rentals, Main St., Rangeley (207-864-0935; crussel@megalink.net; www.rlrentals.com). Agency owner Connie Russell manages the rental of vacation homes throughout the Rangeley Lakes area. Rates range from $500 to $2,500 per week, and many of the owners do permit animals. "I've seen an increase in requests to bring pets," Connie explains. "I have posted pet rules, and I find that telling renters what is expected eliminates 90 percent of potential problems." Check out the Web site for up-to-date property listings.

OUT AND ABOUT

Appalachian Trail. This world-famous trail begins (or ends, depending on how you look at it) in Maine, at Baxter State Park, and continues all the way down to Georgia. Dogs are allowed on the trail, except in a few designated areas like Baxter itself. Many hikers say that the Maine stretch is the most difficult; it's usually not recommended for beginners. In the western lakes and mountains region, the most popular sections are the **Bigelow Mountain** range and, right below it, **Saddleback Mountain** to Route 4. The Appalachian Trail Conference, a nonprofit organization that founded and manages the trail, recommends that dogs be on leashes at all times.

Bald Mountain Reserve, Bald Mountain Rd., Oquossoc (207-778-8231). You can boat, fish, hunt, camp, and swim at this 22,000-acre park in the Rangeley region, but by far the most popular activity is hiking. Start with the 1-mile-long summit trail, which affords fantastic views. The reserve also has miles of shoreline on ponds and lakes, and a primitive camping area (call 207-364-5155 for more information).

Bigelow Preserve, accessible from Rte. 27 or from Long Falls Dam Rd., Stratton (207-778-8231). From mayflies to moose, if it lives in Maine, you can find it at Bigelow. This expansive and remote 36,000-acre preserve encompasses 30 miles of the **Appalachian Trail** (see above listing), 20 miles of designated snowmobile trails, and the entire Bigelow mountain range, including the peaks of **Avery, Cranberry, Little Bigelow, The Horns,** and **West Peak.** Primitive camping sites are available free of charge; no reservations are necessary.

Farmington Historic District, Farmington (www.downtownfarmington.com). This area, which includes Academy, Anson, Grove, and High streets, features many structures dating from the 1700s and makes for a nice walking tour. It's also a stop on the 14-mile-long Jay to Farmington Trail.

Farm Loop, Sunday River Inn, Cross Country Ski Center, 23 Skiway Rd., Newry (207-824-2410). Skiers throughout New England know and love Sunday River, a huge resort that anchors the popular ski town of Bethel. Though pets, as you might expect, are not the focus at Sunday River, the cross-country center at Sunday River Inn does have one trail, the Farm Loop—aka "the Poop Loop"—where canines can join their owners on a 1-kilometer Nordic trek. Dogs are also welcome on all the snowshoe trails.

Five Fields Farm, Rte. 107, Bridgton (207-647-2425; www.fivefieldsski.com); $12 all-day trail pass. Leashed pets are welcome at this 70-acre apple orchard and cross-country ski center. In winter, you can stay on the groomed trails and logging roads or venture with snowshoes into the more deeply packed areas. In summer, bring Fido for a day of apple picking. As a bonus, the 450-acre **Loon Echo Land Trust** sits right next door.

Grafton Notch State Park, 1941 Bear River Rd., Newry (207-824-2912; 207-624-6080). Whether you're looking for a pretty picnic spot or a challenging daylong hike, Grafton Notch can deliver. The site's **Screw Auger Falls** and **Mother Walker Falls** are impressive, the **Appalachian Trail** (see above listing) and the ITS 82 snowmobile trail both cross through the park. Other attractions include **Moose Cave** and **Old Speck Mountain.** Pets must be on a leash.

Hemlock Bridge, Hemlock Bridge Rd., Fryeburg. This quaint covered bridge is worth a stop, especially if you're passing between northern New Hampshire and western Maine. You can walk or drive over the bridge, located in a solitary spot down a long, bumpy road off Route 302, then enjoy some privacy while you swim or picnic. (Tip: Use patience once you reach the rustic road—it's a slow 3-mile ride, but worth the effort.)

Holt Pond Nature Area, Grist Mill Rd., Bridgton (207-647-8580). If you can brave the mosquitoes, this tucked-away spot is a real find. (Follow Route 107 to Fosterville Road, then watch for Grist Mill Road. The parking area is about 1 mile down on the right.) Boardwalks and trails wind through quiet wetland and forest areas, allowing for plenty of solitude and wildlife-watching opportunities.

Mahoosucs Reserve. Vehicle access: East 4 Hill Rd., between Upton and Andover (207-778-8231). First-timers may want to start out at the trailhead on Route 26, where you'll find pit toilets, parking, brochures, and trail maps. The **Appalachian Trail** (see above listing) passes through the higher elevations of this 27,000-acre park, where the most popular attractions are **Mahoosuc Notch** and **Cataracts Gorge.**

Maine Nordic Ski Council, P.O. Box 645, Bethel 04217 (1-800-SKI-XCME). Though the ski council happens to be located in Bethel, this organization is a wonderful source of information for cross-country skiers no matter which region you're visiting. They're also savvy about pet-friendly accommodations and trails; check out their Web site for the latest updated information.

Mount Blue State Park, 299 Center Hill Rd., Weld (207-585-2347; 207-585-2261). This park is a hiker's paradise with three peaks—**Bald, Blueberry,** and **Mount Blue**—and countless trails to choose from. First-timers

ENJOY A PICNIC, TAKE A SWIM, AND EXPLORE AT THE HEMLOCK BRIDGE IN FRYEBURG.

should check out the 1½-mile-long main trail, which reaches to the summit. Don't be surprised to see other dogs, horses, bikers, and snowmobile riders. Pets are welcome on a leash, though they are not allowed on Webb Beach. (See "Accommodations—Campgrounds" for information about camping at Mount Blue.)

Moxie Falls, The Forks. There isn't a much better spot for a picnic: With a dramatic 60-foot drop, Moxie Falls is the largest single-drop waterfall in New England. To reach the falls, take Route 15 out of Shirley Village for about 12 miles (the road eventually turns to dirt). Turn left at Moxie Lake, then take the first right. You'll see the sign and parking area on the right.

Nine Lives Thrift Shop, Rte. 302, Fryeburg (207-935-4358; www.harvesthills.org). All proceeds from sales of furniture, clothing, housewares, and antiques at this shop benefit its next-door neighbor, the **Harvest Hills Animal Shelter.** Since opening in 1992, the nonprofit organization has helped more than 9,000 homeless pets find shelter and new homes each year.

Rangeley Lake State Park, HC 32, Rte. 17 or Rte. 4, Rangeley (207-864-3858; 207-624-6080). Fishermen flock to Rangeley Lake for the salmon, though even without a rod and reel you can have a good time exploring the 869 acres of this secluded park. Visitors will find a picnic area and boat launch, as well as a snowmobile trail that connects to the groomed ITS 89 trail. Dog owners must use a leash and clean up after their animals; pets are also welcome at the park campground (see "Accommodations—Campgrounds").

Range Pond State Park, Empire Rd., Poland Spring (207-998-4104; 207-624-6080). Located off Empire Road, this 750-acre park has a picnic area, a beach, a boat launch, a playground, a baseball field, and miles of hiking trails. The area is popular with boaters; and canoeists, kayakers, and sailborders frequently bob in the lake. As with other state parks, dogs are not allowed on the beach, but they are permitted in other park areas with a leash.

River's Edge Sports, Rte. 4, Oquossoc (207-864-5582; www.riversedgesports.com). Say hello to the in-store pup, Dixie, when you stop by here to rent a canoe or kayak (guides are also available if you'd like some help navigating nearby Rangeley, Capsuptic, Mooselookmeguntic, and Richardson lakes). The shop is located right next to a public boat launch.

Sebago Lake State Park, 11 Park Access Rd., Casco (207-693-6613; 207-693-6231). The 1,400 acres of this popular waterfront park are spread throughout the towns of Casco and Naples. The big attraction here is the beach, but pet owners will have to enjoy the other diversions because dogs aren't allowed on the sand (or at the on-site campground). Luckily, there are also plenty of wooded trails for hiking, biking, and cross-country skiing.

White's Marina, 93 Lake Rd. (Rte. 117), Norway (207-743-5586; www.whitesmarina.com). Pets of all kinds are welcome at this marina offering canoes, paddleboats, and other craft for rent, along with a store, gasoline facility, and service department. One caveat: The resident cat, Boris, is not a dog fan, so be sure to give the Whites (marina owners and animal lovers) advance notice if you plan to bring a canine.

QUICK BITES

Beth's Kitchen Café, 108 Main St., Bridgton (207-647-5211; www.bethskitchencafe.com). Locals rave about the sushi at this casual eatery that specializes in fresh veggies, fresh breads, and pastries, plus a casual menu of "create your own" deli sandwiches.

Bridgton Coffee, 248 Main St., Bridgton (207-647-4666). There is more than just coffee at this casual café—you'll also find boxed lunches (perfect for picnics), breakfast sandwiches, soups and chowders, wraps, pastries, smoothies, bagels, and more.

Café DeCarlo, 163 Main St., Bridgton (207-647-4596; www.cafedecarlo.com). "Eat, drink, and get connected" at Café DeCarlo, an Internet café with indoor and outdoor seating. The menu includes specialty coffee, espresso, smoothies, soups, chili, bagels, pastries, fresh-baked breads, yogurt, and muffins. Broadband Internet access is available for $4–8 per hour.

Café DiCocoa and **DiCocoa's Market & Bakery,** 119 and 125 Main St., Bethel (207-824-JAVA; www.cafedicocoa.com). Located next door to each other, these Bethel eateries each offer a delicious break for dog lovers. Pets are welcome at the front-porch seating at the café, which serves up ethnic specialties, salads, desserts, dinners, and weekend brunches. Doggie water bowls are plentiful at the bakery, which also has outdoor seating—it's a relaxing spot to enjoy fruit smoothies, sugary treats, coffee, and espresso.

Center Lovell Market and Deli, Rte. 5, Center Lovell (207-925-1051). This packed shop has everything you might need for a picnic (indoor or outdoor), including chips, fried chicken, beer, sandwiches, pizza, bottled water, and, of course, dog biscuits.

Hodgeman's Frozen Custard, 1108 Lewiston Rd., New Gloucester (207-926-3553). This roadside ice-cream parlor has take-out windows, outdoor tables, wide lawns, and even a covered picnic area. So there's plenty of room for you to enjoy a hot fudge sundae, custard cone, or thick frappe.

Java House, Lower Main St., Bethel (207-824-0562). Pets are welcome at the small outdoor deck at Java House, a café serving breakfast, wraps, soups, chowders, sandwiches, and fresh-roasted coffee in downtown Bethel. They're open seven days a week until midafternoon. The café is open year-round.

Loon's Nest, W. Lovell Rd., Lovell (207-925-3000; www.kezarlake.com/restaurant.html). Located at Kezar Lake Marina, this casual restaurant has two outdoor decks in addition to its indoor dining room. Choose from pizza, lobster, chowder, and other dishes (including fried lobster). A kids' menu is available as well.

Pine Tree Frosty, 55 Main St., Rangeley (207-864-5894). Grab a cool Gifford's famous ice-cream cone or a hot lobster roll, french fries, or fish sandwich and savor your treats while overlooking Haley Pond.

Red Onion Restaurant, 2511 Center Main St., Rangeley (207-864-5022). Everything on the menu here is available for take-out, including fresh-dough pizzas, pasta dishes, steaks, soups, chowders, and sandwiches. The Red Onion staff cater to large groups, vegetarians, and kids. Leashed dogs are welcome on the patio one at a time, on a first-come, first-served basis. The restaurant even offers water bowls and a canine treat—milk bones topped with gravy.

River Restaurant, Rte. 26 at Snow Falls, West Paris (207-674-3800). The River restaurant is an English-style pub that offers casual American cuisine by the Little Androscoggin River. Executive chef Paul Cornish, wife and manager, Hedy, and their staff create all the dishes from scratch, including appetizers, soups, salads, sandwiches, seafood, poultry, and beef. Well-behaved animals can join their owners on the deck for lunch or dinner.

Ruby Food, 78 Main St., Bridgton (207-647-8890). Take out all your Chinese food favorites at this popular Bridgton stop and bring the hot cartons back to your cabin, hotel room, or RV.

HOT SPOTS FOR SPOT

Bethel Outdoor Adventure and Campground—Pet Care, 121 Mayville Rd. (Rte. 2), Bethel (207-824-4224; 1-800-533-3607; info@betheloutdooradventure.com; www.betheloutdooradventure.com). The Parsons family owns this busy campground (see "Accommodations—Campgrounds"), and their sons,

Charles and Jonathon, have opened a pet day-care business for visitors who want to attend a conference, canoe, shop, or enjoy a meal in a nice restaurant.

Bridgton Veterinary Hospital, 213 Harrison Rd., Bridgton (207-647-8804). While you enjoy a vacation in the Lakes Region, your pet can enjoy a stay at this veterinary hospital. Every doggie guest receives one playtime session and three walks per day in the backyard. Food and beds are provided, although you can feel free to bring your own.

House of Stillwater Pet Grooming and Styling, 118 Fairbanks Rd. (Rte. 2/27), Farmington (207-778-3388). A retired schoolteacher and a certified master groomer opened this shop specializing in "tailored styling" for all breeds of dogs. House of Stillwater also offers pet lodging, a pet taxi service from local B&Bs and hotels, and a variety of pet-care products.

Kaylish-Kartel Kennels, 107 Libby Rd., Mechanic Falls (207-345-3258; www.brittanydog.com). In addition to raising champion Brittany spaniels, owner Karen Thorne also runs a doggy day-care and boarding facility with 20 heated and air-conditioned runs. "Lots of people like to go skiing and leave their dog, so we usually offer winter specials," Karen says. "Plus, we live right here, so it's easy to keep an eye on them." The daily rate is $13. Kaylish-Kartel also offers a pick-up and drop-off service for the airport and Sunday River ski area, a 24-hour monitoring system, and a fenced-in play area with wading pools and toys.

Pet Life, North Windham Shopping Center, 770 Roosevelt Trail, North Windham (207-892-8825; www.petlifestores.com). Stock up on all your pet needs at Pet Life, formerly known as the Kennel Shop, where you'll find chew toys, food, grooming supplies, and much more. For information about the retail chain's other locations in Maine, see "Southern Maine Coast," "Greater Portland and Casco Bay," and "Central Lakes and Cities." The company also works with local humane societies by hosting regular adoption events.

Lazy L. Kennel, 188 Scribner Hill Rd., Otisfield (207-539-9188; www.lazylkennel.vpweb.com). Pets get lots of individual attention at this small, family-run facility that can accommodate dogs and cats for overnight stays. There are 12 heated and air-conditioned runs, and a separate cat area, along with a play area where dogs can frolic together.

Little Jungle, 179 Main St., #6, South Paris (207-743-0356). In addition to the traditional pet-shop accessories, medicines, and foods for dogs, cats, reptiles, fish, and birds, the Little Jungle also has a cat rescue center and a doggie deli. The shop used to be located in Norway.

Mexico Pet Shop, 237 Main St., Mexico (207-364-8528). This full-line store carries all the popular brands of dog food, including Iams, Eukanuba, Science Diet, and Agway, in addition to toys, treats, and supplies for all types of companion animals.

ANIMAL SHELTERS AND HUMANE SOCIETIES

Allen Hill Animal Shelter, P.O. Box 492, Oxford 04270 (207-743-7217)

Franklin County Animal Shelter, 550 Industry Rd., Industry (207-778-2638)

Harvest Hills Animal Shelter, 1839 Bridgton Rd., Fryeburg (207-935-4358; www.harvesthills.org)

Maine Humane Center, 279 River Rd., Windham (207-892-8007)

Maine State SPCA, P.O. Box 10, Windham 04062 (1-800-482-7447)

Responsible Pet Care, 132 Waterford Rd., Norway (207-743-8679)

Somerset Humane Society Animal Shelter, P.O. Box 453, Skowhegan 04976 (207-474-6493)

IN CASE OF EMERGENCY

Bethel Animal Hospital, 179 Walkers Mill Rd., Bethel (207-824-2212)

Bridgton Veterinary Hospital, Rte. 117, Bridgton (207-647-8804)

Countryside Veterinary Hospital, 1035 Rte. 2, Rumford (207-369-9969)

Farmington Veterinary Clinic, 246 High St., Farmington (207-778-2061)

Fryeburg Veterinary Hospital, 203 Bridgton Rd., Fryeburg (207-935-2244)

Naples Veterinary Clinic, 3 Lambs Mill Rd., Naples (207-693-3135)

Norway Veterinary Hospital, 10 Main St., Norway (207-743-6384)

Sacopee Veterinary Clinic, 142 Main St., Cornish (207-625-8505)

© BIKERIDERLONDON/SHUTTERSTOCK.COM

Central Lakes and Cities

This region is literally the heart of its state, from the capital city of Augusta and other busy urban centers to colleges and universities like Bates, Bowdoin, Colby, the University of Maine, and the University of Southern Maine. In many ways, it is a more diverse region than the others around it, attracting a wide variety of business travelers, vacationers, students, culture vultures, and sportsmen.

You'll find a museum around every corner here, along with vast lakes, snowmobile trails, and cheery public parks. Chain hotels outnumber their independent brethren, especially in the cities. Still, a decent number of small campgrounds, motels, and B&Bs welcome guests—and their dogs—to explore the outer reaches of this somewhat overlooked section of Vacationland. While other travelers are crowding along Maine's seacoast or flocking to the western mountains, you and your four-legged friend can fish the lake by day and check out the cosmopolitan scene by night.

ACCOMMODATIONS

Hotels, Motels, Inns, and Bed & Breakfasts

Auburn

Econo Lodge Auburn, 170 Center St., Auburn (207-784-1331; www.choicehotels.com); $69–99 per night. Guests at this Econo Lodge can enjoy free daily continental breakfasts, cable television, work desks, free high-speed Internet access, free local telephone calls, voice mail, air-conditioning, and a wake-up service. Dogs are welcome for an extra $10 per stay (not per night); the hotel has a limit of two dogs per room.

Augusta

Best Western Senator Inn & Spa, 284 Western Ave., Augusta (207-622-8803; 1-877-772-2224; www.bestwestern.com); $116–269 per night. Dogs are welcome in designated rooms at this Best Western hotel, which provides its guests with an indoor lap pool, an outdoor heated swimming pool, a gift shop, a fitness center, complimentary daily breakfasts, free newspapers, free high-speed Internet access, cable television with premium movie channels, and in-room hair dryers and coffeemakers. The spa was voted #1 by *Down East* magazine.

Hampton Inn & Suites, 390 Western Ave., Augusta (207-622-6371; www.hilton.com); $109–131 per night. Formerly known as the Econo Lodge Augusta, this hotel features an on-site Mexican restaurant, a swimming pool, extended-stay rooms with refrigerators and microwaves, a rental-car desk, free continental breakfasts, 116 rooms and suites, and laundry facilities. Pets are welcome, and their owners might be especially interested in the property's picnic tables and barbecue grills.

Best Western Plus Augusta–Civic Center, 110 Community Dr., Augusta (207-622-4751; lsearcy@fine-hotels.com; www.bestwestern.com); $107–154 per night. Located a few minutes from the Augusta State Airport, this two-story Best Western Plus, formerly a Holiday Inn, has 102 guest rooms, a restaurant and lounge, air-conditioning, and photocopying and fax services. It's a popular resting place for visitors to the Civic Center, the University of Maine at Augusta, the capitol building, and Maine General Hospital. Pets are welcome with no extra charge.

Motel 6, 18 Edison Dr., Augusta (207-622-0000; www.motel6.com) $59–79 per night. All Motel 6 facilities allow pets with advance notice; these are simple, convenient lodgings that are pretty much the same at each location. Smoking and nonsmoking rooms are available, as are laundry facilities, air-conditioning, televisions, and phones.

Bangor

Fireside Inn of Bangor, 570 Main St., Bangor (207-942-1234; www.firesideinnbangor.com);

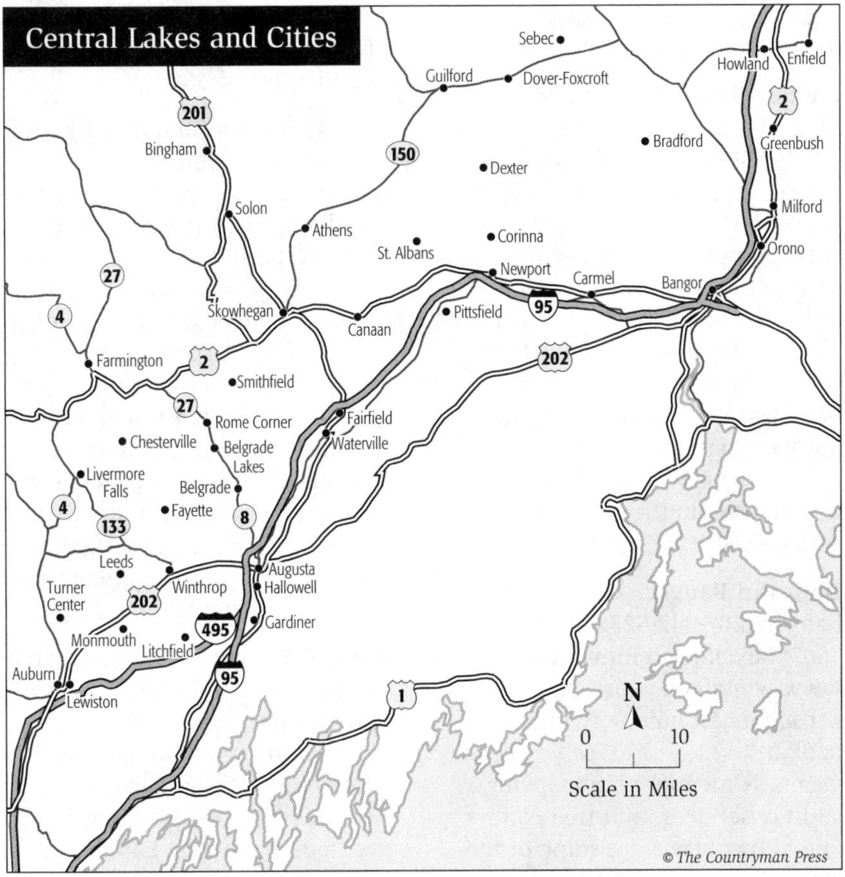

$109–239 per night. Guests with pets get a kick out of a sign hanging in this hotel's lobby: "We've never had a dog who smoked in bed and set fire to the blankets . . . who stole the towels . . . who played the TV too loud . . . So, if your dog can vouch for you, you're welcome, too!" The rooms here are clean and comfortable, with cable television, alarm clocks, data ports, irons and ironing boards, and free newspapers. There are no extra fees for pets, and human guests get a complimentary, official Maine treat: a whoopie pie.

Best Western White House Inn, 155 Littlefield Ave., Bangor (207-862-3737; www.bestwestern.com); $113–167 per night. This family-owned hotel sits on 40 acres of fields and woods. Some of the themed rooms have fireplaces, Jaccuzzi tubs, and massage chairs; all have king- or queen-size beds, televisions with remote controls, in-room hair dryers and ironing boards, and refrigerators. Amenities also include a sauna, laundry facilities, free continental breakfasts, and a Hall of Presidents display. Dogs are welcome for an additional $10 per night, per pet, with a maximum fee of $100 per week.

Comfort Inn, 10 Bangor Mall Blvd., Bangor (207-990-0888; 1-800-338-9966; comfort@midmaine.com; www.choicehotels.com); $99–149 per night. For an extra $6 per stay (not per night), your pet can accompany you at this hotel located just down the road from the Bangor Mall. Guests enjoy free continental breakfasts, a fitness center, an outdoor swimming pool, free daily newspapers, a video arcade, free airport shuttles, and in-room coffeemakers and hair dryers.

Days Inn Bangor, 250 Odlin Rd., Bangor (207-942-8272; 1-800-835-4667; daysinn@midmaine.com; www.wyndham.com); $79–109 per night. An indoor swimming pool, a video arcade, cable television, Nintendo, photocopying and fax services, and free continental breakfasts are some of the amenities at this Days Inn located around the corner from Bangor International Airport (free shuttles are also available). Pets are welcome for an additional $6 per stay (not per night).

Econo Lodge Bangor, 327 Odlin Rd., Bangor (207-945-0111; 1-800-393-0111; econo@midmaine.com; www.choicehotels.com); $59–109 per night. Guests at this Econo Lodge have access to laundry facilities, cable television, Nintendo, nonsmoking rooms, free coffee around the clock, and photocopying and fax services. The Bangor Mall is 5 miles away, movie theaters are just across the street, and Blackbeard's Family Fun Park is next door. Pets are welcome with a one-time fee of $6.

Four Points by Sheraton Bangor Airport, 308 Godfrey Blvd., Bangor (207-947-6721; www.starwoodhotels.com); $150–285 per night. It doesn't get much more convenient than this: The Four Points is connected to the Bangor International Airport via an enclosed skyway. The full-service hotel offers room service, an on-site restaurant and lounge, a 24-hour front desk, a fitness center, a game room, and an outdoor swimming pool. Dogs weighing less than 20 pounds are welcome for an additional $20 per night.

Motel 6 Bangor, 1100 Hammond St., Bangor (207-947-4253; www.motel6.com); $59–79 per night. One well-behaved pet per room is permitted at this Motel 6. Amenities include smoking and nonsmoking rooms, laundry facilities, a "kids stay free" program, cable television with premium movie channels, free coffee in the lobby, free local telephone calls, and vending machines.

Ranger Inn, 1476 Hammond St., Bangor (207-945-2934; www.rangerinn.com); $55–59 per night. Pets are welcome in about 20 of the inn's 89 rooms: "It is more costly to clean the pet rooms, but we find there are so few places that allow pets that we are providing a much-needed service," explains owner Joel Ranger. All rooms have televisions and phones; smoking and nonsmoking rooms and free coffee and ice are available.

Riverside Inn, 495 State St., Bangor (207-973-4100; 1-800-252-4044; www.riversidebangor.org); $99–129 per night. This hotel has an interesting history; owned by Eastern Maine Healthcare Systems, it once served as a nurses' residence for the nearby hospital owned by the same company. The building was converted into an inn about 20 years ago, but it still primarily caters to hospital-related guests during the week and tourists on weekends. Pets are welcome for an extra $10 per night, with a maximum of two per room. Check out the Web site, which features photos of the staff's pets.

Travelodge Bangor, 482 Odlin Rd., Bangor (207-942-6301; 1-800-214-2152); $79–99 per night. Children under 10 stay free and pets are always welcome at this Travelodge. You can get complimentary coffee 24 hours a day in the lobby, and all the rooms have air-conditioning, cable television with premium movie channels, coffeemakers, hair dryers, and alarm clocks.

Bingham

Gateway Recreation and Lodging, Rte. 201, Bingham (207-672-9395; 1-800-440-0053; gateway@gwi.net; www.gateway-rec.com); $75–90 per night or $400–500 per week. Each of these seven housekeeping cabins can accommodate six to eight people; four of the cabins have kitchens, and all are located next to the Kennebec River. Gateway guides can lead guests on hunting, fishing, whitewater rafting, snowmobiling, and canoeing trips. "Well-mannered" pets are welcome to join their owners in the cabins and on explorations of the property's 25 acres.

Brewer

Vacationland Inn, 453 Wilson St., Rte. 1A, Brewer (207-989-5450; www.vacationlandinn.com); $69–235 per night. Pets are allowed with prior notice at the Twin City Motor Inn, where guests will find 123 rooms (some with waterbeds), free continental breakfasts each morning, an outdoor swimming pool, cable television, and an on-site restaurant.

East Winthrop

Lakeside Motel and Cabins, Rte. 202, P.O. Box 236, East Winthrop 04343 (207-395-6741; 1-800-532-6892; info@lakesidelodging.com; www.lakesidelodging.com); $69–99 per night. "We understand that pets are part of the family, and a lot of people wouldn't leave them home any more than they would leave their children," says Sheree Wess, who owns Lakeside with her husband, Andy. The motel and cabins sit next to the Lakeside Marina, where families can rent a variety of boats for fishing or cruising (canoes are free to guests). There's a fee of $10 per night or $50 per week for pets.

Leeds

Angell Cove Cottages, Bishop Hill Rd., Leeds (207-524-5041; angellcove@ctel.net; www.angellcovecottages.com); $95–1200 per week. Located on 50 acres under towering pine trees on the shores of Androscoggin Lake, each of these recently built housekeeping cottages has a screened-in porch, a kitchen, two bedrooms, a living room with a foldout couch, and water views. Each is individually decorated with its own Maine wildlife theme, and linens are provided. Pets are always welcome.

Lewiston

Motel 6 Lewiston, 516 Pleasant St., Lewiston (207-782-6558; www.motel6.com); $59–79 per night. Guests at this Motel 6 location will find interior corridors, free coffee in the lobby, laundry facilities, and cable television with premium movie channels. Children under age 17 stay free with their parents. One well-behaved pooch is welcome per room.

Milford

Milford Motel on the River, 154 Rte. 2, Milford (207-827-3200; 1-800-282-3330; info@milfordmotelontheriver.com; www.milfordmotelontheriver.com); $99–125 per night. The Milford Motel offers standard rooms and larger suites and views of the Penobscot River. Most breeds of "small to medium-size dogs" (call to see if yours qualifies) are permitted, as long as owners keep them off the furniture, use a leash, don't leave them unattended, and clean up any messes. A pet fee may be charged, depending on the size of the dog.

Newport

Pray's Motel, Main St. (Rte. 2), 146 Main St., Newport (207-368-5258; 207-368-4636; www.downtownme.com/praysmotel); $53–62 per night. House-trained pets are welcome at this conveniently located motel in Newport, about halfway between Bangor and Waterville and near large Sebasticook Lake. All rental units have a living room, bedroom, full bathroom, and kitchenette, along with cable television and complimentary coffee. The motel is located next to Pray's Service Station, which sells gas and sundries. Dogs can enjoy romping in the large backyard.

Orono

Best Western Black Bear Inn, 4 Godfrey Dr., Orono (207-866-7120; www.blackbearinnorono.com); $99–169 per night. Convenient to the University of Maine, the Black Bear Inn offers king- and queen-size beds, free continental breakfasts, cable television, and in-room hair dryers, ironing boards, and alarm clocks. The hotel's conference space can accommodate up to 300 people. Pets are allowed but cannot be left in rooms.

University Inn Academic Suites, 5 College Ave., Orono (207-866-4921; 1-800-321-4921; www.universityinnorono.com); $79–149 per night. Formerly known as the University Motor Inn, this motel is located on the Stillwater River and right next to the University of Maine. The 48 rooms are air-conditioned and have cable television; outside, you'll find a heated swimming pool and nearby bike trails.

Downtown Orono is within walking distance. Pets are welcome in designated rooms as long as they are not left unattended.

Skowhegan

The Towne Motel, 172 Madison Ave. (Rte. 201 N.), Skowhegan (207-474-5151; 1-800-843-4405; townemotel@verizon.net; www.townemotel.com); $86–118 per night. Guests at the Towne Motel will find expanded continental breakfasts each morning, high-speed Internet access, a swimming pool, cable television with premium movie channels, in-room coffeemakers and hair dryers, and a location that's close to the Skowhegan Fairgrounds. Dogs are permitted with advance notice in some rooms for an extra $10 per night.

Waterville

Best Western Waterville Inn, 356 Main St., Waterville (207-785-0111; www.bestwestern.com); $79–129 per night. The 86 rooms at this two-story hotel have cable television with remote control, alarm clocks, irons and ironing boards, hair dryers, and coffeemakers. An outdoor pool and a hot tub are surrounded by lounge chairs, and there's also a family restaurant on-site. All types of pets are welcome.

Budget Host Airport Inn, 400 Kennedy Memorial Dr., Waterville (207-873-3366; 1-800-87-MAINE; info@visitwaterville.com; www.budgethost.com); $57–119 per night. Pets are welcome in the Budget Host's 45 rooms for an extra $10 per stay (not per night). Outside, you'll find a large, 1-acre lawn area with plenty of room to run around. Inside, there are typical chain-style hotel rooms; a 24-hour front desk serving complimentary coffee, tea, and hot chocolate; and Internet access.

Econo Lodge Waterville, 455 Kennedy Memorial Dr., Waterville (207-872-5577; www.choicehotels.com); $69–99 per night. Convenient to all the local colleges, this Econo Lodge offers cable television, free coffee in the lobby, free local telephone calls, interior corridors, a wake-up service, vending machines, an outdoor swimming pool, and smoking and nonsmoking rooms. Dogs are welcome for an additional $5 per night.

Campgrounds

Bangor

Paul Bunyan Campground, 1862 Union St., Bangor (207-941-1177; 207-947-3734; www.paulbunyancampground.com); $23–42 per night. Leashed, friendly pets are welcome at this "country oasis within the city." The campground facilities include 52 shady and open sites, heated restrooms, lots of planned activities during the summer, a playground, a recreation hall, a heated swimming pool, a camp store, a dumping station, and paddleboat rentals.

Dover-Foxcroft

Peaks-Kenny State Park Campground, 500 State Park Rd., Dover-Foxcroft (207-564-

2003; 207-941-4014); $15 per night Maine residents; $20 per night out-of-state residents. The 56 sites at this park campground are fairly secluded. Campers have access to bathrooms with showers, a picnic area, telephones, scheduled family programs in the amphitheater, and hiking trails. Pets are not allowed at the beach and must be leashed at all times.

Hermon

Pleasant Hill RV Park and Campground, 45 Mansell Rd., Hermon (207-848-5127; info@pleasanthillcampground.com; www.pleasanthillcampground.com); $24–37 per night or $144–252 per week. Located just outside Bangor, Pleasant Hill caters to RVers (though it does have some tent sites) with paved roads, room for even the largest rig, fire pits and picnic tables, a recreation hall, a camp store, two playgrounds, basketball and volleyball courts, and a fishing pond stocked with trout. Leashed pets are welcome for an extra $10 per night.

Pumpkin Patch RV Resort, 149 Billings Rd., Hermon (207-848-2231; 1-866-644-2267; rvoffice@pumpkinpatchrv.com); $34 per night, $204 per week, or $629 per month. This RV camp offers free hot showers, laundry facilities, an events pavilion, picnic tables, ice and fax machines, Internet access, clean restrooms, and plenty of space for large rigs. Most pets are welcome on a leash; the first pet is free, and any additional animals are $2 per night. Pit bulls and rottweilers are not allowed.

Holden

Red Barn Campground, 602 Main Rd., Holden (207-843-6011; info@redbarnmaine.com; www.redbarnmaine.com); $28–35 per night. Pets are allowed at Red Barn Campground, a facility offering 30 wooded acres, a swimming pool, a playground, a camp store, a designated dog-walking area, a dump station, outdoor games, planned activities, and a restaurant serving breakfast, lunch, and ice cream.

North Monmouth

Beaver Brook Campground, RFD 1, Box 1835, North Monmouth (207-933-2108; camp@beaver-brook.com; www.beaver-brook.com); $28–40 per night. Campers at Beaver Brook can enjoy 191 spacious sites with picnic tables and fire pits, restrooms with showers, a swimming pool, a snack bar, and a camp store offering groceries, ice, wood, and other sundries. Pets are welcome at campsites but not in cabin and trailer rentals.

Stetson

Stetson Shores Campground, Rte. 143, Stetson (207-296-2041; Stetson@gwi.net; www.stetsonshores.com); $25–30 per day or $130–170 per week. The tent and RV sites at Stetson Shores are located on 32 wooded and lakefront acres. Amenities include laundry facilities; flush toilets; hot showers; a camp store; a boat launch; and canoe, kayak, and paddleboat rentals. Pet owners are welcome to bring their furry friends as long as they keep them on a leash and clean up after them.

Vassalboro

Green Valley Campground, 1248 Cross Hill Rd., Vassalboro (207-923-3000; info@greenvalleycampground.us; www.greenvalleycampground.us); $33–36 per night. Green Valley Campground is a family-oriented place with dock space, an outdoor spa, boat rentals, a camp store, laundry facilities, a recreation hall, sports courts, and sites for tents and RVs. Well-behaved pets are welcome, as long as owners agree to clean up after their animals. Dogs are not allowed in the swimming or playground areas.

Homes, Cottages, and Cabins for Rent

Kents Hill

Cornerstone Cottage, 18 Ellis Ln., Fayette (207-897-5485; cornerstonecottage@verizon.net); call for rates and specials. Cottage is definitely a misnomer in this case: Cornerstone is a full-size, luxurious house, complete with country furnishings, knotty-pine walls and bedposts, handmade quilts, three bedrooms and two sleeping lofts, a large deck, a screened-in porch, skylights, and an organic garden with vegetables and fresh eggs. Guests are also free to use the canoe and two kayaks.

OUT AND ABOUT

Capital Park, Augusta. This picturesque 34-acre plot, located between the State House and the Kennebec River in Augusta, has served many functions in its nearly 200-year history as a public park: It was used as a soldier's camp during the Civil War; leased for farming purposes after that, and once was crisscrossed by a busy railroad track. Today, the park serves as a peaceful place to walk, jog, relax, and admire the State House dome and the river. Dogs must be on a leash.

Fort Halifax, Rte. 201, Winslow. A reconstructed building now stands in place of the original Fort Halifax, America's oldest blockhouse, which was nearly wiped out during a 1987 flood. The original structure was built in 1754 by Massachusetts and Maine residents who feared attacks from French troops and Native Americans. Despite the flood, parts of the historic blockhouse remain intact. The site is located about 1 mile south of the Winslow–Waterville bridge. Dogs must be on a leash.

French's Mountain and **Blueberry Hill,** Rome. The Belgrade Lakes region has many beautiful mountain trails, but French's Mountain has the best views of scenic **Long Pond.** To reach the trail, follow Route 27 north out of Belgrade Lakes Village. Drive for about 1.2 miles and turn left onto Watson Pond

Road. Or, if you'd rather not hike to the views, you can drive there: Blueberry Hill lookout is also on Watson Pond Road, and you won't even have to get out of your car to see vistas of Long Pond and **Great Pond.**

Historic Lewiston. Lewiston's Historic Preservation Board publishes a self-guided tour book designed to help you navigate your way around more than 120 of the city's noteworthy historic places. The guide includes information on buildings such as the **Healy Asylum** (circa 1892), the **Church in the Triangle** (circa 1903), the **Empire Theater** (circa 1903), the **J. L. Hayes Store** (circa 1880), and the **Art Deco Block** (circa 1929), to name just a few. For more information, call 207-784-2951.

Kennebec "Whatever" Family Festival, Augusta. For 18 days in early summer, Augusta bustles with fun and activities for kids and adults, locals and visitors. Events vary from year to year but typically include talent shows, fireworks, barbecues, crafts fairs, puppet-theater shows, sing-alongs, trolley rides, road races, golf tournaments, face painting, hot-air balloon rides, and more. For up-to-date information, call the Kennebec Valley Chamber of Commerce at 207-623-4559 or visit www.augustamaine.com.

Lake George Regional Park, Canaan and Skowhegan (207-474-0708). This 275-acre park is managed by a nonprofit organization and offers a boat launch, forested area, and trail for hiking and cross-country skiing. Pets are allowed from September 15 to May 15 in the park proper, but you can hike the **East Side Trail System** year-round. Take Route 2 for about a mile out of Canaan Village toward Skowhegan; you can park at the second boat launch, where you'll also find the trailhead.

Peaks-Kenny State Park, 500 State Park Rd. (Rte. 153), Dover-Foxcroft (207-564-2003; 207-941-4014). This 839-acre park is largely uncrowded (compared to other state parks) and offers miles of hiking trails. Dogs on a leash are welcome everywhere except the beach. There's also a family campground on-site (see "Accommodations—Campgrounds").

Pine Tree State Arboretum, Hospital St. and Piggery Rd., Augusta (207-621-0031). This 200-acre preserve is home to hundreds of cultivated trees, shrubs, and other plants. The arboretum is designed to educate the public and advance horticultural science, but it's also just a beautiful place to wander and enjoy in all seasons. Dogs on a leash are welcome, provided that their owners clean up after them. The arboretum also occasionally hosts pet walks for the local humane society.

Two-Cent Bridge, Front St., Waterville. This free-swinging bridge has earned a spot on the National Register of Historic Places as the last-known toll footbridge in the country. It was built in 1901 to allow pedestrians to travel between Waterville and a paper mill in Winslow.

Window-Shopping in Hallowell. From clothing boutiques to flower, gift, and clock shops, downtown Hallowell has much to offer meanderers on a lazy afternoon. Antiques dealers crowd Water Street, in particular; and Park, Water, and North streets all have plenty to peer at—and eat. Check out Dana's Hot Dogs (under the umbrella) and the unique gifts at Cushnoc Trader.

QUICK BITES

Bagel Central, 33 Central St., Bangor (207-947-1654; www.bagelcentralbangor.com). With take-out service and even a dog tie-out area out front, this sandwich shop is popular with canine lovers. Menu items include bagel and deli sandwiches, pastries, and soups.

Butterfield's Ice Cream, 136 W. Main St., Dover-Foxcroft (207-564-2513). Walk up to the window and choose from 31 homemade, creamy, cool flavors in a cone, sundae, or shake. If you're in the mood for something hot, you can also get burgers, hot dogs, fries, and other fast-food items to go.

Giffords Ice Cream, 503 Madison Ave., Skowhegan (207-474-2257; www.giffordsicecream.com). Order your slow-churned cold treat at the window and relax with the happy crowds at the outdoor tables. Ice-cream flavors include favorites like chocolate chip, black raspberry, and Rocky Road along with more out-of-the-ordinary options such as Maine Black Fly, Cashew Turtle Sundae, and Sunken Treasure.

Grand Central Café, 10 Railroad Sq., Waterville (207-872-9135; www.thegrandcentralcafe.com). In addition to its indoor dining room, this brick-oven pizzeria also has an outside seating area where well-behaved pets are often allowed to sit quietly with their owners. Menu items include gourmet specialty pizzas, brick-oven quesadillas, and hot and cold sandwiches.

Luiggi's, 63 Sebattus St., Lewiston (207-782-0701; www.luigispizzeria.com). Everything on the menu at this casual Italian restaurant is also available for takeout, including pizza, spaghetti, lasagna, sandwiches, french fries, and chicken wings.

Moose Alley, 2809 Main St., Rangeley (207-864-9955; moosealley@me.com; www.moosealleymaine.com). Though the main attractions at this bowling alley are indoors (including pool tables, a dance floor, and a bar), Moose Alley also has a small outdoor seating area with umbrellas. The menu includes bar-and-grill fare such as steaks, sandwiches, and burgers.

Old Mill Pub Restaurant, 39 Water St., Skowhegan (207-474-6627; www.oldmillpub.net). This cozy restaurant is located in a historic mill building beside the Kennebec River. Though dogs aren't allowed on the outdoor deck, you can order any item on the menu as takeout—including lobster rolls, club sandwiches, and pub burgers—and eat at one of the nearby benches along the river. The staff are happy to provide a dish of water upon request.

Sam's Italian Foods, Lewiston and Auburn (www.samsitalian.com). You can grab a sandwich or pizza to go at any of Sam's area locations: 268 Main St., 675 Main St., 902 Lisbon St., and 963 Sabattus St. in **Lewiston;** 229 Center St. and the Taylor Brook Mall in **Auburn;** and 583 Prospect Ave. in **Rumford.**

Simones' Hot Dog Stand, 99 Chestnut St., Lewiston (207-782-8431). In summer, you can usually find one or two outdoor tables here, or you can order Simones' dogs, chili, burgers, salads, sandwiches, and soups to go.

HOT SPOTS FOR SPOT

Animal Crackers Pet Supply Company, 204 Hammond St., Bangor (207-990-3232). Pet owners can browse grooming supplies; toys for dogs, cats, birds, and small animals; crates; collars; and premium dog and cat foods at this cozy shop. "We have everything," says owner Joel Gottlieb. "It's a very small store, but it's filled right to the ceiling."

Barks and Meows, 1014 Western Ave., Manchester (207-623-4976). Owner June E. Gilley, a licensed veterinary technician, makes sure pets get lots of personal attention at this boarding and doggie day-care facility. Dogs and cats alike enjoy TLC for short- and long-term stays.

Bear Brook Kennel, 19 Bennett Rd., Brewer (207-989-7979; www.bearbrookkennel.com). Located behind the Brewer Veterinary Clinic, this overnight boarding and day-care kennel offers 48 indoor/outdoor runs, "presidential suites" with Internet web cams allowing remote viewing, several bedding options (washed and disinfected daily), and grooming services such as washes, cuts, nail clips, and shave-downs. Clients can also take advantage of doggie day care, a retail store, a new cattery, and training classes.

Fin, Feather & Fur Family Pet Center, 245 Center St., Auburn (207-783-6061). This family-owned shop offers a full line of pet supplies, including food and accessories for dogs, cats, fresh- and saltwater fish, rodents, reptiles, and birds. If you run out of anything while you're on the road, take heart that you should be able to find it here.

Green Acres Kennel Shop, 1653 Union St., Bangor (207-945-6841; www.greenacreskennel.com). This is a one-stop business for animals and animal lovers: Take advantage of the full array of grooming services (by appointment), training classes, overnight boarding, and a retail store selling food, pet beds, chew toys, and more. Overnight canine guests have indoor/outdoor heated runs, two outdoor play yards, and scheduled playtimes.

Pet Life, Shaw's Plaza, Western Ave., **Augusta** (207-623-2939); and Promenade Mall, 855 Lisbon St., **Lewiston** (207-777-1376; www.petlifestores.com). Formerly known as the Kennel Shop, Pet Life really is a superstore for companion animals, offering everything you might need from food to silly, squeaky toys. The store also has other locations in Maine: See "Southern Maine Coast," "Greater Portland and Casco Bay," and "Western Lakes and Mountains."

Second Home Kennel, 11 Adams St., Hermon (207-848-2606). Owner Shirley Murden welcomes dogs and cats to this small boarding facility. The 20 dog runs each have a 4-by-6-foot interior and a 4-by-10-foot exterior area; in addition, each dog gets to run around three to four times each day in the 50-by-60-foot fenced-in yard. Cats have their own separate boarding area.

ANIMAL SHELTERS AND HUMANE SOCIETIES

Animal Orphanage, Airport Rd., Old Town (207-827-8777)

Answered Prayer Acre Animal Rescue, Barron Rd., North Anson (207-635-2377)

Bangor Animal Shelter, 541 Maine Ave., Bangor (207-942-8902)

Bangor Humane Society, 693 Mt. Hope Ave., Bangor (207-942-8902; www.bangorhumane.org)

Carsons Animal Shelter, 79 Hoxie Hill Rd., Orrington (207-825-4574)

Charley's Strays Inc., P.O. Box 64, Clinton 04927 (207-426-9482)

Greater Androscoggin Humane Society, 3312 Hotel Rd., Auburn (207-783-2311; www.gahumane.org)

Humane Society of Waterville, 120 Drummond Ave., Waterville (207-873-2430)

Kennebec Valley Humane Society, 10 Pet Haven Ln., Augusta (207-626-3491; www.pethavenlane.org)

Little Wanderers Animal Adoption, 383 Corinth Rd., Hudson (207-327-1422)

Maine Animal Control Association (advocacy), 60 Community Dr., Augusta (207-353-7492)

Milo PAWS, 65 Sargent Hill Dr., Milo (207-943-2324)

PALS Animal Shelter, P.O. Box 6, East Winthrop 04343 (207-395-4274)

Pittsfield Animal Shelter, 3965 Skowhegan Rd., Pittsfield (207-487-5104)

Pupp-A-Mutt Rescue, 29 Pine St., Farmingdale (207-626-7999)

Save Our Strays, P.O. Box 445, Fairfield 04937 (207-877-0060; www.saveourstraysinmaine.org)

IN CASE OF EMERGENCY

Animal Emergency Clinic of Mid-Maine, 37 Strawberry Ave., Lewiston (207-777-1110)

Auburn Animal Hospital, 864 Center St., Auburn (207-782-4466)

Central Maine Veterinary, 10 Business Pkwy., Turner (207-225-2726)

Eastern Maine Emergency Vet, 268 State St., Brewer (207-989-6267)

Penobscot Veterinary Hospital, 411 Davis Rd., Bangor (207-947-6783)

Pine Tree Veterinary Hospital, 220 Western Ave., Augusta (207-622-6181)

Timberland Animal Hospital, 20 Stillwater Ave., Orono (207-827-7177)

Winthrop Veterinary Hospital, 1942 Rte. 202, Winthrop (207-377-2520; 207-623-5215)

Index

C

D

E

H

K

L

M

S

Y

Z